AMERICAN EDUCATION IN FOREIGN PERSPECTIVES

AMERICAN EDUCATION IN FOREIGN PERSPECTIVES:
Twentieth Century Essays

COMPILED AND EDITED BY

STEWART E. FRASER

Professor of International and Comparative Education
George Peabody College for Teachers

JOHN WILEY & SONS, INC.
New York • London • Sydney • Toronto

Library of Congress Catalog Card Number: 78-76054
Cloth: SBN 471 27540 9   Paper: SBN 471 27541 7
Printed in the United States of America

Dedicated to the memory of
HAROLD R. W. BENJAMIN

"Irascible, irreverent but generous critic of domestic and foreign education"

Preface

The purpose of this book is to present a panorama of some of the many facets of twentieth-century American education as seen through the eyes of illustrative foreign commentators. We trust that it will be of general interest to teachers and students concerned with the history and philosophy of education and also to those more particularly concerned with international and comparative studies in education.

The quality and range of articles in the collection should permit it to be used for students specifically involved in the various "foundations of education" courses. A major documentary collection of this type for the first time provides the opportunity for an analysis of twentieth-century American education, *per se*, as seen in foreign perspectives from both its historical and contemporary aspects. Although this volume of essays by foreigners specifically on American education is the first of its particular genre to be published, the general field of assembling "foreign perspectives" on America at large is certainly not novel. This has been a favorite topic of many historians and commentators, both domestic and foreign, of the American scene. However, to date, their volumes, generally, have portrayed the whole expanse of American society and culture, with only limited references made to her schools or universities. This contention can be readily substantiated if we examine some of the major collections of essays on the United States in general, as viewed through "foreign eyes," this literature is considerable and is thoroughly documented.

An early classic in this field, the contemporary analysis by Henry Tuckerman in his 1864 *America and Her Commentators,* merely touches, though felicitously, on but few points of concern to education.

A quarter of a century later, John G. Brooks in his *As Others See Us: A Study of Progress in the United States* (1909) noted a variety of general comments on American culture and intellectual development by various European authors. In 1921, appeared Delaye Gager's *America as Seen by the French* from which came, as an offshoot, *French Comments on American Education* (1925). Gager's works, when placed in juxtaposition with W. J. Osburn's study, *Foreign Criticisms of American Education* (1922), represent the major analyses of foreign commentary on education in the United States during the interwar period.

The more recent and outstanding collection of essays, such as *America Through British Eyes,* (1948), by Allan Nevins ranges the whole social and political scene, but education is almost entirely bypassed. A companion volume by Henry Steele Commager, *America in Perspective: The United States Through Foreign Eyes*, (1947), whose tenth printing was recorded in 1964, similarly, finds space for only one piece on American education out of some 35 essays. In a further important compilation, *This Was America: As Recorded by European Travelers in the Eighteenth, Nineteenth, and Twentieth Centuries*, edited by Oscar Handlin and published in 1949, there is again little reference to education, with only one out of 40 essays directly concerned with this topic.

Perhaps one of the more frank and stimulating anthologies of this kind is the one edited by Franz M. Joseph, *As Others See Us: The United States Through Foreign Eyes* (1959). This book contains some of the most interesting and articulate of contemporary foreign views on America, although only three of the twenty authors are interested in education and, of these, but modest space is devoted to the workings and effects of American schools and universities.

In 1960, the United States Office of Education was responsible for holding a conference on the theme of "United States education as viewed by foreigners." To the conference came 30 specialists representing university administrators, foreign student advisors, college admissions officers, and comparative education specialists. They also met with United States government officials representing the United States Information Agency and International Cooperation Administration, among others. The results of this conference were published under the editorship of Charles C. Hauch, Comparative Education Specialist of the Office of Education as, *Foreign Understanding and Interpretation of United States Education* (1960). The report, although primarily concerned with the interpretation of American education for foreign students, devoted some space to the evaluation of foreign criticisms of colleges and universities in the United States.

However, it is to Willis Rudy that we owe a major debt of gratitude for affording the topic sufficient importance to include it as a principal chapter in his book, *Schools in an Age of Mass Culture* (1965). Rudy's extensive analysis, an "Evaluation of American Education by Foreigners," is carefully documented; and in lively form he presents a running series of commentaries by overseas visitors on the schools of America.

In 1966, a two-volume historical compilation entitled, *Impressions of America*, was published under the editorship of Ralph and Marion Brown. In this book, there are 50 articles by as many authorities; yet the topic of education is of but passing interest to the editors, and only one selection is devoted to this subject. A more recent analysis by Anthony Scarangello of "foreign commentaries," however, at last presents a compilation of student views specifically on American education. This work, *American Education Through Foreign Eyes*, (1967), consists of 80 interviews and commentaries by a group of foreign students recently in the United States. The views given are those of students who have both "endured and enjoyed" American schools and educational institutions. Although they do not necessarily exemplify the most profound or professional criticism exhibited by such distinguished scholars as Harold Laski, André Maurois, or Dennis Brogan, the students' comments are pertinent, refreshing, and valuable for understanding foreign student attitudes and the working of international exchange programs in the United States.

In spite of the various works noted above a variety of comprehensive multinational and intercultural compilations for use in the teaching and the study of *American Education* in both its historical and contemporary contexts are still necessary. The material contained in this collection should contribute toward the achievement of this objective. *American Education in Foreign Perspectives* offers not only interesting commentaries but provides authoritative analyses by professional educators and scholars of worldwide prominence. In addition, the articles are of particular concern to those who study international and comparative education, especially the American student who seeks to gain an unusual perspective of his own educational system through the study of new and critical materials that generally are not presented or, to date, have been little utilized in the standard works on American educational history.

At present more than 120,000 foreign students and overseas educators come to the United States each year, and a collection of essays on American education by previous visitors should be of special interest as an introduction to their sojourn in this country. The need in teaching and research for documentary materials of what might be called a *cosmocultural* nature has long been the concern of thoughtful American educators. This concern has been highlighted and implemented in recent years by a variety of private and governmental agencies interested in extending the scope and application of international educational studies in American schools, colleges, and universities. More recently, it has been illustrated by the passage of a unique law, the *International Education Act* (IEA) *of 1966*, which seeks to increase immeasurably the international dimension in American education at both the undergraduate and graduate level, as well as in the primary and secondary schools. It is, however, an intellectual tragedy of the first order and a misunderstanding of the potential role of international education that the United States Congress to date has not seen fit to appropriate the necessary funds for this pioneering legislation. In 1968, the original IEA of 1966 was extended until 1971. It is hoped that Congress will contribute appropriately in the near future and not be remiss in its duty and responsibility to aid in the education internationally of both United States students and those from beyond her borders.

The nature of course work at American colleges in recent years and the internationalization of the scope of American public education suggests the continuing need of new avenues for presenting documentary and historical material in contemporary studies. The introduction of hitherto neglected material of a cross-cultural, international, and comparative nature into basic "foundations of education" courses is timely and desirable. Therefore, collections on American education of thoughtful, provocative, and critical essays by foreign authors should have a special appeal to both teachers and students interested in developing a *cross-cultural* and *multinational* approach to the study of education in the United States.

The collection does not purport to be all embracive, representing all major national politics, nor does it attempt to include foreign commentary on every facet of American education. However, it does cover many major aspects of primary, secondary and tertiary schooling in the United States, and does include authors from such diverse countries as Australia, Austria, Britain, China, Denmark, France, Germany, Holland, Ireland, Iran, Poland, the Soviet Union, and Sweden. The bias in this particular collection is undoubtedly towards European commentators; however, the extensive bibliography at the conclusion of the book notes the diverse writings and criticisms of other educators and visitors from many countries in Asia, Latin America and Africa. Accordingly we hope that subsequent anthologies of foreign educational commentary can more adequately represent the views of these regions.

The present collection is divided into two parts. The first concentrates on writings which concern American education in general and analyses of the elementary and secondary schools in the United States. The second focuses on higher education and illustrates the diverse nature of collegiate and university institutions in the United States. Both parts are arranged chronologically, commencing at the beginning of the twentieth century with readings selected to illustrate a variety of salient points in the historical development of American education during the present century.

International Center   *Stewart E. Fraser*
George Peabody College for Teachers   Nashville

Acknowledgments

I would like to thank the many publishers, authors, and agents who have given their kind permission to reprint copyrighted material.

In addition I would wish to gratefully acknowledge the considerable assistance and diverse contributions made to this anthology by many of my students and colleagues, and the help and thoughtfulness of Dorothy Reeves, Vada Rice, Marie Williams and Allan Peterson, staff members of the Peabody International Center.

S.E.F.

Contents

Introduction   1

PART I   EDUCATION, GENERAL: ELEMENTARY AND
SECONDARY   19

1. "School Reform"
   By Hugo Munsterberg   21

2. "Some Points of Contrast in the Educational Situation in
   England and America"
   By Michael Ernest Sadler   39

3. "A British View of American Schools"
   By Alfred Mosley   49

4. "American Education: A Chinese Viewpoint"
   By Wu Ting-Fang   55

5. "Educational Thought: Implications for Australia"
   By John George Cannon   61

6. "A Dane Looks at American Education"
   By Johannes Novrup   65

7. "A Refugee Teacher Looks on Democratic and Fascist
   Education"
   By Rudolf Ekstein   71

8. "Unity, Liberty and Education"
   By Dennis W. Brogan   81

9. "The Negro School: A Swedish Analysis"
   By Gunnar Myrdal   95

10. "Do American Schools Educate?"
    By John Garrett   119

11. "Through Soviet Eyes"
    By Aleksei I. Markushevich   127

12. "English and American Education: Depth Versus Breadth"
    By Geoffrey Crowther   135

13. "A Frenchman Appraises United States Schools"
    By André Maurois   147

14. "Some Irish Impressions of Education in the U.S.A."
    By Terrence O'Rafferty   153

15. "In the Schools of America: Notes of a Soviet Educator"
    By Zoya Malkova   173

16. "A Polish Educator's Observations"
    By Wojciech Dindorf   207

17. "A British View of U.S. Education"
    By Arnold Toynbee   217

18. "School Boards Run System"
    By Arnold Toynbee   221

19. "American Education and the World"
    By Edmund J. King   225

20. "Sick Schools: Australian Perspectives"
    By William Broderick   239

21. "A European View of American Educational Philosophy"
    By Brian Holmes   247

PART II   EDUCATION, HIGHER: COLLEGIATE AND
          UNIVERSITY   259

22. "The American Teacher: Training and Employment"
    By Robert Edward Hughes   261

23. "Intellectual Changes"
    By James Bryce   271

24. "English Students in American Universities"
    By A. Georgette Bowden-Smith   279

25. "University Government and Administration: Australian
    Aspects"
    By E. R. Holme   293

26. "University Study of Education: Anglo-American Analysis"
    By Isaac L. Kandel   307

27. "Why I Shall Send My Son to an American College"
    By Emil Ludwig   327

28. "A Hired Man Speaks: Views of a Dutch Immigrant"
    By J. Anton de Haas   333

29. "English As You Teach It in America"
    By Jack Arthur Walter Bennett   345

30. "America Graduate Education: A British Political Analysis"
    By Harold J. Laski   351

31. "Education and the Humanist"
   By *Erwin Panofsky*   365

32. "Americans as Students"
   By *Pierre Emmanuel*   379

33. "A French Professor's Remarks on American Education"
   By *Henri Peyre*   387

34. "America the Magnet: The Lost Foreign Student"
   By *Nuri Mohsenin*   393

35. "The Teaching of Mathematics"
   By *W. Warwick Sawyer*   401

36. "Typical Student in U.S. University Not Scholar"
   By *Arnold Toynbee*   423

37. "Ivy League Land; Not So Much an Education, More a Way of Life"
   By *Michael Beloff and Jonathan Aitken*   427

38. "The U.S.: Mais Oui! Mais Non!"
   By *Alfred Grosser*   443

39. "University and Community: A Southern Exposure"
   By *Elizabeth Jane Howard*   449

Bibliographical Notes   455

Selected Bibliography   469

Index   527

AMERICAN EDUCATION IN FOREIGN PERSPECTIVES

Introduction

> No one can form a shrewd judgment on American education who merely
> sees what he is bid to see, and who refrains from employing his critical
> faculty as well as his organ of admiration. The comparative study of
> national systems of education is a delicate enterprise. The path to truth
> lies between Scylla and Charybdis; between harsh, censorious judgments
> of other people's failings and too ready belief in the superior merits of
> other people's achievements. But the first requisite for the intelligent study
> of a foreign system of education is sympathy. We must do as we would
> be done by.[1]

Most American college students who have survived the early years of
undergraduate study have invariably read Alexis de Tocqueville's
Democracy in America. A smaller number of their more literate colleagues aspiring to a bachelor degree may also have heard of Isaac
Kandel or Robert Ulich and, perhaps read their evaluations and strictures
concerning American education. Kandel and Ulich are representative of
the foreign-born scholars who have made America their home and who
have contributed immeasurably to America's intellectual development.
Their views (respectively from "Britain" and "Germany") on education
and culture in their adopted land are but partial evidence of the constructive but continuing criticism in which academics throughout the
world engage, as they practice their profession of teaching.

But for every well-known de Tocqueville, Kandel or Ulich, there are
countless others from abroad who came to America and whose thoughtful comments on American education are unremembered and largely
pass unnoticed. Foreign observers who, since the early 1800's, have
visited the New Republic, have traveled across America's diverse coun-
tryside and have commented on its culture and "peculiar though various
educational attainments," depending on their points of view. Their accounts, written in both popular journals and learned tomes on the *Americans* intrigued readers, both domestic and foreign, throughout the nineteenth century. Americans, it seems, have an overweening propensity
for inviting both critical and laudatory commentary from foreigners,
tolerating them for the most part, though sometimes, understandably,
becoming highly disturbed by what is said of their schools and colleges,
and of American culture in general.

---

[1] Michael Sadler, 1902, addressing Scottish teachers on his "Impressions of American
Education," in *Educational Review*, Vol. 25 (March, 1903), pp. 218–219.

1

The essays that follow in this anthology are concerned, with the more recent history of American education and more specifically with the educational developments and events that have occurred since 1900. Before reading the writings of these foreigners as they viewed American schools and schoolmen during the past sixty years, it is interesting to review the contributions of some of those who preceded them during the nineteenth century.

Travelers from Europe almost simultaneously with the establishment of the new Republic showed a special interest in the development of an "indigenous culture and native schooling" in America. The British travelers were for the most part patronizing but still curious about their fractious "castoffs." The French were not entirely uncritical towards their somewhat ungrateful "allies," nor were the Germans, Dutch, and Scandinavians indifferent to the land that was soon to be of even greater interest for so many of their emigrating countrymen in the years to come.

William W. Brickman, historian of international education, has made the following perceptive warning about the reports of foreign visitors: "Naturally, these have to be evaluated on the basis of the criteria of reliability, validity, representativeness, and objectivity."[2] He has also noted accurately that in view of the youthfulness of the state of education in the United States, there were really very few historical writings by foreigners on American pedagogy until close to the mid-nineteenth century.[3]

After the end of the Napoleonic Wars, Americans traveled abroad in increasing numbers, chiefly to Western Europe and, particularly, to Britain, France, and the German principalities. The names of Benjamin Silliman, John Griscom, Calvin Stowe, Alexander Dallas Bache, William C. Woodbridge and, of course, Horace Mann, are now well known in American educational history as being among the first successful pioneers from the United States who ventured into both the practice and the study of international and comparative education.

It should not be supposed, however, that Americans unanimously welcomed foreign ideas either imported by foreign commentators or brought back by returning American educators. William C. Woodbridge, an editor of one of America's first educational journals and an extensive traveler in Europe, noted wryly that "We are aware that there is much sensitive-

[2] William W. Brickman, "An Historical Survey of Foreign Writings on American Educational History," *Paedagogica Historica*, Vol. II, No. 1, 1962, p. 6.
[3] *Ibid.*

ness in our country in regard to foreign improvements—and have received some hints of the danger of exciting it."[4] Accordingly, some limitation must be placed on the efficacy, influence and acceptance within America of "foreign" reports on its educational system. Nonetheless, the travel accounts by Woodbridge and other native Americans are important because they provided valuable information that allowed Americans to be knowledgeable about European educational developments.

However, these visits during the 1830's of Americans to Europe were, reciprocated by many "continentals" traveling in America, as shown by the writings of Alexis de Tocqueville in his *De la democratie en Amérique* (1835–1840), Nickolaus Heinrich Julius' *Nordamerikas sittliche Zustände* (1839), and Edouard Ducpetiaux's *Des Progrès et de l'état actuel de la réforme pénitentiare et des institutions préventives, aux États-Unis, en France en Suisse en Angleterre et en Belgique* (1837–1838).[5]

The last-mentioned traveler, Edouard Ducpetiaux, a Belgian prison inspector, in his study of American educational and penal institutions, placed in comparative perspective similar studies made of institutions in France, Switzerland, Britain, and Belgium. Ducpetiaux's visit to the United States in the 1830's was complemented by a similar visit by George Combe, the Scottish phrenologist and close colleague of Johann Spurzheim. It is interesting to note of Combe's observations concerning American education that he was at once generous in his praise and reserved in his criticisms, stating that "American democracy is a phenomenon which has scarcely had a parallel in the world. It is, therefore, of interest in all its features."[6] But, he also noted perceptively that: "One of the most common errors, in my opinion, committed by foreigners who wrote about America, as well as by the Americans themselves, is greatly to overestimate the educational attainments of the people."[7]

Combe noted the wage scales for both teachers and day laborers in America and found the former so grossly deficient, especially in the country districts that he commented: "Probably nineteen-twentieths of the education of children owing to the conditions of most of the common

---

[4] William C. Woodbridge (editor), *American Annals of Education and Instruction,* Vol. I (June, 1831), pp. 243 and 244.
[5] For a more detailed documentary presentation of the nineteenth century American involvement in transatlantic educational exchanges, see Stewart E. Fraser and William W. Brickman, *A History of International and Comparative Education: Nineteenth Century Documents,* Chicago, Scott Foresman and Company, 1968.
[6] George Combe, *Notes on the United States of America during a Phrenological Visit in 1838–39–40* (Philadelphia: Carey and Hart, 1841), p. xi.
[7] *Ibid.,* p. 155.

schools is defective in the extreme."[8] His comparisons were with the rural schools of Scotland, which he knew so well and to which he was a familiar and regular visitor. Combe took foreign educators, including American visitors, to see them in operation. He observed that in American schools there was a dire need for good normal schools in which to train teachers. He suggested that these institutions should instruct in philosophy and "in the art of training and teaching and they must pay handsomely before they will command good educators."[9]

He prophetically warned that Americans, if they could be animated by "enlightened patriotism," should be prepared to accept "large taxation to accomplish this object because on its fulfillment will depend the future peace and prosperity of their country."[10]

Combe's views were supported, for the most part, by the prominent Swedish educator and politician, P. A. Siljeström, the author of *The Educational Institutions of the United States: Their Character and Organization,* (1853).[11] His work represents the first major detailed and analytical work in Swedish on American education. Siljeström, though a critical and careful observer like Combe, was undoubtedly enthusiastic about American education. He states that, "popular education . . . is not only discussed in legislative assembly, but that it forms part of the national life, and is considered an important, nay, the most important concern of the nation, . . . in the depth of American society there are forces at work, which in Europe has as yet produced but very mediocre results."[12]

These laudatory views were offered at the precise time that American educators were traveling across the Atlantic to seek new models for elementary and grammar schools and for teacher training "normal" institutions. A long-time interest by peripatetic American scholars in higher education was maintained in European universities throughout the nineteenth century, but it was not until the termination of the American Civil War that this interest developed in a major fashion.

The period 1820 to 1850 saw many prominent American educators depart for Europe to observe, compare, and learn. This was perhaps America's great initial period of "international borrowing" as practiced by her scholars and schoolmen. Yet, during this very period of borrowing

[8] *Ibid.,* p. 155.
[9] *Ibid.,* p. 155.
[10] *Ibid.,* p. 156.
[11] Published originally in 1852, in Stockholm as *Resa i Förenta Staterna,* 2 vols., Vol. I, *Om bildningen i Förenta Staterna* was translated into English by Frederica Rowan and published in London by John Chapman, 1853.
[12] *Ibid.,* p. v.

and foreign comparisons, the American "common" school was fast becoming a favorite topic of interest for many European visitors, whether from Britain or the continent. And, as Siljeström noted in explanation, because education is the "most powerful means and the highest end that can be proposed for national activity . . . it is particularly discernible that the system of popular schools in America should be known and studied in Europe."[13]

The interest of foreigners in American education around the mid-century was certainly not confined to European observers and travelers. The names of Jose Pedro Varela of Uruguay and Domingo Faustino Sarmiento of Argentina are recorded as those of interested spectators of the American scene. They have at last become familiar and part of the history of both American education and international education. Their adulatory reports of the 1860's concerning the American institutions they visited are part of the documentary record of Latin American visitors to the United States. But even their useful comparative writings on American education were preceded by another Latin American writer of the 1820's who has gone largely unnoticed, Lorenzo de Zavala, a prominent statesman from Yucatan, Mexico, who wanted the benefits of the American common school for his countrymen.

The democratic and popular nature of American education, the efficacy if not the efficiency of her common schools, the localized control of and the decentralized nature of educational administration, all attracted the attention of foreign visitors. These are perhaps the more positive aspects of American education noted by visitors during the early part of the nineteenth century, but similar topics continued to be of interest, and euphemistic remarks were reiterated by travelers throughout the entire century and well into the next. In all, for over 150 years, certain characteristics of American education have evidently remained constant and have repeatedly drawn the attention and consistent reportage of foreign educators.

Henry T. Tuckerman, writing a century ago about "America and her commentators," noted that the country is "one about which the truth has been more generalized and less discriminated."[14] He also suggested that America was a "land whose inhabitants were so uniformly judged en masse."[15] There were thousands of educated foreigners, including both literate men and intelligent women who visited America during the nineteenth century. Some of these came to settle and contribute materially to

---

[13] Ibid., p. vii.
[14] Henry T. Tuckerman, America and Her Commentators with a Critical Sketch of Travel in the United States (New York: Charles Scribner, 1864), p. 444.
[15] Ibid.

their new homeland, while others traveled across the country, principally to gather travel anecdotes. They also contributed to the wealth of commentary on the natural resources of the continent, the cultural needs of its people, and the education of its children. Frances Trollope, Charles Dickens, Frederick Marryat, and Harriet Martineau are among the more distinguished and publicized travelers who came to America. Dickens, who was no friend of the American press, had a warm personal regard for the academics and intellectuals with whom he met, observing that "an educated American" was "the most endearing and most generous of friends."[16] He was one of the sharpest British nineteenth-century critics to visit America; yet, he could find only praise for American colleges, believing that "they disseminated no prejudices; rear no bigots . . . and above all, in their whole course of study and instruction recognize a world . . . beyond the college walls."[17]

In the 1860's, at the same time that Henry Tuckerman compiled his pioneer work on "foreign commentators," a distinguished English churchman, Bishop James Fraser, traveled in America and inspected both United States and Canadian schools.[18] His comparison of educational developments in North America with conditions in England led him to note enthusiastically that the American school was truly a microcosm of American life. He characterized it as a system that contained both "elements of strength and weakness, of success and failure." Bishop Fraser realized that American education was dynamic, evolutionary, and pragmatic, but he also strongly criticized the excessive "spirit of freedom and equality" that left little time for "work to be thoroughly well done." High, excessive ambition with its peculiar American concomitant of sensitivity to praise and blame," was a debilitating feature of education productive of an "excessive and exhausting strain on the mental and physical powers." The American school reflected so many different values and contained the ideals of such a fast-developing heterogenous population that Fraser eventually had to admit that he found it difficult, if not impossible, to stamp the system with "any one discriminating epithet by which to characterize the resultant whole."

Bishop Fraser's observations, for the most part highly laudatory, still accurately reflected the views expressed twenty years earlier by a fellow countryman, Robert Dale Owen, who indicated to Congress in 1846

---

[16] Charles Dickens, *American Notes*, Vol. XXVII, *The Works of Charles Dickens* (New York: Peter Fendon Collier, n.d.), p. 284.
[17] *Ibid.*, p. 210.
[18] James Fraser, *Report on the Common School Systems of the United States and the Provinces of Upper and Lower Canada*, Vol. II of the School Inquiry Commissions, 1866, see the *American Journal of Education* (Henry Bernard, Editor), National Series, Vol. III, 1870, p. 578.

that a desire for education—a goal for knowledge—must be gauged to reach not only "scholars and students . . . but the minds and hearts of the masses." Owen's words were heard by a receptive fertile audience and, two decades later, Fraser was able to note the contributions of educational reformers such as Horace Mann, Henry Barnard, Calvin Stowe, and Calvin Wiley, all of whom were able to persuade state legislators to follow the educational example set in Massachusetts.

Briefly, in evaluating the travelers, particularly those from Britain, we can state that schools and, generally, educational developments in America were regarded with great interest though not always favorably. But usually the travelers, prior to the Civil War, whose views have been portrayed, were thoughtful, well-educated tourists rather than skilled comparative educators.

The post-Civil War period was clearly distinguished from the fifty years preceding it by the greater range and higher professional status and standards of foreign observers. The Civil War, the principles involved, the educational needs for reconstruction, Negro emancipation, and the Freedmen's Bureau, all were responsible for adding to the interest of European, Latin American and, later, Asian educators in visiting America.

The United States, prior to the Civil War was an educational curiosity for most short-term visitors and represented, culturally, a barren desert. However, the immigration Mecca provided by the United States, through the opening of the West continued to draw both capital and migrants and, certainly, both the curious and desperate from Europe. In addition, during the next thirty years, ending with the turn of the century, several thousand Americans became foreign students in European institutions. Their presence also added to the curiosity of German, French, and British scholars and intellectuals with whom they came in contact. The fast-developing interest in American education after the Civil War was evident in a variety of foreign publications: for example, in Sophia V. Blake's *A Visit to Some American Schools and Colleges,* 1867, an excellent account of women's education as it was then developing; in Celestin Hippeau's *L' instruction publique aux États-Unis,* published in 1870, concerning elementary and secondary schools; in F. Migerka's *Das Unterrichtswesen in den Vereinigten Staaten,* 1877, a report on the Philadelphia World Exposition, containing critical evaluations of American schools prepared for the Austrian Ministry of Education; in Léon Donnat's *L'état de Californie: Première partie, l'éducation publique, la presse, le mouvement intellectuel,* 1878, containing a detailed account backed by careful research of California schools and cultural institutions; in Marie-Casimir Landreyt's *L'instruction publique en France et les écoles Américaines*, c. 1883, described by G. Stanley Hall at "light, but readable notes of travel by a lady" on primary, secondary, higher, and professional education; and in Athanasius Zimmermann's *Die Universitäten in den Vereinigten Staaten Amerikas: Ein Beitrag zur Kulturgeschichte*, 1896, a Catholic scholar's study of higher education in the United States with special attention to religious education.

However, in spite of the proliferation of post-Civil War publications by foreigners on American education (partially shown by the authors noted above),[19] only a few exhibited a distinctive research methodology or evidence of a systematic study of American education in a fuller comparative perspective. The principal exception to this tendency was the work of a New Zealander, R. Laishley, who in 1886 described in tabular and comparative form the structure of American educational administration, curricula, and organization in both international and comparative perspectives. In Laishley's *schema*, America was set down in "true" contrast with the leading European nations, and his careful notes on America was one of the best systematic comparative reviews and presentations of international educational systems made during the whole century. Education was carefully dissected into its various component parts and presented in a useful tabular reference form. Laishley's work was intended primarily for his colleagues back home in Auckland, but it represented with its copious supplementary footnotes, one of the most detailed analyses and carefully substantiated comparative studies of education of the "most and advanced nations of the time."[20]

During the nineteenth century, the study and practice of comparative education developed along a variety of paths whose more accurate delineation had taken a full century to clarify. The growing search for higher and more universal education and a conscious need for educational reform was in part responsible for the curiosity about education in "foreign" countries. The multitude of foreign writings during the century, both by interested travelers and professional educators, testify to a developing interest in American education and to the central role it has played in the political and economic development of America. Some writings already have been briefly referred to above; however, they are merely a limited sample of the diverse material that became available to the student of foreign and comparative education by the end of the nineteenth century. By 1900, America had conquered her West and developed an industrial power that was soon to offer its first

---

[19] I am indebted to William W. Brickman for initially drawing my attention to many of these references.
[20] See R. Laishley, *Report on State Education in Great Britain, France, Switzerland, Italy, Germany, Belgium, and the United States* (Wellington, New Zealand: 1886).

challenge to the industrial leadership of Europe. The country had provided a home and haven for millions of European immigrants who, through their children and the public school, were to be spectacularly absorbed into American society. The early role of American education in international and intercultural education was expressed poignantly by the distinguished English educator, Michael Sadler, who stated that the immigrants were the raw materials of American democracy. But, he suggested that "the school is the mill which grinds up these diverse materials into one consistence."[21] The presence of a growing number of American educators abroad, scholars and missionaries in Asia, Africa, and Latin America, and the American post-graduate student in Germany and France evidenced the fast-growing international exchange aspects of American education. International expositions, the developing interests of the United States Bureau of Education, and foreign officials and delegations visiting the United States contributed to drawing a growing and more professional group of observers to the United States, especially after the Civil War. The professional foreign educational commentaries on American education, prior to 1860, were few and far between and, for the most part, of modest distinction. But the last decades of the century saw teams of distinguished foreign educators come both on private visits and as members of official delegations visiting American schools and colleges. These included German visitors and their accounts such as Rudolf Dulon, *Aus Amerika über Schule, Deutsche Schule, Amerikanische Schule, und Deutsch-amerikanische Schule,* 1866; and Emil Hausknecht, *Amerikanisches Bildungswesen,* 1894; the writings of British authors, Amy Bramwell and Millicent Hughes, *Training of Teachers in the United States,* 1894; Sara Burstall, *Education of Girls in the United States,* 1894; David Salmon, *Some Impressions of American Education,* 1899; the Canadian account by Egerton Ryerson, *Special Report on the Popular Education of Europe and the United States of America,* 1868; the Australian comparisons by W. C. Grasby, *Teaching in Three Continents,* 1891; the distinguished French commentators, F. E. Bussion, *Rapport sur l'instruction primaire à l'exposition universal de Philadelphia en 1876;* Marie Loizillon, *L'éducation des enfants aux États-Unis,* 1883; Paul Bourget, *Outre-mer Impressions of America,* 1895; and the many reports of Gabriel Compayré, particularly those written during the period 1893 to 1900, including for example, his *L'enseignment secondaire aux États-Unis,* 1896.

The modest, rustic schools of America of the early 1820's were a far cry from the fast-developing system of public schools, both primary

[21] Sadler, *op. cit.,* p. 220.

and secondary in operation in 1900. By then, the unique American contribution, the public or common school, was firmly established in American society, and the public comprehensive high school for all was in process of development. By the turn of the century, enough of it was visible to capture the imagination of the foreign visitor. However, there was always the "obviously successful rather than the obviously profound" that had the greatest claim for the admiration of the average American citizen. But the foreign observer could not but note that the creation of America and its emerging educational institutions had been subjected to a wider and more strenuous range of pressures compared to those of other nations, particularly European nations. He observed the peculiar situation of America as the melting pot nation with many but diffusive and divisive segments in her social and political makeup. The thoughtful, though critical, commentator came to realize slowly that, by the turn of the century, American education had several clearly identifiable "aims," which, if understood sympathetically, would nullify all but the most rabid and irrational of foreign critics. The four bases on which American education was predicated in 1900 were: (i) the understanding that a self-governing people must be fully educated; (ii) each individual must be given the fullest opportunity for self-improvement and advancement; (iii) education was to be the prime vehicle for the assimilation of immigrants and the foreign-born; (iv) a rigid caste system either hereditary, political, or economic must be prevented or continually modified through a system of free public and compulsory education for all. Actually, a French critic, Christopher Langlois, noted these four fundamentals and accurately summarized and repeated similar evaluations made previously by many of the other commentators who visited America at the turn of the century.[22] If an understanding of these four principal goals of American education was evident in foreign commentaries, then we can assume that, at least, their criticisms were tempered by some understanding of the special political and economic problems of American schools and society.

By 1900, American education had developed certain distinctive characteristics and specific peculiarities on which foreign observers generally commented almost uniformly. The American elementary public or "common" school was recognized as a major and noteworthy force in the assimilation of immigrant children, although its critics pointed out that it offered only a modest educational base composed of "fundamentals" plus some "civics and patriotic studies." The free, public, and

[22] See Christopher V. Langlois, "Notes sur l'éducation aux États-Unis," *Revue Internationale de l'enseignement*, No. 49, 1905, pp. 289–309.

compulsory aspects of American education, although not then extending much beyond the elementary level, at least, provided a significant basis for integrating Americans of all classes and economic backgrounds. The public school, for "all" classes, for "most" religions, and for "some" races was an established fact. The high school was in the process of being universalized, and the concept of a compulsory secondary education for all those who could utilize it up to their mid-teens was soon to become a new but important characteristic of American education. The avenue to higher education, although difficult to traverse, was possible for many American secondary school graduates. Although in 1900, less than five percent were able to go on to college for obvious reasons of financial and family responsibilities, alternative opportunities for "further education" were pioneered well before World War I. The foreigner's picture of the unlimited opportunities in American economic and political life paralleled what he saw of the considerable opportunities for receiving a complete education unimpaired by the discriminatory, caste-like, and selective schools that he saw in Europe, many of which did not prepare students for entering the university. The American system of higher education provided for "further training"—some of a professional nature and much of a vocational nature. However, it still could not afford the "luxury" of a "higher education" for all who deserved it—and it was another half century before this goal could be attempted. The European observer, on the other hand, "knew full well" that a university training was for both aesthetic and practical purposes relating to the professions (especially the distinguished professions such as law and medicine) as well as for developing an intellectual and literate upper class. Hence, higher education for the European had distinctively mixed utilitarian professional, as well as aesthetic and class reasons for its being, although for reasons that were distinctively different from the practical bent that could be found as partial justification for the universities of the United States.

The selection of essays and articles in this book will offer a panorama of American educational development in its many facets with selections concerning specifically elementary, secondary, and tertiary education. As will be apparent, some of these essays discuss the philosophical aspects of American education, while others are concerned more practically with its curricula and effective application. Approximately half the articles concern education in general and the elementary and secondary schools. The second half of the collection deals with various aspects of higher education. The authors whose work is included in this book, for the most part, are (or were) well-known and highly respected as leading educators in their own countries. Many have also become well-known in America for their scholarly contributions. A few of the authors in the collection for some time have made the United States their home and have written as integral members of the American academic community. Yet, their basis for intellectual orientation and their educational backgrounds are such that they are invaluable to this collection as "foreign commentators," in spite of new allegiances and deep-felt attachments to this country.

For every selection included in this book, there are perceptibly a dozen other articles written in a similar vein, some critical, some laudatory. Obviously, the problem of choice and selection has been of concern in this collection; it would have been simpler, for example, to restrict this compilation to either transatlantic commentaries or to the analyses and descriptions of, for instance, British visitors commenting specifically on American higher education. Instead, it seemed desirable to include a somewhat wider range of commentary. Thus, a larger spectrum of analyses on American education is presented, although a balance has not been in any way rigidly observed between the various levels of education. Similarly, it was difficult to achieve a balance between visitors from all major geographical areas: for instance, those representing a European viewpoint as against those with an Asian outlook, or perhaps an African viewpoint balanced with the commentary of Latin American educators. Of greater importance is the intellectual content of the criticisms and commentaries, the level of writing, and the vivid and interesting portrayal of certain principal aspects of American education.

The extensive bibliography contained in this book of English language materials on the topic of "foreign commentary on American education" quickly reveals the capacious treasure house of material available to students interested in learning what others think and have thought of the educational system of the United States. It is also reasonable to anticipate that, for every English language item noted in the bibliography, at least a dozen or more articles have been written in other languages on the now familiar topic of "What I Saw of American Schools." In effect, the selections of this book merely present a sample of foreign views but, it is believed that they are representative of the better, more interesting, provocative, and useful of foreign commentaries.[23]

The ideals, goals, and aspirations of many nations are for some ob-

---

[23] Two of the best interpretations of the nineteenth century interest of foreigners in American education and their contributions to it can be found in: B. A. Hinsdale, "Notes on the History of Foreign Influences upon Education in the United States," *Report of the U.S. Commissioner of Education,* I, (1897–98), pp. 591–629; and W. J. Osburn *Foreign Criticism of American Education,* Bulletin 1921, No. 8, Bureau of Education, Department of the Interior, Washington, D.C. Government Printing Office, 1922, 158 pp.

servers more clearly reflected in the schools. The widespread availability of education, the degree of social and educational mobility, public involvement, and even the curricula and textbooks, all reveal something of a nation's cultural and educational levels whether determined by economic, political, or religious considerations. An analysis of civic and moral education, the absence of religious observances, the streaming and selection of pupils, the availability of higher education may give sufficient indication as to the kind of society in which the school is situated and may allow for an evaluation of the relative role that it plays and the importance that it holds. Thus, it is particularly important for the foreigner to observe, understand, and evaluate carefully and accurately American ideals in education, both on an American "national" basis, as well as on an "international-comparative" basis. A misinterpretation of these national goals or a prejudice against them may mar an evaluation of the importance of what is really going on within the classroom. But we should sympathize with the foreigner in his attempt to equate and evaluate comparatively an all-negro school in Biloxi, Mississippi, and its erstwhile racial counterpart in Harlem, New York. Similarly, the education of a Spanish-speaking Puerto Rican in New York will not necessarily and or uniformly show strong correlation with the schooling of a Spanish-speaking student of Mexican background in Los Angeles. The diversity of American education, the disparate communities that it serves, and the all too apparent over-embracive goals that the schools must espouse are such that perhaps only a Soviet educator, who well knows the polycultural background of his own country, can understand. The Russian also is familiar with the diversities in language, religion, race, and geography that are contributing factors affecting the fullest coordination of national educational goals. Even within Britain the goals of Scottish education do not entirely or necessarily coincide with those of Wales or Northern Ireland, far less with those of England. The diversity of aims between schools in Dublin, Eire, and Belfast, Northern Ireland, though but 100 miles apart, are attested to through diverging goals based on religious and political differences, whose origins are several centuries old.

Thus, it is an interesting and practical intellectual exercise to ask the foreign observer to define what he thinks are the "principal goals in American education?" This is a question that Americans, particularly today, are increasingly asking themselves, although many foreign observers believed that America's communality of goals was theoretically assured politically 200 years ago and, supposedly, there was considerable consensus socially only 50 years ago! Today, there is an ever increasing variety of answers and, certainly, considerable divergencies when the subject of American educational goals is discussed. And yet, amid the utmost diversity, immediately apparent, there are certain fundamentals that appear to have persisted during the past two centuries and that still form a philosophical core to which most Americans can generally accede. Basically, these goals concern the necessity of the school at the elementary level to teach a specific number (although gradually increasing range) of fundamental skills. These goals are then enunciated at the secondary level in the upbringing of young men and women with a variety of intellectual competencies and manual dexterities needed to obtain both financially and socially satisfying employment. Because the United States is both a democracy and a pluralistic society, it is important to all its citizens that equality of educational opportunity be translated into factual nondiscriminatory terms. The school in America, as a common denominator, has necessitated the involvement of the widest range of talents, skills, and aspirations. Unfortunately, as many foreigners quickly note, the school, in spite of all its promises, cannot guarantee that individual aspirations will be properly satisfied or even partially achieved where there is a definite lack of talent or, what is now so prosaically termed, a minimal "achievement potential." The frustrations of society for many children during and after school hours are such that many of the formal processes of learning are immediately or partially negated or diverted into antisocial channels. The decided concern with democratic institutions in America more than a century ago led de Tocqueville to remark on this country's pronounced tendency towards mediocrity. The educational situation today would undoubtedly lead him to comment on the new tendency towards "meritocracy," or perhaps on a graduated system of mediocrity that contains its own plateaus of achievement and, thus, allows American youth to make the most of their educational opportunities while permitting various levels of mediocre though socially accepted achievement plateaus. In de Tocqueville's time, the apparently endless economic opportunities available to the energetic American led him to believe that the "all-rounded person," a mediocre citizen rather than a "superlative" specialist, was a decisive force in allowing Americans to obtain only modest returns from their schools. Today, de Tocqueville would find that the benefits from schooling, particularly high school diplomas and college degrees, have a cash value and are indispensable in the economic and social ratings that come with the new "meritocracy."

De Tocqueville, in his time, would also have argued that America, although a land of inventors, could not produce "great scholars, poets, artists, or authors." This early nineteenth-century observer suggested that, where practical utility was important, Americans excelled, but that, where "meditation and 'the pursuit' of truth for its own sake" predominated, Americans were unsuccessful. This viewpoint, which labels Americans as a practical people, but devoid of sensibilities for the contemplative, to some extent, still influences foreign commentary on American education, particularly higher education. However, the intervening century since de Tocqueville wrote has seen Americans become deeply involved in the development of aesthetic education, the endowment of the performing arts, and a valiant attempt to integrate humanistic and scientific studies in the general education of both her high school and college students.

The endowment of education (particularly higher education) through legislative appropriations and by private philanthropic foundations at least demonstrates to the foreigner that Americans *were* and more than ever *are* prepared to consider education as a form of both personal and national investment.

In 1900 the German educator, A. Wallage, for example, observed that Americans "gladly pay right large costs and without a murmur give to education more than any other country in the world . . . it is in general a striking characteristic of the American people to appropriate splendid sums of money for the erection and maintenance of schoolhouses and equipment."[24]

But the commentator from Europe in 1900 would find it difficult to make the same observations without considerable qualification sixty years later. He would be awed by the developments that have taken place, the diversity of educational institutions, and the materialistic hold (or promise) that they have developed on American life. He would also note that the availability of education in America, although guaranteed at the primary and secondary level for all up to the age of seventeen or eighteen, cannot truly be guaranteed for all those who wish to have a higher education. In the mid 1970's, ten million Americans will probably be enrolled in colleges and universities, assuming that adequate financial provisions have been met in the next few years. However, for the present, it appears that Americans are simply not making sufficient funds available through taxation, bond issues, and investment loans, or foundation grants to guarantee the fulfillment espoused by many educators of a national ideal of a system of "universal higher education."

The enthusiastic note that Wallage uttered in 1900, whether an accurate description or even a comparatively useful one, is in sharp contrast with a Soviet view of American education given some sixty years later. Zoya Malkova, a leading Soviet comparative educator long familiar with

[24] A. Wallage, "Ein Nordamerikanisches Lehrerseminar," *Deutsche Zeitschrift für Ausländisches Unterrichtswesen*, No. 6 (1900), p. 106.

the American educational scene, commented pertinently on the increasing problems of financing American education. She notes the blatant utilitarian and commercial aspects involved suggesting:

A university education in the United States is an expensive thing and by no means can everyone afford it . . . Many Americans who wish to educate their children at a university begin to save money for their studies as soon as the child is born. There are banks and companies that specialize in this type of savings. Here is an advertisement by one of these companies which we heard daily on television:

Are you preparing your son or daughter for college? In every family the cost of education is the largest expense after the purchase of a home. You can avoid worrying if you begin to put away money now and utilize the services of our company.[25]

The author pointedly states that "all types of schools in the U.S.S.R., including the institutions of higher education are free," and that "students" receive government allowances.[26]

It may be beside the point here to note for the Soviet author that NDEA loans and fellowships, work-study programs of the federal and state governments, plus the institutional supported scholarship and assistantship programs in America do provide a somewhat modified picture than what may be implied solely by her statement. But unfortunately, the truth of the matter is that American universities have observed with increasing concern that federal and state governments, at a fully subsidized level, are unable to provide sufficient facilities for every American who wishes to have a higher education. The intervening years between the German and Russian commentaries above represent a span of educational development, school expansion, and concomitant knowledge explosion that surpasses collectively and cumulatively all the earlier years of American education.

The purpose of the documentary collection that follows is to illustrate some of the highlights of American educational history since the turn of the century. The collection is arranged in two parts for the reader's convenience. Part I reflects foreign views of American education in general as well as some particular aspects of elementary and secondary schooling. Part II is concerned with higher education in America, college teaching, the status of professors, and the behavior of students. Although it may be possible, it is not deemed feasible here to provide, in strict chronological or topical order, a collection of articles treating *all* aspects

---

[25] Zoya Malkova, *Soviet Education* [trans.], Vol. V, No. 2 (1962), p. 53.
[26] *Ibid.*

of American education: hence, for convenience, the division into articles on precollegiate schooling and those concerning higher education. Considerations of time and space preclude a complete bibliographical collection, but a perusal of the references given at the conclusion of this book will provide the reader with a variety of excellent articles, many of which could substitute equally well for some of the essays that actually are included in this collection.

Just prior to presenting these articles written during the last sixty years, it seems appropriate to note the thoughtful *caveat* of Robert Edward Hughes concerning the "correct" evaluation of "foreign systems of education." Hughes, an English educator made a special study of American education and placed it clearly in comparative perspective with England and Germany. Not only was his evaluative warning, uttered in 1900, perceptive then but his views on the future course and limitations of international studies in education were also to become topics of controversy among comparative educators. He stated:

Each system of education can only be understood when seen in its own setting. Each is an expression of its nation's genius; it is characteristic of its people. In so far as it is thriving it is truly popular, and only so far as it is popular and peculiar is it national. The 'habitat' of each system is fixed, it is an indigenous product; consequently it is not only unscientific, but it is impossible to measure comprehensively any system of national education in terms of another. These systems cannot be arranged in order of merit. The finer elements, the more ethical and spiritual factors in national culture, defy the balance of the analyst and the scalpel of the anatomist; they are susceptible to no quantitative tests.

Thus the whole drift of our investigations points to this one main conclusion: every country has, in the main, that system of training best adapted to its present needs, and most capable of developing in such a way as to meet future national needs.

Although, however, each system is, as we have said, characteristic, yet they all reveal certain general tendencies which show unmistakably the growth of world-citizenship that is going on all over the globe.[27]

[27] Robert Edward Hughes, *The Making of Citizens: A Study in Comparative Education* (London: The Walter Scott Publishing Company, Ltd., 1902), p. 387.

Part 1

EDUCATION, GENERAL: ELEMENTARY AND SECONDARY

1

School Reform

I feel myself, on the whole, pretty free from autobiographical tendencies; I am quite ready to double the number of my years, at least, before I begin upon memories and confessions. At one point only has the desire for an autobiographical eruption grown in me steadily: I am impelled to tell the story of my school time.

I remember exactly how the impulse took shape in my mind. It was at a teachers' meeting. The teachers were discussing how to relieve the overburdening of the school children, and how to make tolerable the drudgery of the classroom. Some demonstrated that all the trouble came from the old-fashioned idea of prescribed courses: if the courses were freely chosen, according to the talents and interests of the pupils, their sufferings would be ended. Others maintained that the teachers were guilty: that they did not know enough about educational aims, about child study and psychology and the theory of education. What else than drudgery was to be expected, under such inadequate pedagogues? The fight between the two parties went on with an inspiring fullness of argument, and thus I fell into a deep and sound sleep. And the sleep carried me away from the elms of New England to my dear old home on the shore of the Baltic Sea, where I spent my school days. I saw once more my classmates and my teachers; I strolled once more, as a little boy with my schoolbooks, through the quaint streets of Danzig; I passed again through the feelings of more than twenty years ago. Suddenly I awoke at the stroke of the gavel of the chairman, who solemnly announced that the majority had voted for a compromise: the community ought to see to it that both free election and the pedagogical information of the teachers were furthered. At this point the meeting was adjourned, and the teachers went to the next hall for luncheon: there some minor speeches were served up, on the pernicious influence of the classical languages, and on the value of stenography and typewrit-

Hugo Münsterberg. "School Reform," *The Atlantic Monthly*, Vol. LXXXV (May, 1900), pp. 656–669. Reprinted by kind permission of the publishers of *The Atlantic Monthly*, Boston, Massachusetts.

Author (1863–1916): Educated Danzig Gymnasium; Leipzig and Heidelberg Universities; he taught at Freiburg University and later served as Professor of Psychology at Harvard University from 1892–1910.

ing for a liberal education. It was then that the autobiography budded in my mind. My instinct told me that I must make haste in the undertaking; for if I should hear, for some years to come, all these sighs of pity for those who were instructed without election and pedagogy, I might finally get confused, and extend the same pity to my own childhood, convinced that my school life was a deplorable misfortune. I hasten, therefore, to publish this chapter of my life's story as advance sheets, some decades before the remainder, at a period when the gap of time is still small enough to be bridged by a fair memory.

My great-grandfather lived in Silesia. But perhaps it may be too long a story if I develop my case from its historical beginning; I will shorten it by saying at once that I entered the gymnasium in Danzig at nine years of age, and left it at eighteen. I had previously attended a private preparatory school, and subsequently I went to the universities of Leipzig and Heidelberg. It is the gymnasium period about which I want to speak. I have no right to boast of it; I was a model neither of industry nor of carefulness. I was not quite so bad as some of my best friends among my classmates, but I see, with serious repentance, from the reports which I have carefully kept together, that I was not attentive enough in Latin grammar; it seems that in the lower classes, also, my French did not find the full appreciation of my teachers, and I should feel utterly ashamed to report what their misled judgment recorded of my singing and drawing. I was just a fair average. The stages of knowledge which we reached may most easily be characterized by a comparison with the standards of New England. At fifteen years I was in *Untersekunda;* and there is not the slightest doubt that, at that stage, all my classmates and I were prepared to pass the entrance examinations for Harvard College. As a matter of course, German must here be substituted for English, German history and literature for the English correspondents. We should have chosen, at our entrance, that scheme in which both Latin and Greek are taken. The *Abiturientenexamen* at the end of the school time, the examination which opens the door to the university, came three years later. It was a difficult affair, somewhat more difficult than in recent years; and, from a pretty careful analysis of the case, I can say that very few Harvard students have entered the senior class who would have been able to pass that examination respectably. In the smaller colleges of the country, the senior might be expected to reach that level at graduation. No doubt, even after substituting German for English, almost every senior may have taken one or many courses which lie fully outside of the circle in which we moved. The college man who specializes in political economy or philosophy or chemistry from his freshman year knows, in his special field, far more than any one of us knew; but if we take a composite picture of all seniors, the boy who leaves the gymnasium is not at a disadvantage in the comparison of intellectual physiognomy, while he is far less mature according to his much lower age. If any man in Dartmouth or Amherst takes his bachelor's degree with that knowledge in mathematics, history, geography, literature, Latin, Greek, French, and physics which we had on leaving school, he is sure to graduate with honors. Our entrance into the university can thus be compared merely with the entrance into the post-graduate courses. Our three highest gymnasium classes alone correspond to the college; and whoever compares the German university with the American college, instead of with the graduate school, is misled either by the age of the students or by the external forms of student life and instruction.

I reached thus, at the end of my school time, as a pupil of average standing, the scholarly level of an average college graduate in this country. I was then eighteen years of age; the average bachelor of arts is at least three years older. How did that difference come about? The natural explanation of the case is that we poor boys were overburdened, systematically tortured by a cruel system of overwork, which absorbed all our energies for the one goal, the passing of the examination. I do not dare to contradict. But the one thing I may claim in favor of this scheme of overloading is the wonderful skill with which the school administration was able to hide these evident facts so completely from our eyes that neither my classmates nor I, nor our parents, nor our teachers themselves, ever perceived the slightest trace of them. The facts were so shamelessly concealed from us that we poor deceived boys thought all the time that the work was a pleasure, that we had leisure for everything, and that every one of us was as happy as a fish in water.

I think that I spent, during all those ten years, about three hours a day in the fresh air, walking and playing, swimming and skating; yet I found time from my ninth year to practice on the violoncello one hour every day, and the novels which I wrote may have lacked everything else, but they never lacked length. Besides such individual schemes to fill our vacant time, we coöperated for that purpose in clubs, from the lowest classes to the highest: at ten years we played instructive games; at twelve years we read classical dramas, each taking one rôle; at fifteen we read papers on art and literature; and at seventeen we had a regular debating club. And all the time, at every stage, there were private theatricals, and excursions into the country, and dancing lessons, and horseback-riding, and coeducation with the education left out; for the poor overburdened girls helped us to bear the load by suffering in common.

Every one of us had, of course, the minor special interests and amusements which suited his own taste; there was no lack of opportunity to follow up these inclinations; to use the terminology of modern pedagogy, we "found" ourselves. I found myself, too; but—and in this respect I did not behave exactly according to the prescribed scheme of this same pedagogy, I am sorry to say—I found myself every two or three years, as some one very different from the former individual whom I had had the pleasure to discover. In the first years of my school time botany was all my desire. We lived in the summer in a country house with a large garden, and a forest near the garden; and every minute I could spare belonged to the plants which I collected and pressed. It became a boyish passion. If I had to write a novel, this feature of the botanical enthusiasm of the boy would be a very poor invention, if the final outcome were to be a being who has hardly the talent to discriminate a mushroom from an apple tree, and for whom nothing in the world appears so dry as squeezed plants. But I have not to invent here: I am reporting. I thus confess frankly my weakness for dissected vegetables: it lasted about three years. Then came my passion for physical instruments: an uncle gave me on my birthday some dainty little electrical machines, and soon the whole house was overspun with electrical wires. I was thus, at twelve years, on the best road to discover the patent-hunter in my personality, when a friend with ministerial inclinations interfered: we began to study comparative religion, Islamism in particular. Thus, at fifteen years of age we learned Arabic from the grammar, and read the Koran. Now, finally, my true nature was found; my friend wrote prophetically in my album that we should both go out as missionaries to the Arabs,—and yet I missed the connection, and went to Boston instead of to Mecca, and forgot on the way all my Arabic. But trouble began soon afterward: friends of mine found, in digging on their farm, an old Slavic grave containing interesting urns. I became fascinated by ethnological discoveries, and, as important excavations were going on in the neighborhood of my native town, I spent every free afternoon and whole vacation weeks in the ethnological camp, studied the literature of the subject and dug up urns for our town museum, and wrote, at the age of seventeen, a never published book on the prehistoric anthropology of West Prussia. Then the happy school days came to an end, and yet I had not found myself. I have never dug any more. I did not become an ethnologist, and if a visitor to Cambridge insists on my showing him the Harvard sights, and we come into the ethnological museum, the urns bore me so utterly that it is hard for me to believe that in earlier days they made all my happiness. I went, then, to the university with something like a liberal education; supplemented the school studies by some broader studies in literature, science, and philosophy; and when, in the middle of my philosophical studies, I came to psychology, the lightning struck. Exactly ten years after leaving school, years devoted to psychological studies and psychological teaching in German universities, Harvard called me over the ocean as professor of psychology. I thus found my life work; and in all these years I have never had an hour in which I doubted that it was my life work. Yet I did not approach it, in spite of all those various fancy interests, before I reached the intellectual level of the graduate school.

I have spoken of these boyish passions not only to show that we had an abundance of free time and the best opportunities for the growth of individual likings, but for the purpose of emphasizing—and I add this with all the gratitude of my heart to my parents, my teachers, and the community—that the school never took the smallest account of those inclinations, and never allowed me to take the slightest step aside from the prescribed school work. My school work was not adjusted to botany at nine years because I played with an herbarium, and at twelve to physics because I indulged in noises with home-made electric bells, and at fifteen to Arabic,—an elective which I miss still in several high schools, even in Brookline and Roxbury. The more my friends and I wandered afield with our little superficial interests and talents and passions, the more was the straightforward earnestness of the school our blessing; and all that beautified and enriched our youth, and gave to it freshness and liveliness, would have turned out to be our ruin, if our elders had taken it seriously, and had formed a life's programme out of petty caprices and boyish inclinations. I still remember how my father spoke to me, when I was a boy of twelve. I was insisting that Latin was of no use to me, as I should become a poet or a physicist. He answered: "If a lively boy has to follow a country road, it is a natural and good thing for him to stroll a hundred times from the way, and pick flowers and run for butterflies over the fields on both sides of the road. But if we say to him, 'There is no road for you; follow your butterflies,' where will he find himself at nightfall?"

My question was, how our German school made it possible to bring us so much more quickly, without overburdening us, to the level of the American senior. I have given so far only a negative characteristic of the school in saying that it made no concession to individual likings and preferences: that is of course not a sufficient explanation. If I think back, I feel sure the chief source of this success was the teachers. But in regard to the teachers, also, I may begin with a negative statement: our teachers did not know anything about the theory of education, or about the history of pedagogy or psychology; and while I heard about some of them gossip of a rather malicious kind, I never heard that any one of them had read a book on child study. The other day I found in a paper on secondary education a lamentation to this effect: that the American schools have still many teachers who have no reflective theories on the aim with which they teach their subjects, and the educational values which belong to them. The author said: "I shall not soon forget the surprise with which an intelligent teacher said to me, not long ago, 'An aim! I have no aim in teaching; that is a new idea.'" "Such teachers of Latin and algebra," the author compassionately added, "meant that the choice of these subjects as fit subject-matter of instruction was no concern of theirs; they taught these subjects as best they could, because these subjects were in the course of study." Exactly such old-fashioned teachers were ours. My literature teacher was never troubled by the suspicion that literature may be less useful than meteorology and organic chemistry, neither of which had a place in our school; and if some one had asked my Greek teacher, "What is the value of the instruction in Greek? What is your aim in reading Sophocles and Plato with your young friends in the class?" he would have answered that he had never thought about it, any more than why he was willing to breathe and to live. He taught his Greek as best he could in the place to which he was called, but he certainly never took it as his concern to reflect whether Greek instruction ought not, after all, to be discontinued; he left that to the principal and to the government. His Plato and his Sophocles, his Homer and Thucydides, were to him life and happiness, and to share them with us was an instinctive desire, which would have lost its enthusiasm and inspiration if he had tried to base it on arguments.

But this thought has led me from the negative characteristics of my teachers to a rather positive one,—yes, to the most positive one which I felt in them,—to the one which was the real secret of our German school: my teachers were enthusiastic on the subjects they taught, as only those who know them thoroughly ever can be. I had no teacher who hastily learned one day what he must teach me the next; who was satisfied with second–hand knowledge, which is quite pretty for entertainment and orientation, but which is so intolerable and inane when we come to distribute it and to give it to others. I had from my ninth year no teacher in any subject who had not completed three years' work in the graduate school. Even the first elements of Greek and mathematics, of history and geography, were given to us by men who had reached the level of the doctorate, and who had the perspective of their own fields. They had seen their work with the eye of the scholar, and thus even the most elementary material of their science was raised to the height of scholarly interest. Elements taken for themselves alone are trivial and empty everywhere, and to teach them is an intolerable drudgery, which fills the schoolroom with dullness and the pupils with aversion. Elements as the introductory part of a scholarly system are of ever new and fascinating interest, more promising and enjoyable than any complex problems. A great poet once said that any man who has ever really loved in his youth can never become quite unhappy in life. A man who has ever really taken a scholarly view of his science can never find in that science anything which is quite uninteresting. Such enthusiasm is contagious. We boys felt that our teachers believed with the fullness of their hearts in the inner value of the subjects, and every new bit of knowledge was thus for us a new revelation. We did not ask whether it would bake bread for us. We were eager for it on account of its own inner richness and value; and this happy living in an atmosphere of such ideal belief in the inner worth and glory of literature and history, of science and thought, was our liberal education.

I know it would be wrong to explain our being three years ahead of a New England boy merely by the scholarly preparation of our teachers. A second factor, which is hardly less important, stands clear before my mind, too: the help which the school found in our homes. I do not mean that we were helped in our work, but the teachers were silently helped by the spirit which prevailed in our homes with regard to the school work. The school had the right of way; our parents reinforced our belief in the work and our respect for the teachers. A reprimand in the school was a shadow on our home life; a word of praise in the school was a ray of sunshine for the household. The excellent schoolbooks, the wise plans for the upbuilding of the ten years' course, the hygienic care, the external stimulations,—all, of course, helped toward the results; and yet I am convinced that their effect was entirely secondary compared with these two features,—the scholarly enthusiasm of our teachers, and the respect for the school on the part of our parents.

No one can jump over his shadow. I cannot suddenly leave all my memories and experiences behind me, and when I behold the onward rush of our school reformers, I cannot forget my past; I may admire their good will, but I cannot accept their bad arguments. I do not speak here as a psychologist; I know quite well that some consider the psychologist a pedagogical expert, who brings the profoundest information directly from his laboratory to the educational witness stand. No such power has come to me. I do not know whether my professional brethren have had pleasanter experiences, but I have always found Psychology silent as a sphinx, when I came to her with the question of what we ought to do in the walks of practical life. When I asked her about the true and the false, she was most loquacious; but when I came to her about the good and the bad, seeking advice and help, she never vouchsafed me a word. I confess that I have, therefore, slowly become a little skeptical as to whether she is really more communicative with my psychological friends, or whether they do not simply take her perfect silence for a welcome affirmation of all their own thoughts and wishes. I thus come to the question of school reform without any professional authority; I come to it simply with the warm interest of a man who has children in the schools, who has daily contact with students just out of school, and who has not forgotten his own school time.

The most essential feature of all recent school reforms—or, with a less question–begging title, I should say school experiments, or school changes, or school deteriorations—has been the tendency toward elective studies. But I am in doubt whether we should consider it really as one tendency only; the name covers two very different tendencies, whose practical result is externally similar. We have on one side the desire to adjust the school work to the final purposes of the individual in practical life; which means beginning professional preparation in that period which up to this time has been given over to liberal education. We have on the other side the desire to adjust the school work to the innate talents and likings of the individual, which means giving in the school work no place to that which finds inner resistance in the pupil. In the first case the university method filters down to the school; in the second case the kindergarten method creeps up to the school. In the one case the liberal education of the school is replaced by professional education; in the other case the liberal education is replaced by liberal play. If one of the two tendencies were working alone, its imminent danger would be felt at once; but as they seem to coöperate, the one working from the bottom and the other from the top, each hides for the moment the defects of the other. And yet the coincidence is almost accidental and entirely superficial; both desire to make concessions to individual differences. Peter and Paul ought not to have the same school education, we are told; but the essential question what, after all, Peter ought to learn in school must be answered very differently, according as we look at it from the point of view of the kindergarten or from the point of view of professional life; as there is indeed a difference whether I ask what may best suit the taste and liking of Peter the darling, or whether I ask what Peter the man will need for the battle of life, in which nobody asks what he likes, but where the question is how he is liked, and how he suits the tastes of his neighbors. The one method treats the boy as a child, and the other treats the boy as a man. Nothing is common to them, after all, except the result that boyhood loses its opportunity for a liberal education, which ought to borrow from the kindergarten merely its remoteness from practical professional life, and from professional work merely its seriousness. Neither tendency stands alone in our social life. In short, the one fits the mercenary spirit of our time, and the other fits its spirit of selfish enjoyment. From the standpoint of social philosophy, mercenary utilitarianism and selfish materialism belong together; everywhere do they grow together, and everywhere do they fight together against the spirit of idealism. But while they fight together, they march to the battlefield on very different roads.

Practical life demands division of labor, and therefore the specialization of the individual. The argument which urges the earliest possible beginning of this specialization is thus a natural one; and the conviction that the struggle for existence must become more difficult with the growing complexity of modern life may encourage the view that the remedy lies in professional training at the expense of all other education. The lawyer and the physician need so many facts for the efficiency of their work that it seems a waste of energy to burden the future lawyer with the knowledge of natural sciences, and the future physician with the knowledge of history. If this is true, however, we ought to begin still earlier: on the first day in the kindergarten, I should show my little lawyer two cakes, and explain to him that one is his cake, and the other is not,—social information which does not lie in the line of my little naturalist; and I should tell the other little fellow that one cake has plums, and the other has not,—scientific instruction which is without concern for the future lawyer. But even if I shape my school according to such schemes, do I really reach, after all, the goal at which I am aiming? Does not the utilitarian spirit deceive itself? And even if we do not acknowledge any other standpoint but the mercenary one, is not the calculation very superficial? The laborer in the mill may be put, sometimes, by the cruelty of the age of steam, in a place where his personality as a whole is crippled, and only one small function is in use; but the higher the profession, the more nearly is the whole man working in every act, and the more, therefore, is a broad general education necessary to practical efficiency. The biologists tell us that the play of animals is a biologically necessary preparation for the struggle of existence, and that, in a parallel way, also, the playing of the child is the wise scheme of nature to prepare man in some respect for the struggles of life. How infinitely more does that hold for the widening of the mind by a well-planned liberal education!

The higher the level on which the professional specializing begins, the more effective it is. I have said that we German boys did not think of any specialization and individual variation before we reached a level corresponding to the college graduation here. In this country, the college must still go on for a while playing the double rôle of the place for the general education of the one, and the workshop for the professional training of the other; but at least the high school ought to be faithful to its only goal of general education without professional anticipations. Moreover, we are not only professional wage-earners: we live for our friends and our nation; we face social and political, moral and religious problems; we are in contact with nature and science, with art and literature; we shape our town and our time, and all that is common to every one,—to the banker and the manufacturer, to the minister and the teacher, to the lawyer and the physician. The technique of our profession, then, appears only as a small variation of the large background of work in which we all share; and if the education must be adapted to our later life, all these problems demand a uniform education for the members of the same social community. The division of labor lies on the outside. We are specialists in our handiwork, but our heart work is uniform, and the demand for individualized education emphasizes the small differences in our tasks, and ignores the great similarities.

And after all, who is able to say what a boy of twelve years will need for his special life work? It is easily said in a school programme that the course will be adapted to the needs of the particular pupil with respect to his later life, but it would be harder to say how we are to find out what the boy does need; and even if we know it, the straight line to the goal is not always the shortest way.

The one need of my individual fate, compared with that of other German boys, is the English language, and the one great blank in the prescribed programme of our gymnasium was the total absence of instruction in English. Yet I have such unlimited confidence in the wisdom of my teachers that I cannot help thinking they knew quite well how my case stood. When I was twelve years old, I can imagine, the principal of the school said in a faculty meeting: "This boy will need the English language later, to philosophize on the other side of the ocean, and he ought to begin now to learn it, in time for his professional work; to get the free time for it we must eliminate the Greek from his course." But then my dear little gray-haired Greek teacher arose, and said with indignation: "No, sir: the bit of English which is necessary to lecture to students, and to address teachers' meetings, and to write for The *Atlantic Monthly* can be learned at any time, but Greek he will never learn if he does not learn it now; and if he does not have it, he will never get that inspiration which may make his scholarly work worth calling him over the ocean. Only if he studies Greek will they call him to use English; but if he learns only English, he will never have the chance to use it." That settled my case, and so came about the curious chance that I accepted the professorship at Harvard without having spoken a single word of English in my life; and I still thank my old Greek teacher, who is long since dead, for his decision. Yes, as I think it over, I am inclined to believe that it is just so in most cases: if we prepare for the one thing, we shall have a chance for the other; but if we wisely prepare at once for the other, our chance for it will never come. Life is, after all, not so easily manufactured as the advertising circular of a private boarding school, in which everything is exactly adapted to the individual needs.

This elective adjustment of the studies to the later professional work and business of the man plays a large part in the theoretical discussions, and there acts effectively on the crowd through the promise of professional success; but it strikes me that this utilitarian appeal works, on the whole, for the interest of that other kind of electivism which promises ease through the adjustment of the school to the personal inclinations. It seems to me that, in the practical walks of education, this is by far the stronger impulse to election. Even in the college, where most boys have at least a dim idea of what they want to do in life, the election with reference to the later occupation plays usually a secondary rôle; liking is the great ruler. The university method was powerless in the school reform, did it not act as agent for the kindergarten method. This leading plea for electives takes the following form: All instruction must be interesting; if the pupil's interest is not in it, the whole instruction is dead matter, useless vexation. Everything which appeals to the natural tastes and instincts of the child is interesting. Instruction, therefore, must be adjusted to the natural instincts and tastes.

The logical fallacy of this ought to be evident. All instruction which is good must be interesting; but does it follow therefrom that all instruction which is interesting must also be good? Is it not possible that there are kinds of interest which are utterly bad and destructive? All that appeals to the natural tastes and instincts is interesting; does it follow that nothing is interesting which goes beyond the natural instincts? Is it not savage life to follow merely the instincts and natural desires? Is not all the meaning of education just to discriminate between good and bad desires; to suppress the lower instincts, and to reinforce the higher; above all, to awake new desires, to build up new interests, to create new instincts? If civilization, with its instruments of home and school education, could not overcome our natural tastes and instinctive desires, we should remain forever children whose attention is captured by everything that excites and shines. The street tune would expel the symphony, the prize fight would overcome the drama, the yellow press and the dime novel would be our literature; our social life would be vulgar, our public life hysterical, and our intellectual life a mixture of cheap gossip and sensational news with practical schemes for comfort and advertisement. Yes, instruction must be full of interest; but whether instruction is good or bad, is in the spirit of civilization or against it, depends upon the question what sort of interest is in the play: that which vulgarizes, or that which refines; that which the street boy brings from the slums to the school, or that which the teacher brings from the graduate school to the country classroom. The more internal the motives which capture the attention, the higher the mental functions to which we appeal, the more we are really educators. The platform is no variety show; the boys must be inspired, but not amused.

I am not afraid to push my heresy even to the point of seeing with serious doubts the rapidly growing tendency toward the demonstrative method in scientific instruction. No doubt all such illustrations strongly appeal to common sense; our happy children, the public thinks, see and touch everything, where we had only words on words. But the words appealed to a higher power than the demonstrations: those spoke to the understanding, these to the perception; those gave us the laws, these the accidental realizations. No demonstration, no experiment, can really show us the totality of a law; it shows us always only one special case, which as such is quite unimportant. Its importance lies in the necessity which can be expressed merely by words, and never by apparatus. The deeper meaning of naturalistic instruction is by far more fully present in the book than in the instrument; and while it is easier to teach and to learn natural science when it appeals to the eye rather than to the reason, I doubt whether it has, from a higher standpoint, the same educational value, just as I doubt whether the doll with a silk dress and a phonograph in the chest has the same value for the development of the child at play that the simple little wooden doll has. The question of scientific instruction is, of course, far too complex to be analyzed here; the method of demonstrations has some good features; and above all, the other kind of instruction, to be valuable at all, needs much better teachers than those whom the schools have at their disposal. I wish only to point out that even here, where the popular agreement is unanimous, very serious hestitation is possible.

I have spoken of the damage to the subject-matter of instruction, which results from the limitation of the work to personal taste; but there is also a formal side of education, which is to me more important. A child who has himself the right of choice, or who sees that parents and teachers select the courses according to his tastes and inclinations, may learn a thousand pretty things, but never the one which is the greatest of all: to do his duty. He who is allowed always to follow the paths of least resistance never develops the power to overcome resistance; he remains utterly unprepared for life. To do what we like to do,—that needs no pedagogical encouragement: water always runs downhill. Our whole public and social life shows the working of this impulse, and our institutions outbid one another in catering to the taste of the public. The school alone has the power to develop the opposite tendency, to encourage and train the belief in duties and obligations, to inspire devotion to better things than those to which we are drawn by our lower instincts. Yes, water runs downhill all the time; and yet all the earth were sterile and dead if water could not ascend again to the clouds, and supply rain to the field which brings us the harvest. We see only the streams going down to the ocean; we do not see how the ocean sends up the waters to bless our fields. Just so do we see in the streams of life the human emotions following the impulses down to selfishness and pleasure and enjoyment, but we do not see how the human emotions ascend again to the ideals,—ascend in feelings of duty and enthusiasm; and yet without this upward movement our fields were dry, our harvest lost. That invisible work is the sacred mission of the school; it is the school that must raise man's mind from his likings to his belief in duties, from his instincts to his ideals, that art and science, national honor and morality, friendship and religion, may spring from the ground and blossom.

But I go further: are elective studies really elected at all? I mean, do they really represent the deeper desires and demands of the individual, or do they not simply express the cumulation of a hundred chance influences? I have intentionally lingered on the story of my shifting interests in my boyhood; it is more or less the story of every halfway-intelligent boy or girl. A little bit of talent, a pretty caprice favored by accident, a contagious craze or fad, a chance demand for something of which scarcely the outside is known,—all these whir and buzz in every boyhood; but to follow such superficial moods would mean dissolution of all organized life, and education would be an empty word. Election which is more than a chance grasping presupposes first of all acquaintance with the object of our choice. Even in the college two thirds of the elections are haphazard, controlled by accidental motives; election of courses demands a wide view and broad knowledge of the whole field. The lower the level on which the choice is made, the more external and misleading are the motives which direct it. A helter-skelter chase of the unknown is no election. If a man who does not know French goes into a restaurant where the bill of fare is given in the

French language, and points to one and to another line, not knowing whether his order is fish or roast or pudding, the waiter will bring him a meal, but we cannot say that he has "elected his courses."

From whatever standpoint I view it, the tendency to base the school on elective studies seems to me a mistake,—a mistake for which, of course, not a special school, but the social consciousness is to be blamed. I cannot think much better of that second tendency of which I spoke,— the tendency to improve the schools by a pedagogical-psychological preparation of the teachers. I said that, just as I had no right of election over my courses, my teachers had no idea of pedagogy and psychology. I do not think that they would have been better teachers with such wisdom than without it. I doubt, even, whether it would not have changed things for the worse. I do not believe in lyrics which are written after the prescriptions of aesthetics; I have the fullest respect for the scholar in poetical theory, but he ought not to make the poets believe that they need his advice before they dare to sing. Psychology is a wonderful science, and pedagogy, as soon as we shall have it, may be a wonderful science, too, and very important for school organizers, for superintendents and city officials, but the individual teacher has little practical use for it. I have discussed this point so often before the public that I am unwilling to repeat my arguments here. I have again and again shown that in the practical contact of the schoolroom the teacher can never gain that kind of knowledge of the child which would enable him to get the right basis for psychological calculation, and that psychology itself is unable to do justice to the demands of the individual case. I have tried to show how conscious occupation with pedagogical rules interferes with instinctive views of right peda- gogical means; and, above all, how the analytic tendency of the psycho- logical and pedagogical attitude is diametrically opposite to that practi- cal attitude, full of tact and sympathy, which we must demand of the real teacher; and that the training in the one attitude inhibits freedom in the other. And when I see that teachers sometimes interpret my warning as if I wished merely to say, "I, as a psychologist, dislike to have any one approach the science with the purely practical question whether it bakes bread, instead of with a purely theoretical interest," I must object to that interpretation. I did not wish merely to say that the bread question would better be delayed; no, the teacher ought to know from the beginning that if he takes the bread which psychology bakes, indigestion must follow.

Yet I do not mean to be narrow. I do not think that if teachers go through psychological and pedagogical studies they really will suffer very much; they will do with them what they do with most studies,—they will forget them. And if they forget them, what harm, then,—why all this fighting against it, as if a danger were in quesion? This brings me, finally, to my last but chief point: I think, indeed, that great dangers do exist, and that the psychopedagogical movement does serious damage, not so much because it affects the teacher, but because it, together with the elective studies, turns the attention of the public from the only essential and important point, upon which, I feel deeply convinced, the true reform of our schools is dependent,—the better instruction of our teachers. That was the secret, I said, in our German schools; the most elementary teaching was given by men who were experts in their field, who had the perspective of it, and whose scholarly interest filled them with an enthusiasm that inspired the class. To bring that condition about must be the aim of every friend of American school life. That is the one great reform which is needed, and till this burning need is removed it is useless to put forward unimportant changes. These little pseudo-reforms become, indeed, a wrong, if they make the public forget that true help and true reform are demanded. If a child is crying because it is ill, we may keep it quiet for a while by a piece of candy, but we do not make it well; and it is a wrong to quiet it, if its silence makes us omit to call the physician to cure it. The elective studies and the pedagogical courses are such sweetmeats for the school. The schools were bad, and the public was dissatisfied; now the elective studies relieve the discomfort of the children, in the place of the old vexation they have a good time, and the parents are glad that the drudgery is over. And when, nevertheless, a complaint arises, and the parents discover that the children do not learn anything and that they become disrespectful, then there comes the chance for the man with the psychological—and pedagogical—training; he is not a better teacher, but he can talk about the purposes of the new education till all is covered by beautiful words; and thus parents and children are happily satisfied for a while, till the time comes when the nation has to pay for its neglect in failing really to cure the sick child. Just as it has been said that war needs three things, money, money, and again money, so it can be said with much greater truth that education needs, not forces and buildings, not pedagogy and demonstrations, but only men, men, and again men,—without forbidding that some, not too many of them, shall be women.

The right kind of men is what the schools need; they have the wrong kind. They need teachers whose interest in the subject would banish all drudgery, and they have teachers whose pitiable unpreparedness makes the class work either so superficial that the pupils do not learn anything, or, if it is taken seriously, so dry and empty that it is a vexation for children and teachers alike. To produce anything equivalent to the teaching staff from whose guidance I benefited in my boyhood, no one ought to be allowed to teach in a grammar school who has not passed through a college or a good normal school; no one ought to teach in a high school who has not worked, after his college course, at least two years in the graduate school of a good university; no one ought to teach in a college who has not taken his doctor's degree in one of the best universities; and no one ought to teach in a graduate school who has not shown his mastery of method by powerful scientific publications. We have instead a misery which can be characterized by one statistical fact: only two percent of the school-teachers possess any degree whatever. If the majority of college teachers are hardly prepared to teach in a secondary school, if the majority of high-school teachers are hardly fit to teach in a primary school, and if the majority of primary-school teachers are just enough educated to fill a salesgirl's place in a millinery store, then every other reform is self-deceit.

I do not feel at all surprised that many of my brethren who are seriously interested in the progress of education rush forward in the wrong direction. They have been brought up under the prescribed system with teachers who did not know pedagogy, and they feel instinctively that the schools are bad and need reform. It is only natural for them to think that the prescriptive system is guilty, and that pedagogy can help us; they are so filled with aversion to the old-fashioned school that they think only of the matter which they were taught, and the method after which they were taught; but as they have no standard of comparison in their own experience, they never imagine that it may have been the men alone, the teachers, who were responsible for the failures. These friends have never experienced what my classmates and I enjoyed,—prescribed courses with expert teachers. They do not and cannot imagine the revolution as soon as a teacher stands on the platform who has the inspiring enthusiasm for his science which springs from a profound scholarly knowledge. No pedagogical technique can be substituted for this only real preparation of the teacher; and I fear that pedagogy must become a hindrance to educational progress, if it ever causes the principal or the school board to prefer the teacher who has learned pedagogy to the teacher who has learned the subject he is going to teach.

But my German memories not only arouse in me a pessimism with regard to those pseudo-reforms; they give me also most optimistic hopes with regard to a point which may be raised as an objection to my views. The teaching staff is bad indeed, it has often been said, but how can we hope for an improvement? The boys leave the high school at eighteen years of age, the college at twenty-two; how can we hope that an average high-school teacher will devote a still larger part of his life to the preparation for his professional work, and will spend two or three years more in a graduate school before he begins to earn his living? This argument is utterly wrong, as it neglects the interrelation of the different factors. If we had thoroughly prepared teachers, the aims of the school would be reached here just as quickly as in Germany, where, as I have shown, the level of American high-school graduation is attained at fifteen years, and the level of American average college graduation at eighteen or nineteen. Time which, with the teachers of to-day, is hardly sufficient to bring a man through a good high school would then be enough to give him a college education, and the time which to-day is necessary to pull him through college should be enough to give him three years in the graduate school. I was twenty-two when I took my doctor's degree in Leipzig, and so were most of my friends. The change cannot come suddenly; but as soon as the public recognizes in what direction true school reform must lie, it can be brought about by a slow, persistent pushing along that line. If the schools insist more and more on the solid scholarship of the teachers, the time in which the ends of the school are reached will become shorter and shorter: this will give more and more room for the continuation of study on the part of the future teachers, and thus we should enter upon a bene-ficial revolution which would in a short time supply the whole country with efficient teachers. If we look at the situation from this point of view, we can hardly doubt that even those who have only the utilitarian interest in mind,—yes, even those who think of the mercenary aspect only,—that even those must prefer this true reform to the efforts of the "new education" men who operate with pedagogy and elective studies. Those three years which every American boy loses through the bad prepa-ration of his teachers represent a loss for the practical achievement in later life which cannot be compensated for by an early beginning of professional training through electives. It is a loss for the man, and an incomparable loss for the nation.

I merely indicated one other feature of our German education when I disclosed the secret of its efficiency. I said our parents reinforced in us respect for the school, and the home atmosphere was filled with belief in the duties of mothers' clubs and committees for that, and there was little discussion about what children need *in abstracto;* but they made their children feel that the home and the school were working in alliance. We boys took all that as a matter of course, and what it meant I never quite understood before I crossed the ocean. I feel inclined to say that what our school children need is not only good teachers, but also good parents. However, as Lincoln said, one war at a time.

2

Some Points of Contrast in the Educational Situation in England and America[1]

That great inspirer of educational interest, Colonel Parker, used to pray to be delivered from foregone conclusions. Every student knows how hard it is to clear his mind of prepossessions and of bias when he tries to measure the good and the evil in so intimate and intricate a thing as a system of national education. But shall we not do well to be on our guard, not only against foregone conclusions, but also against those which are premature and superficial? We slowly come to understand how hard a task it is to trace the subtle tendencies, and to probe the secret hopes, of an educational system, of which we ourselves, by birthright and upbringing, have had long and close experience. How much more, therefore, is it right for one to shrink from any feeling of self-confidence in reviewing the educational situation in another country, of the inner life of which, deep as his sympathies may be with what he believes to be its central and animating principles, a stranger can at best know so dangerously little.

I need not, therefore, ask you to excuse the tentative form of this address. It would be an impertinence for me to speak to you in any other tones. And the more ambitious my theorizing, the more disastrous would be my fate at the hands of critics who, like so many of my

---

[1] An address delivered at Columbia University, July 18, 1902.

Michael Ernest Sadler. "Some Points of Contrast in the Educational Situation in England and America," *Educational Review*, Vol. 25 (March, 1903), pp. 217–231.

Author (1861–1943): Educated at Rugby, and Trinity College, Oxford; member of the Royal Commission on Secondary Education, 1893–1895; Director, Special Inquiries and Reports in the Education Department, 1895–1903; Professor of History and Educational Administration at Manchester University, 1903–1911; Vice-Chancellor, Leeds University, 1911–1923; Master of New College, Oxford, 1923–1934.

hearers, are steeped in the knowledge of those educational affairs which I have only observed, and that somewhat hurriedly, from the outside.

First of all, let me briefly recall to you certain broad and simple facts which have had a governing influence on your national life and therefore on your national education.

The streams of immigration which trickled into this country in the course of the seventeenth century bore with them strong views, or at least ingrained habits of mind, in regard to the aims, the forms, and the functions of government. But broadly speaking and with due allowance for such disquieting phenomena as Roger Williams in Salem, the various types of political and ecclesiastical affinity naturally sorted themselves out in different localities, so far separated as to allow of the healthy development of somewhat disparate ideals of social order. True it was that, as became plain in the revolutionary struggle at the close of the eighteenth century, a common instinct for independence from European control animated the great majority of the inhabitants of the British Colonies in North America; but there was also, amongst the colonies themselves, an inner conflict of social ideals, which under the stress of later economic development revealed itself in that great struggle between North and South, now hallowed by heroic memories of valor and self-sacrifice on either side and in its issue the seal of the true unity of the American people. These conflicting ideals of social order revealed themselves partly in the unit of local administration—viz., the county and the town; partly in preference (not equally serious on both sides) for this or that form of ecclesiastical organization; but still more characteristically in the very different attitude taken by Virginia and New England toward the task of common education. But it was a matter of no small moment that these differing types of social ideals were segregated from one another at different points in the long Eastern seaboard of this continent. Now in England these two ideals, and the people in whose heart's fiber these ideals were embodied, were intermixed in one small kingdom, and in almost every separate part of it. Hence came the two most important of all the emigrations to America in the early part of the seventeenth century; hence our English civil war; hence, in our despair at reaching an ultimate settlement of these problems of human destiny and of State rights, either by the arbitrament of the sword or even by the process of incessant debate, like that which Sir Walter Scott has pictured for us in the opening pages of *Woodstock*, we in England welcomed the vague political and religious compromise which enveloped us during the later years of the seventeenth and the earlier half of the eighteenth century, and which, by its baffling repression of any tendency to embody unflinching logic in clear-cut schemes for social reorganization, turned the thought of so many of our bolder, and more adventurous spirits to the winning of a new Empire in the East. Hence, too, because we have differed so profoundly on many of the religious and political conceptions which lie at the root of any system of unified national education, we have never yet succeeded in building up one simple fabric of common schools, supported by all, congenial to all, beloved by all. During the last two hundred years there have been two serious attempts to organize English education from top to bottom on the basis of one common principle and of unified conviction. Each of these efforts was inspired by a profound belief in the necessity for a common system of national education, so constructed as to be coherent in form and aim from bottom to top. The first of the two attempts was made by an influential group of leaders in the Church of England at one of the noblest periods in her history: after a long and obscure struggle the attempt was stalemated—necessarily and rightly stalemated—by Dr. Joseph Priestley and the Nonconformist interest. The second attempt was made by Robert Owen on the basis of scientific rationalism illuminated by a truly religious passion for social reform. His attempt was checked—necessarily and rightly checked—by the deeper insight and more spiritual conceptions of the leaders of that movement in English thought and feeling which was interpreted to us by Wordsworth, by Samuel Taylor Colebridge, by John Keble and John Henry Newman.

Again, three times within the last two hundred and fifty years we have drawn very near to the ideal of a system of national education which, by the frank recognition of differences, would have attained administrative and spiritual unity on a higher plane. Three times the attempt has failed—failed partly thru the perversity of narrow-minded partisans, partly thru the disastrous influence of jealousy, but partly too thru the unwillingness of good men, on both sides, to surrender what they conceived to be points of essential principle. These failures to attain comprehension combined with administrative efficiency form the tragedy of English education.

Secondly, the history of education is in large part a study of controlling traditions—social, economic, intellectual, and spiritual traditions. The most significant things in it are often the unconscious things; not the things that we do, but the latent premises which color or govern much of our ordinary thinking—our individual thinking, and still more our group-thinking. In the study of national education one of the most fruitful lines of thought is to investigate the real reasons for the absence of certain obviously desirable things in a national system of education; for example, to consider why it is that in England, until quite recent times, history has been, as a rule, so mechanically and uninterestingly taught, tho we have one of the most heart-stirring histories of all the nations in Christendom; and why, tho our masters of prose and verse are among the most precious parts of our British inheritance, we have, as a rule, done so little to familiarize our children at school with these beloved masterpieces or even to train them to skill and power in the use of their mother tongue.

The study of the history of American education, too, is in large part a study of controlling traditions. But with you, the old tradition, in passing from the old world to the new, suffered a sea-change. Much came; but much of the ancient power of certain subtle, immemorial influences was left behind. It has been on the whole, (at least that is my judgment), good for the world that this was so. One illustration of this weakening of the grip of the old educational tradition must suffice. The early laws of Harvard College (1642–46) required every scholar to be able, before admission, "to make and speak true Latin in prose and verse." But the American climate proved fatal to this transplanted tradition. Yet in England Dr. William Harvey was at the same time writing notes for his lectures in which many of the sentences are a mosaic of English and Latin. "Exempto corde, frogg scipp, eele crawle, dogg ambulat." Forty years later Locke advised English parents to have their boys taught Latin as a spoken language, like French. Early in the eighteenth century the great Dr. Wake, Archbishop of Canterbury, carried on his famous negotiations for religious reunion in Europe by means of letters written—not in French, but—in Latin. A generation later, John Wesley, landing on the continent of Europe, naturally spoke Latin with the cultivated men whom he met. Early in the nineteenth century it was in Latin that Keble lectured on poetry to the University of Oxford, and was followed by his audiences with the delighted and intelligent attention with which we, at a later day, loved to hang on the lips of Mr. Ruskin; and Isaac Williams, most truthful of autobiographers, tells us that when a boy at Harrow, during the last years of the long reign of George III., he was "so much used to think in Latin, that when he had an English theme to prepare (which was very rarely) he had to translate his ideas, which ran in Latin, into English."

Thirdly, you have had to subdue a continent—a work the marvel and the mastery of which we cannot yet fully appreciate. Under the Providence of God two great forces have enabled you to accomplish this work. First, your resourceful endurance, and secondly, applied science. What a brilliant and fertile combination has been this of undaunted courage, adaptive ingenuity and appreciation of the practical value of long and costly periods of unseen, patient, scientific research. And who shall say how much of the last element in the triple thread of American greatness has come to you from Germany? The figure of that wise, learned, patient, soldier–teacher Steuben, devoting himself to the scientific training of the American army during that critical winter at Valley Forge, is a type of what German science has since done in so many other fields of human effort, by combining itself with the resourcefulness, the verve, and the shrewd practical insight of the American nature. And what a wonderful power had Washington of going to the heart of things, and of rising above personal pique or national jealousy in thus discerning the value of a gift which the foreign soldier-teacher had to bring.

Fourthly, you have been confronted by the great task of fusing into one nation, under one flag and speaking one speech, those diverse races which pour into this continent in an almost unceasing stream. The common public school is, of necessity, one of the most important—probably the most important—part of your national machinery for assimilating these extraordinarily varied materials.

Hence the universal recognition in America of the political, practical, and economic importance of a first-rate public-school system for the whole people. Practical necessity, not less than reasoning and human sympathy, has led you to discern the deep significance of national education to a degree which in England the masses of the people have not yet attained. Great indeed and grave is our need for searching and comprehensive educational experiment and reform. But it must never be forgotten, in comparing the position of public education in America with its position in England, that the imperative need for sustained, scientific, unstinted expenditure on the best possible kinds of public education for the whole people has been made, by the obvious facts of the case, more striking and impressive to the whole community here than with us in England. Ours is a scattered empire. Here every freight train is an object lesson in continental geography and in the economic unity of the American people.

From these more general topics I turn for a few minutes to a review of some of the educational facts which seem to have followed from the historical and social development of this country.

(a) Twenty years and more of education on modern lines seem to the traveler from Europe to have given to the United States a strong type of keen-witted, hard-working, self-controlled young men, and a very influential and public-spirited multitude of collegewomen. We in England thankfully recognize the same types in our own midst—but the numbers and the influence of these younger men and women seem to me to be relatively greater here than with us. Here, it seems to me, the young man is having his innings. With us the older men—hale, respected, but just a little cautious—are still at the wickets, adding to their long score. Every now and again one hears in the crowd a muttered wish that they would slog a little harder. But it is a great thing for a country to have so large a number of men old in years and yet able to bear the burden of heavy administrative responsibility.

(b) Schools alone, however, would not have given you your fine type of young men. Something else was needed to produce that. I mean, the sense of wide opportunity. More and more do I come to feel that this is one of the central reasons for certain differences between your secondary schools and ours. An American boy feels that, if he works hard, shows sense, and keeps bright, he is bound to find opportunity of success. An English boy grows up with a puzzled wonder where in his crowded island he will find a promising opportunity for professional success, or even for industrial or commercial effort congenial to his taste and appropriate to his level of general education. This baffling sense of a strangely limited horizon of personal opportunity is one of the subtle causes of our present educational hesitancy. Can you wonder that so many of our most active-minded educators and statesmen feel it essential to the free development of our national vigor and intelligence that our boys should be taught to think of their after-life in terms—not of England alone—but of Empire?

(c) This sense of opportunity which is so characteristic of American life seems to me to be connected with yet another feature of your education. Your boys and girls have much more choice in their studies than, as yet—as a matter of actual practice—ours have. This greater power of choice naturally comes to those who know, or think they know, what they need. The English student is struck by the fact that your American schoolboys and schoolgirls are much more openly critical of their teachers than English boys and girls are commonly encouraged to be. I fancy that the career and happiness of a teacher in America depend much more largely, than with us in England, on the suffrages of those who are taught. This must certainly stimulate adaptiveness on the part of the teachers—tho I am inclined to suspect that there is a rather darker side to the situation than at first sight appears. Anyway, if the jargon of political philosophy permitted it, I should be tempted to define American educational government as a paidocracy—tempered by expert superintendence on short tenure.

(d) It is an old commonplace that schools and colleges exist to prepare us for life. The difficulty is for them to know how to do it when the conditions of social economic life are changing with a rapidity almost, if not quite, unparalleled in the history of human culture. You in America seem to me to be engaged in an immense effort to get your schools and colleges into true gear with the practical needs of life. Hence you are tearing out in all directions those portions of subjects or parts of curriculums which seem to you unessential. But the difficulty is to say with certainty what are the essentials. And, as life is becoming more and more differentiated, there arises a need for much greater differentiation in types of school. Moreover, this differentiation is not a matter of the last few years of high-school or college life. Its demands affect much earlier years of education than those. And the differentiation is required not only by the difference in life-aims of the pupils, but by far more subtle differences in temperament, in mental aptitude, and in ethical need. This is the true cause of the educational unrest which we can see all over the world at the present time. This is a period of educational ferment, comparable, as it seems to me, to that earlier period of educational ferment which preceded the French Revolution. Much that looks like progress and constructive advance in education at the present time is really the working of a critical and destructive movement washing away the more obstinate fragments of an obsolete system of education, which, in its time, had a very real relation to the actual needs of certain kinds of life.

To me, the educational movement now going forward in America seems the most striking and forceful of all the educational movements in the world. It is on the largest scale; it is supported by the most superb liberality; it is the boldest in its ventures; it is becoming—largely thru the influence of the President of Columbia—truth-seeking and truth-inspiring; scientific in its dispassionate self-criticism; and it is supported by the most whole-hearted national enthusiasm. We educational students in other lands hail its great achievements and its still more brilliant future. Silent admiration best befits us when we think of the future of your great universities—and of what their influence already is and will be on their sisters in the Old World. The science and art of education are being profoundly influenced by your work here in the training of teachers; by your experimental schools; and not least by the currents of suggestion and of encouragement which go out from Teachers College and from the Department of Education in this University, at Clark University, and at Chicago. You in America, and not least the educators of the West, are working out fertile experiments in the field of secondary education on modern lines. You from the North are carrying the torch of educational propaganda over the length and breadth of the awakening South. And in the great work at Hampton and Tuskegee there is shaping itself in successful practice that ideal of training which seeks at once to deepen character, to engender loyalty to a great institution, to educate for the practical labors of life, and to avoid, in its cultivation of the powers of mind, of character, and of expression, any disproportionate use of books or of ill-digested ideas, and of the verbal memory.

How different are your educational problems from those which we have to struggle with in England. The strong points of the best types of English education seem to me to be an unhurried, steadfast pleasure in the great masterpieces of literature; its dislike of false sentiment; its reserve and wholesomeness of tone; its shrinking from pretentious philosophizing; the good spirit of its games; the beauty of some of its old buildings and playgrounds; the unselfish and lifelong devotion of its best teachers; the training which it gives in the government of others and in the leading of men; and in its undercurrent of reverence for those deeper, unseen things which lie almost beyond the reach of words.

Its weakness lies in its lack of widely diffused intellectual interest; in its failure to stimulate the brain power of the average boy; in its deficiencies in regard to the professional training of the teacher; in the aloofness of so great a part of the studies in many of our chief secondary schools from the scientific, political, and ethical problems of the present day; in its ignorance of what scientific research and scientific co-operation really mean; in its good-natured reluctance to press to a logical and practical conclusion some things which must be settled one way or the other, and cannot (without peril) be left in the dim region of indefinite compromise; in the indistinctiveness of its intellectual and social aims; in its unwillingness to attempt a bold questioning of the lessons of our history, and to impress definite teaching derived therefrom on the whole of the rising generation of our people; in the resultant confusion of our school system; in the labyrinthine intricacy of its organization; and in its consequent failure to impress itself on the imagination and clear understanding of the masses of the people.

But much of this mischief comes from our having attempted, and rightly attempted, to combine different aspects of truth in our body politic. We have never really unified ourselves. Slowly, very slowly, a sense of real communal unity is developing itself. It showed itself first in the conviction that every good school ought to give to some accredited public authority evidence of the efficiency of its stewardship. We therefore devised the system of examination of certain kinds of intellectual output by external examining authority, because no more intimate or searching form of communal control was acceptable to the individualistic temper of our English middle class. The analogy between external examination and an independent audit of accounts delighted the plain business man. And thus we put on to ourselves, for the best for motives, that Nessus-robe of external examination which English secondary education must, as it seems to me, cast aside at almost any cost if it would regain true freedom for growth and real artistic happiness in the great creative work of teaching.

But different from yours as it is and must be, the educational movement in England is hardly less interesting than that in America, tho in its operations it is far more obscure. It is full of cross-currents; very sensitive to conflicting claims upon its allegiance; tender in its loyalty to the past as well as eager to adapt itself to the needs of the future. We in England have a complex past; we are at the center of a complex empire. Our individual life, our national life, our new imperial life, are each of them strangely full of different elements and of distracting claims. We are unable to put our difficulties into words; yet you will understand that we feel much that we cannot express. We are unwilling to sever ourselves from our old ties, or to dispense with old guides and teachers whom we love for their own sakes, and not only because they have served us so devotedly and well. You must expect us to be slow in our educational changes. England is not lethargic, but profoundly moved by the swirling currents of change in our modern life. It would be wrong for us to break with our past. We can best do our duty for the world in the future if we refrain from impetuous, revolutionary change. But because this is our lot in this time of deep unrest—because there is laid on us the duty of sacrificing much that is good and profitable in the present, in order that we may be faithful to what is true and sacred in the past; because it is now, as ever, our supreme national task to preserve what is good in two ideals which, tho they appear to conflict, are really two sides of one higher truth—for these very reasons we admire the more the superb sweep of your educational advance, your clear administrative aims, and the rich variety of your buoyant life.

3

A British View of American Schools

Together with a commission of thirty English educational experts, I have just completed an investigation of American schools. The most striking facts I have gathered are these:

1. That the people of the United States spend a marvelous amount of money on their public schools, endowing education more lavishly than any other people in the world.

2. They do not spend enough. The salaries to teachers are not sufficient for the service the country desires and should have.

Our tour of investigation began in New York in October of last year. The previous autumn a commission of British trade-union representatives made a tour of the industrial centres of the United States on my invitation to study industrial conditions—a trip the results of which have already been published in this magazine. The investigations by this industrial commission and the recent educational commission were part of a single plan formed a number of years ago.

While in business in South Africa I had unusual opportunities to study the work of English and American engineers. The English engineers were much inferior. They slavishly followed conventional principles. They worked by rule of thumb. They lacked initiative. They showed inability in a sudden emergency to grasp the situation confronting them, to put the right machinery to work, to carry the task in hand in a practical way to completion. Often they attacked engineering problems with no more expert sureness and efficiency than any intelligent business man might have exhibited. The Americans, on the other hand, were alert and up to date, instantly equal to any occasion that might arise. In emergencies they knew at once what to do and what kind of machinery to use; and whenever they attacked a problem, after swiftly arguing the pros and cons they carried the matter through in the straightest way with professional certitude of method. The English engineers

Alfred Mosely. "A British View of American Schools," *The World's Work*, Vol. 7, No. 4 (February, 1904), pp. 4484–4487.

Author (1855–1917): Educated Bristol Grammar School, came to the United States in 1903 to lead and direct a commission of British educators investigating American schools; he served as a member of the Tariff Commission in 1904.

had been poorly trained; the American engineers well trained. American business men whom I met were quite as alert as the engineers. A visit to the United States convinced me that the secret of this national efficiency lay in the American schools.

As the British Education bill was still in the melting-pot a year ago, I postponed the inquiry I had long planned into the details of the American school system and accompanied the industrial commission on its very fruitful visit. On returning to England I placed the matter of an educational commission in the hands of a committee of which Lord Reay, president of the London school board, was chairman, and Mr. Sadler, late of the board of education, a valuable member. As Mr. Sadler is one of the leading educational experts of Great Britain, it was a pleasure to me that his point of view on the project accorded with my own. This committee drew up a list of the heads of various branches of British education, to whom invitations were sent. One or two letters appeared in the public press protesting that Great Britain could learn nothing from the United States in educational matters, but the thirty gentlemen who accepted the invitation felt that any information they might acquire in the United States would undoubtedly be useful, even though the new British Education bill had fixed for a time the status of public education at home. The commissioners all came open-minded to inquire into the strong and weak points of American education, and to see how far the American system might apply, with modifications, to Great Britain.

We began with a ten days' investigation in New York. Thence we went to Washington, where President Roosevelt made us an interesting address, and then we visited the colored school at Hampton, the schools and colleges of Baltimore, Philadelphia, New Haven, Boston, and Chicago. The party then split. Some went south, some as far west as California, some to Canada. The rest came east by Indianapolis, Dayton, and Pittsburgh. The whole country was covered by at least a part of the commission. We are greatly indebted to President Butler, of Columbia University, for a vast amount of assistance. He prepared our itinerary and put at the disposal of the delegates an encyclopedic fund of information. Dr. Maxwell and members of the Board of Education courteously gave us every facility for seeing the New York schools; Mr. Munroe and members of the School Committee did us similar service in Boston; and President Harper and the Board of Education gave us excellent opportunities for visiting Chicago institutions. Everywhere we were met with the greatest hospitality. The delegates, attended and unattended, visited schools to their complete satisfaction, considering the time they had at their disposal.

My own strongest impression was of the amount of money spent on education. East and West it has become quite the fashion for millionaires to make large gifts to colleges, and in every section I visited I found the people lavishing money on their schools. And the expenditure is appreciated. If the buildings and the equipment are on a much more generous scale than in England, there is greater enthusiasm here also. The very atmosphere of American schoolrooms breathes progress. American teachers are more enthusiastic than English teachers; American pupils have a greater thirst for knowledge than English pupils; and there is a closer bond of sympathy here than in England between pupil and teacher.

In essence, the American people have realized better than European the value of education. They have learned to consider it their primary duty to train themselves for the struggle that modern development entails on the individual. They seem to realize, as the English have not begun to realize, that no boy—and no girl, for that matter—can do without such training.

One especially notable manifestation of enthusiasm I found in New York, Boston, and other large cities. On the East Side in New York and at the North End in Boston the schools in the poorer districts are kept open at night to give the children of the crowded tenements a clean and comfortable place to study their morrow's lessons, with some one to help them on difficult points. The children resort to these evening studyrooms in surprising numbers, and the teachers help them patiently and encouragingly.

Manual training is a very important feature in all the schools of the principal cities for both boys and girls. In England some few schools, laying special stress on the subject, teach manual training. Here in the United States the study is general. And my inquiries serve to show that it helps in the pupil's general development; it offers a change from the other work and it brings out individuality. Serving a need of the United States by turning boys with a mechanical turn of mind to the technical schools, it also develops a practical taste among all the children for the mechanical side of life.

As a whole, the Middle West is more intense in matters of education than the other parts of the country. The schools of the Middle West are newer than the Eastern schools and more modern, because they have no traditions to get rid of. There is an even greater thirst for knowledge there than elsewhere, and money is spent to advantage. The schools of Indianapolis are among the best in the country.

I was much struck with the many colleges for the training of teachers. Both East and West are numerous normal schools and such institutions as the Teachers' College at Columbia University; and in the West especially a large proportion of the women graduates of the State universities enter the teaching profession. This training system assures an endless flow of the best class of teachers. In England the proportion of college-bred women teachers is far lower than in the United States, and, on the whole, the grade of teaching by women is lower. But England is considerably better off in its force of men teachers. My severest criticism of the American school system would be that the teaching force lacks men. Few men in the United States go into school-teaching, and these are not the best. The profession in England attracts a distinctly more capable class.

The trouble lies in the salaries. In many cases the actual money pay of teachers is higher here than in England, but reckoning the difference in the standard of living, especially in those articles that are above necessities, both men and women are paid more there than here. Thus men are attracted to teaching in England, whereas in the United States they find better opportunities in other callings. A larger proportion of men would greatly improve the American teaching force, but there can be no such improvement until American communities match the generosity they exhibit in school equipment with generosity in allotting salaries. Nor are the salaries of the women teachers adequate. The people of the United States have an excellent school system because they spend much money on it; they could have a better system by paying more.

The school system I am referring to is, of course, the public-school system. I am not in favor of private schools conducted for individual profit, of which there are more in England than here, because such schools are likely to be conducted for profit rather than for efficiency. Here all classes go to the public schools, with no harmful results, as far as I can learn, and with many benefits. The poorer boy or girl gets some refinement from the more fortunate children; the more fortunate children are in no way harmed. With no distinctions all classes side by side seek the same advantages. And these are many.

In England the average boy of the poorer class goes to work at an early age after a merely elementary education, entering the trade of his father or a trade his father has chosen for him—often independently of the boy's fitness for it. Here the wonderful opportunities for the masses to go on into higher and higher schools and colleges, securing their education free or practically free, render a boy immeasurably better able to choose a calling for which he is fitted. The manual training, too, discovers latent aptitudes. It is safe to say that an American boy has every opportunity to enter any vocation. In no State can any boy say that he cannot secure all the education he wishes.

The girls, too, have better opportunities here than at home. More of them advance into the higher fields of education. The result is that as a whole American girls are distinctly better educated than English girls—not merely because their parents wish it, but because they have, on their own part, a greater appreciation of education and a greater desire for it.

If American teaching fails in any respect, it is in the matter of inculcating the power of correct and accurate English speech. Again and again I heard children in the public schools give ungrammatical answers quite unchecked. The teachers seemed content to receive correct answers to questions in geography or history instead of being dissatisfied until the correct answer had been given in correct language. This was the one serious defect I found in the public schools. The buildings were better in New York and Boston and Chicago than in London; the sanitation and ventilation were better; and I found highly commendable facilities offered in the higher schools for the pupils to purchase healthful food at low prices during the school recesses. The seats and desks are better. Greater attention is devoted to providing such of these as have been scientifically found best fitted for health and comfort. But the speech of the pupil is often bad.

There is, moreover, too little attention paid, in my opinion, to athletics. In England the taste for athletics is carried to extremes. A schoolmaster is not chosen, as here, solely on his academic qualifications: he is asked what his record has been in 'varsity cricket or football, and whether he has taken his "blue." He is expected then to foster the athletic tendencies of his boys. All the boys take part in one sport or another. Here, in the high schools and colleges, small teams and crews of picked youths monopolize the athletics; the other students merely look on. A wider athletic activity would be better.

The most interesting sights we saw on our tour were in the schools of the great cities, especially New York and Chicago, in which the newly arrived immigrant children were receiving their first lessons in Americanism. It was wonderful to see the raw peasant lad from Russia or Germany in a few months after landing sitting in an American school and singing "My Country, 'Tis of Thee." We saw hundreds of these who in a marvelously short time had caught the American spirit and who were daily saluting the flag, considering themselves part and parcel of the American nation. The teachers showed immense enthusiasm in teaching these little atoms of humanity, and the musical marchings in and out of school, and flag salutes, and the songs they taught the children were decidedly effective devices to engender discipline and patriotism. The same spirit is visible everywhere. The United States is handling the immigration problem so successfully by assimilating the second generation of immigrants in the public schools that the American people may well relieve themselves of any fear on the score of excessive inpourings of untrained foreigners. It is an achievement the United States has every reason to be proud of.

Whether it is advisable or possible to adopt in Great Britain any parts of this or other features of American education, the delegates will declare with some authority in their reports next spring. As a layman with no claim to expert educational knowledge, I should say that the American excellences are well worthy of being grafted on the present English systems. After all, we must judge by results. The public education of the United States has had a large part in placing the country in the first rank in the world, industrially and commercially, at the same time maintaining a high ideal of civilization. There is some disposition on the part of English observers to attack American materialism. What materialism I have seen is largely ambition. There is no more of the "dollar-hunting" spirit in the United States than in other countries. The humanities, culture, refinement are not neglected in the schools and colleges. Research and scientific inquiry of the more advanced kinds are perhaps not so highly developed here as abroad, but there is no serious deficiency, and swift progress is being made. England might well learn lessons from the way in which the United States has worked out its problem.

In brief, I might sum up my impressions of American education by a single personal note. I have placed my two sons in the Hopkins Grammar School at New Haven to prepare for Yale.

4

American Education: A Chinese Viewpoint

Out of a total population of 91,972,266 in the United States there were, in 1910, 17,506,175 pupils enrolled. Few nations can show such a high percentage of school students. The total number of teachers was 506,040. Educational efficiency on such a scale can be maintained only by a large expenditure of money, and from the statistics of education I find that the sum received from tuition fees was $14,687,192 gold, from productive funds $11,592,113 gold, and from the United States Government $4,607,298 gold, making a total of $70,667,865 gold. I question whether any other nation can produce such an excellent example in the cause of education.

In every state there are very many schools, both public and private. There are public schools in every town, and even the smallest village has its school, while in some agricultural states, such as Wyoming, where the population is very scattered, teachers are provided by the government to teach in the farmers' homes wherever three or four children can be gathered together. The public schools are free and open to all, but in some towns in the Southern States special schools are provided for the colored people. Having such facilities for gaining knowledge, it naturally follows that the Americans, as a whole, are an educated people. By this I mean the native American, not the recent immigrants and negroes, but even as regards the latter a reservation should be made for some of the negroes, such as Booker T. Washington and others, have become eminent through their learning and educational work.

The distinguishing feature of the school system is that it is cheap and comprehensive. In the primary and high schools the boys and girls, whether they come from the wealthy or aristocratic families, or from more straitened homes, are all studying together in the same class-room,

Wu Ting-Fang. "American Education" *America Through the Spectacles of an Oriental Diplomat* (New York: Frederick A. Stokes Company, 1914), pp. 54–65.

Author (1842–1922); Educated St. Paul's College, Hong Kong. Chinese minister to the United States of America, Spain, Peru, Mexico, and Cuba; Minister of Foreign Affairs and Minister of Justice for the Government of the Republic of China.

and it is known that a President sent his son to study in a public school. There is, therefore, no excuse for even the poorest man in America being an illiterate. If he wishes he can obtain a degree in a university without difficulty. Many of the state universities admit the children of citizens of the state free, while their tuition fees for outsiders are exceptionally low, so that it is within the power of the man of the most moderate means to give his son a university education. Many of the college or university students, in order to enable them to go through their courses of study, do outside jobs after their lecture hours, and perform manual, or even menial work, during the vacations. I frequently met such students in summer resorts acting as hotel waiters and found them clean, attentive, and reliable. During a visit to Harvard University, President Eliot took me to see the dining-hall. Many students were taking their lunch at the time. I noticed that the waiters were an unusually clean set of young men, and upon inquiry was informed that they were students of the University, and that when a waiter was wanted many students applied, as the poorer students were glad to avail themselves of the opportunity to earn some money.

Honest labor, though menial, is not considered degrading, and no American of education and refinement is above doing it. In some of the states in the East, owing to the scarcity of servants, families do their own cooking and other household work. Some few years ago I was on a visit to Ashburnham, Massachusetts, and was surprised to find that my hostess not only did the cooking but also cleaned my room. I was invited to a formal luncheon by a professor, and to my astonishment his two daughters waited at the table. This is not unlike what occurs in some parts of China in the interior. The members of families, although in good circumstances, do their own household work. In some towns, not far from Canton, wealthy farmers and country gentlemen hire out their sons as menials, so that these youngsters, when they have grown up, shall know the value of money and not squander the family wealth. I cite a typical case of a millionaire who had only one son. In order to make him appreciate the worth of money he took his boy to Canton, and allowed him to be hired out as an ordinary servant. The boy was ordered by his master to look after a certain part of the house, and also to take care of a little garden. One day he carelessly broke a valuable gold-fish jar much prized by the family. His master naturally became enraged and reproached him for his negligence. The young man coolly told him that if he would come to his father's house he could replace the broken vessel by making his own selection from his father's collection of gold-fish jars. This irritated the master, who thought that the lad was adding insult to injury. However, ultimately, his master was persuaded to go with him to his father's house, and to his great astonishment he found there many gold-fish jars which were more precious than that which the lad had broken. Household work, however mean it may be, is not considered degrading in China, but the difference between China and America is that in America the people are compelled to do it from necessity, while in China it is resorted to as a matter of policy to make the young men realize the value of money, and not spend it wastefully.

The curriculum prescribed in the schools covers a wide range of subjects, and the graduates are well equipped to face the battle of life. Not only are drawing, sketching and other fine arts taught, but also carpentry and other trades. I was once shown a fairly made box which was the product of a very small boy. I did not at first perceive the use of teaching a boy to do such work in school, but I learned that its object was to instruct the pupil how to think and arrange his materials systematically.

With the exception of those schools established by Christian societies, or endowed by religious sects, all educational institutions, especially those established by the state authorities are secular. Religion is not taught. Neither the Bible nor any other religious work is used in the schoolroom. The presidents, professors, and tutors may be strict churchmen, or very religious people, but, as a rule, they are not permitted to inculcate their religious views on the students. The minds of the young are most susceptible, and if no moral principles are impressed upon them at school or college they are apt to go astray. It should be remembered that men of education without moral principles are like a ship without an anchor. Ignorant and illiterate people infringe the law because they do not know any better, and their acts of depredation are clumsy and can be easily found out, but when men of education commit crimes these are so skillfully planned and executed that it is difficult for the police to unravel and detect them. It has been known that frauds and forgeries perpetrated by such unscrupulous persons were so cleverly designed that they bore the evidence of superior education, and almost of genius. The more a man is educated the more is it necessary, for the welfare of the state, to instruct him how to make a proper use of his talents: Education is like a double-edged sword. It may be turned to dangerous usages if it is not properly handled.

As there is no established church in the United States, and in view of the numberless different sects, it is not advisable to permit any particular phase of religion to be taught. But why not consent to allow the cardinal principles of morality to be taught in every school? The following may serve as examples:

(1) Honesty is the best policy.
(2) Honor thy father and thy mother.
(3) Universal brotherhood.
(4) Love of mankind.
(5) Charity to all.
(6) Purity in thought and action.
(7) Pure food makes a pure body.
(8) Happiness consists of health and a pure conscience.
(9) Live and let live.
(10) Respect a man for his virtues, not for his money or position.
(11) *Fiat justitia, ruat cœlum* (Let justice be done, though the Heavens should fall).
(12) Bear no malice against anyone.
(13) Be equitable and just to all men.
(14) Liberty and freedom but not license.
(15) Do not unto others what ye would not that others should do unto you.

I have jotted down the above just as they occurred to me while writing. They can easily be amplified, and be made the basis of an ethical instruction in all the schools. In any case, every nation should aim at the highest standard of morals.

Co-education in the United States is not so unpopular as in some other countries, and it is increasing in favor. In all the primary schools, and in most of the high schools, boys and girls study in the same class-room, and girls are admitted as students even in some colleges and universities. This principle of admitting the fair sex to equal educational privileges is slowly but surely being recognized everywhere. In some universities the authorities have gone half-way; lectures are given to the girl students in separate rooms, or separate buildings, or halls, are provided for the girl students. With regard to the teaching staff, in the primary schools nearly all the teachers are women, and in the high schools their number is at least half, if not more. In some of the universities there are lady professors or tutors. It goes without saying that girls have the natural talent for learning everything that boys can learn. The objectives raised by the opponents of co-education seem to rest chiefly upon the danger of the intellectual or physical overstrain of girls during adolescence, and upon the unequal rate of development of boys and girls during the secondary school period. It is further alleged that in mixed schools the curriculum is so prescribed that the girls' course of study is more or less adapted to that of the boys, with the result that it cannot have the artistic and domestic character which is suitable for the majority of girls; but why should not the curriculum be arranged in such a way as to suit both sexes? Is it not good for both to learn the same subjects? That which is good for a boy to learn is it not equally advisable for a girl to know, and vice versa? Will not such a policy create mutual sympathy between the sexes? The opponents of the co-education policy assert that it makes the girls masculine, and that it has a tendency to make the boys a little feminine. It cannot, however, be doubted that the system reduces the cost of education, such as the duplication of the teaching staff, laboratories, libraries, and other equipment.

It is objected that the system has done more than anything else to rob marriage of its attractions, by divesting man of most of his old-time glamour and romance. It is claimed that this early contact with the other sex, on a footing of equality, and the manner in which the majority of the girl students more than maintain their intellectual standing with the boys, has tended to produce that contempt of the much-vaunted superiority of man, that, as a rule, is reserved for those post-nuptial discoveries which make marriage such an interesting venture. But they forget that marriages are frequently contracted in places where girls and boys are taught together, and where they have had ample opportunities for knowing each other intimately, and that experience proves that such marriages are happy and lasting unions. It is interesting to observe, however, that as the number of educational institutions has increased, the number of unmarried women has been correspondingly augmented. It is easy to explain this by the fact that a large number of women earn their own livelihood by going into business and the professions. As they become more educated, and are allowed to participate in many of the same privileges as men, it is only natural that they should show their independence by remaining single. The same thing would occur in any country, and we may expect a like state of things in China as greater facilities for instruction are afforded to women. I do not feel alarmed at the prospect; indeed, I would welcome it if I could see my country-women acting as independently and as orderly as their American sisters.

The games and sports sanctioned and encouraged in schools and universities are useful, in that they afford diversion of the pupil's minds from their school work. They should not, however, be indulged in such a way as to interfere with their studies. Take, as an example, boat racing; several months of preparation are necessary before the event takes place, and during a great portion of this time the students do not think much of their studies; they are all mad with excitement. The contest between the two rival parties is very keen; they have but one thought, and that is to win the race. In this way, at least so it seems to me, the main object of recreation is entirely lost sight of; it becomes no longer an amusement, but labor and work. I am told that the coxswain and the other members of the boat race generally have to take a long rest when the race is over, which clearly shows that they have been overworking. I favor all innocent games and sports which mean recreation and diversion, but if it be thought that without a contest games would lose their relish and their fun, then I would suggest that the aim should be the exhibition of a perfect body and absolute health. Let the students, when they come to the recreation ground, indulge in any sport they please, but make them feel that it is "bad form" to overstrain, or do anything which, even temporarily, mars the perfect working of their physical organisms. Let each student so train himself as to become healthy and strong both physically and mentally, and the one who, through reasonable and wholesome exercises, is able to present himself in the most perfect health should be awarded the highest prize.

5

Educational Thought: Implications for Australia

We Victorian teachers are conscientious and skilful exponents of teaching methods. From time to time we modify our attitudes and our methods, but our educational system does not encourage us to think on the philosophy of education and to express our thoughts fearlessly. I have not found that it discourages us from so doing.

American educational visionaries look forward to the day when every teacher will be a thinker who will have a philosophy that will shape and inspire his work. But they are far from the work-a-day world of the schools, they are human, and they are Americans. They see in the student who tickles them with their own ideas an independent and courageous thinker who is capable of working by himself. Too frequently, he is a sorry enough fledgling who parrots a few catch-calls, "a loud-speaker in a robot," or a spry salesman who sticks new labels on old educational goods. He is far more reckless than our careful young schoolroom operatives and sometimes completely irresponsible. And yet, perhaps he has a vision that has not come to us.

Californian teachers ask the visitor what is the philosophy "back of" education in Australia. Well, what is it? I mumbled some commonplaces collected at random in the course of my reading, went away and wondered. Then I asked for the philosophy behind their education. They spoke confidently of "the integration of personality," "the motivation of learning," "socializing the school," and "making the school child-centred." But few of them understood clearly what they were talking about, and I soon saw the cruelty of my question, "What exactly do you mean by that?", and refrained from asking it. I didn't find more thought in their jargon than in my mumbles, but it sounded more impressive at first.

John George Cannon. "Educational Thought" in *Comments on Education in the United States of America and Victoria, Australia* (Melbourne, Victoria: Melbourne University Press, 1933), pp. 24–28. Reprinted by kind permission of the Melbourne University Press, Victoria, Australia.

Author (1902–   ): Educated at Swinbourne Technical College, Hawthorne; Inspector of Schools, Victoria, Australia.

We Australians live in a commonwealth, and we expect our country to provide for the material needs of the people so that every individual will have the opportunity for spiritual growth. We expect each citizen to contribute to the spiritual and physical well-being of himself and others and to observe the laws that are made by his representatives, and we provide checks and penalties which will restrain individuals from anti-social behaviour. We look to our schools to prepare our young people for life in our Commonwealth and to help them to understand the feelings and aspirations of our kin across the seas. We have no strong disrespect for peoples outside our brotherhood of nations, but we are a small, isolated community and we have yet a long way to go along the road to world friendship.

We have a body of knowledge, organized under subject names and set out in courses of study for schools, from the lowest primary grade to the university. We have also generally approved teaching techniques by the use of which our teachers help our children to learn the matter listed under our subject names and to acquire skills, such as reading, writing, and the handling of tools, instruments, apparatus and machines. We hope and believe that the thinking powers and the characters of our children and young people will be developed by the "social contacts" of the schoolroom and the playground, by the teachers' treatment of the subject matter and by the feelings and thoughts that the pupils will generate from their study of records of deeds, descriptions of places and events, and works of literary art.

I now attempt to give a summarized statement of modern American thought on education:—

(1) Education should develop people who will be able to think and work when they are adult members of a society which may be greatly different from the society of to-day.

(2) Education is an experience in which the learner lives to the full extent of his spiritual, mental and physical powers.

(3) Schooling is a part of education, and the learning process inside the school should be the same as the learning process outside the school.

(4) The essence of true education is that the learner works and learns because he sees the purpose of working and learning.

(5) Therefore, all schoolroom situations should arise from the learner's felt needs of the moment.

(6) The "traditional" school was developed in a society of fairly well defined classes, and the curriculums of different kinds of schools were constructed to prepare students for callings such as the church, medicine, law, and office work, or for life in their social classes.

(7) The traditional curriculums were justified by a faculty psychology on which was grounded a complete faith in the theories of mental discipline

and the transfer of training. We now regard this psychology as unsound, but the theories that were based on it remain the only logical justifications of big portions of the traditional curriculums.

(8) During the last fifty years or more, as life was growing more complex, school people altered the curriculum from time to time by adding or removing subjects or by changing the contents of subjects. When these changes were made, sound educational principles were not considered at all or were not followed consistently.

(9) The building up of the curriculum with regard to the content placed the stress in educational thought and practice on the subject matter instead of on the learner. The practice of estimating the teacher's value on the grounds of the apparent degree of success which he achieved in handling the subject matter to his pupils accentuated the wrong stress. The subject matter is really nothing more than the materials on which the pupil learns and develops.

(10) Teachers tried to secure the motive force of interest by providing material rewards, marks and praise, by holding before the children the promise of material rewards to come later in life, and by threats of punishments. These devices merely increased the emphasis on subject matter, and schooling remained distasteful to the learner. Undesirable and harmful effects on the child's personality followed. The only legitimate motive of a thought or action is that it arises from felt and understood present needs.

(11) We don't separate life into compartments the like of school subjects. If, for several years of a child's life, we teach subjects separately in "parcels" constructed by teachers and provided at times set out on a time-table, we cannot expect the child to use parts of these subjects intelligently as life demands them. We must "break down the walls between subjects" and cast aside the subject point of view. We must depart from the whole present arrangement of school work, from the traditional school furniture, from the schoolroom itself as far as possible, and must devote ourselves to helping the child's personality to develop.

(12) True moral training cannot be given under a system of checks and punishment provided by an authority. The teacher and the children must be free agents who have the opportunity of choosing one of several possible lines of action presented by a situation that arises naturally in the schoolroom. After he has chosen and acted, the teacher and the child's schoolfellows will help the child to see the wisdom or the foolishness of his choice, or, if he desires their aid, they will discuss his problem with him before he chooses.

These are the thoughts of the educational thinkers. There are many indications that they mean little or nothing to a very big majority of American teachers and parents. American newspapers, business people and public speakers determine the thought of the people, and they have taught for years that the most worthy aim in life is to obtain material success. From studies of the incomes of thousands of people, education-ists have produced graphs that show that average individual earnings increase considerably with a small increase in the period of schooling and that the financial return from a small investment on education is very large. For years school principals have used these graphs to persuade students to join their schools. Influences of this kind are at work throughout the community. When prosperous professors and other school people, many of whom compete for their positions with the methods of the business world, express their educational beliefs, is it to be expected that the public will regard them seriously? Can we even believe that the people who issue these "thoughts" are serious? There is much evidence that many of them are not.

Many parents and teachers expressed to me the opinion that the universities are a "racket," or conspiracy to swindle. They say that many professors and school people are interested mainly in the production of text-books, newspaper articles and popular lectures for profit and that there is much cynical carelessness in the granting of degrees. They say also that teachers have to adopt or pretend to adopt the ideas fashionable at the moment on pain of dismissal.

These complaints will not hold in many places that I visited, but I did see much justification of them. The widespread public discontent with higher education is healthy, and is an indication that America may really be moving towards the ideals expressed by her thinkers.

"The big hope for the future lies in the school"—one feels rather ashamed as he writes the platitude—and it rests with the ordinary teachers of the schools of the people rather than with the professors and experts. American teachers are faced with the great obstacles of their own limited knowledge, their attitudes of the past, out-of-school influences on the children, and the charlatans who use the words of the great thinkers for profit, but they are virile, courageous, intelligent and open-minded, and they possess a deep affection for the children with whom they work.

6

A Dane Looks at American Education

When I came to the United States I suddenly found myself among a people who lived not in considerations or deliberations, not by speaking about past centuries and what they have given us and still give us, but a people who were fully taken up by what happened—and, especially, what *they* made happen, what they did, and what they hoped to do; a people that almost sensed the beginning of life in the last decades of the eighteenth century, when the industrial revolution took place; a people that frankly state and tell their children that humanity these last one hundred and fifty years has made more progress than in all the ten thousand years before.

Here life of today, even in the schools, plays an overwhelming rôle—airplanes and radio, cars and refrigerators are the delight and pride of the people. Often there is mentioned "our new civilization," and a philosophy of change and of changing times and conditions is on the lips of the common man. One cannot have lived a year in the United States without becoming deeply impressed by it. Here is certainly the place to take old ideas up for new consideration, for new criticism—but perhaps also a place where one can come to a deeper and clearer conception of the essentials in what theretofore has been called "culture."

American educators' almost restless fight *against* old traditions and a secondary school built upon modern life is a most interesting educational undertaking. Radically the American states that the schools shall be of use; what you learn there shall be useful to you—something which can be a means in the daily struggle for existence. I think that this, even if we disagree with the procedure followed, will drive us Europeans to make up our minds why we have some subjects in our schools, and why we do not have some others.

And another thing! When thousands of new young people, boys and girls, stormed the old secondary schools, the walls had to be broken

Johannes Novrup. "A Dane Looks at American Education," *The Clearing House*, Vol. IX, No. 1 (September, 1934), pp. 476–479. Reprinted by kind permission of the publishers of *The Clearing House*, New York.

Author: Member of the faculty of the Folk High School, Askov, Denmark, at the time of writing; graduate student at Teachers College, Columbia University, 1932–1933; Principal of Magleaas Folk High School.

down. The Americans were faced with the task of building new, big, practical buildings. The school plant, as it is often called, was the result. An educator, writing about it, must give expression to his joy and pride by saying: the structures that have been provided and the equipment housed in them constitute some of the wonders of our day. We, who have walked ourselves tired in them, suddenly have *personal* respect for them. How well everything is laid out and arranged—with classrooms and shops, special rooms for typewriting and stenography, for art and music, and for home economics. There are libraries and gymnasiums, rest rooms and emergency rooms, assembly halls with stages.

If we look at what is going on, we discover a big machine working in order to make everything function perfectly. We discover a whole science behind the administration of the school; studies have been made on the length of school days and the size of classes, etc.; psychological findings determine much of what actually goes on; grouping of children in accordance with intelligence, problems of child and adolescent psychology, the construction of a curriculum, in which everything that is to be taught first has had to prove its value—all these matters of importance.

In the theory underlying the junior-high-school movement, we find the idea of guidance playing a big rôle. In the junior high schools, we constantly hear the individual pupil is supposed to find his special curriculum. In order to find the interests, aptitudes, and capacities of each child, exploratory or "try-out" courses in Latin, modern foreign languages, geometry, and applied arts are introduced. Through systematic educational guidance, an opportunity is given to each pupil to discover his dominating interests and limitations with reference to his future vocational activities or the continuation of his education in higher institutions. Provision is made for the rapid advancement of bright groups. The school hopes to help each pupil to select the career that, as a result of the exploratory courses, he, his parents, and the school are convinced is more likely to be of profit to him and to the State. Among the leading ideas in American education, the one of elimination of waste is one of the strongest. Naturally, therefore, science is supposed to furnish the method to be followed. But right here we also stand at one point where our criticism comes in—the overemphasis on science in education. It is, for instance, stated that curriculum construction is a highly technical thing that claims experts in a specific science of curriculum construction. You have numerous professors, assistants, and helpers steadily, scientifically working in this field. You do research work in the selection and arrangements of materials of instruction. We are told about collections of thousands of courses of study to be examined and evaluated.

One of the tasks has been to write new textbooks. Do not be afraid, the educators seemed to assure us, the skills here have been proved to be of importance for all in everyday life. No "highbrow stuff" at all. Pupils do not lose time. What we teach is of direct practical value. We have found out the one hundred additional facts which everybody must know. We have analyzed cookbooks, factory payrolls, advertisements, trade catalogues. We have asked bankers what they think citizens ought to know about banking. The spelling books and readers have to be built upon investigations of the words actually used by children and adults when they write.

In social sciences the problem was more difficult, but serious, scientific attempts were made. One educator tried to examine political platforms from 1860 to 1916 in order to discover the fundamental recurring problems for the course in civics. Others tried by reading newspapers and magazines to determine the "social worth-whileness" of geographical and historical facts. Here, however, curriculum makers tend, more and more, to become analysts of American life; they hope to find out which generalizations and concepts are needed in order to understand contemporary life.

By a similar study of child life it is supposed to become increasingly possible to make textbooks conform to the abilities and attainments of the children.

The task is not only to find out what should be included in the courses, what material should be assigned to different grades, and in what order and arrangement they should be presented, but also to test objectively the results obtained from present instruction, evaluate critically and constructively the scientific investigations of curriculum making and the accomplishments of these new types of courses. And then, finally, when their findings and recommendations have been put into practice, they follow their application in public schools, collect reactions of school people to the proposed program, test results obtained by different organizations of material found to be socially valuable, and finally report these findings periodically to the school public.

It seems to be assumed that the different school systems ought, as much as possible, to coöperate with the specialists in curriculum making. The schools should always follow carefully the new findings and modify their curricula in accordance with these. Their courses of study should be modified continuously. Through a special machinery of curriculum making within each school system, it might be guaranteed that the curriculum of the school keeps pace with the advance of educational science and with the ceaseless change of life.

We get the impression that the American public-school system is, or hopes to become, an apparatus invented and worked out in every detail by professionals, technicians, and experts. Nothing is to be here by accident; everything fills out a place—bought by the sweat of many a professor's countless hours of work.

The large centers seem to be the laboratories. The big leaders are the technicians, the research workers, and the experts. From these laboratories, too, just as in a modern factory, the findings are to be realized through the efforts of the principals and teachers.

An almost amazing example of the degree to which schools are made, constructed, worked out in every detail, we get, for instance, from curriculum construction in Detroit. Many Europeans will first become absolutely mute when they read about the construction of, for instance, a new course of study in spelling. We are astonished by the American phenomenal administrative abilities, their almost frenzied eagerness to organize, to investigate, to solve practical problems, their desire to reach new standards of efficiency. They do not spare anything, neither money nor work.

However, even when I am most optimistic about it, there always arise in my mind two fundamental doubts, a doubt in regard to the kind of people who stand behind the whole movement and a doubt in regard to the teachers who have to give life to this highly elaborated school. I cannot help but ask myself: Is this movement an expression of creative abilities or is it rather an indication of a certain spiritual dryness and narrowness? Is it not more likely a caricature of life, created by our modern "tested-facts" culture, where confidence in man has been replaced by confidence in a method, which has little or nothing to do with real thinking? Is it not an expression of a world which has no clear idea of what direction it wants to go?

Being unable to create a school as a living expression of leading ideas in society as such, they fall back upon the scientific method, they try to construct a curriculum, a kind of machinery to be put to work by a worker, by a teacher. Science without any vision behind it! Is it not only an escape?

And now the other doubt. When we have seen to what degree American education goes out from laboratories and how these laboratories influence teacher-training institutions, what can we expect from the teachers? Can we, with reason, expect that they will be strong and creative enough to use educational science merely as a means? Is it not more reasonable to fear, especially when we know to what degree American people are prepared for belief in "scientific methods," that they in the normal schools will succumb to a spirit of "science" and "tested facts"? How shall a teacher, even if she has had the possibilities of becoming a harmoniously developed human being, be able to escape this belief in what is average, what is "proved"? Every moment her own inner life will be cut into pieces, because she cannot trust herself and feel responsible, but has to build upon measurements and methods, mechanism put in between herself and her pupil, the individual child.

What will be the result of a nation-wide movement where the placement of material, the construction of a curriculum, and continuous improvement and replacement of its different parts play a far bigger rôle than the subject matter itself—a love of it—and than the teachers who have to interpret it, to teach it? How is it possible that a movement such as this can go on without, in the long run, narrowing not only the relatively few scientists, but also—and this is of much greater importance!—the thousands of teachers? How can the school become a truly cultural agency if the teachers are supposed to be workers only skilled to the point and for the purpose of being able to put a curriculum to work? In other words—and this is my real point—is this excellently elaborated curriculum not bought too dearly?

What now is the conception of education underlying this kind of curriculum-construction work? Education, we are often told in this connection, is primarily preparation for life and life is a series of activities. The task of the curriculum maker will be to discover what the activities are which make up man's life. If we find them, we have the objectives of education. The underlying point of view is clearly indicated in such a statement as this, that "the analysis of man's activities, his physical and mental behavior, together constitute something akin to a complete living." In other words, when by an analysis you have found out that a man's activities include so and so many skills, so and so much information, and some satisfaction from music or literature, then you, if an educator, have only to construct a curriculum which meets all these needs and you will have a complete curriculum.

Behind this conception of education we find a conception of life—the belief that we have given our children what they need, if we succeed in giving them a curriculum built upon a complete analysis of men's activities. But even if a mother gives her newborn child the necessary food, will it suffice, if she does not, at the same time give it her love?

There are human beings who cannot consider life merely as a series of needs to be satisfied and abilities to be developed so that a man may be capable of earning a living and have a comparatively pleasant and reasonably spent leisure time. They rather believe that a man first becomes a man at the moment he becomes a part of a whole, or, better, gets something to live for and struggle for because he has come to love something. Such people cannot agree that a school can be created by constructing a scientific curriculum. They think that the curriculum must have a core, that the separate parts of it, in order to be valuable, must be held together by a connective force, just as the child's food is just one special expression of his mother's love. When we teach a boy reading or social science, this must be just one special expression of our love for the child or for the content of the subject we deal with.

This demand will have to be fulfilled through the teacher. Therefore, the education of a teacher or, better, the cultivation of a type of teacher, is a—or perhaps the—deciding factor in education. The teacher shall be, so to say, an incarnation of the curriculum. The inner core in the curriculum as well as in the teacher will, of course, in most cases simply reflect an inner core in society life as such.

As a consequence, I therefore believe that the normal schools have a greater task than to make professional teachers out of thousands of girls. The normal schools should become more independent of laboratories and educational science. They should develop a tradition of their own, should become centers for American life, social and cultural. Here the students, with the help of mature men and women, should have an opportunity to meet the life of today and cultural tradition as a living reality. Professors, for whom ideas are driving forces, can create anew the normal schools, bring the students into an immediate contact with life, open a world for them, and awaken and stimulate interests. Then everything they do later on in the classroom will have a double meaning. Thus this excellently elaborated curriculum will come into its rightful use. Is not a curriculum much more dependent upon the teacher than independent of her? If a teacher is merely mechanical and sweet, I fear that even the best curriculum will fail.

7

A Refugee Teacher Looks on Democratic and Fascist Education

As hard as we tried to avoid fascism and to restore democracy in my small country—far away in Central Europe—it was in vain. So it might seem to be useless that I, one of the refugees, after the complete surrender of freedom in Austria, write about democratic and fascist education in America, the stronghold of individual liberty, and as I believe, the hope of the whole progressive world.

We—coming from Europe—the happy group of an innumerable army of refugees and prisoners, must confess that we did a bad job in defending the culture of our fatherland, defending the freedom of creed, political opinion, free press and free speech, freedom of religious and national minorities. I must admit that all our attempts to solve political, economical or educational problems failed. And yet, coming from Europe, we have perhaps a great advantage which will help us to contribute to the progress of democracy. We faced fascism, we suffered from fascism and we still suffer from fascism, as it is impossible for human beings whose hearts are not made of stone, to forget their relatives and friends, to forget their people facing fear, terror and death day after day.

We had to pay dearly for this experience and we shall make good use of it. We know the enemy. We know his slogans of independence for suppressed nations and we saw his real deeds. We haven't forgotten and we shall not forget. And so it seems to me appropriate to write about this experience and to try to serve my new country as best I can.

Rudolf Ekstein. "A Refugee Teacher Looks on Democratic and Fascist Education," *Education,* Vol. 60 (October, 1939), pp. 101–109. Reprinted by kind permission of the editors of *Education.*

Author Austrian (1912–   ): Born in Austria, educated at the University of Vienna and Boston University; he has held teaching appointments at City College, New York, and New York University; 1947–1957, Teaching Analyst, Menninger Foundation, Topeka, Kansas; since 1957 Coordinator of Training and Research, Reiss-Davis Child Guidance Clinic; since 1959, Lecturer, L. A. Psychoanalytic Institute.

I have mentioned already that there were many problems we couldn't solve. I only want to make some remarks on educational problems, to which I devoted my work and interest.

Usually when we were asked about the aim of education, we answered: We want our children to get the right attitude for life, to have the right personality, to become capable for the struggle of life. This answer would be clear enough if our society wouldn't change, if all institutions would last; in other words, if we had to educate our children always for the same surroundings.

The child is not fit for society and it must be fitted by means of education. To be fit for society means to be willing to recognize the same rules of living as all grown-ups. But the rules, the laws of society are changing in different times and in different countries.

Different goals, different means! So it is right to say that education deals with the problem of bringing up the children, so that they are willing to play our game of life, to recognize our rules and our laws. But we must add also the kind of game we want to play.

Different games, different rules!—Different rules, different instruction. If we want to understand educational problems (I mean thereby all questions concerning the educational means we need to reach a certain goal of education) of democracy and fascism, we have to ask first: "What is their goal of their education?" What is the goal of fascist education? I will try to point it out in a few words.

You will understand the fascist attitude after I have translated the refrain of a song they have to sing now in Germany, Austria and in Czechoslovakia. I saw kindergarten children, school children, boys and girls, Nazi Youth, storm troopers, policemen, soldiers, war veterans and even war cripples, all forced into organizations of the present government, marching—yes, and even kindergarten children marching the goose-step—and singing:

> "We shall go on marching,
> even though all is falling to pieces;
> today Germany belongs to us,
> tomorrow the whole world."

The educational goal of fascism is to have youth willing for marching, fighting, killing; even though all is falling to pieces. The whole population in fascist states has to be ready for war, when the leader orders. The following "whisper" joke illustrates the life of Germans and Austrians: Germans within the frontiers are divided into two great parts. One part marches, the other part sits; not on chairs, but in concentration camps. The Youth has to be prepared, physically and mentally, to obey blindly the so-called leader. This goal of education needs special means.

In that case we should better say "training," as their means of education have nothing to do with intellect and mind.

The fascist means of education are not very complicated. You need only one means, if you want to suppress all intellectual impulses and to revive all aggressive, destroying instincts in young people. This means is called power, unlimited power.

All schools, all youth organizations, all kindergartens, all educational institutions must be in the hands of the government. No private school, no religious school, no free school organizations of the workers. They suppress now the last remainders of free organizations. But they control not only all educational institutions, they try also to destroy the influence of family life.

They say (and they are right from their point of view) we need no special intellectual youth. The teacher must use his lessons chiefly for propaganda. I need not mention that they force all teachers to join the fascist teacher organization. Every school subject can and has to be used for propaganda. In history they are taught that Germany won all wars, that Germany is the greatest nation and only through betrayal, through robbery by their inferior enemies did they lose their place in the sun. History is not used to teach historical facts, but some historical facts (namely they leave those out which don't fit in their outlook) are used to prove that the leader, in reality the fascist system, is right and that children and adolescents should trust him and must obey him. In geography they don't wish to enrich the knowledge of their children about our earth, but they show them all countries which belong "in reality" to Germany, as they want to go on marching, even though all is falling to pieces. That is also the reason that you could buy maps in Germany, in Austria, now showing great parts of Switzerland, Poland, Lithuania, Hungary and so on within the German frontiers; and so also many colonies. But they don't care for the suppressed German part of Italy, as they are not interested to help the German minorities. In biology they are taught the superiority of German blood, of the "Aryan race." A mixture of vague unproved assumptions, nonsense and unjustified presumptions. Children are made to believe that it is very easy to "go on marching even though all is falling to pieces." In German they have to read and to comment on the speeches of the leader. In French or English they read the translations of his speeches. In chemistry they are informed how to produce and to use poison gas. In arithmetic and in algebra they have to be interested in calculating the trajectories of bullets. In science children learn all substitutes they can use in war time, and how to prepare substitute economy in every household. But most of the lessons are devoted to gymnastics: goose step, drill, target practice (all children of certain ages like to play with guns; and it is not too hard to abuse these human impulses), so that they want to "go on marching, even though all is falling to pieces"; and so that they are willing to change their individual personality and private happiness for the fantastic day dream that the whole world will belong to them tomorrow.

They must not think, because the leader is thinking for them. They should not dare to be independent individuals, to look for the truth. They are not supposed to have their own opinion or their own faith. Every teacher has to be a little leader and he has all the power he wants. He uses all his power to produce fear and anxiety in every individual; to suppress every independent emotion, to destroy all independent thinking. They are taught to be heroes, but only under orders. The teacher is not the children's helpful friend who tries as far as possible to work by intellectual means, but the powerful authority, who has to revive all aggressive emotions, gigantic fear of the single individual before the power of his leaders great and small.

But the fascists know that education is not only a matter of school, but of family life and recreation time, too. And so they try to control the whole life of the child. Every boy, every girl is forced to be a member of the Nazi youth movement. And the Nazi youth movement tries to attain what school couldn't complete: to conquer the souls of its members so that it can use their strength and their idealism. All children like uniforms (unfortunately, also many grown-ups) and so you can see our German and Austrian youth marching in brown shirts. And so I saw also Italian black shirts from six to fourteen years of age marching in Venice, marching with rifles and daggers—not with toys, but with real rifles; and I saw boys a little older at about seventeen singing and marching to Ethiopia and Spain. Many of them didn't come back. It is now little help for their mothers to understand fascist education. It is too late, their sons are buried far from their country and can't come back.

And they have in their youth organizations the so-called leader principle. They can't choose their leaders; all leaders are nominated by higher leaders. Every member fears his leader and has to obey. Every group leader fears his district leader and has to wait for orders, and so on up to the top of the pyramid, the highest leaders of the whole system. They do not have to fear other leaders, but they fear too. They fear the whole population. And so they are forced to invent new kinds of suppression, propaganda; and the greater their fear the greater suppression.

But all these means of "education" do not suffice, as there is a great danger. The children, the youth are taught to "go on marching"; but between the different aggressions in Austria, Czechoslovakia, in Ethiopia and in Spain are intervals—and they want now to "go on marching." If there is no possibility to fight against another nation, they have to fight against the enemy within the country. And as there is no enemy, they invent enemies to satisfy the youth. Aggressive emotions of the unsatisfied youth are directed against helpless national and religious minorities, perhaps the most disgusting deed of fascism. And so I saw how the Nazi children, boys of twelve, thirteen and fourteen years of age, were ordered to beat children of religious and national minorities, to steal from the shops of invented opponents of the state. I saw young brown shirts forcing helpless old women and men to clean the streets for hours on end. These events are not exceptions, but conscious actions of the system to divert the discontent.

They try also to control the family life. They can't trust the family and so they try to win the children against their parents. Parents have no influence against the orders of the youth movement leaders. I know for example a case where a mother took everything away from her son which he had stolen during one of the recent Nazi actions and she brought them back crying to those people whom she had known for many years. For fourteen years she tried to give her son the right education, and now he had to go to this group nearly every night and every Sunday. She lost her influence and is worried about the future of her child. They try also to win all parents, and children are ordered to "educate" their parents for the Nazi ideas.

But in the German and Austrian youth there are not only aggressive emotions, but also desires for peace and freedom, for useful deeds and real democracy. And in spite of all fascist education, in spite of controlled press, controlled movies, controlled books, controlled sport, in spite of all propaganda for heroism and renunciation, in spite of all power of teachers and educators, the wish for peace is not dead; they want freedom, their own life, they want democracy. And the fascist system knows it. You will understand now why the "Führer" and the "Duce" recently declared, that in Italy and Germany was real democracy. You will understand why they try to make their youth believe that the other nations want to start war against peaceful Germany and Italy. They try to make the youth believe that they are for peace and democracy; they mix truth and lies. Suppression and propaganda, intolerance, aggression against helpless people, fear and concentration camps are to "educate" their youth and of this education there is no end; it lasts and lasts: kindergarten, school, youth organization, hard labor service, stormtroopers, army, compulsory organizations for recreation time and for all professions to control the whole life for one goal: always ready for war, to "go on marching, though all is falling to pieces." You see how educational questions in fascist states are interwoven with politics. Education is only one of the means of enlarging the power of the system; and the enlarged power has to be used to enlarge power again without limit.

I am very sad that I am forced to give such a bad picture of education in Central Europe. I am not afraid to criticize fascism, but I am sad for Germany and Austria. I owe all I know, all I am able to do to my German education. I love German culture, German science and German art. These years of fascism in my great fatherland are a terrible set-back for the civilization in Germany and therefore for all mankind. This system in Germany and Italy will not last forever; but it will be very hard for us to repair the damage.

And what is the goal of democratic education? We also try to secure our attitude for the next generations. Our conception of freedom is to enrich the life of the individual. The state and its government should be the servant of the people. In fascist states every person is the slave of the power-hungry government. A government "of the people, by the people, for the people" can't exist without free speech, free press, free and secret vote, justice, tolerance, and reasonable solution of economical problems. Democracy insists therefore on having thinking people able to have their own opinion. Democracy is therefore interested in education for culture, peace and freedom. Our educational system tries to make every child able to live his own happy life without injuring the life of others. Democratic education tries to make every child understand the value of human solidarity enriching the life of all.

When I repeat "Democracy," then, I mean—of course—not to include some of the faults of our present institutions. Democracy is not yet finished and will never be finished. Democracy is an attitude to come nearer to the final goal we see—Humanity. We can't stop our efforts as long as there is hunger and unemployment; as long as there is danger of intolerance and war; as long as all our great cultural and scientific achievements are not open for all men and wished by all. We are not so weak that we have to make ourselves believe that our democratic institutions are perfectly accomplished. Only men with the real democratic attitude are also strong enough to see, to admit and to correct their faults or mistakes.

You know perhaps better than I the means of democratic education. We are going mostly along old ways, successful for many generations. We try to teach the truth, how to think, how to use science for the sake of mankind. We try to develop intellect and mind and to prove that crime and war don't pay. To accomplish this we use all we learned from our parents our own teachers and when we are reminded that it would be useful to grasp more modern ways of education, to ask science for help in our responsible task we like to answer: "This education having been good enough for us and our own parents is also good enough for our children." Many persons feel offended if we try to explain to them the value of progressive, scientific education which as one of our youngest sciences has now to fight the same resistances as medicine did some decades ago. Science helps us to prevent and to cure diseases of body and mind. Science should help also to find better means of education for our goal of a democratic attitude.

Since the great discoveries of Professor Sigmund Freud, the Viennese psychiatrist—living now as a refugee in London—we began to get help from psychology and to see how important early childhood and family life are for the whole life of every person. Education begins with mother's milk and even the first experiences of a baby influence his character. All kindergarten teachers, all nurses, all mothers know that education does not start when the child at six years of age starts to go to school, that school is only one part of education.

The family life is very important, probably decisive for the formation of the child's attitude, and his first human relations are very often responsible for his human relations when he is grown up. The infant is helpless alone and needs help and love of his grown-up surrounding. But father and mother know that they have to demand renunciations of their child. Love would be very short-sighted if the child always could do what he wants to do. The infant has to learn to eat in a correct way, to be clean, to talk correctly, to behave himself, to recognize our rules, our laws. He has to suppress or to change many wishes and urges we can't permit in our society and sometimes the way is very hard for the child. We use reward and punishment to reach our goals. At first children do the right thing because they love their parents, because they fear to lose the parent's love and help. They are good children either to get more love or to avoid punishment. They haven't yet adopted our morality. They suppress the wishes that the parents don't like only because the parents don't like them, and not because they condemn them themselves as wrong.

The infant loves his parents and fears also the punishment for wrong-doing. He wants also to be like his parents, as clever as they, as powerful as they and so he starts to imitate them and really to adapt himself to the demands of his parents. And now he doesn't fear so much the punishment for wrong-doings, but much more the wrong-doing itself. The conscience originates from that time. And we all know that pangs of conscience are a better protection for our society and our morality than the strongest laws. The formation of the human conscience is mostly completed before the beginning of school and all the child adds to his knowledge and his attitude only supplements all these things he accomplished in his first four or six years of life. And it is usually very, very hard to correct bad features gained in these first years. The child's early relation to father and mother and other members of the family influences his whole lifetime, and later when the child grows up and realizes that his parents are not as good and clever and powerful as the parents of his early childhood, he tries to find new models, new ideals as a kind of substitute and he divides his feelings towards his father of early childhood between different people and we also repeat constantly these situations of our early childhood. Many, very often used expressions are a proof for that; for example, "The teacher is like a father to me.—We defend our fatherland.—He is the father of our nation.—My boss treats his workers like a father. He wants to live and to die in the country where his father died.—He wants to be a good patriot (derived from *pater*, Latin).—This general is the father of the army." And if we can't find help in trouble we call the mightiest father for help, God the father. Many well-known songs, poems and novels are written proofs of our deep love towards our parents, of our fear to act in ways that would displease our father and mother. We want to be as good as our models, as our father of childhood; but in trouble we would like to be in the same situation as we were as infants, to get protection, help and love from our father. We all have a double soul. We want to be like our idols (sometimes these idols exist only in our imagination) and also to get their help and love and to trust them. And this is true also of whole groups, of whole nations, not only of single persons. In hard times, when we face great problems, when we see little hope we call very often for great leadership in our nation. In good times we are not very interested in great leadership, as we are able to accomplish all talks ourselves. If we can't solve our problems we hope for a great leader to help us; as the infant who calls his parents in danger.

The father is the leader of the minor infant, help in danger and in troubles, but he should show his child how to solve all problems, how to think, how to be independent, how to become a real grown-up. The child loving his parents and wanting to be like them should imitate their independent thinking, their efforts to solve all questions and not to obey them blindly. The leaders of a nation should try to make all members of the nation more and more free and independent. They should think over with them, decide and act with them. Real leadership means to bring up a child, to bring up a whole nation, so that it is able to solve its own problems without a guardian. Perhaps it is easier now to understand one of the great differences between democratic and fascist education. We want to have free children, free persons, able to think and to act alone, able to protect themselves and to defend the liberty of their people.

Fascists want people always being little children, in fear of the powerful severe father and hoping he will help, and be willing to follow him blindly.

But we must remember what we know about the importance of our first experience in the family. We gained our free attitude, our ability to form our own opinion not through intellectual means, but through our love, sometimes also our hate for our educators, our parents, our teachers. But in times of troubles, many adults would prefer the situation of their childhood and only national leaders who use their influence, the love of their followers, to make them free and independent, are capable of saving democracy.

The fascist leaders use all means in family life, in school, in recreation time,—not to educate their people to become grown-ups, but to remain helpless, fearful and minor children. And they have success, as it is much easier to keep people immature and childish in mind, than to go the long way of real education, the way of democracy.

I believe that democracy can be successful. We must only realize that not only teaching and instruction, but also education and guidance, influence and soul are building up the personality, the attitude of our children. We must use the love of our children, their trust in our experience and our strength to make them free and mature for democracy. Perhaps we haven't been successful in Europe, because we didn't understand how to influence the youth. We were talking to their brains; our arguments for peace and freedom were right, but they didn't reach the hearts of our children. And the way to the brain, the way to independent opinion leads through the heart.

The fascists began to influence the heart. They conquered at first the heart to kill the brain, to destroy free thinking and free action.

We also need leaders. But these leaders in school and in public life have to use their love for education and not for training, to bring up free men and not blind subjects of a powerful machine.

Fascist education is no education at all, only using the primitive instincts and wishes of people. They have success, because they don't have to change these wishes. All healthy boys like more or less warlike games, uniforms, guns, danger and secret groups. All children in certain periods of their lives are very aggressive. This is only natural and the task of education is to change these dangerous wishes to an attitude useful for our society.

We must understand the needs of our children and show them that all they want they can find in our democratic culture, but not in fascist barbarism. They want to be courageous and strong. They want to have ideals, good models they can love, trust and imitate.

It is courageous to defend the liberty of every member of the nation. It is courageous to destroy all remainders of inequality between different groups in our nation. It is courageous and dangerous to work on the skyscrapers, on the great bridges and to build great dams. It is courageous to decide independently, to think and to act as a free man; but it is not courageous to follow a leader blindly like a small child. It is not courageous to beat and to torment helpless people. We have real ideals for our children. It is right to love, to trust and to imitate men, like the American officer who recently brought medicine on an airplane to the population of Chile after the earthquake; what he did was more courageous and better than to drop bombs on poor helpless Ethiopians. It is more courageous to risk one's life exploring the South Pole and to fight alone against nature, than to destroy the churches of defenceless and peaceful people. It is more courageous and better to fight for the freedom of slaves, than to burn scientific books and to close scientific institutions. The lives of our great inventors, explorers, writers are much more thrilling than the life of a watchdog in a concentration camp. Our children should understand that democracy means also, if necessary, to defend with all means our freedom and that a free and prepared nation can't be defeated.

In the present fascist states cultural values are meaningless and despised. The fascist youth is taught only to esteem and to worship the men of war, the powerful uniforms and the medals. But the uniforms of today will be forgotten in a very short time and the real heroes of today, scientists, explorers, inventors, writers, artists, all together working for peace and freedom, shall be the leaders of culture.

Fortunately I had the chance to choose between democracy and fascism. I had the chance to select a country, where the great majority of the people have my attitude. I shall not "go on marching, even though all is falling to pieces." I prefer that attitude, which Abraham Lincoln expressed in these words: "As I don't want to be a slave, I also don't want to be a master." I am very happy to work in an American school and I am particularly glad, as this school is interested in progressive education, using the advantages of science to reach the right goal. I shall try my best to go the way of democracy. And I have, in spite of all the dark clouds in Europe and in Far East, still the hope, that the American way of today will become tomorrow the way of the whole world. My hope is America!

8

Unity, Liberty and Education

The word school in America covers every type of educational institution. Being "at school" may mean being at a kindergarten or at Harvard. School, too, has kept much of its Greek meaning. It is a system of organization and training for leisure as well as work. And it has become more and more adjusted to its environment, undertaking to do more than it can (which is very American) and doing much more than it seems to do (which is also very American).

The social and political role of American education cannot be understood if it is thought of as being primarily a means of formal instruction. If it is so thought of, it will be overrated and underrated. It will be overrated because the number of college students or high-school pupils will dazzle the visitor used to seeing opportunities for higher education doled out on a combined class-and-intellectual basis. It will be underrated if, at any stage below the highest (that is, below the great universities), the academic standards are compared with those of a good English, French, or pre-Hitler German school. If these millions of boys and girls are to be judged by their academic accomplishments, they will be judged harshly. But they are not to be so judged, for their schools are doing far more than instruct them: they are letting them instruct each other in how to live in America.

Of those millions, a large section will be the children of immigrants to whom English is still largely a foreign tongue. Of these millions, a very large proportion will be the children of migrants from different parts of the United States. Others will be the children of rural-bred parents, forced to adjust themselves to the new urban world. They have to learn a common language, common habits, common tolerances, a common political and national faith. And they do. It is this aim and this success that justify the lavish buildings of the local high school;

Dennis W. Brogan. "Unity and Liberty," Part 2, Section 5, in *The American Character* [1944] (New York: Vintage Books, 1959 edition), pp. 161–178. Reprinted by kind permission of Vintage Books, New York.

Author (1900–   ): Educated Rutherglen Academy, Glasgow University and Balliol College, Oxford. He also studied at Harvard University, where he received a MA in American history. Lecturer at Harvard University, University College, London, and at the London School of Economics, London University, Fellow of Peterhouse College and Professor of Political Science, Cambridge University.

not merely the classrooms and the laboratories, but the gymnasium, the field-house where basketball can be played in comfort in the depth of the bitter winter, the swimming pools in which the summer heat can be endured.

It is true that the teachers are relatively badly paid and have an inferior social as well as economic standing, insecure tenure and politics making their condition worse. More money spent on men might get better results than more money spent on buildings. But it is easier to get the materials for buildings than the materials for teachers. As long as American society remains individualistic, competitive, confident that the answers to the present are in the future, not in the past, it is going to take more than money to seduce the right men and women in adequate numbers away from the life of action. And, a point too seldom remembered, the necessity for providing teachers for the millions of college students hampers recruiting for high schools. In many cases, the colleges are doing what is really high-school work and it matters comparatively little where the good teachers are, as long as they are teaching.

The political function of the schools is to teach Americanism, meaning not merely political and patriotic dogma, but the habits necessary to American life. This justifies the most extravagant items in the curriculum. Since the ability to play bridge is one of the marks of Americanism in a suburb, it is reasonable that there should be bridge clubs in schools. The main political achievement of the high schools and grammar schools is to bring together the young of all classes and all origins, to provide, artificially, the common background that in an old, rural society is provided by tradition, by the necessary collaboration of village life. The elementary schools—the "grade" schools—do this, too, but as far as an American town is broken up into racial blocs, the Ethan Allen Public School may have mainly Polish pupils, the Zachary Chandler mainly Welsh. Only in the Warren G. Harding High School is a big enough common pool formed in which Americans can be made.

Some of that Americanization is, of course, done deliberately and formally. Mr. Carlton Hayes pointed out long ago that the ritual of flag-worship and oath-taking in an American school is a religious observance. Little boys and girls, in a school from which religion in the old sense is barred, solemnly rising each morning and reciting together the "American's Creed"[1] are performing a religious exercise as truly

[1] "I believe in the United States of America as a Government of the people, by the people, for the people; whose just powers are derived from the consent of the governed, a democracy in a republic; a sovereign Nation of many sovereign states; a perfect union, one and inseparable; established upon those principles of freedom, equality, justice, and humanity for which American patriots sacrificed

as if they began the day with "I believe in God the Father Almighty" or asserted that "There is no God but God."

And that these daily rituals are religious has been at last affirmed by the Supreme Court in a series of cases in which the children of a fanatical sect, Jehovah's Witnesses, had been excluded from schools for refusing to give to the flag honors that, so their parents had taught them, were due to God alone. In 1940, all the Court except Chief Justice Stone held that flag-worship was among the things that were Caesar's. Since that year, however, by a majority they decided that the religious rights of the children were being infringed. What is significant in the cases is not the Court's reversal of itself but the reality of the issue presented to it. For to the Court, and to the overwhelming majority of the American people, the objections of the Witnesses were as unintelligible as the objections of the Christians to making a formal sacrifice to the Divine Emperor were to Trajan and Pliny. The school board of Minersville, Pennsylvania, was faced with a real problem when it was asked to admit that children refusing to take part in the most sacred rite of the day should be allowed to associate with the believing children of the formally unestablished national church of the United States. So, too, was the state of Oregon when it found Catholic and Lutheran children refusing to go to the schools it provided. But in both cases the Supreme Court held, finally, that compulsory Americanism was not Americanism at all, that coerced belief was not what the American people needed to stay united. This was not Germany or Russia but the country of Jefferson and Justice Holmes.

The flag-worship of the American school and the American nation was brought home in war time to the British public in an episode that, if funny, was also very revealing. For the London makers of ladies' underwear who adorned their garments with American flags were innocent of any insulting or even frivolous intention. At the same time, a revue chorus in London was attired in Union Jack handkerchiefs and nothing else—to the public indifference. But the flag in America is more than a mere symbol among many others. It is the regimental color of a regiment in which all Americans are enrolled. Its thirteen stripes and forty-eight stars are symbols far better understood than the complicated heraldry of crosses of Saint George, Saint Andrew, and Saint Patrick imposed on each other in a way that only experts understand. It was Lincoln's task to see that the number of stars in the flag was not dimin-

---

their lives and fortunes. I therefore believe it is my duty to my country to love it; to support its Constitution; to obey its laws; to respect its flag, and to defend it against all enemies." As a result of the current wave of patriotic religion, the phrase "under God" has been inserted into the "American's Creed."

ished by eleven during his term of office. It was the discovery that
the flag flew over Fort McHenry, despite the British fleet, that moved
Francis Scott Key to write:

> Oh, say, can you see by the dawn's early light,
>   What so proudly we hailed at the twilight's last gleaming;
> Whose broad stripes and bright stars, thro' the perilous fight,
>   O'er the ramparts we watched were so gallantly streaming?

What he wrote in 1814, tens of millions of Americans have since sung
or tried to sing. And when Barbara Frietchie in Whittier's poem rebuked
Stonewall Jackson with:

> "Shoot if you must this old gray head,
>   But spare your country's flag," she said,

she was speaking for all Americans for whom the Stars and Stripes
was still their country's flag as it had been, till recently, that of General
Jackson. And the most celebrated ritual moment of the last war was
the hoisting of the Stars and Stripes on Iwo Jima, caught, in a happy
moment, by a quick-witted San Francisco photographer. The three figures, straining to keep the flag erect, were "the Spirit of '76" in action
and symbol.

Thus Americanization by ritual is an important and necessary part
of the function of the American school. And because it is best carried
out in schools, it matters little that the high-school curriculum has been
so widened that it no longer means a great deal that this boy or that
girl was graduated from it—if we are looking for proof of academic
achievement. But graduation from high school is reasonable proof that
a great deal has been learned about American ways of life, that lessons
in practical politics, in organization, in social ease have been learned
that could not have been learned in factory or office.

And if the high school seems to devote too much time and money
to social life, penalizing the poor boy or girl more than a theoretically
less democratic educational system might do, it is thus early impressing
an awkward truth on the boy or girl who is both mediocre and poor.
It also penalizes the really able boy or girl who is not kept in good
enough intellectual training. And if the main business of the school
is, in fact, the Americanization of the children of newcomers, the parents
of "old American stock" have a good reason (to add to less good ones)
for not sending their children to learn what they know already, at the
cost of diminishing their chance of learning what they do not know.
If English is native to your children and to their home, it is not merely
"undemocratic" to object to having their progress held up and their accent
debased by the tone of a high school largely immigrant in composition.

For the task of an American school in many regions is to teach the American language, to enable it to compete with Spanish, with French, with Yiddish, with Polish, with German, with Swedish. Another task is to give, through the language and the literature of the language, a common vocabulary and a common fund of allusion, fable, and sentiment. With a fluid population this has not been easy. And the countless teachers who have labored, pedantically, formally, with complete and erroneous conviction that there were correct standards, have been heroes as important in the mass as was William McGuffey, whose *Eclectic Readers* sold over one hundred and twenty million copies and helped to make the Union. The teachers were heroes because, although English won against all its rivals, it was itself going through important changes, in vocabulary, in grammar, in sound, becoming the new tongue we are beginning to call American. The teachers who stuck by the rules, who worshipped at the New England shrines in Concord, were bound to lose, but their struggle was not pure waste. For the common tongue, hammered out by millions of immigrants, by millions of migrants, would have been poor in vocabulary and structure but for the people Mencken called the dominies and who call themselves schoolmen. The creation of general literacy and a common written and spoken tongue, intelligible everywhere except possibly in the deep South, is an achievement as remarkable as the creation of Mandarin Chinese or Low Latin or Hellenistic Greek, and this tongue is certain to be the new *lingua franca* of the world.

The making of American has been mixed-up in English minds with the making of American slang. Slang, as we should know, is one of the great sources of language. French is improved Latin slang. And slang has contributed a good deal to American. It is a generation since Mr. Dooley said that when his countrymen had finished with the English language it would look as if it had been run over by a musical comedy. Since then it has been run over by *Hellzapoppin*. But it is possible, indeed very easy, to overestimate the role of slang. It is more and more the creation of professional artists, "makers." The Hollywood prose masters provide a current and often short-lived jargon; the boys and girls, men and women, who wish to be on the beam or in the groove, may murmur with admiration: "I wish I had said that." And Whistler's classical answer to Wilde is certainly appropriate: "You will, Oscar—you will!" But not for long. Some slang will enter the language; some words will lose their meanings or acquire new ones; syntax will be loosened up. But formal speech as taught in schools will still be very important. The high-school English teacher, for all her pedantry, is as much a maker of the American language as Messrs. Runyon and O'Hara. Two streams of language may run roughly parallel, but in time they will merge; they will provide America with many interesting variations, do for American what its dual Germanic and Latin character does for English. That time has not yet come, but it is on the way. And the future character of his truly national tongue is foreshadowed in the drawing by Mr. Peter Arno in which an indignant citizen tells another: "I consider your conduct unethical and lousy."

Most American parents do not want, or are not able, to send their children to anything but public high schools, and the life in such a school is a training in life for America. It may be and often is a training in life *against* Europe. For Europe is the background from which many of the children are reacting and from which they must be delivered if they are to be Americanized. For nearly all immigrants, America is promotion, and this promotion is more clearly felt by their children. The old people may hanker after the old country, but the children— whatever sentimental feelings for their ancestral homes they may have, especially when provoked—are, above all else, anxious to be Americans.

Necessarily something is lost here. The least-common-denominator Americanism of the schools is not a complete substitute for a native culture. What the first-generation American children learn to despise may include elements in their moral diet that are not replaced. A new American whose pride in that promotion involves mere contempt for the habits, what Americans call the "folkways" or "mores," of his parents is not necessarily a good American. So attempts are made to instill pride in the ancestral cultures of the European lands from which the immigrants come. The University of Pittsburgh, located in one of the main melting pots of America, has a set of rooms illustrating the culture of various European countries. In the case of the Greeks, the room may instill adequate pride; in the case of the Scots (if any such need is felt) a shrine of Robert Burns may serve. But for many of the peasant immigrants, the old country is backward though beloved, while for their children it is merely backward.

Americanization comes not from preservation of Slovak or Italian peasant culture, but from speedy assimilation to "American" culture. And that assimilation may take the form of distinction in anything that the American world obviously values. In the narrow sense of culture, there may even be a temptation to go for those courses that have no immigrant stigma on them. Thus I was told by an eminent Scandinavian-American that it is difficult to get good students of Scandinavian literature and language at the University of Minnesota, though most of the students have fairly recent Scandinavian connections. They will study French but not Swedish, for "French is not a servant's language."

Latin, emblem of functionless "culture," plays something of the same role; it is a symbol of liberation. It is said that the only high school in New York where everybody takes Latin is a Negro high school.

Study is not the only way up to Americanization, to acceptance. Sport is another—and one that does the job more dramatically for the newcomers gifted with what it takes to excel in competitive contests, with what is needed to win personal and community and institutional glory.

When Fanny Ellsler, the ballet dancer, came to Boston, her performance was solemnly inspected from the highest motives by Emerson and Margaret Fuller. "The dance began; both sat serenely silent; at last Emerson spoke. 'Margaret,' he said, 'this is poetry.' 'No, Waldo,' replied Margaret; 'it is not poetry, it is religion.' "[2] And the great football games of today are religious ceremonies in this sense. It is significant that the graduating classes in Muncie High School a generation ago took such mottoes as "Deo duce" and today take mottoes stressing the "Bearcat Spirit," the "Bearcats" being the school basketball team. But a Greek would know where he was at a basketball game uniting boys and girls, parents and civic leaders, in a common passion for competitive achievement. It may be hard on the academic work of the school. It may even slightly annoy a schoolboy who, as Mr. Burton Rascoe did, combines excellence in gymnastic and music, to find that his views on literature are less interesting to the other sex than his prowess at football. But sport, school sport, college sport, does unite the parents, the children, and the community. And sport is rigorously democratic. The sons of Czechs and Poles can score there, can break through the barriers that stand in the way of the children of "Bohunks" and "Polacks." And although Harvard may secretly rejoice when it can put a winning team on to Soldiers' Field whose names suggest the Mayflower, it would rather put on a team that can beat Yale, even though it is not a "Yankee" team, than go down to defeat with the descendants of generations of Brahmins. And in the Middle West, sport is a real means of promotion. The Ohio high school that produced the great Negro runner, Jesse Owens, was prouder of him than if he had made Phi Beta Kappa at Ohio State; and Hitler would have made a less serious mistake if he had snubbed a great American scholar whose race he didn't like than he did by sulking at the Olympic Games when the Herrenvolk were beaten by a Negro. It is a frontier tradition; Lincoln's great strength gave him a prestige that helped him as a lawyer and politician. The great athlete performing for the glory of the school, college, state, or nation, is a less egoistic figure than the great scholar pursuing his own

[2] Barrett Wendell: A Literary History of America, p. 301.

studies with an undemocratic concentration. And the Negroes, whose greatest hero is Joe Louis, not Paul Robeson, are not substantially wrong so far. In American society as it is, a Negro heavyweight champion, like a Negro tap-dancer, is a better adjusted figure than a great Negro artist—or America is a less maladjusted society for them. Of course, this will not and should not last. The Irish were rising when their great hero became Governor Al Smith, rather than a successor of John L. Sullivan, the "Boston strong boy." But to get asset to a Negro's *right* to be heavyweight champion is something—as those will agree who remember the frenzied search round 1910 for a "white hope" to save the heavyweight championship from the indignity of being held by Jack Johnson. Great Indian athletes like Jim Thorpe, great Negro football heroes like Paul Robeson in his earlier days, the polyglot teams put on the field by the great Swedish coach Knut Rockne for the "Irish" of Notre Dame—these become "All-American" figures in a wider and deeper sense than that in which the Yale of Walter Camp understood the term. Indeed, when Mr. Camp put Paul Robeson of Rutgers on his All-American team, he was marking, very effectively, the rise of the exceptional Negro. And Negro pioneers in big-league baseball, like Satchel Paige (*monumentum ære perennius*), are more important figures in race history than the universally accepted and admired Willie Mays.

The cheer-leaders, the new *"jongleurs de Notre Dame,"* the "major-ettes," shapely young women more or less involved with musical instru-ments, the massed cheering sections of the students, the massed yelling sections of the alumni—these are the equivalent of the crowds at the great Hellenic festivals in which barbarians were not allowed to compete. The Rose Bowl, the Cotton Bowl, the other intersectional games—these are instruments of national unity, and the provision of such instruments is no mean duty of colleges and universities. It is a religious exercise of a kind a Greek would have understood, however remote it may be from the university as understood by Abelard or Saint Thomas Aquinas or John Harvard.

The university, as these men understood it, exists all the same and exists to play a great national part, for the level of academic learning in America is perhaps the only branch of American life where the prom-ise of rapid progress upward has been consistently kept. It is not as easy to define the nature of that progress as it is to affirm its existence.

Things have changed a great deal since the ideal of American college education was "Mark Hopkins at one end of a log and a student at the other." Then the college existed to provide a common background for lawyers and doctors and divines; it was small and select, not select in a social or financial sense, but select in that only those who accepted the old intellectual order of things were catered for. It was a decisive moment when President Eliot of Harvard (which had long ceased to concentrate on providing for a "learned ministry") introduced the elective system. The college abandoned any idea of imposing a hierarchy of subjects. The student could select what he wanted from the menu provided; *à la carte* had succeeded *table d'hôte*. But in newer, less secure, less rich institutions than Harvard, the change went farther than that, for not only was the student free to choose from what was offered—he was entitled to complain if the college did not offer what he wanted to learn, or even what he wanted to learn in the sense that it was all he could hope to learn. As more and more students came to college with varying school preparation, as life grew more complex and the techniques of life and business more impressive in their results, the unity of college life disappeared. Boys and girls were no longer taken in hand by a successor of Mark Hopkins and given a few general ethical and philosophical ideas suitable to a world still pretty much agreed on fundamentals. They were visitors to an institution that seemed to have more in common with the Mark Hopkins Hotel in San Francisco than with the Williams College of a century ago; and from the glass-walled bar, "The Top of the Mark," they could see the modern world, the bridges and skyscrapers of San Francisco, and across the Bay the lights of Berkeley, where the University of California provides for all tastes from addicts of the Greek theater to the most modern biological and physical techniques.

In this necessary adaptation of the old university ideal to the modern American world, much was lost, or not provided; there was not as yet a common standard of reference for educated men; a mass of information was stored and techniques were imparted in institutes physically associated for historical reasons. But of course the universities and colleges, like the high schools, served other than merely academic ends. *Our Town* illustrates high-school mating which would have taken place anyway. *The Miracle of Morgan's Creek* shows a suitor taking cookery so as to be close to his beloved during her high-school career, but he was bound to be close to her anyway. But the college movie, play (*The Poor Nut*), and novel rightly illustrate the more important phenomenon of exogamous marriage, of bringing together boys and girls who otherwise would not meet at all.

Besides all these activities (formally described as extracurricular) there is, of course, a great deal of first-class academic work done. And in one very important field the American public, if it wills, is given admirable opportunities for learning relevant facts about the modern external world as well as about its own past and present. No charge can be less well founded than that which holds the American school of today up to scorn for its uncritical jingoism. It is no longer true that American history is taught as a simple story of black (George III) vs. white (George Washington). A generation of critical scholarship has borne fruit in an objective and even slightly cynical treatment of the American Revolution and other great crises of American history. If the old simple story is still told and believed, that is not the fault of the schools. And contemporary American life is treated with the same candor. Nothing could be in more striking contrast than the legend of Southern life as it is told and retold by politicians and preachers and the grim, courageous, critical studies of the contemporary South that come from the universities, above all from the University of North Carolina.

It is not only American problems that are studied and analyzed with such learning, acuteness, and candor. World problems are, too. There is no country in the world where discussion of the world's affairs is carried on at such a high level as in the United States. (There are also few countries where it is carried on at such a low level, but that is another story.) Serious discussion, in great newspapers and magazines, in forums and on the air, in universities and institutes, is incessant. And it is discussion by real experts. Unfortunately, it is often discussion for experts, not for the people. For them, as the *Saturday Evening Post* rightly pointed out, the most complicated subjects in international politics are just another "study subject," the theme of accurate and objective but rather chilly debate by those who like that kind of thing.

And the very success of the school system in Americanizing the American young may result in the killing of natural curiosity. For example, the cult of the Constitution leads to the exclusive identification of a political concept like "liberty" with the American constitutional system. This being so, a Latin-American "republic" with a paper constitution like the American is regarded as "free" while Canada is not. For Canada is part of an "empire" with a monarch at the head of it. Some two thirds of the American people, accordingly, quite recently thought that Canada pays taxes to Britain; even in the states bordering on the Dominion, about half the Americans thought this! In the same way, the word "republic" has an almost magical significance for the Americans. Plutarch, as Mr. Wells once suggested, had a good deal to do with this; but, whatever the origins of the belief, it is now part of the American credo that only citizens of a republic can be free. And no matter what romantic interest Americans may display in the human side of monarchy, it should never be forgotten that, politically, they regard it as a childish institution. Mark Twain, a very pro-English American, refused for that very reason to write one of his amusing, critical travel books about England. But he did write two books about England, all the same: *The Prince and the Pauper* and *A Connecticut Yankee at the Court of King Arthur.* How deeply anti-monarchical, anti-clerical, anti-traditional, those books are!

And in *Huckleberry Finn*, the traditional American view of royalty as expensive foolishness is admirably set forth in Huck's remark to Nigger Jim: "Sometimes I wish we could hear of a country that's out of kings."

A great many Americans still think like Huck Finn. And it must be remembered that for Americans the great event of their own and of world history was the destruction of the royal power of George III and the establishment of a Constitution guaranteeing to each state "a republican form of government." It is in that light that the modern world is seen by nearly all Americans.

Nothing is more natural and understandable than the American assumption that all modern historical events are either American or unimportant. The Pole who wrote a book on *The Elephant and the Polish Question* was not merely a typical Pole but a typical human being. There are remote academic subjects that we study, and real, living subjects that concern us. "Listen to my bomb story and I'll listen to yours," as they said in London in 1940. Therefore the American conviction that the First World War really began in 1917, and that the Second one began on December 7, 1941, is simply an American example of a general illusion. We know that the Chinese were fighting the Japanese long before we were, but we don't *feel* it. We could remember, if we tried, that the Poles were fighting the Germans a little before the British and long before the Russians or the Americans, but we don't feel any urgency to recall it. The Americans who, in March 1944, learned that their countrymen had bombed Berlin for the first time were astonished. The "We" who bombed Berlin in 1943 included Americans psychologically, but the "We" who bombed Tokyo didn't include British either factually or psychologically. This is all part of human nature. The Russians, with little experience of navigating on the high seas, could hardly be expected to appreciate that crossing the English Channel and invading are not quite the same thing as crossing even a wide river. Julius Caesar's Mediterranean sailors, after all, had to learn that the hard way in 55 B.C. Of course this human attitude can be carried to extravagant lengths. A Frenchman might or might not be amused, but would certainly be surprised, to learn from a handout of the National Geographic Society that it was "Decatur's courage [which] paved the way for colony-minded France to annex most of Barbary to her African empire."[3]

Such an attitude can be very irritating, yet the assumption that world history is part of American history is healthier than any belief that the two are completely separate and that the one is real while the other is merely interesting. It is only when the heads and hearts of the American people are touched that they can be induced to listen to a call from the outer world for leadership. And that leadership will be given only if moral as well as material interests are involved. The only appeal that will be listened to will be the appeal to come over to Macedonia and help.

"It will be no cool process of mere science. . . . The feelings with which we face this new age of right and opportunity sweep across our heartstrings like some air out of God's own presence, where justice and mercy are reconciled and the judge and the brother are one. . . . Men's hearts wait upon us; men's lives hang in the balance; men's hopes call upon us to say what we will do. Who shall live up to the great trust? Who dare fail to try? I summon all honest men, all patriotic forward-looking men, to my side. God helping me, I will not fail them, if they will but counsel and sustain me."[4] Till that note is stuck again, no answer can be expected from the plain people.

But in the meantime millions of young Americans, serving their country, if not any general cause, were exiled in a foreign world for which their training in a sense had unfitted them. Even today, when the necessity of dealing with the outside world has had more than a decade of habit to commend it, the American serviceman, exiled in Toul or Heidelberg, in Cambridge or Wiesbaden, looks more lost, more conscious of his exile, than do, for example, drunk members of the Highland Light Infantry, or the Cameronians, on a station platform in Hamburg, comfortably convinced that wherever they are, there is forever Glasgow. The American's training has unfitted him because it was based on the theory that there is an answer available to every question; all you have got to do is to find the right authority, whether the question relates to the technique of football, of spot-welding, or of love. There is a charming optimism in this view, an optimism that, in America, is justified most of the time. It creates a world in which, as a wise American friend of mine said, there are known Plimsoll lines in most fields of conduct. It is a world in which formal good manners and comradeship are both happily cultivated between the sexes. It is true that the hearty

[3] *New York Times,* February 13, 1944.
[4] Woodrow Wilson: *First Inaugural* (1913).

camaraderie which is so charming at twenty palls a little at thirty and may give superficial justification for the sour remark of a European critic that "what the American woman suffers from is too much poor-quality attention." It may even justify another view—that American men and American women are better company apart than together, and that the men are better company than the women. But these illusions of solutions attained, in politics and in life, are a tribute to the success with which American life has been made attractive to Americans, to the vast majority of Americans who feel at home in America and are consequently swept away from their moorings in a strange world whose standards they cannot understand and from whose apparent moral and political anarchy they long to escape by going home.

9

The Negro School: A Swedish Analysis

Negro Education as Concerted Action

The trend toward a rising educational level of the Negro population is of tremendous importance for the power relations discussed in this Part of our inquiry. Education means an assimilation of white American culture. It decreases the dissimilarity of the Negroes from other Americans. Since the white culture is permeated by democratic valuations, and since the caste relation is anything but democratic, education is likely to increase dissatisfaction among Negroes. This dissatisfaction strengthens the urge to withdraw from contact with prejudiced whites and causes an intensified isolation between the two groups. Increasing education provides theories and tools for the rising Negro protest against caste status in which Negroes are held. It trains and helps to give an economic livelihood to Negro leaders.

In the Negro community, education is the main factor for the stratification of the Negro people into social classes. The professionals who base their status upon having acquired a higher education form a substantial part of the Negro upper classes. And even in the middle and lower classes, educational levels signify class differences in the Negro community. In addition, education has a symbolic significance in the Negro world: the educated Negro has, in one important respect, become equal to the better class of whites.

These tendencies are most unhampered in the North. There Negroes have practically the entire educational system flung open to them without much discrimination. They are often taught in mixed schools and by white teachers; some of the Negro teachers have white pupils. Little attempt is made to adjust the teaching specifically to the Negroes' exist-

Gunnar Myrdal. "The Negro School," in *An American Dilemma: The Negro Problem and Modern Democracy* (New York: Harper and Row, 1945), pp. 879–886, 893–907. Reprinted by kind permission of Harper and Row, New York.

Author (1898–   ): Swedish author and economist; Lecturer in Political Economy, Stockholm University, 1927; Assistant Professor, Geneva Institute Universitaire de Hautes Études Internationales, 1930; Professor of Political Economy and Financial Science, Stockholm University, 1933–1950; Researcher on behalf of the Carnegie Corporation into the Study of American Negroes; Executive Secretary, United Nations Economic Commission for Europe, Geneva, 1947–1957; Professor of International Economics, Stockholm University, 1960.

ing status and future possibilities. The American Creed permeates instruction, and the Negro as well as the white youths are inculcated with the traditional American virtues of efficiency, thrift and ambition. The American dream of individual success is held out to the Negroes as to other students. But employment opportunities—and, to a lesser extent, some other good things of life—are so closed to them that severe conflicts in their minds are bound to appear.

Their situation is, however, not entirely unique. Even among the youths from other poor and disadvantaged groups in the North the ideals implanted by the schools do not fit life as they actually experience it.[1] The conflicts are, of course, accentuated in the case of Negroes. Often they become cynical in regard to the official democratic ideals taught by the school. But more fundamentally they will be found to have drunk of them deeply. The American Creed and the American virtues mean much more to Negroes than to whites. They are all turned into the rising Negro protest.

The situation is more complicated in the South. The Negro schools are segregated and the Negro school system is controlled by different groups with different interests and opinions concerning the desirability of preserving or changing the caste status of Negroes. Looked upon as a "movement," Negro education in the South is, like the successful Negro organizations, an interracial endeavor. White liberals in the region and Northern philanthropists have given powerful assistance in building up Negro education in the South. They have thereby taken and kept some of the controls. In the main, however, the control over Negro education has been preserved by other whites representing the political power of the region. The salaried officers of the movement—the college presidents, the school principals, the professors, and the teachers—are now practically all Negroes; in the elementary schools and in the high schools they are exclusively Negroes. With this set-up, it is natural and, indeed, necessary that the Negro school adhere rather closely to the accommodating pattern.

Negro teachers on all levels are dependent on the white community leaders. This dependence is particularly strong in the case of elementary school teachers in rural districts. Their salaries are low, and their security as to tenure almost nothing. They can be used as disseminators of the whites' expectations and demands on the Negro community. But the extreme dependence and poverty of rural Negro school teachers, and the existence of Negroes who are somewhat better off and more inde-

[1] Caroline F. Ware, *Greenwich Village* (1935), pp. 455–461.

pendent than they, practically excluded them from having any status of leadership in the Negro community. In so far as their teaching is concerned, they are, however, more independent than it appears. This is solely because the white superintendent and the white school board ordinarily care little about what goes on in the Negro school. There are still counties where the superintendent has never visited the majority of his Negro schools. As long as Negro stool pigeons do not transfer reports that she puts wrong ideas into the children's heads, the rural Negro school teacher is usually ignored.

In cities the situation is different. Negro elementary and high schools are better; teachers are better trained and better paid. In the Negro community teachers have a higher social status. As individuals they also achieve a measure of independence because they are usually anonymous to the white superintendent and school board. In the cities, the white community as a whole does not follow so closely what happens among the Negroes. The Negro principal in a city school, however, is directly responsible to white officials and watches his teachers more closely than do superintendents of rural schools.

In state colleges the situation is similar, except that the professors have a still higher social status in the Negro community and except that the college tends to become a little closed community of its own, with its own norms, which tends to increase somewhat the independence of the teachers.

In the private colleges there is much more independence from local white opinion within the limits of the campus. A friendly white churchman belonging to the interracial movement recently told the students of Atlanta University, in a commencement address, that the teachers there enjoyed greater academic freedom than their white colleagues at the Georgia state institutions, and this is probably true. The influence exerted by the Northern philanthropists and church bodies who have contributed to the colleges—often exercised through Southern white liberals and interracialists and through outstanding conservative Negro leaders—is, to a great extent, effective as a means of upholding the independence of Negro college presidents and professors.

As conditions are in the South, it is apparent that this influence is indispensable for this purpose. Neither the Negro teachers themselves nor any outside Negro institution could provide a power backing effective enough to keep off local white pressure. This outside white control gives the Negro teachers a considerably greater freedom even to inculcate a protest attitude—if it is cautiously done—than is allowed in publicly supported educational institutions. But it is inherent in the Southern caste situation, and in the traditions of the movement to build up Negro education in the region, that even this control is conservatively directed when compared with Northern standards.

In spite of these controls, strongest at the bottom of the educational system but strong also in the higher institutions, there is no doubt, however, that *the long-range effect of the rising level of education in the Negro people goes in the direction of nourishing and strengthening the Negro protest.* Negro-baiting Senator Vardaman knew this when he said:

> What the North is sending South is not money but dynamite; this education is ruining our Negroes. They're demanding equality.[2]

This would probably hold true of any education, independent of the controls held and the direction given. An increased ability on the part of the Negroes to understand the printed and spoken word cannot avoid opening up contact for them with the wider world, where equalitarian ideas are prevalent. But in the South there is not much supervision of Negro schools. And as we shall see later, Southern whites have been prohibited by their allegiance to the American Creed from making a perfected helot training out of Negro education.

Education in American Thought and Life

Even where the Negro school exists as a separate institution it is, like all other Negro institutions, patterned on the white American school as a model. It is different only for reasons connected with the caste situation. Even in their thinking on education, Negroes are typical, or overtypical, Americans.

As background for our discussion we shall have to remember the role of education in American democratic thought and life. Education has always been the great hope for both individual and society. In the American Creed it has been the main ground upon which "equality of opportunity for the individual" and "free outlet for ability" could be based. Education has also been considered as the best way—and the way most compatible with American individualistic ideals—to improve society.

Research in, and discussion of, education is prolific. In America, pedagogy anticipated by several generations the recent trend to environmentalism in the social sciences and the belief in the changeability of human beings. It gave a basis for the belief in democratic values and expressed the social optimism of American liberalism. The major American contribution to philosophy—the theory of pragmatism—bears visibly

---

[2] Cited by Ray Stannard Baker, *Following the Color Line* (1908) p. 247.

the marks of having been developed in a culture where education was awarded this prominent role. And it was in line with American cultural potentialities when John Dewey turned it into a theory of education. No philosopher from another country would be likely to express himself as he did in the following:

> The philosophy of education is one phase of philosophy in general. It may be seriously questioned whether it is not the most important single phase of general philosophy . . . the whole philosophic problem of the origin, nature, and function of knowledge is a live issue in education, not just a problem for exercise of intellectual dialectic gymnastics.[3]

At least since the time of Horace Mann, Americans have been leading in the development of pedagogical thinking. The marriage between philosophy and pedagogy in Dewey and his followers has given America the most perfected educational theory developed in modern times. Under the slogan "education for a changing world" and supported by a whole science of "educational sociology," it requires that education be set in relation to the society in which the individual lives. The introduction of this value relation into discussions of educational goals and means is a paramount contribution of America. And this has remained not only an achievement of academic speculation and research but has, to a large extent, come to influence policy-making agencies in the educational field. America has, therefore, seen more of enterprising and experimental progressive redirecting of schools than has any other country.

The duty of society to provide for public education was early established in America, and private endowments for educational purposes have been magnificent. America spends more money and provides its youth, on the average, with more schooling than any other country in the world. America has also succeeded in a relatively higher degree than any other country in making real the old democratic principle that the complete educational ladder should be held open to the most intelligent and industrious youths, independent of private means and support from their family. Education has been, and is increasingly becoming, a chief means of climbing the social status scale. It is entirely within this great American tradition when white people, who have wanted to help the Negroes, have concentrated their main efforts on improving Negro education.

American Negroes have taken over the American faith in education.

---

[3] John Dewey, "The Determination of Ultimate Values or Aims through Antecedent or A Priori Speculation or through Pragmatic or Empirical Inquiry," in *The Scientific Movement in Education, the Thirty-Seventh Yearbook of the National Society for the Study of Education*, Part 2 (1938), pp. 475–476.

Booker T. Washington's picture of the freedmen's drive for education is classical:

Few people who were not right in the midst of the scenes can form any exact idea of the intense desire which the people of my race showed for education. It was a whole race trying to go to school. Few were too young, and none too old, to make the attempt to learn. As fast as any kind of teachers could be secured, not only were day-schools filled, but night-schools as well. The great ambition of the older people was to try to learn to read the Bible before they died. With this end in view, men and women who were fifty or seventy-five years old, would be found in the night-schools. Sunday-schools were formed soon after freedom, but the principal book studied in the Sunday-school was the spelling-book. Day-school, night-school, and Sunday-school were always crowded, and often many had to be turned away for want of room.[4]

Campbell observed in the 'seventies that ". . . the blacks are very anxious to learn—more so than the lower whites."[5] Bryce remarked some decades later that "there is something pathetic in the eagerness of the Negroes, parents, young people, and children to obtain education."[6] And Baker wrote at the beginning of this century:

The eagerness of the coloured people for a chance to send their children to school is something astonishing and pathetic. They will submit to all sorts of inconveniences in order that their children may get an education.[7]

As self-improvement through business or social improvement through government appeared so much less possible for them, Negroes have come to affix an even stronger trust in the magic of education. It is true that some Negroes may lately have lost their faith in education, either because the schools available to them—in the South—are so inadequate or—in the North—because they achieve education but not the things they hoped to do with it. This attitude of dissatisfaction is probably part of the explanation why Negro children tend to drop out of high school more than do whites. If both sources of dissatisfaction could be removed, there is reason to believe that American Negroes would revert to their original belief in education. And, aside from such dissatisfaction and even cynicism, the masses of Negroes show even today a naïve, almost religious faith in education. To an extent, this faith was misplaced: many Negroes hoped to escape drudgery through education alone. But it is also true that this faith has been justified to a large

[4] Booker T. Washington, *Up From Slavery* (1901; first edition, 1900), pp. 29–30.
[5] Sir George Campbell, *White and Black* (1879), p. 259.
[6] James Bryce, *The American Commonwealth* (1910; first edition, 1893), Vol. 2, p. 520.
[7] *Op. cit.*, p. 53.

extent: education is one of the things which has given the Negroes something of a permanent advance in their condition.

The American zeal of education has always been focused on the individual's *opportunity*. The stress on enforcing a basic *minimum* standard of education for *all* young people in the nation has been less. In education as in many other fields of culture, America shows great disparity; there are at once many model schools and a considerable amount of illiteracy and semi-illiteracy. Bryce observed:

If one part of the people is as educated and capable as that of Switzerland, another is as ignorant and politically untrained as that of Russia.[8]

And a similar statement holds true today.

This disparity is partly explainable in terms of size of the country and in terms of the administrative decentralization of the school system. But when one observes the tremendous differences in amount and quality of education between some of the cities and some of the rural districts in one single state, as, for instance, Illinois, he cannot avoid believing that more basic still is a general toleration by Americans of dissimilar status between regions and groups of people. In any case, these dissimilarities in educational facilities for whites in different regions are important for the Negro problem. A differential treatment of Negroes as a group has been less spectacular and has seemed less indefensible with this as a setting.

There is no doubt that a change of American attitudes in this respect is under way and that an increasing stress is placed upon the desirability of raising the educational level in the sub-standard regions to greater equality. This change—which is part of a much more general tendency of the American Creed to include ideals of greater economic equalization—has taken form in the proposals for greater federal aid to education. The Negroes' chance of getting more equality in education is bound up with this movement.

Considering the importance attached to education in America, it is surprising that the teacher has not been awarded a higher status in American society. Learning has never given much prestige, and until recently the teacher has been held on a relatively low economic level without much security of tenure, in most places. And even today he is, relatively speaking, not well paid, and his tenure is not secure, particularly in the South. Teachers in America have not even been allowed to have as much power over the government of their own schools as they have in comparable countries. Their status as employees is stressed. This applies to all teachers, though in different degrees. The teachers

[8] Bryce, *op. cit.*, Vol. 2, p. 320.

in grade schools, mostly women, are socially and economically placed at a disadvantage compared with other professionals with the same amount of preparation. The professors at colleges and universities are generally accorded middle class status, definitely below that of a successful businessman.

The Negro community is, in this respect, more similar to northern European societies. The teacher generally has a symbolic prestige from the importance of his calling. Because of the scarcity of business opportunities and of successful businessmen in the Negro community, the teacher is also more free from competition for prestige. It should be recalled, however, that the great personal dependency of the teacher, particularly in the rural South, and her low income tend to deflate her position in the Negro community.

Another peculiarity of America, which is not unconnected with the relatively low prestige of the teachers and of learning, is a common tendency to look upon education as something produced by the school and finished by graduation. The ordinary American does not conceive of education as a process which continues through adult life and is dependent upon the individual's own exertion. To few Americans does it seem to be an important goal in life continuously to improve their education. Few schools on any level direct much of their attention to preserving and developing the "educability" of the student. The very perfection of text books and too much teaching is likely to make the student more passive in his attainment of knowledge. Too little is generally asked of the students; too much—in teaching—is required of the teachers. This is, perhaps, one of the reasons why the final educational results do not measure up to the great amount of funds and time which go into schooling in America. In this respect the Negro schools do not differ from white schools. In fact, they can, even less well than white schools, afford to disregard the more formal requirements and go in for experimentation.

In this connection should be noted the relative absence in America of a civic adult education movement upheld by the concerted efforts of the people themselves. We have related this to the relative political passivity of the American citizens between elections. The government of American municipalities does not decentralize power and responsibility to a great number of boards and councils, and does not offer, therefore, much opportunity for participation to the ordinary citizen. This decreases the functional importance of civic adult education, as does also the relative absence of organized mass movements. If this is true of the white Americans, it is, of course, much more true of the Negroes, particularly in the South where they are largely disfranchised. Lack of participation in the wider community must depress interest in continued self-education, except when it is vocational or professional and motivated by narrow considerations of individual economic advancement.

America is, however, prominent in the type of passive mass education through such agencies as the radio, press, popular magazines and movies. The rise of the Negro population, not only to literacy but to a real capability of consuming the spoken and printed word, and the increasing efficacy of those agencies, must have a strong influence in raising the culture level of Negroes. Through these media, they are made more American.

The Whites' Attitudes Toward Negro Education

There are apparent conflicts of valuations between whites and Negroes in regard to Negro education. These conflicts, the interests involved, and the theories expressing them determine the forms of Negro education. But the situation is not so simple as just a difference of opinion. In fact, many whites are as eager to improve Negro education as is any Negro, and there are some Negroes who are rather on the other side of the fence, at least for the purpose of an opportunistic accommodation. The situation is complicated by the fact that both whites and Negroes are divided in their own minds. They harbor conflicting valuations within themselves. Only by keeping this constantly in mind can we understand the development of Negro education and correctly evaluate future prospects.

The American Creed definitely prescribes that the Negro child or youth should have just as much educational opportunity as is offered anyone else in the same community. Negroes should be trained to become good and equal citizens in a democracy which places culture high in its hierarchy of values. This equalitarian valuation is strong enough to dominate public policy in the North, in spite of the fact that probably most white people in the North, too, believe the Negroes to be inferior and, anyhow, do not care so much for their potentialities and possibilities as for those of whites. In the South the existing great discrimination in education is an indication that another valuation is dominating white people's actions. But it is a great mistake to believe that the American Creed is not also present and active in the motivations of Southern whites. Behavior is as always a moral compromise. Negroes would not be getting so much education as they are actually getting in the South if the equalitarian Creed were not also active.

By itself, the interest of upholding the caste system would motivate Southern whites to give Negroes practically no education at all or would restrict it to the transmission of only such lowly skills as would make

Negroes better servants and farm hands. There is no mistake about this interest; it is real and has economic importance. Charles S. Johnson gives an account of it as it appears in the rural South:

> Literacy is not an asset in the plantation economy, and it was not only discouraged but usually forbidden. The belief that education spoiled the slave carried over with but little modification for many years into the belief that education spoils a field hand. The oldest members of the community are illiterate, and in those working relations which reveal least change from the past this lack has proved no important handicap. Reading and figuring carry elements of danger to established relations. Since the detailed direction of planting and handling of accounts are the sphere of the planter, theoretically it is he who can profit most from the technique of literacy. Too much attention to reading about the outside, and particularly to figuring, on the part of Negro tenants, would surely make them less satisfied with their status and bring them into harsh conflict with the system. The need of enough education to read and figure arises largely among those families desirous of escaping from the dependent relationship under the old plantation system.[9]

The poorer classes of whites in this respect have interests similar to those of the planters. They are in competition with Negroes for jobs and for social status. One of the things which demarcates them as superior and increases the future potentialities of their children is the fact that white children in publicly supported school buses are taken to fine consolidated schools while often Negro children are given only what amounts to a sham education in dilapidated one-room schools or old Negro churches by underpaid, badly trained Negro teachers. The observer, visiting Southern rural counties, gets clear statements of these interests on the part of all classes of whites who want to preserve the traditional caste order. The segregated school system of the South, in addition, allows a substantial saving by keeping Negro education low.

The caste interest is not merely economic. The whites have told themselves that education will make the Negro conscious of "rights" which he should not know about. It will make him dissatisfied where he has been happy and accommodated. It will raise some Negroes above many whites in culture. It will make many more Negroes "uppity" and obnoxious. The supremacy of individual whites is bound up with Negro ignorance. If the Negro stays in the only "place" where he should be, then he does not need any education. These opinions also make sense in the light of the white caste's undoubted interest in keeping education away from the Negroes.

The white people have among themselves all the power, and so their

[9] Charles S. Johnson, *Shadow of the Plantation* (1934), p. 129.

convergent interests have molded Negro education in rural districts. The low standard of Negro schools is the result. But even in the rural South the observer sees the impact of the American Creed. Often it is revealed only in a bad conscience. This is apparent everywhere. In most localities there also seems to be a gradual improvement of Negro schools. In practically all places no obstacles are placed in the way of outside help if it observes the proper Southern forms, and it will even be encouraged either verbally or by "matching" it with local financial support. The scattering around the entire region of the Rosenwald schoolhouses is a case in point. Exertions by the Negroes to collect money among themselves for educational purposes are never discouraged but applauded by almost everybody. This is not said by way of excusing the bald and illegal discrimination in the rural school systems in the South, but only to stress the fact that the white caste interests are practically never driven to their logical end.

In the urban South, whites of the employing class do not have the same material interests in keeping the Negroes ignorant. They have rather to gain if their Negro servants and laborers have at least some education. The poorer classes of whites have scarcely any such gains to reap, however. They are interested in keeping Negroes as much as possible out of competition on the labor market. The general interest of keeping the Negroes down to preserve the caste order intact is present in the cities too. It is shared by all classes, but, of course, felt most strongly by the poorer whites. City populations are, however, more closely integrated in the life of the nation: the regional traditions are somewhat weaker, the cultural level among whites is higher, the American Creed is stronger. So we find that Southern cities offer the Negroes a substantially better education. In the Border states the integration in the national life and the strength of the American Creed are still stronger, and we find also that the educational facilities available to Negroes are more nearly equal to those of the whites.

The primary rationalization of this gradual deviation in the South from the policy representing the crude caste interest is usually phrased in the popular theory of the American Creed—that education of the youths of the poorer classes is beneficial not only to themselves but to society. Thomas Nelson Page presented the liberal Southerners' attitude toward the education of the Negro masses many years ago:

There is much truth in the saying that unless the whites lift the Negroes up, the Negroes will drag them down, though it is not true in the full sense in which it was intended. It is not true to the extent that the white must lift the Negro up to his own level; it is true to the extent that he must not leave him debased—at least must not leave him here debased. If he does, then the Negro will inevitably hold him, if not drag him down. No country in the present stage of the world's progress can long maintain itself in the front rank and no people can long maintain themselves at the top of the list of peoples if they have to carry perpetually the burden of a vast and densely ignorant population, and where that population belongs to another race, the argument must be all the stronger. Certainly, no section can, under such a burden keep pace with a section which has no such burden. Whatever the case may have been in the past, the time has gone by, possibly forever, when the ignorance of the working-class was an asset. Nations and peoples and, much more, sections of peoples, are now strong and prosperous almost in direct ratio to their knowledge and enlightenment. . . .

Viewing the matter economically, the Negro race, like every other race, must be of far more value to the country in which it is placed, if the Negro is properly educated, elevated, and trained, than if he is allowed to remain in ignorance and degradation. He is a greater peril to the community in which he lives if he remains in ignorance and degradation than if he is enlightened. If the South expects ever to compete with the North, she must educate and train her population, and, in my judgment, not merely her white population but her entire population.[10]

This has been the main argument through decades for improving the educational facilities for Negroes in the South. Usually it is restricted by assertion of their lower capability of responding to education. Usually also it is qualified by the insistence on a particular kind of education as more suitable for Negroes.

There is petty pressure on Negro education in the South, but the truth is that the *Southern whites have never had the nerve to make of Negro education an accomplished instrument to keep the Negroes in their caste status.* It would have been possible, but it has not been done. The Southern whites' caste policy has been halfhearted all through, but particularly so in education. The explanation is again that they are also good Americans with all the standardized American ideals about education. The interest of educating the Negroes to become faithful helots has been obvious, but the Southern whites have not even attempted to make it effective in practice. Instead, they have merely kept Negro education poor and bad. And even on that point they have been gradually giving up resistance to the command of the Creed. This is the deeper dynamics of Negro education.

"Industrial" *versus* "Classical" Education of Negroes

Quite independent of how the specific value of "vocational" or "industrial" education, as compared with a more liberal education, is viewed, there is no doubt that the popularity among whites, now as earlier,

[10] Thomas Nelson Page, *The Negro: the Southerner's Problem* (1904), pp. 295–297.

of the former type of Negro education is mainly motivated by the interests of preserving the caste order. "Industrial" education for Negroes in the formula upon which Southern whites have been able to strike a compromise between their belief in education, which stems from the American Creed, and their interests as white Southerners in preserving the caste order of the region.

The argument runs: The Negroes are, and must be, servants, farm laborers, and industrial workers; they should, however, be trained to do their work better; then, in their "place," they would be better citizens too. What is needed, consequently, is a Negro education which bothers less with bookish learning and more with life in a humble status, daily duties, and the building up of character; the Negroes have to begin at the bottom and they will probably stay low, but they should be given the chance of moving upward slowly. The advocate of improved industrial training of Negroes also stresses the very material interest of the better class of white people to have more efficient servants. The play of these arguments can be observed today, when, for instance, one accompanies the State Agent for Negro Education in a rural county trying to persuade the local white leaders to spend money to improve Negro education.

The formula, "industrial education for Negroes," thus has a different meaning for different white people. There are some who have a genuine belief in the superiority generally of a practical stress in all public education. There are many more who see strong particular reasons for this educational goal in the actual situation of Southern Negroes. Many have their primary interest in improving Negro education as such and know that it is politically much more feasible if it is proposed in this way. To many the formula is, however, only a rationalization for discrimination and for holding appropriations low for Negro schools.

Industrial education becomes a byword. In the mind of one man it meant that the negro should be taught only to know the relative distance between two rows of cotton or corn, and how to deport himself with becoming behavior behind the chair while his white lord and master sits at meat; while, in the mind of another it stood for the awakening of the best powers and possibilities. To the white man of the South it may have meant that the negro was to be made more serviceable to him and more easily amenable to his imperious will. To the white man of the North it may have meant that the black man was to be made a competent worker, equipped with intelligence and skill such as are demanded of Northern workmen. However variant may have been the interpretations of the meaning of industrial education, there was a general agreement to discredit the higher culture of the race.[11]

[11] Kelly Miller, *Out of the House of Bondage* (1914), pp. 151–152.

This has, among other things, the implication that *in the South the problem of "industrial" versus "classical" education for Negroes is not, and has never been, discussed merely in terms of pedagogical advantages and disadvantages.* The political caste problem is always and necessarily involved. And the type of education to be given Negroes is always and necessarily connected with the amount of education and the financial obligations to be undertaken.

Two factors complicate the issue even more: the high relative costs of modern vocational education and the white laborers' fear of the Negroes as competitors. In the period immediately after the Civil War, vocational education was—a fact now often forgotten—motivated also as a less expensive way of giving Negroes some schooling. General Armstrong, when founding Hampton Institute, stressed the agricultural and vocational line, not only for the reason that such a training best fitted the occupational possibilities of the freed slaves, but also because it allowed the students to earn something toward their maintenance at school. In his appeals for funds for Tuskegee Institute, Booker T. Washington likewise always emphasized this element of economy, and particularly how the students, by their own work, erected many of the buildings and provided much toward the support of themselves and the school.

The pedagogical aim of vocational education outside agriculture in those days was to continue and build up the artisan tradition from slavery and to turn out young Negroes skilled in the old handicrafts— train them to be carpenters, masons, blacksmiths, shoemakers. When, however, the Industrial Revolution finally hit the South in full force, the demand of efficient industry was no longer for the artisan but for the skilled machine operator. The old handicrafts became relatively less important. Even agriculture did not show much demand for skilled Negro labor. On the plantations the employers continued to be best satisfied with the ignorant field hands who were not disturbingly ambitious, and the trend toward increased Negro landownership turned downward shortly after 1900. If Negroes—outside domestic service—were to be given effective vocational education, this would require such an elaborate equipment for the schools that it would become more expensive than "classical" education.

At the same time and partly for the same basic reasons, the interest of the white workers against allowing Negroes to acquire skills became stronger. In agriculture and in the stagnating crafts, new skilled Negro labor was not welcome; in industry it became a principle that all skilled jobs should be reserved for the whites.

What if the industrial education of the Negro should be found to conflict with the interests of the white laborer or skilled worker? Does any one suppose that it is the purpose of the South so to educate the Negro (or even allow him to be so educated) as to enable him to take the bread from the white man's mouth? And does any one suppose that the laboring white man of the arrogant and aggressive Anglo-Saxon race will stand tamely by with folded arms while there is danger of its being done? This is the central point of the whole situation.[12]

By and large, *in spite of all the talk about it, no effective industrial training was ever given the Negroes in the Southern public schools,* except training for cooking and menial service. The expensive vocational training, which conflicted so harshly with the interests of the white workers, has never become much more than a slogan. Negro education has mostly remained "academic" and differs only in its low level of expenditure and effectiveness.

Even at the well-endowed centers of Hampton and Tuskegee, the industrial training offered was in demand almost solely because of a need for teachers in the lesser schools, rather than because of the needs of modern industry. This explains why they have been able to realize, in some lines at least, the vocational idea as well as they have, without coming into greater conflict with the interests of white workers. The schools to which those teachers have gone, and are now going, are usually not nearly so well equipped that they could be called "vocational" in any serious meaning of the term. They usually are poor schools, not deserving much of a classification into their "vocational" or "classical." A few exceptional schools excluded, they offer at best some training in domestic service for girls—which, for understandable reasons, meets more encouragement and less fear of competition—of a poor training in the technique of rapidly disappearing handicrafts, sometimes adjusted slightly to modern times by courses in "automobile repair work" or the like.

The discussion of whether Negroes should have a vocational or a liberal schooling is thus only in part a real issue. Partly it is a cover for the more general problem as to what extent Negroes should have much education at all. The lines are blurred because the argument for vocational education is used both by the people who want to have more education for Negroes and by those who want to restrict it. The main conflict is between the ever present equalitarian American Creed, on the one hand, and the caste interest, on the other. The actual situation

<hr>

[12] Winfield H. Collins, *The Truth about Lynching and the Negro in the South* (1918), pp. 154–155.

is different between regions; opinions are divided and confused within almost every individual. Let us, as an example, have a Southern liberal survey the field of opinions, as he sees it, and attempt to formulate his own attitude:

It is surprising to note the prejudice with which a great many southern whites view the whole subject of Negro education. Their sincere opinion that the Negro should not be given educational opportunities comparable to those which are provided for the white children is at least partly due to the strong belief that better facilities in the colored schools would not yield a proper return in human values. This belief is a heritage from slavery. Of course there is also the attitude that the educated Negro will lose the humility which has characterized his relations with the southern white man ever since Reconstruction. The white laboring man is no doubt influenced in his opposition to better educational facilities for Negroes by the fear that Negroes will enter skilled trades and thereby create a new and very effective rivalry in a field in which the whites have not had as much competition as they have where the task requires less training and education. However, certain farsighted leaders and some others realize that the Negro must be given better schools. They believe that improved colored school facilities will benefit not only the Negroes but also the whites. They feel that the colored man is entitled to a good high school education in subjects which may be selected with a view to the peculiar social situation in the South. The Negro must be trained for the jobs which are available under present conditions. Cultural training in the arts and sciences must for the present be subordinated to an education which is more suitable to his needs. In this way the greatest number will be benefited. The curriculum for the colored schools needs a great deal of study with a view toward revision.[13]

Negro Attitudes

The attitudes of the whites are of greatest importance for the growth of Negro education, as they have all the power. The Negroes are, however, not without influence, partly because the whites are divided among themselves and divided in their own conscience. The remarkable thing is that the Negroes are split in much the same way and on the same issues.

It is natural, to begin with, that the American Creed interest is more stressed with the Negroes. Deep down in their souls practically all Negroes feel that they have the right to equal opportunities for education. And the sanctity of the American Creed gives them the opportunity to express this opinion and to press the whites for concessions. The stress on education in American culture makes the Negro protest most respect-

[13] Charles S. Mangum, Jr., *Legal Status of the Negro* (1940), pp. 132–133.

able. But the observer finds also that there are a few upper class Negroes who express about the same opinion as whites, that common Negroes do not need and should not have much education. This is rare, however, and the opinion has to be concealed.

Much more important is the split in the Negro world as to what kind of education is desirable. On the one hand, they sense the caste motivation behind most whites' interest in industrial education for Negroes. They know also that they can hope to win the respect of the whites and take their place as equal citizens in American democracy only if they are educated in the nonvocational cultural values of the broader society. On the other hand, they see the actual caste situation as a reality and know that many lines of work are closed to them. In order to utilize fully the openings left, and in order eventually to open up new roads into industrial employment, they often conclude that Negroes are in particular need of vocational training. They realize also that the great poverty and cultural backwardness of their people motivate a special adaptation of Negro education. On this point there is a possibility of striking a compromise with the liberal white man. In the North most Negroes will not make this concession, and by no means all Negroes, perhaps not even a majority, in the South are prepared to take the stand. Even the ones who do, stress at the same time the necessity of raising educational opportunities and of improving the schools.

Concerning the content of teaching in other respects, Negroes are also divided. On the one hand, they are inclined to feel that the Northern system, where a standardized teaching is given students independent of whether they are whites or Negroes, is the only right thing. On the other hand, they feel that the students get to know too little about Negro problems. They thus want an adjustment of teaching toward the status of Negroes, usually not in order to make the Negroes weak and otherwise fit into the white man's wishful picture about "good niggers" but, on the contrary, to make Negroes better prepared to fight for their rights. They feel that education should not only be accepted passively but should be used as a tool of concerted action to gain the equal status they are seeking. For this reason many, if not most, Negro leaders desire that Negro students should get special training in Negro problems.

Du Bois, who originally was the most uncompromising advocate of the idea that no difference at all should be made in teaching Negro and white students, later came out with the opinion that the Negro student should not only be taught general history and social subjects as they were taught to white students, but also Negro history and Negro problems and, indeed, a special race strategy for meeting their individual and collective problems in America. Negro youth should even be taught to have pride in Africa.[14]

This opinion, except perhaps for the last point, is not commonly shared by most Negro intellectuals. The institution of "Negro History Week" has emanated from such attitudes. Negro colleges and high schools are devoting an increasing interest to Negro problems. White interracialists condone these things. Other whites do not care but feel, as we have said, that it is the Negroes' right to discuss their own problems if they want to.

There is a further controversy as to whether Negro education ought to be segregated or not. In the North the official opinion among whites is that segregation is not compatible with equality, but, as we have seen, much segregation is actually in effect as a consequence of residential segregation and of gerrymandering districts and granting permits to transfer. In the South direct segregation in schools is a necessary means of keeping up the tremendous financial discrimination against Negro schools. In recent years not even Southern liberals—with some rare exceptions—have stated that they favored mixed education. Segregation is usually not motivated by financial reason but as a precaution against social equality.

Negroes are divided on the issues of segregated schools. In so far as segregation means discrimination and is a badge of Negro inferiority, they are against it,[15] although many Southern Negroes would not take an open stand that would anger Southern whites. Some Negroes, however, prefer the segregated school, even for the North, when the mixed school involved humiliation for Negro students and discrimination against Negro teachers. Du Bois has expressed this point of view succinctly:

. . . theoretically, the Negro needs neither segregated schools nor mixed schools. What he needs is Education. What he must remember is that there is no magic, either in mixed schools or in segregated schools. A mixed school with poor and unsympathetic teachers, with hostile opinion, and no teaching concerning black folk, is bad. A segregated school with ignorant placeholders, inadequate equipment, poor salaries, and wretched housing, is equally bad. Other things being equal, the mixed school is the broader, more natural basis for the education of all youth. It gives wider contacts; it inspires greater self-confidence; and suppresses the inferiority complex. But other things sel-

---

[14] A vigorous and detailed plea for giving the Negro special training to meet special problems may be found in Carter G. Woodson, *The Mis-Education of the Negro* (1933).
[15] See, for instance, Robert R. Morton, *What the Negro Thinks* (1929), p. 114.

dom are equal, and in that case, Sympathy, Knowledge, and the Truth, out-weigh all that the mixed school can offer.[16]

Other Negroes prefer the mixed schools at any cost, since for them it is a matter of principle or since they believe that it is a means of improving race relations.

Trends and Problems

Schrieke, surveying Southern education a few years ago, sums up the situation in the following words:

> . . . although there is some sort and some amount of Negro education everywhere, Negro education still does not have a fixed, legitimate, acknowledged place. It is realized that something must be done in order to keep the Negro satisfied and in order to uphold the American slogan of free schools for every child, but it is rare that a community has any real interest in planning or building a wise system of education for the race. Politically, it is not generally admitted that the Negro has a right to schools or to other public services. . . . The Negro is still not recognized as a citizen despite the Civil War amendments.[17]

This somewhat pessimistic evaluation is warranted by the facts. The educational facilities for Negroes, particularly in many rural regions, are scandalously poor. The white community often blinds itself to the entire matter. But in appraising the situation, it is equally important to recognize that there are dissimilarities in the level of educational facilities offered Negroes, and that there is a definite tendency upward.

This trend is gaining momentum and is pushed not only by Northern philanthropy and the intervention of federal agencies, but also by the growing force of Southern liberalism. The rising educational level of the whites in the region gives an increasing basis for understanding the necessity of doing something for Negro education. The skillful strat-egy of the N.A.A.C.P. is probably going to enforce a raise in the wages of Southern Negro teachers over the next decade and will, if it does not open the door of the graduate schools to Negroes, at least compel the Southern states to initiate some sort of graduate training in the state-supported Negro colleges. In the beginning this graduate training will perhaps be merely a sham gesture, but a basis for further advance will have been created. Segregation will probably be upheld on all levels while discrimination is being fought and decreased. Segregation will less and less be a means of economy; gradually it will, instead, become

[16] W. E. B. Du Bois, "Does the Negro Need Separate Schools?," *Journal of Negro Education* (July, 1935), p. 335.
[17] B. Schrieke, *Alien Americans* (1936), pp. 166–167.

a financial burden. It is not unlikely that segregation will then start to break down on the highest level. In the total view, the prospects are thus not entirely discouraging. In fact, *there have never been, since Reconstruction, fewer reasons for a defeatist attitude in regard to Negro education in the South.*

In spite of much and heated discussion regarding the type of Negro education, its actual development has never followed any plan or theory. The main problem has always been not what sort but *how much education the Negro should have and how much he gets.* Even today the chief problem is how to get increased appropriations and improved standards. As we have hinted, the theory of "industrial" training for Negroes has had its main function in being a bait for the powers of the purse in Northern philanthropy and in Southern public budgets. And the truth is that *any type of improved education for Negroes is salutary.*

There is an immense need of *new school buildings* for Negroes, particularly in rural districts but also in most Southern cities. There is also need for new *equipment* of all sorts, for *consolidated schools* and for *school buses.* After the close of the present war there is going to be, in all likelihood, a great necessity for public works to mitigate unemployment, and much of this activity is bound to be directed upon erecting buildings for public schools.

The only sound and democratic principle for distributing the benefits of the post-war public works policy in various districts and groups would be to build for those districts and groups in the nation whose old buildings are worst. Such a policy would, in the South, mean concentrating almost the whole activity on building Negro schools and other buildings for Negroes. The old Negro schools are generally so bad and inadequate that this kind of public construction would suffice to occupy the unemployed for quite a while. Such a policy will probably not be followed for political reasons. It is, however, not only a Negro interest but a general democratic interest that his policy be pressed, so that Negro schools get the maximum out of any post-war unemployment emergency. As communities usually want to have buildings erected independent of their purposes if they do not have to pay for them—because they mean work and income for the community—and as Southerners are not likely to object too much if Negro school buildings are built with federal money, it should be taken up for deliberation whether it would not be a wise policy to distribute federal aid to education in the form of taking over the responsibility for erecting and furnishing the buildings.

A second most important condition for progress is to improve *the standards of Negro teachers.* This has been seen by the Northern foundations and also by many of the Southern state authorities, and much effort has gone into improving teacher training in the South. Southern state and private Negro colleges largely serve this purpose. Many of the small Negro colleges in the South are inadequate and the whole system needs to be systematized. Many of them will, perhaps, succumb in the financial strain of the present War, and this might turn out to be a blessing in disguise if the remaining colleges are increased and improved correspondingly. The establishment of a new model teacher-training college in the South would be a great service which a farsighted federal policy could undertake in order to equalize education opportunities for Negroes. Meanwhile the raised salary scales, to which the South will be compelled, will probably raise the standards of training Negro teachers. Negro teachers need not only better training and higher salaries; they also need more security of tenure. If the rural teacher could be given a greater independence and a higher prestige, this, by itself, would make her a better teacher and, particularly, increase the influence of the school over the community.

If the federal government undertakes further financial responsibility for education, it will be up against a problem which has been bothering the philanthropic foundations for a long time, although it is seldom discussed openly: How is it possible to aid without decreasing local responsibility? In the author's judgment, *Northern philanthropy in its grand-scale charity toward the South, incidental to its positive accomplishments, has also had a demoralizing influence on the South.* The South has become accustomed to taking it for granted that not only rich people in the North, but also poor church boards, should send money South, thus eternally repaying "the responsibility of the North for Reconstruction." Thus far, rich people in the South have been less inclined to give away their money for philanthropic purposes.

For these moral reasons it is important, when the federal government steps in, that local financial responsibility be preserved as much as possible. *The ideal solution would be that the federal government pay certain basic costs all over the country,* such as original building costs and a basic teacher's salary. It is, of course, of special importance that, as far as possible, *absence of discrimination be made a condition for aid.* Otherwise the idea will become established that Negro education is the business of the federal government and less a concern of the state and the municipalities. In this sense there is a danger that the Negro people might become "the ward of the nation."

Our assumption was that, to improve Negro education, larger appropriations, better buildings, more equipment, better paid and trained teachers are essential. By this we did not want to discount altogether the problem of the direction of Negro education but only to retain true proportions. The main fault with Negro education is that it is under-nourished and inadequate. As it is improved, however, the problem of its direction becomes important. Even when Negro education is on a low level, as in most rural districts at present, it is, of course, important not to have misdirected. But the choice seems, for the most part, still to be between an antediluvian "industrial" education and an equally antediluvian "classical" education.

The Jeanes teacher movement and other constructive attempts in Southern Negro education have tried to work out a makeshift policy in which the emphasis is laid upon maintaining and enriching the relations of the student to his community. This is all very well, and entirely in line with modern educational theory as it has been developed in America. But one main point seems forgotten. With the present trends in Southern agriculture and American agricultural policy, it is fairly certain that many of the children born in a cotton county today are going to live and work not in cotton districts but in Northern and Southern cities. Many of the children born in a Southern city are going to live in the different environment of the Northern metropolis. If the American economy and economic policy are not going to stagnate, Negroes are going to work in new occupations within the next generation. *What is needed is an education which makes the Negro child adaptable to and movable in the American culture at large.*

Even the Negro child who will stay in Southern agriculture will need to use various types of machinery, to follow popular journals in his field, to deal with credit institutions and government agencies, and successfully to take part in organizations. He needs to be able to read, write, and reckon, and to be lifted so high above illiteracy that he actually participates in modern American society. Before all, he needs not to be specialized, but to be changeable, "educable." And *he needs it more than the white child, because life will be more difficult for him.*

The right balance between "industrial" and "classical" education can be struck if due weight is given to the prospect of mobility and change. The masses of Negro children are going to be laborers on the farms and in industries; some are going to be skilled laborers. We do not know where and in what occupation they are going to work, but we know there is going to be much moving around. They need to be taught skills; but the value of any vocational training should be judged in terms of the extent to which the skills acquired are transferable into skills in other trades. They need to be familiarized with the printed word and culture that is found in books, and, indeed, to get as much of the general American culture as they possibly can.

Meanwhile, Southern Negro schools are going to remain inadequate. The North will continue for many decades to get untutored and crude Negro immigrants from the South. These uneducated masses of Southern-born Negroes will be a heavy burden on the social and economic order in the North. It is, therefore, an interest for Northern cities, and not only for the migratory Negroes, that *a program of adult education be instituted to teach the migrating Negro masses the elements of American culture and also, perhaps, elements of vocational skills.*

More significant in the dynamics of Negro education than the low average standards in some regions are the high standards in others, and the general trend toward improvement. The American nation will not have peace with its conscience until inequality is stamped out, and the principle of public education is realized universally.

10

Do American Schools Educate?

The whole theory of modern education is radically unsound. "Fortunately, in England at any rate, education produces no effect whatsoever." This weighty dictum fell from the lips of Lady Bracknell in Wilde's *The Importance of Being Earnest.* Whether the good lady would be as forthright today in denunciation of the theories and results of education on either side of the Atlantic, it is impossible to guess. It is, however, certain that she lacked that essential humility which must characterize the observer who dares to put pen to paper about another country's educational system, after a visit which was as crowded as it was brief. Whatever is written here in way of honest doubt is qualified by warm admiration of the buoyant belief in education, the eager experimentation, and the astonishing vitality which characterize the American scene in schools and universities alike.

One of the surprises facing an inquiring pilgrim from Great Britain is the emphasis placed in the United States upon what the Harvard Report on General Education in a Free Society styles "the ideal of commonness," and the extent to which "social indoctrination" and "the civilizing work of preparing for American life" have gone. A possible explanation is, of course, that America is still faced with the problem of welding a nation out of many nationalities, a consideration which prompts the conscious use of education as an instrument to produce right-thinking and coöperative citizens of a great democracy.

On our side we distrust a use of the schools as training grounds for children as social beings, and note with dismay that the most highly "progressive" teachers make no bones about educating children, not for society as it is, but for society as they mean to make it. We see danger

John Walter Percy Garrett. "Do American Schools Educate?" *The Atlantic Monthly,* Vol. 191 (February, 1953), pp. 68–72. Reprinted by kind permission of the publishers of *The Atlantic Monthly,* Boston, Massachusetts.

Author (1902–   ): Educated Trowbridge High School, Exeter College, Oxford; Assistant Master at Victoria College, Jersey C. I., Royal Naval College, Dartmouth; Crypt School, Gloucester; Head of English Department, Whitgift School, Croydon; Page Traveling Scholarship to the United States, 1934; Headmaster, Raynes Park County School, 1935–1942; Headmaster of Bristol Grammar School, 1943–1960, Smith-Mundt Fellowship in United States, 1952.

in a too conscious indoctrination of any political ideals, and believe rather that the good is often better achieved as a by-product. The citizen of the world is more likely to emerge from a proper study of history than he is from a course in international understanding, and the man of civic virtue from living in the ethos of a good community than from a course in citizenship. The Squire in *Tom Brown's School Days* wanted his son to "turn out a brave, helpful, truth-telling Englishman, and a gentleman, and a Christian." The Harvard Report defines the good man as one who possesses "an inner integration, poise and firmness, which in the long run come from an adequate philosophy of life." Expressed differently, the two statements boil down to the same thing, and the Tom Brown of our times, whether his home is in New England or Old, is more likely to achieve the way of life appropriate to a democracy by exposure to the right atmosphere than by any "social indoctrination" through teaching.

The diet most suited to the taste of the nonacademic pupil is much more carefully catered for in America than in Great Britain. The system is more flexible, and the interests and aptitudes of the individual child at fifteen are more important than the dictates of the timetable. More thought has been given to how to reconcile the interests of the fast and the slow, how to give a fair deal both to the quarter in the high schools who proceed to further education, and to the three quarters who leave school without a university career. A brave and determined attempt is being made to find a binding understanding of the society which the two groups will possess in common despite their different interests and abilities. More has been done in finding new and authentic treatments of traditional subjects for the less able.

In England the course given to the children who leave the modern secondary schools at fifteen is still too often a watered-down version of the academic course of the grammar schools, whose function, substantially, is to educate the cleverest children for entrance to the universities. When the Harvard Report says: "The tendency is always to strike a somewhat colorless mean, too fast for the slow, too slow for the fast," it is making fair comment on the uneasy compromise existing in Great Britain. When it continues: "The ideal is a system which shall be as fair to the fast as to the slow, to the hand-minded as to the book-minded, but which, while meeting the separate needs of each, shall yet foster that fellow-feeling between human being and human being which is the deepest root of democracy," it proclaims a Utopian ideal which so far has eluded both countries.

The quotation rightly implies that America still falls far short of the ideal, in varying degrees in varying States. Mississippi, able to spend a fifth as much per pupil as New York, must clearly present a less rosy picture. But Americans are still far ahead of us British in constructive *thinking* about how to pursue the two goals simultaneously. It is when the Harvard Report asks the question, "How can general education be so adapted to different ages and, above all, differing abilities and outlooks, that it can appeal deeply to each, and yet remain in goal and essential teaching the same for all?" that different answers are likely to come from the two sides of the Atlantic.

Theory does not always produce the results it desires or deserves. Because in these days education has no enemies, it is the more important sometimes to defend it from its friends. If the slower children have a fairer chance in the United States, it also seems clear to a sympathetic observer that a far greater number of clever and intellectually able children have a better deal in the United Kingdom. In the best American schools, whose pupils are trained for and accepted by such universities as Harvard, Columbia, Yale, Princeton, Chicago, and the University of California, and such colleges as Williams and Amherst, the same standards probably obtain as in the best schools in Britain. But the number of such schools is in smaller proportion to the total of those to be educated.

It is furthermore difficult to resist the conclusion that the independent schools set a far higher standard of intellectual attainment than the public schools. President Conant in his enthusiasm to establish the case for the lawyer's son to rub shoulders with the artisan's son in their formative years perhaps gave more support than he intended to those influences which were hostile to independent schools. The hope is that public schools will so improve their standards that parents will feel that a real alternative exists. The development of state secondary education in the United Kingdom since 1902 has owed much to the example of standards set and maintained in the independent schools.

Nothing surprised me so much in America as the comparative indifference concerning the education of the exceptional child. When I used the term, I was told that in its American connotation it described, not the child endowed with rare intellectual gifts, but the child handicapped or in some way underdeveloped mentally. The euphemism is revealing of the difference between the two countries. The emphasis of the American system is on the social and average; ours, at least until 1945, has been fundamentally intellectual and geared for distinction.

Is there a moral to be found in comparing the publications which set forth the life stories of candidates for the Presidency of the United States? Where Andrew Jackson's in 1828 was dignified and written for an electorate which could read, Harry S. Truman's "biography" was presented in comic strip technique, all the more terrifying for being adroitly done. Does this mean that a man who aspires to the Presidency can only hope for success in so far as he can persuade his countrymen that, far from being exceptional, he is actually the common man whose century this is supposed to be? England's Labor Party has improved on the original dictum, which originated in America, by saying: "If this is the 'century of the common man' it must be made the century of the common child." It will be—if our levelers go their purblind way. A more profitable ideal would be to set about making this the century of the uncommon child, and to plan how to increase their number.

The root fallacy seems to be a refusal to admit that there must always be a governing class, and that men are not all capable of appreciating the best even when they are exposed to it. The evidence of newspapers, advertisements, cinema queues, radio, the near pornography of the book-stalls, the so-called "comics," and the recreations preferred by the majority prove that education, however well intentioned, can produce standards of taste and good judgment in only a minority. As Matthew Arnold said, "the highly instructed few, and not the scantily instructed many, will ever be the organ to the human race of knowledge and truth. Knowledge and truth, in the full sense of the words, are not attainable by the great mass of the human race at all."

It is the task and the responsibility of the small creative minority to hold fast to standards, to hope to widen the area of their acceptance, and to ensure that the salt of the centuries' heritage of culture shall not lose its savor. Equality of opportunity there must be, regardless of the parents' ability to pay. That is no longer a question of debate. What we have to guarantee is that the best quality of leadership shall be available for the service of the state from whatever class it may come, and that the most satisfactory means of education for its attainment are accessible. If society is to avoid the creation of a community content to glide along the easy current of life, education has to produce a minority of leaders whose influence is rationally persuasive rather than dictatorially dominating.

The question which now has to be posed is whether education in the United States is calculated to produce an elite of leaders of high intelligence. The highly trained mind must be a prerequisite of all leadership. On the report of a boy just leaving elementary for junior high school, I read: "Emphasis has been placed on helping him to assist and carry out his responsibilities as a member of a group." Splendid! But he was eleven years old, and after a weekend in his home, I could not discover that he had ever learned to read a book. My godson, before he went to Eton, had done four years of Latin, three of Greek, had read all Jane Austen, most of Dickens and Scott, and a good deal of Shakespeare. He was also a good member of a group, a quality which had been added as a by-product of his education.

A professor with whom I had the privilege of staying told me regretfully that his son was a typical American boy in that he never tackled books at a higher level than comics and magazines. At a famous private school, whatever literary values were inculcated in the classroom, on the bookstall in the school shop I found a remarkable range of cheap novels, each in its provocatively pornographic dust-wrapper, with titles such as *Nude in Mink, The Harem,* and *Sin in Their Blood.* A member of the school told me that all the boys bought such trash, and added: "The trouble about this place is that there's so much learning there isn't time for living." His complaint seemed unfair when he added that the school authorities paid $2000 for an orchestra for the school dance! Is this the boasted American maturity?

The books on the school bookstall seemed to stimulate sexual appetite rather than to provide healthy meat for good minds. On a tour of America Sir Richard Livingstone found "the clever children an underprivileged class." An American undergraduate described "our high school products" as "well-adjusted morons." This judgment is of course too sweeping. Another critic said that "when he leaves school the American is socially more mature than the Englishman, intellectually less mature." This is probably true if the emphasis is upon social adjustment rather than upon intellectual development.

Young Americans are certainly kept less at the stretch than young Britishers. One teacher in Kentucky excused the weight of American textbooks on the ground that they never had to be taken home for purposes of study. A family in California told me that if homework was ever set, it was the parents who in effect did it. As with us, the one-eyed television set is threatening the kingdom of the blind. I very much doubt whether this leeway of learning is ever made up. At eighteen, Americans are intellectually anything from eighteen months to two years behind our young people, and at the universities they have to make up two years of education which in England they would have done at school. They arrive at college without the preparation for work at that level which the specialized work in the last two years at school gives to the English student.

While the B.A. degree is rarely the intellectual equivalent of ours, the postgraduate schools in the United States are probably better than ours. The difference is a matter of spread over the years. A similar result may be achieved in the end, but it takes a much longer time to attain it—which is of course a privilege of a wealthy nation. It must be remembered, however, that the greater length of time may be justified because American schools certainly do better by the average boy. Each nation is conditioned by what is practicable and what is desirable.

An American teacher after a year on exchange in Great Britain once summed up the difference between the two systems to me in the words: "Your system produces snobs, ours slobs." The Labor Party in Great Britain would presumably agree with the first statement; and when I look for any hard core of learning in the American high school, I am inclined to see something in the second. I saw little emphasis on the necessity to hold on to the centuries-old tradition of exact, precise, and thorough learning. The syllabus often contained little to bite on, little to discipline minds. The use of Latin and even mathematics was called into question because transfer values had been repudiated. A publishing company reduced Shakespeare's plays to comic strip technique, where the verse, written as prose, emerged in balloons from people's mouths. "Classics Illustrated" justify their vandalism because they are directed "toward familiarizing school-children with the literary classics in a form that will be appealing and 'easy to take.'" Such snippets of culture may be justified for children who cannot read, but they are inappropriate if able minds are to be extended and toughened.

It is difficult to resist the conclusion that in the modern American school the snail's pace becomes the school's pace. Neither can the able child outstrip his companions by a double promotion, because of the custom of classing children by age groups and advancing them by age rather than performance. If "tensions" might result by allowing the clever to outpace the dull, frustration and boredom must be the lot of the able child who is held back. Perhaps that is why there is so much talk about adjustment in America!

The phrase "easy to take" extends to pupils' choice of the subjects of their study in high school. Backward children can take high pride and discover their confidence in subjects which are unsuitable for their brighter brethren. But it is nothing short of idiocy to pretend that a training in typewriting is equal in cultural value to a study of the *Odyssey* or that the child who is exposed to the one is likely to have the same value for the community (qualities of character being equal) as the child who masters the other.

Neither is "Education in the U.S.A.," published by the Federal Security Agency, reassuring on the intellectual pabulum offered. It is hoped that a high school pupil will "acquire the basic tools of learning; the methods and significance of science; prepare for, get, and hold a job; develop and maintain good mental health and physical fitness; be a good consumer; develop insight into ethical values and principles; grow in appreciation of beauty in the arts in nature; be a good citizen; be a good family member; use leisure time wisely." The aims are unexceptionable, but are they not what Johnson called "an ill digested piece"?

Subsequent study of the publication fails to reveal any priorities or any indication of comparative importance. Much is made of the Health Services. "The mental and emotional health of teachers and students is being given careful consideration." By the same doctor? Surely those who are fit to teach can look after their own mental and emotional health, and surely much that is called health instruction constitutes an impertinent invasion of the responsibilities of parents. If the state controls all, the state can demand all.

A Californian mother summed up the compulsory subject of "Health and Safety" as meaning that a child could "mend a fuse, walk across a street, and know how to avoid V.D." The captions to attractive illustrations run: "School programs are adapted to meet the child's needs" (perhaps a lesson in wise shopping?); "Schools provide rich environment for the children" (teacher and class appear to be concentrating attention on a canary in a cage); "Education for intelligent participation in family life" (teacher and class beholding what appear to be plates of cereals); "Home Economics classes encourage students to care for and repair clothing" (young men apparently pressing trousers, preparatory to dating?); "An opportunity to engage in creative activities" (since when has listening to gramophone records been a *creative* activity?). All this is admirable, but does it add up to education? All the children look happy and have photogenic smiles that would make the sunshine jealous. But if they are being prepared for life, is happiness enough?

The heresy of free activity has much to answer for in both our countries. A current story in Great Britain tells of a teacher, who was being inspected, saying to her class, "Now it is time to start arithmetic." Whereupon the inspector interrupted, "How do you know that the children want to start arithmetic?" If the child is to choose and dictate its requirements, what is the merit of maturity? If education is to teach children that they can abandon whatever they find difficult, what sort of preparation for life are we giving?

Children are naturally addicted to egotism, and education should assist their emancipation from its tyranny. Progressive education and free discipline seem something like a reversion to barbarism, as well as a calculated debasement of cultural values. One American teacher told me that the word "progressive" had been omitted from the title of his school because it might lead people to include the school in "education's lunatic fringe." Now that university authorities have found that some of their college entrants are incapable of self-expression on paper, and of tearing the guts out of a book presenting difficulty, there are signs of an overdue reaction against the solemn nonsense of these traitors to true education.

We have them on our side of the Atlantic as well, and both countries are faced with some parallel problems. How can schools be financed from public funds and yet be kept free from the dead hand of bureaucratic tyranny? Do those who pay the piper call the tune? I was in one school which had been done to death by remote control from an office desk. What is the limit to administrative pipe dreams? What is the correct emphasis—extravagant buildings, or a salary scale for teachers which will win them the respect which the community gives to other professions? All schools in the United States are much better housed and equipped than the vast majority of ours. I often wondered what American teachers and pupils would make of some of the small, dark, and ill-ventilated classrooms at Eton and Winchester. But, let us make no bones about it, men not walls make a city, and any school is as good as its staff. Recruitment of men and women of ability and virtue, to what is in very deed a vocation, is the consideration which must perforce override all others in both our countries.

A Cambridge don asked Erasmus: "Who would put up with the life of a schoolmaster who could get a living in any other way?" and Bacon was of the opinion that "to have commandment over children, as schoolmasters have, is a matter of small honor." How wrong they both were. To those who have heard the call, it is a life of unique honor, limitless fulfillment, and weighty responsibility. The job of the teacher is to excite in the young a boundless sense of curiosity about life, so that the growing child shall come to apprehend it with an excitement tempered by awe and wonder.

11

Through Soviet Eyes

On December 12–13, just as they were bringing to a close their month's tour of U.S.A. schools, a team of 9 educators from the U.S.S.R. stopped in Washington, D.C. In those 2 days they held a press conference, visited the National Education Association headquarters, and did a little sight-seeing; but they put most of their time into sessions with Commissioner of Education Derthick and staff members of the Office of Education, which had sponsored the visit as the second half of an exchange that last spring sent 10 U.S.A. educators to the U.S.S.R.

Both at their press conference and in the daylong discussions in the Office of Education, the visitors told some of their impressions of American schools, although they emphasized that they had not yet had time to synthesize their impressions and crystallize their opinions, and that they would formally prepare a more thoughtful report when they had returned home. But they informally and frankly spoke of the similarities and dissimilarities they had noted between our educational effort and theirs, of the things they had liked and the things they hadn't. To the extent that space here permits, their comments are given as they were repeated by the interpreters; but many of the paragraphs here are "composites" of statements made by more than one person or of answers to several questions. Chairman Markushevich made the main report, but it was supplemented by brief talks from all the other members.

About the American System

Our impression of the American system of education is not something we can set forth in a few words. However, the American system does

Aleksei Ivanovich Markushevich. "Through Soviet Eyes," *School Life*, Vol. 41, No. 4 (January, 1959), pp. 8–10; 23. Reprinted by kind permission of the editors of *School Life*, Washington, D.C.

Author: Mathematician; graduate of Central Asian University, Tashkent, 1934; post-graduate studies at Moscow University, 1935; University Professor since 1944 at Moscow University; Professor of Physico-Mathematical Science since 1944; RSFSR First Deputy Minister of Education since 1958; full member since 1945 and Presidium member since 1959 of RSFSR Academy of Pedagogical Sciences; member of the Communist Party since 1951; Chief Editor of *Children's Encyclopedia*, a frequent visitor abroad as member of Soviet Educational Delegations to Finland, 1953; to China, 1956; UNESCO International Conference, 1958; to the United States, 1958; to UNESCO International Conference, 1960, at Geneva I.B.E.

seem to us to be much more unified than it did at a distance. In its great scope and in its effect in raising the educational level of all the people, it shows itself to be based on goals akin to ours; for we, too, wish to make education available to everyone. And everywhere we have found two trends: First, a widespread public interest in education, and a general desire to raise the level of education; second, an increasingly critical point of view toward many educational practices that hitherto have been accepted as sound. Both of these trends seem to us to be positive factors because only through critical appraisal of our performance can we hope to improve.

About What They Were Shown

Quite naturally, our American colleagues have shown us what they think best—the schools and developments of which they're most proud. We've seen many admirable things—fine school buildings, equipment, and shops; dedicated teachers and enthusiastic children. In general, we've seen fine large schools, with 2,000 or 3,000 students apiece. But whenever we've asked to see something that may have been considered less than top bracket our American hosts have always been quick to gratify us. Yesterday, for instance, outside Milwaukee, we were taken to see a 1-room school—at our request. There we saw one energetic young woman working with 30 children in all 8 grades. It was clearly a hard job, but she was clearly doing the best she could. Yes, we have 1-room schools in the Soviet Union, too, but never for more than the first 4 grades.

About Practical Training

We were impressed by the way in which some of your schools give students an opportunity to get a realistic combination of theory and practice. We noted it especially in home economics, automation, and hotel and restaurant management; and we found the training in the building trades especially reflective of the high level of education in the United States. The work experience programs you have for preparing technicians—we saw them in action at General Motors and Allis-Chalmers—impressed us a great deal.

In some cases, however, it seemed to us that practical training was really available only to those who were willing to stop studying and start working. In our own country we aim at combining practical education and study for everyone. We do it—and this point we want to stress—not only for practical results in our labor force but for what we consider sound educational reasons: it is part of our pedagogical faith that productive labor is part of education, that practical work contributes just as much to the education of a person as the theoretical training he gets in a classroom. The reforms we contemplate to make shortly in our own system are designed chiefly to accomplish a more rational combination of school instruction and practical work, and will in no way reduce the amount of academic education a student gets.

About TV

In our opinion TV has a great future in teaching, both directly and through extension; and here, in the United States, we have found many ideas for using it, as well as other media, as an educational tool.

About Ability Groupings

Segregation of children by ability is one of the distinctive features of the American schools. Of course we noted many interesting variations of it—in Chicago and San Angelo, for instance—but in one form or another it seems to prevail generally. This is one point on which our

---

USSR Team

THE MEMBERS of the USSR team of educators were:

A. I. Markushevich (chairman of the team), first deputy minister of education, Russian Socialist Federated Soviet Republic.

S. K. Kartsev, director of training programs of the Labor Reserves of the USSR.

A. S. Makhov, scientific collaborator in the Academy of Pedagogical Sciences, RSFSR.

N. V. Mostovets, inspector of the Ministry of Education, RSFSR.

K. R. Rashidov, assistant minister of education, Uzbek Republic.

S. S. Sagindykov, member of the board of the Ministry of Education, Kazakh Republic.

S. G. Shapovalenko, corresponding member of the Academy of Pedagogical Sciences.

A. A. Smirnov, vice president of the Academy of Pedagogical Sciences and director of its Scientific Research Institute of Psychology.

D. N. Taptykov, chief of the Division of International Relations, Ministry of Education, RSFSR.

Their tour began in Washington on November 16 and continued to Princeton, Boston, Detroit, Dearborn, Ann Arbor, Lansing, Chicago, San Angelo, El Paso, San Francisco, Berkeley, Salt Lake City, Milwaukee, Mapleton (Wis.), Washington, and New York City. On December 18 they flew back to Moscow.

two countries definitely differ. In the Soviet Union, where we do not consider ability groupings significant, we mix the children in school just as they must mix with each other in life.

Then, of course, as a concomitant of ability grouping, you make much use of psychological tests—intelligence tests, aptitude tests, and achievement tests. We, however, don't use such tests at all; we tried them for 20 years and came to the conclusion that they do not measure adequately. We have other means of measuring ability; and because we don't go in for segregating by ability, our need to measure is not so great.

We evaluate our students by the work they do, the interests they show; we have a whole series of extracurricular institutions where students can develop their talents. For instance, we have training programs outside the school system and we have the technical stations—some for the budding chemists, some for the naturalists, and so on—where students can explore problems and set up projects; and from which they carry their work to a national exposition for display. We have also music and art clubs for children whose talents run in that direction.

About Mathematics

I must say [*this is the chairman's statement: he is a mathematician and was the principal spokesman on the subject*] that in the classes I observed the teachers presented their subjects with skill and knowledge and the students were enthusiastic. But when I compared the tempo of instruction here with the tempo in the Soviet Union, it seemed as if I was watching a slow motion movie. Your usual training in mathematics seems to present students only with standard problems: if the problems are changed in any way, the students are lost.

In the elementary schools the pupils are hampered by an unnecessary difficulty: They have to translate all measurements into the English system. In the Soviet Union, before the Revolution, we had the same problem, with three systems of weights and measures—the old Russian system, the English system, and the metric system. Believe me, it was a great relief to the children when they were relieved of the first two!

About Science and Math Curriculums

One big difference between our two countries is that in the U.S.S.R. we require all our students to take both science and mathematics for several years, whereas you permit them to choose how much if any.

In the United States chemistry is usually taught in the 11th grade, for 1 year; but in the Soviet Union it begins in the 7th grade and continues for 4 years. [*In the U.S.S.R., secondary education begins with the 5th grade and ends with the 10th, but Soviet children go to school 6 days a week.*] In the United States physics is taught only in the 11th or 12th grade; but in the Soviet Union it begins in the 6th grade and continues for 5 years. As for mathematics, all secondary school graduates complete a full course, including plane and solid geometry, more algebra than the algebra 1 and 2 given here, and trigonometry.

The freedom of your students to elect subjects results in your having many graduates who know nothing of science and mathematics. From data that's been given to us, only 10 percent know trigonometry and solid geometry, and a similarly small proportion know physics and chemistry.

The Soviet system proceeds from the position that a high knowledge of science and mathematics is an attribute of an educated person. I [*the chairman*] have a hard time conceiving of an educated person who doesn't know science and mathematics. I don't mean that he must necessarily put those subjects to practical use in his work. I'm talking about the ideological thinking, discipline, and intensive training that such subjects give.

About the American People

We have seen nothing of the iron curtain that is said by some unknown evil spirit to hang between our two countries. We remember the warm reception we have been given everywhere. We have come to feel that Americans are close relatives of the Russian people.

About Peace

Teachers here, like teachers in the Soviet Union, are bringing up children in the spirit of peace. And the American people, too, are working for peace.

In a small school in Salt Lake City we saw a colored film that had been prepared for the parents and told all about the activities of the school. In it were some of the drawings the children had made—drawings that portrayed some of their real wishes. One of these showed the U.S.A. and the U.S.S.R. as two land masses, side by side, joined with a kind of line. And along this line were written three words we can't forget: Understanding, Friendship, Peace.

Aesthetic Education

We were favorably impressed by the musical education provided in the secondary schools; in fact, we were favorably impressed with the aesthetic education generally. We'll never forget a wonderful concert for children in Chicago—a concert that combined a music appreciation lesson with a symphony concert, for the conductor was not only a fine conductor but a fine teacher.

[*One of the team, however, had a word of advice about art in our schools.*] America has a great history in the arts and has produced many great painters and other artists; we have seen and admired their works in your museums. But in one school we visited we saw an exhibit of 8th grade art. I personally could not understand a single piece, for they were all made up of lines and dots meaningless to me. I asked the teacher what these drawings meant. "I don't know," she said, "you'll have to ask the children." And as the children had gone, I was never enlightened. In a country such as yours, with so great a tradition in the arts, children should be discouraged from abstract art.

About Belles-Lettres

From what we observed, we are inclined to think United States education in world literature casual and incomplete.

When I [*the chairman*] looked over the collections in high school libraries, I usually missed many of the works that I think should be available to high school students. I'm not talking about Russian literature—that would be immodest—but I'm talking about Stendhal, Flaubert, Anatole France, Balzac. And the American students I talked to seemed less interested in and knew less about foreign literature than Soviet children of the same age. In San Angelo I talked to one of the outstanding students and learned that he knew of no French writer in the 19th century; an 11th grader in Boston who impressed me with his intelligence knew of not one single Russian writer. When I asked him if he knew of any French writers of the 19th century, he could mention only Hugo.

About History

I [*a member of the team who is also a historian*] noted that American children are well-grounded in the history of their own country—and that is commendable, that is as it should be. And they knew some world history, too, though to a much lesser degree.

But apparently the United States school pays little attention to the history of the Soviet Union—and even less to the history of Kazakhstan, my own republic, though great events are happening there. In the courses of history that I observed, the history of the Soviet Union is referred to as "Russian History"—an outmoded term.

About Many Other Matters

You have asked us to point out what we judge to be defects, and in our efforts to oblige you we may have obscured one principal fact:

that we have had many, many favorable impressions in addition to those we have already mentioned.

We have noted the wonderful work you are doing with retarded children. We have admired the great scope of your program of evening studies, where both young and old can complete their education. We have been impressed by your interest in sports, and by your fine physical education facilities. We have seen that your teacher-training institutions are working just as hard as ours to prepare good teachers, and we salute the dedicated spirit of your many splendid teachers.

Above all, we've been favorably impressed by the wonderful children we've been meeting everywhere—friendly, free, and relaxed. And we count as one of the greatest benefits of our visit the friendly contacts we have established with our American colleagues in education.

12

English and American Education

For the past three years I have been engaged, with my colleagues of the Central Advisory Council on Education in England, in a comprehensive study of the English educational system. I had some of my own education in the United States, and I have been a frequent visitor to America ever since. This double experience has bred in me a growing sense of astonishment that two countries which share the same language, so many of the same cultural traditions and ways of life, whose political, religious, and social aspirations are so largely identical, should have educational systems so utterly different as to provide almost no basis for a comparison between them.

That is a strong statement, and my present purpose is to try to justify it. Let me first say, however, that I have no intention whatever of trying to show that one national system is, on balance, better than the other; only that they are much more different than is usually realized.

The American and the English educational systems are different in purpose, structure, and method. Let us start with purpose. The two systems grew up in response to very different pressures and needs. In America, you have always been very conscious of the need to build up a new society. You have wanted to construct something bigger, richer, better than you have. This is said to arise from something in the American national character, but that seems to me to turn the logic upside down; it is the American national character that has arisen from the circumstances in which the American people have found themselves. From the start it was necessary to create a supply of ministers of religion, of lawyers, and of skilled artisans—I place them in the order of importance in which they were regarded at the time. Later on there came the obvious necessity of incorporating the great waves of immigrants

Geoffrey Crowther. "English and American Education: Depth Versus Breadth," *The Atlantic Monthly*, Vol. 205, No. 4 (April, 1960) pp. 37–42. Reprinted by kind permission of the publishers of *The Atlantic Monthly*, Boston, Massachusetts.

Author (1907–   ): Educated Leeds Grammar School, Oundle School, Clare College, Cambridge University, as well as Yale and Columbia Universities; President, Cambridge Union, 1928; Commonwealth Fund Fellow, 1929–1931; joined staff of *The Economist* in 1932 and served as editor from 1938–1956; Chairman, Central Advisory Council on Education, England, 1956–1960; Chairman, *The Economist* Newspaper Ltd., London, England.

into your society. Still later came the great task, in which you are still engaged, of knitting your varied economic, social, and racial groups into the harmonious and balanced society in which the principles of democratic government can work properly.

Consciously or unconsciously, American education has at all times been designed to serve these social purposes. It has been regarded as an instrument by which society can build its own future. From its nature, it has inescapably been concerned with the rank and file of the people. Its chief concern for many generations has been to do something to the masses—and I think the word is *to*, not *for*—in the interests of the American dream.

All this, of course, is platitude in America. What may not be quite so familiar is the contrast in the historical situation in England. We have never been very conscious of the necessity to build a new society. At all relevant times we have had a fully developed society already in being. And at all relevant times we have also, I am sorry to say, been on the whole pretty satisfied with the society we have. For most of the last two hundred years, American education has been designed to do a job of construction; English education has been designed primarily for maintenance, with improvement coming second. In the very latest period, perhaps, those attitudes have started to change. As with so many aspects of education, there seem to be the first signs of a tendency to change sides. Your education is becoming socially more conservative just when ours is becoming more consciously radical.

But that is a speculation for the future, on which I will not enlarge. I am talking of the influences of the past, which have shaped the structures of today. American education has always had to concern itself with the common man in his multitudes. The concern of English education has until very recently been with the maintenance of society, in the words of the old prayer which you will often hear in school and college chapels, "that there may never be wanting a succession of persons duly qualified to serve God in church and state." This is a conception which does not necessarily embrace the education of the great mass. There is a fine, rich, broad educational tradition in England. But it is not a tradition of education, above the minimum level, for the multitude. Post-primary education has always been thought of as a privilege in England; it was not until 1944 that the principle of secondary education for all was established, and it is hardly yet fully effective.

Let me pursue this contrast a little further. Let me give you two of the consequences, of which I would guess that one will shock you, while the other may perhaps surprise you more favorably.

I will start with the shocker. The consequence of our different attitude is that the sheer size, the volume or quantity, of English education is very much smaller than American. The age at which the legal compulsion to attend school expires is still only fifteen. Moreover, that is an effective leaving age, and more than four children out of five in fact leave school before they are sixteen. Of the sixteen-year-old age group— those between their sixteenth and seventeenth birthdays—only 22 percent are still in full-time education. In the seventeen-year-olds, the figure falls to 13 percent of the boys and 11 percent of the girls. Among eighteen-year-olds, it is 8 percent of the boys and 5.5 percent of the girls.

What strikes Americans, I find, as even odder than these figures is the fact that we are not, as a nation, greatly disturbed by them, although many of us think they ought to be larger. But we cannot assume that public opinion is on our side. I am very doubtful whether there would be any support in public opinion for a policy of keeping the majority of children in school after sixteen, and I am certain that you would find hardly anyone in England who believes, as you do, in keeping all children at school until eighteen. Our college students represent about 3 percent of each age group, and there is an expansion program in hand that will raise it to about 5 percent. Anybody who suggested that we needed any more than that would meet with the strongest resistance, and not least from the universities themselves.

This attitude does not arise from any lack of love for our children. It is not because we think we can't afford it. The proportion of our national income that we spend on general welfare services—social security, health, and the like—is about the highest in the world. It is not from lack of generosity or lack of means that we confine education after the middle teens to a minority. It is because we sincerely believe that it is the right thing to do, in the interests of the children themselves. After all, there can be no absolute rules about education. Nobody believes that any child should be allowed to leave school at twelve. I do not suppose a time will ever come when, even in America, it will become legal or compulsory for everyone to stay in full-time education until twenty-five. Where you fix the age between those limits is surely a matter of judgment. And why should it be the same age for all children? Our belief in England is that, balancing what can be got out of school against what can be got out of life, the average boy or girl has probably had the optimum dose after eleven years of schooling—and do not forget that we begin, by legal compulsion, at the age of five. Eleven years, after all, is one year out of every six or seven of the average lifetime.

Now let me give you the other side of the medal. Because education after fifteen or sixteen is confined to a minority, that minority gets every assistance that the state can provide. It is nowadays, to an overwhelming extent, a minority chosen for intelligence and attainment. There are, of course, still the independent schools, where very substantial fees have to be paid. But the pressure of numbers upon them is such that a stupid boy or girl will have great difficulty getting in. And in the state schools, selection is by merit only. But once selected, a boy finds himself with his foot not so much on a ladder as an escalator. He will have the best resources of the best schools concentrated on him. If he can secure a place in a university, and that also is a matter of selection by merit, the state will pay his tuition fees and his living expenses, not only during the session but during the vacation as well. There is no such thing as working your way through college in England. We do not need a National Merit Scholarship scheme because we have one already. Nor is this a recent thing. It has been expanded in recent years, but it has always existed.

Let me move on to structure. The outstanding difference here lies in the fact that we have a very much smaller degree of local control than you do. There are about 50,000 school boards in the United States, each of them, I suppose, more or less free to run the schools as it thinks best. That gives a total population in the average school board area of about 3500 persons. In England there are about 130 local education authorities, which gives an average population per area of about 300,000. Moreover, there are two other differences, apart from this sharp difference in size. Your school boards consist, I believe, in most states, of persons specially elected for the purpose, with no other duties. In England the schools are run by the county council, or the borough council, which is the general-purpose government of the area.

Second, your school boards raise their own money by direct taxes, or at least the greater part of it. In England about 70 percent of the expenditure of the local education authorities is met out of grants from the central government in London. There are advantages and disadvantages in this. It means that we do not have the enormous range in standards between rich areas and poor areas that you do. It means a much greater degree of standardization of conditions of employment among the teachers, and therefore of interchangeability between school and school and between area and area. But it also inevitably means a greater degree of uniformity imposed from the center. We think our system is decentralized, because it allows much more local freedom and variety than exist in the school systems of most Continental European countries. But there is no doubt that it is much more highly centralized than the American system.

The other great difference under the heading of structure is the principle of selection upon which our system is based. All children, except the minority in fee-paying schools, go to undifferentiated schools from the age of five to the age of eleven. At eleven or thereabouts, a proportion of them, varying from area to area but averaging between 20 and 25 percent, is selected for what we call grammar schools, which include children to the age of eighteen, though not all the pupils stay that long. The remainder go to what are called secondary modern schools, which include children to age fifteen and increasingly to sixteen, but no older.

You will see from this description that the crucial time for an English child is at the age of eleven or a little more. The selection test then applied—the famous or infamous eleven-plus examination—is supposed to be a classification purely by ability and aptitude, without any suspicion of being derogatory to those who are not selected. But, of course, everybody wants to be selected, and with the growing pressure of numbers as a result of the post-war bulge of population, the selection has been getting steadily more competitive. As the result of agitation, the Labor Party has adopted the policy of abolishing the eleven-plus examination by sending all children at that age to the same schools, the so-called comprehensive secondary schools. The Labor Party has moved toward this system in several of the areas where it controls the local council, and even in Conservative areas there is a distinct movement to experiment with systems that do not involve sending children to different schools at the age of eleven.

I have several times seen this movement quoted in America as evidence that English education is turning away from selection. I think this is a grave misunderstanding. The public objection to selection at eleven is social and political, not educational. It is an objection on the part of parents to having their children sent to different schools, not to their having different educations. And the remedies that are being applied are wholly in terms of institutions, not in terms of the education they provide. I know, for example, one large new comprehensive school built by a Labor council. Every child entering that school is tested and placed in one of fifteen "streams," differentiated by the children's intelligence and aptitude. This selection is done by the teachers; the parents have nothing to do with it; and the children are not even supposed to know which stream is which in intelligence grading. A child placed in one of the top streams will have an almost wholly different education from a child placed even in one of the middle streams. If this is not selection, I do not know the meaning of the term. But this is what we mean by a comprehensive school. Many people in England will tell you that the comprehensive school has been copied from the American comprehensive high school, some meaning it as a compliment, some as the reverse. I have often told them that they could hardly be more mistaken.

Nonselection—if that is the opposite of selection—as it is practiced in America is totally unknown in England. By nonselection I mean the principle of treating all children alike, allowing them to sort themselves out by their choice of courses, by what they find easy and difficult, or by their varying ambitions—with counseling assistance, no doubt, but without any compulsory segregations. I am sure that your system seems as odd to us as ours does to you. There is no retreat from selection in England; the only change is that a growing number of people—but still a minority—think that the selection should be within a common school, not between schools.

The differences between the two countries in educational method make an enormous subject, and I must restrict myself to four points out of many that it would be possible to make.

The first of these differences in method lies in the position of the teacher, in the relative positions of the teacher and the textbook. One of the things about American education that most strikes the English visitor is the importance you attach to textbooks. We have no parallel to that. To begin with, I do not think there are more than two or three, at most, of the local education authorities in England that tell their schools what textbooks to use. That is left to the teacher, occasionally the principal, or the head of department in a large school. And in the higher grades, more often than not, there is not a textbook at all. A teacher will often recommend a book as covering the subject pretty well and as being useful for reference but will not make any attempt to go through it chapter by chapter.

This system places a much greater responsibility on the individual teacher, and I have often been asked in America whether we do not have a lot of trouble with it. So far as the political and social responsibility of the teacher is concerned, I cannot recall having heard of a single case arising through a teacher's being accused of using a book which seems offensive or objectionable to somebody in authority. That is partly, perhaps mainly, because our system of large authorities and rather remote and indirect public control puts the individual teacher largely out of the reach of vigilance committees, whether of parents or of the local chamber of commerce. There is also a strong tradition against anything that smacks of political interference with the schools.

Educational responsibility, however, is another matter. Quite clearly, a system like ours, which places so much responsibility on the individual teacher, cannot work well unless the average standard of intelligence, knowledge, and teaching competence is high. Up to the present, we have been able to maintain that standard. It is partly, of course, a matter of numbers. In the whole of England last year there were only some 260,000 schoolteachers. We were a little short, but 300,000 would have given us all we need. And this is in a country about one quarter the size of the United States. I do not know how many schoolteachers there are in the United States, but I am very sure it is many more than four times 300,000. I do not see how you could possibly have coped with the enormous increase in the American school population in the past forty years without being willing to take thousands of young men and women who needed close support from a textbook before they could teach. Indeed, under the pressure of rising numbers in the schools, I fear we shall find before long that we shall have to give the teacher more assistance, and that implies more external control on his teaching. This particular contrast is not, however, entirely a matter of numbers. It is partly also the result of a different tradition of teacher training, which, in England, has always laid a much greater emphasis on the content of what is to be taught than in America and much less on questions of pedagogic method.

The second difference in method is the absence in England of the course system which is so universal in your schools and colleges. Indeed, the word "course" has a wholly different meaning in the two countries. If you asked an English school child what courses he was taking, he wouldn't know what you meant. If you asked him what subjects he was taking, he would answer English, Latin, mathematics, history, and so forth. But that would not mean, as it would in America, that those were the subjects he had chosen to take. They would be the subjects that his form, or class, was taking, and therefore that he was taking with the rest of the class. Until the boy is about fifteen or sixteen, it is unlikely that he or his parents have had any say in the choice of form in which he is placed. And at no age does he have any say in deciding the curriculum of that form. At the higher ages, there is a choice between three or four different curriculums, but each curriculum has to be taken, within narrow limits, as it stands.

Here, indeed, is a contrast with the American system. Perhaps it is not quite so sharp a contrast in practice as it is in principle, as I observe that, more and more, those American boys and girls who have ambition to gain admittance to a good college find their choice of courses in high school made for them by the college entrance requirements. But there is one important consequence for teaching that is worth bringing out. In an English school, in any year but one (and that one is what we call the fifth form year, about the age of fourteen or fifteen), you can assume that the pupils who are taking a subject in one year will be taking the same subject next year. The study of a subject can therefore be planned as a continuous process over a period of years. That is what we mean when we use the word "course." We mean a whole balanced curriculum of six or seven or eight subjects, planned to continue over three or four or five years. Once a boy or girl enters on such a course, he or she will normally pursue it to the end. And all the boys and girls in a course will take substantially the same subjects, with perhaps slight options, as between a second classical or a second modern language. You will therefore understand how bewildered we are when we contemplate one of your neat, packaged, self-contained, nine-month courses, such as high school physics. It is no good asking an English schoolboy when he enters college how many years of French he has had at school. Two boys might both truthfully answer nine years. But they might mean totally different things, and neither one would mean what you thought he meant.

How, then, do we measure what a student has accomplished, if we cannot count up the number of courses he has satisfactorily taken? The answer is that we rely, to an extent wholly unknown to you, on general examinations. Every year—sometimes every term—the pupil has to take a written examination in all the subjects of the curriculum, and his further progress depends, sometimes entirely, on his performance in that examination. Most of these examinations are set and assessed within the school itself, by his own teachers. But at three crucial points in his career the examination is set and assessed by an external body. The first of these is the eleven-plus examination, which determines to which sort of secondary school the child should go. The second comes at fifteen or sixteen and is called the Ordinary Level of the General Certificate of Education, set and assessed by one of nine examining boards closely associated with the universities. This examination can be taken in any number of subjects from one upwards, but the most usual practice is to take it in from five to nine subjects. Third, there is the Advanced Level of the General Certificate of Education, which is taken at eighteen or thereabouts and which plays a large part in university entrance.

I have been describing the practice of the grammar schools; that is, the schools for the brightest 20 to 25 percent of the children. Examinations, especially written examinations, play a much smaller part in the life of the less intelligent children. Even in this case, however, they play a much larger part than they do in America; and there is a rising demand for public examinations, at lower standards of intelligence than those of the General Certificate of Education, for these less gifted children. I cannot honestly say that the children themselves clamor for examinations, but employers do, and therefore so do the parents. All the questions that Americans ask and answer in terms of the number and variety of courses a student has taken we ask and answer in terms of the examinations he has passed.

I have left to the last what is the sharpest difference of all between our two systems. This is our system of specialization, in which England is, I think, unique in the world. A student will take the examination for the Ordinary Level of the General Certificate of Education at the age of fifteen or sixteen in a wide range of subjects drawn both from the humanities and from the natural sciences. But once he has passed that examination, he will specialize. That is to say, he will devote two thirds, or perhaps even more, of his time in school to a narrow range of subjects. In one boy's case it may be physics, chemistry, and mathematics; in another's it may be chemistry and biology, or it may be history or modern languages and literature, or classical languages and philosophy. But, whatever the choice, the greater part of the pupil's attention, in the classroom and in his private study time, is given to his specialty, and he will take the advanced level examination at eighteen in his special subjects only. When he gets to the university, the specialization is even more intense. The range of subjects does not usually get any narrower, but the student gives 100 percent of his time to it.

I have found that to Americans, and indeed to educationalists from every country in the world except England, this seems a very strange system indeed. Perhaps you will have difficulty in believing that I really mean what I say. So let me cite my own case, though it is now more than thirty years old. I was a modern languages specialist. For my last three years at school, from the ages of fifteen to eighteen, I studied mostly French and German language and literature, perhaps three or four hours a week of history, and one hour of Scripture on Sundays. For another two years at Cambridge, even the history and the Scripture were cut out, and I studied French and German exclusively. Five years of my life were given to those languages. My experience was perhaps a little extreme; I think the admixture of general and contrasting subjects would nowadays, in a good school, be a little bigger. But the difference would not be great. The English boy or girl is a specialist from the age of fifteen or sixteen.

The advisory council of which I am chairman was specifically requested by the Minister of Education to review this system of specialization. We examined it most carefully and discussed it at great length, both with witnesses and among ourselves. In the end we came to the conclusion that we wanted to see it continued. We found that it was being pushed too far, and we have made a number of suggestions for removing what we think are abuses. But we have reported in favor of this system of specialization. And that is a unanimous conclusion reached by a council made up of educators of all kinds. Perhaps you will find that fact as extraordinary as the system itself, and I must try to give you some of our reasons for thinking that, in this matter, we in England are in step and the whole of the rest of the world is out of step.

Let me begin by telling you of one argument that we reject. This is the argument that every intelligent citizen, or every educated man, ought to know something about each subject in a range so wide that it compels a balanced curriculum; that no one can afford to be ignorant of history, government, science, languages, and so forth. To this, we would give our answer in two parts. First, it is true that there are certain elementary skills and knowledges that everyone must have—reading, writing, arithmetic, and several more. But these essential elements can be, and should be, provided by the age of sixteen. If you go on with them after that age, you will be wasting your time, because the knowledge you instill will be forgotten unless it can be attached to the main intellectual interest of a boy's or girl's life, which begins to emerge at about that age.

The second part of the answer is that it is only when you have got these essential elementary skills and knowledges out of the way that you can confront the real task of education. The acquisition of factual knowledge is by itself a poor test of any education and a lamentably poor test of the education of boys and girls of seventeen and eighteen. It has been said that the process of education is not to be compared to that of filling up an empty pot, but rather to that of lighting a fire. The proper test of an education is whether it teaches the pupil to think and whether it awakens his interest in applying his brain to the various problems and opportunities that life presents. If these have once been done, then factual knowledge can easily be assimilated. If these have not been done, then no amount of nodding acquaintance with widely varying field of human knowledge will equip a boy or girl with an educated mind. We in England argue the case for specialization not primarily on the score of the information it provides but because it awakens interest, teaches clear thinking, and induces self-discipline in study.

We believe that, if you can find which of the recognized intellectual disciplines most arouses a boy's interest—we confine his choice to five or six recognized disciplines, chosen for their intellectual content, not for their vocational value—if you can let him spend his time on what interests him, but insist that he must work hard at it, go deep into it, follow it up in the library or the laboratory, get around behind the stage scenery that defines the formal academic subject, you will really be teaching him how to use the mind that God has given him. This sort of intensive study takes a great deal of time, and that is why it can only be applied, for any one student, to a restricted range of subjects. No doubt you will say that the boy must be very narrow as a result. That may be. Are you sure that being narrow is worse than being shallow?

I find that English education has a high reputation among Americans. I am often asked, for example, whether it is not true that the eighteen-year-old boy in England is a year or two ahead of his American contemporary. I always answer that question, or assertion, by asking some others. What boy? If an English boy is still at school at eighteen, he is necessarily in the upper quartile in intelligence. Are you comparing him with the average American high school graduate, who is of average intelligence? And ahead in what? In the subjects to which he has been giving nearly all his time and attention for two years? It would be strange if he were not a long way ahead in those. Or over the whole range of a broad curriculum? He has been taught different things, by different methods, with a different purpose in view, in a different sort of school. There is no fair basis for a comparative judgment.

13

A Frenchman Appraises United States Schools

Any Frenchman who studies the structure of American education is at first much surprised. He beholds innumerable universities and colleges that seem prosperous and well attended; he is told that 30 percent of the youth get the benefit of a college education and that the proportion will soon reach 50 percent. Yet when he asks "What is the curriculum?" the answer is: "It all depends on the university you speak of. Which colleges do you mean?" He then realizes that many of those institutions are private, being administered either by a board of trustees or by a church, while others are controlled by the various states of the Union. He is informed that there is no uniform program; that in many places a student himself chooses, from a vast catalogue, the subjects he wishes to study, as he would make his own menu in a cafeteria; and also that a doctor's degree does not have the same value when conferred by a comparatively unknown university as it has when bestowed by Harvard or some other institution held in high repute.

How is that possible, the visiting Frenchman asks. Does not the Ministry of Education in Washington determine the programs of exams for the whole country?

When he is then told that Washington has nothing to do with education except for statistics and that the subsidies of the Federal Government are given through the states, his astonishment increases. He has been accustomed in his own country to a complete centralization. First the French Revolution, and later Napoleon, built the University of France, primary, secondary, and superior education, into one solid body, controlled by the Minister for National Education. Napoleon's ideal would have been to see all young Frenchmen of the same age doing at the same time all over the country the same Latin lesson or the same problem of geometry. The rigidity of the system does not in 1961

André Maurois. "A Frenchman Appraises United States Schools," *The Saturday Review*, Vol. 44 (April 15, 1961), pp. 54–55. Reprinted by kind permission of the publishers of *The Saturday Review*, New York.

Author (1885–1967): French scholar, novelist, and essayist; member of the Academié Française.

come quite up to Napoleon's dream, but the unity of programs remains complete. Whether a young man studies in Paris or in Caen, Grenoble or in Aix, he must study the same subjects and his diploma will have the same value as any other diploma. Every year a General Competition takes place between all French *lycées* (high schools). The best pupils of each *lycée* write on the same day on the same themes a French composition, a Latin version, an essay on philosophy, etc. The prizes are solemnly handed over, at the Sorbonne, by the President of the French Republic. On that day Napoleon's dream comes true and it often happens that small provincial towns outrank Paris.

Is French unity better than American variety? The advantage of the French system is to force upon all a basic culture without which it would be for a Frenchman impossible to get a bachelor's degree and to have access to higher education. Yet I realize the French plan would never work in the United States. You cannot impose on Mississippi a type of university that suits Massachusetts. Between populations, traditions, needs, the differences are too wide. America is a continent. Moreover, one cannot compare the American system, whose object is to give the same education to all children, with the French system, which, after each cycle, requires a successful examination before allowing the pupil to proceed. As to superior education, in France it is intended for a small intellectual elite. French universities are similar to American graduate schools. The first two years of an American university would be in France the last two years of a secondary school.

A second deep-seated difference between the two countries is this: In America, where education is meant to be essentially democratic, all school children, whatever their I.Q.s, are treated about the same way. I heard American teachers say, "Let us beware of being ostensibly partial to brilliant minds; slow-witted pupils might then acquire an inferiority complex." Their unconfessed desire is that the bottom boy should feel equal to the head boy. In some extreme cases a dunce may be told to stay in the same grade for a second year, but an American educator doesn't take such a decision without reluctance. The child might feel humiliated. The less gifted child is given easier work suitable to his interests and abilities.

In France, high school years are a permanent ordeal by examination. Every week there is a test, either in French composition, or history, or mathematics, and each boy is told his position on the list. The bottom ones will not get on to the next grade. The French baccalaureate is a difficult examination which at the end of the secondary education eliminates 40 to 70 percent of the candidates. Once a Frenchman has got his bachelor's degree, there begins the time of entrance examinations for the specialized schools which give access to all high positions in France. The *Ecole Polytechnique* and the *Ecole Centrale* remind one of MIT or Cal Tech. Big business in France is run mostly by former students of the *Ecole Polytechnique,* so-called X, and they surround themselves with other X. From the *Ecole Normale Superieure* come the best professors and lecturers in humanities and sciences; that school has an immense prestige. *The Ecole d'Administration* trains future ambassadors, administrators, treasury experts. To sum up, the first twenty-five years in the life of a Frenchman who has both ambition and talent resemble an obstacle course whose successive hurdles are competitive examinations. The good point about this plan is that most men in high positions possess real culture; the danger is that the student who shines in competition will not necessarily become an efficient man of action.

Whenever I explain the French organization to American educators, they reply: "We do it in a different way but we also select the best. In point of fact it is not easy to enter any of our really first-class universities. There is a long waiting list and it takes a brilliant school record to get in. Only *you* seem to throw back the mediocrities to outer darkness. *We* think that brilliant universities are needed for brilliant students and mediocre universities for mediocre students. In America bad students will be accepted by bad universities, where they will feel more comfortable and usurp nobody's place."

Let us add that one of the aspects of American education makes a great impression on a Frenchman; it is the social side of college life. A French university is not a small and self-sufficient society. It is a group of buildings where students attend lectures or work in a laboratory. The student body is not self-governing. There are few social activities. Our students have more time for their studies; they are perhaps less prepared for "togetherness." While I was in America, I happened to take part in a debate with high school boys and girls fifteen or sixteen years old. I was deeply impressed by their ease and poise, their respect for the rules of public discussion, and the interest they took in current affairs.

Here we come to a third difference. Most French educators would say that current affairs are out of place at school. My own master, the philosopher Alain, used to say, "Education should be resolutely in arrears." He meant that the task of school and university is to transmit to the young generation the culture patiently accumulated by centuries. If in school one does not study Homer and Plato, Shakespeare and Molière, Dickens and Tolstoy, there is a good chance he will never read them at all. If one neglects history in favor of current affairs, first he will never know history, and second he will not understand current affairs. The part of schools is not to expedite current affairs but to initiate students in timeless affairs.

The British professor Whitehead remarked that "there can be no successful democratic society till general education conveys a philosophic outlook." In France the last year of a secondary education is mostly devoted to philosophy and for many students, assuming the professor of philosophy proves worthy of his subject, that is the most important year of all. I remember with gratitude how I then found in Alain much more than a professor; I mean a master. I am afraid in America philosophy is more or less left to specialists, whereas it should teach all men the art of thinking and the art of living. Technical power without moral power is dangerous. According to his philosophy—or his faith— man can use or misuse the new forces modern science places at his disposal. In times as difficult as ours men should be made worthy of their increased strength. A modern country needs: a) skilled workers able to apply the new techniques; b) research workers able to improve them; c) philosophers able to teach how to ally efficiency and wisdom. America produces, better perhaps than we do, the first two types. Maybe she doesn't attach enough social importance to the third type.

A heated debate has been taking place in France for some time between the champions of technical studies and those of classical studies. Before the French Revolution education was entirely in the hands of the Church. Jesuit colleges in the seventeenth and eighteenth centuries formed all great French writers; Greek and Latin were then the basis of education. The results proved good. Not only Corneille but also Voltaire was educated by the Jesuits. Today the need for scientists and technicians has become so urgent that more time must be given to scientific studies. It is possible, in a curriculum so heavily loaded with mathematics, to find time for ancient languages? Many doubt it, but surely some sort of literary culture is still necessary. In order to lead men, whether it be in industry or in public services, one must understand them, their feelings, and their passions. Where does one learn to know men if not in the works of philosophers? I once heard a great French administrator tell younger men: "You will never be able to govern France if you have not read Balzac." He was right. Moreover, a literary and artistic culture is necessary to enjoy all forms of leisure: theatre, travel, and music.

The question is: what form of culture? Can modern languages supply at least part of the enrichment ancient authors brought to the minds of former generations? I believe it. Any translation is a useful exercise and increases the nimbleness of a mind. But a language should be studied long enough for the student to reach the point where he really enjoys books and conversation. A foreign language should be chosen very early in life and studied for many years. To study it for only two years is useless. I must say that in many American universities, and especially in girls' colleges, I found the French department very efficient.

A reform of the French educational system is now in process. The main object is to open more widely the doors of secondary schools and universities. Legally all schools are open free of charge to all young Frenchmen; in fact the percentage of workers' and farmers' children is only 7 percent in secondary schools, 2 percent in universities. Why? Certainly not because there are not excellent students among them. Many men of genius came from the popular classes. Why then, do they not avail themselves of their chances? Partly because a taste for culture develops more readily in cultured surroundings, but mostly because a workman or a farmer wants his son to earn a living as soon as possible. In America unions help, because they want to keep young men outside the labor market as long as possible; in France there is a very little unemployment. Yet the nation has no right to waste some of its best minds.

Until now a young Frenchman has been able to leave school at the age of fourteen. From now on it will be sixteen, and later eighteen. Classes of "orientation" will channel the pupils according to their capacities toward classical, scientific, or technical education. Unfortunately, the reform is made very difficult by the lack of adequate teachers. Many causes converged to increase the number of teachers necessary: (a) the high birth rate, which makes today's France a very young nation; (b) the democratization of education and the extension of the school years; (c) the development of new sciences. We are experiencing an acute shortage of teachers in mathematics, physics, biology. Private industry kidnaps a good many scientific graduates. Teachers are tempted to accept better pay. The result is that classes are much too numerous, that there is no one to take the place of a sick teacher, and that one has to trust students to very young teachers who possess neither the necessary diplomas nor the experience. Therefore it is imperative in France, as in the United States, to better the position of the teacher, both in prestige and in salary.

Because we lack technicians we may be tempted to sacrifice humanities to technical education, but we must remember that no technician will be an efficient leader of men if he has no general culture. Robert Hutchins gave this example, which I could match in France: "When the California State Board of Education, desirous of meeting the needs of the Aircraft Industry, asked the industry to recommend specific courses, one manufacturer replied that he wanted students who had more mathematics, history, literature, and English composition." I agree with that manufacturer. If a student knows how to think and how to work, has a good command of language and has grasped the foundation of mathematics, then he will easily learn any new technique.

French school children have been accustomed for years to long hours in the classroom and heavy homework, with very little time for sports and outdoor life. Part of the new reform might be to give more time to games and sports. An experiment is being conducted in one of the newly built *lycées* (the one at Vitry), with sixty children who will devote twenty hours a week to classroom lessons, three hours to manual work, and seventeen hours to games and sport. Homework would be abolished, an innovation that goes against a centuries-old French tradition. (As a child I had to work very hard before and after supper, until 10 P.M.) The Vitry children are forbidden to take schoolbooks home with them. We shall see how it works.

As to the difference between French and American students, I should sum up by saying that French students are generally one or two years ahead of American students in general culture, but that American students seem more unspoiled, keep a fresher mind, and know better how to get along with people. It would be madness to ask either nation to act or teach according to the tradition of the other.

14

Some Irish Impressions of Education in the U.S.A.

I arrived from Ireland in Washington, D.C., on the 4th April 1960, and left the U.S.A. on the following 10th June, having spent almost the entire intervening period in visiting schools of all kinds, from kindergarten to University, in Washington, D.C., North Carolina, Texas, New Mexico, Los Angeles, San Francisco, Seattle, Chicago, Buffalo, Boston and New York city. Throughout the tour I had many discussions on education problems with educators and with members of the general public. I had also, thanks to the State Department and the American Council on Education, the privilege of visiting a number of Americans in their homes.

Life in the U.S.A. is a veritable kaleidoscope, of which the facet that impressed me most strongly was the extraordinary friendliness of the American people. Not for a single moment had I the feeling that I was being passed along in a perfunctory way, as might not unreasonably be expected at the hands of persons who are continually dealing with a multitude of visitors, domestic and foreign. On the contrary, there could be no mistaking the genuineness of the welcome one is accorded.

The Structure of the American Educational System

Unlike the systems of Ireland and France, the administration of education in the U.S.A. is quite decentralised, even more so than in England or West Germany. In the U.S.A. Federal (that is, central government) responsibility in education is limited in the main to the assembling and publishing of educational information (a function which, incidentally, appears to be performed well and thoroughly). Otherwise, public educa-

Terrence O'Rafferty. "Some Irish Impressions of Education in the U.S.A.," *High School Journal,* Vol. 45 (December, 1961), pp. 98–118. Reprinted by kind permission of the editors of the *High School Journal.*

Author (1905–   ): Educated at National University of Ireland, Dublin; Professor in St. Patrick's Training College for Teachers, Dublin; State inspector of High Schools; Chief Inspector of High Schools; Secretary Penement Head. Department of Education, Dublin, Eire, President 1965–1966 of the Irish Historical Society; Member of the Royal Irish Academy.

tion there is almost entirely in the hands of each individual State. Indeed, even within each State responsibility for the provision of education is extended in turn to the counties and school districts. Moreover, so far from there being any incipient trend towards centralisation, tradition and opinion flow strongly in favour of continued local independence. To the European, accustomed to think in terms of a national authority in such matters, the intensity of Americans' feeling in this regard is startling. Fear of "control from Washington" appears to be deeply embedded in the American character, and where, as at the moment in education, a crisis in local financing is threatened, this fear is aggravated by any talk of a need for Federal subsidies.

For this localism there are a number of obvious historical reasons, on which it is not necessary to dwell here. Among its virtues is the existence of an unparalled civic spirit. Americans generally are not only proud of their local educational institutions (as distinct sometimes from the education provided by these) but take a lively and practical interest therein, so much so as to render the finding of the financial sinews of public and private education a much less difficult task than it would otherwise be. One result of this attitude is that the U.S.A. is the home of private educational endowments.

It is a stock joke among Americans that when two of them are introduced these immediately found an organisation for the promotion of something or other. Certainly the country is prolific in useful educational and cultural bodies. Of these, the parent-teacher associations, which operate at local and national levels and in which the parents (usually mothers) appear to predominate, are an outstanding example. As far as an onlooker may judge, their concern is not so much the rights of particular parents as such—those rights are rarely challenged, in theory at any rate—but rather improved provision for schooling and other educational matters of public interest. A teachers' body of nation-wide importance is the National Education Association.

Recent years have seen an intensification of public interest in schooling and it is no exaggeration to say that the U.S.A. is at this moment in the throes of an educational upsurge, a mighty wrestle with an immense problem. In all parts there is a drive for more and better teachers and schools. The university Departments of Education, which have become the chief suppliers of qualified teachers, are straining every nerve to meet the demand. Discussions with Deans of these Departments and with school superintendents and school authorities generally cannot fail to leave an impression of the utter dedication of these men to their task. This drive has enormous achievements to its credit during the last few years, but is probably still far from its peak. The people of the U.S.A. are becoming very conscious that no longer can more and better education be thought of lightly as for leisure, but rather that it is the cutting edge of national survival.

On the debit side of localism is that teachers' salary scales vary not only from State to State, but from county to county and school district to school district within a given State, in accordance with the taxable capacity of the area concerned. The better qualified teachers are thus attracted to the better off centers and the less qualified or unqualified become relegated to peripheral points. This is a serious matter, for talent which would respond to good teaching may thus be in danger of neglect. Moreover, the poorer the area the less are the children's chances of further education and so it is due to such children that what education they do receive be of the best quality available. The problem is similar to that which obtained in Ireland some years ago, in the period before recruitment of untrained primary teachers had ceased. At that time there was a tendency here for the remoter areas to run short of trained teachers.

This situation in the United States is an interesting instance of a conflict between the tradition of local independence and the exigencies of the great national responsibility which leadership of the free world has thrust, willy-nilly, upon that country. That the issue will ultimately be resolved satisfactorily is certain, if one may judge from the vigour and confidence with which it is being approached.

Public and Private Schools

To Irish eyes a second strange feature of the American educational scene is the distinction between "public" and "private" schools. Perhaps the question most frequently put to me was whether there are both "public" and "private" schools in Ireland. In reply I was wont to explain that, with the exception of our vocational schools, which in origin are "public" foundations, Irish schools are at the same time both "public" and "private," since none is a State foundation but all receive State assistance and employ State-paid staff.

American "public" schools, from elementary to university, are public schools in the primary sense of the term, that is, they are established, controlled and entirely supported by the public authorities. The public elementary and high schools are open gratis to the children of all citizens of the State concerned, but the "private" schools, while usually having to satisfy the State or other accrediting authority as to the suitability of their accommodation, curricula, staffing and so on, received no public assistance and so have to keep going by means of endowments, subscriptions and tuition fees.

This difference in treatment arises mainly from the constitutional confining of State assistance to schools from which the teaching of religion is excluded. The pattern, therefore, is the French one of public school and *école libre*, but there are some important distinctions between the French attitude and that obtaining in the U.S.A. There is general goodwill towards the "private" schools, as there is a strong strand of American tradition in favor of having education remain outside public control.

While there are some schools which elect to remain independent for the sake of so being, the great majority of the "private" schools are Catholic foundations, as might be expected in view of the Catholic principle that education should be informed and vivified throughout by religion. It is interesting to note that the Catholic schools generally have a high reputation, among all sections of the community, for their spirit of application and discipline, so much so that they receive many non-Catholic pupils.

Many Americans, accustomed to the idea of an absolute dichotomy between Church and State, were puzzled by the Irish practice of full (and of course impartial) State assistance to all denominational schools by contrast with the American principle, a curious instance of differing interpretations of the constitutional separation of Church and State which is common to both countries.

Conduct and Discipline in American Schools

In the schools I visited, which were of all shades and varieties, including an elementary school containing children of twenty-three races and situated in a poor quarter of a very large city, I did not come across any sign of rudeness or brashness. No doubt there are many "tough" pupils and "tough" schools in the great cosmopolitan cities of the U.S.A., as there are in all the great cities of the world, but my invariable experience was that American youth is very well-behaved and attentive in the classroom and extremely polite and helpful on the campus. In view of the "blackboard jungle" type of sensationalism which has received so much publicity, this testimony may sound strange, even to American ears, but there it is.

A noteworthy instance of training in civic spirit and helpfulness is the not infrequent practice in suburban schools of having the senior pupils take charge of the traffic outside the school gate after the last class so as to ensure a safe crossing of the road for the younger children.

The Standard of American Education

As a former teacher and former State inspector of secondary (*Americanice* high) schools, it is second nature to me to believe that, given reasonably good accommodation and equipment, almost all else is merely incidental to the work done in class. It was, therefore, my principal care, with the permission of the school authorities and teachers, to get down into the classroom, remain there during the entire period, see how the individual children tackled the work set them and finally question the pupils generally with a mind to comparing their answering with what might be expected from Irish, and, as far as my knowledge and experience went, other European children of the same age group. As there are no school inspectors in the U.S.A., this was a novelty to many teachers, but one and all welcomed the idea.

How do American and European standards compare?

As every school inspector knows, one cannot speak of "the standard of education" in any wide area, not to mention a country of continental size in which the system is decentralised. To do so would be as absurd as to say of any particular country that it has "the best (or the worst) system of education in the world." The most that one can generalize about the standard of education in the United States is that it is uneven.

With those reservations, I would say that in the elementary schools I saw, in which I concentrated on English and arithmetic, there is not much to choose between the U.S.A. and ourselves. This was so even of the multi-racial school already referred to. One could readily imagine its staff of excellent teachers busy at their task and, ignoring the various physiognomies and hues, the children busy at theirs in some large school in Ireland.

In subjects other than the two mentioned, American elementary schools have a somewhat broader curriculum than ours, or rather teach the usual subjects in a wider connotation. History and Geography, for example, extend far into the realm of sociology, including a good deal of civics and a mass of general information and activities.

In the main, however, my attention was given to high schools, as that type of school had for many years been my professional interest.

That very American institution, the high school, is neither our secondary school nor the French *lyceé* nor the German *gymnasium;* nor is it our vocational nor the English secondary modern school. It is called upon to perform the functions of all of these, for it would be entirely in conflict with the American concept of democracy to have any but a single school, even at secondary level, for all types of pupil. Anyone who has been to the U.S.A. and has, so to speak, felt the pulse there will be aware that whatever advantages may be claimed for the system of eleven or twelve or thirteen plus, any attempt at assigning American children to two different types of school on a discriminative basis would not be tolerated by their parents or by public opinion.

There has, however, been great confusion, even in the United States, over the issue of the high school, with its comprehensive curriculum and virtually indiscriminate admission, versus the European selective secondary. Often both the defenders and the critics of the American high school fail to distinguish between the principle of its being comprehensive and the quality of the work actually done therein.

Now, while in the matter of organization there may be some drawbacks to the comprehensive school, educationally there is nothing wrong in principle with the idea of a single school for all pupils of a particular age group. Common sense will tell us that normally there is no necessary loss or gain as between having the pupils in separate classrooms under one roof and having them in separate buildings. Comprehensive secondary schools have long been the rule in Scotland, a country with a reputation for high educational standards. What matters is what happens within the school, and there is no law of nature whereby a selective secondary school must cater more successfully for all its pupils than a comprehensive high school for its pupils of talent. Much will depend on the quality of the teachers and on staffing and organization. The real issue, therefore, is whether the American high school is performing well and fully its general function, that is, the preparation of all its pupils for their place in society, and its special functions, the provision of an intellectual discipline of a reasonable standard for the academic type of pupil and the catering for a diversity of abilities other than academic.

Two differences between the European and American systems, with at first sight the advantage to Europe, strike the observer immediately. In the first place, the American high school course is normally a four year one and so the European pupil who completes his secondary schooling has usually spent a substantially longer period at the secondary than has his American counterpart at high school. In this regard it may be mentioned that in many parts of the U.S.A. junior high schools are being established with the part purpose of lengthening the high school course at the lower end.

More important than even the extra year, however, is the fact that the European secondary school pupil carries all or most of his subjects abreast for five or more years, with a fairly stiff final examination, whereas usually the young American has no final general test, but achieves his high school rating by class attendance, often for less than four years, in his several subjects and by concurrent end-of-semester house examinations.

It might therefore be expected that on leaving high school, at eighteen years of age or so, the average American pupil would be less profoundly versed in the more intellectual disciplines e.g. the vernacular and its literature, mathematics, science subjects, Latin, a second European language, history and geography, than would the European, although the former's programme of general studies and activities might have been of a wider range.

But this is not the whole story. I overheard an American youngster with European experience remark, "Yes, those European kids know a lot of stuff out of books, but they don't know how to talk to people," and there is some wisdom in this dictum. Before entering the high school classrooms or attempting to make any detailed comparisons, we must examine further the structure of the American system.

"College"

The American education system, and in particular the place of the high school therein, cannot be properly assessed without an understanding of the term "College" in the American sense. "To go to College" is the ambition of most American parents for their children, but it is not easy to find a cut-and-dried definition that will distinguish between "College" and "University," as American opinion itself is imprecise in the matter. Roughly speaking, "College" applies to the "Liberal Arts" course up to the primary degree, with many "Colleges" not empowered to award degrees beyond that stage. A "University" there includes a "College," but provides also a postgraduate curriculum in "Liberal Arts" and the professional courses. When, therefore, one speaks in the U.S.A. of our Irish University Colleges, the American hearer has difficulty in grasping that each of these is a complete university in the American sense. So much is this so that one is finally driven to say "Cork University" and "Galway University," but again this has the disadvantage of making confusion worse confounded in the case of University College, Dublin and Trinity College, for "Dublin University" is often taken to mean, not Trinity College, but University College, Dublin, with the converse of equally frequent occurrence.

However, that may be "College," that is, a two to four years course in "Liberal Arts" or in a mixture of "Liberal Arts" with some preliminary ingredients of the professional course, if any, to be taken later, is generally obligatory as a preliminary to professional courses. For teaching, business and other professions which are as much an art as a technique, "College" may, however, comprise a full professional course.

A shortcoming in the system of entrance to "College" is that, as already mentioned, there is often no leaving certificate or matriculation examination as we know them. Students are usually admitted by the College authorities on the basis of their high school records. This method of selection can at its worst degenerate into little more than an assessment of the applicant's attendance record at high school classes. Moreover, some students, if not admitted to the College of their choice, keep applying to various Colleges until they are accepted somewhere. Not a few of these triers are ill-fitted academically for their prospective courses. (For such some Colleges provide a "grind" colloquially called "bonehead English.")

Large numbers, therefore, fall by the wayside in the first year or two of College, especially as many students, finding part-time employment as waiters or the like in the evenings or the weekends, have little time to devote to extra-class study.

Nevertheless, the whole idea of "College" as a cultural course in the absolute or as a pre-professional requirement is Newman's ideal put into practice on a very large scale, although Newman might not approve of the intellectual content of some of the courses concerned. "College" is undoubtedly a very important contribution to the general level of American culture. That Europe could not afford such a procedure is simply Europe's loss.

The great numbers at "College" give a swollen figure of university attendance in the U.S.A., 30% or more of the age group 18 to 22 as against the European figure of 5% or so. For this reason no valid comparison between European and American university undergraduate standards is possible, since when one speaks of 30% of an age group and of 5% of the same age group elsewhere, one is speaking of two quite different things. Any random comparison would be unfair, as the margin between the really good European students and the remainder of the 5% is small, whereas in the U.S.A. the margin is the difference between, say, 1% and the remaining 29%, within which range there is room for standards to fall very low. If a comparison is insisted upon, all that can be said is that it is well known that at the postgraduate and professional level the quality of American published work, not only in science, but in such traditional subjects as English literature, history, Latin and so on, is at least the equal of that of any country.

From all this it may be surmised that in the U.S.A. there is no very clear-cut dividing line between the standard at the top level of the high school and that to be found in the lower reaches of "College." A virtue of this, or perhaps of the American democratic idea, is that American College and University staffs think it useful to consult from time to time with their high school confrères. The very constructive discussions that result, at one of which I was privileged to be present, make for the allaying of mutual prejudices and a greater mutual understanding. They are a particularly pleasing feature of the American education system.

Before leaving the subject of "College" and "University," it may be worth mentioning that where a student fails to secure admission to a public College within his own State and has to find a place in a public College elsewhere or in some private College, the all-inclusive cost of his College education, allowing on the one hand for the high income level in the U.S.A. and on the other for the high cost of living there, is probably about three times what it is in Ireland. This accounts to some extent for the large number of American students who have to "work their way through College." Many American parents, unaware that the problem of university accommodation is even more acute in Europe than in the U.S.A., speak seriously of sending their children to an Irish or other European university.

American high schools and their curricula must therefore be viewed in the larger context of high-school-cum College. The high school students who proceed to College, a large proportion of the total, receive there something that European secondary school pupils either miss altogether or swallow at a less mature age, for "College" as a largely cultural pre-professional university course can hardly be said to exist in Europe. Those American students, therefore, who survive to become the finished product of their universities ought to be, and no doubt very often are, better educated men and women than their European counterparts.

The Curriculum and Work of the High School

To come down now to the high school classrooms, there is in the United States, as in all countries, a chronic shortage of fully qualified teachers of mathematics and science subjects. This, of course, is merely an extension of the pattern of industry and business. Again, as in almost all countries except Ireland, there is a substantial shortage of qualified teachers of subjects other than the two mentioned. That said, it may at once be added that in the U.S.A. high schools generally there is good and thorough teaching. Weak classes there are, but I did not come across any listless teacher. On the contrary, among all those I met there was a spirit of commitment to what they regard as an urgent national responsibility.

Moreover, the classwork there generally is often much more attractive, much less humdrum, than in European schools. Here the traditional method of teaching Latin is rarely enlivened by such a "project" as the making of plasticene figures of Roman soldiers, generals, senators, matrons or the like, or the demonstrating of how Hannibal won Cannae.

Such digressions from the conning of the parts of irregular verbs help to maintain lagging interest. Diversions of the sort can of course be too frequent, and in fact there is at the moment a strong movement away from "Deweyism" (so called from Dewey, an educational figure who is taken to have preached that the child should be given his head in whatever form of activity he or she prefers) and towards the traditional processes of teaching and learning, towards subject content rather than teaching methods. But while "Deweyism" can be and, it is widely alleged, has been overdone, a happy mean is preferable to the violent swing of the pendulum to which teaching methods are too often subject. Incidentally, I should perhaps mention that I saw a high school freshman (First Year) Latin class in which the teacher combined the use of mechanical aids and traditional methods and that, with a long experience of inspecting the teaching of Latin in Irish schools, where the grounding given is often very good indeed, I have never seen a better First Year Latin class. As a matter of special interest it may be added that the only Greek class I happened to see in the States made an equally good showing. Admittedly the pupils concerned were—heretofore a rarity in the United States—selected groups of what we would call very good Honours standard.

Mechanical Aids

Mechanical aids, especially the film and the recording machine, are widely employed. One use of the recording machine is the reproducing of the parts taken by the various members of the class in the play that is being studied. Mistakes in pronunciation and in dramatic emphasis can thus be noted by the offender. This emboldens the girls to improve their efforts, but the boys seem less open to its influence. At any rate the boys I heard under the test were inclined unblushingly to repeat their errors. Another advantage of these machines is that in large schools they save the time and voice of the teacher by repeating to a number of classes the instructions for homework, based on the textbook.

The more one sees of educational films, however, the more one doubts the efficacy of some of them. For example, in a Domestic Science class (the American term is Home Economics) there was a lesson on how to wrap a parcel properly. The film had everything to make it attractive, a mellow speaking voice, coloured ribbons, a pretty label addressed to an aunt and so on. It ended with a neatly and prettily wrapped packet. In reality, however, it appeared to be so much time lost, for the children were quite passive and the teacher would have to do it all over again, with many of the pupils only attaining perfection after first doing wrongly now this part, now the other. (It occurred to me incidentally that it is doubtful if any European school would regard teaching how to wrap and tie a parcel as its functions. Perhaps, however, the Americans are right in defining education somewhat more broadly than we.)

On the other hand, some of the history and geography films could not but enrich the students' knowledge and imagination beyond what the best teacher could achieve. It should be mentioned also that educational films dealing with the part played by the U.S.A. in world history are characterised by an objectivity that does great credit to the spirit of American education.

Textbooks

A matter worthy of special note is the quality of the textbooks. They cover their subjects lucidly and thoroughly and are illustrated and produced most attractively. Teachers and pupils are expected to use them to the utmost and this they do. It could, however, be contended that the very excellence of the textbooks is in some degree a drawback. At any rate, one receives the impression that overuse of them tends to take from the intellectual effort that should be involved in classwork.

An example might illustrate the matter better than I can explain it. In the course of questioning a highly intelligent sophomore (Second Year) high school English class which had been in the hands of an able and earnest teacher, I asked for the names of four English poets of the first rank. A few pupils volunteered Longfellow, but eventually the names of Shakespeare, Wordsworth, Shelley and Keats were elicited. The class knew quite a lot about these, when and where they lived and died and so on, including a good deal of information that I had forgotten or never knew, but on being asked to quote a few lines from any one of the four, they were unable to do so. The textbook had supplied a plethora of information about the poets, but it could not, of course, teach appreciation of their work. That process must depend, not on any textbook, but on the teacher's art of imparting to the pupils his own feeling for poetry. Part of his method in this regard should be to have them repeat and learn by rote some of the best poems or lines, so that they would come to appreciate these in the same way as one comes to recognise good painting by looking long and often at good paintings.

An Irish pupil might well experience the converse of the method in question. An anthology, not a textbook, would be put into her hands. The notes on the lives of the poets and on the meaning of difficult references would, as likely as not, be in small print at the back, where she might or might not read them. At the end of the school year she might not on the spur of the moment be too sure of when or where Wordsworth died, but very probably she could repeat some of his best sonnets and under a good teacher would have come to realise that in these she had acquired a possession for ever.

Once again, however, it must be stressed that any generalization is dangerous. While the learning of poetry by rote is customary in Irish schools, the incident cited is not necessarily typical of American practice. It is introduced here merely to show the undesirability of overmuch dependence on any textbook, however good.

One educator (the term used in the U.S.A. for what we would call an educationalist—the latter word has a slightly pejorative nuance there) felt strongly that Latin should be compulsory for all high school students. "But" I asked, "how could you possibly find enough qualified teachers for this?" "We wouldn't need qualified teachers," he replied. "The textbooks are so good that a little Latin on the part of the teacher would go a very long way!"

The Latin textbooks are very good, but those for the teaching of science subjects are, as might be expected, a sheer delight to the eye and the mind. At the risk of apparently contradicting the opinion expressed above, it must be said that it would be almost impossible for a reasonably intelligent American schoolchild not to acquire a good elementary knowledge of the natural sciences and, more important, an interest in them, from the textbook alone.

The Courses Taught in High School

To go into any further detail on teaching method might be tedious to the reader. In any case, the finer points of method will vary with the individual teacher, but it may be repeated that the teaching generally is good and thorough, sometimes indeed inspired, as, for example, when a class of young children, tired of routine, were asked to take the floor to a musical recording, with each of them expected to create his own individual dance form and rhythm.

It is not teaching method that strikes the visitor as unusual, but rather the impact of public feeling on method and organization. The philosophy that insists on a comprehensive post-primary school is also behind the view that even within the comprehensive school there should be no clear-cut distinction between the kind of courses taken by the more and by the less able pupils, lest any such form of separation might set a headline for social segregation. European educators, accustomed to the dual stream, or "Pass" and "Honours" classes, or whatever it may be called, would probably have little fear on this score, as their experience will have been that the boy or girl of "Pass" standard usually feels more relieved than otherwise at not having to attempt the "Honours" course. Certainly his or her personality will not suffer unduly thereby, if my recollection of my own secondary school days is not awry. American parents, however, are sensitive in this regard, and it is only recently that a movement towards "streaming" on the basis of ability has set in, following on a pronouncement in its favour by the distinguished American educator, Conant.

All this boils down to the fact that in the U.S.A., as in every other country, the system of education does not exist in a vacuum, but strongly reflects the outlook of the community. It would therefore be foolish to suggest the importing into the American system of full-fledged "Pass" and "Honours" streams or nationwide State examinations. The vastness of the country would render the latter measure, at any rate, unworkable. Nevertheless, to a visitor, who of course may well be insufficiently informed, it does seem that there is place for more widespread testing, on a regional basis, in a broad front of academic subjects at a given moment towards the end of the high school course. Where this is absent there is often no adequate incentive for the abler student to show his academic paces. Sometimes, therefore, it can happen that it is only in the Junior (that is, Third) year or so of College, when many of the weaker brethren have fallen by the wayside, that such motivation, as Americans would call it, comes into play.

For those capable of benefiting from a solid high school course in the traditional disciplines a more protracted course in these would be called for by such a final year general test, and for such students this would be educationally sounder than the present system of credits for having at various stages of the high school course attended for a limited number of semester hours at classes in a variety of subjects of which some may have no great intellectual content.

It is desired to stress that this view relates only to students of higher ability. As circumstances are, the present arrangement appears to be the more suitable and perhaps indeed the only feasible method of catering for the majority of the millions of students concerned.

No General Comparison Possible

Speaking generally, one might perhaps conclude that the comprehensive character of the American high school demands of it a wider scope and a greater flexibility than the European *lycée* or *gymnasium* or secondary school, which latter institutions are dealing with a selected group. No valid comparison can therefore be made between the two types. Each has sprung from a different concept and so has a different function.

The European secondary school pupil probably knows more about less, but with this less comprising mainly academic knowledge. As against that, American pupils address themselves in an easier and more familiar way to the teacher, without bashfulness but without disrespect, and have had more training in what is there called "life adjustment." The European pupil would probably be the better of a little more assurance, while it might be to the advantage of the American pupil to concentrate on a narrower and more academic front.

With the greatest hesitation, I would venture the opinion that while the European tradition has been to stress the intellectual and to neglect the psychological and physical in education, American practice may be suffering from an insufficient recognition of the place due to the intellect in the curricular hierarchy. *Pace* the wisdom *ex ore infantium* already referred to, it is the primary function of a high school to impart "a lot of stuff out of books." (The practical application of this in the case of individual pupils will, of course, depend on many factors.)

Many Americans themselves have come to this conclusion, and it is partly for this reason and also, of course, partly because far away hills are green, that the American public generally has an excess of deference for a European education and is sometimes inclined to speak slightingly of its own system. The main cause, however, of the disesteem in which many of them hold the schooling given there is not so much by reference to the high schools but rather that the system generally has for a number of years been subjected to a fierce barrage of the "Why can't Johnny read?" type.

The Problem of Reading

Now Johnny generally *can* read, and that at quite an early age. At least that was my experience. Incidentally, Johnny can also do his arithmetic pretty well. Over and above good written work, I saw excellent practice in mental arithmetic in several elementary or as they are there called, "grade" or "grammar" schools. (For the benefit of the American reader it may be mentioned that "grammar" school of the European side of the Atlantic is the academic type of secondary school. Such confusion in educational terminology, of which there is much, can be very misleading.)

There are, however, two kinds of Johnny who at the age of ten or so cannot yet read. One is the "poor little rich boy" who up to then has been at a nursery type of "private" school where the pupils are kept occupied somehow but receive no regular or skilled instruction. This sort of school is found in all countries. The trouble with it is that if Johnny or Seán or Jean or Giovanni, spoiled at home, complains loudly enough that he does not like the teacher, his parents threaten to remove him and the school has to relax its discipline or lose the tuition fee on which it depends for its existence.

The other type of Johnny, who is peculiar to the U.S.A., is a more serious problem. He is the great mass of young Puerto Ricans or Chinese or Slavs or Negroes or other (not usually Irish or Italian any more, except for the occasional colony of Italian or Irish extraction which has remained at a low social level) whose parents, other than those of the Negroes, are recent immigrants or first generation but not yet assimilated Americans, and who are condemned to spend their childhood in an extremely crowded and squalid quarter of one of the great cities. While there is also the question of the education of the rural or recently rural Negro in the South and while there exist here and there some pockets of near-illiterate whites of what is called the "hillbilly" type, in the main the problem is an urban one. Often the parents speak no English and the child very little. In such circumstances it would be more than surprising if these pupils could learn to read English (which is what is meant by "learning to read") before eleven or twelve years of age.

These immigrants or unassimilated first generation Americans live together in such large colonies in the cities that they present an educational problem that will take at least a generation to resolve. A further difficulty arises from the constant drift of Negro families to the northern cities. These also tend to dwell in colonies except where, as in Washington, the capital, they are up to 60% to 70% of the population. Unlike the others mentioned, the poorer Negroes speak English, of a sort, and while their intellectual potential is said to be no different from that of the white races, most of them have no educational tradition or background. One can, therefore, find in the same school district an all-white, or mainly white, elementary school where the answering is superior to that in the neighbouring "coloured" or mainly "coloured" school, although the staffs of the two schools are of equal calibre.

In the deep South the question of State provision of additional schools and teachers is, of course, complicated by the "integration" problem.

Novel Aspects of American School-Life

Often, also, the question, "Why can't Johnny read?," like so many rhetorical questions on education, does not mean what it says. Rather does it mean, "Why can't he read easily and fluently, and why does he not care for reading?" Where the latter is the case, it is certainly not for lack of a school library, for American schools are extremely well supplied in that respect. Nor is it for lack of urging on the part of the teachers, although there is a certain tendency in American schools to emphasise the importance of "looking up references" rather than of sustained reading. The great reason for Johnny having no taste for reading is the tremendous emphasis in American life on physical activity of some kind and on the watching of games on the campus or of "westerns" and the like on television. In school life particularly, games are part of the picture to a degree that is almost incredible to Europeans who have not been there to see this for themselves. This is partly because the Americans are still to a great extent endowed with that pioneering, active nature and exuberant vitality that is at the root of the nation's greatness, partly because the average boy or girl in any country, if accorded the degree of liberty given to American children, would scarcely choose reading as a principal pastime and partly because of the enormous prestige enjoyed by schools which distinguish themselves in games. It is a point of honour for an alumnus to be a vociferous and lifelong supporter of his school's team. Inter-school and inter-varsity football and baseball attract huge crowds, and favourable notice of even a high school boy in football or baseball may open the way for him to a lucrative profession as a player or coach.

A somewhat different aspect of school life there is the important place given to the national flag. All schools fly the Stars and Stripes, as do many churches. In Ireland the general feeling would probably be that to fly the flag on schools or churches would savour of an over-emphasis on nationalism. Not so in the U.S.A. There an outward (and, it may be assumed, inward) emphasis on the flag and, perhaps to a slightly lesser degree, on the Constitution, is held and felt to be a matter of supreme importance. One reason for this is that the U.S.A. is still absorbing powerful streams of immigrants of many origins. The task is to weld all these into one nation, and the flag, being the obvious national symbol, is put forward as such at the most impressionable age. In this the Americans are probably wise in their generation. It will be recalled that when the Comte de Chambord was offered the throne of France but would not stomach the tricolour, Marshal MacMahon remarked to him that if the fleur-de-lys were to be run up, the soldiers' rifles "would go off of their own accord."

That the American constitution and American history are also stressed very heavily in the schools is similarly understandable, particularly as the history of the country, brief though it be, can boast of a large number of very remarkable leaders renowned for their efforts, not in war, but in the cause of peace and concord.

The flag, constitution and history probably fill part of the void created in the public schools by the absence of religious teaching there. It is, however, to be noted that they are given an equally important place in the private schools.

Another powerful unifying influence is the almost exclusive use of the English language as a medium of instruction in the elementary school, whatever the child's home language may be. One reason for this is the difficulty of finding teachers with a command of any of the various other vernaculars.

A drawback to this justifiable effort to mould the citizens of the U.S.A. into one homogeneous whole is that sometimes values tend to get mixed. An instance of the kind, I was told, is the disproportionate interest of history students in the American Civil War (or, as it is called there, the War between the States). Such, however, is a comparatively small matter in relation to what is fundamentally a good and simple people who are by no means given to chauvinism and who perhaps get their national values less confused than any other nation one may care to name. There seems to be no feeling, at least in educational circles, of that sense of superiority which history tells us was the national vice of Spain, France and Britain in turn during their periods of world leadership. The absence of a superior attitude among the people of the U.S.A. and their acceptance of themselves and of others as they find them is probably due in the main to their innate sense of the fundamental equality of man, wherever he may be found. It may also be due in part to their realization that the "fortress of America" is not all-sufficient in the face of a rival who controls almost half the world and is in possession of weapons of immeasurable destruction. On the other hand, it would seem that the American people, to whom the idea of using their giant strength for the purpose of imperialist expansion is anathema, are, rightly or wrongly, quite certain that their might and resources are such as to forbid any total cataclysm. In Chicago, an obvious target of immediate attack, it was interesting during the days of the recent "summit" conference débácle, when it could be thought that almost anything might happen, to observe this quiet confidence on the part of all sections of the population, from university professors to taxi-drivers.

The Special Contribution of the U.S.A. to Education

The special American contribution to education may not be, as is sometimes claimed, the comprehensive high school. It may rather be, firstly, that such a high proportion of young people go to "College" and, secondly, that a complete course of high school education is available gratis to all, in so far as room can be found in the schools (and each year sees a greater and greater provision of places). It is not, however, to be supposed that everyone between the ages of 14 and 18 who could attend high school is doing so. The bootblacks of not more than 15 years of age who are to be seen plying their trade in public places from Monday to Friday[1] are evidently not at high school or any school. Again, of those who do attend high school, probably more than a third leave before completing the course. A large number take up fulltime work at 16, while others leave high school at that age to attend part-time at vocational schools during their industrial training. Finally, the price that has to be paid by Catholics and those of other religious denominations who believe that the teaching of religion should be an integral part of education is the building, staffing and maintenance of their own schools. Here it may be permitted to a friendly visitor to wonder whether a great and godfearing people might not find some alternative to the official exclusion from the curriculum of such formative institutions as its public schools of the teaching of eschatological values, which in the belief of very many millions of the American people are the supreme values. For the moment strong family religious traditions doubtless continue to hold the fort, but if the young mind eventually becomes a no man's land of the spirit, it could quickly be occupied by many evil forms of materialism.

Vocational Education

As vocational education has been mentioned, a few words on it may not be amiss. In Ireland vocational, as distinct from technical, education is generally understood as referring to full-time continuation pre-technical courses for the 14–16 age group. In the U.S.A., as in most countries concerned, vocational education usually means the kind of part-time education that goes with post-16 industrial training. In those countries it is often provided by and within the factory. Where in the U.S.A. it is given in a school, on a part-time release basis, it falls mainly into two sections—business training of many varieties and manual skills with a good intellectual content. As far as I could judge within the time at my disposal, the work done is of a highgrade character and the teaching excellent, although in the manual skills the student material is not always of the best, a result of the attraction of "College" for students of high quality.

I would have liked to have visited many vocational schools but time forbade. It was likewise not possible within the time available to make any assessment of the position in modern language teaching. The five

---

[1] There is no high school on Saturdays. This loss of morning classes over a period of years is substantial.

or six French classes I saw were in the hands of good teachers who spoke French well. Unfortunately, the great distance from Europe and the great expense of the journey there are serious (but evidently not insuperable) obstacles to the attainment of oral fluency.

Conclusion

These are a few impressions, based in part on notes taken at time, but they are no more than that. Certainly they are not intended to be categorical judgments, for it is a safe rule in education that the more categorical the critic, the more likely is he to prove ill-informed.

I should add that at no time did the State or other authorities even hint that they expected me to give any account of what I had seen or thought, but it seemed a pity not to jot down some comments while my memory of the visit was still fresh.

Like our Gaelic poets of old time, let me repeat at the end what I have said at the beginning. My most vivid impression was of the overwhelming friendliness I was privileged to experience. There is a book called *The Ugly American* which everywhere stares at one from bookstalls, evidence enough that complacency is not an American vice. Indeed, as far as that goes, the people of the U.S.A. seem to be over-critical of their own achievements in the enormous educational responsibility which is theirs and which they are facing with a vigour and resolve that is worthy of their best traditions. To return, however, to "The Ugly American." I met none such, but did meet a large number of people of all creeds, classes and colours whom I would be proud to have as friends. There is room for a book to be called "The Good American" which would do justice to this great people.

15

In the Schools of America: Notes of a Soviet Educator

I

Bravo, Soviet Friend!

A huge spaceship stands on the launching pad. An elevator flies upward, its doors fling open, a crane removes the covering from the top of the ship. All is ready for the reception of the "astronaut." The eyes of the little Americans, girls and boys, stare with delight at the preparations for the flight.

"Are you ready to fly?" asks the guide.

"Yes," is the friendly response of the children as they clap their hands.

Such scenes were repeated daily at the model of the spaceship launching area that was being demonstrated at the exhibit of "Technical and Artistic Creativity of Soviet Children" in the United States of America. The exhibit was organized at the beginning of 1962 in conjunction with the agreement on cultural and scientific exchange between the Soviet Union and the United States, and was shown in three American cities— New York, Minneapolis and Washington—with three weeks in each city. The author of these notes worked as a guide and specialist in public education at the exhibit.

It was gratifying to observe the delight and interest with which the Soviet exhibit was received in the United States. The exhibit was in progress for nine weeks, and for nine weeks the flow of visitors continued. There were so many of them that in New York people were obliged to wait in line for a long time in order to get into the exhibit. Our exhibit in Minneapolis set a unique record. According to the management of the local museum where the exhibit was presented, more people were attracted to it than to any other single exhibit in the history of the museum.

Zoya Malkova. "In the Schools of America: Notes of a Soviet Educator," [from *Narodnoe Obrazovanie*, 1962, Nos. 11 and 12] in *Soviet Education* [trans.], Vol. 5, No. 2 (November, 1962), pp. 50–59; No. 4 (December, 1962), pp. 55–62. Reprinted by kind permission of the editors of *Soviet Education*, [trans] New York.

Author: Doctor of Pedagogical Sciences of the Soviet Academy of Pedagogical Sciences, Moscow, U.S.S.R.; a frequent official visitor to the United States; Chief of the Department of Foreign and Comparative Educational Studies of the Academy.

The exhibit was beautiful, gay, and of interest to everyone—both adults and children. There were especially large numbers of the latter. They came singly, with their parents, and with entire classes. They were, of course, attracted first of all to the working models of trains, planes, ships, satellites, atomic power stations, and many others.

"Miss," said a boy pulling at my sleeve, "please show me that machine over there," and he pointed to a huge model of an excavator which took up half of the hall. I know that this boy has been coming to the exhibit practically every day and that he has seen all the models in action more than once. But his eyes are so pleading and his voice so entreating that I go over and start the model. A huge crowd gathers in an instant. The excavator's crane turns, the scoop rises, and then the whole excavator, waddling from side to side like a huge monster, takes a stride forward.

"Gee!" resounds loudly. Thus American children express their highest degree of delight and surprise.

The artistic work of Soviet children aroused great interest among the visitors. The Americans stood for long periods in front of drawings and funny figures made of cones, acorns and straw that had been done by pre-school children. Artistic articles made of wood and bones, sculptures, pictures and embroidery, sent by schoolchildren from all the union republics of our country, were examined with delight.

Americans went to the exhibit not just to see the displays. Many of them came in order to talk with Soviet people. It must be said that American propaganda gives very distorted information about the Soviet Union. Daily, from the pages of newspapers and television screens, Americans are deluged by a flow of fantasies, lies and distorted facts about the life of the Soviet people. This misinformation often is so crude and stupid that even relatively simple-minded people see the threads that knit it together. Americans came to the exhibit to obtain, as they would say, information at first hand. Filled with all kinds of fantasies from newspapers and doubting them, they usually began their questions as follows: "Is it true that in Russia . . ." and then some cock-and-bull story would follow. How many times at the exhibit did the guides' clothing become subjected to careful examination? "The skirt you're wearing—is it Soviet?" asks an elderly American woman, draped with bright beads, as she captiously felt the material of my skirt. "Is the blouse also from Russia? The shoes?" I take off the shoes and show her the factory mark—"Paris Commune."

"Just think," exclaims the woman, "you dress the way we do!"

But people such as this lady, who ask whether or not Russians wear factory-made shoes and whether homes have radios, are becoming fewer.

Americans themselves ironically call such people "provincials." A thin "beep-beep-beep" above the heads of Americans in 1957 awakened them. They suddenly became aware of a technologically powerful country, which yearly shakes the world with new achievements.

Now they want to know "everything—everything about Russia" (that is what they call the Soviet Union): "What is communism?" "What is the meaning of 'from each according to his abilities'?" "If there is no private property in the country, what induces people to work?" A countless number of questions every day! And the most frequent one: "Do the Russians want war?"

The question of war and peace is now of concern to all Americans. There was a time when America, protected by the oceans, considered itself invulnerable. But now war threatens even their little house with the traditional lamp in the large window. This threat of war became more apparent when the Government of the United States made the decision to renew testing of the atomic bomb. We were witnesses to the fact that American women in New York carried placards reading "No to the hydrogen bomb!" and "Stop the insanity!" American university students organized a march on Washington protesting atomic armaments. People came to the exhibit wearing buttons that shone on their jackets and sweaters with the words: "No to war!" "Peace or pieces?" and "Ban the hydrogen bomb!"

The question "Do the Russians want war" was asked of us by all— young and old, people far removed from politics and public figures. After hearing a decisive "No" as the answer, and an account of the sacrifices endured by the Soviet people during the last war, Americans would say: "Yes, peoples do not want war. We can and must live in peace. In order to do so we should know one another better. We need cultural exchanges, we need exhibits such as this one."

The exhibit "Technical and Artistic Creativity of Soviet Children" was accepted by the majority of Americans as a step toward mutual understanding, and the work of the exhibit was rated highly. The pages of the visitors' book glow with words with large exclamation marks: "An outstanding exhibit!" "Remarkable!" "Fantastic!" "Beautiful!" And these of course are the exclamations of children: "Great!" "Terrific!"

There are more lengthy remarks: "Beautiful and disturbing—these are the only words that can express my reaction to the exhibit." "The exhibit demonstrates that your people are simply great," and "Bravo, Soviet friend! Send us more of these exhibits!"

"My 7th grade, now studying geography, has looked at your remarkable exhibit with enthusiasm and delight. We want to know you better and be friends. York Sempan, geography teacher."

And here are some remarks by children: "I think the exhibit is great. I've picked up a lot of information here, Ricky Karten, 6th grade."

"Soviet children do very good work and these are the best educated children of all the ones I know. Rene Zapotti, age eleven."

"I was very pleased, and your children are great. Boy, age ten."

"I thought the children in Russia were simpletons, but they are talented," wrote a young man.

The visitors' book is full of such remarks. They constitute 90 percent of all entries and indicate that simple Americans want to know as much as possible about the Soviet Union, that they dream of peace, hate war and want to live in peace with the Soviet people.

These remarks are also indicative of the high estimates that Americans place on the Soviet system of education. So at this point I shall move on to what was of chief interest to me in the United States—the schools.

At the Textbook Stand

There was a section at the exhibit that was not bright with colors, that did not include a working model of a pneumatic hammer or elegant works of art made of bones. But this section was always full of people, and lengthy conversations and heated discussions were held here. This section was called "Public Education in the U.S.S.R." Interest in it was not accidental. Since 1957, one of the most popular themes in the American press has been the "Challenge of Soviet Education." The Soviet system of education was discussed as the basic reason for the success of science and technology in the U.S.S.R. At the same time, criticism began of the American schools. Many books appeared which spoke of the crisis of the American school, of the fact that it does not provide its pupils with fully adequate knowledge. Many famous persons made declarations concerning the superiority of Soviet schools in comparison with American schools and the challenge presented by the Soviet Union to the United States in the area of education. Their sensational declarations spread throughout America. That is why every American, even though he was far removed from pedagogy and schools, knew something, had heard something about the "challenge of the Soviet schools" and was interested in visiting the section for public education to see personally what it was that helped the Soviet Union to catch up with the United States in the areas of science and technology.

The "Public Education" section included charts, diagrams and figures that demonstrated the achievements of public education in the U.S.S.R. Films about the Soviet school were shown, and examples of school textbooks were displayed at a large stand. This stand attracted special attention.

A young American woman in shorts (the customary wear of American women in warm weather) is in a great hurry. But she cannot go by the stand with the textbooks. "Tom, come here," she calls to her small son. "Look," and she shows him a textbook.

"They solve problems in multiplication in the first grade!"

"Isn't this a mistake?" says a girl wearing glasses, bringing me a book with a label in English on it which states: "Physics textbook, 6th grade." "Do your pupils really study physics in the 6th grade?" Having received a positive answer she exclaims, "This is unbelievable! Our 6th-graders don't even know the word 'physics.'"

A tall graying woman removes a textbook from the stand entitled *Native Speech* [Rodnaia rech'], for 1st-grade use. She spends a long time leafing through it and then approaches me.

"Is this book to be read in the 1st grade?"

"Yes."

"I suppose that it is used by only the most able pupils?"

"Oh no! This book is read by all pupils. Some are a little better, others worse, but all of them read it."

Surprise shows on the face of my partner in conversation. It grows and is accompanied by loud exclamations when she discovers that texts in *Native Speech* are excerpts from the works of Russian classics—by Pushkin, Tolstoy, Nekrasov, and others.

"I am an elementary school teacher," says the woman. "Do you realize that your children in the 1st grade read texts that are read with difficulty by our school children in the 6th grade? How do your teachers achieve such success? How do they teach the children to read?"

I begin to explain how our youngsters acquire reading skills. More and more people join our conversation. There is a constant flow of questions: "When do children begin attending school?" "How large are the classes?" "How long do they stay in school?" "Do they get homework?" "How is their progress evaluated?" "Do the children like to read?" "What is done with a pupil who cannot read?"

Some of the people involved in the conversation had heard of the recently published book by Professor Trace entitled *What Ivan Knows That Johnny Doesn't*. In this book the Cleveland professor of English makes a careful analysis of textbooks and curriculums in the humanities of Soviet and American schools. This the conclusion he reaches (used as an advertisement on the book cover): "While American children climb the hill with Jack and Jill, Soviet children of the same age apparently study the height of this hill, its minerals, and its physico-political role in international affairs. . . . Our children are behind Soviet children not only in mathematics and natural science. By the time the American 4th-grader learns to read 1,500 words from the standard reader, the Soviet child in the 4th grade can read at least 10,000 words and is ready to dig into history, geography, and natural science. The fact is that when Ivan is reading Tolstoy, Pushkin and Gogol, Johnny is still reading the adventures of Jerry and the little rabbit who jumps about 'hop-hop-hop.' The Soviet schoolchild begins English as a foreign language in the 5th grade and studies it for six years. By the 10th grade he may, possibly, read more in English than the American child is required to do in the 12th grade" [Retranslation from the Russian—Ed.]

Leafing through the Soviet textbooks, my schoolteacher friends say: "Yes, Trace does not exaggerate, Trace is right." Our conversation is interrupted suddenly by an angry man. A stack of algebra, trigonometry, and physics textbooks are in his hands.

"Are you going to maintain that all pupils in your schools study these subjects? Do you really think that all people are able to understand physics and solid geometry?"

The American is not pacified by my explanations.

"Do your schools include pupils who do not keep up?"

"Yes."

"What do you do with them?"

I tell him of the methods used by our teachers to encourage pupils, to evoke in them an interest for knowledge. Then I tell him of the system of mutual assistance, where the better pupils help the lagging ones.

"It is the state that forces them to help the lagging pupils," remarks the man. "As an individual I cannot understand why these talented children should waste their time on the lagging pupils when they could spend it on their own studies and achieve much better results."

Yes, it is difficult for us to understand one another. The American schools base their work on a completely different philosophy. But I shall come back to this later.

The Americans, particularly young people, always stopped at the stand with the sign: "All types of schools in the U.S.S.R., including the higher educational institutions, are free. Students at higher educational institutions receive government allowances." They would stop and sigh: "How lucky your students are."

A university education in the United States is an expensive thing and by no means can everyone afford it. This cost of instruction at good universities approaches 2,500 to 3,000 dollars a year. Many Americans who wish to educate their children at a university begin to save money for their studies as soon as the child is born. There are banks and companies that specialize in this type of savings. Here is an advertisement by one of these companies which we heard daily on television: "Are you preparing your son or daughter for college? In every family the cost of education is the largest expense after the purchase of a home. You can avoid worrying if you begin to put away money now and utilize the services of our company."

How many sweet and intelligent boys and girls came to the exhibit who spoke of their inability to go to college, or their having to drop out, because of the absence of funds. These are the thousands of capable Americans of whom President Kennedy once spoke when he lamented the loss of potential Einsteins.

The Americans were greatly interested in our pre-school institutions— the kindergarten. There are hardly any in the United States, if we exlude the small number of private kindergartens. Many Americans would come to the exhibit with erroneous impressions about our pre-school institutions, impressions they received from newspapers and magazines, where the Soviet kindergarten is depicted as some kind of a monster that tears children away from their parents and conducts communist propaganda. But seeing films about kindergartens and learning that children in kindergarten are fed four times a day, that they have a good time, play, sing, and dance, the visitors quickly change their minds. "Yes, kindergartens of this type are wonderful things!" The Americans were astounded by the insignificant sum that parents pay for the upkeep of their children.

Young mothers were especially attracted by the kindergartens. "I am a teacher," a young woman with two children tells me. One child was sleeping in the carriage and the second was holding her hand. "I worked for a year, and then the children came. I had to give up my work. There was no one to leave the children with. I can't afford a housekeeper; they're too expensive, and there aren't any kindergartens. So I stay at home."

The visitors would leave, carried away not only by the exhibit itself, but also by the system of education in the U.S.S.R. and by the work of the Soviet school. Most of them understood that the complicated models and artistic creations that they saw at the exhibit could have only been made by children who had been well educated, who possessed skillful hands and clear heads. The Americans wrote of this also in the book for visitors.

No matter where we were in the United States—on the streets, in museums, schools or private homes—the overwhelming majority of Americans displayed in their attitude toward us, Soviet people, great hospitality and sincere friendship. We were given broad opportunities to familiarize ourselves with the school system of the United States. We were able to visit various types of schools, to attend classes, and to converse with teachers and students. We learned about the work of out-of-school children's organizations, visited universities and teachers colleges, local departments of education and central administrative organs. In learning about the American school we first of all wanted to determine its more characteristic traits. At the same time, remembering V. I. Lenin's words that we must bring back from abroad with full arms all that is favorable, we tried to find everything that could be of use to us—to Soviet educators.

Problem Number One

Meeting with American educators of various ranks, from ordinary teachers to heads of sections of the ministry of education (for the sake of simplicity we shall refer to the Department of Education, which is part of the Ministry [sic]) of Health, Welfare and Education, we would pose the following question: "What is the basic problem facing American schools?" To this question everybody would reply in the same way: "Money."

The lack of sufficient funds is really the number one problem of American schools. The United States has a so-called decentralized system of school administration. This means, first, that the selection of textbooks, the drawing up of curriculums and other factors in the work of the school are matters that are resolved by the local community in which the school is located. Second, schools exist on funds that are collected as a tax on the local population. The school budget is made up of the following parts: 55% from the tax on the population; 41% from the state; and 4% from the Federal Government.

Until recent times this system of decentralization was lauded in every way. It was said to be the most democratic system. Only recently has the opinion been expressed that this system is more suitable for the eighteenth century than for the twentieth.

The division of American cities into poor and rich areas is very clearly seen. When showing us a city the Americans would usually say, "The rich live here." And we would see splendid residences, far from the dust and smoke of the city, in the suburbs, and hidden by clumps of trees. "And this is where the poor live." This could be guessed without explanations: ramshackle houses squeezed against each other, garbage containers under windows, laundry on the lines, and children playing right on the streets.

It is quite obvious that if schools exist on the basis of local resources, then the schools in wealthy areas are in better material circumstances than in poor areas. Actually, in the suburbs, to which businessmen and the highly paid intelligentsia have moved, the yearly expenditure for each pupil is twice that of the expenditure in the poor areas. This is what we were told at the National Education Association. It was enough to look at the exteriors of schools to sense the difference. In wealthy suburbs we saw magnificent schoolbuildings built in the contemporary style. This is usually a group of one-storey buildings connected by passages. These schools have plenty of light and air. Modern materials are used in construction; they are light, strong and beautiful. The construction of schoolbuildings in the United States is guided by the rule that it is better to spend more initially and then not have to expend money on current repairs. The planning of a school is well thought out. There are many rooms for various purposes. Classroom furniture is light and movable. Some schools have swimming pools. Americans show these schools with pride, and they have reason to do so. The buildings are really beautiful. However there is one "but." You will see such schools, as a rule, only in wealthy areas.

We visited a seventy-five-year-old school in the large city of Minneapolis. Three classes study in one room at the same time; a library of 200 books is located in a small storeroom. In other schools we saw pupils studying on the stage and in the corridors because there were not enough classrooms. According to official data, the schools do not have room for two million pupils. The situation is particularly bad in the southern states of the United States. We were shown a chart at the Ministry of Education that indicated the percentage of illiterate or partly literate in the adult population. The figure for the southern states is 20 to 25 percent.

Money is needed to build schools—much money. Local school communities cannot cope with this problem on their own. That is why the American public is now demanding, with greater frequency and persistence, that the Federal Government increase its share in the financing of schools. And not just schools. There is nothing in the United States that resembles our out-of-school institutions. The few centers for children that exist depend upon private contributions and experience an acute need for funds.

The Congress of the United States has more than once considered legislation for increasing school allocations. But it has been rejected every time: congressmen, half of whom are people with an income greater than fifty thousand dollars a year and a fifth of whom are millionaires, do not wish to spend money on public education.

In an Elementary School

I went to one elementary school, where I was very gladly received, nearly every day over a period of three weeks. The children became used to me and, when meeting me on the street, they would greet me as they would their own teachers with: "Hi, Mrs. Malkova!"

The school is a one-storey brick building in a poor area. The people who live in this area are Negroes, Puerto Ricans, and whites, all of them at the lowest rungs of the social ladder. The school has 750 children ranging in age from five to twelve years. Compulsory education in the United States begins at the age of six. But part of the children attend preparatory grades before enrolling in the 1st grade. These are called "kindergartens" in America. But they have very little in common with our kindergartens. The school that I visited had three preparatory grades. They function three to four hours a day. Looking through the glass door of the class, you can see tots drawing, listening to a teacher's story, or singing. These are "kindergartens"—preparation for formal instruction in the 1st grade.

The elementary school in the United States is usually of the six-year type and exists apart from the secondary school. One teacher teaches all subjects in each class. True, the pupils get a new teacher every year, since teachers specialize in a definite grade and do not "lead" pupils through the six years in a row.

The school has a good library with a large reading room. But it does not have workshops, study halls, or laboratories. All study activity takes place in the classroom.

Each classroom is an independent unit. It has chests for storing teaching aids and simple instruments, a wall closet for the children's clothing, shelves under the windows for textbooks and books, and also a wash basin.

The furniture in the classrooms consists of little tables and chairs which are grouped either in a semicircle or are scattered chaotically around the room. Each classroom reflects the tastes of the teacher. In some classes I saw small sofas with covers and a mountain of pillows, or tables covered by a white embroidered tablecloth. Everywhere the walls are decorated with the children's drawings, their various other efforts, posters entitled "Winter," "Our Breakfast," "What We Know About Animals," and so forth. The classrooms usually have two or three blackboards, and in front of the main one is the mandatory fixture in every American school—the national flag.

The school day begins at 8:30 A.M. The 1st and 2nd grades begin their classes a little earlier because there are two sessions of these grades. Once a week the school day begins with a general meeting of pupils—the assembly. All the children gather in the auditorium of the school, sing the national anthem, and swear the oath of allegiance to the flag. Then follows some kind of performance—the 6th grade depicts a scene from the "Life of Lincoln," the 4th grade relates the story of their trip to the zoo and the habits of the animals, and so forth. Sometimes a guest of the school addresses the assembly—which is what happened with me, for example.

The school day ends at 3:00 P.M. There is a thirty-minute lunch period in the middle of the school day. Most of the pupils eat in the school lunchroom. For thirty to forty cents they get a small carton of milk, a "hot dog" (that is what the Americans call their most popular food—a hot sausage on a bun), and jelly. School ends an hour earlier on Wednesdays. The school gives the churches a special period for religious instruction. Usually, however, school is let out at three o'clock. Only the prolonged-day groups remain. These groups now exist in a number of schools located in poor areas of large cities.

Special teachers take charge of the prolonged-day groups. Pupils get sandwiches and milk in the classroom itself and then special activities are organized with the children (music, dances, and handicrafts for the boys).

The 750 girls and boys in the school are assigned to classes according to a whole series of classifications. First of all, the school has a class for the mentally retarded children, a class for children with poor eyesight, two classes for the so-called emotionally disturbed children. The remaining children are assigned to classes in accordance with their "intelligence quotient" [*koeffisient umstvennoi odarennosti*].

More than a half-century ago American pedagogy came to believe deeply in the theory of intellectual endowment and since that time has built its work on this theory. According to the theory, people are born with definite intellectual abilities and only one-fourth of the people can cope with intellectual activity. At that time, half a century ago, measurements were established—tests for measuring the intelligence quotient. The overwhelming majority of American schools now use these tests and assign pupils to various classes in accordance with the test results.

We examined dozens of tests that were being used in the schools. They included the following problems: find the words similar in meaning; insert the suitable word missing from the sentence; underline the number that does not fit into the given sequence of numbers; and so forth. Dozens of specialists, American and English, have proved convincingly that if the tests measure anything it is certainly not innate intelligence, but only the skills acquired by the child in classifying the systematizing, and his store of words.

Obviously, in taking these tests the best results are achieved by children from well-to-do families, where parents could afford to buy them toys and books, in short, to develop their children. A low intelligence quotient is received, as a rule, by children from poor and, particularly, Negro families. Many progressive educators in the United States with whom we spoke protest strongly against measuring the intelligence quotient of pupils, and consider this system faulty because it categorizes, without foundation, a large number of children as slow and deprives a great many children of an education.

Frankly, we Soviet educators were staggered by the harshness of this system. A youngster enters the 1st grade and takes his first step in school. But already in October, on the basis of his test results, he has been labeled "slow" and assigned to a specific class.

The school referred to above has the following gradations in the 1st grade: 1–1, 1–2, 1–3, and so forth up to number 7. The "intellectually gifted children" are in the 1–1 and 1–2 sections, then follow the "average," and at the very end the "slow" children whose quotient was lower than ninety.

The labels "able" and "slow" have a tremendous influence on the status of the children and on the work of the teachers, even of those who are against the system. As a teacher once said to us: "I am against testing. But knowing the intelligence quotients of the children in my class, I cannot force myself to be unbiased. I still look at them through the prism of this confounded quotient." We saw what this system of classifying children by abilities leads to in practice when we attended classes.

"Here Are the Slow Children"

We heard this phrase from a teacher every time we prepared to attend a class with an index of 4, 5, or lower. The teacher conducts his class with this thought in mind. It is considered that the "slow" children are incapable of abstract thinking, that the teaching materials must be simplified for them, and that these materials must have a greater share of practical elements.

We came to class 1–5 on a winter morning. It was cold; snow, unusual for Americans, was falling. But the children, as always, wore sneakers, socks, and light jackets.

The class began with the traditional anthem and oath of allegiance to the flag. Then a girl dressed in a bright red, wide skirt, from under which peeped the hem of her petticoat, showed the class a white cup and related that it had been given to her by her mother, that coffee was drunk from the cup, and that such cups were made in a factory. A boy showed a picture of a house, which he had drawn, and related that his family lived in that house, that the house was large and old, and that he was afraid to use the dark stairway at night.

The teacher placed before each child a thin magazine consisting of several pages. This periodical is published once a month and is used as a supplement to the textbooks. We saw such magazines in all of the classes. They contain stories about things in the children's environment, and there are technical and political articles for the upper-grade students.

The magazine for the 1st-graders had pictures of various buildings. The children would examine the pictures and relate the use to which each building was put. "This is a skyscraper," said a boy, pointing to the picture of the famous hundred-storied Empire State Building. "Do people live here?" asked the teacher. "No." "And what do people do in this building?" Silence. Several of the children are resting on the little tables, others are rocking in their chairs. "People work in this building," prompts the teacher. "You don't know the word 'to work,'" she continues. "I'll write it on the board. Let's read this word and Mike will try to find it on a card." The boy approaches the cards and searches for the word for a long time. He finds it with the help of the teacher.

We saw the same in the 2nd grade. Singing of the anthem and the oath, the magazine-textbook with pictures of various machines. The teacher wrote several words new to the children: "machine," "strong," and "shadow." The children read them and found them on the cards.

Then the teacher distributed the readers. They read the text in which the same words were repeated in various combinations:

"Listen Jane," said Dick, "I have a ball, I can play ball. Come and play ball with me" "I can't play ball," said Jane . . . , and so forth.

Reading in most American schools is taught with the method of "whole words." We were told that up to the 3rd grade pupils were not taught the alphabet and sounds. They learn the word as a whole as, for example, they memorize hieroglyphics in some Eastern languages.

Instruction in reading is a slow process. The texts are so arranged that words are repeated and there are not more than three to five new words on each page.

While examining the readers we were struck by the poverty of content and the simplicity of the texts. We began to understand the exclamations of surprise of American teachers when they learned that our 1st-graders read excerpts from Russian classics.

The problem of reading instruction is considered to be a most serious one in American schools. A large portion of American schoolchildren cannot read when they finish elementary school. This is a result, first of all, of the "whole word" method, the fallacy of which has been written and spoken about by many American educators. This also implies, I think, that American schoolchildren write very little.

The American schoolchild's notebook is a thick folder, the pages of which are fastened with metal rings. This notebook is for recording episodes and for tests. The children write with a pencil, as they please. As far as exercises and problems are concerned, the teacher mimeographs them beforehand—as a rule, the schools are equipped with mimeograph machines. All the pupils have to do is to place the required number or word in the blank space provided.

Such mimeographed sheets undoubtedly save time. But it is also true that the schoolchildren do little writing and, as a result, are slower in learning to read and spell. It is not surprising that even in the higher grades of secondary schools (10th to 12th grades) we saw groups learning to read.

The inability to read handicaps the study of other subjects. We talked with a teacher in a 6th grade with an index of 5 about the teaching of social studies. She told us that the pupils learned all the material by listening to the teacher. "That's because they can't read the textbook," she explained. "It's true that at times I ask one of the better pupils in the class to read a paragraph from the textbook out loud. Or I simplify the textbook material and mimeograph it so that the children can read it."

An 8th-grade teacher of natural science in another city and another school told me the same thing. "My goodness!" he exclaimed when we asked whether pupils used their textbooks at home. "They can't read. All of the material is covered only in class."

A characteristic trait of the American school is work on so-called "projects" or "themes." Every teacher, in planning his work for the year, selects five or six projects or themes. Work on these themes, according to the educators, should combine various subjects into a unified whole. The themes generally combine social studies, English, drawing, and handicrafts. In the 4th grade, for example, one such integral theme was "Our City in the Past and Present" The children divided into teams dealing with "Transport," "Communications," "The Professions," "Religion," and so forth. The teams are supposed to read the literature, meet with specialists, make up albums with magazine clippings, draw illustrations, make models, and the like.

In fact, the latter—drawing and handicrafts—supplant all the other forms of work. The class was turned into a workshop for an extended period. Whenever we would come in the children would be painting, building, or drawing, but would not be writing or reading. Observing this class during its period of work on its theme, I would continually think of the lines from a book called *A Teacher Analyzes the School Crisis* by an American teacher, Wilma May: "Our children spend too much time in the building of little houses at the expense of time assigned for arithmetic, reading and writing." [Retranslated from the Russian—Ed.]

While telling us about the work of the class, the teacher explained the following: "This is a class of slow children; they can grasp things only in practice. In building this," and she pointed to a model of a covered wagon in which nineteenth century American migrants traveled and which seems to be a symbol of masculinity in the United States (these wagons and wheels adorn the entrances of restaurants, parks, and private homes), "the children can learn more than they would by reading books."

Regarding the children as "slow," teachers in classes with an index of 4, 5 or lower teach arithmetic according to a reduced syllabus. The demands on the children's knowledge here are not great.

Upon hearing that we were going to a lesson in class 3–4, a young schoolteacher, stressing each word, warned us: "Bear in mind that these children are slow." We sat at a low table at the end of the room and began to watch the "slow" ones. Sweet and shining faces, laughing eyes turn to us from time to time. There are thirty-three pupils in the class; sixteen of them are Negroes. We noted an interesting pattern: the higher up the ladder of class "ability," the fewer Negroes.

The children have pieces of paper with printed homework in arithmetic. The teacher attempts to check the answers, but unsuccessfully. There is a terrible noise in the classroom and even the voice of the teacher cannot be heard.

The teacher distributes pieces of paper with a new problem to solve: "One fishbowl contains three fish (a drawing of a fishbowl with the fish), and another has five (again a drawing of a fishbowl). If we remove the fish from the first bowl and place them in the second, how many fish will there be in the second bowl?" Amidst the noise, singing, and shouting the class solved the problem in twenty minutes.

The 6–4 class had a young man as a teacher. The class had thirty-four pupils, twenty-six of whom were Negroes. The teacher explains the division of a multi-digited number by a two-digit number, and divides 7,426 by 12. The pupils sit quietly but are indifferent to all that is taking place. Five or six of them listen and do the work.

Boys sit with their coats on at the back of the room, waiting for the bell. The girls, opening their handbags, look at themselves in their mirrors, file their nails, and comb their hair.

Having finished his explanation, the teacher gives the following problem to the class: "8,274 pieces of candy were divided among 42 classes. How much did each class get?" Another three pupils open their notebooks. The rest continue to occupy themselves with their own affairs.

The teacher walks around the class, observes how the problem is being solved, and quietly passes by those who are not working. Not a single remark!

We were astounded by this, shall we say, mild, neutral position of the teacher in the class which we observed fairly frequently. As we noticed, the teacher seldom uses methods to force the pupil to work, to encourage and stimulate him. Being under the influence of the theory of innate endowments, the teacher does not attempt to somehow pull up the pupil, to give him complicated problems. His reasoning is simple: "What can you expect from this boy? He has an intelligence quotient of 75." The boy looks upon himself in the same way, since all of the children know whether they are "able" or "slow."

The indifference of teachers is also attributable to the fact that it is school practice to transfer all pupils to the next grade. At the end of the year the teacher effects not a transfer but a so-called reorganization of the class. He writes a report on each pupil, similar to the following: "Williams reads poorly. He is poor in arithmetic. But his quotient is 80. In the 2nd grade he should be placed in the 6 (or 7) index group." And there he will study in accordance with an even lower level syllabus, with very low demands on the quality of his knowledge.

We were invited to a conference of teachers and parents in New York where pressing school problems were discussed. In their speeches many said: "The elementary school is the root of all evils. It does not provide the basic knowledge. The children cannot read, write or count. They are not prepared to continue their studies in the secondary school."

To get a complete understanding of the American elementary school we must become familiar with yet another part of it—the work with "I.G.C."

I.G.C.

Those three letters—I.G.C.—were to be seen on classroom doors. They are constantly being mentioned in conversation by American teachers. The children also say: "We are from the I.G.C. class." They are the initial letters of three words—intellectually gifted children. According to American standards these are children with an intelligence quotient higher than 110 to 120. They are assigned to separate classes where the content and methods of instruction are very much different from the ones described above. Attending these classes and talking with the children gave us the impression that their knowledge is at the level of knowlege of our good pupils.

In the I.G.C. classes we saw real exercises and serious work in arithmetic and the native language. When at these classes we almost felt as if we were back in our own school. Class 4–1 had 22 pupils, including only seven Negroes. A spelling lesson was in progress. The teacher would pronounce a word and the pupils would name its letters. From time to time the teacher would ask them to make up a sentence with this or that word, change the tense of its verb, and explain the forming of tenses.

The pupils found the prefix and root of the word "triangle," and discussed the origin of the prefix. The teacher imperceptibly moved from grammar to mathematics. The pupils discussed various geometric figures and determined their properties.

Class 6–1 has 24 students, five of them Negroes. The arithmetic lesson is progressing at a quick tempo. The teacher reads the problem and the pupils make brief notes on their sheets. One boy is at the blackboard. Two or three minutes pass; several persons raise their hands and supply the answers. The next problem follows; brief notes; answers. There is no waiting for the late ones; the solutions are arrived at quickly, without explanations, without long notes, and almost orally. The syllabuses in I.G.C. classes are rich and serious. The teaching of mathematics, for instance, is conducted in accordance with a new syllabus, the basis of which is the theory of numbers. The teaching of arithmetic has been reorganized to accord with this theory, beginning with the 1st grade.

Foreign language instruction is introduced in the I.G.C. classes of the 3rd and 4th grades, with the broad utilization of television and radio. Independent work by pupils plays a large role in these classes.

Just as in the grades for the "slow," the teacher plans a series of integral themes for the year. But while studying these themes attention is concentrated on independent work in reading and the writing of reports and compositions.

Reference books, encyclopedias, and dictionaries are prominently displayed in these classes. The pupils utilize this literature in class or in the library when writing reports. Once a week a class is held in the library. The children are taught to use catalogues, to find needed information, make notes, etc.

Pupils in the higher—5th and 6th—grades, while studying the natural sciences, do two or three so-called projects per year. The project is a small "research" paper on a subject selected by the pupil and usually related to the syllabus. We saw finished projects by 6th-graders on the subjects of "Space," "Atomic Energy," "Man's Nervous System," and others. These reports present material gathered from books, reference works, and museums. They include charts, diagrams, drawings, and descriptions of small experiments conducted by the children. Bibliographic information is attached to the reports. It is interesting to note that American teachers, as a rule, do not evaluate the pupils' responses in the classroom. Only tests and independent "research" papers are evaluated.

The school year is divided into three or four periods. The evaluations of schoolwork are recorded on a special card for parents at the end of the year.

When one moves from a class for the "slow" to an I.G.C. class one gets a literally physical sense of the difference in the level of knowledge, the demands made by the teacher, and the atmosphere prevailing in the classroom. We also felt this difference sharply when we visited schools in the wealthy suburbs.

Montgomery County is one of the most fashionable suburbs around Washington. Here, in beautiful residences surrounded by green lawns, live highly-placed officials, businessmen, lawyers, and university professors. They have built schools for their children that match their residences. The teachers here are well qualified and children are not divided according to abilities. Only within the classroom are the children grouped according to progress in their studies. Thanks to the small number of pupils in each grade, the teacher can organize work with separate groups. For example, at an arithmetic lesson of the 5th grade nine pupils were working independently with problem sheets. The ten remaining pupils were working under the supervision of the teacher.

Learning to read is also fully individualized. There is no common textbook. Each pupil makes his own selection of a book to read. Having read it, he discussed it with the teacher, shows her his record of books read and the list of unfamiliar words that he is compiling. Each pupil must read thirty to forty books during the year. He draws illustrations for some books or makes a dramatic presentation to the class.

In the natural sciences each large topic is covered through the same sort of independent work as we had seen in the I.G.C. groups.

The teacher also behaves differently in these schools. He is active; he employs many methods to stimulate the pupil, to force him to work. The parents are sent not only the children's grades but also their work.

We observed the same kind of educational work in private schools. These are institutions where an education costs up to 2,000 dollars yearly. They are accessible only to children with very wealthy parents. There are no "slow" ones here either, and each child gets his needed share of attention and encouragement from the teacher.

We also had the opportunity to become acquainted with the secondary schools of the United States, but we shall talk about this in the next article.

II

In the Junior High School

The junior high school in the U.S.A. consists of the 7th, 8th, and 9th grades. Teenagers from 13 to 16 years of age study here: 16 is the age up to which education is compulsory in most of the states.

The school, in which I spent many pleasant days meeting with constant attention and a willingness to be shown everything, occupies an old but sturdy building. On both sides of the long corridors are classrooms with glazed doors. The corridors are lined with students' wall lockers. American schools do not have cloakrooms for general use. Each student has his own locker, which he keeps locked and in which he stores his clothing and private belongings.

A departmental system is used in the school, and plates on doors indicate "Mrs. Lacy—English Language," "Mr. Crop—Natural Science." But there is no laboratory for physics or chemistry. A small room contains a pets' corner. The third floor contains well-equipped rooms for home economics classes. Downstairs are wood and metal workshops, a drafting room, a gymnasium for girls and boys, a cafeteria and an auditorium. The school is clean, but rather dark. The school is cleaned by five persons. It is centrally heated, and the heat is unbearable in spite of the snow and freezing weather. Not only the children but also some of the teachers are dressed in short-sleeved blouses and shirts.

The children, 950 of them, are as a whole from families, as it is said in America, of the lower middle class. Their parents are bus drivers, unskilled workers, airport service personnel and store saleswomen. All the students study the same subjects: in the 7th grade—English, mathematics, natural science, world geography, shop (boys), home economics (girls), physical training, music and art; in the 8th grade—the same subjects except that American history is substituted for world geography; and in the 9th grade—social studies, which includes the selection of a vocation, traffic rules and the country's economy. The first elective subjects appear in the 9th grade—typing, chorus and physics.

But the identical subjects do not at all indicate that everyone receives the same knowledge. As in the elementary school, students are assigned to classes according to their abilities as shown in test results. Each level has three classes for slow students, three for average students, and three for above average students (the school has a total of 27 classes). The students study subjects with identical titles but their contents, scope, depth and requirements are different in the various groups.

The school principal, in describing this system, calmly stated these words, which to the ear of a Soviet educator sounded simply blasphemous: "The students from the slow group will become unskilled workers anyhow. That is why they do not require the same depth in the study of subjects as is required by the able students. We adapt the subjects to the children's needs and abilities."

We saw this system in operation in our visits to the school. We observed how the "slow" students in the 8th grade were engaged in "consumers' arithmetic" and were calculating the price of Christmas dinners and presents. At the same time, their "able" friends in a neighboring class were engaged in mathematics in accordance with a new and recently developed syllabus, including rational and irrational numbers, equals and non-equals, an introduction to statistics, graphs and elements of trigonometry.

As in elementary school, all students here are promoted to the next grade. The school principal said: "We feel that there is no value in keeping students in the same grade for a second year. We promote everyone, but make the notation that, for example, an 8th grade student is on 4th grade level as far as his arithmetic is concerned."

Independent project work by students in classes for the "able" occupies an important place in the junior high school, as well as in the elementary school. The point system is also made a part of it. In class 8-1, the English and social studies teacher (these subjects are usually taught by the same teacher) selected the theme of "The Civil War in America." She gave each of the students a sheet on which was indicated the time to be taken in studying this theme, what the students were to do and the point value of each assignment. The sheet, for this example, included the following statement: "1) Compile a chronological table—50 points; 2) draw a map of military operations—50 points; 3) describe one of the episodes as if you had witnessed it yourself—100 points; 4) read these books (a list of books is given) and write a review on one of them—100 points; 5) construct a model (a list is given)—from 50 to 100 points," and so forth. Some tasks are compulsory for all, others are not compulsory and are completed by the students who wish to obtain a much higher grade.

Having received their instructions, the students work independently in the classroom or may go to the school library. They must prepare a brochure with tables, charts and stories—always with references to source materials and a bibliography—by a certain date.

Independent work by students in natural science is organized in approximately the same way. But we were surprised by the absence of a laboratory in the school. The students can only observe the demonstration of experiments in the classroom but cannot perform the laboratory work themselves. While studying natural science they are restricted to books, encyclopedias and petty practical tasks which do not require equipment and can be completed at home.

Practical subjects are compulsory for all students in the 7th and 8th grades: shopwork for boys and home economics for girls. As we became familiar with the workshops we felt that their equipment could be richer, inasmuch as shopwork in American schools has a history of more than half a century. We were surprised by the small amount of mechanical equipment.

Boys in the workshops work on individual tasks and projects. These are articles for personal use and for the home—lamp bases, benches, shelves, etc. Group work is rare. Sometimes something is made for the school. We asked what we later understood to be a naive question for America: "Do the students ever make socially useful articles?" The principal looked at us in surprise. "Of course not. Because then the students would be competing with adults and depriving them of work. No trade union would permit this."

We were very pleased with the home economics rooms. Here, in contrast with the workshops, the equipment was modern: stoves, work tables, wash basins, and sewing machines. The girls learn to sew, cook, keep house efficiently, and how to dress in good taste. In the 8th and 9th grades the girls take a course in child care, family relationships and hygiene. American girls, as we gathered are being prepared for marriage practically from the diaper stage. All education, not only within the school but also outside of it, is so structured that it appears that the sole goal of women is to marry and create their own home. It is not surprising that American girls of 12 or 13 years of age already look like little women. We saw girls, sitting right at their desks, with painted lips and eyes and with manicures. And it is not surprising also that there are, in the fullest sense of the word, few girls in technical colleges.

"We call the junior high school a school for exploration, a school for selection," the school principal said to me. "The student in the 9th grade must make his choice for his future: Should he prepare himself for college or will he choose another path leading to a working trade or office vocation? Counselors help him to make his choice."

There are two counselors at the school. Both of them, after several years of teaching, completed a special course at a university. There they studied psychology, testing methods, vocational orientation methods, etc. The school, as was stated above, has 950 students. "Of course we are not in a position to work with individual students, as it should be," said a psychologist. "Our fundamental task is the group testing of students and the checking of tests and control over the conduct of their personal affairs."

The psychologists' office has large file cabinets containing information on the students' personal affairs: the condition of health, progress in studies, subjects studied, participation in competitions, election to office in student government, and many, many other facts dating back to the 1st grade. These files contain numerous records of test results. In the 8th and 9th grades tests for determining aptitudes and vocational interests are added to those for determining the intelligence quotient. At the same time, a course in "Learning About Vocations" is conducted in the 9th grade. All this comprises the so-called vocational orientation of students.

At the end of the 9th grade, the counselor arranges a meeting with the student and his parents. The aim of this meeting is to advise the student what to pursue after the 9th grade. But the results of this meeting have already been determined a long time ago—in the 1st grade—when the students were divided into groups according to "abilities" and when instruction had begun in different ways. The "able," having been solidly prepared, demonstrate better knowledge during tests and are recommended for the academic sector of the high school, which leads to a higher educational institution. "Unfortunately, however, our recommendations very often do not carry any weight," sighs my partner in conversation—the counselor. "Money is the chief counselor. If parents can afford to pay for their son's university schooling, he will choose the academic course. If they do not have the money. . . . " and the counselor gestured with his hands. He continued: "Each person in our country receives as much education as he has money for." We were convinced of the truth of these words at each step we made—for example, when we visited a high school.

"Social Dynamite"

The high school (10th to 12th grades) is a many-faceted school. There are usually three divisions—academic, general and vocational. These fully correspond with the division of students in the elementary and junior high school into the "I.G.C." [Intellectually Gifted Children], average and slow. The subjects studied, their contents, the demands upon the students' knowledge differ in the separate divisions as previously.

An elective system for subjects exists in the high school. Characteristically, more subjects are compulsory than non-compulsory for the "able" students. This relationship is exactly the opposite in the non-academic divisions. Here, for example, is what the syllabus of a 10th grade, which I visited, looks like.

The compulsory subjects for students who have chosen the academic course are: English, a foreign language, geometry, chemistry, modern history, military training (for boys). Elective courses are: typing, art, drawing, chorus and orchestra.

The only compulsory subjects in the general course are: English, physical training and military training. The elective subjects are: a foreign language, world history, business correspondence, the printing trade, biology, general natural science, sewing, cooking, typing, art, drawing, chorus and orchestra.

The compulsory subjects for students in the third—the so-called fundamental—course are: English, mathematics, physical training and military training. The elective subjects are: business correspondence, sewing, cooking, art, drawing, chorus, orchestra and typing.

The essence of the matter is that under the one roof of a high school there are various types of schools, each preparing students in a different manner although all students receive a diploma certifying to their completion of high school. It is interesting to note that in suburban schools, where the well-to-do live, 85 to 100% of the students are in academic courses. Almost all of them go to college after being graduated from high school.

The atmosphere in the school is "adult." Perhaps it is because the school has only the upper grades and the children are reserved. Their appearance, particularly that of the girls with fashionable hairdos and abundant makeup, is somehow no longer that of schoolchildren. College methods of instruction are used extensively—lectures, seminars and discussions with the teacher on a subject being covered.

Compositions on freely selected topics and essay writing occupy an important place in the literature classes. "Our chief aim," said a teacher in one of the Montgomery [a Washington, D.C. suburb] schools, "is to teach the children to express their own thoughts" While studying physics, chemistry and biology, a student has the right to intensify his studies in the subject which interests him most. That is why we saw children in these schools studying biochemistry, microbiology and other subjects which ordinarily are not part of the usual high school curriculum. Meetings with specialists and summer classes with university teachers are arranged for these students. In the latter case, students from various schools are combined.

The school which I visited over a long period of time was in a Negro area. Only 20% of the students are taking the academic course here, and only 15% of the graduates go on to a university. The school is large: 1,500 students, from 16 to 18 years of age. There are 300 students in the 12th grade. Only 40 of them study physics. The rest limit themselves to courses in general science which, we became convinced, had a descriptive character.

An interesting conversation took place between myself and a physics teacher after I had attended several of his, I must truthfully say, good classes. But I was again struck by the teacher's indifferent attitude in the class. The lesson proceeds at a quick tempo and the teacher is not even interested in whether or not everyone has solved the problems or completed the report.

"If a student does not keep up with your class, what do you do with him?" I asked the teacher.

"I tell him 'Goodbye' "—and the teacher waved his hand. "If he can't keep up in physics, let him choose another and easier subject."

Students are not encouraged to study difficult subjects. "I teach biology in the 10th grade," said an old teacher to me. "The courses are for the slow—this is a dilution of the curriculum. And even in this course I have children who are outstanding and talented. It would be better for them to study more serious things."

"Then why don't they study them?"

"Why?" the teacher shouted at me angrily, as if I were in some way guilty. "Ask our counselors 'why?' They are the ones who create the flow. They say that these children will not go on to college. Well, what of it!" the teacher shouted again. "Is that any reason to keep them on a watery soup? I am an old teacher and do not understand this."

One of the most vulnerable spots in the American school is the absence of students' interest in knowledge. Teachers complain about this constantly. We saw some students wearing buttons reading: "I hate school." These buttons startled us in spite of the fact that we had become used to seeing inscriptions on buttons and right across the fronts of shirts and blouses, such as "I am an alcoholic. Well, what do you want from me?"; "I like boys"; "I'm from the gang of cheaters"; "Let's do the twist."

Considerably more than half of American students leave high school without having studied physics, chemistry, algebra, a foreign language and other general education subjects. Students select other subjects instead of these, often substituting chorus for physics. We must give American schools credit for the excellence of their choruses and orchestras. These functions included in the schedule, are regularly conducted with special teachers, and listening to the performances of school choruses and orchestras is a real pleasure.

Students in non-academic courses are not only deprived of a good education but are also deprived of the training necessary for getting a job. The schools have workshops where upper-grade students make articles of greater complexity than children in junior high schools. But all this is amateurish production—far from the reality of modern production. The school workshops do not to any degree provide the training which is demanded by modern industry.

Trade union bosses object sharply to vocational training in schools; we were told by a school principal. They maintain that graduating students will compete with adults, thereby depriving the latter of their jobs.

One of the main reasons for the tremendous student drop–out rate after the 9th grade is the dissatisfaction with the school, which provides neither a good education nor vocational training. Barely half of those in the 9th grade eventually graduate from school. Boys and girls leave school and begin to look for work. However, they are not met with open doors but with signs reading "No work." Where there is work there is a demand for people with good training, which these young people do not have.

Graduates completing the non-academic course also find themselves in a similar situation. They swell the ranks of those already unemployed. The percentage of unemployed among young people is twice as high as among adults. Among Negro and Puerto Rican youth the number of unemployed reaches 70%. A condition has developed in the country which the well-known educator James Conant described as "the accumulation of social dynamite in cities and areas of poverty" which is ready to explode.

President Kennedy, troubled by this same problem, recently delivered a special message in which he spoke of growing unemployment among young people and the necessity of resolving this problem in some way.

The American School Is Being Reorganized

"Every Soviet student knows this course. Do you?" We saw this screaming caption on the cover of a physics textbook when we visited a special school in New York for students gifted in the areas of mathematics and physics. This is but a small touch which characterizes the feverish attempts to improve the work of American schools, particularly in the area of teaching the natural science disciplines.

Four years ago, subsequent to the launching of the first Soviet satellite, commissions comprised of well-known scientists and educators were formed in the U.S.A. which developed new courses in physics, chemistry, biology and mathematics. New textbooks and teaching aids were written; films and other visual aids were developed. We must note the high scientific level of these courses and the rejection of obsolete principles.

In the physics course, for example, students are not given prepared facts; the course is so structured that students have to conduct investigations and acquire knowledge on their own. The purpose of this course is to develop the students' scientific thinking. Many topics are excluded from it but, instead, the number of laboratory tasks and mathematical calculations are increased. Physics is being taught in 500 experimental schools in accordance with the new syllabus. The teachers in these schools have taken additional university credits to improve their qualifications. Despite the common practice whereby teachers themselves pay for courses to improve their skills, physics and mathematics teachers from the experimental schools studied at government expense.

The initial result of work according to the new syllabuses demonstrated that the reorganization of teaching is being retarded by a shortage of teachers and their insufficient qualifications. One fact alone—more than half of the mathematics teachers do not have the necessary training—indicates a great deal.

Recently, in connection with the shortage of teachers, experimental uses of television, teaching machines and programmed instruction have become especially popular. We saw movable television sets in many schools which could be easily transported from one classroom to another. Programs that supplement school courses are shown on television, in accordance with a schedule. We observed how children in an elementary school, through television, learned songs and saw a program of "Mexican Dances" (when they were studying this country).

Closed circuit television systems, intended for just several schools, are to be found less frequently. This is purely educational television. We attended a lecture on geometry which was being televised. Students listened to the lecture in a hall. Then they dispersed to their classes to do their practical assignments. The superintendent of the school district which had such a television system evaluated its merits in the following manner: "We feel that one good teacher gives more to 300 students than 10 mediocre teachers, each working with 30 students."

Teaching machines are still at the experimental stage. We became acquainted with these machines at a branch of the National Education Association. The basis for these machines is the psychologist Skinner's theory of confirmation. The mastery of materials, in accordance with this theory, takes place considerably faster and more effectively if the learners immediately receive confirmation of the correctness of their solution of set tasks.

We saw a machine which, theoretically, should teach spelling. A sentence with a word missing appears in a slot in front of the student. On the right, in another slot, is a list of three words, one of which is written correctly; the others contain errors. The student has to press a button opposite the word which he considers to be corrrect. If he is correct, a green light goes on and a new sentence appears in the slot. The machine has a time counter which indicates each student's length of work.

After we had inspected all the machines, we were led to the last exhibit displayed at this branch. This was a thin board. We read the note on the board and laughed together with our hosts: "This is the most effective teaching machine. To be applied against that part upon which the student sits."

The theory behind programmed instruction is the same as for teaching machines—to enable the student to go through a course independently and in a way whereby he receives confirmation of his progress in the mastery of the course. However, the authors of programmed instruction have rejected unwieldy and expensive machines. The study material is given in portions (programs) to the student in special textbooks. The programs are so set up that the student himself can check up on his mastery of the material.

The attempt to overcome the teacher shortage and increase the proportion of the independent work by students is being promoted in the U.S.A. by the popular Trump Plan. It is named for its author, the well-known educator Lloyd Trump. Trump and his associates came to the conclusion that 60% of the study materials can be learned by students independently. Some of the material can be mastered in large groups and some requires a teacher to work with small groups of students.

So-called "team teaching" has been introduced into the practice of a number of schools. The teachers of one subject form a team and divide the work in accordance with their abilities and interests. One reads lectures for a large group of students; others conduct practical tasks and give guidance to small groups. One knows grammar best and teaches it; another is stronger in literature and takes this area upon himself. These teaching teams include teacher aides, who perform the purely technical functions that do not require special training: they do clerical work and find the errors in compositions, while the teacher just checks them for substance.

There are other plans for improving the work of the school. However, all these attempts to raise the level of instruction are not aimed at the whole mass of students but only those possessing a high intelligence quotient. No wonder that one of the main problems of the American school is to improve the methods by which students are divided according to ability, and Congress, which usually does not allocate a cent to schools, recently became generous and allocated supplementary sums for the testing of students.

"Smile"

Student behavior in the American school appears to be rather strange to a Soviet teacher. They do not rise when the teacher enters or when reciting. Each one sits as pleases his fancy during the lesson. Some lie on the desks, others practically put their feet on the desk. The lesson goes on, but the children stand up, walk about and leave the classroom. This type of discipline is supported by the theory that the child should not be repressed; let him feel free during the lesson and then his thoughts will work freely too.

Perhaps this is fine in theory, but in practice this simply leads to bad discipline. We saw classes where the teacher could not work because of the children's laxity. Student discipline in big city schools is particularly bad. Teachers in New York and Chicago experience tremendous difficulties. The matter has gotten to the point that legislation for corporal punishment has been introduced into the State Senate of New York. We noted that these punishments are not at all rare. While taking children on a tour around a museum, a teacher will take a misbehaving boy into a corner, slap his face and threaten: "And you'll get more!" We often asked school principals whether or not corporal punishment was being applied. We did not hear a categorical "No" in reply but an evasive "Perhaps—with the parents' permission."

Student behavior in schools in smaller cities is better. Superficially, the children are courteous and one constantly hears them say: "Thank you," "Pardon me" and "Please." This surface propriety, we feel is the results of the broadly disseminated theory in the United States that a man's success in life depends not on his knowledge or skills but on whether the man can get along with people. The results of a survey have been broadly publicized which, it is claimed, indicate that success in life depends 85% on the ability to conduct oneself properly, to be lively, courteous and well dressed.

"No matter how you feel, smile. Smile! A smile is success in life." Such posters hang in schools, in offices, in taxis and at railroad stations. However, the surface courtesy is deceptive. I was talking with a counselor in a school where at each step one hears "Thank you" and "Pardon me." Our conversation is interrupted by a policeman. "Again," sighs the counselor. "Well, what is it?" "A week never goes by without some kind of incident," he explains to me. This time a student in the school had stolen an automobile.

Figures are incontrovertible. They show that crime among teenagers in the United States grows with each year. Practically every day newspapers report violence, killings, burglaries and other crimes committed by school-age children. When we became acquainted with the conditions in which American children grow up, we came to the conclusion that it would be difficult not to become a criminal under these conditions. The theme of violence resounds everywhere persistently—in books, the movies, television and in games.

The first thing you see in bookstores is a stand of books with colorful, glossy covers. There isn't a cover where someone isn't being stabbed, killed or shot. These are books about "strong" people who kill at every step. Alongside this stand, a prominent space near the entrance is taken up by a section with a notice reading "For Men Only." Here are books and magazines with the purest pornography. We have already written a good deal about American television. But the most vivid description does not indicate one-tenth of what actually exists. One must see these television programs in order to understand how harmful any and the best of man's inventions can become when they become subservient to the dollar. From six in the morning to late at night, television screens show unceasing fights, killings, poisonings, thefts and arson. We sometimes joked, sitting before a television set at night: "We will count up to the twentieth killing and then go to bed." In half an hour we could already go to bed.

The bestial faces of murderers, their victims in pools of blood, and vampires with bared teeth drinking people's blood look down upon you from the publicity posters of movie houses. Some posters have the warning: "Those seeing the film up to the end will receive a prize."

The movie *Wax Figure Museum* was being shown to children in an overcrowded hall. The content of the film is not involved: a wax figure museum had burned and its owner, in re-establishing it, kills people and covers them with wax. A continuous flood of murders, together with all the finest details, takes place during the course of two hours.

This cult of violence and murder resounds everywhere. We visited an amusement park for children. Even the innocent carousel had not escaped the general fate. A child does not simply sit on a horse but has a pistol in his hand and, as he rides along, shoots at figures of people in black masks. Such a situation gradually instills the outlook that killing and violence are normal phenomena, that killing a person is a natural and simple matter. From the point of view of ordinary common sense, all this seemed horrible and inexplicable to us. We often spoke about this with American intellectuals. Many agreed with us: "Yes, it is horrible. This is shameful for a civilized nation.

"Can't anything be done against this obvious corruption of children?"

"Something is being done; committees have been established in some cities which convene meetings and write protests. But those who produce films and television programs receive large revenues. And the dollar in our country is stronger than the arguments of reason."

Our partners in conversation continued to tell us how they as individuals, in their own families, strived to protect their children from the corruptive influence of television, films and books. For example, they do not buy television sets and, actually, we did not see television sets in many of the homes of the intelligentsia. But quite frequently we received other answers. We were told: "You are outraged by books about killings? But have you seen the good books in stores? This is, in fact, our freedom—the freedom of choice. I, for example, do not read the books and did not see the film which you spoke about and which is, in fact, horrible."

"Well, all right," we would say, "you do not look. But what about the children who are still unaware of what is good and what is bad?"

"Don't you see," they persuaded us, "that in order for children to become highly moral people, they should go through all obstacles and temptations?"

"Well and if they don't hold out?"

At this point, our conversation partner would become quiet. The answer was obvious: these children swell the ranks of teenage criminals, which are growing from year to year.

Where Can the American Boy Make a Radio?

American society, in attempting to fight against the growing criminality of youth, now talks a great deal about the necessity for the organization of children's out-of-school time. Various kinds of clubs and neighborhood centers are being established for school-children in the large cities. We visited several such centers and were staggered by their poverty.

The center in one of the areas of New York is located in a basement. There are several smallish rooms for home economics, photography and drawing. A large hall is both a place for sports activities and evening dances. There are two teachers. The equipment is pitiful and primitive; poverty stares from every corner. We were heartened only by the teachers' dedication and love for this cause. We became interested in whether or not this center had technical groups.

"This center is supported by private contributions," explained our leader—an energetic young man. "They are not large and we cannot afford to buy equipment for technical groups."

"What if a boy wants to assemble a radio—where could he do this?" asked one of our comrades, the director of a station for young technicians which has all the necessary equipment, at the disposal of Soviet children, for the most complicated construction.

This question nonplussed the American teachers. They began to confer and then said:

"At home, buying the necessary components."

"And who will help him?"

"His father."

"But if his father is not a specialist?"

"What if the neighbor is not a specialist?"

"Then perhaps a neighbor."

"Then he will not assemble the radio."

Our comrade put this question everywhere—in schools and in children's organizations. The responses were the same. Children's organizations in the U.S.A. are supported by philanthropy. It is well known that one does not thrive on philanthropy.

We became acquainted with the more popular out-of-school organizations in the U.S.A.—the Scouts, Young Farmers' Club [4-H], the Young [Men's and Women's] Christian Association. We were left with the impression that all discussions and all activities in these organizations revolved around where and how to get money.

Exhibits of children's work are organized once a year. We were at one of these exhibits. We saw beautiful flowers, huge fruits and articles for home decorating. But we were struck by the complete absence of work connected with technology. We did not see radio, airplane models or machines—nothing of that which usually fills children's exhibits in our country. And this was not accidental. For technological creativity materials, equipment and specialized leaders are needed.

Who Must Educate?

We got into a conversation with an 8th grade supervisor. She complained about the lowering of morals, that children become interested in sexual matters too early.

"We saw several girls with painted lips in your class. Why do you allow this?" we asked.

"This is not my business," replied the teacher. "I have no right to interfere if the family does not object."

We became convinced that the viewpoint among American teachers is that the moral education of children is the business of the family and the church. The church in the U.S.A. is an influential force. Despite the formal separation of the church from the school, religion actively interferes with the schools's work. To begin with, parochial schools exist in the U.S.A. Catholic, Protestant and other churches have their own schools and their own colleges where teachers are trained. But the church does not limit itself to these. It wants to embrace all children with its influence. I do not speak of the fact that in many public schools meetings and meals in lunchrooms begin with a prayer or a Bible reading. But schools also assign time in their schedules for children to go to church once a week. Each church has its Sunday School. While adults listen to the service, children study in the classes. The studies are placed on a broad footing, with textbooks, tests and promotions.

When we came to a lesson in the first grade of a Sunday School, the children there were occupied with art. They were drawing illustrations for Biblical stories; some were preparing a visual aid: "The Tomb of the Lord." In a class for older boys and girls a discussion was being held on "the role of the church in contemporary society." I do not know exactly what percentage of schoolchildren attend Sunday School. But as far as we were able to observe, Sunday Schools are being attended by an overwhelming majority.

We once asked a teacher—an intelligent and educated man—why his daughters attend Sunday School. His answer is typical for Americans: "The church fills the moral emptiness in our society; it provides the foundations for moral conduct."

The church in the U.S.A. has evidenced particular activity during recent years. The matter has come to the point where it is demanding subsidies for its schools from the government.

We must note that an interest in questions of ideological education has now increased in the U.S.A. Indicative of this was a conference held in Washington in April of this year [1962]. At the conference it was noted that American youth is not ideologically educated, that it is not able to value the "advantages" of the American way of life and is quite unprepared to counter the influence of communist ideas. Conference participants talked about improving the teaching of history and social studies. There was talk about improving the recently introduced course on "Communism" in the schools.

The content of this course is such that it should be called "Anti-communism." It is a clot of lies and distorted facts about the Soviet Union, about its politics and about the lives of Soviet people. One is swept with a sense of outrage and concern when one becomes acquainted with the textbooks of this course and sees films that supplement it. For this course can only contribute to inflaming hate between peoples and to a sharpening of relations rather than peace.

Intelligent American teachers understand this and are outraged by the introduction into schools of this provocative course in anti-communism.

Meetings with American Colleagues

These meetings occurred often: at exhibits, in schools, in homes and at lectures. And no matter where we met, we always found a common language.

The majority of American teachers impressed us as being people dedicated to their cause and liking children. Many of them give all their strength to the school. But their work is poorly rewarded. American teachers became very surprised when they learned that the work of the teacher in the Soviet Union is remunerated in the same way as that of the doctor, the lawyer and the engineer. A teacher's salary in the U.S.A. is the lowest in comparison with other specializations that require higher education. Teachers, particularly men, are obliged to take supplementary jobs after school. We visited the family of a natural science teacher. He works in school during the day and in the evenings knocks at the doors of homes, publicizing the wares of an electric appliance company. According to official statistics, 72% of the teachers do this.

The working day of the American teacher begins at eight o'clock in the morning and continues until three o'clock, with an hour's break. He has five to six classes every day during which he may teach mathematics and light athletics, English and singing.

American teachers evidence great interest in Soviet schools. We gave many lectures on public education in the U.S.S.R. Dozens of questions followed each lecture: What are the requirements for becoming a teacher in the U.S.S.R.? How does a teacher work in a class comprised of students with various abilities? Why are you against determining intelligence quotients? What is the reason for the school reorganization? How is schooling tied in with production work? Why is work compulsory for students who will be going on to a higher educational institution? What is a collective; does a conflict arise between the collective and the individual and how is it resolved? Why are Soviet schoolchildren better trained physically than American children? What do Soviet children know about the U.S.A.?—and a host of other questions.

Many teachers would come to us and ask us for advice: "We want to study the Soviet school. Will you recommend the literature"; or "I have to make a speech about the education of children in Soviet schools. Tell me, how is a collective established?"

We talked a lot about peace and about what the school can do to strengthen friendship between nations. The American teachers agreed that the future of the world depends a great deal on how youth is educated. They often expressed a negative attitude to the course on anti-communism and spoke about the necessity of giving students true facts about the Soviet Union. But, they would add, under present conditions in the U.S.A. not every teacher would decide to talk about the Soviet country objectively. This is not without danger. "In one school," we were told, "a teacher received a reprimand simply because she stated that the territory of the U.S.S.R. is larger than that of the U.S.A." The John Birch fascist organization is gathering strength.

We were all the more happy to meet courageous teachers who invited us into their classes to talk with the children and to tell them the truth about the Soviet Union; to meet teachers who protested against atomic armament and teachers who were on strike in order to achieve better living conditions.

16

A Polish Educator's Observations

In one of the talks in the Report on United States Education radio series delivered over Voice of America last year [1961], Professor James Conant, former president of Harvard University, comes to the conclusion that the United States educational system, although extremely different from the European, and although sharply criticized by many, is the best system for the United States, and that it does not need drastic changes in the direction of Europeanization in order to meet the goals which its contemporaries set for it.

Professor Conant's is but one of the voices heard in the enormous discussion in recent years in newspapers and on radio and TV programs. Never before have Americans been so vitally interested in what goes on in the schools, and never before have there appeared so many arguments pro and con on the condition of education in the United States. One of the problems of utmost importance in these discussions is that of increasing emphasis on the subjects of chemistry, biology, and physics. These three subjects, embraced under the common title of *science*, have long constituted and still constitute one of the weakest areas in the twelve-year U.S. public school system.

Here are a few facts related to the progress of science education: in 1900, secondary schools were only beginning to teach chemistry, biology, and physics as separate subjects. In 1930 the study of natural science was gradually entering the elementary-school program. In 1941, deterioration of teaching standards brought about a return in many schools to the practice of treating science as a single subject. And in 1957, Sputnik exerted a powerful influence to raise the level of these combined subjects in educational programs.

Wojciech Dindorf. "A Polish Educator's Observations," *Educational Forum*, Vol. 29, No. 18 (January, 1965), pp. 189–198. Reprinted by kind permission of the editor of *The Educational Forum*. (originally published in *Nowa Szkola*, October, 1962, pp. 41–47)

Author (1931–   ): Teacher of physics in Opole Teachers College in southwestern Poland; awarded the degrees of Magistrar of Science and Magistrar of Education; member of the Polish Physics Association and of the Society for the Popularization of Science. During 1961–62, he visited the United States and participated in the International Teacher Development Program of the United States Office of Education.

This word Sputnik, appearing suddenly in almost all discussions, came to symbolize, the new trend in American education—a trend of thinking about education more seriously, talking about it more loudly, and acting in its behalf more energetically. For Americans, Sputnik came as a genuine shock which they frankly admit they will not soon forget. The fall of 1957 made Americans realize that Europe extends considerably beyond France and Germany; that the frontier scientific progress from which one may learn much of importance is by no means limited to the fifty states of the United States. Thus in the future, an incident like the following will not happen any more: for a U.S. educator to show a movie camera to Japanese teachers or a tape recorder to European teachers visiting the United States and to ask them: "Do you know what this is?" This was precisely the kind of question asked a group of several hundred teachers from numerous foreign countries paying a six-month visit to numerous American schools. I was one of them.

The United States public school system is so intricate that I have grave misgivings about my ability to give you a clear notion of it without oversimplifying or generalizing overmuch. Considering the breadth of the subject and the scope which an article on it may have, I will touch only on certain problems dealing with elementary and secondary schools there.

The 175-year-old U.S. Constitution does not mention education. Matters which it neither mentions nor forbids are left to the competence of the individual states. Thus the entire responsibility for the condition and progress of U.S. education depends primarily on State officials—that is, in the United States, fifty ministries of education (called "State Departments of Education") direct the destinies of the free public elementary and secondary school systems. These departments also decide the age limits of compulsory school attendance. (In most states, ten years of schooling starting at age six is required.) These departments also decide which subjects and how many hours of each are to be taken, as well as the requirements for public-school teachers.

This local board of education holds authority over schools in an area known as a *school district*, which may include only one school (as in small, widely separated communities) or over a hundred schools (as in a large city). About 50 percent of these districts have fewer than fifty pupils, but only one-half of one percent have over 25,000. The tendency of the smaller districts to consolidate has resulted in a 50 percent decrease in the number of districts in the last decade: at present they number nearly 50,000. Local boards are chosen by the local citizens and are typically composed of a superintendent and several administrators. This local board has the greater share in financing school operations—56 percent against 40 percent state support and four percent federal support.

It is no exaggeration to point out that the school principals have a primary authority in U.S. schools. Within a loose framework, which is proposed rather than imposed by the state departments and local boards, the principal organizes the school program according to his abilities and those of his teaching staff, the local school budget, the needs of the community, and the like. The result is that schools differ extensively from one another—even schools in the same school district!

Alongside the U.S. public school system, about 20,000 elementary and secondary schools remain practically outside all government control. These are the private schools, run by various religious and secular organizations. About 18 percent of young people attend them. Tuition fees for these schools are often higher than for university courses; their curricula sometimes approximate those of good European schools. As a rule, they are not coeducational. About 10 percent of elementary and 20 percent of the secondary schools are now under private control.

The highest school office is the *U.S. Office of Education* in the Department of Health, Education, and Welfare. This office occupies an enormous modern building in Washington, D.C., with (according to 1960 data) over a thousand employees and an annual budget of $9,600,000. Its head is called the *Commissioner of Education*. In general, it gathers and disseminates statistics and information, directs educational research, supplies advisory and consultation services, and distributes foreign and domestic scholarships. In no sense does it issue rulings or decrees about the control or administration of schools. While this is probably the institution with the best orientation to the complex of U.S. education problems, it probably exerts the smallest influence on them.

I seem to remember reading somewhere that the American school is the least controlled institution, but the teacher is the most controlled worker, and there is a good deal of truth in this. The school with great independence; the teacher with a minimum of authority—this is the character of U.S. education in a nutshell. It is extremely difficult to generalize about U.S. schools: school attendance requirements, the curriculum, teacher qualifications, the textbooks, the length of class periods, pupil regulations—these are different in different states, and even in different schools in the same state.

Two systems predominate in the twelve-year public school: 6-3-3 (six years of elementary school, three of junior high, and three of senior high—the latter approximating the *gymnazyum* or *lycée*); or else 8-4 (elementary and *lycée* respectively). A clear-cut distinction between elementary and secondary school appears only starting with ninth grade.

Out of every 1000 pupils beginning school (according to 1959 statistics), only about 580 finish grade 12; for what is required is not to complete a certain number of grades or to acquire a certain stock of knowledge, but rather to remain in school until age 16. (Even this requirements is not always fulfilled!)

Here are several interesting observations I made while visiting U.S. schools.

I observed dozens of lessons, and I saw hundreds of classrooms in many different schools, Nowhere did I see any benches. The children (25 to 30 per class) sit individually in chairs at little tables constructed of bent metal tubing and wood or plastic. These units are not always arranged in rows facing the blackboard; indeed, the blackboard often occupies several walls. I have seen these units arranged in fours facing each other. Each foursome usually included one good pupil whose task it was to help the slower ones (homework is relatively rare). This was one solution to the problem of the slower pupil. Another solution is to group the class members according to their rate of learning into faster, middling, and slower, the teacher working with each group in turn. This is especially common practice in the lowest grades. For example: a group of first-graders is sitting at a round table, each reading silently from a separate book—the faster ones. Around another table sits a group wearing earphones plugged into a tape recorder and listening to a story the teacher taped previously—the middling ones. In another corner of the room sit the ten slower ones. Surrounding the teacher in a semicircle, they follow the movement of her lips, repeating in a whisper: "Water, W-A-T-E-R. . . . Butter, B-U-T-T-E-R. . . . Mother, M-O-T-H-E-R. . . ." After a while they go to do silent work, and the teacher listens to the faster ones reciting on the story they've just finished.

If there are enough pupils in the school, three parallel classes may be formed according to this faster-middling-slower distribution. Here as elsewhere, the ability grouping is determined by tests taken by each student several times a year. Courses of study and requirements set for students differ substantially in these parallel groups. Further, a student making little headway in class 5-B may be transferred to class 5-C. This type of demotion occurs much more often than does not going on to the next grade. This simple system does not wholly solve the problem, because in groups A, B, or C there are apt to be those for whom arithmetic comes easier than English. Therefore each class may be further divided into various groups for lessons in different subjects. While this most certainly presents serious problems for the teachers, the pupils view these divisions quite passively, treating such a state of affairs as altogether normal. They may pass to a lower group with the knowledge and approval of their parents, and without meeting jeers from the better students. Often they are really the school heroes, since it is frequently from these classes that most of the best football or baseball players come.

In the elementary school, children spend the whole day (8:30 A.M. to 3 P.M.) with one teacher, except for gymnastics and (sometimes) singing or music. In class they feel very much at ease. They get up from their chairs during their work; without asking permission, they leave to go to the washroom or to get a book from their hall lockers. Yet the children do not take advantage of this freedom—all of this takes place quietly. They dress altogether as they please; they carry no bags with slippers in them, nor do they generally change footwear in school. They write with what they please (pencil or ballpoint pen) and how they wish (about 25 percent of those I saw are left-handed). In the first grade, I have seen little girls with manicures and pedicures; and at which grade they start using cosmetics it would be hard for me to say. Smoking is prohibited on the school ground—even teachers are forbidden to smoke in the halls.

In many schools, a bell rings only for the start of school and for lunch. Lessons last around fifty minutes. During recesses (from four to thirty minutes) the pupils remain in the building. Air conditioning (in operation summer and winter) is supposed to replace the fresh air for them.

Nowhere did I see (and I have strong professional attitudes against cheating) any one prompt or copy from someone else. I did see a teacher, wanting to check the exercises which he had assigned the previous period, read off the correct answer and then ask if those who got that answer would raise their hands. Several hands went up. A student answering a question does not rise; he does not even alter his usually comfortable (sometimes almost reclining) position. The teacher does not note anywhere his appraisal of the student's answer; he asks only for the purpose of getting the pupil to repeat the material, or to inspire a discussion. The teacher teaches. To evaluate the pupil's knowledge as well as the teacher's skill, tests supplied by the state or district board of education are used. Oral examinations are used almost nowhere at any teaching level.

The elementary-school curriculum generally consists of the English language (not going much beyond reading and writing); U.S. history; geography (in a very limited sense); natural science (so-called general science, including elementary biology; physics through meteorology and astronomy; geology; and very little chemistry); arithmetic; drawing;

handicrafts; singing; music appreciation; and physical training. Religion is taught only in private church schools. I noticed particularly that the elementary-school curriculum does not encompass the teaching of a foreign language. Gymnastics is limited to between three and six hours a week. The children devote much time to drawing; they paint rather well; they sing frequently. They go to school eagerly, and they like it.

Schools are in session five days a week; Saturdays and Sundays are free. A school year includes about 180 teaching days. Teachers in elementary or secondary schools (and also many colleges) work 25 to 30 hours per week. The number of hours of work beyond the required norm (around 25) depends on the needs of the school and has no relation to the salary scale.

It is a fact that in the elementary schools one teacher teaches virtually all subjects. This has a decided influence upon the quality of teaching, which is sometimes incredibly low. There is much recent talk about an experimental attempt to correct this condition: team teaching is what the Americans call this new method of elementary-school teaching. As its name indicates, it is a matter of teaching as a team, an arrangement which permits the teacher who feels quite sure of himself in physics, for example, not to teach the history in his class. This is a most significant move in its effect on the role of the teacher—a role which is emphatically otherwise different from the teacher's role in our own country [Poland].

In the United States, school is considered to be a service institution: children must be taught. Thus the entire burden of teaching is borne by the teacher alone. We must remember that there are no outside incentives for pupils as, for example, the pupil's awareness of his subject-matter deficiencies, the parents' signature in the daily report booklet, and the physical punishment which Polish students often receive from parents for poor schoolwork. As a rule, there is also no homework in the form of written compositions, or (to put it bluntly) any obligation to learn actual material found on a given number of pages in a textbook. Further, textbooks and notebooks are typically locked up in school lockers. The severe teacher, the exacting teacher are quite unfamiliar types to American young people.

Let us return to the team teaching experiment. In a large room, one teacher is teaching a biology lesson to a combined group of classes 3A, 3B, and 4C. Other teachers who would have had a free period at this time now occupy themselves with smaller groups or even individual pupils, helping the slower ones or arranging special work for the most capable. I saw one of these experimental centers, consisting of 7500 pupils, a complex of public schools in one section of Pittsburgh.

That Americans consider this experiment important is indicated by the fact that the Ford Foundation had granted $400,000 to this center for a three-year period. It is still too early to predict the future of this new system, yet it is beginning to solve the problem of a shortage of qualified teachers; it makes teaching somewhat easier and more attractive; more essentially, it promises to give good results.

Let us turn now to the secondary school. The basic principles of high-school organization may be expressed as follows: the conditions and curriculum must be such that each pupil may develop his interests as much as possible. Each standard curriculum required for thousands of pupils and aimed at average abilities will include, from the viewpoint of any individual pupil, ingredients which are too easy for him and ingredients which are too hard for him; no two pupils exist with identical study habits or identical learning abilities in all directions.

As in the elementary school, all responsibility for the education of the young falls on the school and the teacher. One should give the pupil as much as possible, but in such a form as not to tire him overmuch; one should give him what he likes; one should not take up too much of his time after school; after all, his family may have plans for the rest of the day. The notion that the pupil's homework has a minor influence on his progress in learning is a generally accepted one. (Occasionally parents are of a different opinion, and one may find then a pupil bent over a book at home. This is exceptional, however.)

Here is how the school meets the need for individualized teaching. Each pupil is required to take certain basic subjects, as well as to choose from among others proposed by the school which fall within the pupil's personal interests, the whole program to total a given number of units. (The *unit* or *credit point* is 180 class periods of lessons in a given subject, five periods per week throughout a school year.) Among the required subjects are (usually): English language, two units; elementary algebra, one unit; U.S. history, one unit; one of the three sciences (biology, chemistry, physics), one unit; and physical training, one or two units. These plus the elective subjects must total 13 to 15 units in order for the pupil to graduate. The course content of the elective units may be very broad or very narrow: this depends primarily on the school's finances and the schoolrooms available.

Larger schools (numbering sometimes several thousand pupils) use a somewhat different system. Here ninth-grade candidates are given a choice among the courses of study offered, each course having largely different sets of required and elective subjects. The courses are typically:

(1) the academic course, laid out for those headed for college in the future;

(2) the general course, which gives a general education;

(3) the business course, for those who will seek employment in business or industry; and

(4) the vocational course—a trades course.

Finishing any of these courses means only finishing secondary school. There are no final certificates of mastery; and vocational diplomas for technicians and repairmen are only received after additional schooling or from specialized vocational schools.

Simple arithmetic shows that the American pupil is required to take slightly more than half as much school work as the *lycée* pupil in Poland. Further, if we compare the U.S. pupil's total time in elementary and secondary study with the typical Polish pupil's, I should estimate the ratio as one to three. These differences are clearly reflected in the level of general knowledge of high-school graduates.

The 16 units sufficient for graduation do not, strictly speaking, guarantee the right to enter college. Schools of higher learning generally have different requirements as to the number and kind of credits. Thus knowing which department of which college he is aiming for early enough, the pupil arranges his program to fulfill the requirements of that institution. In most cases, the pupil finishes high school with from one to three more than the required number of units. His choice of college must sometimes be made at the beginning of ninth or tenth grade. In other cases, the pupil chooses his course according to the credits he already has, or else he makes up the needed credits in his senior year.

The school principal or the PTA [sic] may increase the required minima of units for certain subjects. Most often, physical training is increased to two or three units. These hours are spent for the most part in sports: basketball or football (which young people go overboard for anyway). Each pupil takes four or five subjects a year. Typically, physics is taught only in grade twelve, chemistry in grade eleven, biology in grade ten. The math requirement for pupils not preparing for technical or physico-mathematical studies is limited to elementary algebra—or sometimes merely arithmetic. A complete picture of a typical American secondary-school curriculum includes driver education. Most high-school graduates receive, along with their diplomas or certificates, a driver's license. This is much better than in our country [Poland].

Many changes are being made in most school curricula. In the pre-Sputnik curriculum (like that above), only one credit in the three sciences was required. Foreign language study was less common. Russian history, the Russian language, world history or world geography, new science teaching methods are emphases or additions of recent years. Universities have worked out new textbooks, and U.S. industries for example, Bell Laboratories, are producing new audio-visual aids. All these trends are in the direction of modernization and raising of standards. Americans may owe much to the creators of the first artificial moon.

At a certain time preceding a new school year, each pupil is required to determine his program for the next grade. With a guidance counselor's advice based on test results, his parents' wishes, his own interests, his future plans, and the list of subjects which the school offers, the pupil registers for the following year, selects his courses, and agrees to complete the required number of selected subjects. Of course, the pupil's interests and plans may undergo some change from year to year. He may then change to a different course, leveling out the possible curricular differences in the years that remain.

Registration completed, the school principal produces a schedule for the following year and informs the teachers what subjects and grades each will teach. A high-school teacher is prepared to teach two or possibly three subjects—a necessity in that system. A specialist teacher in the field of geography, for example, could hardly find enough classes in any school for a full program. Teacher education under such a system is so comprehensive and intricate that it would require a separate discussion.

In the American school, a very important and responsible function is fulfilled by the guidance counselor, in other words, a guide, advisor, or preceptor. He is a regular school employee but without teaching duties. The number of pupils per counselor varies greatly, between 400 and 1200. The boys' counselor is always a man, and the girls', a woman. A good counselor is the pupils's confidant and, as I came to realize, may often know more about the pupil's private concerns than the pupil's parents, often mediating parent-child conflicts which sometimes occur. Although I didn't get to see conflicts between pupil and teacher, I gathered that these are rare.

The system of national standardized tests chosen by the board of education by which the teacher as well as the pupil may be evaluated, the absence of a recitation grading book in the teacher's hands, his social position—he doesn't earn a great deal—the highly permissive school regulations make for treating the teacher as an older "buddy." I never saw a teacher call a class to order or interrupt a pupil's nap; and the title *Miss* or *Mr.* often preceded the name of the pupil called upon—a title the pupil would rarely be called by in any other circumstances.

Boards of education are busy with research into general educational and teaching problems at all levels, special guidance reports, the employment of psychologists, consultants, psychiatrists, and specialized teachers whose duty it is to help the guidance counselors. These teams prepare tests to measure the intelligence, ability, and interests of pupils. They conduct pupil testing programs several times a year, beginning generally with grade six. Test results are turned over to the guidance counselors, who add them to the personal records of their charges.

Yet I still have not touched on many matters connected with the school system. In this necessarily brief article I have had to omit reference to teaching aids, school texts, school buildings (with interesting construction designs), teaching through the mass media of TV and radio, teacher education, vocational training, and the whole field of higher education. I hope to return to them in the future.

I wish to conclude, with pleasure, that everywhere I went, in every school and every home, I was met as a teacher from Poland with an extraordinarily sincere welcome. In hospitality and sincerity my American colleagues broke the record. Everywhere—at official meetings as in private conversation—they emphasized the communion which exists among educators all over the world; they spoke of the ideals which unite us: the attainment of a fuller life through universal education, and a strengthening of peace among all men on earth. Another statement was always added: "Say *hello* for us to all your teacher-friends in Poland." This is what I am doing here, and with genuine pleasure.

17

A British View of U.S. Education

Educational policy is an important public question in the United States, but it is something more than an exclusively American national affair. The rising generation in the United States, and in the Soviet Union, seems likely within its lifetime to have a decisive say in the determination, for good or evil, of the long-term destinies of the human race.

The populations of these two countries, even together, are but a small fraction of the population of the planet, and they will be a smaller fraction of it by the end of the century, if the statisticians' predictions are correct. But the United States and the Soviet Union command between them about 80 percent of the effective power in the world. This means that current educational issues in the United States are matters of world concern.

The American people has always been egalitarian-minded; it has now become affluent, too; and this is making it practicable for the United States to apply its egalitarian ideal to education on a large scale. The target today is education for everybody up to the stage of graduation from the university. It is only at the post-graduate stage that it is still acceptable for education to be specialized, and for the openings to be severely limited to students who can show that they are capable of profiting.

Short of the postgraduate stage, the United States is now aiming at providing for every boy or girl those educational amenities that in Europe, from the Renaissance until the early twentieth century, were enjoyed by the aristocracy and the upper-middle class as a matter of course, but by these higher-income brackets only.

Like the eighteenth-century European aristocrat, the U.S. citizen feels that a higher education is one of his human rights. He would be indignant if he were to be told that a higher education is his not as a right, but only if he succeeds in passing an exacting intellectual test.

Arnold Toynbee. "A British View of U.S. Education" and "School Boards Run System" in *Globe and Mail* (Toronto) July 29 and 30, 1963. Reprinted by kind permission of the publishers. The Observer Foreign News Service, London, England.

Author (1889–   ): Statesman, historian, and author; educated at Winchester College and Balliol College, Oxford, Director of Studies, Royal Institute of International Affairs, London.

Americans in general combine a high regard for education with a low regard for intellectual ability.

While a majority of U.S. state universities and colleges impose intellectual tests on candidates for matriculation, some—mostly in the Middle West—are bound by law to accept any candidate who has graduated from a high school within the state's borders. The faculty in these state universities is free only to weed out intellectual incompetents in their freshman year.

Thus, as a tribute to U.S. democratic egalitarianism, coupled with an aristocratic disdain for intellectual standards, the faculty in these Middle-Western state universities is compelled to waste several months on this frustrating process. This is a tax on time and energy, and a formidable handicap to the raising of state universities' intellectual standards.

An attempt is now being made to remove this handicap, or to reduce it. Some states—California, for instance—are setting up a number of two-year state colleges; and these will relieve the pressure on the state universities by drawing off many of the weaker candidates for a university education. Already the University of California accepts only the top 12 percent of the candidates for admission.

The eighteenth-century European aristocrat expected to pay his way at the university. It was his ability to pay that gave him his entree. As a matter of fact, at an Oxford or Cambridge college down to 1914, and perhaps even down to 1939, a commoner did not pay his own way entirely. Like a scholar, though to a lesser extent, he was partly paid for out of the college's income from endowments. The present-day U.S. citizen's education at the high school stage, and at the pregraduate university stage, is also partly paid for by people other than the student's parents. It is paid for not out of the bequests of medieval benefactors, but out of current taxes.

The American people, which is being indoctrinated by the U.S. medical profession with a horror of "socialized medicine," has accepted "socialized education" as a matter of course. In the United States "socialized education" is a going concern on a scale that dwarfs that in any other country.

Yet even at a state university, the taxpayers' contribution does not cover the whole of a student's costs. A state university does not charge tuition fees for students domiciled in its own state, but there are appreciable incidental expenses, particularly for sport and other extra-curricular activities; and, since the American way of life is lavish and costs are high, the maintenance of a child is a considerable financial burden for an American parent. Scholarships are still relatively rare in the United States.

Consequently, the incidental costs of an American university education, even at a state university, put this stage of education out of reach of families in the lower income brackets.

Perhaps about one-third of the rising generation receives a pregraduate university education of one kind or another. This is, of course, an enormous proportion of the population, judged by the corresponding performance of any other country to date.

I have been told by a leading authority on the subject that the 18 million Negroes in the United States have more students at universities than the total present number of university students in Britain. Even so, the United States is still far from having achieved her ideal of a university education for everybody.

18

School Boards Run System

If I were a teacher is a U.S. public school, I should be envious of my British and Continental European opposite numbers. I should envy the British teachers for their national salaries scale, for the national Ministry of Education's effective control over the local education authorities, and for the National Union that defends the teachers' rights.

In the United States the Federal Government has hardly begun to gain a foothold in education. The state legislatures do control the state colleges and universities; but they have no control over the private universities within their boundaries, and the control they exercise over education at the pre-university stage seems to be perfunctory even by British standards, while by Continental European standards, it is almost nonexistent.

In Britain, the Ministry of Education controls the local education authorities through the purse. The local authorities cannot do without grants from the national treasury to supplement their locally raised funds. In the United States the local school boards are largely independent financially, paying their way from locally raised taxes. Consequently they are virtually sovereign authorities, and they behave as such—sometimes arbitrarily and tyrannically.

For these school boards are mostly small-scale bodies, and the men and women elected to serve on them are, on the average, perhaps not fit to exercise the formidable power they wield. When this power is abused it is the teachers who are the immediate victims; but in the long run, the victimization of teachers has a serious effect on the whole nation's welfare.

Like the teachers, the faculties of the state colleges and universities are subject to the public authorities' pressure; but the university faculties' situation is relatively not so bad. They are partially protected by their collective academic prestige and by the support of their alumni.

The most distinguished of the state universities also possess considerable private endowments that make them not wholly dependent on the state legislature's periodic grants. In some state universities the board of regents is not periodically appointed by the state legislature, but is

Arnold Toynbee "School Boards Run System," *Globe and Mail* (Toronto), July 30, 1963.

a self-co-opting body. However, only a few years ago the regents of some state universities imposed a loyalty oath, and dismissed any professor who declined to take it.

The political position of public school teachers is worse than that. Politically, a public school teacher is perpetually on the defensive. He never knows whether a child may not carry home to its parents some story of something "pink" the teacher is alleged to have said in class. The parents may then complain to the school board, and the school board may arraign the teacher, and perhaps reprimand or dismiss him— and if he were to be dismissed on the charge of having expressed "pink" sentiments at school his chances of being employed in any other school might be poor.

If a British school board behaved like that it would have to reckon with the national Ministry of Education and the teachers' union, and, if it were convicted of having acted improperly for ideological reasons it would be the school board, not the teacher, that would get into trouble.

Such cases do occur in the United States. It is difficult to judge how frequent and how typical they are, but it is clear that the public school teacher's profession is a politically dangerous one. I also suspect that a school teacher need have little fear of trouble for airing conservative or even Facist views instead of liberal ones.

Parents who disliked seeing their children indoctrinated at school with the ideology of, let us say, the John Birch Society, might be shy of complaining to the school board about this, for fear they would be branded as being "pink." The sovereign U.S. local school board is, in fact, a fortress of McCarthyism that has not yet fallen, and the U.S. people can hardly afford to leave this fortress permanently standing.

Though a majority of the school boards perhaps have in common the same conservative ideology, they are in competition with each other for hiring the best teachers, and the richer school boards are able to secure the best teachers by outbidding the others.

School boards differ greatly from each other in affluence owing to the topographical structure of U.S. society. Since the original Americans have been outnumbered by the influx into U.S. cities of immigrants from Europe and of Negro migrants from the South into the great industrial cities of the North, the well-to-do minority of the urban population has tended to move out beyond the administrative limits of a city and to incorporate a number of new miniature municipalities in a ring round the old city's outskirts.

Since the average wealth of their ratepayers is exceptionally high, they can afford to pay their teachers higher salaries than can be afforded by the school boards of slum districts. So the slum districts, which particularly need the good teachers, are apt to lose them to the suburban districts.

What was once said by a British member of parliament about the power of the British Crown is applicable to the power of the U.S. school boards today. Their power, like King George III's, "has increased, is increasing, and ought to be diminished." Ought not the states to exercise a stricter control over the school boards? Constitutionally, this is the state governments' right, and therefore their duty as a matter of crucial importance to the nation.

19

American Education and the World

Every favoured visitor to the United States, when once he has recovered from the delirium induced by American hospitality, goes through a lengthy period of contradictory experiences. He is impressed by the vastness, the beauty, the variety and the monotony of the continental slice. He wonders at the grandeur of natural resources and of human ingenuity. He is confused by the nation-wide scale of enterprises and the petty repetitiousness of small-time parochialism. He is torn between the universality of friendly welcome and the intense loneliness of those who happen to be by-passed. But amid all these contradictions one thing stands out; a passionate committedness to the future, relying on a sometimes unquestioning trust in American enterprise in education.

What is this enterprise? Where is it seated? What are its inner resources? What are its aims? Nearly always the ready answer is that they are discernible in the school. Yet if the survey attempted in this article has meant anything, it must suggest that schools take on their possibilities and limitations from their context—in America as everywhere else. The American school's circumstances are in headlong change. To be true to those, the school's momentum must be equally dynamic.

In fact, we ought to remember *ad nauseam* to think not of "the American school" generically but of "American schools"—differently situated, differently composed, differently financed and administered, differently oriented and vasty different in their achievements or the services offered. We cannot think timelessly, but in real terms of real people— here, now, and especially tomorrow.

American books about schools, school practices, school aims, however, commonly continue to talk in universalist terms. They read like ancient devotional books intended to serve disembodied souls with few daily problems, little family or social context, and only the thinnest public

Edmund J. King. "American Education and the World," in *Society, Schools, and Progress in the U.S.A.* (Oxford: Pergamon Press, 1965), pp. 219–236. Reprinted by kind permission of the publishers, Pergamon Press, Oxford, England.

Author: Educated at University of Manchester and London University; Reader in Comparative Education, King's College, London University. He has served as visiting professor at the Universities of Tokyo, Syracuse, Harvard, British Columbia, and Puerto Rico.

commitment to a world which is too dangerous to meddle with. Better save one's soul (or at any rate avoid controversy) by staying uninvolved in any but the most transcendental terms. Of course, professorial platitudes are challenged less if thus presented; and profitable textbooks can be smoothly distributed from college to college or school system to school system. But is this pragmatic trueness to context? Is it really the logic of local self-determining ruggedness? Is this what the little red school-house finally gave to the world?

In point of fact the little red school-house (both literally and ethically) is likely to be encountered only among the Amish, the Mennonites, some exclusively Negro sections and some poor white backwaters. The yearly struggle of the Commonwealth of Pennsylvania to enforce compulsory attendance above the age of 14 on conscientious objectors among the strongly Christian "Pennsylvania Dutch" is evidence that the old static idea lives on, but that modern America cannot logically tolerate it in fairness to the children. Are schools only an extension of the family, the kitchen and the workshop? Are they solely a supermarket for the personal shopper? If so, who chooses the range of choices? And whose labour or skill makes the choices available? *To Whom do the Schools Belong?* asked Professor W. O. Lester Smith in England and Wales. The same question is urgent in the United States, with the implied corollary "—and what for?"

It is useless to give the teachers' college textbook answer that the schools belong to the children. Manifestly, they do not. They cannot. Obviously some "child-centred" communication and acting-out of perception is pedagogically necessary if only to secure and retain children's interest. In pioneering or efficiently exploiting interest-centred methods of schooling, American educational innovators have performed a world service; but there is nothing sacramental about method. Pedagogy is the servant of purpose and principle. It is the spirit of innovation or trueness to a developing context that really moves education; methods and institutions appropriate to one circumstance are deadening in the next. This very conviction brought the Pilgrim Fathers to Massachusetts; and a similar faith brought millions of immigrants to a land open to new perceptions. So even in the children's school preserve there can be no timeless inviolability of procedure. Still less can there be any unchangeable content, or indifference to a rampagingly different context around the schools. Schools are like parents. Some "over-protective" parents smother their children's development, though allegedly devoting their own lives to them. That is only another form of selfishness, reinforced by ignorance of the more truly educative environment surrounding everyone. Supposing the schools really did belong to the children,

children's very needs would similarly require the fullest barrage of contextual influences.

Therefore any one classroom in any one school in any one place is doomed to atrophy unless the children there are becoming aware of their home, their circumstances, their country and their world. Theoretically this outward-rippling exploration takes place in the United States. In fact, relatively few Americans know their local, regional or national context in any but the most superficial sense. Seeing before them universal automobiles, universal stores and commodities, and the universal possibility of going somewhere else, they tend to assume that (apart from minor idioms of custom or legislation) the American way of life goes on much the same everywhere. Commuting past Harlem, or journeying through the picturesque Cumberland Mountains, they view the "inevitable" ghetto with some detachment; they may not even see poor white destitution and ignorance.

Leaving aside such extremes, it is more unlikely still that in their travels they cast a penetrating eye upon the vagaries of local "autonomy" or its implications for America's entirety. As for those thus eyed, they frequently repudiate whatever constructive criticism is ventured by other Americans, calling it "un-American," "egg-head," "socialist" or even "communist." No less a person than ex-President Eisenhower has been called "a dedicated agent of the communist conspiracy." People may criticize in their own backyards; but not even Americans may criticize across the fence. Any attempt to penetrate the daily America of most other Americans is bedevilled by conservative entanglement. Customs and institutions survive into the later twentieth century from pre-industrial English villages, with the peculiarly self-righteous but blinkered ignorance to be expected in them. The administration and opportunities of the schools perpetuate this conceptual foundation.

In practice, of course, the schools are public institutions in a quite different sense from any purely localized or regionalized interpretation. Barnard, Mann and others vindicated the school as a publicly supported (i.e. tax-maintained) public instrument whether parents willed so or not. Through their revolutionary application and extension of European school discoveries to people and purposes beyond the vision of the Europeans, they opened the whole future to all American children. They did not relent before parental or managerial obduracy. They processed the books, the teachers; they provided and standardized the buildings and equipment; they planned ideal curricula with day-to-day objectivity but long-term perspicacity; they built modern America out of people who did not know America; they laid the foundation for nationality of a new kind by establishing the people's schools across the country.

On this public elementary instruction were founded the railroads, the "know-how," and the technology that not only became the workshop of the world but gave the entire world the possibility of a quite reoriented life pattern.

These men and women pursued the children's and "the people's" interests by a public overview of opportunity, need, and method. They did not behave like villagers or a world-renouncing priesthood. Administration, expertise and policy of the type and elevation required lay far beyond the ordinary parent's or the ordinary teacher's competence. Despite myriads of local and temporary setbacks, and despite the decrepit persistence until now of contradictory influences, the American public school ideal discovered appropriate instrumentation. It has therefore prevailed to be an inspiration and conceptual model for mankind. The United States' "great experiment" in nation-building, in claiming a future far beyond its own realization at the time, is centred on the public school. More than any other country, the United States has a nationhood achieved by conscious contrivance, with the school as its mainspring. If American democracy had done nothing else, it could be fiercely proud of this.

The American School and Its American Alternatives

"The school," we find ourselves saying once again; but that generalization seems less reprehensible now because we remember the immense variety of experimental adaptations for any one age range, the great extension and branching-out of later opportunities, and the restless endeavour to perfect in higher education the potential of the most elementary beginning. Unfortunately, the more enterprising the better American schools and colleges became, the further the others were left behind—in financial resources, in committedness, in awareness. Yet even the best of school systems in the United States or anywhere else has been surpassed in power and cultural influence by its own products and implications. This is a world-wide tendency worth a fuller examination; but it applies with most crucial reference to the American school system.

The recognizably respectable teacher (often associated with a venerable church role) once known in pre-industrial days, when "school" meant one kind of prescription in one place, has long ago given way to the paid professional expert whose learning can be challenged and whose service can be assessed. For the progress of education this has been a good thing. Instead of being a multipurpose friend, father and civic guide, the teacher has in some ways become a greater help by restriction of his function to one area of specialized competence—provided that his professed field is firmly grounded, and surrounded at all points by true awareness of the world.

Even so, teachers are not the unchallenged giants of knowledge and morality that they were once expected to be. Moreover, the teacher, being one of a particular group amidst a majority of educated people (including the children's parents and a multiplicity of competing specialists in other occupations which may have creamed off the potential teaching force anyway) is relatively diminished in stature. Though the children are longer in school nowadays, they may spend an equal length of time before radio and television sets or with the comics. By these means and through the press, "experts" give facts and opinions in a way that the teacher could not—often far more persuasively. The pupils' own mobility and resourcefulness are an unspoken challenge to school. When school is finished, and throughout life, the extracurricular adult education of not supposedly educational forces communicates information, normative data and values. Books, magazines, advertising and the example of neighbours add their influence. It is not suggested that these are bad, of course; but they are manifold in quantity and intensive in quality. They may reinforce the school's message; more often they are competitive. Career experience and job requirements tend to be more persuasive still.

These are all extra-scholastic influences which we can see at work in any country of the modern world; but there is no country in which their cumulative importance is greater than in the United States—not because of any shortcomings in the teaching profession but because of the inevitable evolution of technology and urbanization. However, in the United States the absence of an overall direction of education endeavour (such as a Ministry of Education might provide)—without even an approximate consensus of opinion about educational priorities—leaves the field clear for alternative persuaders. As the commercial corporations and the controllers of the mass media are so gigantic, and are necessarily given to simultaneous co-ordination of long-term planning on a nation-wide basis, they inevitably have hegemony in a way that no district, state or existing national body can have. As these topics have been developed earlier, it suffices here merely to mention them.

If we ponder over their importance as they deserve, these extra-curricular influences already condition the school in the present. Yet the keenest and most powerful competitors of today's school as anyone can imagine it are the implications of the future. Some attempt to adumbrate these was made earlier. Clearly, if the school is already becoming only one of many contestants in the cultural arena of the present, when we look towards the future we can see a more devastating comparison still. The continued efficacy of the schools will be altogether dependent upon their competence to serve unprecedented needs. What is more, their work will feel its way forward temporarily and on a hypothetical basis, with the schools' justification further dependent on a "fulfilment education" given continuously to adults throughout a scarcely foreseeable future. This cannot lie within the purview of purely local responsibility, any more than hurricanes and floods can be safeguarded against by a few sandbags before the door or a few ropes and rocks securing the roof. Far-ranging vigilance over many lands, electronic sensitivity and long-range prediction are the essence of any security that may be afforded. The same is as true of education as of everything else. Long-range calculations so complicated as to need computer analysis are the daily stock-in-trade of every modern business. Unseen but powerful, they lie behind every can of meat, every book, every child.

Freedom for Personal Choice

Strange inconsistencies appear in anyone's life and character. No one will presume to take Americans to task for being as human as everyone else. Looking back we see that one of the greatest American contributions to mankind was not the idea itself that ordinary people count but the implementation of the idea, and the devising of apparatus to require that implementation. People needed to have guarantees for the opportunity to become fully developed, to contribute their hunches significantly to the community's deliberations, and thereafter adapt daily living circumstances to whatever unprecedented challenge arose. According to this view, identity of interest is not required; in fact it is undesirable. Every man is his own frontier. His birthright is to have an unhampered view, free scope for his arm, equal prospects for his dear ones, and an ultimate collective protection against unprovoked disaster.

However, gone for ever are the days when great events or issues could be simply or distantly seen. Thermonuclear annihilation may be less than 4 minutes away. There need be no questions; there can be no personal or community reply at that stage. Yet every question asked about everything in homes, schools and political decisions in the United States (as in every democracy) leads on potentially to a chain-reaction of responsibility for whatever happens. Even if people shut their minds to the unbearable gravity of this responsibility for choice, they cannot possibly close their eyes to the facts of life surrounding the choice.

Apart from the risk of nuclear war as an imminent threat, there is the long-range responsibility for avoiding a build-up of antagonism in which large-scale destruction seems inevitable or worth risking. Inflammatory situations develop all over the world all the time because of the hunger of most of mankind (now 3280 million), and because of their understandable wish to share the knowledge possessed by prosperous nations, which would enable them to seek pacific remedies for their plight. Before our children pass middle age, mankind will have doubled in size, mostly in poor countries.

Supposing they did not have warlike inclinations, the choice all these people face in organizing their lives is between one polarity in the United States and another in the U.S.S.R.—China complex, with Europe as a possible buffer or third way in between, trying to preserve the ancient prescriptions of civilization in a less streamlined idiom. Time does not wait, with the world's population increasing by 65 million a year—and all needing food, government and education. No modern, responsible American can remain unalerted to all these risks, unless he is being denied the very birthright for which this country stands. Is he too inconsequential to be kept aware, to act out the implications of his knowledge, and to make its purport felt?

Complement or Conformity?

Obviously, these questions can and must be asked of all citizens in every democracy. Most people have not proceeded as far as the United States in the direction of educational implementation; but this is precisely the point—the United States has relied on *educational* implementation of its purposes. We are therefore entitled to inquire how effective that implementation has been or can be in American circumstances. For we outsiders are would-be learners from the United States; or else we must look (like everyone else among mankind) for something more reliable outside the United States. Americans will make their own decisions; but the rest of mankind are entitled to make theirs on the basis of the evidence.

Outsiders see the gravest risk to American education in the inequality of opportunity so widely prevalent. (Mr. Fred Hechinger of the *New York Times* in his *Big Red Schoolhouse* said that nothing resembling equal opportunity existed in the United States—and he was referring not to coloured people but to white.) A second grave risk, not altogether separable from the first, is a prevalent tendency among the educationally handicapped in the United States to see everything in black and white, true–false, pure–impure, American and anti-American terms. Only children (who may be of any age) see things with such circumscribed lack of subtlety; and no really well educated American does so. There is no other country in the world where international or social discussion is more shrewdly or sensitively carried on at the topmost level; but this very kind of discussion (on the assumption that all hunches have the right to be reckoned in) is the very thing stigmatized by local or conservative opinion as revealing the diabolical perverseness of Washington "socialists" and eastern professors. Conclusions carefully arrived at are stated to be "false" (just like that) or even "a pack of lies" arising from the wish to subvert "the real America."

There is no need to go back to McCarthy (who still has his loyal supporters). At the 1964 Republican conference in San Francisco, the watching world was told that "extremism in the defence of liberty is no vice." Governor Rockefeller was barracked and howled down when he begged his fellow delegates to repudiate such "communist and Nazi methods" as wearing down opposition (within his own party) by "midnight and early morning telephone calls." He also referred to threats of violence which he himself had received. Some distinguished scholars in the United States, of unimpeachable American loyalty, have similarly been subjected to this incessant attrition by telephone calls at all hours by a roster of women conservatives for no better reason than that they have worked with UNESCO and other "communist" organizations. This was an attempt to "drive them out of town"—as far as these patriots could think!

Several county school systems in the United States have in fact been forbidden to make any teaching reference to UNESCO or other international organizations to which the United States Government lends notable support. This has happened not only in anti-evolution fundamentalist centres but in California itself—the seat of the first meeting of the United Nations! Obscurantism of this kind plays false to the American past, undermines the future of the United States in the world and denies American children their birthright of knowledge and decision-making. In a graduate class of my own in an American university in 1956, only two students knew what UNESCO was, although American generosity towards overseas programmes is an example to the world.

Though clear-sighted American writers often refer to the brooding sense of violence still lurking in the backwoods of their country (and at the back of some ignorant minds), it would be grossly unfair to suppose that these outbursts and examples of persecution truly represent "grass roots" opinion. In matters of segregation, political decision or educational choice "the people" are often stampeded by professional "leaders" (Russians would call them "activists") brought in from somewhere else. Any observer not primarily concerned to apportion blame but more eager to pinpoint the locus of critical decision will note this phenomenon time and again. If professionals can thus persuade conservatively, why must it seem so evil that really educated and dedicated school people make sober recommendations in their field? Medical practitioners and engineers make recommendations in theirs! It is all the more astonishing that "the people" in any one district or state should truculently resist progress, because that frequently represents no more than catching up with more realistic neighbours in the United States, having nothing to do with any possible example from foreign parts. A remarkable beginning would be made if all teachers, parents and administrators really knew their United States.

Professionals and Citizens

A beginning of self-knowledge and responsible choice could be achieved in the schools. But the schools have their being in a public world dominated already by experts and prestige personalities. Idiosyncrasies and selective privacy may be suspect or clandestine for social reasons, as many a collegian or co-ed will tell you. Firms invade privacy not only by television advertisements and the "hidden persuaders" of relatively obvious kinds but by the inevitable process of predicting production requirements. These then become normative habits for the consumer and convey their own system of values. Possibly little harm is done this way, though pessimists think so. In any case, the citizen is a cipher in the calculations of the expert. Senator Goldwater turned over the conduct of his 1964 Republican nomination campaign to a computer. No criticism is implied. So much of life and its decisions is "bugged" (to use the graphic American term for being subjected to electronic surveillance) that it becomes hard to know what is the citizen's choice and what the specialist's echo. Whatever the schools can begin, or find basic information for, will reach maturity in a world such as this.

Of course, we must not overlook the critical but cheerful American intellectuals' scathing reaction to these phenomena. They know. They are not spoofed. But have they the effective opportunity to disengage themselves and take control of American affairs? Is all their flow of critical information going to run into the sand? Can they carry the American people forward, or even convince them? In the United States there is a widespread survival of the Arminian (and Puritan) creed that God materially rewards the good. Wealth and charismatic eminence may therefore be outward signs of inward grace; whereas towards mere cleverness there is ambivalence, if not mistrust. It may be more rewarding on earth (as in heaven) to pay tithes to local church or civil leadership than cleverly to claim a soul and mind of one's own—in other words, than to claim the heritage of the Pilgrim Fathers, the Founding Fathers and the common people's school.

The Common School and the "Dialogue" of Democracy

Before that can happen nowadays it is prerequisite that *everyone* should have the most alert and thorough education available, particularly in a country so totally committed in principle to the idea of education as a birthright and the major public instrument. Giving everyone the basic opportunity and the essential data are only the beginning, of course. The Soviet system believes it does this for its citizens. The distinctively American difference has been to provide for nearly everyone the political, legal and educational opportunities which Europeans dreamed of for the minority from the time of the Greeks onwards—but which they never really succeeded in providing for the ordinary people. This endeavour, even partially fulfilled, is rightly a source of pride to the American people; but once again it differs from communist commitment to education only in its restless determination to provide opportunity for *constructive difference*. Merely parochial difference and difference-through-backwardness are not constructive; they have become a denial of the basic freedom for personal choice. Even more antidemocratic is an insistence that respectability is determined by one faction, or one district, or one state.

In so far as these observations impinge on the government of school districts, and on some states' effective unawareness that the world is in motion, they may be called political. But some such observations are merely technological or social. Already militating against the honourable ideal of personal integrity and uniqueness is a growing idea that the private lives and opinions of employees are a proper concern of corporation managers. Others think they may be a normal concern of the community, whether that is the sorority, suburbia, or local government. The McCarthy episode showed that they might become a congressional concern, with perhaps more justification in so far as politics were politically scrutinized. But when purely personal preferences, intellectual interests and social relationships are politically or industrially blackguarded by having pejorative labels stuck on them, that is a graver matter for the country as a whole, as well as for individuals. It is gravest of all when any possibility of change is outlawed in advance by being stigmatized as "socialistic" or "atheist." Such benightedness is a denial of America's most characteristic contribution. It makes impossible the continuation of what R. M. Hutchins called "the great dialogue"—the most important thing that active nonconformity can bring about.

Commerce, Science and Politics

There is hardly an American enterprise of industry or commerce (including agriculture) that is not totally dependent on all-American planning, interchange and skill. This is manifestly true in times of complete peace. The unstable international situation, entirely apart from military considerations, makes it still more necessary to think "all-American" about external trade relationships, investment, American skill and the security of American domestic living standards in peace time.

If there were war or even large-scale build-up of weapons, the obvious concentration of resources and planning in the hands of the military, the President, or Congress would push centralized control far further than the most mammoth-like corporation trust could ever aspire to. Already, great corporations do not wait upon local enterprise in education; they push it, finance it, reward it, supplement it or supersede it if inadequate. When corporations look abroad at "formidable commercial competition" in Europe or Japan, they inevitably demand and secure people highly educated according to precise specifications—if they can.

Moreover, many of those space and para-military projects which have directly or indirectly brought such prosperity to American heavy industries, electronic enterprises and supply agencies are themselves bound to pre-empt a still greater proportion of scientists, technologists and managerial potential. Present demands affect far more than school expansion. In 1964 Dr. James Killian's committee on the supply of scientific manpower reported that changes in long-term government policy were having unpredictable effects on the supply of highly educated personnel for the scientific and engineering community in the civil sector. The government's existing sponsorship of some 60 percent of *all* those engaged in research and development also implied an entirely new concept of responsibility of the recruitment and balanced distribution of available talent. A longer view was called for, not for political reasons but to complete the logic of national security abroad and economic security at home. This is the language of the whole world, not just of the United States; but it was not the language in which ancient educational prescriptions were once laid down.

The American School and the World Example

Most of the effective decisions referred to here and earlier are purely domestic decisions for the citizens of the United States and their leaders.

But these decisions are crises in the educational arena of the whole world, which has long been indebted to the example of the determined revolutionaries and patient administrators of the United States.

The United States is a world power far more potent than military might could make it. The outside world is dazzled immediately by its technological "know-how," its high standard of living, its ability to dispense financial investment and technical aid. It is at this level, at the summit of its achievements, that the outside world most readily but most superficially admires the United States. If American hegemony of the Western World is to continue, the progress of the United States must maintain its momentum. This it cannot do by "father-will-fix-it" methods in technology or education. There is something far deeper than technological expertise in the American example. Responsible political choices at home and abroad depend upon a kind of penetration and awareness which most American educators have by implication, but which they have not made explicit.

This awareness is transcendent in world terms. Like the Declaration of Independence it thinks, talks and acts in terms of "all men." It is not messianic presumption which makes American stamps show the Statute of Liberty with the caption "liberty for all," but rather a deep conviction that inner security for Americans depends on the prevalence of humane régimes outside. Equally, the triumph of a humane example abroad depends inescapably upon the universality of sound political, social and educational principles within the whole of the United States. No amount of gimmicks or rocketry can be a substitute for these.

Fundamentally the message of the United States to the world is that government and learning are based upon the daily exercise of opportunity by responsible citizens. Idealism and pragmatism found a new home in the New World and produced a robust race. Of that race the most vigorous offspring have been institutions bearing the likeness of their ancestors yet capable of venturing upon unrecognizable endeavours. Among these the common school and the widespread access to useful higher educational opportunity are the most remarkable—partly because of idealist commitment to a principle, partly because of pragmatic readiness to evolve.

The fierce criticism by Americans of so many points in their educational system shows a healthy recognition that evolution has lagged behind the ideal, behind need. If that were not so, there would be no necessity to spend so much money on restorative programmes nor so urgent a determination to reform (like Dr. J. B. Conant) the education of the educators. Though this really does look like a purely domestic matter, it is of much more widespread importance than many will recognize. Let us consider once again American know-how in technology, management and research. If Americans recognize that continued progress in these fields, with an effective supply and distribution of suitable personnel, depends upon radical reorganization as well as on more intense efforts, that recognition is promptly forced upon all outside observers too. If these observers also note that resistance to educational progress or reorganization widely prevails in the United States, what are they tempted to conclude? That the revolutionary drive and all the frontier-seeking in education have lost their momentum? Or that the much-vaunted institutions are not really serviceable today?

Now this brings us back to the world's avid reading of so many American books and the world's readiness to use American devices. These seem to offer quick access to high living standards with first-class citizenship or nationhood. If, like the governmental and ecclesiastical apparatus of the Old World, the organization of the New has lost its elastic adaptability, has the time come for another large-scale departure from a dispensation that has had its day? If people so decided, they might feel that they were making a point of principle. They might look far away from the United States for a preferable principle. They might, indeed, think they discerned within the United States alternative operative principles: those of big-business monoliths, social conformism and personal dependence upon "leadership"—a most popular but most dangerous catchword in the United States. In either case they would be rejecting the old, "legendary" America of freedom to espouse the reality of mechanized control.

It is at this point that the most serious misgivings set in. The glories of the American educational system are historic. In the world circumstances of today they are largely potential and conditional glories, rather than inevitable or even actual at all points. Yet it is an integral part of the American message that all points count. Herein lies a matter of principle, which every immigrant seeking naturalization is required to understand fully as he accepts the whole American way of life with the loyalty of conversion. Is it asking too much of born Americans to manifest the same recognition? If it is too much, then the Presidential and congressional upgrading campaigns will be doomed to failure, the endeavours of foundations and powerful individuals will be unavailing, and the world will regretfully mourn the passing of a fundamental American principle.

In truth, of course, the principle is almost universally accepted as a matter of commitment. What has gone wrong is the implementation. The apparatus of the seventeenth and eighteenth centuries has survived into the twentieth. The schools which in the nineteenth century were required to give ordinary people a publicly provided educational minimum, then a good secondary foundation, and finally a higher complement if they could claim it, are now being transformed into a multipurpose and nationwide apparatus of a quite different kind. They are variously expected to be bastions of the Pentagon, trainers for technology, suppliers for commerce and industry, and social therapists for the world of automated riches and leisure. Whatever we or the Americans as a whole decide about their schools, this last catalogue of demands is a reminder that the world in which the school system evolved during the past century has since evolved further and faster. If only the implementation, and not the principle, has fallen short of expectation, the prospect is still hopeful.

At this point the interests of the world and of the American people coincide to a large extent. The questions asked are not prompted by alien sympathies; they concern achievement. They are questions of quality, of mechanics, of administration. They query only the present idiom for implementing time-honoured but necessarily adaptable principles. How is America to achieve modern self-recognition? What of priorities? How can the nation direct itself? What is to be the "image," the civilizing and peace-securing example for the world?

For answers to some of these questions there must be concerted endeavours and far-sighted striving together. For this enterprise at present no official mechanism or agreement exists. To reach purely American decisions today is a grave responsibility for the loyal and alert American. Today he must inevitably measure decisions by the criteria of the world outside, and by all the tomorrows of mankind. No other nation has ever before been so pivotal to civilization—at any rate in so far as that has turned upon the schools. It is on schools that mankind increasingly depends for reorientation. With these thoughts we do not attempt to transform the role of the United States; we simply return to the universalist tone of her basic Declarations.

20

Sick Schools: Australian Perspectives

"From Australia? You couldn't have come to the States at a better time. All the issues that have ever bedevilled American education are in full voice at the moment. In the schools you'll see every form of teaching from ultra conservatism to ultra modernism.

In the staff rooms you'll see every brand of educational philosophy from Plato to Jacques Barzun being thrashed out. The only constant in the whole system is change. If you don't take sides, but watch and listen you'll have a rewarding experience, believe me."

The speaker was a veteran professor of education from New York's Columbia Teachers' College. My wife and I, who were just embarking on a tour of leading American schools, found his words prophetic. As spectators we saw more of the game than most of the participants.

What we saw was a grim wrestling match for control of education at all levels. This article is an attempt to identify the wrestlers and to predict the results of the contest. Until Sputnik went into orbit in 1957 most people in the United States believed that they had the finest educational system in the world. True, there had been voices of dissent, but these had been labelled "knockers" and dismissed as examples of unAmerican activities.

When Sputnik shattered this complacency these "knockers" found themselves prophets in their own land. Titles such as these moved into the best seller lists: "Why Johnny Can't Read," "Quackery in the Public Schools," "Educational Wastelands."

Typical of the reaction to Russia's demonstration of technical and scientific leadership was the statement of Admiral Rickover made in the first moments of shock:

None of us is without guilt. But now that the people have awakened to the need for reform, I doubt whether the reams of propaganda pamphlets

William Broderick. "Sick Schools," *The Age* (Melbourne, Australia), November 24, 1965, pp. 13, 15. Reprinted by kind permission of the publishers of *The Age*, Melbourne, Victoria, Australia.

Author (1912–   ): Educated University of Melbourne, B.A., B. Education, senior lecturer in English and Head of the English Department Ballarat Teachers' College, Ballarat, Victoria, Australia.

stating that all is well with our schools will ever again fool the American people into believing that education can safely be left to "progressive educators."

The mood of America has changed. Our technological supremacy has been called into question, and we know now that we have to deal with a formidable competitor.

Parents are no longer satisfied with "life-adjustment" schools. Parental objectives no longer coincide with those professed by "progressive educationists." I doubt that we can ever again be silenced.

So here we have an identification of the wrestlers. On one side is the group known as "progressive educators," on the other side are people like Rickover who believe in solid, European-type studies.

At this moment in American educational history the "progressive educators" are held guilty of seriously weakening academic studies in high schools and colleges throughout the land.

Put simply, the case against them is this: By pandering to sentimental theories about children they have thrown out or watered down such solid subjects as mathematics, science and modern languages; in their place, they have inserted driver education, family relationships, local history, civic development pep club, freshman problems, marching band, and dozens of similar "life-adjustment" offerings.

The average American high schools are very pleasant places in which to idle away one's adolescence. Their function is to make children happy, socially mature, outgoing. No one is to be made to feel inferior or superior (except in sport). In a sense they are not educational institutions at all but co-educational youth clubs.

In fact, most of the schools are anti-intellectual in tone. Clever children are cut down to size by providing them with subjects which do not call for intelligence or application. This fact explains the awful cloud of boredom that one encounters in so many classrooms in the United States.

Never-ending, shapeless "nattering" about "family relationships," "dating patterns," "democratic procedures" occupy most of the school day. My wife one day was asked to join a class of 14-year-old children to answer questions about "family relationships" for an hour. All the questions put to her were on the subject of dating practices in Australia: When did dating commence? Was necking allowed in cars on the campus? How many dates a week did the average fresher high schoolgirl have?

The American girls were astonished to learn that their Australian counterparts wear school uniforms, use no make-up, are interested more in passing French, mathematics and other subjects, at an external examination than in making passes at boys and that "dating patterns" are non-existent. "I'd hate to go to school there," one girl exclaimed. "All you could do is learn things."

And the implications of this comment sum up the prevailing attitude of people steeped in the "progressive" philosophy of education. School is not primarily a place where formal learning takes place. It is a co-ed centre where one "adjusts to one's peers and the community and where one explores one's personality"—to quote the words of one high school catalogue.

Martin Mayer in his book, *The Schools,* says standards are low in American high schools because of the legacy of progressivism's pseudo-science of educational research which insists that children not learn ahead of schedule. Children, he says, are held back because of the cloying concept of "readiness" which lays down that Johnny can't read until he is six and a half and can't do algebra until he is 14 or 15.

To reinforce the inhibiting effect of "readiness," intelligence testing has been invoked: "Mary has an I.Q. of only 85. We can't teach her anything." So all the Marys—whose I.Q. is in most cases a measure of their lack of skill in English—are left to drift aimlessly along in an environment that offers no challenge.

In the course of our travels around the States we spent a week teaching at Melbourne High School, Florida. This is one of the most dynamic schools in America, where really solid work is being done—some of it at college level. Dr. B. Frank Brown, principal of the school, was one of the first men to respond to the challenge of Sputnik.

Almost overnight he lifted the level of instruction significantly by eliminating life-adjustment courses, abolishing grade levels and introducing independent and individual work for suitable students. I asked him his opinion of I.Q. as a means of gauging a student's suitability for independent research.

"I.Q. is meaningless in assessing the ability of students to undertake this programme," he said. "What we look for is Quest Quotient, that is, the ability to quest, inquire, investigate, explore. Without this nothing else is of use."

In the year following Sputnik, the Federal Government entered the educational field with its National Defense Education Act, plainly designed to encourage efficient teaching of science, mathematics and modern languages. Ten million dollars were to be spent on education from elementary to graduate schools.

Schools like Melbourne High, with its accent on science and mathematics, were given liberal funds to build science and language laboratories and to develop stiffer courses in mathematics. The big foundations added their weight in the resuscitation of American education. The Ford Foundation, the Carnegie Foundation and the Rockefeller Foundation have all lavishly aided science and mathematics at every level.

The Eisenhower Administration, set up a committee on National Goals to see what could be done to rehabilitate American education. The committee reported that what was needed was "excellence." Excellences in this sense meant above-average ability in mathematics, science and the languages likely to be useful in the next war.

In 1962 John Gardner published a book entitled simply, *Excellence*. What was needed, Gardner said, was to identify the gifted student and then give him an education "in depth." "Gifted" in Gardner's sense means cleverness at mathematics, science, and modern languages.

It does not mean gifted in art, literature, music, history, or any other discipline, except the three mentioned above.

So the Federal Government has given an unequivocal answer to Herbert Spencer's question: "What knowledge is of most worth?"

One of the depressing results of the answer is that subjects at the bottom of the hierarchy of esteem are neglected and their practitioners made to feel guilty and unwanted. Art teaching for example, so alive and vital in England, is formal and lifeless in the States. Music, too, is a subject that seems to have been squeezed out. In all the schools we visited in America, we cannot recall hearing one music lesson.

Another depressing feature of most high schools is the introversion and provincialism of the curricula. American history, for instance, is taught in courses in grades V, VIII, and XI—and again in college. The only time we could find any treatment of the history and geography of other countries was in optional survey courses which aim to teach the geography of the world and its history from the earliest beginnings to the present day—in one semester (six months).

This type of shallow "butterfly" course gives many students the mistaken idea that they know all there is to know about history and geography. Some compulsory courses prescribed by State legislatures are jingoistic and lacking in objectivity.

The compulsory "Americanism versus Communism" course is as objective as one imagines its Russian counterpart to be. "Problems of Democracy," another compulsory course in most schools, was described to me by one teacher taking the course as "unsubtle brainwashing that even the kids can see through."

One aspect of American education that would worry Australian teachers is the number of administrators who supervise the teachers' work. Martin Mayer in *The Schools* states: "Attempts to control a teacher's daily work are more prevalent in the United States than elsewhere.

In America nearly ten percent of the staff is engaged in full-time supervision."

In more popular language, there are too many chiefs and not enough Indians. Everywhere we went we saw people in cushy jobs earning higher salaries than the hard-pressed teachers in the classrooms, and enjoying more prestige and authority. Many of these administrators were ex-coaches. All of them carried important titles such as curriculum co-ordinators, guidance counsellors, study consultants, administrative assistants, &c.

While teachers taught through the entire day in these high schools without even one free period, the administrators sat in their well-appointed offices and made up new courses of study for them to teach, or advised students individually on how to "adjust" to their fellows or to the class situation. As a result of this system, good teachers quickly drift out of the classrooms into more rewarding occupations.

Admiral Rickover, one of the most trenchant critics of "progressive" education, reserves his scorn for the ill-educated, non-teaching school administrator whom he finds endemic and ubiquitous. He recommends a surgical operation to remove them from the educational body.

When pressures are developing in Australia for more local control of education, it is interesting to note that in America, where local control is very powerful, the movement there is towards central control. More than any other nation the United States has made local control the central feature of its school system.

The result is what James Conant calls a Noah's Ark of education—"a happy confusion of 35,000 independent school systems in which standards vary so widely than an A grade in one school may be worth a D grade in another." Admiral Rickover states that local control is the greatest obstacle to school reform. In his book, *Swiss Schools and Ours; Why Theirs Are Better*, Rickover writes: "I know of no country that has brought off successfully a really thorough reform of the school system without making use of some national standard that sets scholastic objectives."

In the wealthiest school districts such as Beverly Hills in Hollywood and Winnetka in Chicago the schools are superbly staffed and high standards are maintained. On the other hand, some rural schools in Alabama are slums in every sense of the word.

Unquestionably the academic standards of the vast majority of American high schools are much below the level of English grammar schools. We encountered in every high school that we visited the inevitable big crop of children in upper forms who were functionally illiterate—that is they were reading on grade II or III level.

Most of them were aggressively resentful of all school activities except sport and social engagements. In some school systems where the leaving age is fixed at 17 or 18, these youngsters were, in effect, prisoners exerting a harmful influence on their fellows, and learning nothing.

Most of these "slow learners," to use the euphemism of the administration, are located in high schools in the slum areas of the big cities. The demise of the apprenticeship system, child labor laws and union pressures all combine to turn these youngsters into school-hating conscripts.

It is well to remember these children when pressures to push up the school-leaving age in this country become more insistent. Are the progressive educators then the only ones to blame for the current low standards in U.S. schools? It is not as simple as that. They are the popular scapegoats, but others too are not without sin. In truth, the whole American community is guilty. By opening the doors of the high schools to mediocrity as well as to talent, the Americans at the beginning of this century sealed the fate of academic education.

Local education authorities, consisting mostly of tradesmen, insisted that the schools be "practical" in the worse sense. They insisted that their children pass, and that promotion be automatic. By hiring teachers on annual contracts they saw to it that teachers who tried to insist on high standards were not re-employed.

What the high school has done supremely well is to produce millions of students with one face. Despite the 35,000 different school systems, American students give the impression of being rolled off the one assembly line. All have the same stock ideas, the same prejudices, the same jargon, the same lack of curiosity about what is happening overseas.

The schools by encouraging conformity through "socialization" and life adjustment have made the individual feel a misfit and individuality an un-American activity.

What is needed now is a massive attempt to stimulate heresies, to encourage heretics, to foster the off-beat and the eccentric, and to make individuality a prized social attribute. There are sufficient Babbitts in the U.S. What is needed there is a multiplication of the Admiral Rickovers of this world.

What the high school has failed lamentably to do is to produce scholars, and more important for national survival it has failed to produce scholars in the quasi-military subjects of science, mathematics and modern languages. The progressive educators merely gave the demands of the pressure groups a philosophical form.

In the matter of quantity American education has done well. What is lacking is quality. How can the school system be rebuilt to embrace quality as well as quantity? Democracies work slowly and education is one of the slowest-moving agents in a democracy. There will be no instant quality education for all. There is too much demolition to be done before construction can start.

The first thing to go will be local control. Selective use of Federal funds will be used as an instrument to bring the old "life adjustment" board of education into line. Education is too vital to be left any longer to parish-pump tradesmen. Under the National Defense Education Act the Federal Government has infiltrated into education in all areas and at all levels.

It is determined to use its powers to pick out the gifted and to see that the schools to which they are sent are excellent at teaching the hard disciplines of mathematics, science and modern languages. Schools are anxious to reform so that they can participate in the Federal largesse. Philosophers have now built a new philosophy to justify the new direction dictated by the need to see that Johnny knows as much as Ivan.

It could well be called excellentism. But the new name can hardly disguise the fact that America, realising she has thrown out the baby with the bath water, now has decided that mediocrity is not democracy and that scholarship, so highly prized in European schools, is the most practical thing when all is said and done. It is so practical that national survival depends on it.

Ironically, all the pressures in Australian society today are tending to push us along the educational path that America is so anxious to desert.

21

A European View of American Educational Philosophy

Twelve years ago in the Boyd H. Bode Memorial Lectures which I had the honor to deliver at Ohio State University I asked American critics of American education to provide a rationale for the practical proposals they were then making to reform the school curriculum. I wondered whether they were able to justify a curriculum centered round selected subjects or disciplines without returning to a neo-liberal arts theory of curriculum of the kind held by Aristotle and succeeding generations of European educators. I doubted very much whether such a theory of acceptable basic and unacceptable non-basic disciplines would meet the needs of American schools.

I doubt whether A. E. Bestor, A. Lynd, Hilda Neatby, Robert M. Hutchins, and other critics to whom I referred took up the challenge. Nor am I immodest enough to think that *American Criticism of American Education* sparked off a spate of discussion in England about curriculum reform. Certainly in the last ten years English and American philosophers of education have analyzed in considerable detail terms such as: *field of study, area of study;* and how these differ from a *discipline.* One outcome of this philosophical discussion implies that practical curriculum reform can be based on choices made from a number of logically related disciplines. Those subjects which have been taught in school for many years but which under this critical analysis do not meet the criteria of the basic disciplines, may under pressure for time in the school year be rejected. These forms of analysis are obviously important if the position held by Bestor and others is examined.

Brian Holmes. "Comprehensions and Apprehensions Concerning American Educational Philosophy" Chapter II in *International Education: Understandings and Misunderstandings,* Stewart E. Fraser (editor), Nashville, Peabody International Center, 1969. pp. 29–40.
Author: Educated at University College, London and the Institute of Education, London University; lecturer in education at the Durham Colleges, and since 1953 has been on the staff of the Institute of Education where he is Reader in Comparative Education. He is treasurer-secretary of the Comparative Education Society of Europe.

This philosophizing, using the refined tools of analysis has been made, it should be noted, from the basis of a particular frame of reference which if not strictly Aristotelian is nevertheless European. The frame of reference itself determines the kinds of questions philosophers of education have asked and the kinds of terms they have chosen to subject to critical analysis. In other words conceptual analysis has, in many cases, not made any more explicit than the critics of American education have done the set of assumptions from which analysis is launched. In other words analysis has not been adequately matched by processes of synthesis.

Conceptual and linguistic techniques are without question important and in need of development. The schoolmen, committed broadly to an Aristotelian logic, debated endlessly. But, as Bertrand Russell has said, modern logic has to advance in the teeth of opposition from those who held that the syllogism was the basis of logical disputation. Yet while there is constant need to refine the techniques of philosophical disputation there is also needed a clarification of the systems of philosophy without which techniques are no more valuable than the metre rule, or the swinging pendulum, or a pound of platinum are to the physical sciences. Refinements of technique carried Newtonian science to the edge of theoretical breakdown in the late nineteenth century. A new cosmology was needed before science could again make a major leap forward.

My request today therefore is that American philosophers of education continue to search for a new rationale for American education. Success would mean that a new system of philosophy would evolve to give general answers to the main philosophical questions and to major socio-political issues of the day. There is need in other words for serious normative studies which will help professional educationists and laymen to decide what "ought to be the case" and to know possible alternatives to any consensual normative position. Lawrence A. Cremin's attempt in *The Genius of American Education* to find a new rationale for American education no doubt failed, but the question he asked was of fundamental importance and should be pursued with vigor. Such a claim should not be interpreted to mean that when new assumptions answering major questions are put forward, critical analyses of them are not needed. The process of testing new ideas needs to go on, and indeed may be of greater educational and social value than the present somewhat exclusive interest in the analysis of familiar terms in education.

There are two main reasons why this approach to philosophizing in education has become urgently needed. The first reason is that Europeans have had to depend heavily on American writers for an educational theory which will make it possible for them to make sense of practical reforms. The applied philosophy of Harry S. Broudy, Joe Burnett, B. O. Smith, Hilda Taba and Ralph Tyler, to mention a few, in the field of curriculum reform is symptomatic of this dependence. Present moves in curriculum change in England today, indeed, remind me of much of the work which was being done in the U.S.A. during the 1930's. Even a superficial analysis of some new English Certificate of Secondary Education syllabuses with some of the proposals put forward by schools engaged in the *Eight Year Study* would justify a more careful comparative investigation of the source of English curriculum theories for the less academically inclined school child.

The changing European curriculum is only one of many institutions which are in process of reform. Under the impact of industrialization, the growth of new aspirations, and the expansion of numbers many educational institutions are undergoing reform. In many cases American prototypes provide the basis of institutional innovation. The organization of the second stage of education, the development of new types of teacher education and the structure of higher education are areas in which the influence of American innovations during the period 1920 to 1950 are being felt, particularly in England. There is no doubt also, for example, that French educationists responsible for the Langevin-Wallon reform proposals immediately after World War Two were influenced by the progressive education movement. Again the interchange of Dewey's ideas with those of English educationists such as Margaret and Rachel McMillan and J. J. Findlay could no doubt be documented. This community of outlook was shared by progressive educators throughout Europe.

What Europeans need today is a new rationale which will enable them to run comprehensive schools, *écoles uniques,* and *einheitschulen.* Unfortunately there is evidence to show that American philosophers of education have not made pragmatism acceptable to many European educationists. In the field of Comparative Education, for example, Friedrich Schneider's constant reference to the inadequacy of Anglo-Saxon pragmatism serves to make the point. The reliance in East European and Soviet literature on the main theories of social change advanced by Marx in seeking to develop comparative studies is somewhat modified now by a willingness to investigate functional relationships in various educational systems in a more pragmatic manner than was the case a few years ago. Russell's reference to Dewey as an apologist of American commercialism is symptomatic of the view taken by many European philosophers of the materialistic philosophy of the U.S.A. Yet, at the same time, there is a tendency to regard all Americans as pragmatists, whether they be followers of recognized spokesmen of the tradition such as Peirce, James or Dewey, or whether they be neo-Thomists existentialists, perennialists or neo-classicists. In other words, Americans are thought to hold to certain assumptions about the nature of knowledge, the characteristics of the desirable society and the qualities of individuality which place them in a particular and in most respects different, category or framework of thought from those which prevail in Europe. Parenthetically European philosophers of education sometimes consider the conceptual analysis by Americans of terms such as "activity," "creativity" and "democracy" as less than adequate.

The second main reason why attention should be given to the creation of a new rationale is because since the Second World War American institutions have been in the process of subtle but radical change. In addition, the conditions under which they have had to operate have changed considerably. Among the important innovations are the programs supported by the 1958 NDEA Act, the 1965 Elementary and Secondary Education Act and the 1966 International Education Act; not to mention those which followed the 1954 Supreme Court ruling on segregated schools. The new wealth of America stands out as one of the very significant new conditions, but perhaps the most important of all is the country's involvement in world affairs. The center of the world stage is occupied by the U.S.A. Its political, economic and cultural policies are followed by most Europeans with the closest attention. Polarization of reaction towards these policies is inevitable. Negative responses can, no doubt, be explained as due to a misunderstanding of America's motives and objectives. At the same time it is possible that concepts appropriate to the welfare society and the new frontier need to be worked out with care. A new theory of internationalism for Americans may well be in process of formulation. The present debates about Vietnam suggest the quest for it has begun. They reflect a more fundamental concern for a system of philosophy which will help Americans to decide what they ought to do—whether to commit themselves more deeply in world affairs or withdraw to a pre-war isolationism; whether to pay more attention to qualities of leadership than to skills of mass participation; whether to promote the gifted or provide massive aid to the underprivileged and disadvantaged.

In goal orientated pluralistic societies analytical philosophy alone cannot provide answers to these and other major questions. Normative studies are needed too. The objective of such studies should be to discover a new, or to reformulate an old, system of philosophy which will serve to provide guidelines for action. Will an up-dated pragmatism suffice for America? Or are any of the traditional or up-dated European philosophies suitable? The search for alternatives among American philosophers of education seems to me to lack important comparative dimensions. At present, due no doubt to the need for survey courses and appropriate textbooks in philosophy of education, it seems to be leading to a confused eclecticism. Idealism, existentialism and materialism have within them several schools of thought. The great European idealist philosophers and their assumptions can be identified, so can the materialists and the more recent existentialists. But it is also necessary to make clear the national characteristics of these philosophies. When speaking of idealism, for example, are we referring to Descartes' system which is now peculiarly French, based as it is on a belief in the ability of individuals to think for themselves and reach certainty through such logical thinking? Or is it an Hegelian form of idealism which has, and does, appeal to the West Germans? Hegelianism postulates absolutes which transcend men but towards the achievement of which men should strive. How different from this form of idealism is the idealism of Englishmen who have been influenced by Locke and Berkeley? And again Marx and Lenin provide an absolutist framework which enables us to make sense of Soviet materialism but which is in many important respects very different from the absolutism of German idealism.

The importance of recognizing that these systems of philosophy are reflected in national systems of education lies in the relationships which exist between theory and practice. While it would certainly be foolish to assert that there is a one to one relationship between ideology and educational policy and practice, nevertheless systems of philosophy do influence the work of teachers and give to it a particular national flavor. Rarely is it possible to criticize educational practice without calling into account some aspects of the theory behind it. To hope that undesirable foreign practices can be avoided in spite of the fact that the theoretical foundations of them are accepted is a dangerous illusion.

Whether traditional systems of philosophy can be so improved as to serve the need of America in the mid-twentieth century and subsequently is doubtful. Yet philosophers of education need a coherent, consistent system of philosophy. Confused eclecticism places them at a technical disadvantage. The practical implications of accepting a consistent form of European idealism, materialism or existentialism may be unacceptable. Finally the search for a non-American alternative may lead to failure on the part of professional colleagues and laymen to appreciate, let alone accept, the philosophizing of academic philosophers.

The international dimension of America's role today probably makes it necessary for philosophers to look seriously at non-Western systems of thought. Buddhism, for example, influences much of what goes on in education in Ceylon. Other forms of Buddhism can be applied to education in Japan. Islam, with its sectarian differences, circumscribes debates about education in many countries. There is need to reveal through philosophical analysis the major differences between these systems and those of Europe and North America. I have pointed out elsewhere that theoretical or rational constructs, based on philosophical forms of inquiry would help comparative educationists to establish bench marks for the comparison of value systems. Such constructs would be complementary to those prepared on the basis of empirical techniques—questionnaires, attitude tests and the like.

In short the comparative dimension of the philosopher of education's work is becoming increasingly important in face of America's world commitment. The assumptions of his own system should be examined carefully and compared with the assumptions of a system of philosophy which may be regarded as representative of a selected foreign country. Unless he adopts a philosophical position from which to use the tools of analysis the analysis itself will be sterile. If the position or cluster of theories he accepts is itself sterile or inappropriate to the conditions of the day then the value of critical analysis will be very strictly limited. The contexts of analysis should therefore be (a) logically consistent within a philosophical system, (b) sociologically appropriate and (c) capable of international-comparative application. For example, what does democracy mean to a French Cartesian? Or to a follower of Condorcet? What does equality mean to a British empiricist or follower of Locke and J. S. Mill? What meaning can be given to the Japanese concept of charisma?

Needed today are philosophers who will break the bonds of technique and move into the field of speculation in search of new answers to philosophical and socio-political questions. The need is as great, if not greater, than that which faced the early pragmatist in the late nineteenth century. Then according to Philip Wiener in *The Evolution of Pragmatism* men such as Chauncy Wright, William James, Oliver Wendell Holmes, John Fiske, George Mead attempted in a rapidly changing world to make sense of the assumptions which were informing their own professional work. One of them found in pragmatism a rationale for law, another for medicine and Dewey attempted to provide one for education. Is a new pragmatism needed? Or are today's problems such that an entirely new set of assumptions are needed if in the future Americans are to have a system of philosophy to which, in face of difficult problems and decisions, they can turn with some confidence for guidance?

Another task is for philosophers of education to build up rational or theoretical constructs of normative patterns, value systems, or acceptable systems of philosophy which can be used to make sense of national systems of education. The arbitrary character of the choices which will have to be made in order to proceed should be recognized. The techniques of analysis are, however, well developed and the possibilities are excellent of establishing constructs useful in comparative education studies.

Given a system of philosophy from which to work, with what kinds of questions should philosophers of education concern themselves? At present two tendencies can be discerned. Some philosophers start from philosophical questions and analyze in great detail the meaning of terms associated with them. Such starting points lead almost inevitably to esoteric discussions designed to improve techniques of analysis. Logical consistency is examined. Distinctions between meanings are drawn. Attention is paid to the characteristics and types of definition. The "meaning of meaning" and the nature of knowledge are proper subjects of inquiry. Such philosophers are the pure physicists of education not the engineers; their work is perhaps less system oriented than the next group of philosophers of education; they are perhaps less committed to education and to the achievement of stated goals and objectives.

Philosophers of education are social engineers insofar as they clarify the aims and goals of educational systems and make explicit the implications of accepted premises. As such many of them believe that the starting points of philosophical analysis should be educational issues, problems and assumptions. Among such exponents two categories of questions have received considerable attention recently. There are first of all classroom or school terms such as learning, teaching, subject disciplines, authority, discipline and its sanctions, the curriculum and so on. The second category of terms relate to the educational system as a whole. In this group, terms such as equality, social disadvantage, selection, organization and structure fall.

Among English philosophers of education there are those who hold that, because the tests of education are intrinsic to it, there is little purpose in going beyond them since education has its own goals and the achievement of them can be judged in educational terms. This form of assessment is based on means-ends relationships. Additional forms of inquiry would evaluate the internal consistency of educational ends. An assessment of the consistency of institutional practices to achieve these ends, though desirable, is hardly a task for the philosopher.

The belief that education can be judged solely in educational terms would, of course, be rejected by most pragmatists and by comparative educationists who follow the lead given to them by Sir Michael Sadler who held as very important tests of an educational system which were intrinsic to it. His view that educational processes could only be understood in the light of the relationships between education and other aspects of society has had a profound effect on comparative educationists. The tests of a good education are in terms of ends-means relationships but the goals are not only internal to education but external to it. Education promotes democracy, political stability, higher standards of living and greater social harmony. Political, economic and social class tests can therefore legitimately be applied to education. To be sure, it is important to make plain the criteria on which these tests are based. Against what criteria can social harmony be measured? What are the constituents of political stability? How can economic standards of living be measured? One task of the philosopher of education would be to examine these indices, make them much more explicit than at present so that the testers may devise empirical instruments which are reliable and valid. Again the comparative dimension of the problem of establishing by philosophical methods instruments to evaluate educational achievement on an international basis should be considered most carefully. Unfortunately these tasks are not always regarded by philosophers as legitimate and psychometrists all too frequently assume that they are unnecessary.

There is a range of problems which appears to be neglected at present by philosophers of education. These are the major socio-economic and political issues of the day. Most of them arise from processes of rapid and asynchronous social change. The assumptions and theories relating to social change need critical examination. Traditional theories abound. Most of them emphasize the lag between technological development and the value system of a pre-industrial society. It is a viewpoint which does not run contrary to the main thesis of this paper. One contention of this paper is, however, that too little attention has been paid to the lag beween political changes and value systems which were appropriate in the age of imperialism. Concepts of leadership, democracy, elitism, governing and non-governing elites and mass education need to be subjected to further logical analysis. In very general terms this has been done. A comparative international dimension has perhaps been lacking. Moreover, perhaps not enough attention has been given to an analysis of logical coherence and consistency (or lack thereof) in national value systems of the post World War Two period. There is need particularly to identify normative inconsistencies and to clarify through philosophy public and professional debates. I think particularly of the debates which took place in England at the close of the war. The issue was planning. Should England's post-war society be subject to total planning, to partial planning or to none at all? The philosophical debate between Mannheim on the one hand—arguing in favor of a democratically planned society— and Hayek and Popper on the other, arguing in favor either of *laisser faire* or a modified process of piecemeal social engineering, had real political significance. It was central to the opposing policies of the Labour and Tory parties. The issue was domestic. The provision of a rationale in terms of which it could be debated at various levels was extremely important. The debate has had considerable implications for philosophy too.

Today many of the most pressing problem for which national solutions are needed have an important international component. Consider for example the issues arising out of technical assistance programs. One of them arises from intercultural conflicts in which in any country three or four competitors are to be found. The indigenous culture faces that brought to it by the technical expert whose cultural assumptions may be in conflict with those of a former colonial power and in competition with those of another contemporary great power. For example, the technical assistant from America may meet in an indigenous culture some elements of a European culture and competition from Soviet advisers. In this situation the teacher or adviser should examine the bases of his own assumptions: compare them with the assumptions which inhere in the indigenous culture, the assumptions of the European system which until recently prevailed and the value system of Soviet experts.

The object of philosophical analysis should be to point out the areas of major disagreement and the possibilities of normative adjustment. Only after careful and critical analysis of terms drawn from politics, education, economics, religion and sociology in comparative perspective should the effectiveness of proposed policies be examined. Anthropologists doubtless are needed to examine the value system of many indigenous cultures but philosophers should, it seems to me, take seriously the task of studying in terms of present political and educational needs the philosophical assumptions of the major world religions, e.g., Buddhism, Hinduism, Islam and the secular traditions, for example, of Confucianism and Shintoism and their derivatives.

Such philosophical investigations, necessary though they are, are not themselves a sufficient basis on which to build educational policy. Investigations based on means-ends and means-outcomes relationships will almost certainly be interdisciplinary and contain important empirical components. It is important to point out that empirical techniques reflect a set of philosophical assumptions just as much as do the techniques of critical philosophical analysis. Failure to grasp this fact helps to explain the defects of several large-scale comparative education studies recently completed. The International Educational Achievement project lacked such a philosophical base, consequently the empirical techniques employed in it, though in themselves carefully examined and modified for comparative use, were often inappropriate.

In conclusion I should like to mention a problem of international significance which in my judgement should concern American philosophers of education as well as empirical investigators. A crucial issue for the U.S.A. in light of its bilateral commitments to involve itself in the defence of territories abroad concerns political stability. To examine the theoretical constituents of political stability would involve the acceptance of a political science theory on the basis of which a number of hypotheses could be given precise meaning. Tests could then be devised which would enable them to be studied empirically.

Of the many theories of government available I suggest by way of example those put forward by V. Pareto in his monumental *Mind and Society*. There he maintained that important to the maintenance of political stability in the balance of *Lions* and *Foxes* is the composition of political and social elites and the provision of opportunities for the circulation of elites. He examined the psychological bases of human and group action and categorized political leaders as either Lions prepared to use force to gain and hold on to power or as Foxes who seek cleverly to persuade and manipulate without resort to force. According to Pareto, there should be a balance in a governing elite. An accumulation of Lions in the non-governing elite or among the masses may lead to revolution against a government unable, because it lacks Lions, to reach firm decisions and stand by them. Too many Lions in a government would make it possible for Foxes among the masses to overthrow by force a manifestly unsuitable government.

Crudely stated in this way such a theory may suggest little scope for careful philosophical analysis. But meaning has, however, to be given to many key terms: "residues," "derivations," "governing elite," "sentiments," "non-governing elite," "stability," "revolution" and so on. Criteria need to be established which will make it possible to use these terms unambiguously in comparative studies. The qualities of mind and disposition associated with Lions and Foxes should be analyzed. This example suggests that to be effective, philosophers of education need to analyze their social and political terms within a stated cultural context or against a known political theory. Unless this is done their discussion of words such as "democracy," "authority," and "permissiveness" will be of little value in comparative and international studies.

Follow-up studies should be empirical. For example, how do national systems of education operate as agencies of selection? How do they pick out future members of the governing elite? Which qualities are important in selection procedures? Those of the Lion or those of the Fox? And after selection what qualities of leadership are inculcated through the educational system? Are the qualities of Lions emphasized or those of the Foxes? What kind of balance is drawn in the educational system? Has France habitually picked out through her educational examination system potential Foxes and encouraged in them the qualities of mind associated with them? To what extent have the English Public schools in the past paid attention both to Lions and Foxes and selected out for political leadership positions both the intellectuals and the rugby players? Or again how far have Americans disregarded in the past the role of the schools as agents of selection of a political elite? What qualities of character and intellect have other agencies of selection emphasized? What in these terms are the implications of the gifted child movement? And the effort made by President Kennedy to draw more intellectuals into government? What implications are there in these terms for education in light of present American debates about Vietnam?

Some evidence from history may throw light on these questions. In the newly independent countries where missionaries shouldered the burden of education until recently it is all too evident that future political leaders were the products of the mission schools. What kind of person was selected by these systems of education? What attitudes and character traits were encouraged among young people who were later to lead their countries to independence? And against this form of selection what was the role of other agencies such as the armed services and the trade unions? Were the seeds of post-independence unrest and revolution sown by systems of education?

What are the consequences of drawing sharp boundaries between the governing and non-governing elites? To what extent does an educational system inhibit the circulation of elites? Are American intellectuals politicians? Are politicians capable of offering cultural leadership? The divorce in the nineteenth and early twentieth century between the German academics and the politicians was doubtless a serious factor in the collapse of effective paraliamentary government before the Second World War.

These hints at possible lines of approach in the study of relationships between education and political stability are intended only to reveal the extent to which comparative studies focused on major and pressing socio-economic and political studies need to be sustained by interdisciplinary studies and among these some of the most important are those that can be pursued by philosophers of education either collectively or as individuals. I hope they will accept such challenges. I feel that Dewey would have recognized the need to internationalize his work and would have responded to the challenge.

Part 2

EDUCATION, HIGHER: COLLEGIATE AND UNIVERSITY

22

The American Teacher: Training and Employment

The American Teacher.—Americans themselves are generally agreed that the weakest point in their system is the teacher. There are 400,000 primary teachers, and of this huge army it is impossible to make any general statement except that in variety it is unexcelled. The contrast that we have observed running all through the American system between the work of the best schools and that of the worst schools will find its natural explanation in the remarkable variations in academic qualifications and professional skill of the American teacher. On the one hand is a teacher who has received a Secondary School training, supplemented by a two, three, or four years' course in the State Normal School; on the other hand is the poor, broken-down relative of a powerful school manager, thrust into the school for the brief period it is annually open, with absolutely no professional or academic qualification whatsoever for the high post of teacher; and these are privates in the same great army.

No one can use stronger words than the American official on the gross way in which the interests of the school and its children are made subservient to personal considerations by unscrupulous school managers. "With all deference to the faithful and conscientious ones, in many instances the school fund is being wantonly and unrighteously wasted. Men and women who have made a failure of their own lives and enterprises are to-day occupying these positions (Directors of Schools)" (State Superintendent of Colorado, *C.R.*,[1] 1896–97, p. 1,283); and Judge Draper writes, "Men engaged in managing the organisations of the different political parties have undertaken to control appointments in the

[1] *C.R. Commissioners Reports,* material found in the annual reports of the U.S. Commissioner of Education, Washington, D.C.

Robert Edward Hughes. "The American Teacher," in *The Making of Citizens: A Study in Comparative Education* (London: The Walter Scott Publishing Company, Ltd., 1902), pp. 150–158.
Author: Educated at Jesus College, Oxford University, 1890–93, BA, M.A., and at London University.

TABLE 1 STATISTICS OF NORMAL SCHOOLS IN THE UNITED STATES
FOR 1897–98[2]

	Public Normal Schools	Private Normal Schools	Total
Number of normal schools	167	178	345
Teachers instructing normal students	1,863	1,008	2,871
Students in teacher's training courses	46,245	21,293	67,538
Male students	12,578	10,597	23,175
Female students	33,667	10,696	44,363
Number of normal graduates	8,188	3,067	11,255
Male graduates	1,543	1,689	3,232
Female graduates	6,645	1,378	8,023
Volumes in libraries	566,684	194,460	761,144
Value of buildings, grounds, apparatus	$19,980,222	$5,047,507	$25,027,729
Value of benefactions received in 1897–98	336,185	240,203	576,388
Total money value of endowment	1,472,865	2,311,594	3,784,459
Appropriated by states, counties, and cities for buildings and improvements in 1897–98	417,866	—	417,866
Appropriated by same for support	2,566,132	19,696	2,585,828
Received from tuition and other fees	514,562	648,459	1,163,021
Received from productive funds	57,648	38,759	96,407
Received from other sources and unclassified	307,409	191,995	499,404
Total income for 1897–98	3,445,751	898,909	4,344,660

interests of their party machines, and the downright scoundrels have infested the school organisation in some places for the sake of plunder." It is this deplorable state of things that is driving democratic America into the arms of the bureaucrat.

Let us now first see what the means are for equipping the American teacher for her work. To fill up the vacancies in an army of 400,000 teachers, annual recruits to the number of 60,000 are required. There

[2] A.E., B. A. Hinsdale, *American Education*, p. 377.

are in the United States 167 public normal schools primarily intended for the training of teachers, and supported either by the State or city. These have 46,245 students, and turn out annually 8000 students who have completed the course. Besides these there are 178 private normal schools with 21,293 students, which supply annually 3000 more completed students. Thus the normal schools under present conditions can supply about one-sixth of the annual demand. It must not be overlooked, however, that it is the *trained* teacher who is most likely to remain in the profession, so that the proportion of trained teachers is certainly greater than would be indicated by the annual supply from the normal schools.

One the other hand, it must be stated that many of these normal schools are such in name only. "The normal school does some of the work of the high school, but mingles with it professional training for teachers. . . . There are schools of this character at New York and Philadelphia.

"At New York the course lasts four years and is much like that of a high school, except for two hours a week given to pedagogy in the third year and three hours in the fourth year, out of which last time is taken for a very little practice in teaching. At Philadelphia all the actual practice that falls to the lot of each student is one single week, and she watches the teaching of another student for a week before that." And Professor Hinsdale thus compares the American with the Prussian normal school:—

While the German schools confine themselves exclusively to training intending teachers, including, to be sure, much academic instruction, American schools generally do a large amount of miscellaneous teaching. To a great extent they parallel the work of the high schools, and to some extent even the elementary schools. In the second place, this wide range of work accounts in part for the much greater size of the American schools. In 1888 only five of the 115 normal schools of Prussia had upwards of a hundred pupils, while one had less than fifty, but several of our State schools count more than a thousand pupils. It must always be borne in mind that a large proportion of these American pupils are in no proper sense normal pupils. In the third place, there is necessarily a great disparity in the size of the respective faculties. An ordinary Prussian normal school requires but nine teachers, including the two in the practice school, while our normal school staffs often number fifty or sixty persons. It is clear, therefore, that we have not yet realised the pure normal school type as Germany, for example, has done. Nor can it be doubted that our schools, as institutions for training teachers, have often suffered greatly from their overgrown numbers and large classes. (Hinsdale, A.E., p. 378)

Of State normal schools New York now possesses 12, Pennsylvania 13; West Virginia, North Carolina, Missouri, and Wisconsin have 7 each.

The New York State normal schools cost the State £105,000 per annum. Of this amount, £6,119 was devoted to the provision of libraries and text-books. The practising schools, kindergarten, primary, inter-mediate, and academic, absorbed £5,704. These schools turn out annually 860 graduates, of whom 714 are women. The cost of each graduate to the State is from £80 to £100.

It is impossible to say what proportion of American teachers have received the benefit of any kind of professional training before beginning to teach.

It is confessed on all hands that the professional efficiency of the American rural teachers is generally very low.[3] Even in the towns and cities not one in four of the teachers has received any kind of training. In many States a majority of the primary school teachers have received no education whatever further than that provided in the primary schools. While the fatal belief of American democracy persists, "that anybody is fit for anything" (J. S. Mill), the necessity of training the teacher will not be popularly recognised. An American head-mistress, when asked whether she believed in the necessity of training for teachers, replied emphatically *no,* and gave an utterly ludicrous reason for the faith in her (Dr. Rice, *The Public School System of the United States,* p. 58). Even in cities like Chicago we are told by Dr. Rice that there are many teachers absolutely destitute of any professional training, and some of them who have never been through even a secondary school course. In Massachusetts, admittedly the first State in educational effi-ciency, 38.5 percent only of all the teachers have passed through a normal school (Hinsdale, *A.E.,* p. 376).

Over half the teachers of the State of Pennsylvania are only provision-ally certificated, and nine thousand of them have received no other education than that provided by the common school. This professional weakness of the American teachers has led to two developments—

1. The appointment of an expert to take charge of the city or county system, whose chief duty it is to train the teacher professionally.
2. The growth of subsidiary means of training by which the teacher

---

[3] "In America," says M. Levasseur, "the masters are as a rule young; they have energy and enthusiasm, but they lack skill and experience; the 'elective' system exposes them to frequent changes, and moreover in the country the school year is very short: all these reasons give rise to the abuse of the Text-book method, and to the idea which teachers and pupils share, that all is done when the text-book has been recited to the last page" (*L. Enseignement primaire* p. 394.)

is able during school vacations, and at other times, to attend special courses and conferences on pedagogical subjects.

The American teacher knows her weakness, and is most ready to learn. "I am convinced," says Mr. Findlay, "that there is in the minds of American teachers a desire to learn about education, a humility with reference to their present knowledge of the subject which contrasts favourably with the attitude of the successful teacher in European countries." (*Report of the Royal Commission on Secondary Education,* "A Report on Certain Features of Secondary Education in the United States of American and in Canada.") And the President of Haverford College, who has made a special study of the English system of schools, is still more pointed:—

Our system has a tremendous and overflowing vitality, which promises more for the future than the well-fitted machinery of England. Did you ever live in a country town during the week of a teachers' institute? It is a greater attraction than the new railroad or the circus. The air is saturated with educational questions. The teachers, often of the same social grade as the best of the residents, are received into the homes and made the central features of the excitement. Better still, have you ever been to a State or national education convention? The discussions do not strike one as being in the least shallow or vaguely general. . . . Thus our country is permeated with educational life. England does not know much of it. Her teachers do not read professional literature, as ours do. They do not communicate popular enthusiasm for education as ours do, although they are often more highly trained—President Sharpless, of Haverford College, on the "Relation of State to Education in England and America" (No. 87, in publications of the American Academy of Political and Social Science).

The school superintendent, like all other American institutions, varies enormously. He is often merely an artful politician, a skilful wirepuller, and absolutely destitute of any educational qualification for his high post. He devotes a small portion of his time to this work, and his main interest in the school is concerned with helping his political friends. But of that type of superintendent we will say nothing more here. We would rather devote our attention to the skilled experts who are generally found at the head of the large city organisations. Too often their tenure of office is as uncertain as that of the teacher, and the wonder is that these distinguished men are content to fill such precarious posts. Many of these higher posts are held by women; thus two State superintendents are women. Out of 836 cities that have superintendents, 18 are occupied by women, who also occupy 256 county superintendentships.

The superintendent is the head of the city administrative machine for education. He generally examines and appoints all teachers, has a considerable voice in the selection of textbooks, and prescribes not only the course of study for the schools, but details the methods to be pursued. The result is that oftentimes the efficiency of a school is estimated by the care and faithfulness with which the superintendent's instructions have been carried out. The results are often admirable, and generally very much better than could be anticipated, were the quality of the staff and their previous professional training alone considered. But in the case of the trained, skilful, and resourceful teacher, so little is left to his own individuality that the system often becomes very galling, and indeed something like tyranny arises.

To supplement the training of the teacher a number of characteristic institutions have arisen in America. Such are the Teachers' Institutes, Summer Schools, and Reading Unions. The Institute may be confined to the teachers of a single city, county, or State, or may be constituted by an amalgamation of two or more of these units. It consists of a series of conferences, lectures, and discussions, in which the chief officials and teachers take part. It may extend from a couple of days to weeks. Attendance is often compulsory. In the State of of New York as many as 106 Institutes were held in one year, and attended by over 16,000 teachers. The total cost was £7000. The Summer School is an attempt to combine the advantages of the normal school and the Teachers' Institute, and is generally held in the normal school during the summer vacation. It is estimated that half the total number of teachers in the United States attend either one or other of these various organisations for subsidiary training.

We have already said something as to the peculiar qualifications of many American teachers, and an obvious question is, How do such people get into the profession at all? It has been already pointed out how the locality controls the school, and how strongly and zealously the local rights are defended.

The appointment of teachers is in the hands of the local managers, whether these be the District School Trustees or the City Council. They alone fix the qualifications of the teacher, as a rule. They also fix the time during which the certificate of qualification is valid.

Hence we get the most extraordinary variety of certificates. This town certificates its teachers for one year, that one for three, and so on. In a few of the more progressive States an attempt has been made to introduce a certificate which shall be valid for the whole State, and for life; but only about one in every thirty teachers, even in New York State, holds such a certificate.

The school managers sometimes fix a very low standard for their teachers. The fact is, they have to cut their coat according to their cloth.

TABLE 2   AVERAGE ANNUAL SALARIES OF TEACHERS AND SUPERVISING
OFFICERS IN CITIES OF OVER 100,000 INHABITANTS

City	Number of Teachers and Super- vising Officers	Paid for Supervising and Teaching	Average Salary
San Francisco, Cal.	1,070	$940,820	$879.27
Denver (District No. 1), Col.	292	243,650	834.42
Washington, D.C.	1,061	801,016	754.96
Chicago, Ill.	5,535	4,937,362	892.03
Indianapolis, Ind.	627	399,928	637.84
Louisville, Ky.	394	408,237	687.27
New Orleans, La.	691	319,000	461.55
Baltimore, Md.	1,855	1,084,109	584.42
Boston, Mass.	1,832	1,952,483	1,065.77
Detroit, Mich.	832	571,813	687.27
Minneapolis, Minn.	782	530,474	678.36
St. Paul, Minn.	572	334,465	584.73
Kansas City, Mo.	508	336,844	663.08
St. Louis, Mo.	1,670	1,013,853	607.09
Omaha, Neb.	394	259,131	657.69
Jersey City, N.J.	582	354,410	608.95
Newark, N.J.	748	518,695	693.44
Buffalo, N.Y.	1,234	793,412	642.96
New York, N.Y.	10,008	8,127,067	812.05
Rochester, N.Y.	765	396,922	518.85
Cincinnati, Ohio	910	790,342	868.51
Cleveland, Ohio	1,234	883,077	715.62
Alleghany, Pa.	393	246,330	626.79
Philadelphia, Pa.	3,471	2,422,820	698.02
Pittsburgh, Pa.	912	641,789	703.72
Providence, R.I.	680	451,833	664.46
Milwaukee, Wis.	862	581,037	674.06

(*C.R.*, 1898–99, p. 1,477.)

The pay of the average American teacher is very low. For men it totals up to £109 per annum, and for women £93 per annum; that is, were the monthly pay continued throughout the year. The average monthly pay is highest on the Pacific Slope, namely, for men, £11.72; for women, £10.18; and lowest in the South Atlantic States, where it is for men, £6.22; for women, £6.29.

In a city like Chicago, where a working man receives on an average two dollars a day, men and women teachers in primary schools begin with £80 for the first year, and ultimately reach a maximum of £155. . . . The so-called School Cadets—pupil teachers in fact, whose employment was a necessity in years past in Prussia—also receive three shillings a day for their work, which they perform under the supervision and guidance of a regular teacher. (Prof. Waetzoldt, C.R., 1892–93, p. 567.)

In Massachusetts, which employs 989 males and 10,244 females, the average salary of the males, who are generally principals, is £28 per month, and of the women £10 per month.

It is to be remembered, too, that deductions from salary are made for absences from school,[4] and that as a rule no pensions are awarded to the American teacher.

The proportion of the sexes in the army of American teachers was in 1897–98—

Male	—	—	—	—	131,750
Female	—	—	—	—	277,443

For previous years the numbers were:

	1870–71	1879–80	1889–90
Male	90,293	122,795	125,525
Female	129,932	163,798	238,397

The average professional life of the American teacher is said to be about five years; of the country teacher, only about two years. In Minnesota, in 1892, out of 6,560 teachers:

937 had been in the same post for more than 3 years;
397 had been in the same post for more than 2 years;
641 had been in the same post for more than 1 year;

and the remainder were all new appointments. Indeed, it has been said that there is no profession of teaching in America. Teaching is simply used as a means to some higher end—marriage in the case of women, and some other professional career in the case of men. The American teacher seems to lack the sense of professional unity. There are no purely teachers' associations in America as there are in France, England, Ger-

[4] In the city of New York the *fractions of salary fortfeited by teachers or other school employees*, owing to absence from duty, together with 1 percent of all the salaries, which is retained for the purpose, are sufficient to create a fund for the retirement of old or incapacitated teachers, which fund has assumed considerable proportions—about $65,000.

many, Holland, and Belgium. This is a great loss. Until professional unity has been developed, it will be impossible to retain the best minds as teachers. At present the American teacher is entirely in the hands of the superintendent, and will remain so until the professional instinct has led to co-operation and self-help. It is a professional corps of teachers that is America's great need, and no army of expert officials will ever fill this gap.

23

Intellectual Changes

The Outlook has asked me to set down on paper some of the changes in the United States which have struck me on revisiting that country. Thirty-four years have passed since I first saw it, and twenty-one years since I spent in it a time long enough to form impressions. The invitation interests me, for much has happened in the period over which I can now look back. Yet it is with diffidence that I comply with the request, because the older a man grows the more does he feel the difficulty of discerning and interpreting social phenomena, and because every time an observer visits America he finds many more phenomena to study than he had found before. My friends, however, say that if it is worth while to discover and point out the changes that are passing on a country, this is most easily done by the visitor who comes at long intervals. As one who has been away from home for some years notices on his return changes of which the members of his family are scarcely conscious, as he sees that the slender youth has filled out into a man, and that the dark locks of thirty have begun to silver at fifty, so he who comes back to any country after a long absence is struck by novel aspects of things which the home-stayer, living continuously among them, has scarcely observed, because the process of change has been slow and unobtrusive.

Accordingly, I shall try to enumerate sundry differences between the United States of 1905 and the United States of 1870 or 1883. About some of them I may be mistaken. Some, again, may be superficial or transient, and yet they may deserve to be remarked, because one may thus be led to think of the underlying influences that are at work. All the changes of which I am about to speak have come gradually and naturally. In retrospect, one can see that they are such as might have been expected to come, though most of them were not in fact predicted.

James Bryce. "America Revisited—Changes of a Quarter Century," *The Outlook* (March 25, 1905), pp. 733, 736–738, 740.

Author (1838–1922): Lawyer, university professor, parliamentarian, and author; Regius Professor of Civil Law, Oxford, 1870–1893; entered Parliament for Aberdeen, 1880; in 1905 appointed Irish Secretary; educated at the Glasgow High School, University of Glasgow, Trinity College, Oxford, and Heidelberg; Ambassador to the United States, 1907–1913.

One exception, indeed, there is. One new and large fact has appeared which nobody looked for, a fact due partly to a sort of contagion spreading from Europe, partly to an unpredictable series of historical accidents (if anything in history is an accident). Of this new fact more hereafter. The other changes seem due to causes which were already at work forty years ago. They have moved on broad and well-marked lines. Most of them show a relation to one another which makes them appear part of the same great movement. Some—and these are of peculiar interest— show that America is being more and more drawn into the general current of the world's movement, not always, perhaps, to her advantage. . . .

All the changes I have been enumerating tend to make men occupy themselves more than ever with their work and with material interests in general. It is true that they have more money, and some of them more leisure. Hours of labor are shortening, as they have shortened, and more generally, in Australia. But as labor is more intense while it lasts, leisure is necessarily given chiefly to amusement. Such conditions may seem unfavorable to intellectual progress. But here comes in another remarkable change, which casts a new light upon the landscape and fundamentally affects our estimate of the prospect that lies before the nation.

There has been within these last thirty-five years a development of the higher education in the United States perhaps without a parallel in the world. Previously the Eastern States had but a very few universities whose best teachers were on a level with the teachers in the universities of Western Europe. There were a great many institutions bearing the name of universities over the Northern and Middle States and the West, and a smaller number in the South, but they gave an instruction which, though in some places (and especially in New England) it was sound and thorough as far as it went, was really the instruction rather of a secondary school than of a university in the proper sense. In the West and South the teaching, often ambitious when it figured in the program, was apt to be superficial and flimsy, giving the appearance without the solid reality of knowledge. The scientific side was generally even weaker than the literary. These universities and colleges had their value, for their very existence was a recognition of the need for an education above that which the school is intended to supply. I ventured even then to hazard the opinion that the reformers who wished to extinguish the bulk of them or to turn them into schools, reserving the degree-granting power to a selected few only, were mistaken, because improvement and development might be expected. But I did not expect that the development would come so fast and go so far. No doubt there are still a great many whose standard of teaching and examination is that of a school, not of a true university. But there are also many which have risen to the European level, and many others which are moving rapidly towards it. Roughly speaking—for it is impossible to speak with exactness—America now has not less than fifteen or perhaps even twenty seats of learning fit to be ranked beside the universities of Germany, France, and England as respects the completeness of the instruction which they provide and the thoroughness at which they aim. Only a few have a professorial staff containing names equal to those which adorn the faculties of Berlin and Leipzig and Vienna, of Oxford, Cambridge, Edinburgh, and Glasgow. Men of brilliant gifts are scarce in all countries, and in America there has hardly been time to produce a supply equal to the immense demand for the highest instruction which has lately shown itself. It is the advance in the standard aimed at, and in the efforts to attain that standard, that is so remarkable. Even more noticeable is the amplitude of the provision now made for the study of the natural sciences and of those arts in which science is applied to practical ends. In this respect the United States has gone ahead of Great Britain, aided no doubt by the greater pecuniary resources which not a few of her universities possess, and which they owe to the wise liberality of private benefactors. In England nothing is so hard as to get money from private persons for any educational purpose. Mr. Carnegie's splendid gift to the universities of Scotland stands almost alone. In America nothing is so easy. There is, indeed, no better indication of the prosperity of the country and of its intelligence than the annual record of the endowments bestowed on the universities by successful businessmen, some of whom have never themselves had more than a common school education. Only in one respect does that poverty which Europe has long associated with learning reappear in America. The salaries of presidents and professors remain low as compared with the average income of persons in the same rank, and as compared with the cost of living. That so many men of an energy and ability sufficient to win success and wealth in a business career do nevertheless devote themselves to a career of teaching and research is a remarkable evidence of the intellectual zeal which pervades the people.[1]

The improvement in the range and quality of university teaching is a change scarcely more remarkable than the increased afflux of students. It seems (for I have not worked the matter out in figures, as I am giving impressions and not statistics) to have grown much faster than

---

[1] Many subjects are taught to large classes at the best Eastern universities for the study of which hardly any students can be secured in England.

population has grown, and to betoken an increased desire among parents and young men to obtain a complete intellectual equipment for life. The number of undergraduates at Harvard is much larger than is the number who resort to Oxford; the number at Yale is larger than the number at Cambridge (England). Five leading universities of the Eastern States—Harvard, Yale, Columbia, Princeton, Pennsylvania—count as many students as do all the universities of England (omitting in both cases those who attend evening classes only), although there are twice as many universities in England now as there were forty years ago, and although the English students have much more than doubled in number. And whereas in England the vast majority go to prepare themselves for some profession—law, journalism, medicine, engineering, or the ministry of the Established Church—there is in America a considerable proportion (in one institution I heard it reckoned at a third or more) who intend to choose a business career, such as manufacturing, or banking, or commerce, or railroading. In England nearly every youth belonging to the middle and upper class who takes to business goes into a commercial office or workshop not later than seventeen. In the United States, if he graduates at a university, he continues his liberal education till he is twenty-one or twenty-two. This practical people do not deem these three years lost time. They believe that the young man is all the more likely to succeed in business if he goes into it with a mind widely and thoroughly trained. To say that the proportion of college graduates to the whole population is larger in America than in any European country would not mean much, because graduation from a good many of the colleges means very little. But if we take only those colleges which approach or equal the West European standard, I think the proportion will be as high as it is in Germany or Switzerland or Scotland and higher than it is in England.

This feature of recent American development has an important bearing on the national life. It is a counterpoise to the passion, growing always more intense, for material progress, to the eagerness to seize every chance, to save every moment, to get the most out of every enterprise. It tends to diffuse a taste for scientific and literary knowledge among a class to most of whom, in other countries, few opportunities have been opened for acquiring such a taste. It adds to the number of those who may find some occasion in their business life for turning a knowledge of natural science to practical account, and so benefiting the country as well as themselves. Nor is its social influence to be overlooked. One is frequently impressed in America by the attachment of the graduates to the place of their education, by their interest in its fortunes, by their willingness to respond when it asks them for money. In the great cities there are always university clubs, and in some cities these clubs have become centers for social and political action for good public ends. Not infrequently they take the lead in municipal reform movements.

When I pass from the places set apart for the cultivation of letters and learning to the general state of letters and learning in the community, it is much more difficult to formulate any positive impressions. One feels a change in the spirit of the books produced, and a change in the taste of the reading public, but one cannot say exactly in what the alteration consists, nor how it has come, nor whether it will last. Having no sufficient materials for a theory on the subject, I can venture only on a few scattered remarks. Literary criticism, formerly at a low ebb, seems to have sensibly improved, whereas is England many people doubt if it is as acute, as judicious, and as delicate as it was in the 'sixties. The love of poetry and the love of art are more widely diffused in America than ever before; one finds, for instance, a far greater number of good pictures in private houses than could have been seen thirty years ago, and the building up of public art galleries has occupied much of the thought and skill of leading citizens as well as required the expenditure of vast sums. Great ardor is shown in the investigation of dry subjects, such as questions of local history. The interest taken in constitutional topics and economic questions, indeed in everything that belongs to the sphere of political science, is as great as it is in Germany or France, and greater than in Britain. This interest is, indeed, confined to one class, which chiefly consists of university teachers, but it is a new and noteworthy phenomenon. Few people thought or wrote on these matters thirty years ago.

On the other hand, it is said, and that by some who have the best special opportunities for knowing, that serious books, i.e. books other than fiction and the lighter form of *belles lettres,* find no larger sale now, when readers are more numerous and richer, than they did in the 'seventies. No one can fail to observe the increasing number and popularity of the magazines, and it seems likely that they are now more read, in proportion to books, than they used to be. The same thing is happening in England. It is a natural consequence of the low prices at which, owing to the vast market, magazines containing good matter and abundant illustrations can be sold. It may also be due to that sense of hurry, which makes the ordinary American little disposed to sit down to work his way through a book. Both these factors are more potent in the United States than they were ever before, or than they are in Europe.

If in America as well as in England the growth of population has not been accompanied by a growing demand for books (other than fiction), let us remember and allow for the results of another change which has passed upon both countries. It is a change which is all the more noticeable in America because it is there quite recent. It is the passion for looking on at and reading about athletic sports. The love of playing and watching games which require strength and skill is as old as mankind, and needs no explanation. So the desire not to play but to look on at chariot races and gladiatorial combats was a passion among the people of Rome for many centuries. The circus factions at Constantinople have their place in history, and a bad place it is. But this taste is in America a thing almost of yesterday. It has now grown to vast proportions. It occupies the minds not only of the youth at the universities, but also of their parents and of the general public. Baseball matches and football matches excite an interest greater than any other public events except the Presidential election, and that comes only once in four years. The curse of betting, which dogs football as well as horse racing in England, seems to be less prevalent in America; nor do the cities support professional football clubs like those which exist in the towns of northern England and even of Scotland. But the interest in one of the great contests, such as those which draw 40,000 spectators to the great 'Stadium' recently erected at Cambridge, Massachusetts, appears to pervade nearly all classes much more than does any 'sporting event' in Great Britain. The American love of excitement and love of competition has seized upon these games, but the fashion, like that of playing golf and that of playing bridge, seems to have come from England. It is a curious instance of the more intimate social relations between the two countries that speak the same language that fashions of this kind pass so quickly from the one to the other, and do not pass from either to Continental Europe. There has been no development of the devotion to athletic sports in Germany or in France coincident with that which is so marked a feature of modern England and so novel a feature in America.

No subject fixes the attention of social philosophers in Europe who seek for light from the New World more than does the problem of divorce. The states of the union have tried many experiments, and some rash experiments, in this field. The results, momentous for America, may be instructive for the rest of mankind, and are being watched with curiosity by European sociologists. Mr. Gladstone was so profoundly interested in the matter that whenever conversation turned upon the United States he began to inquire about the divorce laws and their working. Such information as I could gather does not enable me to say whether the position is substantially different from what it was twenty years ago, when the legislation which so many observers regret had, in most states, come into operation. There does, however, seem to be a growing reaction against the laxity of procedure in divorce suits, as well as against the freedom granted by the states which have gone farthest; and though little is heard of the proposal that Congress should receive power to pass a general divorce law for the whole country, the suggestion that efforts should be made to induce the states to introduce greater uniformity, and to make the procedure for obtaining divorce less liable to abuse finds increasing favor. It is encouraging to note a stronger sense, among thinking men, of the evils which laxity tends to produce.

Serious as these evils are, the general moral standard of the United States still appears to me, as it did twenty years ago, to be, on the whole, higher than that of Western Europe. (The differences between France, Germany, and England are not so great as is commonly supposed.) Even in the wealthiest class, where luxury weakens the sense of duty, and lays men and women most open to temptation, there are apparently fewer scandals than the same class shows elsewhere. Nor is the morality of any country to be measured by the number of divorces. Its condition may be really worse if people cynically abstain from obtaining divorces where there are grounds for obtaining them. Although there is more wealth in America than in England, luxury is less diffused, and that idle and self-indulgent class which sets a bad example to other classes is relatively smaller.

Among minor changes which the traveler notes, he must not forget the growth of what may be called aesthetic sentiment. The desire to have beauty around one, to adorn the house within and the grounds without, if not new, has developed apace since 1870. In one respect it is much more active in the United States than in most parts of Europe. We have in England, so far as I know, none of those Village Improvement Societies, which have arisen in some of the Northern States, and especially in New England. Neither has any English city surrounded itself with such a superb ring of parks and open spaces, some hilly and rocky, some covered with wood, some studded with lakes, as Boston now possesses. America used to be pointed at by European censors as a country where utility was everything and beauty nothing. No one could make such a reproach now. One melancholy exception may, however, be referred to. Niagara has lost much of the charm that surrounded it in 1870. Hideous buildings line the banks of the rivers below the falls, almost as far down as the railway bridge. The air is full of smoke. Goat Island has, indeed, been preserved; the Canadians have laid out a park just below the Horseshoe Fall; and the volume of the green flood that rushes over the precipice has not been visibly diminished by all that is now abstracted to work the great turbines. But the wildness of nature and the clear purity of the sky have departed. It is a loss to the whole world, for the world has no other Niagara.

The sentiment which seeks to adorn cities and improve the amenity of villages is near of kin to the sentiment which cherishes the scenes of historical events and the places associated with eminent men. Here, too, one feels in the United States the breath of a new spirit. Reverence for the past and a desire to maintain every sort of connection with it has now become a strong and growing force among educated people. A slight but significant illustration of the changed attitude may be found in the disposition to expect university and (in some places) judicial officials to wear on formal occasions an official dress. Thirty years ago no such dress was worn by any functionary in the United States except the judges of the Supreme Court sitting at Washington.

I must pass over many other points in which new facts, disclosing new tendencies, present themselves to the observer's eye. One among them is the attitude of the churches towards one another, and the wider channels in which religious opinion now flows. Another is the position of women, with the remarkable growth of women's clubs and societies. People who seemed to be impartial told me that this had not brought women any more into politics, as a similar change has done in England. They said, indeed, that the woman suffrage movement, which at one time seemed to be rapidly advancing, had of late years experienced a check. But I am far from trying to reckon up all or even most of the changes of thirty-five years. Sensible of the difficulty of conveying to my younger readers an idea of the impression that America made on European travelers just after the war, still more sensible of the still greater difficulty of conveying the impression which America, now far faster and more complex, makes on the traveler today. I attempt no more than to indicate some of the more obvious differences between those days and the present . . . .

Perhaps I have been overbold in venturing, after a brief visit, to record so many impressions, hastily formed, upon large questions. But I am encouraged by the kindness wherewith the comments on American affairs, which I made sixteen years ago, have been received. And it is hard to resist the temptation to express one's admiration for the richness and variety of the forms in which civilization has developed itself in America, for the inexhaustible inventiveness and tireless energy of the people, for the growing passion for knowledge, the growing desire to diffuse happiness and enlightenment through every part of the community.

24

English Students in American Universities

The recently-formed Association for the International Interchange of Students has declared itself prepared to provide all information required by those who are attracted by the idea of an academic *Wander-Jahr*. But the regulations and requirements are so entirely different on the two sides of the Atlantic, that the personal experiences of a student who had to undertake the arrangement of her own American degree course without previous assistance may possibly be of some interest, and even of use, to those students who contemplate a similar enterprise.

A student familiar with the regulations and life of the Scottish and the younger English Universities would find the transition to an American "Campus" less striking than one from Oxford or Cambridge, but probably even then there would be difference enough in the general environment to render him grateful for any chance scraps of information which might help him to adapt himself to it. If it is becoming easier year by year to get information in this country as to the respective opportunities and advantages offered by the bewildering number of American Colleges, it is still somewhat difficult to get really comprehensive and unbiassed advice. This is not entirely the fault of the advisers. There are so many things to be taken into account, and the personal element counts for so much on the Faculties, that conditions change very quickly, and past experience, even of comparatively recent date, may be quite misleading, and, moreover, the intending student should be quite clear as to the special object of his *Wander-Jahr*.

In order to get experience which shall be distinctively American, it is almost necessary to look beyond Harvard and Yale to the great State Universities, or to such institutions as Leland Stanford or Chicago. In

---

A. Georgette Bowden-Smith. "English Students in American Universities," in *An English Student's Wander-Year in America* (London: Edward Arnold, 1910), pp. 1–21.

Author (1873–   ): Educated at Cambridge University and Cornell University (M.A. 1908). After teaching in England she went to China in 1921 and taught at various schools including Pei Hud School, West City, Peking, until her retirement in 1960 to the Russian Orthodox Mission, Peking.

Columbia may be seen a most interesting development of the City University, though it must not be forgotten that New York City has also a College of more recent date and still more democratic tendencies than the old foundation of colonial days. At the University of Virginia he may study the effects of degree requirements so high that only the barest minimum percentage of students succeed in graduating. At Oberlin or Brown he may share the refreshing freedom and irresponsibility of the smaller Institution to which young men and women come from outlying farm-homes, rather to "see life" than to devote themselves to more serious academic pursuits. At Minneapolis or Madison he may admire the crowning efforts of a whole community determined to secure the fullest benefits of the highest education for the greatest number, and will inevitably envy the lavish and splendid generosity which has secured the finest Campus on the Mississippi shore, and has housed the Library between the lakes of Wisconsin in marble halls. At Cornell he may watch the diversified activities of a foundation that certainly does its best to make good the boast of its founder: "I would found an institution where any person may find instruction in any subject."

There is something very attractive and inspiring in a College life in which the students turn to such varied schools as those of History and Analytical Chemistry, Classics and Electrical Engineering, Philosophy and Agriculture, and where the advanced degrees may be taken either in Arts or Philosophy, Civil Engineering or Veterinary Science. In any case, the student who desires to enlarge his circle of thought by a year in the United States will not be thinking entirely, perhaps not even mainly, of such advance in his own special subject as he might have gained in his own University. Rather, he will welcome the intercourse with fellow-students whose circumstances and point of view differ most widely from his own, and he will seek a more intimate acquaintance with American institutions and methods than can possibly be gathered from any course of reading, however thorough. Meantime, he will no doubt wish so to plan his *Wander-Jahr* that it affords reasonable facilities for profitable work along some definite line, and here no doubt the Association will give most valuable assistance.

At present, the entrance and degree requirements of American and English Universities are so different that it is not altogether easy for a student to pass satisfactorily from one to the other. It must be frankly admitted that it is far easier for an English student to pass for a year to an American College than *vice versa*. It is true that an American can take an English University year and count its "credit" towards his own degree, but the computation is an exceedingly delicate one. The unit of degree credit in the States is the actual hour spent in the classroom or laboratory, with the proviso that in certain subjects two hours of lecture or seminar count as one point in the final reckoning. In spite of this equalizing safeguard, some lectures are eagerly sought after as "snap-courses," whilst others have the academically unenviable distinction of being "regular cinches"—i.e., of enabling the wary student to make the maximum amount of credit with the minimum output of energy. A student must "carry" a certain number of hours per semester, and he may not overstep a maximum in order to graduate. It can easily be imagined that an American passing to Oxford, and having to certify to his "Dean" that he was "carrying" the required number of lectures, would be quite likely to find himself overburdened with reading. Nor do American Colleges permit such intense specialization, even in the senior year, as is required for any Cambridge Tripos.

Should an American wish to spend an additional year abroad, he is, of course, far more attracted to Germany than to the older English Universities, while the younger have hardly as yet made their reputations. On the Continent a man can take his Ph.D., and have competent and sympathetic direction in research. This will no doubt be the case in a few years in Manchester and Birmingham, and even London, but, except in certain lines, the research student—unless so advanced that he only needs the facilities of laboratory and library—does not get in England the advice and encouragement which are the characteristic notes of the graduate departments of an American University.

The comparative expense of an English academic year is much greater. A stranger has not the same chance of a Scholarship or Fellowship as a foreigner has in the fierce competition of the transatlantic Colleges for promising students, and he has to return after his year abroad with "nothing to show for it"—a serious drawback in a community which has formed "the degree habit." A stranger may, too, in the absence of any regular organization of the student life, drop out of sight. A new-comer may be classed with other new-comers, and a graduate student from the other side will be apt to resent this. In an American College all "Classes"—i.e., each "Year"—is most thoroughly organized, and remains a decidedly self-contained unit. The graduate candidates for advanced degrees are also organized, and enjoy many privileges, and constitute the élite of the "Campus." From the American side one hears complaints that Rhodes' scholars have in some cases failed to enter into the ordinary student life round them. Experience in both English and American Colleges leads to the suspicion that absence of class organization may in many cases be answerable. It must be most difficult for a student passing from an organized College life, in which each individual has his special status, to take kindly to the purely fortuitous constitution of a society in which there are no bonds save those of personal relationships.

If, on the contrary, an English student wishes to pass to the United States, and take a fourth year for it, the way is delightfully open. The American Colleges spread their nets abroad in all waters, and bait them well with Fellowships. In the academic world there is no Monroe doctrine of exclusion. No University in the States cares where its Fellows come from, but looks to it sharply that they are such as shall do it honour. In the Universities there is no room for the cry "America for the Americans." The number of foreign Fellows is not more striking than that of foreign-born Professors and Presidents. The many Canadians holding high University positions is specially significant. It is true that Canadian mothers still impress upon their sons and daughters that no temptations must draw them south of the line of the St. Lawrence, but year by year, the very ablest and most energetic are being beckoned by the wider spheres and higher emoluments across the boundary-line. It is one of the many indications of the extreme artificiality of that line—a fact to which the average Englishman insists on shutting his eyes.

If the English student goes to the States as a Fellow, his course will be mapped out for him, he will find a most hospitable welcome, and if only moderately tactful he will fit into his new environment with very little difficulty. He will find his Professors most anxious to assist him in every way, and he will marvel at the amount of time and thought they are prepared to give him. There can be little doubt that the advantages of a year's research in America are greater than those of a fourth year in England, even leaving out of account the enlarging and enlightening effects of transatlantic experience. Even in the case of a Fellow, however, it is advisable for the English student to bring some personal recommendations from his old University, and to have some reference there known to a member of the new. The very different implications of the degree course on either side sometimes render it necessary to have some outside statement as to capacity and attainment.

This is, of course, far more necessary in the rather exceptional cases in which an English student does not wish to specialize in his own field, but to take work in another. Although technically the courses at Oxford and Cambridge are "undergraduate," they correspond in actual demands to the more specialized work of the junior and senior years of an American College, and even—though without the necessary original "thesis"—to that for the A.M. or second degree. If the new Association for International Interchange of Students could do something to establish some sort of equivalence between the English and American standards of academic "credit," it would be of great advantage to both sides. A student who has only examination results to show may be landed in serious difficulties by the "accrediting" system, by which pupils from schools stamped by University approval and under University inspection matriculate without any examination for College entrance.

It takes a stranger a little time to find out how regulations—in older communities rigid as the laws of Medes and Persians—in newer lands yield to pressure if that be applied at the right moment and in the right way. On the contrary, it is a little disheartening to discover that a "class" which cost much hard work to secure, and ranked at home fairly high, represents nothing worth having abroad, and that a testimonial—so kind that its possessor is somewhat shy of presenting it—is tossed back with the comment, "*That* won't do you much good!" Patience and perseverance, however, will untie the knots of most American red-tape.

After many rather trying interviews, one student was admitted to graduate work in Philosophy on quite inadequate and irregular grounds, partly because one kind-hearted Professor said she "looked intelligent," and partly because she asked whether, if the disgrace of failure fell on herself, and not on the Philosophical Department, she "mightn't at least have a shot at the A.M."; but she nevertheless found, at the end of the first semester, that she was allowed to work exactly as she pleased. The case was further complicated by very ancient and poor school work. The much-harassed Dean of the Graduate Department, with his office thronged with waiting aspirants for advanced degrees, must have regretted that he had not checked proceedings at an earlier stage. Modern languages were easily provided for, but classical requirements were more troublesome. The Dean asked, "What did you do at school?" and the English student could only answer, "I can now do so-and-so," which didn't advance matters a bit.

"How much Latin did you read at school?"

"Very little, but"—with the courage of despair—"I could deal easily with any Latin charters for my historical work."

The Dean shook his head.

"Have you read Cæsar at school?"

"No; I only read what I wanted in illustration of my work the last two years."

"How many books of Virgil did you read at school?"

"Two, I think"—here the student had a sudden inspiration, and added: "But I read all the others for my own amusement afterwards," hoping that would at least imply a certain amount of intellectual effort.

The Dean shrugged his shoulders hopelessly, and wearily dismissed the unfortunate applicant to the Philosophical Department.

This student was lucky in that she had selected a College specially founded "as an institution where any person can find instruction in any subject." She found she was not the only student who had tried to shelter under its broad principle. In the early days of Cornell—so the story goes—a teamster in a Western State came to offer his services to the University, and upon being asked what he wished to study, he replied that he wished to learn to read. Upon being told that the public school was the place for that, he was very indignant, and quoted Mr. Cornell's words: "I would found an institution where any person can find instruction in any study."[1] The teamster does not appear to have succeeded in entering for his degree on that application. The English student was more fortunate, and has often had reason to bless the memory of Ezra Cornell.

The actual arrangements for registration are very businesslike and easily made. A few yards of duplicate cards, perforated at intervals and bristling with printed directions, are served out to all students, and after stating all the relevant personal information demanded—or as much as can be truthfully given—the various cards are torn off, handed in for the stamp of the various departments, and, after the fees have been paid, the final approval of the Registrar: whose authority is supreme, whose methods are autocratic, whose ways are beyond the highest research, who has been known to threaten a student with expulsion for having in his possession an extra card, sent out by his own office by mistake—or perhaps for looking at him "in that tone of voice"— and who has a song all about himself at the Senior Singing in the last week of the academic year, which is an honour shared by none of the Deans, not even by the President himself. It is never without a tremor that the student approaches the Office, not even on Commencement, when there is still one last chance that the Registrar may not have seen fit to provide the actual sheepskin, for which the newly-made Bachelor or Master exchanges the dummy roll he has received at the hands of the President.

The expense of a College year in the States, even with the return passage, and including a fair amount of travelling, is extraordinarily moderate. The Fellowships do not as a rule cover board entirely, unless the student is content to live very roughly. The tuition fee at Cornell is only $75 (£15 12s. 6d.). Board can be had from $150 (£31 5s.) a year. There are graduation fees, and the various "Class" and "Club" dues mount up expenses a little, but extras are on the whole insignificant. In most of the Eastern Colleges the fees are "a good bit" higher. In the West, again, they are lower, and the State Universities tend to be

[1] A. D. White, *My Reminiscences of Ezra Cornell*, p. 21.

almost entirely free to their own citizens. The student who wishes to live economically will be more comfortable in a "Dormitory" or "Hall of Residence," and under University management, than in a private boardinghouse. The system of sharing rooms is, however, almost universal, at any rate in the poorer Colleges, and intending students ought to get someone on the spot to make early arrangements, or they may not get very satisfactory quarters—according to English ideas.

The actual necessities of life are well cared for, and the food provided is usually excellent in quality, and well served. At most Colleges there is a well-equipped student hospital, where non-infectious patients are taken at small cost. Every student, whether "Frosch" or Graduate, is medically examined on entering. As a rule, gymnastics, and in Colleges holding the Morrill land-grant military drill for the men, is compulsory. Those who are pronounced unfit by the doctor are placed on a special régime of exercise, and have to report themselves from time to time to the medical officer. No one likes to be stamped as a "Physical Wreck," and both men and women do all they can to get registered as fit for the gymnasium, and the general standard of health is said to rise during the College years. The student has to fill up a very searching form at the first test, with columns for details as to family diseases and previous physical record. It must be admitted that there is nothing to prevent perfunctory dealing with this medical *questionnaire*, and that the double-rooming system renders it almost impossible to deal satisfactorily with any infectious complaint. Still, the care for the physical welfare of the students contrasts most favourably with English *laissez-faire* in this most important respect.

The English student will probably have some difficulty in getting used to new methods of work. The hours are long: eight o'clock sees the busy stream of students separating on the Campus to fill the various lecture-halls and laboratories. During the Summer School it is not unheard of for a lecturer to put on an extra class at 7:30 A.M. For an hour at 12:30 or 1 the Campus is almost deserted, but even before the clock has struck, the busy stream is flowing back again, or the sergeants are mustering the men for drill. The laboratories empty again at 6, but there are evening Seminars, and the Research Students are busy with their experiments, and the University Library is usually full till the closing gong sounds at 10 or 10:30. As is the day, so is the semester. The short English Term seems a thing to laugh at when a Mid-West University, Purdue, works steadily from Christmas to June without a break. However, the long hours do lend themselves to a somewhat easy pace. Excellent as the lectures are in matter and style, they cover extraordinarily little ground sometimes, and there is not that sense of fierce drive during working hours that marks the British Honours Schools. It must always be remembered that the real "honours" work is done in America only at the graduate stage, and it is therefore most undesirable for a foreign student to register in undergraduate courses.

At the same time, no English student should omit "visiting" some of the undergraduate lectures. They are not only models in method, but afford the very best illustration of American determination to bring the highest culture within not only the reach, but the grasp, of all. This is specially striking in the Philosophical Department. Psychology is one of the alternatives "required" in many places for the first degree, and is, of course, treated from the experimental standpoint. Readers of American Pedagogy, Ethics, or Æsthetics, or even of American literature generally, must be struck by the preference for the psychological aspect and treatment of a subject, and by the conspicuous absence of that slipshod, vague, quasi-psychological terminology which is unfortunately characteristic of a certain type of English work. The Head of one American Psychological Department has worked out a most excellent introductory course. The lectures, chiefly of the nature of demonstrations—in working through the "Senses" and "Affection"—lay a firm foundation for future work. The first lecture lays stress on the fact that psychology is one of the natural sciences, and that to study psychology is to learn to psychologize—not to absorb a certain number of facts ascertained by the observations of others. As a rule, pupils in High Schools have already been introduced to the subject, but, nevertheless, it is deeply interesting to watch a crowded audience following the lectures with real enthusiasm and comprehension. The thorough grasp of the perceptive processes which results is in itself an excellent mental discipline, while it also enables students to deal with any psychological literature, and to prosecute the study of the more complex problems of the science with a saving hold on fundamental data. The Demonstration lectures are followed by a unique undergraduate Laboratory course, in which students work through the elements of the science by direct experiment. Those who intend to specialize in the subject attend further courses on Systematic, Comparative, and Abnormal Psychology: they read the History of the Science, and are assigned some original problem.

Similarly we may hear a "recitation" in Metaphysics, when perhaps an idealistic scheme of the universe will be gradually catechized into an apparently raw lad, which may be a revelation of Socratic success in drawing out unsuspected depths of thought in most unlikely quarters.

There is, of course, another side to the question. It may often appear to an onlooker that all the work is being done by the teacher. It is the elementary system sublimated to University level. It must be remembered that the American College has no desire to cater only for the intellectual élite. There can be no "democratizing" of the highest education without the conscious and deliberate use of the best pedagogical method, and this intention does throw the heavier burden on the teacher.

The American College is quite aware of the dangers inherent in the "Lecture system." There are too many students to make it possible to have much written work, and papers are corrected by "junior instructors"—a process not too far removed from the "monitorial" supervision of Bell and Lancaster. It is especially in the Arts courses that the difficulty is most apparent. President Schurman, of Cornell, says:

> The course in Arts is believed to be easier than the course in engineering, or medicine, or law. This disparagement is probably well founded. Art students have not a definite goal before them like students in the professional and technical courses, and lazy students take advantage of the elective system, which is peculiar to the course in Arts. The evil may not be a serious one, and the character of the student population of Cornell and the all-pervading spirit of hard work are sufficient to correct defects in any College, once the Faculty is aware of their existence and determined on their elimination. Perhaps the Professors and instructors can improve their methods of teaching, making the work more interesting, stimulating, and vital. Perhaps they can get into closer personal touch with their students. It is indispensable that somehow, in the class-room or out of it, they give the students individual attention and training. Nor should undergraduates be given opportunities to shirk their regular work. It is little less than pathetic to read in the Harvard Report (and the implied criticism is not more deserved by the Harvard Faculty than by others) that "students themselves express the opinion that the instructor or assistants should, by means of frequent 'quizzes,' or conferences, keep them in their work, and enable them to read with greater understanding."[2]

The "quizz" consists of a fairly long string of questions to be answered in class, and represents little but memory work. The same is true of the periodical "tests," in which, should a student gain a certain percentage of marks, he is exempt from any final examination. The questions are always so marked that 100 percent is possible. Good students expect to make over 90 percent, and it is not unusual for one who gets under that number to interview the Professor and demand the raising of the marks. When the marks are handed round—it is not etiquette to announce them publicly—the Professor will sometimes add: "If anyone thinks their marks too low, I shall be glad to talk the matter over with them." To a stranger this seems to open the way for rather undesirable elements, and, indeed, the tide of opinion is not setting strongly against "exempts." Of course, the strain of work is enormously lessened by not

[2] *President's Report, 1906–7.*

having to prepare for a final examination. In some courses "tests" may even be given fortnightly, and it must have been possible for some students to cram for these, and relieve their minds to such good purpose that the final mental residuum was not very great. On the other hand, in all work in which further advance implies and involves what has gone before, this mental discharge at short intervals may be defended from more than one point of view. Both the "quizz" and the "test," however, are apt to be irritating to students accustomed to work steadily along their own lines and on their own plans towards a final issue, which is really the most complete mastery of their subject of which they are capable.

If in certain respects the American student takes his work somewhat easily, the labours of the Professors are enormous. The vacations are very short, and most men take additional work in the Summer Schools. Nearly all are engaged in literary production, and all are most generous in putting themselves at the disposal of their students. Superficially, an English student is inclined to feel at first that there is a certain aloofness in the attitude of the lecturers to their classes. The English lecturer seems rather a guide, walking some way ahead, indeed, but still on the same road. The American takes the position of the man on the platform in the middle of a maze, authoritatively directing the movements of those wandering below. This attitude is, however, merely a matter of the classroom, and in his own office the patience and generosity with which a Professor will meet the most elementary difficulties are really wonderful. In the absence of any tutorial system, the professorial office hours are an enormous boon to the student. The graduate, above all, will never fail to meet with the utmost consideration and kindness, and the most insignificant individual will be able to profit to the full by that stimulation and encouragement in his work which can come to most students only through intercourse with those who are themselves original investigators.

It is just in this touch of original work that the English student will find American experience most inspiring. It is possible to ridicule the minute points raised by some of the "theses" for the second degree, and to criticize the literary form of some of the University publications, but the list of degree subjects on any Commencement programme represents a very respectable amount of patient investigation, and does, moreover, imply the firm conviction that the true aim of the student is not to absorb, but to achieve some new advance in the frontier of human knowledge. The student finds, too, that the University deliberately aims at leading all to this position.

"Let us frankly recognize," says the President of Cornell, "that freshmen have just come from the High Schools, where their training has consisted almost exclusively of drill in languages and mathematics, and of memory work in history and in English. The ideal, therefore, should be that the first year of freshman work should only slightly depart from the methods of the preparatory school, but yet should introduce the student into the larger atmosphere of the University, and successively each year in College should depart a little farther from the more elementary methods of teaching, and should gradually lead the students up to the work of the senior year, which would in large measure consist of investigation and elaboration under the direction of teachers, and in association with graduate students as fellow-workers."[3]

It is believed to be only through a strong graduate department that a University becomes a place "in which the spirit of inquiry is in vigorous activity, and controls the intellectual life of the community." Through the corporate work of the "Seminar," which tends to take the form of more or less original research, the graduate enjoys the inspiration of intellectual comradeship in fresh adventure. The atmosphere of the graduate school is regarded as highly beneficial to the Professors themselves.

The almost universal confession of Professors is that if it were not for graduate work, they would fall into ruts in their undergraduate classes. The Professor needs contact with more mature minds than those of the undergraduate; he needs the stimulus of necessity to keep abreast of the literature of his subject; he needs the free criticism and discussion of his statements which he can get only from graduate students. The teacher of graduates cannot presume to speak *ex cathedra;* he is a coworker with his students in the discovery of truth. It is in the graduate department pre-eminently that the teacher can walk naturally in the footsteps of Socrates.

A Professor thus engaged in investigation cannot fail to be a better teacher of undergraduates than one who is not so equipped. He may, indeed, not be so good a drill-master, but he will give to his students a better understanding of the *spirit* of his science, and of the direction in which it is advancing. He makes it possible for the undergraduate to feel the inspiration and zest of an individual search after truth, and to learn the methods by which advances in knowledge are effected. Nor does it matter that the specific knowledge which may be the subject of his graduate work differs from that which he communicates in his undergraduate classes; it is the *spirit* which he gains by these investigations that counts.

Thus for its effect upon the teacher alone the seminary of research has an importance far out of proportion to the small number of students who may be taking work in it. It compels the teacher to go forward. It surrounds

[3] *President's Reports, 1906–7.*, "Reaction of Graduate Work on the Other Work of the University," p. 58.

him constantly with competent critics. It forces him to submit his work to the judgment of keen minds. When we cease to grow ourselves, when we lose interest in new ideas, we at the same time become incapable of arousing enthusiasm in students, and we seem to lose our insight into the manner in which ideas are communicated to, or developed in, them. As long as one is doing serious work in his own department, no matter how humble in character, he is not likely to be the slave of formulas or to become a pendant; but the moment he relaxes, the process of crystallization begins. The only hope for such a man is to get at work once more, and do something on his own account. In the great majority of cases, the result is not important for the learned world; but it is highly important for the man's own intellectual life, and for his power of teaching. So long as the graduate student is with us, the Professor cannot safely cease to be a student himself. The ordinary man tends to become unproductive when limited solely to undergraduate teaching. The stimulus afforded by sharing in the productive work of a graduate department affords to most teachers the necessary conditions for keeping intellectually alive. And the so-called fine teacher of undergraduates who is not interested in scholarship and does not keep alive in his subject is nowadays a natural object of suspicion. Where there is no enthusiasm for ideas on the part of the teacher, there will be no response on the part of the student.

Furthermore, the intimate personal relation into which a teacher is brought with his graduate students, his constant contact with the fresh ideas of young investigators, prevents him from growing stereotyped and rigid in his views. This intellectual old age is more to be dreaded by the teacher than physical infirmities. Now, Dr. Osler has recently admitted that it is possible to escape the intellectual death which old age tends to bring by 'running with the boys'—by keeping one's mind young and fresh through intimate association and intellectual companionship with the vigorous and daring thoughts of younger scholars. It is the graduate work, and the graduate work alone, which supplies the conditions for this intercourse.[4]

Through membership of the Graduate Club, the students will be brought into a certain amount of social intercourse with all those engaged in the research work of the University, and will learn to appreciate something of what is being done in fields other than their own, and to admire that fine determination of American students which drives them back to a University to work for an advanced degree, taking their place contentedly beside far younger people, "in the seat of the unlearned," after years of independent work in the world beyond the "Campus."

The English student will also be impressed by the resolute overstepping of limitations. Even below the graduate school an American University expects its students to deal with books in the original. There

---

[4] *Op. cit.*, p. 55 *et seq.*

are even special courses for the training and practice in rapid reading of German, or Latin, or Greek, and the former is naturally part of the indispensable equipment of the research student. In most branches he will find himself called upon to wade through any number of German *Jahr-Bücher* and dissertations, and he may regret that he is not occasionally called upon to read an English article, if not from patriotic motives, at least for the sake of variety. He may begin to believe that the Arctic Circle is not the only sphere in which British discovery lags behind.

Meantime, both on and off the Campus, the student will find his *Wander-Jahr* rich in fresh experience in unlooked-for directions and in new friendships. Though the lines of English and American development have diverged widely enough during the last three hundred years, and though misunderstanding arises easily enough between them, the common bond of language and literature, and the common heritage which Old England bequeathed to the New, make friendships possible between the two races as between no other. One has, of course, friends of other nations and other tongues, but in whole tracts of life they are separated from one. With one's American friends one is not conscious of any such break in completeness of fellowship. The memories of friendly hands and hospitable homes that the English student brings back with him are not those of an altogether foreign land or of an alien community; they differ only in degree, and not in kind, from those he would gather in Canada or Australia, and will be the most precious gifts of the American University to the English student.

25

University Government and
Administration: Australian Aspects

The present system of University government in the United States has the great merit of making the Universities conspicuous among the institutions which legislators and wealthy persons should endow; of providing the readiest means whereby to inform both types of benefactor how academic financial needs should be met; of keeping rich or influential men active both in University management and among possible benefactors or before legislatures; of securing financial advice from experts; of giving the widest public scope to the talents of some academic personage of distinction, chosen as President worthily and expertly to represent the University before the world, and of setting him apart to think sedulously about the systematic development of the University, upon the understanding that he shall be responsible, above all others, for its right administration.

I believe such merits to be quite real, in American conditions. Despite frequent gibes at "tainted money," or "the cent that is clapped on each gallon of oil after the millions have been given," or the fears that "they are cornering our education, like everything else," the American people sincerely admires generous gifts to Universities. The money is there, and not unlawfully obtained. It represents material success, national as well as personal. Its purely personal use is despised. Its hoarding is abominated. Its employment in some ideally-motived way is held to be very honourable. To found or endow a University is the form of social distinction that has not only the most outspoken but also the most heartfelt and most enduring approval of Americans. The cause of the higher learning has everyone's support, so far as it is understood.

E. R. Holme. "University Government and Administration," in *The American University. An Australian View* (Sydney: Angus and Robertson, Ltd., 1920), pp. 29–51. Reprinted by kind permission of the publishers, Angus and Robertson, Sydney, New South Wales, Australia.

Author (1871–1952): Educated at The King's School Parramatta, University of Sydney, B.A, 1891, and at the Universities of Paris and Berlin; Assistant Master of the Sydney Church of England Grammar School, 1891–1894; Lecturer in English, University of Sydney, 1894–1908; Assistant Professor, 1908; and McCaughey Professor of English language, 1921–1941.

That is the greatest American idealism which has any fixed form. In a play which I saw in New York the hero, who was sorely tempted to fail in his patriotic duty during the war, was straightened partly by the reminder that his grandfather had founded a University. The vast audience knew then that the ideal, selfless, patriotic motive must triumph—as it duly did—in the young American. Such an appeal to common sentiment would probably be unintelligible or ridiculous outside America.

The men who can afford to dream of themselves putting such ideals into practice may have to satisfy their ambition by making minor gifts and by serving on University governing bodies. In the course of their work as University "Trustees" or "Regents" they often subscribe to make up, among members of the governing body itself, deficits they have risked to maintain or expand the work of their University. They collect large sums by personal application to others of their class or to those richer still. One such man told me how he had raised $1,500,000 for his small University in this way. What he gave himself in addition I did not like to ask. But, as he was rich, the amount was probably large.

In the State Universities the obtaining of gifts is more than ever the President's task. Yet the principle that other members of governing bodies must get as well as spend money for their Universities is valid in the support of all Universities, States as well as Endowed. One President of a State University recently received a private benefaction of about $1,000,000 for the benefit of women-students. He reminded the giver that there were men-students also, and is presently to receive as much for them. The Governing Body of a State University may not be able to draw on the wealth of its individual members to any great extent. But it represents the fixed idealism in the people of the United States, and can thus secure very large legislative endowments. A State's honourable position among its fellow-States is generally felt to depend upon the scope and efficiency of its University. Public opinion is continually being led in this direction by the authorized spokesman of the University—the President.

The title "President" is almost universal. But "Provost" or even "Chancellor" may be used instead. It represents a universal system, and an academic type of which Australia has no experience. In theory—and in practice, subject to rare exceptions—the occupant of the office is as eminent for scholarship as for executive ability, and fitted for leadership as much by the largeness of his mind as by the strength of his character. No other gift or grace could be amiss in him; but his faculty of self-expression in words must be strong, because he is to embody somehow in his own person all that the University ought to stand for in public consciousness. Once dedicated to this high duty, he is to live in and for the University as a whole; and he may exercise a practically supreme authority over all whom it contains. In some of the best Universities, both State and Endowed, he is fully a member of the governing body, but in all cases he attends its deliberations. He may take part in the teaching of the University, but very often is solely occupied in its general control, inspiration and representation. Ideally, he should combine the qualities of the administrative and the educational expert with those of the statesman and leader of men.

Considering the rare balance of qualities which such an office demands, it is remarkable how many great Presidents there already are in American academic history, and what fine combinations of head, heart and practical abilities an observer of the greater American Universities will remark in the men now attempting to realize in their practice the American ideal. It is probable that the wonderfully large and original development of the American University system has owed much of its possibility to the American form of academic government, which has grown up very independently of British or other European precedents. It may be that that form will have to continue because it still best suits American conditions. The University of Virginia, not very long ago, found reason for adopting it after experience of another that lasted for the better part of a century. But, in recent years, it has been fiercely attacked in the United States itself. There is almost revolutionary zeal against the Presidency through much of the American academic body. "Presidency," said one of the best of Presidents, "is an example now of opprobrium without power." There are times when one feels that an office in which some good men do not appear happy and against which so very much is now being alleged—both on principal and as regards practice—cannot be far off some important modification of its character.

Here again a right judgment, for a foreigner, depends upon knowledge of history. The term "President" has become the commonest in the United States to indicate, in a dignified way, any delegated but revocable supreme authority. It stands for a national idea of organization for business efficiency. This has passed on into the Universities, which have suffered the influence of modern competitive methods in business. So far as such methods are practised, an American University President may be essential to academic management. But in a wider view, President Eliot wrote:

> Common experience during the last fifty years teaches with certainty that the efficiency of any corporation—financial, manufacturing or commercial— depends on its having one responsible head. . . . A university cannot be an exception to this rule for securing efficiency.

Against that business analogy, with its autocratic bias and its confusion of unlike organizations for unlike purposes, much of the academic world in America is now in revolt. Yet all other forms of University government have disappeared before this one in the United States.

The original of the modern University President was the first "College President," who began by being a copy of an Oxford or Cambridge College head and then became, very largely, a secondary school Headmaster after the English Public School kind. This the University President still essentially remains. He alone of all the masters sits with the governing body in its deliberations; he settles the educational policy of the whole institution after consultation, such as he may think profitable, with his assistants; he engages and dismisses the staff (subject, of course, to confirmation by the governing body); he is paid a good deal more than any other member of the staff; he gets the credit for the institution's success and, ultimately, must pay with his position for its failure; in the meantime he *is* the institution, to the outside world, as neither governing body nor any other man or body of men can be. A really great and good man of some quite rare type can, on these terms, do valuable work and make his whole institution happy. But even in Public Schools with the English tradition, under the best of Headmasters, the assistant-master pays in loss of prestige, and stinting of salary, for the pre-eminence of the Headmaster upon whose favour he depends so largely, and in whose shadow he is too much obscured. And the Headmaster occasionally comes to sad ruin—which might have been avoided if he had been called less to regard himself as the one pillar of his world.

Something similar occurs with the American University President and the American University Professor; but, the scale being larger and the system more diversely tried, the results may be more serious. American University history is strewn with wrecks of Presidents whom their burden broke. A successful one has written: "The biography of American College Presidents has, on the whole, been a history of burdened hearts, often breaking." I was told that the average life of a President, as such, is but eight years, though it is a satiric saying among University men that, whatever virtues a President may possess, resignation is not among them. Some of the best-esteemed University professors of to-day cannot be induced to take Presidencies.

But the wrecks of presidential careers are accompanied by others that are professorial. A President mostly has the power, if he has the will, to remove a professor whom he does not like, or whom his governing body thinks to have objectionable opinions—or, even, whom students, parents, benefactors, or public demand as their victim. To what extent cases of unjust dismissal occur cannot be safely estimated. To what extent dismissals are unjust will depend on the principles of tenure concerned. A President, for example, has been known to maintain that for every professorship there should be an initial competition, and thereafter a continuous competition; so that, if the President sees a man whom he thinks able to fill it better than its present occupant, he may decide the competition again in favour of the outside competitor. For one cause and another, an Association of American University Professors has been formed. It investigates and publishes the facts about all cases of dismissal, and is generally regarded as exercising a good influence.

But, however the situation is modified by good Presidents, good governing bodies, good University traditions and outside influences, it is not good in itself: the very idea of a University is obscured and may be falsified by it. The heart of a University is its teachers and their students. Between them takes place all that the University does for the increase of knowledge in the world, and for its diffusion among long-trained and otherwise qualified learners. The teachers are the leaders in all the work of search, evaluation and exposition. They must bear the whole responsibility of this kind. Much more, too, is inevitably added. Upon them depends, greatly, the conduct of students, the organization of studies, the selection of apparatus and other equipment, the formation of the whole higher teaching profession, much of the recruiting of their own body—most, indeed, of what is vital to the good name and development of the University. Even in America, a very large share in University administration must be taken by the professors, though the American system allows them to avoid it more than does the British. University teachers cannot be reduced to the status of employees of an administration without losing, to a great extent, the sense of their responsibility for the University itself. A University is not a business concern employing certain experts, called professors, like a public company or (as the Americans term it) a corporation. University government is not, in principle, that of a Board of Directors and a Manager or Managing Director—or, in American phrase, a President. The false analogy with business has done much harm among Universities. Modern America, with a kind of national passion for "big business," has a University system in which it has prevailed to an unusually dangerous extent. But it is well known among British Universities. A writer in the Educational Supplement of *The Times,* for April 4, 1911, discussing "Modern Universities and their Government," dealt very ably with this aspect of his subject, as seen from the strictly English point of view:

The directorial view of University government is not only a novel view, it is also highly misleading. For there is no real analogy between the board of directors of a trading company and the governing body of a University.

Since the trading company exists for the sake of the financial interest of the shareholders, which the directors represent, and not for the sake of the scientific interests which the company's experts represent, it is natural and right that the board should have the determining voice. But a University does exist primarily for the sake of the interests which the experts represent— namely, the cultivation and the diffusion of knowledge; it does not exist primarily for the sake of the interests which the Council represents—namely, the economical administration of public and trust funds. In the one case the experts exist for the sake of finance, and in the other the finance exists for the sake of the experts.

From the British (including the Australian) point of view, the American University presidential system is historically interesting, and perhaps warranted by its results, in American conditions; but is otherwise to be condemned as improper for a University, because its principles are those of autocracy (though its practice need not be and often is not), and its effect mostly is to set one learned and thoughtful man an impossible task while exempting nearly all the others on the staff (which ought to contain none but such men) from any comparable responsibility.

I know that these generalizations need to be qualified in many ways as regards particular institutions; and that the American professor has, by custom of the best Universities, a position of more security and more academic authority than is legally his. But he has not—and he cannot have, though he want it ever so badly—the same security, and the same authority, and the same power to take part in University government, as he would possess under the British University tradition. To that tradition the American University Presidency is now alien. So far as it is educational, it belongs rather to the tradition of the secondary school, where one directive mind can cover, more or less, the whole field of studies, and where an autocratic method carries less danger of hindrance to learning. The rest of it is, in great part, derived from the cult of business efficiency.

The Vice-Chancellorship in Great Britain is always very different from an American Presidency, and does not always mean the same thing in any two institutions. In Scotland, the Vice-Chancellor is merely the deputy for the Chancellor. For convenience sake, the Vice-Chancellorship may be combined with the "Principalship"—the real chief executive office. The term "Provost" may be used instead of "Principal," as at Trinity College, Dublin. Queen's University, Belfast, has a President—but he is called "Vice-Chancellor" too. London University has a "Principal" as well as a "Vice-Chancellor," and, though the two offices might be combined in the Scottish manner, they are not, and the executive function resides in the "Principal." At Oxford and Cambridge heads of colleges become "Vice-Chancellor" in rotation. There has been talk of making some radical change as, even, by appointing someone permanently to that office—which is rather a burden on the college head and perhaps needs more consistently effective exercise than it can have under the present system. It is not capable of being used for any sort of domination.

A man of autocratic temper might dominate and act the Headmaster for a while in a Scottish Principalship—possibly even in a modern English University Vice-Chancellorship. But he would raise such opposition among the rest of the staff that in the long run he would be forced out. He could not force others out, except by irritating them into resignation. The British University Head is but *primus inter pares* as regards the professional staff or most of the teaching body. He has one sort of effective share in the government of the University, and the staff has another. Their co-operation is practically compulsory; and domination by him is practically impossible. So jealously is any presumption on his part regarded, that complaints are to be heard against the present business committee of the Universities Bureau of the British Empire (a Committee of Vice-Chancellors and Principals) because it contains no representatives of teaching staffs as such.

The British system, therefore, has no office at all identical with that of the American President; and it is, for its own conditions, clearly the better for that. It does not risk the lapse of the University's head into the position of an executive clothed with the delegated powers of the governing body, and insensibly attracted to the attitude of the employer.

But British University Government is of diverse types, and always different from the American. The only comparable English kind is that generally exemplified by the provincial Universities of England. It is complicated and clumsy, but the English people understand how to make that kind of machine work, though an American would have less patience with it. The English writer already quoted gives its full analysis, which I follow. The supreme authority "nominally resides in a very large body known as the Court, or Court of Governors," usually including "all large benefactors and representatives from very numerous public bodies," and its possible "hundreds of members" are "necessarily ignorant of the matter they theoretically control." Hence its proceedings are only formal. "The real governing authority rests in every case with a smaller body known as the Council," composed partly of certain representatives of the Teaching Staff, and perhaps also of some endowing public body, but mainly elected by the Court. The election is only nominal, and "normally means" that the elected members are "annually nominated by the Council itself or by the few leading spirits who draw up the list of names to be submitted to the Court." So this effective governing Council is largely "a self-electing or self-renewing body."

Below the Council comes the Senate, consisting of all the professors of the University. It is the chief academic authority. The Guild or Convocation of graduates has no real power. There are "certain orders of academic business reserved for the initiation of Senate and not to be dealt with by Council except on the recommendation of Senate." But the ultimate effective control rests with Council. Such a system of government "can be defended only on the assumption that the lay Council will always recognize the limits of its own knowledge." Everything depends on the relations of the Council and Senate, whose links are the Vice-Chancellor and the professorial representatives on the Council.

The American Endowed University is governed by what may generally be classified as a "Board of Trustees"; the State University by a "Board of Regents." The method at once suggests, but wrongly, the British Council. The "Board of Trustees" used generally to be a close corporation: its members sat for life, or until resignation, and it perpetuated itself by co-opting the new members it required. But the general practice is changing to that of election by the graduates for vacancies as they occur. The "Board of Regents" has *ex officio* members—e.g., the State Governor—and other members who may be appointed by the Governor, or elected by the Legislature, or elected by the people like other legislators, or like judges. But the professors have traditionally no representation on these "Boards," except through the President, who always attends them. The theory is that the President is the link between the "Faculty" (in the sense of teaching-staff) and the Board. This he might be, if he were elected by the teaching-staff, responsible to it and removable by it. But he is not. Indeed, he is responsible to none but the Board. The Board is generally large and quite miscellaneous. Its members may live widely scattered. Frequent general meetings may be impossible. An executive committee only will enable it to attend regularly and often to urgent business. So long as the President holds its confidence and favour, he practically can exercise, if he will, almost all the absolute powers which it possesses. A wise man does not do this; and often to do it is practically impossible, because certain schools (such as Medicine and Engineering and Law) are entwined with powerful professions, and have asserted a kind of autonomy. But the inevitable result is to bind the President far closer to the Board than to the staff, and to give the University too much the feeling of being ruled monarchically by the delegate of a rather remote and absolute authority.

Sometimes the effect produced is expressed by the American metaphor of the "department store" ("a department store President" or "a department store University"). In any case the tendency of the system, to separate President from Teaching Staff and prevent their full and equal co-operation, is regrettable. So the most respected President of Cornell University, Dr. J. G. Schurman, has declared "The only ultimately satisfactory solution of the problem of the government of American Universities is the concession to the professoriate of representation in the board of trustees or regents"; and he shaped the policy of his own University in this direction. The representation has been granted.

The defects of the American system are historical. Harvard's first governing body was "a large group of the leading persons in the little colony" and the President. Its effective government now is a Corporation consisting of the President, Treasurer, and five Fellows elected for life. Vacancies are filled by co-optation approved by the Board of Overseers, which now represents the original governing body. It consists of thirty members, with the President and Treasurer. The members are elected by the graduates, and hold office for six years. A traditional Harvard jest is that they "overlook things and their actions are oversights." The Board is too large and too infrequent in its meetings to exercise detailed control. But it has a certain reviewing power, and it could force the retirement of a bad President. This bicameral system has worked sufficiently well, judged by results.

The Harvard model has been largely used in America. Yet it is not typical. Yale, which followed it closely at first, has developed a different form and one outwardly much more democratic. But the general tendency has been towards reduction of the size of governing bodies, or restriction of the active management to a small executive committee; again, towards diminution of the official and political elements, and towards the election by graduates of at least a part of the membership— in some cases even the whole. The example of Cornell has created a new tendency to associate the teaching staff also with the general control. Many local and temporary devices for giving the staff some informal but effective voice with Trustees or Regents are being invented and tried. But the old bad tradition of its exclusion from the supreme authority is not yet broken. Hence the American University professor cannot sufficiently feel himself a free citizen of a republic of learning— which a University ought to be—but has too much reason to believe himself regarded as the servant of a lay oligarchy whose expert representative is, or can be at any moment, an autocrat. The modern English system, despite its gross defect of excluding graduates from all share in University government, and its risky conventional balance of power between Senate and Council, is far preferable—at least for Universities of the British tradition.

The Australian University has known members of governing bodies who tried to defeat the object of the more liberal Australian constitutions by demanding that professors be treated merely as employees. But their effort to import the American principle, now widely condemned in America, happily failed. It will surely not be made again. The example of America cries loudly against it.

The American presidential system, in a University of any size, demands a considerable force of administrative assistants for the President. This, together with the American love of system in business and the American esteem for the work of the organizer and administrator, has produced a whole academic army of administration, and has altered the character of certain traditional academic offices. For example, there are Deans of Faculties who once were professors, and may still keep a more or less uncertain hold on teaching, but who are mainly sub-presidents of large academic departments. One of them will be acting-President if the President is away. All of them will be very busy in administration. They will be paid more than professors—sometimes a good deal more. If successful, they have a certain chance of becoming Presidents somewhere. Then there are Deans of Women and Deans of Men—to look after the morals and manners and habits and plans of students. There are Deans of Extension and Sub-Deans and Junior Deans, and Student Advisers, and Secretaries of Faculties, and Registrars, and Business Managers and Comptrollers; Directors of Physical Culture, Recorders, and many more. In comparison of all this the primitive Australian administration seems like some relic out of prehistoric times.

Perhaps there is too much administrative machinery in America. Certainly some of it appears over-valued. To pay a professional Dean more than a Professor is to weaken the vital principle that teaching and the increase of knowledge are what a University exists for. To tempt good scholars out of professorships into administrative work, by means of apparently higher positions and actually higher salary, is surely bad policy. American academic critics are right when they claim that all Deans should be elected by the teaching staff, and not merely appointed on the nomination of the President, as is now the case. And at least some of the work done in supervision of undergraduates is again part of the secondary school operations of the American University—a burden that might well be avoided, if it could be; a burden, anyhow, that the Australian University does not assume.

The typical American system of University government is open to vital objections from the Australian point of view, and could be adopted in Australia only as a largely undemocratic and wholly foreign method, forcibly imposed upon the comparatively democratic British method which we inherited in the ordinary course of our history, and have developed freely to suit our own conditions. The addition of a Presidency of the American type to the machinery of an Australian University might be the cause of temporary progress, even in the learning and teaching values of the University. The "Committee System," on which Australian Universities are still being managed, has its own grave disadvantages. In particular, it limits initiative. Busy men on a governing body of a more or less miscellaneous character and of unwieldy size, snatching an hour or two once a month or so in which to consider the affairs of the University, cannot safely initiate much, or be other than rather abstracted and spasmodic in their thought for the University. Members of Professorial Boards and Faculties look at University development with great interest so far as it concerns their own or collateral departments, but have a somewhat suspicious reserve as regards the claims of other departments. The professorial representatives on the governing body are necessarily often drawn from among those who teach utilitarian subjects, so that pure scholarship and science run great risk of insufficient regard and support, such as a good President would know they must have. At any time a committee of professors, or of University teachers generally, is very keen and critical in its discussion of new ideas but slow and tentative in applying them. Where rapid decision and action produce the best results, an American President may easily surpass, in effective enterprise, an Australian professorial or other academic committee. Yet I am quite satisfied that the American Presidency ought not to be imported into any Australian University, however unsatisfactory the system now in operation.

As for the British (or, more specifically, English) Vice-Chancellorship, it is an office of much value, not dangerous to academic freedom, not in the least foreign to Australian University tradition or method, and already promisingly (although too tentatively) approximated in two of our Universities. There is no need to copy either the name or the schedule of duties of an English Vice-Chancellor. The thing to achieve is the separation of a qualified officer of the University from all routine work, in order that he may think far more disinterestedly and comprehensively for the University than any departmental Head can do; also, in order that he may be free to study it in the detail of its parts and in the relations of its parts to one another; again, in order that he may have time and opportunity to read the now very extensive literature of University development, to visit other Universities and compare them with his own, and to become familiar with the ideas of every leader in scholarship and science and administration that the Universities of Australia contain; finally, in order that the governing-body of his University may be assured that its chief executive officer is what I may term a scholar of comparative University systematization as well as an expert in its own system, able valuably to supplement the skilled counsel of the professorial representatives.

Such an officer would be the properly authorized representative of the governing body in the business relations of the University, and in those of a social or ceremonial kind which did not require the personal attention of the Chancellor or his deputy. The University would thus be more continuously and effectively represented, as an institution of innumerable relationships, both public and private, than it can be now by any Chancellor or Dean or Professor for whom such representation cannot be a duty of first obligation. I have found it of the utmost advantage to go straight to the President in an American University, or to the Principal, or Vice-Chancellor, or Provost, or President in a British University. There, in one person, I found the mind of the University, at least in some of its essentials; the lore of the University, in far greater sum than I could have collected from many departmental sources; and the general authority which, whatever its deficiency in detail, was greater than resided in any other paid officer of the University. I felt that, if I had been an intending benefactor of one of the Universities, I should have been just as glad of the existence of this kind of University head as I was when I had for my only object to learn a great deal in short time and accurately.

The creation of Australian offices of this kind should be considered. The term "Principal" is not appropriate except under the special Scottish tradition. At London, it is part of an academic constitution unfit for imitation almost anywhere. Birmingham gives the only applicable precedent for its use, outside Scotland. The term "Provost" (pronounced as English, not French) is traditionally suitable. "Warden" and "Rector" are too ecclesiastical for Australian conditions. The term "Warden" has also been applied in some Australian Universities to the presiding officer of certain graduate bodies. Outside the Universities it is used to designate the magistrate of a Mining Court, and the heads of certain religious or philanthropic institutions. "President" is too American and misleading. Undoubtedly, the best course would be so to alter existing Australian academic nomenclature as to substitute "Deputy-Chancellor" for "Vice-Chancellor" in its present uses, and release the term "Vice-Chancellor" for employment in a manner that accords with English University tradition. Our Universities, like the modern English Universities, owe a great deal to the Scottish model, but they are just as much historically a part of the modern English University growth as Manchester or Liverpool or Sheffield, all of which have Vice-Chancellors of a kind which is essentially the kind we need. If we use the regular English term, we shall be better understood in all the British Isles. At the present time our administration is supposed to be even more primitive than it really is. From this point of view the University of Western Australia, with its useful administrative office of Vice-Chancellor, appears to English University men, better (or, at least, more normally) organized than any other Australian University.

Any such Australian "Vice-Chancellorship" ought perhaps to be definitely limited in status so that it may rank on an equality with, and not higher than, an elective Faculty Deanship or Chairmanship of the Professorial Board. The salary, or perhaps the salary with allowances (for hospitality and other such duty), should be higher by, at least, fifty percent than is normally paid for a professorship—on the declared ground that the Vice-Chancellorship should be financially the more onerous position. In Australia the best way for a governing body to appoint a Vice-Chancellor would probably be on the nomination of the Faculties, voting together not as bodies but as individuals. Like a Dean and a Chairman of the Professional Board, the Vice-Chancellor might be subject to re-election or replacement from time to time. The new office should neither carry with it the Registrarship nor cause any loss of range or status in that.

The American system of Deanships has some attraction from the Australian point of view. The Australian Dean is democratically elected by his Faculty, and is charged with its representation in various ways. He adds this work to his regular duty as professor. It is often very burdensome. To be a good Dean, a professor may have for the time being to sacrifice his ambition as a scholar or man of science. Permanent Deanship has been connived at for some such reason and with some such result. Overwork among Deans of large Faculties is the rule, especially since curricula have extended, options have become numerous, and the Dean has been compelled to act largely as an adviser of students upon the courses they should take. Yet the Australian Deanship is an honorary office. Its occupant gets only his salary as professor. Australian practice could be improved by utilizing American precedents. The Dean should always be elected by the Faculty, as now. But in a large Faculty he might be given either an honorarium or the assistance of a Junior Dean—or, at least, the assistance of a secretary. In some special case it might be desirable to release a professor from teaching-work so that he might act as Dean and director of his department, on his normal salary; and provision should be made to render this possible. No harm can come from an administrative Dean so long as he is elected by his colleagues, for a limited term, and does not cease to be a professor.

There is no such thing in an American University as a Dean without a secretary, stenographer and typist; though sometimes one person combines the three functions. It is doubtful whether any Australian Dean has such necessary assistance, except at his own expense. My impression is that in no respect is the Australian University system more undeveloped than in the lack of sufficient clerical assistance for its officers engaged in any kind (even the honorary kind) of administration. The loss of time and waste of labour at present endured would nowhere be tolerated under the more businesslike American University system.

There are student "advisers" now, in name as well as in fact, in practically all Universities except those of Australia. It appears to me that some Australian Universities require them, if only in the form of an occasional "Junior Dean." Their principal function should be to advise upon curricula; but some of them might have the wider scope of employment agents for graduating students.

26

University Study of Education:
Anglo-American Analysis

The most significant development in the whole field of education in the United States has been the organization of facilities and opportunities for its study. It is difficult to realize, however, that this development has taken place in less than the twenty-five years that have just passed. By the close of the nineteenth century grudging recognition had already been given in a number of colleges and universities to the study of pedagogy or education, but the subject either was treated as an appanage of the chair of philosophy or, where it was taught in a separate department, was given only by one or two men. The view of Josiah Royce, expressed in 1891, was shared by many who professed the long, or even the recently, established subjects considered worthy of college or university study. "To sum it all in one word," wrote Royce, "teaching is an art. Therefore there is no science of education . . . But, on the other hand, if the teacher wants aid from the scientific spirit, and counsel from scientific education, there stands ready to his hand such assistance as, above all, psychology has to offer to the educator who desires to become a living observer of the minds of children, and such assistance, too, as ethics may suggest to the man who is strong enough to grapple with deeper problems."

The next thirty years were to disprove Royce's statement and to establish the fact that, while the practice of education is an art, the foundations for its successful pursuit rest on scientific bases. In spite of the discouraging attitude of colleges and universities to the study of education, the view was soon accepted that a modern university must be

Isaac L. Kandel. "University Study of Education," in *Twenty-five Years of American Education: Collected Essays by Former Students of Paul Monroe*, edited by I. L. Kandel (New York: The Macmillan Company, 1926), pp. 29–54.

Author (1881–1965): Educator and author, born in Rumania, educated at the University of Manchester, 1904; Classics Master, Royal Academical Institute of Belfast, 1906; he came to America and attended Columbia University, receiving a Ph.D. in 1910; served as Assistant Editor of Monroe's *Encyclopedia of Education*, 1909–1913; Staff member, Carnegie Foundation, 1914–1923, and served from 1923 as Professor at Teachers College, Columbia University; Editor of the *International Year Book of Education*, 1923–1944, and *School and Society*, 1946–1953.

an "institution where any person can find instruction in any study," and that from the standpoint of the public the scientific study of education is as urgent as the study of law, medicine, and engineering. It was still necessary, however, and at the beginning of the period no easy task, to prove that the study of education included more than the mere preparation of teachers. The keynote of the new movement was probably sounded by Dean J. E. Russell when in 1900 he wrote that "University departments of education have as their special function the investigation of educational foundations, the interpretation of educational ideals, the invention of educational methods, and the application of educational principles. The science of education . . . needs to be developed and made over to fit modern conditions." In 1896–97 the material was not available to carry out such a program. Although 220 out of 432 institutions were reported by the United States Commissioner of Education as offering courses in pedagogy, these consisted only of "elements of theory and practice of teaching," or of "psychology, history of education, child study, and school management," or of "the science, art, and history of education." At best the work hardly rose above the standards of the regular normal schools. Not only did the subject lack content and rely on borrowing extensively from other fields of science, themselves still young, but few specialists were available to teach it. So long as the subjects consisted mainly of theory which was little more than sophisticated practice, or was based on a few principles of psychology which on the whole had little bearing and applicability in the classroom, or derived its aims and ends from a metaphysical philosophy unrelated to the needs of a developing society, its claim to scientific character could not be established. Neither the formalism of Herbart nor the mysticism of Froebel furnished the basis for further progress, but that progress was demanded is indicated by the prevalence during the last decade of the nineteenth century and the early years of the twentieth of a kaleidoscope of changing fads and fancies, each guaranteed to solve the problem of education—until the next appeared. That the subject of education did ultimately emerge from the realm of tradition and vague expectations and fulfill the vision that was in those who, like Dean Russell, early saw the possibilities of a scientific basis for it, was due largely to the stimulus derived from the faith of the American people in education.

The Public and Education

The most striking difference between the administration of education in the United States and in European countries is the absence of a centralized authority. Constitutionally the direction of education is left to each state. Since, however, this direction was, and in many states still is, but lightly exercised, education becomes a matter of local concern. To this fact is due the great variation in educational progress throughout the country, but while it is responsible for standards in certain sections lower than those that prevail under more centralized governments, it has also been responsible for the attainment of standards considerably in advance of those that prevail elsewhere. This point was shrewdly brought out by Sir Joshua Fitch, who wrote, in 1901,

There is no uniformity in the methods or machinery of education in the States. But in its stead there prevails much of the local patriotism, which makes each of the leading communities proud of its own institutions, and keenly solicitous to produce such examples of good work may prove worthy of imitation in other states and cities . . . Hence America may be regarded as a laboratory in which educational experiments are being tried out on a great scale, under conditions exceptionally favorable to the encouragement of inventiveness and fresh enthusiasm, and to the discovery of new methods and new truths.

Such experimentation and enthusiasm, however, are due not to the desire for novelty; they have their roots in the popular attitude to education. Without a centralized authority to which to look for direction and guidance, local communities were compelled to seek their own educational salvation. Out of this variety of standards and experimentation based on local initiative and independence, leadership in education went from time to time to the most progressive and resulted in a search for and encouragement of a more scientific study of all phases of education.

Democracy and Education

Fundamentally the essence of American education rests on a demand for equality of opportunity for every boy and girl for the best possible types of education. The absence of social stratification, with opportunities for advancement through education mainly, furnishes for the American educator one of the most searching problems with which the European educators have not been called upon to deal until recently. The system has to provide not merely two or three types of education, but types to suit the needs and ability of each individual. The absence of one type of education for the masses and another for the leaders has made it incumbent on the student of education to make every year of schooling as rich and fruitful as possible. The problem of education is thus to train good citizens and at the same time to furnish freedom for individual development. In the secondary field the fact that the secondary schools are open to all has given rise to a new situation to which the traditional conceptions of a liberal education are no longer applicable, a problem that is further complicated by the fact that such education must look to the needs of an industrial and commercial society. The traditional views on culture are thus in the melting pot, and a new conception must be evolved suited to modern needs and modern conditions. Both elementary and secondary education have in their recent development demanded a new orientation of educational aims and values and a sounder and more reliable psychology of individual differences, new principles of curriculum-making, and more effective methods of instruction.

Professionalization of Education

A further problem was set by a demand from the public for better results. It was felt with the increasing cost of education, which set in at the beginning of the present century, that the schools did not accomplish what they set out to perform. Many pupils did not advance through the schools; many dropped out before completing the minimum expected even in elementary education. This demand directed attention to a reexamination of aims, processes, and methods, and in turn posited the development of a scientific attitude and scientific methods of investigation and research. Allied to this problem and equally influential in leading to a similar demand for scientific inquiry was the changing attitude on discipline. A society founded on faith in individual freedom refused to tolerate a type of discipline in the schools which rested on obedience to authority. Hence the task devolved on the educator to discover a substitute to replace external pressure and the imposition of the teacher's will.

From another aspect another influence was brought to bear on the student of education to approach his subject scientifically. Education rests on popular control and free discussion with great local freedom. The faith in education is widespread, but the educational administrator can only turn this to account if he brings to his task not merely a knowledge of education but an equally sound and thorough equipment in the principles of administration. Since educational progress rests on popular will and consent, the administrator must understand his public and educate it up to new standards, and in a society where business efficiency is one of the cardinal virtues he must be no less efficient in the conduct of his office than the director of a large industrial concern spending an equal amount of money. Education has become one of the largest enterprises of the country for the management of which mere empiricism and routine will not suffice. A new field has thus been opened in the second half of the period under discussion, which requires a sound equipment not only in framing educational aims and policies but also in the principles of management and administration.

The attitude of the American people to the universities, and especially to those that are maintained by public taxation, has resulted in a demand for service which has given them a new status in national life, barely realized in the European universities during the War. The agricultural colleges and experiment stations have for many years devoted themselves to the task of bringing their scientific knowledge and equipment to bear on the practical work of the farmer. A similar function has been expected of the departments or schools of education in colleges and universities, a task which has had the advantage of keeping such departments in close touch with practical everyday problems of the teacher and administrator and has provided them in turn with extensive laboratories both for experimentation and research. The study of education was thus saved from becoming academic and cultivating idols of the den.

Finally, as a result of improving standards in the training of teachers, higher salaries, greater security of tenure, and the establishment of pensions, the occupation of teaching has changed from a craft to a profession. It may at once be admitted that improvement in these respects has not been uniform, that many thousands of teachers are still inadequately prepared, that annual appointments still prevail, and that salaries are grudgingly paid, but the fact remains that the tendency is strongly in the direction of professionalization. This development has been at once the result and the cause of the improved status of education as a professional study. Nowhere is this more obvious than in the recent program of educational associations, national, state, and local, which have assumed an increasingly technical character and, as was recently noted by an English observer, give little attention, as contrasted with English organization, to questions of group welfare. The absence of stratification within the different grades of teaching and the opportunity open to every serious student of education have both stimulated the progressive study of education as the chief avenue for advancement. The same effect has been achieved by the slow but gradual disappearance of "politics" from the conduct of educational affairs. At the same time the teacher is being given greater participation in the administration of professional matters; even though this may be provided legally in but few systems, the day when courses of study and methods are prescribed from above is gradually disappearing. Such encouragement of initiative, with promotion made dependent on improved training and study, has stimulated the establishment throughout the country of institutions for the advanced study of education.

Teachers in Service

The past twenty-five years have witnessed a radical change in the improvement of teachers in service. At the beginning of the period the teachers' institute was still popular, though ineffective. Offered for but a few days each year, the courses of such institutes were haphazard, unorganized, and unconnected frequently with the requirements of classroom procedure, with inspirational lectures and entertainments to offset the meagerness of the programs. Their professional content and value were slight because teachers came unprepared and were not expected to show any results. While the short-period institutes have survived, their character has changed; the work has become more highly technical and specialized to meet the needs of particular groups of teachers and with a special bearing on the problems in which the teachers are daily interested.

Institutes are, however, being replaced by opportunities for more intensive study conducted in some cases by teachers' associations, in others in connection with local normal schools, teachers' colleges, and education departments of universities. The work here offered, while not restricted to professional studies, largely revolves round these. It may include cultural courses, but in general covers courses in methods in special subjects, the organization of the curriculum, training for positions as principals and supervisors, and professional studies in general, such as principles of teaching, philosophy of education, psychology, and tests and measurements. While much of this work is of an undergraduate character, it serves not merely to improve the service of the teacher but to promote a professional attitude, and to prepare for further advanced work.

The effect of such organizations for the improvement of teachers in service becomes obvious in the increase of teachers attending summer schools maintained by normal schools, teachers' colleges, and universities. The long summer vacation combined with a growing practice of local boards to subsidize the attendance of their teachers either by scholarships or bonuses or by increases in salary contingent on successful work in the courses pursued, has increased the enrollment of summer schools in many cases beyond the capacity of the institutions to deal satisfactorily with the large numbers that present themselves. In 1921 a total of 253,111 students, the majority of them teachers, attended summer schools in 410 institutions; of these 241 were universities and degree-granting colleges, attended by 143,154 students. Here again the work is predominantly of an undergraduate character, although a large proportion of the students attend for graduate study. The majority of the courses selected are professional. Whatever the nature of the studies, however, and whatever the standards, the distinguishing feature is that the teacher acquires the habit of further study and the supply of students serves both to raise the standards of professional attainment, and by its wide ramifications in which practice and theory react upon each other, the professional study of education is constantly vitalized and compelled to justify itself by its practical applicability. As in engineering and medicine, the pressure of practical situations, which are brought to a focus in the needs of teachers in service, has prevented the professional study of education from becoming too academic. It would be difficult to find in any other profession or in any other country, except in England and Scotland where similar work has recently been begun, such intense desire, as shown by teachers in summer schools, to keep abreast of the latest developments in their subject.

The stimulus obtained from the "refresher" courses in summer schools, local institutions, and extension work is further strengthened by the enlistment of teachers in the revision and improvement of courses of study and in other ways in which their practical experience is helpful, by the increasingly frequent publication of official circulars and magazines dealing with current movements in education, and by the coöperation of teachers with local or university bureaus of research.

The greatest obstacle to the development of a profession of teaching at the beginning of the period under consideration was the absence of anything to encourage the exercise of initiative on the part of the teacher. Originating at a time when the facilities for training were inadequate, a system of local centralization developed in which the superintendent undertook to prescribe with meticulous detail not merely the course of study but also the methods of instruction. The result frequently was rigid uniformity within any one system, a tradition, which like the system of payment by results in England, long hampered educational progress even after the requirement of normal school training had been established in the larger areas. The change came but gradually and is not yet generally prevalent. Teachers are, however, being given more opportunities than formerly to coöperate in the drafting of courses of study and greater initiative in the employment of methods of instruction.

Although formal agencies have been established in eighty-six school systems for the organization of such channels of coöperation, the informal selection by the superintendent of committees of teachers of recognized ability for specific purposes has been found more effective than the elected teachers' councils. The important contribution of such systems of coöperation lies in the improvement of professional standards and in the promotion of professional study. If teachers are to enjoy opportunities to make available their knowledge and experience, it follows that such contributions can only be of value and carry weight if based on a thorough appreciation not merely of the problems involved but of the need of a scientific attitude in education.

It may be objected that, with more than 150,000 untrained and relatively unprepared teachers employed in the schools of the country, it is premature even to-day to talk of the professionalization of teachers. But, as Sir Michael Sadler has pointed out, democracy in its advance presents a ragged edge; the great hope of a democracy, and particularly a democracy without a centralized authority, lies in experimentation and variation, and the advance so far made by those teachers who are in the van of progress marks the route yet to be traveled but free from the handicaps and obstacles encountered by the pioneers.

Agencies for Research and Investigation

The absence of a centralized national authority, while it has had the advantage of placing the responsibility for educational progress on local bodies, meant also the absence of an agency for setting standards and for investigation. The only guidance and direction available were afforded by a comparison of the efforts and results of the work achieved by the local systems themselves. The great service of the United States Bureau of Education, handicapped though it is by a lack of compulsory powers, has lain largely in the collection of information on the progress of education throughout the country and in directing attention through its reports and bulletins to progressive movements in all branches and fields of education both here and abroad. Early in the course of the past quarter-century the need was felt for something more than generalized reports and statistics to enable the school systems to evaluate their achievements and defects. Professor Royce had already advocated, in the nineties, the appointment of consulting psychologists to devise and recommend better methods of instruction; and this suggestion was repeated by Chancellor in one of the earliest books on school administration. In 1905 Professor G. H. Locke urged the importance of the investigation of school systems by outside agencies—"a thorough study of the system of schools in a city, its organization and administration, its curriculum, indeed the methods by which the city undertakes to afford opportunities for education to its boys and girls." Such investigations, he suggested, might properly be undertaken by departments of education in colleges and universities—a practice which would at the same time keep such departments in close touch with practice. A similar suggestion was put forward in 1907 by Professor M. V. O'Shea—"What we need to do is to see to it that departments of education are first of all investigating institutions."

Excellent though these suggestions were they were compelled to wait for their success for the development of an adequate technique that would raise the results of any investigations above the level of mere personal opinion. Nothing had as yet been done in discussing in the field of educational administration such questions as the standards of buildings and equipment, the selection of textbooks, reports and accounting, educational finance, rating of teachers, and similar questions. Statistical technique in educational psychology was in its infancy and little had yet been accomplished in devising standard tests and measurements. Nor was there any definite agreement on the aims and purposes of education, although guidance was to come shortly from the work and writings of John Dewey. Investigations by external authorities were, however, beginning to be demanded, in some cases by the public in order to discover the status of their school systems, in others by the superintendents and teachers, in self-defense. The first survey, made in Montclair in 1911, represented the personal opinion of one expert; within less than four years the character of surveys was changed and personal opinion, however expert, yielded to objective standards based on a completely developed technique of tests and measurements; quantitative methods were substituted for qualitative methods and personal opinions, and while the results are not yet sufficiently extensive and advanced to furnish the basis for a clearer statement of educational aims and ideals, the procedure of the classroom has been greatly affected by the movement.

The development of the survey as a method of educational accounting and control is dealt with elsewhere * * * . From the point of view of the present essay its significance has lain in the stimulus that it has given to and the demands that it levies upon the student of education in all its branches—administration, psychology, methods, curricula, and so on. Educational theory can no longer be based on authority and tradition; it must be related to practical needs and must constantly be infused with a critical and inquiring attitude of mind. The survey movement is the American substitute for governmental inspection; but summarizes in itself all the differences that distinguish a system of education centrally organized and slowly responsive to changing conceptions and requirements in education from a system that is based on variety and local initiative, that is self-critical and perhaps too alert and too sensitive to the varying demands of rapidly changing social conditions. Whatever the weaknesses, however, the survey method has changed the professional study of education from an academic and theoretical study to a laboratory science. In a more real sense than was ever dreamed of by Sir Joshua Fitch in 1900, the schools and school systems of the country have become the experimental stations of a vast array of organizations for the study of education; and experimentation by trial and error methods is being replaced by experimentation under the control of scientific methods.

The conduct of surveys was in the early stages intrusted to a few individuals, but in the later development it has become an important coöperative enterprise, requiring a large force of collaborators, a long period of time, and the expenditure of large sums of money. These requirements were in many cases met by the entry into the field of educational inquiry of wealthy private foundations. Thus the General Education Board, established in 1902, has conducted a number of local and state surveys and has contributed considerably by a wise expenditure of funds to the improvement of education in the South; the Carnegie Foundation for the Advancement of Teaching, established in 1906, has conducted important surveys in a number of fields—standardization of colleges, legal and medical education, the professional preparation of teachers, and the organization of education in a state. The Russell Sage Foundation, established in 1907, very early gave a much-needed impetus to the quantitative and objective study of education and has made several important surveys. Finally, one of the youngest of these foundations, the Commonwealth Fund, established in 1918, is subsidizing valuable studies in educational finance, the organization of the content in several subjects, and investigations in educational psychology. The developments of the last decade have justified the anticipation of Professor J. H. Tufts in 1909 that "if we can show that we want to do something worth doing, that we know how to set about it, and that we are broad enough in our vision to look beyond our machinery to the larger personal and social welfare, means for investigation will not be wanting."

Such foundations, however, are interested in the main in pointing the way and in opening up and stimulating new fields of inquiry. There still remains the desirability of establishing permanent agencies of investigation and research. The more progressive communities in the United States are ready to welcome the scientific collection and interpretation of statistical and other data referring to schools, while trained educators are equally ready for opportunities in the practical field for scientific research, the results of which may be utilized for the formulation of educational policies. The occasional survey, while it was of great value, only pointed the way to the creation of permanent local bureaus of reference and research. New York City was the earliest to establish such a Division of Reference and Research in 1913 and has been followed by a number of other important centers, both city and state. The character of the work of such bureaus varies; in some cases the whole field of education is covered; in others only the administrative and statistical aspects; in others again only measurements and tests. The university departments of education, particularly in the state-maintained institutions, have also recognized their opportunities and obligations in this direction and both informally through individual members of their faculties and through formally organized bureaus have entered the field of coöperative research in education. In this way they serve as centers for the direction of inquiries into problems submitted to them by local school systems, for the collecting and interpretation of data, and for the publication and dissemination of results; in a number of instances opportunities for purely experimental work are furnished by schools attached to such departments. The first bureau of this type was established in 1913 at the University of Oklahoma and has been followed by the creation of bureaus in other universities and in teachers' colleges.

The work of both city and state bureaus and of university bureaus of research culminated in the organization in 1916 of a National Association of Directors of Educational Research, now the Educational Research Association, whose aims are the promotion of the practical use of quantitative methods in educational research and the improvement of the efficiency of educational administration, supervision, and teaching by means of scientific methods.

Only a reference is necessary to the numerous professional associations for the promotion and discussion of educational research. A comparison of programs of the societies that were in existence at the beginning of the past quarter-century and at the end of this period will serve to indicate the road and distance that the study of education has traveled. The Proceedings of the National Education Association, of the Department of Superintendence, and of the National Society for the Study of Education tell their own story. More recently there have been established the National Society of College Teachers of Education, the Educational Research Association, Section L, of the American Association for the Advancement of Science, the National Conference on Educational Method, and numerous local societies, all devoted to the advancement of the study of education on a scientific basis, to the improvement of all branches of education, and ultimately to placing the vocation of teaching on a professional footing.

The Formal Study of Education

The account of the study of education up to this point has dealt in the main with the factors that contributed to its development as a result of the public attitude to education, and of the practical demands of the schools themselves. It is difficult in dealing with any applied science to disentangle the share contributed from practical needs and situations and the share derived from pure science. So in the field of education it is not a simple matter to apportion equitably the stimulus that has been given to its development in the last twenty-five years by the necessities of classroom procedure and of administration on the one hand and the formal organization of and research into the different branches of the subject that have taken place in the universities. It is not necessary here to indicate the growth in the number of graduate schools of education, the number of courses offered, and the enrollment of students. From the point of view of this essay, greater interest attaches to the development of the content and subject matter subsumed under the general term of education.

At the beginning of the period under discussion the study of education, whether in normal schools or in colleges, was limited to a few fields and with very little differentiation. Virtually the only specialization possible was between preparation for service in the elementary or in the secondary field. The subjects of study were included sometimes under the blanket term "pedagogy," sometimes "school management and pedagogy"; in a few places courses in history of education and psychology or child study were gradually beginning to appear. No provision was yet made for training the supervisor, principal, superintendent, or any of the other specialized workers in education; training for these fields was to be obtained by experience. The courses offered by Teachers College, Columbia University, for 1897–98 may be taken as an adequate and representative summary of the status of education as a special study at that time:

Psychology and General Method
Advanced Psychology and General
  Method
Child Study
Primary Methods
History of Education (2 courses)
Philosophy of Education and
  School Management
School Supervision and School
  Management
Elementary Methods
Principles of Art Education
Methods of Teaching English
  Literature
Methods of Teaching English
  Composition
The Teaching of History in Secondary Schools
Methods of Teaching Mathematics
  in Elementary and Secondary
  Schools
Kindergarten Department (11
  courses)
Methods of Teaching Domestic
  Science
Methods of Teaching Sewing

Within ten years these courses had become so differentiated that the following list could be compiled in 1905–06:

Child Study
Genetic Psychology
Mental Development
Educational Psychology
Principles of Education
Philosophy of Education
Educational Theory
History of Education
Educational Classics
General Methods

Special Methods
School Management
School Supervision
Elementary Education
Secondary Schools
School Systems
Contemporary Education
School Law
School Administration
School Hygiene

With these were continued the courses in methods of special subjects.

Five years later it became possible to consider seriously the problem of research within the field of education. Hitherto the various studies were isolated and unconnected subjects within the larger field. After 1910 the field gradually became so wide and its subdivisions so highly specialized that no student could be expected to master them all. The rapid development of facilities for the graduate study of education leading to advanced degrees may be said to have begun at that time. The reasons have already been suggested in other parts of this essay. The publication of Monroe's *Textbook in the History of Education* in 1905 had already indicated the possibilities in that field and had stimulated a number of special studies and contributions, which gradually led to the expansion of the subject into a number of highly diversified courses, including new research into the historical development of education both in this country and elsewhere and establishing the value of the historical outlook as an important method of approach to the study of principles. The work of John Dewey opened up a new field of inquiry into the philosophical and social bases underlying education and, while it has not stimulated any considerable contributions in philosophy of education, it has influenced most of the investigations made in the last decade or more on principles of education, the course of study, and methods of instruction. At the same time this field of study and inquiry has been compelled to take into account the extensive contributions which have been made since 1902 by the psychologists, for whom a new field was opened up by Professor Thorndike both in educational psychology and in educational statistics. An entirely new subject has been added to the list, as a result of Dewey's emphasis on the social aspects of education, under the title of Educational Sociology—an inquiry into social and group life and its effect on educational aims and purposes.

The same period has also witnessed the development of a specialized study of educational administration, which resulted from the revelation of the general ignorance of such matters as the classification of pupils, retardation and elimination, school finance, adequate accounting and reports, and in general the absence of a suitable relation between the hours spent for education and the products of the schools. The practical demands for expert guidance, as revealed by the surveys, have led to the development of specialized training for expert administrators and superintendents in such problems as the following:

Problems of teaching, involving the study of methods employed with a view to improving the results achieved; problems of supervision with the confident expectation that the efficiency of teachers might be increased through the methods which were employed; the classification of children; the fiscal administration of schools, including cost accounting, budget-making, salaries and salary schedules, the distribution of state school funds; the development of adequate systems of taxation; the development of building programs; studies of equipment to be provided; the setting up of an adequate attendance service; the methods of handling school publicity; the installation of an adequate system of records and reports; the development of a set of rules for boards of education; the revision of sections of city charters dealing with education; the codification of state laws for education; the development of an adequate health service; the reorganization of curricula for the training of teachers; the organization of a rural community in relation to a modern rural school; and the like. (Based on G. D. Strayer, in *Studies in Education,* Educational Monographs of the Society of College Teachers of Education, Number XI, 1922, p. 98.)

The opportunities for specialization in elementary, secondary, and rural education have similarly been expanded and fructified by the recent developments in psychology, philosophy of education, and social studies. Each field has been analyzed in turn, its needs and problems have been appraised, and technical courses have been elaborated for the specialists. In another direction, the practical-mindedness of the American public and a desire to give a suitable equipment to each boy and girl for a life career have led to the development of specialized training for teachers and organizers of vocational and agricultural education and in home economics, all of which have been specially stimulated and fostered by federal subsidy.

The emergency created by the War was for the nation as a whole more revealing than any survey; the mass of facts collected in connection with the organization of the army and other activities revealed deficiencies in American education, hitherto suspected, perhaps, but not statistically verified. The lack of preparation of a large percentage of the teachers, the importance and needs of rural education, the prevalence of physical defects and inadequate provision for health education, the problems of immigrant and adult illiteracy, and the low standard of education in general were revealed, and, while alarming, have had the effect of emphasizing the need of further study and improved training both of teachers in general and of experts in the different fields here mentioned.

What this specialization in the various branches of education has resulted in may be indicated by the organization of the College of Education of the University of Minnesota, which may be regarded as typical of the organization in other state universities and a number of the larger private institutions, offering both undergraduate and graduate work. The following departments are there maintained: history and philosophy of education; educational administration; theory and practice of teaching; trade and industrial education; agricultural education; home economics education; art education; physical education; public school music; bureau of educational investigation.

The following list of courses offered by the School of Education of Teachers College, Columbia University, is presented for purpose of comparison with the courses listed earlier and to indicate the ramifications in the professional study of education as organized to-day. The various branches may be found in many other institutions, and, although the number of courses is not so extensive elsewhere, the general range and scope are representative.

History and Principles of Education
History of Education
Play Materials for Young Children
Experimental Playground
Plays, Games, and Dances of Early Childhood
Beginnings of Music for Young Children
Beginnings of Fine and Industrial Arts
Biological Materials for Elementary Schools
Regional Studies in Science
The Library in the Modern School
Teaching English to Adult Immigrants
Teaching English to Foreigners
Literature of Upper Elementary Grades
Literature of the Primary Grades
Geography for Teachers and Supervisors in Elementary Grades
Phonetics
American History for Elementary Teachers and Supervisors
Teaching of Civics in Secondary Schools
Household Arts for Rural Communities
Industrial Arts for the Elementary Grades
Industrial Arts for Social and Religious Workers
Industrial Arts for Special Classes

Teaching Industrial Arts in Elementary Schools
Mathematics of the Elementary School
Teaching Applied Mathematics
Teaching Applied Mathematics in Evening Schools
Educational Hygiene
Health Education
Practice Teaching in Connection with Education
Hygiene of Childhood and Adolescence
Principles and Practices of Scoutcraft
Recreational Education
Recreational Leadership and Games
Clubcraft
Club Leadership
Principles of Education Administration
Consolidation and the Rural High School
Democracy and Education in Europe
Problems of Advisers of Women and Girls
Educational Publicity
Theory and Practice of Teaching in Elementary Schools
Principles and Practice of Teaching in Elementary Schools
Measurement and Experimentation in Elementary Education
Illustrative Lessons in Citizenship
Supervision in the Elementary School
Socializing the Elementary School Curriculum
The Technique of Teaching
Methods of Teaching in Special Classes
Observation Experimentation and Teaching in Special Classes
Organization and Supervision of Special Classes
Subject Matter and Methods of the Primary School
History of the Family as a Social Institution
Education of Women
History of Education in United States
Observation of Teaching of Young Children
Fundamentals of First Grade
Practice in Teaching of Young Children
Conservation of the Child and the Home
Philosophy of Education
Foundations of Method
Ethics and Educational Problems
Educational Psychology
Psychology of Childhood
Psychology of Adolescence
Psychology of Exceptional Children
The Psychology of Thinking
Introductory Course in Mental Tests
Psychology of Habit, Skill, Practice, and Memory

Mental Measurements
Methods in Religious Education
Field Work in Social-Religious Centers
The Use of the Bible in Religious Education
Problems in Missionary Education
Rural Education
Rural Education and Country Life
Field Work: Rural Education and Rural Sociology
Rural Sociology and Economics
Field Work in Rural Community Surveys
The Preparation of Rural Teachers
Rural School Supervision
General Methods for Secondary Schools
Teaching in Junior High Schools
Supervised Observation and Teaching
Teaching Secondary School Subjects
Experimental Teaching in Secondary Schools
Improvement of Instruction in Secondary Schools
Problems in Administration for Heads of Secondary School Departments
Administrative Problems of the High School
Organization and Administration of Secondary Education
Organization and Administration of the Junior High School
Extra-Curricular Activities in Junior and Senior High Schools
Social Organization of the Secondary School
Field Studies in Extra-Curricular High School Activities
Introduction to Sociology
Introductory Educational Sociology
Practical Applications of Sociology
Sociological Foundations of Civic Education
Education in Citizenship for Foreign-born
Fundamentals in Civic Education
Vocations for Girls and Women
Vocational Education
Vocational Education in High Schools
Administration of Vocational Education
Vocational Guidance
Prevocational Training in Junior and Senior High Schools
Science in Secondary Schools
Teaching Biological Science in Secondary Schools
Teaching Physics in Secondary Schools
Laboratory Projects in Automobile Mechanics
Teaching General Science in Secondary Schools
Teaching Chemistry in Secondary Schools
Problems in Teaching Science in Secondary Schools
Teaching English in Secondary Schools
Teaching English in Elementary and Normal Schools

Practicum. Teaching English in Secondary Schools
Supervision of English in Secondary Schools
Experiment and Research in Teaching English
College Teaching of English Composition
Development of Theory of Composition
Teaching French in Secondary Schools
Teaching and Supervision of Geography in Secondary Schools
Regional Geography
Teaching Foreign Languages in Secondary Schools
Problems in Modern Language Method
Teaching History in Secondary Schools
Experimental Lessons in History
Education for Citizenship
Teaching History in Normal Schools
Practicum. Literature of American History
Practicum. Industrial and Social History in Schools
Teaching and Supervision of Latin in Secondary Schools
Advanced Course in Cæsar and Vergil
Teaching Algebra in Secondary Schools
Teaching Geometry in Secondary Schools
Advanced Course in Teaching and Supervision of Mathematics
Practicum in Health Education
Administration of Hygiene and Physical Education
Major Course for Superintendents of Schools
Research Course for School Superintendents
Practicum. Cost and Financing of Public Education
Practicum. Comparative Education
Major Course for Elementary and Primary Principals and Supervisors and
    Critic Teachers in Training Schools
Criticism and Supervision of Instruction in Elementary Schools
Measurement and Experimentation in Elementary Education
Experimental Supervision and Teaching of Classroom Studies
Supervision in Primary Grades
Major Course for Normal School Teachers, Supervisors, and Administrators
Research Course in Elementary Supervision
Research Course in Professional Education of Teachers
History of Education
Historical Development of Modern Elementary Education
Historical Development of Public Education
Practicum. History of Education in the United States
Historical Study of the Problems of Secondary Education
Practicum. Current Problems in Supervision and Training of Teachers of
    Young Children
Study of Curricula for Young Children
Philosophy of Education
Practicum. Philosophy of Education

Practicum. Historical Relations of Philosophy and Education
Major Course in Mental and Educational Tests
Practicum. Statistical Methods in Education
Advanced Educational Statistics
Clinical Psychology
Mental Adjustments
Mental and Vocational Tests
Reconstruction of the Elementary School Curriculum
Reconstruction of Junior and Senior High School Curriculum
Psychology of the Elementary School Subjects
Educational Psychology—Advanced Course
Practicum. Problems of Social-Religious Work
The Curriculum of the Church School
Supervision of Religious Instruction
Principles of Religious Education
Practicum in Religious Education
Introduction to the Psychology of the Christian Life
Problems in Missionary Education
Major Course for Rural Community Workers
Major Course for Directors of Rural Education in Normal Schools and Teachers Colleges
Major Course for Supervisors of Rural Schools
Major Course for High School Principals
A Research Course for High School Principals
Administrative Problems of the High School
Practicum. Educational Sociology
Community Socialization
Applied Sociology: Special Education for Adults and Community Groups
Public Opinion. Adult Education
Sociological Foundations of Curricula
Problems of Curricula
Training Supervisors for Americanization of Foreigners
Research Course for Administrators of Vocational Education
Major Course in Administration of Vocational Education
Practicum. Vocational Guidance
Seminar. Historical Foundations of Modern Education
Seminar. Elementary Education
Seminar in Normal School Education
Seminar. Philosophy of Education
Seminar. Educational Psychology
Seminar in the Teaching of Mathematics
Seminar in Religious Education
Seminar. Rural Education
Seminar. Rural Sociology
Seminar. Secondary Education
Seminar. Educational Sociology

The study of education has emerged from its swaddling clothes in the period covered by this essay; neglected and hidden under the ægis of other subjects or departments, education has become in most universities the field through which the greatest service is done to society. Statistical presentations might have indicated the number of students, both undergraduate and graduate, engaged in this study and the amount and cost of buildings and equipment devoted to its pursuit, but nothing speaks so eloquently as the list of courses here given of the vast field for human endeavor that has been made explicit in the past twenty-five years. The schools need well-prepared teachers, but society needs still more the guidance and direction of specialists and experts, and if faith is to be cultivated in them, it can only come, as it is more and more coming, through the existence and cultivation of a scientific study of the subjects that they profess. This has been made possible in less than half of the twenty-five years here discussed. If only passing reference has been made to the dark spots that still exist in education in the United States, this has not been done to glorify the advances made in the study of education, but in the belief that the instruments already perfected will remove the deficiencies that still remain, and find new fields to conquer.

27

Why I Shall Send My Son to an American College

My son is eight years old—a blond young rascal, but of sound charac-ter. Recently when I surprised him poring over the globe, absorbed in the study of a map of America, to which country I was about to travel, I said to him, "In twelve years I shall send you there."

He looked mildly surprised, and wisely kept his opinions to himself.

As a matter of fact, my plan is to send him first for two years of study to a German or Swiss university. Here he will build a solid founda-tion of classical culture, which, more than any other learning in the world, gives to youth a trend towards high idealism and right thinking. In these schools, too, he will take unto himself protective antitoxins which will guard him against certain dangers that threaten in America. For if a twenty-year-old European goes to America unprepared for what awaits him there, he will be drawn into the vortex of incredible tumult; its confusion may well overwhelm him. The heaviness of the German nature, brought into sudden contact with the lightness and swiftness of the American, inclines towards a loss of balance which may be more than temporary.

Therefore—why do I wish to send my son to an American college when he is twenty?

The first reason is that learning there is a cheerful and happy thing. In America, students no longer study in dark, Gothic halls, as they do in Germany; they no longer sit at old-fashioned desks, in half a hundred rows, one primly behind the other. They sit informally and at their ease, in classrooms which are flooded with light. The American student is not bent over his books for five weary hours at a time. He is at his books for an hour or two and then he has change and recreation in exercise or play.

Emil Ludwig. "Why I Shall Send my Son to an American College," *The American Magazine*, Vol. CXII, No. 1 (October, 1931), pp. 29, 96, 100.

Author (1881–1948): Swiss writer of German origin, naturalized in 1932; educated at Breslau and Heidelberg; biographer, playwright, and political essayist; visited the United States on a private visit in 1931; his publications included studies of Napoleon, Lincoln, Hindenburg, and Mussolini.

This speedy alternation of work and play was largely responsible for the splendid physical and intellectual development of the ancients. We strive for it as an ideal in Germany, but here it must fight an uphill battle against age-old tradition and reaction, and it is coming into its own very slowly and with difficulty.

The wide gap which separates teacher from pupil, and which is a result of our respect for authority and our belief in obedience, has been bridged in America, and there exists a splendid comradeship, without lack of respect. Because of this easy comradeship, there have arisen between teacher and pupil a cordial affection and mutual confidence. When I was a student, I would never have dared go to my teachers for advice as to how I should conduct myself in certain affairs that had to do with my debts or with my sweetheart. I believe, however, that the American teacher, partaking as he does of play and sport with his pupils, is just the man to whom those pupils turn for advice.

The second reason why I shall do my best to send my son across the ocean to study is the competitive system, which is much stronger in America than in Germany. We are all, to be sure, familiar with the evil outgrowth of such competition—that is, the tendency, deplored by all of the highest-type Americans, to overpraise and overvalue "the tallest," "the handsomest," "the richest," "the swiftest," and so on. This is the system at its worst. But at its best the competitive system in American physical training, which is given infinitely greater emphasis there than in Germany or even in England, does awaken in the student the ardent desire to prove himself as among the foremost in prowess. In spiritual and intellectual matters, the thing is not so simple; excellence is not so readily obvious. A creative spirit proves itself only after years, while any afternoon suffices to bring proof of physical superiority.

The third reason why my son is to study in America is the great variety of races which come together in close and friendly communion in that country. All together they are building a new race, and yet the student of physiognomy knows them as the descendants of a dozen older races. Nationalistic and racial hatreds, such as the various nations of Europe cherish and tend, are in America—at least, among the whites—unknown. The son of an Italian immigrant associates on terms of perfect equality with the sons of Norwegian, Irish, German immigrants. The thought never occurs to him that the others may be better than he, or not so good. Such thoughts burden the social intercourse of innumerable students of European schools. Whoever has not been born in the country, who does not know to perfection its mother tongue, will never be accepted in the full spirit of trust and confidence and love.

My son is to understand that the people of all nations are equal and have equal rights; he is to learn this in a country where all nations together are building a new nation. That coöperation, that working together of all nations, is the great school of tolerance and understanding which is open in America to youthful hearts.

My boy is to learn there a similar tolerance in regard to class and caste. I realize that this tolerance does not obtain universally, even in America; I have found many of our own social prejudices in your country. A few years ago, when I asked the head of a certain college whether sons of working men studied at his institution, he denied it with evident indignation. But the lesson that a young man can learn only in America or in Soviet Russia is that, in these countries, everyone works, including the rich.

The old ideal of the European young man was the "dandy," a foppish fellow who dressed himself in the latest mode and whose chronic state was one of idle boredom. The War suppressed this trend toward dandyism, but did not destroy it. No country of Europe has, up to the present, held the idler in social disrepute.

The scorn of idleness I hold to be the greatest American invention.

When I asked one of the richest men in New York why, white-haired and bent with years, he still went downtown every day, he answered, "Because, if I didn't, I should be forgotten in a year."

The greatest European criticism of America is, of course, the accusation of an insatiable materialism. America is "Dollar Land" to many Europeans. Which, of course, implies that in Europe things are very different, that in Europe the all-important things are things of the spirit.

As a matter of fact, the all-important thing in Europe is money; the difference is only the engaging frankness and *naïveté* with which, in America, you admit money to be one of the two very foundation stones of a good life—the other is health—while, in Europe, all of this is veiled and disguised.

Thirty years ago, as a young piano student, I must needs hand my "professor" his monthly stipend in a sealed envelope which contained my father's visiting card, slit to hold the coin with which he was paid. Even today, any European scholar who changes his profession to enter industry will never admit the greatly enhanced compensation which industry pays him as his motivating force. He will say, instead, "I hope, with my specialized knowledge to serve mankind in some practical way." But not long ago, when I renewed acquaintance with an American professor in the offices of a newspaper of which he is now editor-in-chief, he said, with a smile, "I am getting five times as much money from the newspaper as I used to get in my academic pursuits."

My son has been brought up as a pacifist. He has never possessed a box of lead soldiers to play with, and he has no flags or banners. When he was only four, he was taught that the people of all nations are equal and that war is a crime. But in our schools he would be surrounded by disquieting talk about parties, about worldpower, about revenge, about hate against other nations.

Such talk as this he will not hear in the schools of America. When he sits with his friends over a glass of wine—and in the year 1943 he will be doing that—he will not be forced to sing songs in which a neighboring country is held up to scorn and hate. The wish for power, among his American fellow students, will not express itself in terms of the wish to butcher. Living with the youth of America, my son will learn that money is better than war, that peace is better than money, and that health and love of his fellows are better than anything else. He will understand this fully only when he becomes familiar with the history of America.

One day my son will stand before the gigantic marble figure of Abraham Lincoln in that pillared portico in Washington. He will gaze into the wise and melancholy face and ponder on the significance of this man's life and death.

In Europe, it is the kings and warriors who, in gigantic statues of bronze and stone, dominate the public squares, occupy the highest and holiest places. In no country there does the great lover of his fellow man occupy the place of greatest honor. Shakespeare, Voltaire, Goethe, Dante—in every country, their monuments are smaller, the places in which they stand are more secluded and inaccessible than the monuments and the places accorded to kings and warriors.

It is only in the United States that the greatest monument in the country is a monument to a man who, in his own time, was not acknowledged as a statesman, was scorned as a commander, was blamed by millions for having brought about warfare. In Abraham Lincoln, the nation honors, if I read aright, its great ideal, its great symbol, the perfect prototype of the Man of the People, the hewer of wood, the teller of stories, the friend of every oppressed human soul, whether black or white; the man who, in the nation's crisis, held that nation together infinitely more by the greatness of his spirit and his understanding and his love than by any intellectual gifts as a leader and a statesman. Voluntarily, almost instinctively, the nation has chosen this odd, rough man as its ideal and its prototype. And today the nation seems mirrored in him, just as truly as he is mirrored in the waters of the long lake which lap the stairs of his temple. . . .

When, after long and earnest gazing at this monument, my son will go back to the confusion of the streets and their thousands of unfamiliar faces, he will see among those throngs more happy and cheerful men and women than he would find in any city of Europe.

There is nothing easier, of course, than to caricature this typical American cheerfulness. In Germany, we like to feel amused at this American idea of "keep smiling." Why not be honest about it? Why not admit that a stronger love of life, a stronger will to enjoy, is at the bottom of all this? We like to say that people in America hurry and worry more than we hurry and worry in Germany, and that all the haste and excitement are in futile pursuit of money and transitory pleasure. In the midst of the depression, I saw these Americans by the thousands playing baseball in their open squares, all merry, all absorbed in their play, or in their observation of others' play. In our country, there is no national sport in the enjoyment of which young and old, rich and poor, are at one; and the overfilled beer gardens of a Sunday give no reassurance of common repose or refreshing recreation.

The famed "American haste" is nothing more than a mere matter of European prejudice. When I go to the desk of an American bank or post office or business organization, when I visit the big stores, the official in charge, or the sales person, greets me in a spirit much more quiet and serene than would be the spirit of a similar type of worker in Berlin. He greets me as quietly and serenely as I would be greeted in London. In America no one is brought up to be obsequious or subservient; all of these workers seem to me to be taking part in a big game which begins anew every morning and in which, at the close of the day, one counts oneself among the winners or the losers.

This spirit of a game which all workers play together seems to me to engender greater friendliness and joy in living than can possibly be engendered by our never-ending desire to dominate or be dominated. I saw the president of one of the greatest business organizations of New York in a most friendly and informal chat with the youngest and humblest among his employees. I saw no one bow low, be subservient, rush to open doors, click heels in obeisance. A natural self-respect seems to obtain in every circle. . . .

Some evening my twenty-year-old son will ascend to the highest pinnacle of the city of New York—and in 1943 there will be none much higher than the mighty turret of the Empire State Building. He will gaze down, from the balcony, on this gigantic city with its millions of souls, and he will ponder on the evil necessity which forces these millions to live so herded together; he will ask himself if these things cannot be changed and bettered.

The social order will have changed, in one way or another, by then.

But, whatever the change, my son will see above him, as recently I saw, the lighted peak of the tower, and he will know that however high we stand, the ideal is still beyond us, unattainable, but sending out its golden beams as an augury of hope. The emotion that was in my breast as I stood there, where he will stand, was one between humility and pride. It is my hope that both humility and pride will remain always in the youthful heart of America.

To awaken in my son this pride that is without aggresiveness, this pride that is in part compounded of humility—that is the main objective towards which I shall be aiming when, in twelve years, I shall send him to an American college. For myself, I am decided. The question remains: Will that blond young rascal who is my son abide by my wishes, or will he—as is the immemorial habit of youth—decide to do exactly as he pleases, even if the doing should lead him exactly contrary to his father's wishes?

28

A Hired Man Speaks: Views
of a Dutch Immigrant

I

Since 1915 I have held appointments as full professor in four American universities and one European university. I am not an executive—not a president, nor a dean, nor even an assistant dean; merely what may be called a hired man.

The first commencement address through which I suffered was a pathetically insistent plea urging the listeners to accept the proposition that America had the most remarkable education system in the western world. I listened; I was impressed, but not convinced. As a matter of fact thirty-five years of intimate contact with the system have failed to convince me. I have conscientiously tried to find out what is wrong with the system. These are my observations.

It seems to me that we are suffering from three distinct maladies. Each of them is sufficiently serious to cause pernicious anæmia in any educational system. We lack clearly defined objectives. We sacrifice contents to method. School administration is a poorly coordinated mixture of two methods of management, the one admirable adapted to industrial concerns, the other suited to a church dramatic society.

All this may sound flippant, but, believe me, I am serious. More than that, I am worried. On every hand I can see influences at work which promise to make matters much worse before they may become better.

The three diseases are so clearly related and interact upon each other to such an extent that it is almost impossible to separate them in our

Jacob Anton de Haas. "A Hired Man Speaks," *The Atlantic Monthly*, Vol. CLXII (July–December, 1938), pp. 815–822. Reprinted with kind permission of the editors, *The Atlantic Monthly*, Boston, Massachusetts.

Author (1883–1963): International trade scholar and author; born in Amsterdam, where he received his elementary and higher secondary schooling; educated at Stanford and Harvard; Special agent in Europe for the California Commission on Immigration, 1914; Adjunct Professor, University of Texas, 1915–1917; Professor, University of Rotterdam, 1919–1921; Professor, New York University, 1921–1927; Professor at Harvard University since 1927; Lecturer, U.S. Naval War College since 1928; Consultant War Department, 1940 and 1941; Office of Coordinator of Inter-American Affairs, 1941–1943.

discussion. My reactions may be understood more clearly when I explain the aims of the system of which I am the product. In Holland we have, as here, three types of schools—the elementary, the secondary, and the university. Their positions are clearly defined and separated.

The elementary school has as its purpose to give to the pupils a command of the tools with which to acquire knowledge, and a rudimentary acquaintance with the world in which they live.

The secondary schools have the purpose to impart such information as any person needs to possess to be fully aware of the physical, cultural, political, and economic world—in other words, the indispensable minimum of knowledge for a modern person.

The university, on the other hand, provides for specialized professional training and for research in all fields of knowledge.

The real backbone of the system is the secondary school. Here the pupils learn four modern languages well enough to be able to read, write, and speak them. They study chemistry, physics, mathematics, botany, sociology, economics, civics, astronomy, drawing, geography, and history. Throughout the five years of this school the subjects are coördinated with each other. No subject is dropped after having been taken up, and when the five-year course is completed the student passes a searching examination covering nineteen different subjects. It consists of a two weeks' written test, followed by a two weeks' oral test. The examinations are given by a committee selected by the central office of education from high school and university faculties. Practically all my teachers in the high school held doctor's degrees in the subjects they were teaching, and taught only the subject in which they were trained. And we learned by the only process that has yet shown results: we learned by constant drill and hard work.

Of course, we did not enjoy this rigid discipline. There was mighty little time left for play or for spectacular athletic feats. But we seemed to survive, and I never heard of any student having a nervous breakdown. I believe that life insurance statistics do not show an abnormally high rate of early deaths among the alumni of the system.

When I was working my way through an American university by teaching French and German in a secondary school, the principal came to me one day very much disturbed. The teacher of chemistry had fallen ill and there was no one who could take his place. The honor was therefore conferred upon me. 'Can you do it?' he asked. And I, by that time sufficiently Americanized to know what answer was demanded, responded with sadness in my heart, but with the expected confidence in my tone: 'I can try.' And so I became the expert in chemistry.

The new work thus wished on me was appalling enough, but what made it really difficult was the comforting statement that followed the assignment: 'After all, they are not here to learn chemistry, but to learn the laboratory method!' That was indeed a new slant on my problem. I was greatly puzzled. In my crude innocence I had always believed—in fact, had been encouraged to believe—that one studied a subject in order to acquire accurate knowledge of that particular field. Evidently I had always been wrong. One studies a subject to learn some kind of method. Now for two years in my high school I had spent four hours a week in a laboratory in a course of elementary qualitative analysis. But I must confess I never knew there was such a thing as a laboratory method which one could acquire by the mysterious process of not learning chemistry.

Being young and anxious to learn, I asked for advice from others. I made a most surprising discovery: every subject was apparently taught for some equally mysterious purpose. One studied mathematics, not to learn to add and subtract, or to solve complicated mathematical problems—heaven forbid! One studied mathematics to discipline the mind.

French was studied, like Latin, not to learn the language in order to enlarge one's cultural horizons—that was an exploded and antiquated notion; foreign languages were studied to enable the students to understand their own language.

How could I undertake to teach chemistry under these circumstances, not having the remotest idea what was to be found at the end of the road along which my poor students and I were to travel? I asked for more advice. I found it in the Department of Education of our university. My visit to one of the leading men in the department gave me much to think about—but clarified nothing.

I was told that although I knew a good deal of chemistry I was totally unfit to tell others of my knowledge, since I did not possess the right method. 'You mean the laboratory method?' I asked hesitatingly, conscious of my inferiority. 'Young man, that is a by-product. What I mean is that with the right method any good teacher can teach almost any subject. Before you undertake to teach chemistry, you need, not more knowledge of chemistry, but knowledge of teaching method.'

After thanking my learned adviser, I returned to the school and taught chemistry. To this day I don't know whether the students learned the laboratory method, nor whether my method was right or wrong. But this early experience has not been forgotten.

II

Curiously enough, thirty years later I heard it stated that the function of a university professor could be reduced to that of a traffic policeman;

given the right kind of book, all he needs to do is to direct the discussion. Again method!

It is an old axiom that the good teacher must so direct the study of his pupils that he may in time become superfluous, but it has taken the American system to discover that a teacher with real knowledge of the subject to be taught can be dispensed with altogether—given the right book and the right method. I have observed this philosophy in operation, and to me it seems to be the expression of a sense of inadequacy and defeat. The pupils do not learn any chemistry. They fail to acquire a knowledge of languages or of history. Is the system a failure? Mercy, no! You expect the wrong thing. You are ignorant of the true purpose behind it all. We do not teach a subject to accomplish such a crude and banal result as the conveying of knowledge of the subject! We have outgrown that notion long ago. We are teaching all these things in order to give something far more valuable, far more intangible—the right attitude of mind, the right method of approach; by means of these acquisitions the whole complicated world of facts will just open up before the students. We give them the keys that will unlock all intellectual mysteries.

I have always been skeptical of all this. I have had a suspicion, which has grown into a conviction, that the setting up of an intangible aim finds its explanation, not in a clearer vision of the purposes of education, but in a desire to set up an aim of values which defy measurement. No one can now be charged with failure. Who, indeed, can determine whether the student has gained in 'intellectual grasp,' 'social awareness,' and all those other intangibles now regarded as educational aims?

The teachers now teaching in our grammar schools and high schools are inadequately equipped with a knowledge of the subjects they are required to teach. Many of them are called upon to teach subjects with which they have only the most superficial acquaintance. They have spent so much time in departments of 'education,' learning how to teach, that they have been deprived of an opportunity to learn what to teach.

There is no short cut in educational procedure. There is no escaping the fact that acquiring knowledge is a slow, laborious process, and takes drill, hard work, and competent guidance. The overemphasis of method would not be so disastrous if along with it had not come an overemphasis of the wrong method. Our educational system has sold out to the demands of big business. To the business 'executive' the slow process of arriving at sound conclusions by a thorough investigation of all available facts is always annoying. He is a man of action; he demands action, and 'action now.' His success is due largely to this decisiveness. Since in many business situations one guess is as good as another, the ability to find a short cut is at a premium. A rough examination of facts—a decision based on a hunch—is frequently the only method that can be used because there is little time to do the job of deciding more thoroughly. If he guesses right, the executive gains a reputation of deep insight; if he guesses wrong, he can often find an alibi in labor trouble or an unwise policy on the part of the federal administration.

The business man is not hesitant in expressing his contempt for the theorist, for the man who refuses to act until he has exhausted all means of acquiring information upon which to base a decision. What the world needs, so he tells his fellow members of the Chamber of Commerce, is leadership—men like himself—doers, not thinkers: we need men who abhor hesitation and approach all questions 'realistically,' unhampered by accurate knowledge. In colleges that train youth for the business world it is proper that these principles should be accepted. But when these principles are set up as guides in the teaching of literature, art, and the sciences it is another matter. In cultivating the garden of our mind we are mainly concerned with the beauty of the flowers, not with the marketability of the fruits.

The purse strings are controlled by the 'leaders,' and endowments must of necessity be secured from the same sources. The needs expressed by them become the end of our educational systems. We are now training for leadership. And the school authorities feel obliged to offer apologies if, in spite of their devoted endeavors, some of the human material emerges, not as doers, but as thinkers.

No longer does the student labor to gain in understanding, to see the world in all its complex interrelationships, to enlarge his horizon, to gain in wisdon. He studies to become an effective doer. Impatient with time-consuming and action-retarding investigation and thought, he is encouraged to seek short cuts, gradually becoming imbued with the principle that it is better to act unwisely than not to act at all.

The modern school no longer believes there is a satisfaction that comes from knowing a thing thoroughly, from the successful accomplishing of a task. We are modern now. No one can be expected to have the slightest interest in anything whose practical use is not immediately clear to him. The student is being trained to act. He is encouraged to ask, 'How does this knowledge contribute to effective action? Of what possible use can it be to me?'

Nowhere else in the world have I ever heard the question asked, 'What is a college education worth?' Our educational institutions prepare impressive statistics to prove the correlation between a college degree and earning power in such widely separate fields as selling automobiles and preaching the gospel. But what sane person could ever have doubted that a man with more knowledge than the average would be in a position to get ahead a little faster in whatever he undertook? And when we consider that the school system—to some extent, at least—eliminates the worst numskulls, can anyone be surprised to discover that the more intelligent students who get a degree, if only in virtue of academic longevity, will make a somewhat better showing? However, to the business man, with his awe for statistics, such graphs and colored charts are convincing. Now that we have shown our financial backers that the acquisition of knowledge has proved not too great a handicap in the one field in which our real interest is centered—the field of money making—we are ready to proceed.

But notice what standards we have set for ourselves. We have completely capitulated. We are committed to a training for action. We ourselves have set up earning power as the test of educational success. I wonder where Shakespeare would have been classified, or if college statisticians would have conveniently neglected to include Spinoza in their calculations so as not to spoil the convincing character of their success curves.

But our 'educators,' who are ever looking for more intangible objectives, have grasped with avidity this new motto, 'Training for Leadership!' What a blessing from heaven! How can anyone tell whether the product is finished? How does one become a leader? What qualities are demanded besides ruthlessness and lack of consideration for others? Here indeed is a smoke screen behind which failure may be hidden.

Our educational system now has as its motto, 'No one can be expected to learn unless he sees the value of what he is about to learn.' The next step is: 'We will arouse your interest by showing you how the knowledge may be used.' And the next step becomes inevitably: 'No one can acquire knowledge unless he can do something about it while he is learning.'

So the small child studying Greek history is given a project to carve a Greek temple out of soap, and in the more advanced stages the student is asked to render decisions concerning the conduct of the United States Steel Corporation without his ever having seen a steel plant.

To mature minds such mental exercises are undoubtedly stimulating, and a splendid training for young executives; to the immature the effect is fatal. Like the morons driving high-powered engines of destruction on the public highways, they develop a conquering sense of power without a corresponding sense of their own limitations. The individual is given a deep-rooted confidence in his own judgment. He becomes the judge of values. What he considers worth-while is the criterion. Given the right I.Q., he can't go wrong; or, in the words of the title of Pinero's ultramodern play which reflects so subtly the philosophy of Fascism, 'Right you are if you think you are.'

III

Our theory is complete. Action, knowledge for action, knowledge through action, knowledge is action. And the world is reaping the whirlwind which it has sown.

If there is one thing the world does not need it is more leadership. The battle being waged politically and internationally is essentially one between leaders craving action and those who know too much to act. Nor have we been wholly unaware in this country that something is not quite right. The egocentric mentality of youth, who more than ever before are convinced that this is the day when 'youth will be served' and that the world is largely if not entirely run for their benefit, has led to some protests. But our educators are undaunted. If something is wrong it can easily be corrected. What we now need is more attention to 'character building.' Thank heavens, another intangible.

Now to me all this seems absurd. I am old-fashioned enough to adhere to the old notion that character is, as it were, the subtle essence of a person's inherited chracteristics, his environment, and his habit of life. I have always thought that honesty with one's self, intellectual honesty, was the first step on the road to character building, and that a decent regard for others, born of a clear understanding of their problems and desires, though different from our own, was the next step.

But I am wrong again. We are now, so the newspapers inform me, going to give special attention to character building. I can just imagine a teacher saying to a group of undisciplined and spoiled young brats, 'Now, children, we are going to devote the next half hour to character building.'

Have we gone insane? Maybe not quite, but we are certainly on the road. And don't blame the teachers altogether. They are usually quite helpless. Many, if not most of them, are definitely opposed to all this falderol and firmly believe in the old way of acquiring knowledge. They still believe that an individual needs certain fundamental knowledge to fit into society, that this knowledge can be acquired only by hard work, and that the by-product is a character formed by intellectual honesty and disciplined thought and action. But they are helpless. Why?

Enter the executive.

To any visitor from abroad, the most impressive thing in the United States, next to the wonder of sky-reaching and unoccupied steel structures like the Empire State Building, is the group of business executives. Nowhere else, per worker employed, do we find so many mahogany desks and Oriental carpets devoted to the use of executives as we do in this country. It is indeed fortunate that our industry can afford to bear this burden of administrative overhead, but to the ignorant visitor from abroad it looks like a top-heavy structure. As one visitor said to me, 'You have gone administration mad.'

I do not know anything about these matters, and, not possessing adequate statistical data, am not prepared to render judgment. All I ask is that you look at your local schools some day and compare their administrative burdens with those of, say, twenty years ago. Principals and vice principals, curriculum directors, psychological advisers, stenographers and filing clerks—I shall not undertake to enumerate them. We of the old school wonder why all this is necessary. Why all this elaborate office machinery, why all these files and files of cards and folders, why all this entourage of the executive? Under the system of which I am a product no such executive staff existed, nor does it exist to-day. What do they all do? How do they occupy themselves? There is only one way they can keep busy. They supervise, check, correct, direct, and improve method.

The American system sets up, not the world and its requirements as the standard, but the child. Thus, as the child passes along the assembly line, the progress of the product must be constantly inspected, just as they do it in the Ford plant.

The process starts with the psychological test. The child's I.Q. is registered. And that is only the beginning. From then on, the teacher's time is occupied far more with checks and counterchecks and inspections than with acquiring more knowledge of the subject or with teaching. And my observation is that most of this record compilation is totally useless.

Some years ago our daughter, attending a public high school, was not receiving very good grades in arithmetic. We went to the school to see if possibly the teachers could suggest some way in which we could assist her to make a better showing. We were ushered into the august presence of the chief executive. A clerk was summoned, and a search was made in the elaborate filing system that lined the walls of an adjoining room. Triumphantly a folder was extracted and placed on the desk. Deep silence and a close examination of the statistical data followed. Then came the pronouncement: 'You have no cause for worry; her I.Q. is all right!' This certainly soothed my ragged nerves; but I had never doubted her I.Q. I did not even know what it was or where she carried it. I wanted to know about her arithmetic. It was explained to me, in that condescending and kindly fashion which the expert so frequently assumes when addressing the rank outsider, that my worry regarding arithmetic was quite irrelevant. Her I.Q. being what it was, the system being what it was, the outcome was assured. The assembly-line technique would not fail her.

We removed our daughter from the assembly line and from the further administrative protection of this perfectly systematized educational factory and sent her to a school where they did not know the difference between an I.Q. and a bullfrog. She is doing excellent work now, unhampered by executive interference and periodic inspection.

To use, if I may, an unacademic expression, 'How do they get that way?'

That is not difficult to answer. Once you make method the center of your system, the need for constant supervision, checking, and revision of technique becomes easily evident. Teaching now becomes a matter of organization and administrative control and not of knowledge. The professional administrators, through their constant contact with State Boards of Education, state legislators, and town officers, have learned about all that politicians can teach. They, and the select few among the teachers' colleges, have by now secured a strangle hold on a substantial part of the educational system of the country.

They speak the language of business and of politics. Their importance and indispensability increase with the dimensions of the administrative force. In order to demonstrate that they are wide-awake and 'on the job,' they must constantly place before the controllers of the purse strings a new theory—a new experiment. The business man understands this. He would not offer you a 1936 Ford in 1937. It is not difficult for him to grasp that a school must be similarly 'up to date.' He is baffled by the pseudo-psychological lingo of the expert 'educator,' but it has a strange fascination for him.

Now the poor teachers are caught. They cannot refuse to accept the new ideas. Their advice is usually not asked and certainly not followed. They dare not protest. The 'administrator' has too much knowledge of the methods of business administration. He speaks of 'coöperation' and interprets it, as the business executive, to mean, 'I'll tell you what to do—you just do it.' Should the teachers protest, they would soon discover that the school administrator has also learned the good American method of management by 'shake-up.' As one reorganization plan follows closely upon the heels of another, with no one knowing where the lightning will strike next, intelligent opposition is effectively unnerved.

Our universities have, on the whole, been little affected by all this, probably owing to the fact that the administrative direction has not been in the hands of professional administrators, or of those trained in schools of education where method was set up as superior to contents.

Yet it would be incorrect to assume that the universities have escaped entirely. To be sure, the academic independence of the university professor has been preserved to a most surprising extent; but subtle influences are at work to undermine it. The largest single danger in our university life comes again from the tendency to copy the pattern of management of big business. In our universities in Holland, all important decisions are made by the faculty or its representative body, the senate; and each professor in turn, in the order of seniority, occupies the post of presiding officer of this body.

When entering upon his activities in an American university the professor discovers that democracy has no place in the educational world. To be sure, faculty meetings are held, but in too many instances they are merely opportunities for the members of the faculty to blow off steam, and are intended only too often merely to give the impression that faculties are being consulted. Decisions are made in many institutions by the superexecutives. That is the way the Standard Oil Company operates, so who can doubt that the same method will also bring the best results in directing the work of a university?

This suppression of the democratic principle is most in evidence in our state institutions, where more or less successful business men are often brought in to direct the affairs of the institution. This is quite logical to the man who worships method. Is not the 'method of management,' like the 'method of teaching,' of universal application?

IV

Is there a remedy? I believe there is. I also believe it will not be applied. The first curve will lie in a clearer and more courageous definition of what we hope to achieve. Since our plan of operation is what it is, we must continue to face the need for elementary courses in our institutions of higher learning. But we should make a sharp division between those courses which are merely supplying what the students failed to receive in preparatory school and those which are of true university character.

Now there is every reason to encourage as many as are willing to come to expose themselves to the elementary subjects; and two years of college should be enough to satisfy this demand. But the point is that we must stop avoiding the issue. They come to learn. Then let us not find alibis. Let us tell the youngsters, 'We think this is what you need to learn to be an intelligent, modern citizen of the world. Now go to it. We don't care whether it will increase your earning power. In fact, we are mean enough to hope it will not. Neither are we going to tell you that you come to college not to learn but to make "social contacts." This is not a country club.'

If any students are left in the institution after the first two years, we may then decide who is fitted by intellectual capacity, knowledge, and general adaptability to continue and get the benefit of specialized professional training.

As far as the administrative side of the university is concerned, it is not too much to ask that the democratic spirit about which we hear so much in this country be reflected in the one place where it can exist most naturally. If, because of their size, universities in this country need business managers, let us have them, but let us separate as sharply as possible the academic from the administrative functions. The able-bodied, able-minded, and full-grown men who constitute the faculty can safely be granted the democratic right of sharing more fully in directing the policies of the institution than is now generally the case.

But most of our trouble does not lie in the universities, but in the grammar and high schools. There the first step in advance must be found in better pay for the better-trained teachers. Once the quality of the teaching staff has been improved, more democratic control of the schools by the teachers must be introduced. And this implies that the pernicious interference in school matters by high-strung Parent-Teacher Associations must end. These associations have undoubtedly done some good in isolated instances, but in many cases they have merely added to the dark fears that surround the underpaid teachers. They have only too often opened wide the gates for lay interference with the school system, and have frequently proved the means of shouldering upon the schools the burdens of neglected parental responsibilities. If your teachers know their jobs, if they have been selected because they have had the necessary equipment and experience, why not leave them alone? Would you organize a family doctors' association to supervise the operating-room technique of your physicians?

Once the teachers are free from outside interference and from the fear of arbitrary executive discipline, once they know their subjects thoroughly, I have little fear that they will find it necessary to hide behind method and intangible aims to cover up the lack of results. They themselves will insist that one studies a subject to learn it, and that one learns it because it is better to know the world in all its aspects than to be ignorant. And Johnnie, working late hours to keep up with his lessons, will in time discover that there is a joy in learning things for the sake of learning, that the most effective way of arousing one's interest is to complete successfully a distasteful and difficult task; and his character will develop as the by-product of disciplined living and thinking.

But I have been dreaming of a world that will never be. I am sorry if I have spoken out of turn. We have the greatest school system in the world. A recurring world crisis is upon us, and battleships must be built. We cannot now consider increasing the pay of our teachers; nor is it necessary, for in the immortal words of a legislator of Massachusetts, the cradle of our American culture, 'Teachers is cheap.'

29

English As You Teach It in America

Dear P——:

I shall soon be leaving your hospitable shores, after five very full months here. If ever I am to comply with your suggestion that I set down my impressions of your universities, it must be now. But I do it only on condition that you come to England, when the world grows sane once more, and comment as freely as I am doing—"nothing extenuate or set down aught in malice." I certainly don't want to perpetuate the bad English tradition—I suppose Mrs. Trollope began it—of lecturing Americans as if they were cowboys in search of culture (you remember the Oxford don who described Harvard as a place he had last heard of "twenty years ago"?).

True, I shall make various contracts with English methods and modes of thought; but I am well aware that these methods are not necessarily the image of perfection! Again, my visits to American colleges have not been official, or even orderly. I think you agree that the dozen institutions I have seen, from coast to coast, are fairly representative; but I fully realise that my judgments can only be tentative—which is another way of saying that there is much greater variety in American standards and achievements than you would find in the same number of colleges in England.

One thing the teachers of English in both countries have in common: their subject is a comparative new-comer to the academic world. Indeed, the usual order is reversed, for English was firmly established as a teaching subject earlier in American universities than in England. The Oxford English School, in its present form, is barely fifty years old; that of Cambridge is even younger. So there is a fair basis for comparison with your achievements here.

Jack Arthur Walter Bennett. "English as You Teach It in America," *College English*, Vol. 2, No. 7 (April, 1941), pp. 675–681. Reprinted by kind permission of the editor, *College English*, Chicago, Illinois.

Author (1911–   ): Author and English scholar; educated at the University of New Zealand and Merton College, Oxford; Fellow of Queens College, Oxford, 1938–1947; Head of Research Department and later Director, British Information Service, New York, 1940–1945; Fellow and Tutor Magdalen College, Oxford, 1947–1964.

In both countries, too, the early development of the subject was considerably quickened by the boom in Germanic philology in the nineteenth century. The pioneers in this study were Germans, and the early teachers were inevitably influenced by German methods. In England, there was some reaction against these methods about the turn of the century, and with it a change of emphasis from philology to literature—partly because most of the claims in the field of philology had been pegged out, and partly, I suspect (the laws of Supply and Demand operate even in the groves of Academe), because of the growing number of women students, who were supposed to be better fitted for the study of literature.

Fortunately, most English universities agreed that "Eng. Lit." began at least as early as Chaucer; and in an academic system that had been based for centuries on a knowledge of Greek and Latin, it did not seem unusual that students of English Literature should be required to learn the grammar of the language in which the earliest documents of that literature were written. Such a pre-requisite was, in fact, almost a guarantee of respectability. The result is that "Language" and "Literature" have generally been on speaking terms. There has been coordination rather than conflict. "Pure" philology has perhaps suffered, and nothing has quite taken the place of the effective discipline it can provide; but most students are made incidentally aware of its larger lessons of historical continuity and development; and they have a better understanding of the sound and meaning of our early literature than they could ever get from translations or modernizations.

I would not trouble to repeat these simple facts if it did not seem to me that there are some signs in America of a separation between these two partners, which almost amounts to a divorce. I know that courses in Old and Middle English are included in most syllabuses. But I got the impression that they were treated a little grudgingly, a little skimpily, and that for most undergraduates they did not mean much else besides Chaucer and *Beowulf*. A few other couples, once happily married, seem about to break up; and I wonder if you do not make this process of divorce too easy in America. The polite name for it is "specialisation"; but the methodology of scientific research does not always apply to the teaching of English. If we separate "Speech" from language, "Dramatic Art" from literature, the study from the practice of "Creative Writing," we are surely leaving each partner too poor to pay expenses. It was a surprise to find that undergraduates could take courses in "Speech" without studying phonetics or the history of the English language in America; and that a young novelist could obtain a degree in "Imaginative Writing," without knowing anything of the history of the Novel. I agree that his novel might be none the worse, and perhaps better, for this ignorance. That raises another issue, which I must remember to touch on later.

Fundamentally, this separatism (and if it is not confined to America) seems to be due to a dislike of the historical method as being dry-as-dust, academic, irrelevant. Here I've only time to point out that this historical approach has been adopted, in different degrees and ways, by some of the greatest artists of our time—amongst them Eric Gill, Picasso, Joyce. I realise, of course, that historical consciousness is of varying strength and found at various levels in different countries, and that it is expressed in a wide variety of ways. Most American students, for instance, seem "alive" to American literature, past and present; but they do not seem equally aware of the growth of what Mencken calls the American language. Perhaps you will have to wait until such works as the *Dictionary of American English* are completed, for such a consummation. But when courses in the American language become general, I hope that they will be linked closely with the study of American literature.

I was struck by other differences in emphasis that seem to spring from an historical consciousness that is characteristically American. The Renaissance, for example, often bulks larger in your courses than it does in England, where the word itself has almost gone out of fashion in literary criticism (perhaps because of the current inclination to modify the violent contrasts between the Middle Ages and the Renaissance drawn by the older text-books). I take it that this different emphasis exists because America itself was one aspect of the Renaissance—and, for that matter, of the Reformation; perhaps your country, which has not yet been stained with the grayness and disillusion that has pervaded Europe since the last war, and which still represents a brave new world to many, is intuitively more sympathetic to the multi-coloured life of the Renaissance period and all the energy and enterprise it generated. Again, I found that attention was focussed on Victorian literature much more often here than in England. One reason, presumably, is that American literature came of age last century, sometimes modelling itself on Victorian examples, and American writers were in closer contact with their English contemporaries than they have ever been, or wished to be, since. A less conscious but equally powerful reason may be that something of Victorian idealism and individualism (which in one direction produced the doctrine of Free Trade, in another Samuel Smiles's *Self-Help*) still survives and even flourishes here: your climate of opinion enables you to understand the Victorians better, perhaps, than we can. I pass over the materialistic suggestion that this period was the only one left to be sliced up for research, and that American scholars, with characteristic foresight, got in first. It does not take account of all the facts! Whatever the reason, the results have been abundantly worthwhile: the attention recently paid here to Matthew Arnold, for example, must put English critics to shame.

But it is perhaps a consequence of the pre-occupation with these two eras that American advances in the field of English medieval literature, where for long American scholars have been in the van, seem to be slackening. The doyens have retired, and there are few to take their place—and this at a time when texts and other material are more accessible here than ever before, as the progress in other medieval studies, as symbolised by *Speculum*, clearly indicates. The halt, I am sure, is merely temporary; but I feel that it is directly connected with the small amount of attention paid in ordinary courses to pre-Chaucerian language and literature. I realise that it is largely a matter of balance, and that the process of adjustment must always be delicate. But one does not have to be a neo-Thomist in order to be qualified to emphasise the value of the study of medieval literature at this point of time.

You will have one weighty retort to this criticism: "lack of time and lack of teachers." I admit the force of this argument, and agree that it would be fatal to overcrowd syllabuses any further. I am not advocating expansion, but a more economical use of those resources you have. Most teachers I have met agree that the freshman composition courses, for example, entail much useless drudgery, and that it would be more appropriate if this work were done before the student enters college. Such a change would at once free part of your faculties for more productive work, and raise the standard of teaching. As it is, these courses surely tie the freshman down to earlier habits of study intead of preparing him for a more critical and comprehensive approach. Many (though not all) of the "Readers" designed for these courses seem suited to the schoolroom rather than to the library. Feeding the young on gobbets must surely delay for them that recognition of the individuality of a book or an author which is one of the prime pleasures of literature. These *biblia abiblia* usually involve the dissection of many good books to make a few heavy ones. That they are, supposedly, remunerative is nothing in their disfavour. Dr. Johnson would certainly have approved of any desire their compilers may have for pocket money—but I doubt whether he would have felt that these selections were the best way "to teach the young idea how to shoot." Frequently extracts from living writers give an air of contemporaneity; but they may also give a false prestige to the writer chosen, and a limited or even misleading view of his work. They may even defeat the very purpose for which they are intended: they may help to reduce all literature to an academic study. Examinations are a cruel necessity, and the less they lay their dead hand on current books the greater the student's capacity for testing his own standards of enjoyment.

The question, "Should there be courses in contemporary literature?" leads me inevitably to the feature of some of your curricula which most interests an English visitor: the Schools of what is rather ambiguously called "Creative Writing." I presume that one purpose the founders of such schools had in mind was to banish the notion that literature stopped with Tennyson, or even with Whitman. I heartily sympathise with this impulse: it is obviously good that students should realise that writing is a living art, and that they should have some contact with contemporary writers. But, clearly, in the work of these schools everything depends on the teacher. He may be a good novelist or poet or journalist, but this does not necessarily mean that he will be a good critic. He may have a strong influence over his pupils, but this may merely turn them into his imitators or idolaters. He may not want to teach at all, but may be tempted by the prospect of security; even if he does no harm to his pupils, he may do harm to himself. Besides, any attempt to teach the art of imaginative writing surely presupposes an agreed aesthetic—and discovering that usually turns out to be a full-time occupation. Incidentally, I've still to learn how one works out the equation that x poems $= y$ short stories $= 1$ novel $= 1$ degree.

But to criticise these schools of writing is not my main concern; they can be judged only by results. They interest me insofar as they form another characteristically American phenomenon. They could never have arisen here but for the widespread eagerness to write, which has no parallel in England, where writers are still drawn from a comparatively restricted class, and where very few go through the equivalent of that "sodajerking" stage which seems an accepted part of American education. The mere variety of human experience which the young American writer contrives to assimilate is probably one reason why American novelists are more popular in England than English novelists are in America.

I'm not going to expatiate on the American fondness for research—another feature of your educational system that sometimes intrigues visiting scholars. Most of the research students I met seemed to be well-trained and to be doing useful work. I did sometimes feel that graduate courses consisted of rather heavy façades to ordinary workaday programmes (just as I felt that the criticism in some college literary journals hid rather commonplace judgments behind sententious phrases). But the real perversions of graduate study seem to be flourishing in nonliterary fields. Why must guileless physical educators be compelled to write high-sounding dissertation like: "A study of the movement pattern of football guards leading interference," or: "A study of the effects of hard usage upon the feet of college women"? I think we must all disabuse ourselves of the notion that research is the goal to which education must aspire. Otherwise, before long we shall be identifying culture with *PMLA* or the *Review of English Studies*.

Your facilities for research are proverbial, and I have nothing but admiration for them and for the enthusiasm behind such projects as the American dictionary and the linguistic atlas. I hope that in the future they will lead to even closer cooperation between American and English scholars (we could probably learn much from you, for example, in the study of dialects), and that intercourse between them will not be confined to hurried dashes to the Huntington or the Bodleian.

But in the last analysis it is the quality of the average student, and not of the professional researcher, that we must consider. I feel that your colleges would gain greatly if their standards of entrance were more uniform; yet from the almost infinite variety of your undergraduates you perhaps reap something in human value that the more rigid academic systems of Europe do not always preserve. Education is the real criterion of a nation's claim to be a democracy. One inevitable consequence in England of the present war will be the further democratisation of our university system. In this respect it is likely to approach increasingly close to yours. If this is the outcome it may well compensate for the loss of buildings, books, and some of "the last enchantments of the Middle Age."

30

American Graduate Education:
A British Political Analysis

Graduate work in the American university has two major sides. On the one hand it is professional training for a vocation like law or medicine. If the standard of this training inevitably varies from place to place, few serious observers would deny that, at its best, it is far ahead of any similar training in Europe. A great law school, like that of Harvard or Yale, Wisconsin or Columbia, will turn out students who, at their best, are likely not only to know more law than, say, an average law teacher in a British University, but also to have a far more critical mind about the problems of the law. These best students will have helped to produce, with no more than occasional professorial advice, journals of a quality good enough to be cited with respect by the most eminent American judges. Their teachers will naturally be considered for the highest judicial positions. Mr. Justice Holmes was a professor at the Harvard Law School when he was called to the Supreme Court of Massachusetts; so was Professor Felix Frankfurter when Mr. Roosevelt nominated him to the Supreme Court of the United States. Professor W. O. Douglas went from Yale, through the Securities and Exchange Commission, to the Supreme Court as the youngest judge who had sat there since the famous Story; Dean Charles E. Clark and Professor Thurman Arnold went, by way of Yale also, to the United States Circuit Court of Appeals. Dean Harlan Stone of Columbia University Law School went therefrom, first, to be the Attorney-General of the United States, and thence to the federal Supreme Court of which he became Chief Justice. Nor is it unimportant to note that when Mr. Taft ceased

Harold J. Laski. "American Graduate Education," from "American Education," in *The American Democracy: A Commentary and an Interpretation* (New York: The Viking Press, 1948), pp. 370–380. Reprinted by kind permission of the publishers, The Viking Press, New York.

Author (1893–1950): Educated Manchester Grammar School and New College, Oxford; Lecturer in History, McGill University, 1914–1916, and in History and Government, Harvard University, 1916–1920; Lecturer in and later Professor of Political Science, University of London since 1920; Vice-Chairman, British Institute of Adult Education, 1921–1930; Member, National Executive, Labor Party; Vice Chairman, 1944–1945; Chairman, 1945–1946.

to be president of the United States, he became professor of constitutional law at the Yale Law School, and later returned to Washington to become the only ex-president of the United States who also occupied the great post of Chief Justice. These are merely instances of a general habit of mind.

There have, of course, been professors of law in British universities of the highest intellectual distinction. Blackstone and Dicey, Sir Frederick Pollock, and that greatest of all English historians since Gibbon, F. W. Maitland, were all for many years professors of law. But of them all, Blackstone was the only one to reach the Bench, and this was less because he was an eminent Vinerian Professor at Oxford, than because, in between, he was a member of Parliament and Solicitor-General. No doubt it is true that a number of English judges have lectured upon a part-time basis in English law schools, like Lord Wright, who was an early and brilliant lecturer on commercial law at the London School of Economics and Political Science. But they invariably do this only while they are establishing their position at the Bar; it is a temporary financial expedient and no more. And even if, in the last thirty years, there has been a tendency for the Lord Chancellor to offer the dignity of King's Counsel to a few law teachers of exceptional eminence like Dicey, this remains infrequent; and I am, I think, right in believing that between Blackstone and the present time Sir Henry Maine is the only great jurist—an English lawyer uses the term to denote a lawyer remote from practical experience—to whom high judicial office has been offered; and it must be remembered that he had served a full term as legal member of the Viceroy's Council in India. The main road to the Bench in England lies, first, through the House of Commons, and next through actual practice; a "writing" lawyer may even find himself at a disadvantage, since the habit is to think that a barrister is free to publish because his desk is empty of briefs. England supports one law review of real distinction, and another, not yet of equal standing, which is still struggling to live. The Cambridge Faculty of Law produces an annual number of a law review, and the London School of Economics and Political Science an "Annual Survey" of judicial and administrative decisions and of statutory enactments. Books, mainly textbooks, apart, there are hardly half a dozen really eminent names in the whole range of its legal literature since Bentham and Maine.

The contrast with the law schools of the United States is startling. It is startling in the quality of teachers; it is startling in the volume and distinction of their published work; and it is startling in the light of the achievement of American students at their best. The big law firm in New York or Boston or Chicago jumps at the chance of getting one of the top men from a good American school; so, too, especially in recent years, has the administration at Washington or New York. It would be easy to name a score of young graduates who went from Harvard directly to a post of real significance in the office of the Attorney-General or of the Secretary of Labor, in the Department of the Interior or the Department of State; a journey, I suggest, that would be almost unthinkable in England. The professor of law on a faculty, with a high standing in the profession, is a man held in high esteem; even his favourite pupils are sought after. Judges will eagerly canvass his opinion of their decisions; they are not unlikely themselves to write against him in defense of themselves. In the result, a good American law school is not merely a place where law is often admirably taught; it is also a place where a good deal of important law is likely to be made. As a consequence, no one who knows the dozen or so major law schools can really doubt that they are far more alive, far more able to elicit eager interest from their students, far more likely to be engaged in significant research, than all the English law schools put together. I hazard the guess that Professor Sheldon Glueck of the Harvard Law School has done more, in his own department, for the serious study of criminal law in its results upon convicted defendants than all the law schools of England together with the work of the Prison Commission, the four Inns of Court, and the Law Society. There is nothing that remotely compares, either in fullness or precision, with the crime surveys of Cleveland and of Boston, or of similar studies, like those of procedure and bankruptcy and freedom of speech, which have been undertaken either singly or in co-operation by American professors of law. Nor can I omit to emphasize that no generation of students seems to leave the better schools without receiving from their teachers an inspiration to study some problem in law reform.

Of the position of the medical schools I am not, of course, competent to make a judgment in similarly comparative terms. But there is, I believe, no shadow of doubt that American medical education, at its best, is at least as good as that of any other country. It is indeed notable how considerable a proportion of the eminent figures in modern American medicine have bred teachers in the university schools. The fame of the Johns Hopkins Medical School, in the days of Welch and Osler and Adolf Meyer, hardly yields precedence to that of the University of Vienna in its greatest days. It is, moreover, suggestive that, almost a generation before Great Britain, the better American schools had realized the significance of social and industrial medicine, and the value of the history of medicine in its community setting as a clue to the secret of its progress. In this regard, it is not too much to say that

the works of Henry E. Sigerist at Johns Hopkins marks something of
an epoch in the development of medical education; as those of Bernhard
Stern have done at Columbia University. Dr. Sigerist and his colleagues
realized, what only an occasional figure had recognized elsewhere, that
if medicine is put in its proper historical background, much of its failures
and successes begin to be understood. Nor is there much doubt that
the policy of whole-time professorships to which medical men of the
first quality are called while they are young enough to do pioneering
in research has had great advantages in making the university schools
of medicine, at any rate at their best, something akin to what the Graduate School of Medicine in London was intended to be.

Broadly speaking, the university professional schools have been a remarkable success. The general standard of their teaching is extraordinarily high; the level of student interest is exceptional; and the schools
manage not only to produce research work of outstanding distinction,
but imbue a considerable proportion of their students with the sense
that an interest in the social responsibilities of the *métier* they follow
is part of the obligation they assume when they decide to follow it.
The comparison, in this regard, between the law schools of America
and the law schools of Britain is all to the former's advantage. The
British law school has not yet found any creative place in the system
of training either for the Bar or for the solicitors' side of the profession.
The American law school has made itself not only the main source
from which the best lawyers and the best judges are likely to be recruited, but also a vital instrument in the struggle for law reform. The
kind of criticism which judicial opinion and legal administration ought
perpetually to encounter is something that the British university law
school has hardly even begun to recognize that it ought to undertake
as part of its normal function; that function has been primary in the
work of an American law school, at any rate of the first rank, for something like fifty years. And if it be said that the British law schools
have produced great scholars, Maine, Maitland, Pollock, Holdsworth,
to take some outstanding examples, the answer is the simple one that
the American schools have produced Holmes, Ames, Thayer, and Pound,
quite apart from their additional claim to have set the criteria of criticism
in issues of contemporary doctrine in work like that of Thomas Reed
Powell in constitutional law, of Francis H. Bohlen in the law of torts,
of John Chipman Gray in the law of real property, of Frankfurter, in
his academic period, in the vital field of administrative law, of Chafee
in the field of civil liberties. And this is quite apart from the work
done by the university law schools in the important field of legal administration, which in Britain has mostly been left either to an occasional

government committee or to some solitary investigator who, like Sir Edward Parry, was driven to furious protest by daily experience of the urgent need for reform in one aspect of the work of the court over which he presided with such distinction. Lawyers with the deep social responsibility of Parry are as rare in England as jurists with a passion, like Bentham, to adapt law to the needs of a new time.

It is curious to note how different are the habits, and the results, of the non-professional graduate schools from those of their professional analogues. To understand this difference the graduate school must, however briefly, be set in its historical background. It was far from infrequent for American scholars of a century ago, men like Ticknor and Everett and Bancroft, to spend several years in Europe in preparation for the life work they intended to undertake. For the most part they were in comfortable circumstances. They accepted the New England tradition, so finely exemplified in Parkman and Prescott, that private wealth ought to admit its obligations by devotion to the cultivation of knowledge. Not a few of them were deeply perturbed by the mainly English criticism that the American contribution to letters and learning was, compared with its wealth, of relative insignificance; and since many of them were still in thrall to the idea that American scholarship was a minor branch of English scholarship, they were, in no small degree, moved by a desire for intellectual independence. That attitude was emphasized in a famous appeal of William Ellery Channing,[1] and later in the acid but brilliant phrase of James Russell Lowell in which he referred to "a certain condescension among foreigners." The desire for cultural independence coincided with, was even, perhaps, an outgrowth of, the persistent attempt of American economists, especially after the war of 1812, to plead, like Henry Carey, for a new political economy which would suit American conditions and therefore reject the postulates of the classical political economy which the predominance of England had fastened upon Europe.[2] And it was, no doubt, greatly aided by the rise of the new West, and the sense there that neither the habits nor the forms of eastern culture, so obviously tied to European, above all to English, models, would suit the circumstances of a new America. Even if they were criticized and disliked, there can be but little doubt that the growth of the West had an immense influence on American ways of thought.

Slowly before the Civil War, but with remarkable acceleration after it, this attitude coincided with the discovery of German university schol-

[1] *Remarks on National Literature*, in *Complete Works* (London, no date), p. 101.
[2] See Dorfman, *The Economic Mind in American Civilization*, Vol. II, Chap. xxix.

arship, with its immense achievements and elaborate organization. Many of the younger students began to visit the German universities and to take their doctorate degrees in Germany. When Johns Hopkins University was founded, research there began to be built around the seminar, with the conception of the professor, surrounded by his band of devoted pupils, working at some problem he thought important in a coherent and systematic way. It began to be the custom to train the student for scholarship by an elaborate discipline in methodology and bibliography, in the proper grasp of the way to handle original sources, in the belief that true learning emerged from the intensive cultivation of a small field of inquiry rather than from embarking, before the student was ripe enough for investigation, on some massive issue beyond his powers and experience. To this, I think, must be added the important inferences that the young scholar's work ought to be worthy of publication, that if he took one part of a field, his neighbour in the seminar might well take a related part, which enabled each to stimulate the other—the real beginning, I suspect, of the modern craze for co-operative research—and that a period of devotion such as this to original research was the necessary prelude to the work of university teaching. The publication in 1883 of the first series of the Johns Hopkins *Studies in Historical and Political Science* was a landmark in the academic history of the United States. Within a decade the doctorate in philosophy had become the well-nigh indispensable passport to the right to teach in an American university.

The popularity of the system grew by leaps and bounds. A university soon became an institution which could take pride in its ability to attract graduate students. Research achieved a status equal with teaching in importance; the tradition became established that there was little or no hope of a permanent university position without the degree of doctor of philosophy. Teachers were appointed in the belief that, where they went, research students would follow; it even became increasingly necessary for the teacher to publish in order that his name might be continually in the minds of students who were uncertain what university to choose for their graduate work. Or, if he did not publish, he needed the kind of influence with his colleagues in other universities which enabled him to secure posts for the students who were registered under his supervision. Once, moreover, the doctorate had become a passport to a college post, it began to be a distinction universally sought. The members of the faculty of a normal school desired it as a means to promotion. A teacher in a high school would regard it as the key which unlocked the door to a principalship. It became necessary to invent ways and means of helping along the young men and women in quest, in ever-increasing numbers, of their Ph.D. Not everyone could be given a scholarship, still less a travelling scholarship. But there could be teaching fellows, who combined some form or other of class work, quarter-time or half-time, with their research; there could be university assistants, who paid their way through college by taking off the professor's hands the laborious work of holding the "quiz" or a class or reading his examination papers for him; or there could be the research assistant to the professor, who hunted down references for him in the library, made notes at his indication of significant material he desired to use but had not the time to go through for himself, read his proofs for printers' errors, and compiled the index to his book. I have even known research assistants who read and digested for their professors books in languages the professors could not read, so that, on publication, they could not be accused of overlooking important foreign work they ought to have known. And in between the performance of such labours the assistant went on with his own researches. First, as a rule, he took the master's degree, an examination in a field of studies connected with the subject on which he thought of specializing. Then he prepared for and took his general examination, an oral examination in which a group of professors "grilled" him, much in the manner of continental Europe, to be sure that his background knowledge was adequate for the work on which he proposed to embark. After this, he would begin preparing his thesis, which might take him anywhere from two to five or six years, according to the time at his disposal and his habits of work.

The range of academic studies, moreover, which now shelter themselves under the wings of a university institution has increased at an almost terrifying speed. There is the vast area of commerce, both territorial and functional; there is the complex called "home economics," which may include the analysis of family budgets or the examination of the machinery most suitable for dish-washing in small restaurants. There is the immense area called "education," on which one student may be working at the history of the methods of teaching elementary arithmetic, another on professional solidarity among teachers in England, a third on tendencies towards centralization in the state educational system of Illinois, and a fourth on what French critics think of the American educational system. The study of Romance philology may take one man to the examination of what Dante has to say about each species of the animal kingdom mentioned in his works, and another to an analysis of the use in French of the infinite, instead of the finite, verb. A group of students may take the problems of reconstruction in the South after the Civil War, and each give attention to their impact upon a particular state. Another group may study the drift to administrative centralization in one or a number of states. As each new specialism pushes its way to university recognition, it is hardly unfair to say that its teachers feel they have won for it its full status when one of their students has received his doctorate in the subject.

The writing of a thesis goes through a physiological rhythm almost as regular as the circulation of the blood. The student chooses his "topic" in consultation with the professor who is to supervise his work. It is curiously rare for a student to know what it is he wants to write about. Far more usually, he accepts the professor's suggestion, and he then decides upon a theme from a list of possible subjects which the wise professor keeps, as it were, in stock; or he works upon some project the material of which may ultimately be the basis of a chapter, or a paragraph, or a footnote in the *magnum opus* the professor is writing. The subject once chosen, the student compiles a bibliography of whatever exists about his subject, with special reference to manuscript material or to remote sources, like old newspapers, not previously used in work upon his theme. He goes through all the obvious material conscientiously, taking careful notes as he reads; if the manuscripts are in Europe, in the British Museum, for example, or the Bibliothèque Nationale, he tries to get a scholarship to London or Paris, or to get a loan against his future, to consult them; or he may be fortunate enough to persuade a wealthy university to have photostatic copies made that he can peruse at leisure in its library. After more note-taking, he begins to arrive at a scheme of work which he will probably amend somewhat in the light of discussion with his supervisor. He then begins the heavy work of writing his thesis, consulting at intervals his supervisor or other professors from whom he may get ideas or counsel. As he writes, he will support each statement he makes with a footnote showing the source from which it is taken, until, not seldom, the text itself seems like a small island, surrounded by a veritable ocean of references. And when the last chapter is done, he will conscientiously add the most comprehensive bibliography he can compile, perhaps classified with a minute precision that would evoke a smile of approval from the shade of that ingenious librarian who invented the Dewey decimal system. The thesis submitted, he is examined upon it by a small committee of professors to whose hands is entrusted the fate of the research and its author.

Not even in Germany has so massive a system been evolved, so intricate and so terrifying, in order to help a young man or woman learn how to write a book. It has evoked an endless stream of protests, of which, perhaps, the acid essay of William James[3] is the most famous. But no criticism has yet proved powerful enough to stay its torrential

[3] "The Ph. D. Octopus," in *Memories and Studies* (New York: Longmans, 1912).

movement; it has been said that in the year before the outbreak of the Second World War more than three thousand doctorates were granted in the United States. I have myself calculated that in one Midwestern university alone, and that by no means the largest of its area, over six hundred doctorates were conferred from 1919 to 1939. Sometimes the university requires that the theme be printed; most of them today more mercifully asked no more than the submission of several typewritten copies, one of which will remain on file in its library. But few of them are published in the ordinary way; only a minute percentage, when published, ever reach the dignity of a second edition. Out of 459 numbers in the John Hopkins' series, which represents the best work of all its graduate students in the social sciences for sixty years, only fifty-four are out of print; and the demand for these is apparently not ample enough to justify reprinting. Out of 380 numbers in the well-known Columbia University *Studies in History and Economics and Public Law*, published between 1893 and 1903, only nine appear to be out of print, and only one volume seems to have gone into a second edition. Much the same is true of similar series published under the auspices of Harvard and Yale Universities.

Obviously enough, statistics for this character tell but a small part of the significance of any volume. Few people would, or could, rightly expect that a learned and heavily documented book could normally expect to have a wide sale. Its author is almost certain to be unknown; his theme is likely to be narrow; nor is he likely to have made any exciting discoveries or put forward any important generalizations. Yet, when all this is granted, the picture remains a disturbing one. A student writes a book not because he feels called to write that particular book, but because he is bound to write a book in order, broadly speaking, to have a certificate of competence which entitles him to begin or to continue teaching in a university. He rarely conceives of the subject he takes as the preliminary study for some great book he has at least the ambition one day to write. He rarely even seeks to approach it in an original way. It is often thorough, often useful, now and again it may shed some new ray of light of real significance upon its subject. It is but seldom that its author finds inspiration or even stimulus in doing it. It is a task that must be got through; it is a means of opening a gate, a possible road to promotion. Rarely, indeed, does he see the bridge between his particular field of study and the next field. Rarely, either, does he inquire whether what he does is important in itself or likely to be the basis upon which some later scholar may build more important work. His anxiety is to get the work done so that he may enter the stage of work where he has become his own master.

I do not want for an instant to paint a picture that is out of perspective. Everyone knows that remarkable books have been written for the doctorate, and that some of them rank as indispensable in their field. But that is not because they were written for the doctorate; it is because they were written by remarkable men and women. The system as a whole holds hundreds of students in bondage every year to an idea that is wholly illusory. Some of them are fundamentally incapable of writing a good book. Others are not yet mature enough to write one. Others, again, have no desire to write a book and learn little or nothing from their effort to write it. And the system develops habits of its own. It begets what the French call the *fureur de l'inédit*. It begets the obligation not to write upon a topic, however important, upon which someone else is known to be writing; hence the publication every year, in the learned American journals, of long lists of subjects already pre-empted. It begets the passion for footnotes, the conviction that no statement will be believed unless it can be referred to an earlier writer or document, and it gets, perhaps above all, what can only be termed bibliographical elephantiasis. No doubt there are supervisors work with whom is an illumination the light from which will give vision to the student for the rest of his days; no one who worked with Frederick J. Turner, or with Carl Becker, but must have felt the excitement of seeing how the great artist hews from the rough stone a portrait which comes to life, just as no one can have submitted an idea for critical examination to William James, or to Morris Cohen, without the joy of seeing how a great swordsman can cut it to pieces. Quite obviously, a man who is born for thought or learning, whether in the humanities or in the sciences, will find the Ph.D. a hurdle he can take in his stride; and there will always be some for whom the system leads to association out of which solid work, even occasionally inspired work, will emerge.

Yet, granted all this, the system has now become a vast machine which kills the very purposes it was intended to serve. It leads to premature and excessive specialization. It leads to the production of a fantastic mass of minute researches of which but a small part has any special significance either for the author or for the public they are intended to reach. In the social sciences especially, it breeds a race of researchers who cannot see the woods for the trees. But its worst effect is, I think, that in all save the really exceptional scholar, it becomes a form of escapism which makes for unreal thinking and ineffective teaching. It makes for the first because the intense concentration on a small theme seems to breed a type which becomes afraid either of large generalizations or considering issues which reach beyond its boundaries. He becomes unaccustomed to the co-ordination of his specialism with the larger problems of which it is a part. There even comes a time when he resents being asked either to let his mind play freely over a large realm of ideas or to show an awareness that the need to arrive is not less important than the preparation for the journey. And he becomes, only too often, an ineffective teacher, because his training inhibits him from realizing that the one thing his students want to know is how the subject helps to explain the kind of world in which they live. He thinks that the more he detaches himself from such an explanation, the more scholarly his treatment ought to be regarded. He begins by taking no risks because he is uncertain; he ends by taking no risks because he has ceased, by use and wont, to have any convictions at all. He becomes a purveyor of information, most of which is easily available in books, which he retails afresh every year in much the same way as an automobile dealer sells his cars.

It would be an immense boon to American education if the Ph.D., together with the immense administrative apparatus it has come to involve, were got rid of altogether. Most of the labour it involves is not in any real sense, educational. Most of the men and women who have something real to say in their chosen field of study would say it anyhow, whether there were a degree or no; and its existence leads a multitude of people to try to say something when they are uneasily conscious either that they have nothing to say or that what they are asked to examine is not in fact worth, as a problem, the immense effort they have to spend upon it. I think it is reasonable to insist that most of the creative minds in American universities are aware that this is the case; but they shrink from the effort involved in a sustained attack upon what has now become an immense vested interest in the university. Not least among the evils is the fact that it tends to destroy the reflective mind, the mind that broods over a large range of facts until, by a flash of insight, a relation is seen between them from which they come to have a new meaning. In place of the thinker, it puts the card index; in place of the play of ideas, it puts the footnote and the bibliography. Nothing invented since the Inquisition has had so sterilizing an effect upon that habit of free speculation and eager debate of first principles out of which the scholar is most likely to transform information into wisdom.

Two other features of the university system deserve a word. The first derives directly, the other indirectly, from the institution of the doctorate. The first is the use of volume of production as one of the main indices to promotion. Unless a teacher makes his mark early, either by a promising piece of work or by the quality of his personality, there is a constant drive to publish, especially in a large university, lest his claim to promotion be overlooked. The result is that the learned journals of the United States are full of what can only be called machine-made research in which the habits of the aspirant to a Ph.D. are prolonged year after year until the teacher is satisfied he can climb no higher. He is afraid of being labelled as "unproductive," so that, year after year, he will devote his leisure to grinding out articles which are only too often dead even before they have reached the printed page. And because most of the scholars who edit the journals are aware that the articles are insignificant, the question of whether to publish them or not tends to become either the presence of some unpublished document or the tabulation of some material, the first of which will only very rarely have importance, and the second of which will give a precision, the labour of which is out of all proportion to its value, to some simple platitude which everyone knew before. It may be a letter, say, of Robert Southey saying that he has received a parcel of books for which he had asked, or it may be a table to prove that in a New England village there are more Packards above the railroad tracks per family than there are below them. The point I am concerned to make is that the whole academic atmosphere tends to lead to the insistent cult of the insignificant, and those who are driven to the practice of this cult are bound themselves, before long, to become insignificant too.

The other feature which needs emphasizing is the cult of the textbook. This depends upon a number of factors. The need for a doctorate tends to make the achievement of a permanent university post something that few teachers will reach before their thirties. By this time they may well be married and have family responsibilities. They find it difficult to live in any real comfort on their salaries. They know that the author of a successful textbook will certainly earn a far greater reward than he is likely to do in the normal way if he gives his time to serious research. His needs are great; the publisher's offer is tempting. He knows that it is, of course, a gamble, but if it is a successful gamble he can buy a new car, or take his family away for the summer vacation instead of spending hot and tiring days in New York City or Chicago, or get someone in "to do the chores or look after the children" so that his wife may have some time in which to call her soul her own. The result can be seen in the catalogue of any educational publisher in the United States. Each has his history of America, his government of America, his geography of America, his principles of economics, his textbook of statistical method, or of accountancy, or of ancient history, or of medieval history, or of modern history. Once there is a large potential audience to whom teachers can address textbooks, they will be published almost beyond computation; and since the appetite grows by what it feeds on, one success is only too likely to lead to another venture, in the hope that it may be repeated. These books vary very little from one another. They usually crowd such a mass of information into their six to eight hundred pages that the student loses himself in their midst. And, worst of all, the need to get the book used in as large a range of colleges as possible leads to the suppression of any ideas that have colour or vitality or a bias that might offend. Nor must it be forgotten that one of the inevitable results on the student is that he expects to find in the textbook all he needs to know about the subject, and he tends to regard with horror the notion that he may reasonably be asked to read the original authorities out of which the subject gained its existing contours.

31

Education and the Humanist

Even when dealing with the remote past, the historian cannot be entirely objective. And in an account of his own experiences and reactions the personal factor becomes so important that it has to be extrapolated by a deliberate effort on the part of the reader. I must, therefore, begin with a few autobiographical data, difficult though it is to speak about oneself without conveying the impression of either false modesty or genuine conceit.

I first came to this country in the fall of 1931 upon the invitation of New York University. I was then professor of the history of art at Hamburg; and since this Hanseatic city was always proud of its cosmopolitan tradition, the authorities were not only glad to grant me a leave of absence for one semester but subsequently consented to an arrangement whereby I was permitted to spend alternate terms in Hamburg and New York. Thus for three successive years I commuted, as it were, across the Atlantic. And when the Nazis ousted all Jewish officials in the spring of 1933, I happened to be in New York while my family were still at home. I fondly remember the receipt of a long cable in German, informing me of my dismissal but sealed with a strip of green paper which bore the inscription: "Cordial Easter Greetings, Western Union."

These greetings proved to be a good omen. I returned to Hamburg only in order to wind up my private affairs and to attend to the Ph.D. examinations of a few loyal students (which, curiously enough, was possible in the initial stages of the Nazi regime); and thanks to the selfless

Erwin Panofsky. "The History of Art," in *The Cultural Migration: The European Scholar in America* (Philadelphia: University of Pennsylvania Press, 1953), pp. 82–83, 95–111. Reprinted by kind permission of the publishers, University of Pennsylvania Press.

Author (1892–1968): Historian, educated in Germany; privatdozent at Hamburg University, 1921, appointed professor, 1926; came to the United States in 1931 to teach at New York University; in 1935 invited to join the humanistic faculty of the Institute for Advanced Study, Princeton University.

efforts of my American friends and colleagues, unforgettable and unforgotten, we could establish ourselves at Princeton as early as 1934. For one year I held concurrent lectureships at New York and Princeton universities, and in 1935 I was invited to join the newly constituted humanistic faculty of the Institute for Advanced Study which owes its reputation to the fact that its members do their research work openly and their teaching surreptitiously, whereas the opposite is true of so many other institutions of learning. I, too, have thus continued to teach in various places, with special regularity in Princeton and New York.

I am telling all this in order to make it perfectly clear that my experiences in this country are somewhat atypical in regard to both opportunities and limitations. As to the opportunities: in contrast to nearly all my colleagues, including the American-born, I was never hampered by excessive teaching obligations and never suffered from a lack of research facilities; in contrast to so many immigrant scholars, I had the good fortune of coming to the United States as a guest rather than a refugee; and, be it said with deepest gratitude, no one has ever made me feel the difference when my status suddenly changed in 1933. As to the limitations: I neither know the South beyond Asheville, N.C., nor the West beyond Chicago; and, much to my regret, have never been for any length of time in professional contact with undergraduate students. . . .

I have just mentioned that the American scholar more frequently faces a nonprofessional and unfamiliar audience than does the European. On the one hand, this can be explained by general considerations. For reasons insufficiently explored by anthropologists, Americans seem to be genuinely fond of listening to lectures (a fondness encouraged and exploited by our museums which, unlike most of their sister institutions in Europe, think of themselves as cultural centers rather than as mere collections), and of attending conferences and symposia. And the "ivory tower" in which a professor is supposed to spend his life—a figure of speech, by the way, which owes its existence to a nineteenth-century conflation of a simile from the *Song of Songs* and Danaë's tower in Horace—has many more windows in the comparatively fluid society of this country than in most others. On the other hand, the larger radius of professorial activities results, to some extent, from the specific conditions of academic life in America. And this brings me to a brief discussion of what may be called organizational questions—a discussion which will somewhat transcend my subject because what applies to the history of art applies, *mutatis mutandis,* to all other branches of the humanities.

One basic difference between academic life in the United States and

Germany (I wish to limit myself to firsthand experience)[1] is that in Germany the professors are stationary and the students mobile, whereas the opposite is true in the United States. A German professor either remains in Tübingen until he dies, or he is called to Heidelberg and then, perhaps, to Munich or Berlin; but wherever he stays he stays put. It is part of his duties to give at stated intervals, in addition to specialized lecture courses and seminars, a so-called *collegium publicum*,[2] that is to say, a series of weekly lectures dealing with a subject of more general interest, free of charge and open to all students, faculty members, and, as a rule, the general public; but he rarely ascends a platform outside his permanent habitat, except for professional meetings or congresses. The German student, however, his *abiturium* (final diploma of a recognized secondary school) entitling him to enroll at whichever university he pleases, spends one semester here and another there until he has found a teacher under whose direction he wishes to prepare his doctoral thesis (there are no bachelors' and masters' degrees in German universities) and who accepts him, so to speak, as a personal pupil. He can study as long as he wishes, and even after having settled down for his doctorate he may periodically disappear for any length of time.

Here, as we all know, the situation is reversed. Our older colleges

[1] My comments on the organization of German universities (largely identical with that of the universities in Austria and Switzerland) refer, of course, to the period before Hitler whose regime destroyed the very foundations of academic life in Germany and Austria. With some reservations, however, they would seem to be valid also for the period after 1945 when, so far as I know, the *status quo* was more or less restored; such minor changes as have come to my notice are mentioned in notes 2 and 4. For further information, see the fundamental work by A. Flexner, *Universities, American, English, German* (New York, London, Toronto, 1930); and the entertaining account in E. H. Kantorowicz, "How the Pre-Hitler German Universities Were Run," *Western College Association; Addresses on the Problem of Administrative Overhead and the Harvard Report: General Education in a Free Society*, Fall Meeting, November 10, 1945, Mills College, Cal., pp. 3 ff.

[2] Specialized lecture courses are given *privatim*, that is to say, the students have to register for them and pay a moderate fee (about 60 cents) per weekly hour for each semester. Seminars, on the other hand, used to be given *privatissime et gratis*, that is to say, the students did not pay any fee while the instructor, and he alone, had the right to accept the participants according to his requirements. Now, I learn, seminars (except for the most advanced ones, given for the special benefit of candidates for the Ph.D.) are subject to the same fee as the *privatim* lecture courses; but the instructor still enjoys the right of admission. In addition to the fees for individual courses, of which he must take a minimum number while their choice is his own affair, the German student of a humanistic discipline pays only a registration fee for each term, plus an "admission fee" which includes permission to use the library and seminars as well as the right to medical service, etc.

and universities, all private and thus dependent on that alumni loyalty which in this country is as powerful a force as public school loyalty is in England, reserve the right of admission and keep the undergraduates for four entire years. State institutions, though legally obliged to accept every accredited student from their state, maintain at least the principle of permanency. Transfers are looked upon with marked disapprobation. And even graduate students stay, if possible, in one and the same school until they acquire their master's degree. But, as if to make up, to some extent, for the ensuing sameness of environment and instruction, both colleges and universities freely invite guest lecturers and guest professors, now for one evening, now for some weeks, now for a term or even a year.

From the point of view of the visiting lecturer, this system has many advantages. It widens his horizon, brings him into contact with colleagues and students of greatly different types, and, after some years, may give him a delightful sense of being at home on many campuses much as the itinerant humanists of the Renaissance were at home in many cities or courts. But from the point of view of the student—the student, that is, who plans to take up humanistic scholarship as a profession—it has obvious drawbacks. More often than not he enters a given college because family tradition or financial reasons leave him no other choice, and a given graduate school because it happens to accept him. Even if he is satisfied with his choice the impracticability of exploring other possibilities will narrow his outlook and impair his initiative, and if he has made a mistake the situation may develop into a real tragedy. In this event, the temporary contact with visiting lecturers will hardly suffice to counterbalance the crippling effect of an unsuitable environment and may even sharpen the student's sense of frustration.

No sensible person would propose to change a system which has developed for good historical and economic reasons and could not be altered without a basic revision of American ideas and ideals. I merely want to point out that it has, like all man-made institutions, the defects of its qualities. And this also applies to other organizational features in which our academic life differs from that in Europe.

One of the most important of these differences is the division of our colleges and universities into autonomous departments, a system foreign to the European mind. In conformity with medieval tradition, the universities on the European continent in general, and those of the German-speaking countries in particular, are organized into four or five "faculties": theology, law, medicine, and philosophy (the last-named frequently divided into mathematics and natural science as opposed to the humanities). In each of these faculties there is one chair—only exceptionally more than one—devoted to such special disciplines as, to limit the discussion to the humanities, Greek, Latin, English, Islamic Languages, Classical Archaeology, or, for that matter, the History of Art; and it is, in principle, exclusively of the incumbents of these chairs, normally full professor (*ordinarii*), that the faculties are composed.[3] The full professor forms the nucleus of a small group of what, very roughly, corresponds to associate professors (*extraordinarii*) and assistant professors (*Privatdozenten*)[4] over whom he has, however, no formal

[3] After the First World War the German *Privatdozenten* and *extraordinarii* (cf. following note) won the right to be represented on the faculty by delegates who, of course, occupy their seats as representatives of their group, and not of their discipline, and are elected for only one year; when I was in Hamburg they even had to leave the room when matters pertaining to their discipline were discussed. As to the *etatsmässige extraordinarii* (cf. again the following note) the custom varies. In most universities they have a seat on the faculty only if their discipline is not represented by an *ordinarius*.

[4] This correspondence is indeed a *very* rough one. On the one hand, the academic status of a *Privatdozent* (our "instructor" has no equivalent in German universities) was and is more assured and dignified than that of even our associate professors without tenure in that he enjoys perfect freedom of teaching and is as irremovable from office as the full professor. On the other hand, this office carries, as its name implies, no remuneration (until quite recently in certain universities). Having granted the *venia legendi* (permission to teach) on the basis of his scholastic merits (documented by a *Habilitationsschrift* and a paper read to the faculty) rather than having been "hired" to fill a gap in the curriculum, the *Privatdozent* can claim only the fees paid by the students for his *privatim* lecture courses and seminars (cf. note 2). He receives a fixed salary only if he either obtains a *Lehrauftrag* (commission to teach) in a specified subject or accepts an assistantship, in which case he shoulders a goodly part of the work involved in the administration of the seminar or institute. Otherwise he depends on outside income or such subventions as may be obtained from official or semiofficial foundations. The somewhat paradoxical nature of this arrangement became especially apparent during the difficult period after the First World War and may be illustrated by my personal experience. I had become (upon invitation) a *Privatdozent* at Hamburg University, founded as late as 1920, in 1921; and since I was the only "fulltime" representative of my discipline (other lectures and seminars being given by the directors and curators of the local museums), I was entrusted with the directorship of the nascent art historical seminar and had the unusual privilege of accepting and examining candidates for the doctorate. I received, however, no salary; and when, by 1923, my private fortune had been consumed by the inflation I was made a paid assistant of the very seminar of which I was the unpaid director. This interesting post of assistant to myself, created by a benevolent Senate because the salary attached to an assistantship was somewhat higher than a *Lehrauftrag*, I held until I was appointed full professor, skipping the stage of *extraordinarius*, in 1926. Today, I learn, the *Privatdozenten* in some West German universities receive a stipend *ex officio;* but this entails a restriction of their previously unlimited number, the extension of the minimum interval between doctorate and admission to a *Privatdozentur* from two years to three, and the introduction of an intermediary examination after which the candidate bears the beautiful title *Doctor habil* [*itandus*]. The *extraordinarii* fall into two very different classes. They are either older *Privatdozenten* to whom a professorial title has been given by courtesy and without any material change of status, or *etatsmässige* ("budgeted") *extraordinarii* whose position is similar to that of the full professors, except for the fact that their salaries are smaller and that they have, as a rule, no seat on the faculty (cf. preceding note).

authority as to their academic activities. He is responsible for the administration of his seminar or institute; but the awarding of degrees and the admission or invitation of teaching personnel, regardless of rank, is decided upon by the whole faculty.

To one accustomed to our system of self-governing departments operating directly under the dieties this time-honored arrangement sounds rather absurd. When a candidate submits a doctoral thesis on the development of the diacritical signs in Arabic, the full professor of the history of art has a voice in the matter while the associate and assistant professors of Islamic Languages have not. No full professor, however unsuited for administrative work, can be relieved of his duty to conduct the affairs of his seminar or institute. No *Privatdozent*, however unsuccessful, can be discharged except by disciplinary action. He can neither be assigned a specific lecture or seminar course (unless he has accepted a special *Lehrauftrag* comparable to the contract of a "Visiting Lecturer" here), nor can he legally be prevented from giving any lecture or seminar course he pleases, regardless of the comfort of his full professor, as long as he keeps within the limitations of his *venia legendi* ("permission to teach").[5]

But here again the American system has the faults of its virtues (among the latter, incidentally, is a most healthy elasticity which permits, for example, older graduate students to do some teaching, either in their own university or in a neighboring institution). The American associate or assistant professor has a full vote at departmental meetings; but he must give the courses which the department assigns to him. The affairs of the French Department cannot be interfered with by even the fullest professor of modern history or *vice versa;* but just this perfect autonomy of the departments entails two grave dangers: isolation and inbreeding.

The art historian may know as little of the diacritical signs in Arabic as the Arabist does of Caravaggio. But that the two gentlemen are bound to see each other every fortnight at a faculty meeting is good for them because they may have, or develop, a common interest in Neo-Platonism or astrological illustrations; and it is good for the university because they may have well-founded, if divergent, views about general policies which may be profitably discussed *in pleno*. The professor of Greek may know nothing of Chaucer and Lydgate; but it is useful that he has the right to ask whether the professor of English, in proposing a nice young man for an associate professorship, may not have inadvertently overlooked some other young man perhaps less nice

[5] Cf. preceding note.

but possibly more capable. In fact, our institutions of learning are becoming more and more acutely aware of these two dangers, isolation and inbreeding. The University of Chicago has attempted to coördinate the humanistic departments into one "division"; other universities try interdepartmental committees and/or courses; Harvard goes so far as to make a permanent appointment in, say, the Department of Classics only after convoking an "*ad hoc* committee" composed of Harvard professors other than classicists and classicists from institutions other than Harvard. But to coördinate sovereign departments into a "division" is about as easy as to coördinate sovereign states into an international organization, and the appointment of committees may be said to indicate the presence of a problem rather than solve it.

Needless to say, this difference between the "departmental system" and the "chair system," as it may be called, reflects not only a divergence in political and economic conditions but also a divergence in the concept of "higher education" as such. Ideally (and I know full well that the European ideal has undergone, and is still undergoing, no less significant a change than the American reality), the European university, *universitas magistrorum et scholarium,* is a body of scholars, each surrounded by a cluster of *famuli.* The American college is a body of students entrusted to a teaching staff. The European student, unsupervised except for such assistance and criticism as he receives in seminars and personal conversation, is expected to learn what he wants and can, the responsibility for failure or success resting exclusively with himself. The American student, tested and graded without cease, is expected to learn what he must, the responsibility for failure or success resting largely with his instructors (hence the recurrent discussions in our campus papers as to how seriously the members of the teaching staff violate their duties when spending time on research). And the most basic problem which I have observed or encountered in our academic life is how to achieve an organic transition from the attitude of the student who feels: "You are paid for educating me; now, damn you, educate me," to that of the young scholar who feels: "You are supposed to know how to solve a problem; now, please, show me how to do it"; and, on the part of the instructor, from the attitude of the taskmaster who devises and grades test papers producing the officially required percentage of failures, passes, and honors, to that of the gardener who tries to make a tree grow.

This transformation is presumed to take place in the graduate school and to reach perfection in the following years. But the sad fact is that the average graduate student (a really superior talent will assert itself in the face of any system) finds himself in a position which makes it more difficult for him to achieve intellectual independence than for a certain group of undergraduates—those, that is, who, owing to their high scholastic standing, are freed from compulsory classes during their senior year.

It is the chairman of the department who assigns to the graduate student a number of courses and seminars each term (and far too many in most cases), in which he has to struggle for high marks. The subject of his master's thesis is, more often than not, determined by one of his instructors who also supervises its progress. And at the end he faces an examination, concocted by the whole department, which no single member thereof could pass in creditable fashion.

There is, by and large, any amount of good will on both sides; kindliness and helpful solicitude on the part of the teacher and—I speak from happiest experience—loyalty and responsiveness on the part of the student. But within the framework of our system just these engaging qualities seem to make the transformation from student into scholar so much the harder. Most graduate students in the humanities are not financially independent. In a society which, for good and sufficient reasons, rates the scholar considerably below the lawyer, the doctor, and, quite particularly, the successful businessman, it takes a strong will and something akin to obsession for the scion of a wealthy family to break down the resistance of his parents, uncles, and club friends when he proposes to follow a calling the highest possible reward of which is a professorship with eight or ten thousand dollars a year. The average graduate student, therefore, does not come from a wealthy family and must try to prepare himself for a job as fast as he can, and this in such a way that he is able to accept whatever offers. If he is an art historian, he expects his teachers to endow him with the ability either to enter any department of any museum or to give any course in any college; and the teachers do their best to live up to this expectation. As a result, graduate student and graduate teacher alike are haunted by what I should like to call the specter of completeness.

In German universities this specter of completeness—or, to be more polite, the preoccupation with the "balanced curriculum"—does not exist. In the first place, the freedom of movement enjoyed by the students makes completeness unnecessary. The professors lecture on whichever subject fascinates them at the time, thereby sharing with their students the pleasures of discovery; and if a young man happens to be interested in a special field in which no courses are available at one university, he can, and will, go to another. In the second place, the aim of the academic process as such is to impart to the student, not a maximum of knowledge but a maximum of adaptability—not so much to teach him subject matter as to teach him method. When the art historian leaves the university his most valuable possession is neither the fairly uneven acquaintance with the general development of art which he is expected to acquire through lecture courses, seminars, and private reading, nor the more thorough familiarity with the special field from which the subject of his thesis has been taken, but an ability to turn himself into a specialist in whichever domain may happen to attract his fancy in later life. As time goes on, the world of the German art historian—and this writer is no exception—tends to resemble an archipelago of little islands forming, perhaps, a coherent pattern when viewed from an airplane but separated by channels of abysmal ignorance; whereas the world of his American confrère may be compared to a massive tableland of specialized knowledge overlooking a desert of general information.

After the final degree—and this is another important difference—the German art historian, provided he wishes to enter the academic career, is on his own for some time. He cannot be admitted to a teaching position before at least two or even three years have passed and he has produced a solid piece of work, the subject of which may or may not be connected with that of his doctoral thesis. And after having received the *venia legendi* he is, as mentioned earlier, at liberty to teach as much or as little as he sees fit. The young American master of arts or master of fine arts, however, will, as a rule, at once accept an instructorship or assistant professorship which normally entails a definite and often quite considerable number of teaching hours and in addition—owing to a recent development which I consider unfortunate— imposes upon him the tacit obligation to prepare himself, as speedily as possible, for a doctor's degree as a prerequisite of promotion. He still remains a cogwheel in a machinery, only that he now grades instead of being graded, and it is difficult for him to achieve that balance between teaching and research which is perhaps the finest thing in academic life.

Too often burdened with an excessive "teaching load"—a disgusting expression which in itself is a telling symptom of the malady I am trying to describe—and no less often cut off from the necessary facilities, the young instructor or assistant professor is rarely in a position to follow up the problems encountered in the preparation of his classes; so that both he and his students miss the joyful and instructive experience which comes from a common venture into the unexplored. And never during his formative years has he had a chance to fool around, so to speak. Yet it is precisely this chance which makes the humanist. Humanists cannot be "trained"; they must be allowed to mature or, if I may use so homely a simile, to marinate. It is not the reading matter assigned for Course 301 but a line of Erasmus of Rotterdam, or Spenser, or Dante, or some obscure mythographer of the fourteenth century, which will "light our candle"; and it is mostly where we have no business to seek that we shall find. *Liber non est,* says a delightful Latin proverb, *qui non aliquando nihil agit:* "He is not free who does not do nothing once in a whole."

In this respect, too, considerable efforts at improvement have been made in recent years. Most art departments no longer insist on absolute omniscience in their M.A.'s, M.F.A.'s and even Ph.D.'s, but allow one or two "areas of concentration." A breathing spell between the end of graduate school and the beginning of a "career" is provided, in a number of cases, by the Fulbright Fellowships (which are, however, limited to study abroad and are administered, as far as the final decisions are concerned, by a political rather than scholastic agency). The same Fulbright Fellowships are also open to scholars already in harness, if I may say so, and these can furthermore obtain a year or two of unimpeded research by winning such awards as a Guggenheim Fellowship or a temporary membership with the Insitute for Advanced Study which considers this kind of service as one of its principal functions. Grants of this type, of course, take the incumbent out of teaching altogether. But even the problem of balance between teaching and research has, fortunately, begun to attract some attention. A few universities, notably Yale, make use of special funds to cut the teaching obligations of promising young faculty members in half for a number of years without reducing their salaries.

Yet much remains to be done. And nothing short of a miracle can reach what I consider the root of our troubles, the lack of adequate preparation at the high school stage. Our public high schools—and even an increasing number of the fashionable and expensive private schools— dismiss the future humanist with deficiencies which in many cases can never be completely cured and can be relieved only at the expense of more time and energy than can reasonably be spared in college and graduate school. First of all, it is, I think, a mistake to force boys and girls to make a decision between different kinds of curricula, some of them including no classical language, others no mathematics to speak of, at an age when they cannot possibly know what they will need in later life. I have still to meet the humanist who regrets that he had to learn some mathematics and physics in his high school days. Conversely, Robert Bunsen, one of the greatest scientists in history, is on record with the statement that a boy who is taught nothing but mathe-

matics will not become a mathematician but an ass, and that the most
effective education of the youthful mind is a course in Latin grammar.[6]

However, even assuming that the future humanist was lucky enough
to choose the right curriculum when he was thirteen or fourteen (and
a recent survey has disclosed that of the million high school students
in New York City only one thousand take Latin and only fourteen
Greek), even then he has, as a rule, not been exposed to that peculiar
and elusive spirit of scholarship which Gilbert Murray calls *religio gram-
matici*—that queer religion which makes its votaries both restless and
serene, enthusiastic and pedantic, scrupulously honest and not a little
vain. The American theory of education requires that the teachers of
the young—a vast majority of them females—know a great deal about
"behavior patterns," "group integration," and "controlled aggression
drives," but does not insist too much upon what they may know of their
subject, and cares even less for whether they are genuinely interested
or actively engaged in it. The typical German "Gymnasial-professor"
is—or at least was in my time—a man of many shortcomings, now pom-
pous, now shy, often neglectful of his appearance, and blissfully ignorant
of juvenile psychology. But though he was content to teach boys rather
than university students, he was nearly always a scholar. The man who
taught me Latin was a friend of Theodor Mommsen and one of the
most respected Cicero specialists. The man who taught me Greek was
the editor of the *Berliner Philologische Wochenschrift,* and I shall never
forget the impression which this lovable pedant made on us boys of
fifteen when he apologized for having overlooked the misplacement of
a comma in a Plato passage. "It was my error," he said, "and yet I
have written an article on this very comma twenty years ago; now we
must do the translation over again." Nor shall I forget his antipode,
a man of Erasmian wit and erudition, who became our history teacher
when we had reached the stage of "high school juniors" and introduced
himself with the words: "Gentlemen, this year we shall try to understand
what happened during the so-called Middle Ages. Facts will be presup-
posed; you are old enough to use books."

[6] It may not be amiss to reprint in full Bunsen's statement, transmitted by an
ear-witness who was a biologist: "Im Anschluss an Gauss kam Bunsen auf die
Frage zu sprechen, in welcher Weise man einen für Mathematik besonders begabten
Jungen erziehen solle. 'Wenn Sie ihm nur Mathematik beibringen, glauben Sie,
dass er ein Mathematiker werden wird?—Nein, ein Esel.' Für besonders wichtig
erklärte er die Denkerziehung durch die lateinische Grammatik. In ihr lernen die
Kinder mit Gedankendingen umgehen, die sie nicht mit Händen greifen können,
die jedoch einer Gesetzmässigkeit unterliegen. Nur so lernen sie es, mit Begriffen
sicher umzugehen." Cf. J. von Uexküll, *Niegeschaute Welten; Die Umwelten
meiner Freunde* (Berlin, 1936), p. 142.

It is the sum total of little experiences like these which makes for an education. This education should begin as early as possible, when minds are more retentive than ever after. And what is true of method it is also true, I think, of subject matter. I do not believe that children and boys should be taught only that which they can fully understand. It is, on the contrary, the half-digested phrase, the half-placed proper name, the half-understood verse, remembered for sound and rhythm rather than meaning, which persists in the memory, captures the imagination, and suddenly emerges, thirty or forty years later, when one encounters a picture based on Ovid's *Fasti* or a print exhibiting a motif suggested by the *Iliad*—much as a saturated solution of hyposulphite suddenly crystallizes when stirred.

If one of our great foundations were seriously interested in doing something for the humanities it might establish, *experimenti causa*, a number of model high schools sufficiently endowed with money and prestige to attract teaching faculties of the same caliber as those of a good college or university, and students prepared to submit to a program of study which our progressive educators would consider exorbitant as well as unprofitable. But the chances of such a venture are admittedly slim.

Apart from the apparently unsolvable problem of secondary education, however, the immigrant humanist, looking back over the last twenty years, has no cause for discouragement. Traditions, rooted in the soil of one country and one continent, cannot and should not be transplanted. But they can cross-fertilize, and this cross-fertilization, one feels, has been initiated and is in progress.

There is only one point which it would be disingenuous not to touch upon, though it may seem indelicate to do so: the terrifying rise of precisely those forces which drove us out of Europe in the 1930's: nationalism and intolerance. We must, of course, be careful not to jump to conclusions. The foreigner is inclined to forget that history never repeats itself, at least not literally. The same virus produces different effects in different organisms, and one of the most hopeful differences is that, by and large, the American university teachers seem to wrestle against the powers of darkness instead of ministering to them; in at least one memorable instance they have even found the support of an alumni committee the voice of which cannot be ignored in the land.[7] But we cannot blind ourselves to the fact that Americans may now be legally punished, not for what they do or have done, but for what they say

[7] See the report of the Yale Alumni Committee "On the Intellectual and Spiritual Welfare of the University, Its Students and Its Faculty," reprinted in full, e.g., in *Princeton Alumni Weekly*, LII, No. 18 (March 29, 1952), p. 3.

or have said, think or have thought. And though the means of punishment are not the same as those employed by the Inquisition, they are uncomfortably similar: economic instead of physical strangulation, and the pillory instead of the stake.

Once dissent is equated with heresy, the foundations of the apparently harmless and uncontroversial humanities are no less seriously threatened than those of the natural and social sciences. There is but one step from persecuting the biologist who holds unorthodox views of heredity or the economist who doubts the divine nature of the free enterprise system, to persecuting the museum director who exhibits pictures deviating from the standards of Congressman Dondero or the art historian who fails to pronounce the name of Rembrandt Peale with the same reverence as that of Rembrandt van Rijn. But there is more to it.

The academic teacher must have the confidence of his students. They must be sure that, in his professional capacity, he will not say anything which to the best of his belief he cannot answer for, nor leave anything unsaid which to the best of his belief he ought to say. A teacher who, as a private individual, has permitted himself to be frightened into signing a statement repugnant to his moral sense and his intellect, or, even worse, into remaining silent where he knows he ought to have spoken, feels in his heart that he has forfeited the right to demand this confidence. He faces his students with a clouded conscience, and man with a clouded conscience is like a man diseased. Let us listen to Sebastian Castellio, the brave theologian and humanist who broke with Calvin because he could not dissimulate; who for many years supported his wife and children as a common laborer rather than be disloyal to what he believed to be true; and who, by the force of his indignation, compelled posterity to remember what Calvin had done to Michael Servetus. "To force conscience," Castellio says, "is worse than cruelly to kill a man. For to deny one's convictions destroys the soul."[8]

[8] R. H. Bainton, "Sebastian Castellio, Champion of Religious Liberty, 1515–1563," *Castellioniana; Quatre études sur Sebastien Castellion et l'idée de la tolérance* (Leiden, 1941), pp. 25 ff.

32

Americans as Students

The audience of a summer-school course in Comparative Literature falls into several distinct categories. To begin with, there are more women enrolled than men; in a practical world, men are less attracted by literary subjects. Year after year, I found roughly the same ratio of ladies of ripe and respectable age (and one faithful auditor who for three summers never missed one of my lectures). Nothing is more moving than the attention with which they listen and the conscientiousness with which they work their way through reading lists. When, as sometimes happens, they are bewildered by ideas that are new to them, they make a valiant attempt to understand them and to fit them into a framework of their own.

Among the persons taking the course for credit are to be found a few high school teachers, graduate students, and a large but fluctuating number of undergraduates who from time to time bring along their friends. I have always felt a great deal of respect for the high quality of those secondary school instructors who, in order to refresh their minds during the summer, sacrifice two months of vacation time. And my respect would turn into admiration whenever I learned that so-and-so, who was a teacher or a graduate student, worked in a factory at night to balance his budget.

The most conscientious and mature students are not always the most brilliant or the most original. Their papers, for instance, are solidly based on facts and readings: all you asked for is there, but seldom more. They seem no longer to feel the need of expressing their own ideas, and prefer simply to present in orderly fashion what they have learned.

Pierre Emmanuel. "Americans as Students," *The Atlantic Monthly*, Vol. 194 (1954), pp. 59–62. Reprinted by kind permission of the publishers, *The Atlantic Monthly*, Boston, Massachusetts.

Author (1916–   ); Formerly taught mathematics and psychology at a French secondary school; author of some twenty-five volumes of prose and verse; when this article was written he was in charge of the English language broadcasts of the French government radio station, Radiodiffusion Française; he has also taught regularly at the Harvard Summer School, and has been visiting professor at Brandeis University, Jones Professor at Buffalo University, and Turnhill Memorial Lecturer at Johns Hopkins University. He is currently Director, International Association for Cultural Freedom, Paris.

Their own reflections on the subject are adequate, intelligent, and neutral. I suspect them of being somewhat wary of the reader's moods; they know the minimum required to obtain a good grade, and they are unwilling to take chances.

The most exciting members of the summer school are the undergraduates. Here we find the budding genius who writes poetry or short stories, feels the world just doesn't understand him, dreams about suicide, speed, violence, and calls himself an existentialist on the faith of a few scattered readings or a lecture on Sartre; the Harvard junior, specializing in political and economic theory, who, thanks to literary history, enthusiastically discovers that social change goes hand in hand with transformations in the moral world; the son of European immigrants in search of his origins; the young Jewish student who becomes fully aware of his Hebrew heritage after reading Hersey's *The Wall;* the 200 percent American who sees in Europe's complexity a sign of her hopeless decadence and, as a contrast, sings fervent hymns in praise of the pioneering spirit, which in his eyes the businessman symbolizes; the sophomore from Smith or Wellesley, whose quiet and honest efforts bear witness to the fine teaching methods employed by these two institutions; the Radcliffe girls, whose zeal for work does not dampen her imagination and insights and who seems to reach maturity more quickly than the average girl; the "progressive college" girl, more loaded with "problems" than the ass in the fable was burdened with relics, who is up-to-date on everything, from Anouilh to Schönberg, not to mention the Marquis de Sade and Heidegger; the girl starving for love who has been cloistered in some out-of-the-way campus for nine long months and now has a heyday, brushing through the boys and finding herself a new meal ticket every night; the Southern girl, at once an anarchist and a Puritan, torn by inner conflicts which, she discovers to her own surprise, make her astonishingly sensitive to certain tragic European destinies; and many others, each one infinitely individual in the midst of a world where everyone fancies that he resembles everyone else.

What is the intellectual background of the twenty-year-old student in America? It is a varied and confused one, whose extent does not always compensate for the absence of the indispensable. I believe that I am not going too far in saying that education at the high school level is mediocre. The fault does not lie with the teaching staff. The tenets of democratic egalitarianism are so strong in the United States that they assume a downright metaphysical importance. The postulate goes this way: All minds must have an equal chance at the start. They are like fertile fields; all that needs to be done is to sow them with method and prevent their differences from growing more marked, since differences contradict the principle of fundamental equality of all brains. This pseudo-Cartesian illusion leads to the adoption of the least astringent of all methods: that of the potpourri.

The criterion of immediate usefulness partly sterilizes education, turning it from a cultural undertaking into mere social adaptation to the American kaleidoscope. Often I have been fascinated, in my conversations with American students, by the bits of knowledge emerging without reason from the recesses of the mind, floating at the surface, then vanishing as others take their place. In his first or second year of college an American student does not assimilate what he learns as efficiently as a French student in the last two years of the French *lycée*, which corresponds roughly to high school. The freshman is thus faced with the following alternative: either he makes the effort of acquiring the basic patterns which he lacks and which his secondary schooling should have given him, or he will launch out on a random quest into realms that are too vast for the limited scope of his actual comprehension.

This absence of basic information is particularly noticeable in the fields of literature and history. Instead of being concentrated, channeled, continually kept aware of that "spiritual duration" which is manifest in the evolution of thought, the attention roams distractedly and fails to grasp the unity of culture: only scattered components remain in the mind—ruins, one might almost say. At best, when the youthful mind strives to connect these *disjecta membra* without having in its possession the means necessary to resurrect them—the historical sequence, the sense of time, the network of causal relations—the student is led to formulate hazardous inductions, fantastic or superficial comparisons, pitiful attempts at synthesis which bring out clearly the disparity between the desire for an integrated kind of knowledge and the fragility of its foundations.

Of course the best students, gifted with a natural inclination for culture, strive as much to acquire knowledge as to develop the critical sense necessary to its organization. Those who come from the great American universities where the intellectual traditions inherited from Europe are still being upheld are helped in this task by methods more rigorous than elsewhere. At times I have observed, when comparing undergraduates from different institutions, variations in the level of the education received so great that they would be considered scandalous in France, where there exists only *one* form of education at university level, whether it is being dispensed at the Sorbonne, in Strasbourg, or in Algiers.

In a French *lycée*, every student spends four hours a week, for five years, learning the literary history of his country; and he spends as much to gain a general notion of his country's and the world's political history. Education is designed to provide the mind, at a very early stage, with the notion of a lasting temporal structure as well as of a logic of history. This conception may be open to debate, but it is an efficient one and it has the advantage of forming into a continuous progression everything that has happened in Europe since the time of the Roman Empire.

In France, I admit, the teacher's authority forces upon the child's mind a uniform mold into which are cast abstract notions which actually he will experience only later. Having a fifteen-year-old boy comment on Pascal and Rousseau according to a method which an adult mind alone can master would be a dangerous absurdity if it were anything but a temporary means of relating a mass of intellectual facts to a broader historical scheme. The strongest objection one could make to such a system of education is that it dismantles the classics in order to build up literary history with the broken fragments. The student does not read all of Montaigne, for instance, but forever dissects the same excerpts, which have been passed on from anthology to anthology over the last two centuries.

In America, you may be a citizen of the United States, a well-fitted part of the nation's machinery, and yet remain a complete stranger to almost all of its history. Such a thing, barring a few special cases, is unthinkable in France. In the United States, everyone blends into the community which he chooses to join as an individual. On the soil of Europe, on the other hand, everyone thinks of himself as a mere shoot of a thousand-year-old tree, and the European's manner of thinking, whenever he evolves a personal one, begins at the point where his predecessors have left off.

On American faculties may be found some of the best specialists in European history and literary history, the most eminent proponents of Comparative Literature; yet a certain state of mind still remains to be created among the students, a sense of historical space which would enable them to move about effortlessly in the dense universe of systems and works. I am far from suffering from that date-fetishism, common among Frenchmen, at which Mark Twain poked fun in such an amusing manner. But I do believe that if we wish to avoid making fatal blunders, we must know the historical context in which Montaigne, Locke, or Schiller places himself. Human thought is not made up of juxtaposed monads; it is a complex of relationship that must come out of the knowledge of certain specific facts and synchronisms.

Too many American students neglect the compass which history gives them, for the sake of a personal approach to the classics. This adventurous exploration has its good points, of course. You read the works from the first page to the last, instead of limiting yourself to so-called "significant" excerpts. Instead of telling the student, "Read chapters such and such of *The Social Contract*," it is advisable to let him discover the work as a whole and in its newness, without weighing it down with interpretations, and above all without approaching the work through them. The contrary method leads a great many French students to content themselves with the commentaries before they even have caught a glimpse of the object to which these are applied.

How quickly the American student makes friends with a book or a man and treats them as if they were his contemporaries! He hardly knows the background from which they arise: they surge out of his own mental world, haunt him, call forth in him an instantaneous and, frequently, a passionate reaction. A fortnight later, however, others have taken their place; it is love at first sight, but indifference rapidly follows.

And when the boy and, particularly, the girl student look at the authors on the program with the eyes of their own "problems"—that is, with a psychological narcissism that has been aggravated by a watered-down form of psychoanalysis—the result of their investigation is likely to be ludicrous. I shall not even mention a certain perverted manner of reading, feet resting on the table, while phonograph or radio is blaring. True, all the reading gets done, but against a background of inner vacuousness, and all that remains in the memory is a kind of gelatinous magma. When the time has come to discuss the text in class, each phrase begins to float outside of its context; and the student, as if he could not wait to do his own thinking, lets himself be carried away by entirely personal associations of ideas which he attributes to the author under discussion. The two favorite expressions used by the American student to preface his comments are "It seems to me . . ." and "I think . . ." These clearly reveal his individualism. No attitude is more praiseworthy, as long as you are wary of using it as a basis for hasty generalizations.

Here is an illustration—a charming one—of this undaunted self-confidence. The incident took place on a beach on Cape Cod. One of my students had been invited, as had I, by some common friends; she brought along the Modern Library Nietzsche reader. A few days later, she was to give a report on the philosophy of the father of Zarathustra. As she lay on the sand, basking in the sun, she leafed lazily through the book. That was the moment she picked to ask me to sketch for her a broad outline of Nietzsche's philosophy! I began as best I could—most clumsily, I must say—trying to illustrate what I was saying with a few excerpts hastily—too hastily—picked.

After ten minutes, she interrupted me with the inevitable opening words, "It seems to me . . ."; and then she started to build an entire system before my eyes, naïve and at the same time brilliant in spots. This she took for the master's thought. Need I mention that she came from one of those "progressive" colleges where any sophomore is encouraged to think of herself as sufficiently endowed with genius to reinvent, by starting from almost nothing, a world that some titanic creator spent a lifetime shaping? My pretty student, having concocted her picture of Nietzsche in a few moments, now read him through the image which she had constructed, and she retained from his words only enough to add a few concrete touches to that image. Yet her account was not lacking in interest, for it contained flashes of intuition which a more sustained analysis would certainly have brought into sharper evidence. You may be sure, however, that as soon as she had finished her work, she forgot her subject as lightly as she has learned it. For her, it had merely been an exercise in scholastic rhetoric.

It is said that American students do not like to think. It would be better to say that they do not know how to think, through ignorance of a small number of rules which secondary schooling should have trained them to use. First of all, certain rules of attention. A good half of my students never took any notes: listening was a part of their soliloquy, and what they heard of my lectures was but an echo distorted by their inner dream. Their chief difficulty seemed to be to get out of themselves; as a result, what they were being taught was shredded into vague impressions on the surface of their minds.

Others, no less tormented by the desire to unbosom themselves, would be pathetically on their guard to keep from saying anything that concerned them intimately; and since they were unable to forget themselves for one minute, their monologue would quickly stop short. Those who were capable of abstracting themselves from their little private universe were also the most thoughtful ones, and consequently those most aware of their lack of discipline. Despite the extent of their information, they realized that without structures, knowledge is only chaos.

In the course of the summer, the students had two weeks to write an essay on some general theme. Although confused and badly presented, their ideas were not devoid of substance. One hardly could reproach American students with lacking personality, but most of the time it remains in a primitive state. On the day of the final examination, everything was changed. When the white sheet of paper stared up at them, most of the unhappy victims remained defenseless. The first two years, I had chosen a significant sentence from the works of the authors on the program, one that summarized the tendencies of the course, and I had asked the candidates to comment on it by referring to what they had learned. Their collective failure—the graduates floundered no less than the undergraduates—assumed the proportions of a downright rout. The blue books handed in could not even be called rough drafts: they were, at best, vague cogitations jotted down as they came to mind.

What are the reasons for this? In the first place, the subject suddenly paralyzed their minds. During the course, they had accumulated notions which no general idea helped to relate; they had listened to me day after day, as one lets oneself be carried downstream by a river. It was thus impossible for them, in the space of three hours—or, let us say, twenty minutes: long enough to map out a general outline—to bring together all their scattered ideas and to organize them into a coherent whole.

I was so dismayed by this result that, the third year, I decided to assign six questions: three general ones and three dealing with a brief text to be commented upon. The answers and comments were successful, with the exception of one, which I had not discussed in class. It had to do with a sentence from Malraux's *Man's Fate*, a book that all had read. Most of the students committed the same error as those of the two preceding years. All they kept in mind was the name Malraux, and they began to disgorge whatever they knew about him.

However, American students possess some very positive qualities. The foreigner appreciates these all the more since, from the very first, he finds himself surrounded by an atmosphere of confidence. The most valuable perhaps, in my opinion, is a certain psychological liveliness: feelings interest them more than ideas. They attach more significance to what the hero of a novel—and even its author—does than to what he thinks. The delicate distinctions of the heart frequently call forth unexpected responses in these young adults; they discover a language fitting their own emotional experience, which up to then has not found a voice. Hence the freshness with which they become acquainted with their classics: no prejudice to mar the purity of the encounter.

They look at all books as if they had been written yesterday, and attempt to find in them a convenient mirror which they question—in vain sometimes, but always sincerely. They try to project what they feel or have guessed abut themselves into all things, and, by means of examples drawn from external sources, seek to justify inner urges which they usually keep secret because their moral environment frowns upon them. Trapped in a conventional and gregarious society, they take advantage of their college years, with a kind of nervous haste, to have a little taste of everything in order to satisfy their unruly appetites, as if compelled to learn as much as possible about themselves before it is too late. Hence the professor, if he wants to fill his role successfully, must try to get to know his students intimately, to understand their personalities even more than their immediately recognizable gifts and abilities. This explains the importance—absolutely inexistent in France—of working in small groups or under the guidance of a tutor. In a way, the American student expects his teacher to become his mentor, a kind of intellectual director of his conscience. Such relationships can be fruitful and satisfying for both parties concerned, but I need hardly point out that they are sometimes dangerous.

Here we face defects which, in most American students—to a varying degree, of course—are the counterpart of their good traits. Whereas Europeans go through their critical stage of adjustment at the very beginning of adolescence, it seems that Americans experience this crisis at a later period. At the age of twenty, their personalities are too much concerned with themselves, their doubts, their fears before their environment, and not enough with the mainfold aspects of the external world. Before another man's thought, their attention is held only by the echo of their own haunting ego.

In my opinion, the faults which I have pointed out are by no means congenital. Social environment certainly accounts for a good many; but its influence is furthered by the system of education that has grown out of it. This vicious circle cannot easily be broken. It is in high school that students must be trained to use that objective type of attention without which each new bit of information merely adds to the chaos of thought. Such training is out of place at the college level. At the age of twenty, the mind has already contracted fatal habits. Secondary education has the duty of teaching adolescents to organize what they know and to express it in coherent terms.

33

A French Professor's Remarks on American Education

Education is one of the few ways, and perhaps the surest of those few ways, in which we can hope ever to transform the world into a more tolerable abode, and turn man into a creature fully worthy of the name. Americans have always revered education and, more than any other people, they have attempted to extend it to the whole of their population. Yet they are also harassed with doubts as to the degree of their success, quantitative and qualitative. Have they given enough people an adequate amount of knowledge and of wisdom? Have they not diluted the essentials of education overmuch by being content with providing everyone with a mediocre education, since they lacked the manpower, the material means and perhaps the genuine will, to give everybody an adequate education, and to select the able students for a preferred, hence more arduous training which might turn them into leaders of thought, of imagination, of action?

The challenge of the "Sputniks" brought to a climax much criticism of American education which, since Woodrow Wilson, John Maynard Hutchins, Walter Lippmann, Arthur Bestor and others uttered it, had remained unheeded. A French professor, who has chosen to teach in this country because he has always had faith in its youth and in its energy is not going to jump on the bandwagon of much inconsiderate and hasty faultfinding with his adopted country. Let us not foolishly and masochistically repudiate the good which has been accomplished, and which must not be "interred with the bones" of Leika, the Russian dog catapulted into space. But let us not, on the other hand, underestimate the power of that dog. Our profession has often had the courage to shun idle boasting and to distrust charts and data about the ever-

Henri Peyre. "A French Professor's Remarks on American Education," in *Quality and Quantity in American Education,* 46th Annual Schoolmen's Week Proceedings (Philadelphia: University of Pennsylvania Press, 1958), pp. 55–61. Reprinted by kind permission of the University of Pennsylvania Press, Philadelphia, Pennsylvania.

Author (1901–   ): Educated at the Ecole Normal Superieure, Paris, and University of Paris; taught at Universities of Lyon, Caire, and since 1939 Sterling Professor of French and Head of the French Department of Yale University.

swelling numbers of our college boys and Ph.D's. It knows that the goals of excellent education are not easily reached, and must always be set higher. It responds with constructive humility to the challenge now thrown at us by other countries and by America's manifest destiny, which is to help the world save itself in the second half of this century, the American half-century.

It has been pointed out lately that much of what we envied in the Russian educational system (hard work, stress on tough subjects, mental discipline, large role assigned to science and languages) had had its sources in the educational system first developed by Napoleonic France, later adopted and improved by Germany. Much is probably excellent in French secondary education; but discipline, uniformity, unity, the emphasis on general and on pure science, have not necessarily produced in France a disciplined people, political stability, fiscal discipline or the greatest physicists and chemists of our age. Let us not propose one nation as a sole model to be revered by others. In any case, an educational system should be, and usually is, an internal secretion of a country, a reflection of its history and of its aims, clearly or dimly perceived. Exotic plants can be grafted to the native stem only with the greatest prudence.

On the other hand, a country which has, today, to assume the leadership of a large part of the world cannot be content with complacency or with provincialism. Education at its best is a liberation from fear, superstition, egocentric prejudices. It may gain from studying what has been attempted elsewhere and from the constructive strictures of foreign educators in its midst.

I came to teach in America as a young man, not to escape the ridden and culture-soaked European continent, but to discover something new over here. I taught for a few years at Bryn Mawr College: a Frenchman is naturally convinced that sentimental education should be acquired soon after the intellectual training; and feminine colleges can teach a young French male not only sentiment, but prudence, diplomacy, patience, and the value of frustration and sublimation. I returned to my native land, taught in several countries, observed and compared. At the age of thirty-eight, I came back to America and threw in my lot with the educators of this country. Doubtless, more than by material advantages, libraries easy of access, or the gentlemanly sport of faculty meetings where one learns how to be suavely bored and to call it an instructive experience, I was attracted by the youth of this country, its energy, its freshness, its receptivity to the teachers' sermons of all kinds, and by the freedom from traditions and from fixed syllabi which prevails over here. The lack of standardization, even if it occasionally carries with it a lack of standards, is a welcome novelty to a European-trained educator who feels free to initiate reforms and to experiment. A certain informality, through which professors are treated like big brothers by students, or like male nurses every ready to listen and to confess, has its charm after the august but cold reverence shown to scholars in Europe. Knowledge in America, when it is not destined to learned conventions where one makes a point of showing how smart it is to know more and more about less and less, is made directly relevant to life. An undergraduate may call us up at our home to ask if we think he would learn more, on the vexing question of how to treat his date from Vassar, from reading *Othello* or *Manon Lescaut* or Proust's analysis of Swann in love. How many young tourists to France have brought their dollars and their illusions to that country because they were convinced that most French girls resembled Madame Bovary or the heroine of *La Dame aux camélias!*

The drawbacks of such freedom are, however, real. There is often no core of knowledge assimilated by all the students of several comparable schools; no common stock of allusions to the Bible, to ancient mythology, and European history; little effort made at integrating the fragments of learning picked up at random or according to the teacher's whim. Secondary education is so varied in those respects that colleges have to spend one or two years reteaching fundamentals of grammar, of calculus, of history, of literary analysis to young people who should come with that preparation. Moreover, while there prevails a fine democratic informality on our campuses and students may say everything in discussion courses, in their college papers, even in the essays that they hand to us, they actually fail to say much, or to think boldly and with originality. Their meekness, their gregariousness impress their teachers as extraordinary marks of humility in a nation which some Europeans believe to be addicted to boastfulness.

The differences between American and European education are to be explained in part by the divergent aims pursued in the two continents. In Europe, in France in particular, the aim was traditionally to train civil servants, teachers, doctors, lawyers, diplomats, army officers. It was easy for gifted boys to receive the best education, even in the eighteenth century, and to rise to the top. Yet on the whole it was not a mass education, but that of a cultured class, consisting chiefly of state officials. Business men counted but little, and were normally considered as men who could not ascend to the loftier level of a liberal profession. Technical and vocational training was relatively neglected. Such a system, however, offers dangers in the modern world. It is no longer possible to be placidly content with traditional humanism, which left out too many barbarians from outside (underprivileged lands, Asiatics, Africans) and too many barbarians from inside (workmen, peasants).

This country has boldly attempted to pursue new goals. It has insisted upon education being practical at all costs and upon its enabling boys and girls to take up a trade at once and make money on it. Extreme vocationalism, however, has its dangers. Those who go to the top in life are seldom those who were narrowly prepared for one job alone and acquired the needed know-how. The humanist who is not starch bound by traditions and complacency is often a more flexible individual, and one far more likely to succeed, than the narrowly trained specialist. The evil of training specialists is that we tend to make them, and ourselves, believe that most problems in life are susceptible of being solved through accumulation of quantitative data and by experts. One tends to overlook the fact that an insight into the emotions and the ideas which have always moved men is ever more essential than technical knowledge. "Think how" matters more than "Know-how." An excess of vocational specialization brings us close to the level of the animal, the bee, the ant, the beaver, which can do one thing to perfection, but one alone. It turns us into what a Spanish thinker has called "barbarians of specialization." In our offices, factories and even on our campuses, the need today is for men who think freely, against the tide, who venture on the borderlines of charted lands of knowledge, who attempt paradoxes, not out of a desire to outsmart their colleagues, but because paradoxes often become the truths of tomorrow.

A European professor who lives in America soon comes to develop a genuine admiration for businessmen; they work far harder than he does, they are harassed by arduous problems and often, martyrs of the modern world, their heart collapses at forty-five or fifty from the tension undergone. They have to meet a payroll, to avoid being in the red, to practice the exhausting art of lobbying, to face the demands of labor unions and the resistance of consumers to publicity and gadgets; they worry about how to spend their expense account or how to keep their wives happy with mink coats and platinum rings. A number of them, and the scions or great business barons who once developed railroads, oil wells or glass works, go into politics or accept embassies abroad. Their civic devotion is admirable; but their performance sometimes is less so. At a time when this country needs representatives abroad and statesmen at home with almost superhuman gifts of imagination, intelligence and tact, it must be confessed that it finds those giants with difficulty. One of the reasons is perhaps that government and diplomacy are not just another type of business. They require very different gifts, a readiness to face the unpredictable, an independence from quantitative

data and economic charts and diagrams, and acceptance of the fundamental irrationality of man, and even of woman (the more reasonable
and calculating sex) for which their training has failed to prepare them.
The reading of novels would perhaps reveal more of life, in its baffling
unpredictability, and of human nature, to businessmen than the memo-
rization of statistics and the study of marketing.

Behind American education, there lurks probably a philosophy which
differs from that which underlies education in old countries like France.
Man is innately good or can become so, and the child is essentially
right. From Rousseau and Wordsworth, that romantic view of the goodness of man appears to have come down to a country which once was
the paradise of austere Puritanism. Even Freudianism, which has tried
hard to demolish that myth, has not yet convinced Americans that the
child is a prey to evil instincts, erotic urges, preyed upon by lurid vices.
Hence, while in France parents do their very best to have their children
behave like them, in this country it is the children, despots of the home
and noisy possessors of playgrounds, who force their parents to behave
like them. The purity of the child must at all costs be preserved. Studies
are made easy for him. He has counselors at every stage; grammar,
declensions, geography, physics are made entertaining; soft chairs are
provided in libraries so that he may doze after three or four pages
of reading; illustrations enliven textbooks which might be too forbidding;
novels are cut up into comics so that images may succeed one another
before his eyes quickly enough so that none of them will provoke a
thought. Clifton Fadiman has branded that fault in American education
as "the decline of attention." The student is invited or forced to passively
absorb what is offered to him. He will thus be less resistant, in life,
to the lures of publicity and to the hammering of slogans. He will be
a docile consumer of goods, but untrained to discriminate and apt to
leave his personality undeveloped. Yet the modern world, as every commencement speech these days recalls to us, needs nonconformists.

The opportunities offered to American education at the present time
are unequaled. There are many excellent teachers, first rate schools and
American universities rate among, not only the richest but the best in
the world. But the demands made by this challenge of history to the
United States are such that the good achieved is not enough. Europeans
often prove severe in their criticism of America, but behind their severity
there is much disappointed expectation. They would wish Americans
to be even superior to what they are now. And indeed they could be.

There is so much to learn in the modern world, ten times more
geography, physics, sociology, economics, history than a century ago;
there are so many more languages, national cultures to be informed

about, so much in the exterior world and in the nether world of man's subconscious, that twice as much time at least than ever before should be devoted to education. If that is not possible, at least the American child should be made to start his schooling earlier, to study more intensively while at school, to waste no time by going straight to hard subjects, and to pursue his education after college, through reading and thinking assiduously after twenty-five. That education should include much precise knowledge and the accumulation of facts and precise data, but distrust the worship of facts and stress ideas and that inventive faculty called imagination. It should turn out men of affairs and scientists and engineers, to be sure, but also first-rate educators and many more men apt to be diplomats, statesmen, even—for the work stands badly in need of rehabilitation—politicians. "Politics are more difficult than physics," Einstein used to say, "and the world is more apt to die from bad politics than of bad science." The American of tomorrow should be informed on the rest of the world and eschew provincialism; he should face the future with the audacity and the energy which have always characterized his nation but not ignore the best in the legacy of the past which still lives in and around us. He should fulfill the wish expressed by Margaret Fuller when he distinguished three kinds of Americans and placed at the top "the thinking American, a man who, recognizing the immense advantages of being born to a new world . . . yet does not wish one seed from the past to be lost."

34

America the Magnet: The "Lost" Foreign Student

In recent years, American educators and others involved in technical assistance programs in the less developed nations of the world have shown growing concern over the problem of students from these countries who do not return to their native lands after completing their studies in the United States.

No one really knows the extent of this problem nor the percentage of students that stay here, and, to date, no method for obtaining such information easily and accurately has been developed. So far, the number of students who do not return is really not large enough to cause undue alarm. Nevertheless, it is not a negligible problem and steps should be taken to remedy it.

The reasons for denationalization, or alienation of foreign students from their home country, are complex and varied. With a few exceptions, foreign students who remain in this country come from middle-class families. Because of the favorable financial, social and political status in their home country, the students from the wealthy and powerful upperclass families usually return home, where opportunities for their advancement are far more attractive than in the United States. Upperclass students rarely would achieve the same class status here, but a student of a middle-class background can fit into a correspondingly similar class in the United States because of his educational training and profession.

Insofar as the fields of study are concerned, graduates of engineering and physical sciences seem to stay in greater numbers than those in other fields of studies. The students in other fields (with the exception

Nuri Mohsenin. "The 'Lost' Student: Cause and Cure," *Overseas*, Vol. 2 (November, 1962), pp. 2–6. Reprinted by kind permission of the publishers, of *Overseas*, the Institute of International Education, New York.

Author: A native of Teheran, Iran, spent nine years in the United States of America as an undergraduate and graduate student. He taught for three years at the University of Shiraz, Iran, and the University of Beirut, Lebanon, before returning to the United States: currently Associate Professor of Agricultural Engineering at Pennsylvania State University.

of medicine) usually find it more difficult to get employment in the United States.

Though each individual who prefers to remain in the United States may give many reasons for his decision, the main factors usually are cultural isolation and alienation, lack of employment or research opportunities in the field of specialization, higher standard of living in the United States, lower pay scale versus higher cost of living and various personal reasons such as religious and political affiliation.

Cultural Isolation

One of the most important factors influencing the student's decision to live and work in the United States is the problem which sociologists have called "cultural isolation." A young, impressionable and idealistic student who lives in this country for a number of years may change completely in his outlook, attitudes and habits. Most of these changes have come about by simply living in this country rather than by any formal training. They are the outcome of being in another environment which might, in certain cases, be completely different culturally, socially and economically from that of his own. The student begins to react differently to both familiar and unfamiliar situations and adopts a new frame of reference drawn from specific areas of American culture.

When he returns to his home country, he may find himself as much an alien among his own people as he was when he first entered America. Often the political, economic, and social conditions of the country are such that his government, despite the desperate need for trained and technical personnel, cannot take advantage of his training. Such factors as graft and corruption, a high degree of bureaucracy, lack of administrative efficiency and resistance toward change and innovation—basic characteristics in most underdeveloped countries—are additional reasons for the student's discouragement, frustration and disappointment. There are several personal factors contributing to this problem of cultural isolation; the student's age, his previous home life and past experience and the extent of study and education in the United States are, however, of prime importance in determining the degree of his cultural isolation.

Lack of Employment Opportunities

It has been argued that American education, particularly in the fields of engineering and physical sciences, is too sophisticated for students from the less developed countries. Engineering education in this country is now placing more emphasis on basic and fundamental sciences. This trend is dictated by the rapid advancement of technology in such fields as nuclear physics and space exploration and the control of such accrediting agencies as the Engineer's Council for Professional Development. We cannot expect American engineering schools to set up special curricula for the limited number of foreign students without getting involved in some sort of double standard. Besides, the application of fundamental and basic courses is universal, and it is up to the student to mobilize the best of his ingenuity in applying these fundamentals to many of the diverse and unique problems which he may face in his home country.

Sophistication comes about when the student starts on a graduate program leading toward advanced degrees. Most of the students coming from underdeveloped countries would like to continue their studies through the doctoral degree not only to be able to stay longer in America and thus obtain more practical and academic training, but also to receive the doctoral title which gives them higher social status and better employment opportunities upon returning to their home countries. In some countries, a doctoral degree is essential for university teaching.

The tendency to stay for an advanced degree frequently leads the student into rather exotic fields and areas of specialization which have little or no application at the present time in the country to which the student is expected to return and work. With all the opportunities available in this country for research and teaching in the fields of engineering and physical sciences, we cannot expect very many foreign students with Ph.D. degrees in these fields to go back to their home countries and, after "string pulling" and lobbying, settle for inconsequential desk jobs or, if lucky enough, teaching positions in high schools at substandard salaries.

More Comfortable Life in America

Although the higher standard of living in the United States is one of the factors influencing the decision of some foreign students to remain in America, its relative importance has been overemphasized. Most of these countries are inherently rich, and if the conditions were such that the Western-educated man were given a fair share of his country's wealth, sometimes he could live at a higher material level than in the United States. Despite the numerous mechanical and electrical machines, appliances and gadgets available to the American family, very few of these machines can take place of the cheap human labor which is plentiful in the less developed countries. With such help, a man can put his time into more constructive work than "do-it-yourself" projects around the house.

What is most appealing to a serious and sensitive visitor from these underdeveloped countries is not the comforts of life and the high American standard of living in terms of physical and material things, but the atmosphere creating the peace of mind which enables a man to concentrate on his own work and to be more efficient and more productive.

Frequently there are employment opportunities available for the American-educated student upon returning to his home country, but the scale of pay is so low that with a high cost of living it is virtually impossible for him to live and support a family merely on his earned salary. In many cases the parents must continue supporting their Western-educated son after his return home. If he comes from the lower economic class and cannot expect this supplementary living allowance from his family, he will generally try to find a job in another country where he can live the better life that his Western education has shown him to be possible.

Personal Reasons

Students sometimes emigrate because of their political or religious affiliations and the attendant fear of persecution and discrimination by the ruling majority or the government in power. In this category would be the former member of the Communist party from a country where communism is outlawed, the pro-Western student whose country is now under a communist regime, the Palestinian Arab and the Middle Eastern Armenian who belongs to a minority group and fears discrimination upon returning to his home country.

In some cases the reason for staying in America, or going home and then returning to the United States, is the inability of the foreign student's American wife to adjust herself to the social and economic conditions of her husband's homeland. This is particularly true when there are children involved, and the parents are concerned about their upbringing and education.

Proposed Solutions

From the reasons mentioned above, it seems clear that the core of the problem is the long residence of the student in a rich and highly complex society, which changes him to such an extent that he cannot readjust himself to the less economically-developed society from which he came.

Many of the shortcomings in government, education and the standard of living which are discouraging to the American-educated foreigner are accepted by his fellow countrymen. These men may also be dissatisfied, frustrated and unhappy, knowing that a better life is possible, but since they have not had the experience of a Western education and have not earned advanced degrees, there are not many opportunities for them in foreign countries. These men stay home and either conform to the status quo or attempt to fight the situation and hope it will improve.

If the core of the problem is the student's leaving home and studying in a country far more economically advanced than his own, then the obvious solutions are 1) to expand the educational facilities in the home country, 2) to send the student to study in the regional universities close to home and 3) to send to America only graduate students who have already established their roots in the home country.

The primary reason for the large flow of students from the less developed countries to America and to other advanced Western countries during recent years is the lack of educational facilities at home. In one of the Middle Eastern countries where admission to the university is through entrance examinations because of the limited facilities, only one out of 50 students who are capable of doing college work is admitted to the school of medicine. In engineering and agriculture, these figures are about one out of 30 and one out of 20, respectively. Since vocational training in these countries is virtually unknown and the little which is available does not carry the weight and the social status demanded by high school graduates, those who are not admitted to the local universities look for college education elsewhere. Ususally, the first choice is America, the second is Europe and the third is one of the neighboring countries.

What the U.S. Can Do to Keep Foreign Students Home

Perhaps the most effective way of spending the American dollar in underdeveloped countries is through education—training the people of the country to solve their own problems. The millions of American dollars which have been given to these countries for military purposes, as well as for huge and ambitious projects such as the construction of dams in remote parts of the country, are intangible aids which may win the friendship of only a few men in the higher government echelons. A fraction of this money spent on education would buy for the United States the more valuable and needed friendship of the common people in these underdeveloped countries.

American aid for education should be concentrated in the three following areas: the introduction of vocational training as it is known in this country, the establishment of land-grant type provincial colleges and the development of graduate programs and research facilities within the large universities to offer advanced degrees.

Limited programs of this type in the past have pointed out many problems which have been discouraging for both the Americans and the foreign faculty members. One of the most common problems is the oppostion of European-educated professors, who welcome American aid in terms of equipment, buildings and libraries but oppose any changes suggested by their American counterparts in their inefficient and antiquated teaching and their outmoded administrative methods. On the other hand, some of the American faculty members recruited for academic work abroad have not been the best available insofar as competence in the field of specialization, understanding of the people and the problems, and interest and dedication to a foreign assignment are concerned. This has created many unpleasant problems jeopardizing American prestige and leadership in these countries, where people are most critical of and sensitive to their relationship with foriegn experts.

These problems can be solved partly by paying more attention to the selection of American personnel for overseas assignments, by establishing new institutions which will differ from the traditional European-style universities and by training a new core of young teachers to take up teaching and research responsibilities. The most outstanding graduates in each field would then work as assistants to the American professors for a few years before being sent to the United States for advanced degrees. Such a plan has been tried at the American University of Beirut in the newly established College of Agriculture. Under this plan, the American staff is being gradually replaced by the Lebanese who are working for advanced degrees in this country.

Establishment of Regional Universities

Recent establishment of new land-grant type universities in India, Turkey and some other countries under the Unites States university-to-university program is a positive move toward this proposed educational development in the less developed countries.

Some of the problems associated with the establishment of American-style colleges and universities in some of the less developed countries, such as the high cost of the program, difficulties in recruiting a competent yet devoted American faculty, language barriers and problems of cross-cultural communication, bureaucratic red tape and the lack of cooperation from local governments and the local universities, can be overcome by training foreign students in regional universities administered and financed by Americans. In such universities, there are fewer language and other communication problems, increased possibilities to recruit more competent faculty members because of the more favorable location and few readjustment problems for the foreign students upon returning to their home countries.

An example of such a regional university is the American University of Beirut. This is an American institution which, for the past 100 years, has trained many leaders in medicine, education, engineering and other diciplines for the Middle Eastern countries. During the academic year 1957–58 this writer had the opportunity to meet and get to know a number of foreign students coming to this university from the countries of the Middle East and North Africa under an ICA (now AID) program. Except for a few who have come to America for advanced degrees, these students have returned to their homelands, and some are holding highly responsible positions.

If government and private agency funds are to be used in training foreign students, some carefully selected advanced graduate students and teachers may be brought to this country for practical training and observation, not only to learn American teaching and research techniques, but also to work for advanced degrees. In selecting these trainees, attention should be given to those whose roots are already established in their home countries by means of local undergraduate training, a suitable job and, preferably, a few years of government civil service. In graduate training programs leading to an advanced degree, the student should be encouraged to choose an area related to a situation in his home country and, if possible, even use data gathered under the conditions existing at home. This is a more realistic approach than having the student work on a project which supports a graduate assistantship but has no practical application in the student's home country.

These proposals may help alleviate the problem of the non-returning foreign student and provide a deeper and more realistic basis for international educational exchange.

35

The Teaching of Mathematics

American teachers of mathematics are in much the same position as an army attacked by superior numbers from all directions. This is not to say that they should be resigned to defeat. On many occasions outnumbered armies have secured brilliant victories by vigorous and unconventional action. The reason for emphasizing the adverse factors are, first, to make clear that the situation is quite out of the ordinary, that it will not yield to routine procedures, and second, to establish some system of priorities—of all the tasks which confront us, how shall we select the essential ones on which we should concentrate our limited resources? For the greatest mistake an outnumbered army can make is to spread itself too thin, to attempt to hold all positions and to end by holding none.

The criticism most frequently heard in the past few years has been the lack of "Modern mathematics"—the curriculum does not reflect the mathematical research of the present century. This last statement is true enough, but it is rather like telling a man who has forgotten to put his trousers on that his tie is not straight. Imagine a visitor from the past, a mathematician educated in the 1880's. He knows nothing of the content or the spirit of modern mathematics. Will he therefore be satisfied with what he finds in the schools? Not in the least. He has been trained to solve problems; he has all the standard methods and theorems at his finger tips; he is ingenious in coping with the unexpected; his whole attitude is one of attack. But he finds hardly anyone in the schools who can solve the problems in the bible of the 1880's, Hall and Knight's *Higher Algebra.* Instead, algebra is taught as a series of isolated, museum exhibits: a student can obtain a high grade by doing ten routine applications; he is then free to forget it. Ingenuity, original

W. Warwick Sawyer. "The Teaching of Mathematics," *The Education of the Secondary School Teacher* (Middletown, Connecticut: Wesleyan University Press, 1962), pp. 209–233. Reprinted by kind permission of Wesleyan University Press, Middletown, Connecticut.

Author (1911–   ): Educated at Cambridge University and has taught in England, Ghana, and New Zealand. He came to the United States in 1957, spent a year at the University of Illinois, and then was appointed Professor of Mathematics at Wesleyan.

discovery, the readiness to attack the subject for oneself—these are rare indeed. The curriculum is quite as defective in ancient mathematics as it is in modern.

These weaknesses are accentuated by the package system. Traditionally, the subjects are separated in time: instead of teaching algebra, geometry, and trigonometry concurrently, the student encounters these subjects in separate years. At the end, he does not know any of them. He graduates on the basis of grades earned in subjects he has already forgotten. When students preparing to become teachers are told that a competent teacher has the whole of high school mathematics in his mind, they usually regard this as an extremely novel idea. If an incoming student is asked to write briefly the main theorems he remembers from Euclidean geometry, a very meager harvest commonly results.

The curiously static teaching of algebra is also reinforced by the separation of mathematics from physics. Where these two subjects are taught together, each helps the other. In dealing with a problem in mechanics, the student has to formulate it algebraically, with symbols for the unknown forces, and then solve the resulting system of equations. The mathematical formulaton makes physics more systematic. The physical problems illustrate the mathematical concepts and show mathematics in action, instead of as a museum piece.

To anyone familiar with education in Europe, the most startling feature of traditional American education is the intellectual vacuum in grades four through eight. These are the most wonderful years in the life of a child. The storms of infancy are behind; adolescence is yet to come. Children are eager to learn, ready to play with ideas, fascinated by the patterns of the universe. As intellectual nourishment for these beautiful years, the traditional curriculum provides commerical arithmetic, moving at a snail's pace, completely devoid of beauty or surprise, and culminating in the three cases of percentage. In the same years, on the other side of the Atlantic, an able student acquires a more thorough knowledge of algebra, geometry, and trigonometry than most high school students obtain here. Unless one believes—which nobody does—that American children are biologically inferior to European children, and are intellectually retarded by four years, it is clear that we tragically underestimate our students. Particularly the abler students, with an excess of unused and undirected mental energy, are liable to become bored, idle, troublesome, or delinquent. But even the weaker students have a right to something more stimulating than percentages, and (later on) that desert of boredom, "general mathematics."

Grades four through eight have a double significance. They represent the strategic point at which a given effort will produce the maximum response. Much teaching at college level is merely a waste of time, a belated attempt to change attitudes already firmly established and to convey knowledge that should have been acquired years before. The same can be true of high school teaching. There are some high schools where an atmosphere of intellectual inquiry prevails and useful work can be done. But there are many at which the students are already "too old at fourteen." There are many pressures on the students; they are too busy; their attitudes are formed. Grades four through eight may thus be a period of make-or-break, the last opportunity of influencing the student effectively.[1]

This phase of education is thus of central importance for anyone concerned with the future supply of mathematicians, scientists, engineers, teachers and so forth. But this aspect—the public aspect, which regards the student as someone who may be needed by others in the future—this is only one half of the story.

Even if there were no shortage of mathematicians, if industry had reached the final goal of automation and supplied all our wants without effort on our part, one would still wish to see a change in grades four through eight. For the intellectual awakening of these years is a thing good in itself. You cannot help feeling this as you observe the interest and the eagerness that young students display when some topic intrigues them. This is what a good society would wish its children to experience; this is what parents should hope to provide for their children. It seems, incidentally, not easy to provide; education swings uneasily between the anti-intellectuals, who seem to feel that the less you know the better, and the academic pedants, whose philosophy appears as a mixture of sadism and masochism—"It doesn't matter what the students are doing, so long as they don't like it."

The provision of intellectual stimulation in the elementary grades is a central task but it is also an extremely difficult one. The whole weight of tradition is against it. The purpose of arithmetic lessons a century or so ago was to produce clerks who could keep accounts accurately. The mood of the early twentieth century led to a relaxation of actual arithmetical achievement, and the arithmetic texts became essentially without purpose. They had inherited the one aim of accuracy, and this they failed to achieve. I do not know any arithmetic text, used here in the period 1920–1950, which seems to have the object of stimulating

---

[1] A high school teacher conducted a poll of her students. She asked them, "Do you like or dislike mathematics? Which teacher caused you to like or dislike the subject?" *The replies did not mention the name of any teacher in high school.* Whether the student had come to love mathematics or to hate it, this feeling had already been established in elementary schools.

interest and intellectual curiosity. Indeed, arithmetic lessons have proved a most effective way of destroying children's power of independent thought. A very young child looks at things and seeks to understand them. After a few years of school he no longer does this. Instead, he tries to remember a rule; he usually remembers a rule that does not apply, and makes a statement that is sheer nonsense. Vision is destroyed in the elementary school, and the process of destruction often continues in high school and in college.

The increased demand of industry for mathematicians and scientists is a factor, partly adverse and partly favorable. It is adverse insofar as industry tends to absorb those who might make a contribution to teaching. It is favorable insofar as industry's demand for skilled employees constitutes a powerful force, making the improvement of education an urgent question of practical politics. The strength of this force can hardly be overestimated. For the role of mathematics in society has completely changed since 1945. Prior to that time, a mathematician was in almost the same position as a classical scholar; he had the choice of doing research and discovering more mathematics, or of teaching other people mathematics; he lived in a closed circle. Insurance absorbed some mathematicians, and industry a few—much fewer than most people realized. An extremely competent report[2] to Congress in 1941 estimated that industry in the United States could absorb *ten* mathematicians a year. A country as large as the United States does not have to organize to produce ten mathematicians a year. They happen spontaneously. Before 1945, in almost every country, the supply of mathematicians exceeded the demand. This was shown by the fact that students with good mathematical degrees went into occupations where mathematics was not used at all. There was an element of realism behind the neglect of mathematics in American schools. No one, here or elsewhere, foresaw the change that was coming.

After 1945, the demand for mathematicians far exceeded the total available. Statistics have been thrown around, estimating how many tens of thousands of mathematicians industry could absorb in the coming years. Even so, the figures correspond to a very small proportion of the population. To the best of my knowledge, no one has suggested that a quarter of a million mathematicians, or any number near to that, will be needed in the present century. It could therefore be argued very reasonably that the education of future mathematicians is a highly specialized problem, that provision should be made for these exceptional

[2] By Dr. Thornton Fry. Reprinted in *American Mathematical Monthly*, XLVIII, No. 6 (June-July 1941), Part II Supplement.

individuals, the general scheme of education remaining as it is. But this overlooks another aspect of the revolution. Electronic computers and automation do not merely create a demand for skilled workers; they also make obsolete unskilled and semiskilled workers. The industrial revolution in fact is moving toward its logical conclusion, in which every mechanical task, whether physical or mental, will be performed by a machine. Surveys of employment already show the first signs of this process, a shortage of highly skilled workers alongside a surplus of the unskilled and untrained. As far ahead as we can see we can expect this situation to continue and to become intensified.

This development cannot fail to influence education. A person whose services are in strong demand is secure and influential; a person on the edge of unemployment is insecure and his opinions are little regarded. In the society that is now passing, a certain shrewdness and common sense were often enough to take a man into the ranks of the secure and influential. It seems likely that much more will be required in the society of tomorrow; that shrewdness without a considerable background of knowledge will be insufficient. The first to appreciate this change will undoubtedly be professional people and executives. Suburban schools will begin, as they are already doing, to provide a richer curriculum in the elementary grades, and to attract competent teachers by giving higher salaries, by relieving teachers of all unnecessary clerical duties, and by providing scope for experiment and individual initiative. Other areas will then be faced with the choice of similar changes or accepting the exclusion of their children from the key positions in society. One section of the nation that is clearly unwilling any longer to accept an inferior position is the Negro community. The demand of Negroes for the best possible education will be intensified, and the present waste of Negro ability will, in all probability, be brought to an end.

One aspect of technology is its perpetual and ever-accelerated change. A few years ago there was a bottleneck caused by the shortage of computer programmers. This led to devices by which the machine did much of the work of programming itself; the detailed drudgery was transferred from the human being to the machine. Thus a new industry demanded a new skill, and within five years the industry had so transformed itself that this new skill was no longer needed. This development is typical of this age. Change is constant and rapid. Students in schools today are preparing themselves to perform unknown tasks in industries not yet invented. This implies the emergence of a new branch of the teaching profession, inside industry, with the task of perpetually retraining engineers and technicians. This new branch of the profession makes exacting requirements—the ability to learn new ideas quickly, to disentangle the essentials from the complicating nonessentials, and to put these ideas into a form which can be readily grasped by those who are not specialists in that particular field. Similar qualities are needed for institutions that will surely become a permanent feature of the landscape—summer schools and academic year institutes, designed to keep teachers aware of new developments in knowledge, both pure and applied.

In a primitive tribe, boys and girls commit to memory the precepts of the elders. In this way they absorb the traditional wisdom and also the traditional mistakes of their society. Education in a modern society differs remarkably little from education in the tribe. It too passes on wisdom and folly, and this must be so, for we have no way of identifying the unconscious errors in our own reasoning; we have no rule for distinguishing farsighted generosity from idealistic illusion, or justifiable caution from mean and self-destroying suspicion; we have no way of telling how much of our science is in fact tribal superstition, and how much of our superstition may be science. At times, when we consider the record and prospects of mankind, we may wish that the slate of memory could be wiped clean, that the continuity of history could be broken, and that a generation could grow up, uninfluenced by parents or teachers, and able to look at life with the eyes of the newborn and see it as it is. This experiment will certainly not be tried, and if it were tried, the result might be a world even worse than the one we have now. Children are born capable of adapting to almost any order of society. The one thing they cannot endure is anarchy. Thinking has to be within some framework, within some tradition. Each generation, of necessity, faces a painful search to separate the truth from the falsehood in the tradition received and a struggle to decide which parts of that tradition shall be passed on to the next generation. In an age of stability the search and the struggle are limited in scope; in an age of change, they dominate the scene.

We are living in an age of exceptionally rapid and continued change, an age which calls above all for independence and openness of mind, for resourcefulness and initiative, for flexibility. It might seem that our prospects are almost hopeless, for the tradition in the American teaching of mathematics and science lacks precisely those qualities; it is dominated by rote learning and the quiz, by the memorizing of words and isolated facts, rather than an understanding of general laws and the reasons for the facts. Yet this reflects a paradox in American culture, for the temper of American thinking is rational and analytic. Where a European will ask, "What is the history of this thing? How has it been done in the past? How does that limit our action in the future?"

an American will say, "Never mind the past. How should this thing be done? What is the logical way of doing it?" It is indeed strange that minds accustomed to this heroic courage in thinking about the infinitely complex problems of human society should recoil in terror when asked to give a logical account of some simple theme in arithmetic, such as the procedure for multiplying twenty-seven by thirty-eight. But it is so. The overwhelming majority admit, without shame, that they are afraid to think about arithmetic, and prefer to rely on the rules handed down by the elders of the tribe. The salvation of mathematics and science in American schools lies in breaking the barrier between these subjects and the general culture, in allowing them to become subjects for discussion and thought, in the same way that matters of current interest are topics for discussion and thought.

We certainly do not lack for tasks. More mathematics needs to be taught, as a subject unified in itself and related to other sciences, in a more lively and enterprising manner, to students at a younger age, by scholarly teachers who are themselves continually extending their own knowlege. We have a big advance to make, and we begin farther back than many other nations. This is the challenge. It is a considerable but not a superhuman task.

The Criteria for Decisions

In view of the variety of the problems confronting us, it is not surprising that a variety of solutions are proposed. These solutions correspond, as a rule, to the activity of the proposer. One professor may be dealing with Ph.D. students who hope to do research work in pure mathematics; another professor may be teaching freshmen engineers. It is inevitable that the ideas of each will be influenced by his circumstances: each will tend to imagine mathematics in terms of the themes he teaches; each will make proposals designed to make his work more effective. And each may easily forget that the other exists at all. The divergence of viewpoints just instanced is merely one example out of many; mathematicians differ in innumerable ways. To the teachers, looking at the disputes, it seems that mathematicians are completely unable to make up their collective mind. The teacher, with a very limited mathematical training, has to decide which mathematician to believe. The school principal is often in an even worse position, with no mathematical training at all. The professor of mathematics in a teachers' college stands at the junction of the two worlds, between the embattled specialists and the bewildered teachers. By what criteria can he make his choice?

To a certain extent the choice makes itself, as soon as one recognizes the existence of diversity. It is clearly not the business of an educational system to identify itself with any one kind of specialist and to despise all the others. Society both will and should continue to produce pure and applied mathematicians, mathematical physicists, scientists who are not mathematicians but who use some branch of mathematics in a routine manner, engineers, teachers, and many others. All of these stand in different relationships to mathematics; all of them see different aspects of the subject. Clearly, schools should be sufficiently flexible to value and to encourage all these varieties of mathematicians and users of mathematics.

It cannot be too strongly emphasized that these different varieties *are* different. The layman usually thinks of mathematics as a subject serving practical ends, and he tends to assume that research mathematicians share this viewpoint. If a pure mathematician speaks of some topic as important, the layman interprets this as meaning that the topic has applications of practical utility. Nothing could be farther from the truth. A pure mathematician works on problems which he considers interesting or beautiful. The mathematics of engineering he frequently finds dull, and tends to despise. One might think that the tremendous development of technology in the United States would have effected mathematicians here, and that American mathematicians would be more interested in practical applications than mathematicians are elsewhere. The reverse is true. In the words of an authoritative report:[3]

As American mathematics grew up during the first quarter of this century to join the older European schools in the front line of mathematical advance, it did so primarily in the purest, most abstract branches of mathematics. . . . With the exception of a few pioneers, mathematicians in the United States did not actively participate in the corresponding development of applied mathematics until the outbreak of World War II.

One should not consider a pure mathematician as being in the least like an engineer. He resembles rather, say, a chess player. You do not expect any economic benefit or scientific advance to come from reading a book on chess. But you may expect to find intriguing and beautiful positions and examples of ingenuity and resourcefulness. The analogy between chess and mathematics is not perfect; indeed, there is nothing that can serve as a complete and satisfactory analogy for mathematics. For each chess problem is more or less self-contained; it does not lead anywhere. On the other hand, every mathematical result is a part of one vast structure. The close of one investigation is the beginning of another. There is no knowing what direction the exploration may take, nor whether some new result may show a connection between parts

---

[3] F. J. Weyl. *A Survey of Training and Research in Applied Mathematics in the United States.* Society for Industrial and Applied Mathematics, 1956.

of mathematics that seemed entirely separate. The pure mathematician engages in this exploration for its own sake, and is rewarded by the richness and intricacy of the patterns he uncovers. The applied mathematician engages in the exploration in the hope that it will lead to other territories outside mathematics. Somewhere, he hopes, mathematics borders on science and technology. But the shape of mathematics is still vague and incomplete; we do not always know where the desired borders are, nor even for certain that they exist at all.

According to the poet Keats, it is inevitable that first in beauty should be first in might. If so, those parts of mathematics valued by pure mathematicians for their beauty should be the same as those valued by applied mathematicians for their power. In the long run, this may be true; in the short run it does not seem to work out at all. Most applied mathematicians must have had the experience of hearing of some new branch of pure mathematics that sounded promising and exciting, but which, after being laboriously mastered, made no contribution at all to the problem in hand.

One might illustrate this by that part of modern algebra which lies close to Galois theory. This theory is built around the idea of symmetry, and it allows one to prove, for example, that the equation of the fifth degree cannot be solved by the methods of elementary algebra, and that there is no general procedure for trisecting an angle with the means permitted by Euclid. This theory affects in quite different ways the mathematician, the teacher, and the engineer. All mathematicians would agree that it is a singularly beautiful and satisfying theory. A teacher has a direct concern in it because it lies near to familiar subjects; a student in a geometry class may claim to have trisected the angle; a student in an algebra class, who has been shown how to solve quadratics, may well ask whether similar devices will work with equations of the third, fourth, fifth, and higher degrees. A teacher should know enough to deal with discussions arising in this way. An engineer, to the best of my knowledge, never meets a problem for which Galois theory is helpful in any way. If an engineer meets an equation of the fifth degree, he will solve it numerically; if he needs to trisect an angle, he will certainly not restrict himself to Euclid's compass and ungraduated straightedge. In some very indirect and general way, the study of Galois theory might influence an engineer's philosophy and assist him in the solution of some particular problem. But this would be a rare event, affecting an exceptional engineer. Put crudely, Galois theory is a central topic for some mathematicians, a topic of interest for teachers, and a waste of time for engineers.

Too often, all these distinctions are slurred over in some slogan such as "modern mathematics." We must be up-to-date. Galois theory is a worthy representative of modern mathematics, a profound and beautiful subject. But one can imagine the growing bewilderment of an engineer who happened to wander into a course on Galois theory, as he tried to see how this type of mathematics could be applied to engineering problems.

It is not only engineers who can become bewildered. A young professor of mathematics at a teachers' college attended a course on modern algebra. He came back somewhat puzzled and reported that the course had not contained any applications. He did not mean simply engineering or scientific applications. The course had contained no applications at all. The lecturer, presumably, had explained what groups, rings, and fields were, and had proved some properties of these. And that was all. But the young professor knew that, if he returned to his college and began to teach modern algebra, the first questions his students asked would be, "What can we do with this? What is it *for?*" He had no idea what it was for. He only knew that people were saying we ought to be modern and this, apparently, was modern.

Much mystification has been caused by the manner in which the campaign for "modern mathematics" has been handled. Recent work in mathematics, of course, has yielded beautiful and valuable results, but one cannot arrange the branches of mathematics in their order of importance simply by giving the dates of discovery. It is necessary to be highly specific; to show for what purpose any branch of mathematics can be used, and by whom.

Mystification is the great enemy of mathematical thinking. Mathematics, above all other subjects, is that in which you expect to produce reasons for whatever you do. The way to avoid mystification is to be extremely explicit.

Mathematics is not an aimless subject. New branches arise, in a way that can be traced, from particular problems in the older branches of mathematics or in the world outside mathematics. Usually one can foresee that these new branches will serve certain purposes and lead in a particular direction. Sometimes, of course, a discovery serves quite unexpected purposes, not dreamed of by the discoverer.

We may then state a principle—almost a platitude, one would have thought, but certainly a principle often ignored in practice: *the work should make sense to the student.* The student should experience the subject, not as a mass of foreign information pressed upon him, but as a natural growth of his own consciousness. He should have some idea, at the outset, of the problem that is being attacked, and why we consider it worth attacking. He should know from which parts of mathematics it arises and to which parts it leads. He should know the purpose of the work, because purposes vary. For example, in some courses we expect to arrive at new results; in others, we know all the results before we start and are trying simply to provide a sounder logical basis for these. As soon as possible after meeting any new concept, the student should meet a worthwhile application of this concept. Then he sees how the work has increased his mathematical power. It is most unsatisfactory if, instead of this evidence of his own experience, he is given some vague, authoritarian justification—"this is the modern way," "this is how great mathematicians do it." The student, in short, should have some indication of where the work he is doing fits into the scheme of mathematics and, indeed, of human knowledge as a whole.

The traditional curriculum had at least this virtue, that its purposes were evident. The purposes were sometimes humble, but at least they were not mysterious. A text on physics, or engineering, or astronomy or surveying or plumbing or sheet-metal work, opened at random, would provide examples of algebra, geometry, trigonometry, and perhaps of calculus. The purpose of modern mathematics, on the other hand, is often obscure to the student. There is an obvious reason why this tends to be so. Twentieth-century mathematics was built on the foundation of nineteenth-century mathematics. But the student is often unfamiliar with nineteenth-century mathematics. Some of it he may have learned and forgotten; some he never knew at all. Thus he cannot possibly see the motivation for more recent work. It is particularly noticeable how calculus plays the role of a connecting link between the older and the newer mathematics. Cantor's work on sets and transfinite numbers grew out of his study of Fourier series. Lebesgue's use of sets was intimately connected with the theory of integration. Hilbert space and Banach space began with the theory of integral equations. Fréchet's work on metric spaces grew from a variety of topics in analysis. Topology was stimulated by the theory of the Riemann surface and of integration over complex numbers. If a student is not aware of these and other connections, he is bound to be mystified. He finds mathematicians treating with great reverence topics that to him must seem trivial and pointless. Topology will appear to him as a matter of Möbius strips, the Königsberg bridges, and the four-color conjecture, entertaining perhaps but of doubtful significance. It is the good student who will be puzzled, the student of integrity, who expects mathematics to make sense. The poor student will be quite happy to jump on the bandwagon, and take the new material on trust. All his life he has taken things on trust, not submitting statements to the court of his inner judgment, but repeating the phrases of the lecturer and the text. This, he believes, is the way to win friends and influence professors. But mathematics cannot be learned so. All the nonsense of the type $(x + y)^2 = x^2 + y^2$ is written because the student writes irresponsibly. He does not feel that he is committing himself to the truth of a statement, with a duty to ascertain the meaning of this statement, and see whether he really believes it. He is merely trying to write something like something he heard some time, and the result is usually as incorrect as the purpose. Indeed, the greatest difficulty in teaching college students is that they are usually so anxious to please and so unwilling to think.

A key principle, then, in any course of mathematics is that *it must encourage and establish the student's habit of examining evidence for himself.*

A future teacher must not only think for himself; he must be prepared to encourage others to do the same. His classroom must not simply be a place where students are told things, but a place where students engage in discussion. Now this is a very severe stipulation, for no one can foresee where discussion may lead. Many teachers, in fact, try to avoid discussion, for fear they may get out of their depth. But free discussion is the essential part of a mathematical lesson. In order to face discussion, *a teacher must know with extreme thoroughness the actual subject being taught and also have a good knowledge of other topics that arise naturally from this subject.* The reason for this, our third principle, is not that the subject necessarily contains vital information. Our concern here is less with *what* is taught than with *how* it is handled. Whatever material we teach, we may wish twenty years hence that we had taught something else. But if we have used this material to form correct habits, if the students are ready to think for themselves, to make conjectures, to debate the evidence for and against these conjectures, to attack nonroutine problems—then they are well armored to face the unknown future.

This emphasis on student thinking, student discovery, student discussion, on the way in which the subject is approached, of course does not mean that the choice of content is unimportant. A student's thinking is inevitably influenced by what he knows, as well as by how he has learned it. We should try to see that material is carefully selected. Nevertheless, the emphasis on *how* over *what* remains: if a student has not learned to think about mathematics, he knows nothing of mathematics. Rote-learned information, whether ancient or modern, is not mathematics, and will in any case be remembered only inaccurately for a short time and soon forgotten altogether.

Thinking is an activity, and one that cannot be produced by compulsion. A teacher, therefore, must seek for subject matter and for methods of teaching that will create in the students a desire to learn. A teacher's selection of material differs both from a mathematician's and an engineer's. The engineer selects material that can be *used;* the mathematician tends to select material that can be *systematically developed.* The teacher's first concern, however, is to *stimulate.* A teacher should choose material that makes children want to think. This thinking should not be a form of self-torture. It should be the natural outgrowth of a child's interest and curiosity. The most depressing thing in our educational system is not the student who decides to terminate his education. It is rather the student who slaves away for the sake of grades, without ever realizing that it would be possible to study a subject for its inherent interest.

The present ferment in education offers some hope of achieving a united society, instead of one divided into two separate camps: eggheads and blockheads. At present, intellectual endeavor is like a play acted in an empty theater or a game with no spectators. The spectators do contribute something to a game. If they are not themselves experts, they at least understand what the experts are trying to do, because they have played the game themselves. It would give tremendous impetus to all kinds of creative work if it were done as part of a general culture, instead of an exclusive, minority undertaking. Such an objective is not visionary; there have, in the past, been societies which attained it. We shall not achieve it, however, by impressing on the public that mathematics and science are important for industry or strategy or what not. Rather we shall achieve it if children themselves take part in mathematical and scientific activities which they enjoy.

Now young children do enjoy mental activity. They enjoy thinking and discovering. But, as has been noted earlier, this enjoyment decreases with the years, and is in fact systematically, though no doubt unconsciously, destroyed by our institutions. Once destroyed, it is almost impossible to restore. If, then, any change is to come, it must come through those who are in contact with young children. Now there are very many teachers of the young. It might be possible to identify high school students who gave promise of becoming brilliant research workers in mathematics or science, and to provide special treatment for them. It would be extremely difficult to identify students who are likely to become teachers of grades four through eight. Very well, it might be argued, wait until teachers' college and deal with the problem there. But teacher's college is already too late. A student who has learned mathematics by rote through twelve grades is not likely to blossom out as a creative thinker in college. This is the essential problem of educational change, the vicious circle we always meet. The reform of the schools can only occur within the schools. Not the least significant aspect of the high school curriculum is the part it plays in determining the outlook of future teachers in elementary schools, for it is they who hold the key position in determining the nature of our future society. A high school teacher has, in fact, great responsibilities in connection with elementary education. He has to co-operate in the transfer to elementary school of parts of the traditional high school curriculum. More important, he has to see that this transfer changes and revitalizes these topics. A mechanical, rote-learning approach to algebra, for example, will prove even more fatal in grade five than it used to be in grade nine. He has to assist those who are already teaching in elementary and junior high schools in his neighborhood. And above all, he has a duty to his present students who may become teachers in the future. As he does not know exactly which students these are, he has an obligation to see that *all his students are able to think and enjoy thinking.*

At this point a certain element of conflict enters. The thinking of mathematicians tends to be logical and abstract. The thinking of the population in general tends to be intuitive and concrete. Only a few seem able to think in the way demanded by a graduate school of mathematics. Almost everyone is able to think, more or less effectively, in the way demanded by everyday life.

Two points of view are therefore current today. Some take as their goal that children should learn to think like research mathematicians as quickly as possible. Advanced mathematics is abstract and general. Therefore elementary instruction should be abstract and general. Others take the opposite view. Let the classroom be full of apparatus which the children can see and touch. Then they will certainly learn to think and some of them, later on, may learn to think more abstractly.

These diverging views directly affect practice. For example, an equation has traditionally been illustrated by means of a balance. An enthusiast for apparatus might well have an actual balance in the classroom and use it to demonstrate the steps of solving an equation. To a purist, this is most distressing. A balance is a *thing*. Mathematics is not about things. It is only obscured by physical illustrations. The proper method (he would say) is to bring in the axiom

$$\text{"If } a = b \text{, then for all } c, a + c = b + c\text{"}$$

and let the students appeal to this axiom every time they add the same quantity to each side of an equation.

There can be no doubt how the methods would compare for teaching effectiveness. The balance, seen and touched, would leave a definite image in the students' memories. It may seem strange to mathematicians, who are accustomed to looking at statements very carefully and remembering exactly what they say, but the fact is that on the next day many students would not be able to reproduce the axiom correctly. Some might have forgotten that an axiom had been mentioned at all. And those who did remember the axiom might very well fail to appreciate its meaning.

My own belief is that there is no conflict between the illustration of the balance and reliance on the axiom. Indeed, probably the most effective way to teach the axiom would be to do a physical demonstration with the balance, and *let the students carry out the process of abstraction and generalization*. The teacher could say, "I have added three pounds to each side and it still balances. Could I have added any number of pounds? How shall we express, in the language of algebra, the conclusion this demonstration suggests to us?" The concrete experience thus becomes a means of recalling the abstract statement.

This belief, that concrete material can help, rather than hinder, the formation of abstract ideas, is held by a number of mathematicians. Professor Marguerite Lehr, in her introduction to Catherine Stern's admirable book, *Children Discover Arithmetic*, says that Stern's treatment of arithmetic has something of the spirit of modern higher algebra. Now modern higher algebra is a highly abstract subject, and Catherine Stern's method is inseparably bound up with the use of measuring rods.

J. E. Littlewood writes in his *A Mathematician's Miscellany*,[4] "A heavy warning used to be given that pictures are not rigorous; this has never had its bluff called and has permanently frightened its victims into playing for safety. Some pictures of course are not rigorous, but I should say most are (and I use them whenever possible myself) . . . pictorial arguments . . . can be quite legitimate . . . For myself I *think* like this whenever the subject matter permits."

S. Ulam, writing about the truly exceptional mathematician, John von Neumann, expressed surprise that von Neumann was apparently able to think without pictorial aids. "It seems curious to me that in the many mathematical conversations on topics belonging to set theory and allied fields, von Neumann even seemed to think formally. Most mathematicians, when discussing problems in these fields, seemingly have an intuitive framework based on geometrical or almost tactile pictures of abstract sets, transformations, etc. Von Neumann gave the impression of operating sequentially by purely formal deductions."[5]

---

[4] (London: Methuen, 1953), pp. 35–36.
[5] *Bulletin of the American Mathematical Society*, LXIV, No. 3, Part 2 (May, 1958), p. 12.

At a conference of mathematicians concerned with summer school institutes, reference was made to a habit that many professors have. The professor finds himself in difficulty in presenting a chain of formal deductions. He makes a little drawing on the blackboard, erases it, and then continues with the formal presentation. But often he makes no reference to the drawing and the help it gives him. The drawing is, so to speak, the professor's own private affair. Only the finished argument, the formal proof, is for publication.

It is a great pity that mathematicians make this particular distinction between public and private life. The whole process of mathematical creation, beginning with "geometrical or almost tactile pictures" and then analyzing these pictures and extracting the essential ideas in a form suitable for abstract development—this whole process is much easier to understand than the final result taken in isolation. A von Neumann or an Emmy Noether may not find it necessary to work in this way, but if most professional mathematicians, as adults, find it necessary to use physical models as an aid to mathematical imagination, then surely children, who are just beginning to build up their system of thinking, are entitled to do the same. Many teachers as college students have suffered in courses that were too abstractly presented. Such a course does not teach a student to think like a mathematician. As a rule it teaches him not to think at all.

We may state our conclusion as a principle. *The most important task of mathematics teaching in elementary and high school is to strengthen intuition. The teacher should feel perfectly free to use drawings, apparatus, and other physical aids to the imagination. The student should be prepared for more formal treatment at a later stage, by having his attention drawn to paradoxes and fallacies in which intuition, pushed too far, leads to contradictions and incorrect results.*

Mathematical Content

If a student in his senior year at high school decides to become a mathematics teacher, to what topics should he be exposed in four or five years at college? What course will best prepare him for his future work?

It is clear that there can be no hard and fast answer to this question. Very much depends on the quality of the student. Is he a first-rate mathematician who has responded to the changing atmosphere of the times and has decided to teach in high school instead of in graduate school? Or is he a student who has drifted into teaching because he has no qualifications for anything else? Clearly very different courses will be appropriate. College should provide the flexibility we hope to see in high school. There should be every opportunity for students to work independently and for able students to forge ahead on their own.

As a rule, the first course taken by students in college should be one of rehabilitation. Its purpose is to free the student of any static, rote-learning habits he may have acquired in high school. The academic content of this course is not important. Any material can be included that is simple enough for students to experiment with, and at the same time complex enough to stimulate curiosity and interest. The essential thing is that the work should proceed by student discovery, that each student shall succeed in solving the problems presented to him so that he gains in confidence and begins to think of himself as an originator and discoverer. The importance of such training has been well explained and demonstrated by Polya. It represents a vital and irreplaceable ingredient in the course. If the student fails to become an independent thinker, he fails in everything. The rest of the work becomes a fake. The student pretends to do mathematics, and hopes the pretense will deceive his professors. It will be quite impossible for such a student to stimulate genuine thinking in children.

Since this initial course is so vital, it should be taught by the best teachers the college has. It is the hardest course of all to teach, since it aims not merely to impart information, but, in a sense, to change the character of the student by awakening powers and energies that have hitherto been dormant. The teacher should have the utmost freedom to vary the content of the course, to individualize instruction, and to adapt his material to the needs and interests of each student.

Earlier, we accepted the principle that a high school teacher must know, thoroughly and expertly, the material he is actually teaching. If, for example, a child in a geometry class produces an alleged trisection of the angle, the teacher should be able, by means of trigonometry and co-ordinate geometry, to calculate by how many parts in a million the construction is in error—and generally be able to decide for himself, by more powerful methods, the truth or falsity of any conjecture produced by a geometry student. This means that the teacher must be able to handle algebra and trigonometry very competently, not merely in the modern sense of knowing axioms, but in the old-fashioned sense of being able to perform calculations. Such facility is only acquired by continual practice. It would probably be psychologically wrong to begin a college course with a review and a reteaching of the traditional high school syllabus. The student is probably hoping for the stimulus of novel material. But every opportunity should be taken to launch the student on investigations that will require the sustained use of elementary algebra or trigonometry. Facility in these subjects is made more than ever necessary by the trend to include co-ordinate geometry in the high school curriculum. Without a good command of algebra it is impossible for a student to work effectively on problems of co-ordinate geometry.

It was mentioned earlier that subjects tend to become fragmented. To avoid this, the topics of the college curriculum should be interwoven. As each new subject is brought in, it should be applied to earlier subjects. Calculus naturally involves elementary algebra and co-ordinate geometry. Through Taylor series one is naturally led to the connection between the trigonometric and the exponential functions. Expressing sine and cosine as algebraic functions of $e^{i\theta}$ reduces all trigonometric identities to algebraic identities. It would be natural to illustrate this by exercises which students work. The use of i naturally raises the questions of the logic involved in the use of complex numbers, and allows one to compare four or five different ways in which their use may be justified—as geometric operations, as matrices, as polynomials modulo $x^2 + 1$, or as an abstract algebra. The use of infinite series leads naturally to problems of convergence and to the theory of functions of a complex variable. Since i can be regarded as a matrix, the use of $e^{i\theta}$ naturally raises the question of exponentials of matrices and of infinite series of matrices. One can show that the methods used to prove the convergence of an absolutely convergent series of complex terms can be generalized to metric spaces, and applied to series of matrices.

The vocabulary of calculus should be established early—differentiation and partial differentiation, integration, differential and integral equations. With the rise of electronic computers the solution of particular differential equations decreases in importance, but a student should be able to visualize the meaning of a differential equation and the way in which a differential or integral equation can be used to define a function. Students should know enough about Fourier series to appreciate their historical significance and to realize how unexpectedly such a series can behave.[6] The student will then be able to see that some of the situations considered in real variable theory are by no means as arbitrary and artificial as at first sight they may seem to be.

Calculus opens the road to all kinds of mathematics. The numerical solution of differential equations leads to the theory of finite differences, a subject that can add considerable interest to the study of elementary algebra, and one that has risen in importance with the spread of electronic computing. From Fourier series one could motivate an introduc-

---

[6] Chapter IV of Piaggio, *Differential Equations*, in the space of three or four pages says enough about Fourier series to act as an eye opener.

tion to Hilbert space and perhaps Lebesgue integration. Much, of course, would depend on the interest of the professor and the ability of the students. One could also turn back toward trigonometry and re-examine this subject, pointing out to students that $\cos \theta$ and $\sin \theta$ are merely co-ordinates of a point on the unit circle. The real problem is to calculate θ which, being the length of an arc, raises a problem of integration. Again, many problems in differential equations can be put naturally in matrix form. Some of these, such as vibration problems in dynamics, show the importance of reducing a matrix to canonical form. The rather old-fashioned symbolic method of solving linear differential equations with constant coefficients provides a natural example of a ring involving an entity, D, which is not a number. One can hark back to trigonometry yet again in connection with matrices. The matrix representation of the orthogonal group in two dimensions gives a simple way of deriving the formulas of trigonometry—one which, indeed, could be used in high school. From the orthogonal group in two or three dimensions, the student might also obtain a first insight into the subject of topological groups.

The curriculum here suggested is vague in outline. To some extent, vagueness is proper to the subject. No one can know the whole of mathematics. Different students will naturally attempt to master different sectors, corresponding to their individual tastes and temperaments. But some of the vagueness in this essay is due to its being a kind of interim report. I am still at work investigating such questions as: "What parts of modern mathematics are both intelligible and useful to a high school teacher?" "What parts of mathematics are likely to become of scientific or technological importance in the next half century?"[7] Teachers and teacher-training institutions have the responsibility for answering such questions. Our viewpoint will of necessity be different from that of most research mathematicians, for they are mostly concerned with the furthering of pure mathematical discovery, while we are concerned with that and also with the education of the future scientist, engineer, and citizen. It is our task to search through the literature of mathematics, of science, of technology, and to select those topics which will stimulate our students and provide them with principles around which future knowledge can be organized.

We would like teachers to know as much as possible. An intuitive treatment of a subject can be taught rapidly; a formal, axiomatic treat-

---

[7] Some discussion of the latter question will be found in my paper, "The Reconstruction of Mathematical Education," *Journal of Engineering Education,* LI (November, 1960), pp. 98–113.

ment requires a considerable length of time. Which is preferable, to teach many ideas in a "sloppy" manner or a few ideas in full-dress development? The correct policy seems to be the following:

All ideas should be presented first in an intuitive manner. Some of the ideas should then be analyzed, in discussion between the students and the professor, until they have been clarified and brought to a rigorous form. This should be done sufficiently often for the students to recognize the process by which loose ideas are tidied up and made rigorous. The students should then be able to appreciate the possibility of axiomatizing those parts of the subject that have been presented only in intuitive outline.

It would be a mistake to cut down the curriculum to what can be treated with complete rigor. At all costs, a student should leave the course full of ideas. It is regrettable if a high school teacher commits an error of logic. But it is a mortal sin to teach mathematics in a way that obscures the generating ideas.

Naturally, the most thorough treatment should be given to those subjects which now are, or are soon likely to be, in the high school curriculum—co-ordinate geometry, matrices, vector spaces, calculus. We can anticipate (very conservatively) the time when intuitive calculus will figure in the junior year, with a more rigorous treatment of calculus in the senior year of high school. High school teachers will need to know epsilontage, and above all, how to make epsilontage intelligible. This can be achieved by a careful study of the process by which a proof in analysis is constructed. This process usually begins with a picture, and ends by translating the pictorial argument into formal deduction. Incidentally, it usually calls for fairly expert manipulation of elementary algebra.

In addition to the thorough treatment of these subjects, there will also be some sampling of topics in mathematics. Here there is no pretense of conquering a territory; merely a solid bridgehead is established. Some small part of the subject is explored thoroughly enough for the student to work problems and exercises—otherwise the student will remember nothing. As mentioned earlier, the student must see how this subject arose, and to what it leads. In this way, the student at least comes to know the general nature of certain branches of mathematics, and sees some of the interconnections between these branches. The connections with high school subjects are particularly important. Two or three years after leaving college a student forgets whatever he has not used. If he is to retain any recollection of more advanced mathematics, the links with elementary work must be securely forged in his mind so that, as he prepares his lessons or answers questions in class, his college work will pass through his mind in perpetual review.

In considering any program for the training or retraining of teachers, one cannot escape a certain sense of frustration. However well and however fast we improve teaching, we cannot keep pace with the demands of the situation. In classrooms throughout the country, hundreds of thousands of students will continue to have their intellect blunted and their enthusiasm destroyed. The ablest students do not constitute the most serious problem; if administration has the vision to let such students read ahead on their own, they will educate themselves and each other. The hardest problem lies in the remainder of the students, from those just below brilliance to those just above mental defect. These need teachers. Nearly all of them will respond to lively teaching and to some explanation of their difficulties. If we could keep them mentally alive, we should be able to draw on them for a future generation of teachers. Our most important problem is to find some way of doing this.

36

Typical Student in U.S. University Not Scholar

Britain in our time, has put herself through a peaceful revolution in university education. Before 1914, Oxford and Cambridge Universities were primarily playgrounds for privileged young people whose parents could afford the fees.

These "commoners" were then in a great majority over the "scholars," whose education was subsidized as a reward for their having passed a severe intellectual test, and who were kept on their toes by the knowledge that their scholarship might be withdrawn if they idled. In English universities today it is the drone student who is a rarity.

The typical university student today is a scholar who is being subsidized out of taxpayers' money because he has been considered capable of profiting intellectually.

In the United States, too, a candidate for a scholarship to a university normally has to pass an intellectual test, as well as a means test, but the scholar is not the typical present-day American student.

Today the American, like the eighteenth-century European aristocrat, does not regard education as being primarily an intellectual activity, but as being an amenity to which he has a right. The primary reason for going to a university is to acquire social experience and aplomb. Intellectual work comes second to that.

This view is shared by the adults who pay, whether as parents or as taxpayers. The school boards that govern elementary and secondary schools, and the state legislatures that govern state universities and colleges, are willing to pay generously for splendid buildings and elaborate equipment; for huge field-houses, in which basketball and football can be played indoors in the winter months, and for the floodlighting of open-air football fields.

Arnold Toynbee. "Typical Student in U.S. University Not Scholar" *Globe and Mail* (Toronto) July 31, 1963. Reprinted by kind permission of the publishers, The Observer Foreign News Service, London, England.

Author (1889–   ): Diplomat, historian, author, educated at Winchester College, and Balliol College, Oxford; Director of Studies, Royal Institute of International Affairs.

But if a rural school board is asked to raise teachers' salaries its reaction is likely to be grudging. As the taxpayer sees it the teacher is economically unproductive and indeed, not a very important feature of the school, because intellectual training is not the primary purpose of American education.

Teachers, therefore, must expect the poor pay that unimportant jobs inevitably bring.

The high school is the weakest link in the American educational chain. The graduate from an average American high school emerges intellectually about two years behind his European contemporary in at least two important aspects—he has not yet learned to express himself effectively in writing, and he has not yet begun to become intellectually independent.

Consequently, the first half of an American university course is largely taken up in learning things that, in Europe, he would have learned at school. Consequently, an American university education is considered not to be complete unless, and until, the graduate has gone on to take a postgraduate course. This will prolong his education until he is rising twenty-seven.

American education is thus "aristrocratic," in the traditional European sense of the term, in several respects. It allows many students who are intellectually unfit for a university education to have one, but it does not ensure that all boys and girls who are intellectually fit for one shall get one. And, for a minority of students that do take the intellectual purpose of education seriously, it caters only by prolonging the period of education far into adult life, when they may be already married with children of their own.

This shortens the effective working life of the intellectually ablest part of the population. It is wasteful of money, ability and time, but it has one advantage—in so far as the present-day American system of education gives the student an intellectual training, it gives him a liberal one, in the sense that the intellectual work required of him covers a wide field, even though it may cover it superficially.

The British method is to impose tests at every rung of the educational ladder. This may ensure that the intellectually fit shall all have a chance of going to the top, but it does this at the cost of forcing the student to specialize at a much earlier stage than in the United States.

But can the present U.S. ideal of education, and the system, survive? The world is becoming increasingly competitive and mechanized, and the key to success is the mastery of science and technology. These are intellectual pursuits, and the intellectual standard required for them is becoming increasingly exacting.

The American people want power. At the same time they dislike and distrust intellectuals. In present circumstances they are going to have to make a choice between reversing their attitude toward intellectuals and renouncing power. It seems improbable that they will choose to renounce power when they have been forced to face the issue; and they may be forced to face it by the educational policy of their principal rival, the Soviet Union.

Since the time of Peter the Great, Russia has embraced the educational system of continental Western Europe—and continental European education is intellectually strenuous by the standards of the English-speaking countries, with the possible exception of Scotland.

In the U.S. education there are signs of an intellectual awakening which may prove to be as revolutionary as the change that has come over British education since 1919. The best of the American private universities have a higher intellectual standard than all but the very best of the state universities. It is true that within a foreseeable time, about 80 percent of America's student population are going to be on the campuses of the state universities. Yet the cream of the private universities will still be a powerful leaven for the lump.

Moreover, there are symptoms of an intellectual awakening in the public schools. For instance, there has been a new move for teaching foreign languages, and high time, in an age in which the United States has become deeply involved with the rest of the world. But in the history of American education this is a remarkable new departure, and it may portend a genuine break with the American people's traditional anti-intellectualism.

In the age of automation, a contempt for intellectual training will have dire personal consequences for the individual who acts on it in his educational career. In the days when the American people were winning the West, easy money could be made by unskilled labor. In the future there is going to be no employment for the unskilled worker, either manual or clerical.

The traditional self-made businessman is being pushed off the stage by the highly trained executive; the unskilled manual worker by the highly skilled technician. The American child who leaves high school at or before the minimum leaving age of sixteen is dooming himself in advance to life-long unemployment.

And so, perhaps, is the student who graduates from the university without having taken the intellectual side of education seriously. In the United States, as elsewhere, the egghead who can keep abreast of the progress of science and technology has turned out to be "the wave of the future."

37

Ivy League Land; Not So Much An Education, More a Way of Life

Ivy League is the New World equivalent of "Oxbridge." It consists of Columbia, Cornell, Harvard, Dartmouth, Yale, Princeton, Brown and the University of Pennsylvania. The only official relationship of these eight schools is that they have all agreed to play a particularly ineffective variety of football with one another. But in the popular mind, and in their own mind too, they represent the pinnacles of the American educational system. And this superior octopus is a beast both to be admired and to be shot at.

Americans like to call America "God's own country." But though since 1776 they have ceased to be the King's own country, they retain their craving for hierarchy. One of the things that most amused us about the American vernacular was their misuse of the word "aristocracy."

"Frank, Harry and Joe are the aristocracy of this year's football team," said one caption to a campus newspaper photograph of three sinister-looking toughs. The reason for this social promotion was that Frank, Harry and Joe were the only players left over from last year.

"Mr. Hickenberg is the great aristocrat of our University benefactors" were the words of introduction to a corpulent local undertaker, whose outsize embalming profits had for years been given to campus building projects.

Of a mid-western debater who produced a corny peroration laced with ham-acted pauses and gestures, we were told by the debates coach, "Jim is an exponent of the ancient aristocratic tradition of American oratory."

Michael Beloff and Jonathan Aitken. "Ivy League Land; Not So Much an Education, More a Way of Life," in *A Short Walk on the Campus* (London: Secker & Warburg, 1966), pp. 57–68; 156–169. Reprinted by kind permission of the publisher, Secker and Warburg, London, England.

Authors: While undergraduates at Oxford University, they traveled to the United States in 1964 representing the University's Debating Team. Jonathan William Patrick Aitken, (1942–   ) educated at Eton and Christ Church College Oxford, Treasurer Oxford Union Society 1963 and Vice-President 1964. Michael Beloff (1942–   ) educated Eton, and Magdalen College Oxford. President Oxford Union Society 1964; he has held a law lectureship at Trinity College, Oxford and now is a writer, teacher, and barrister.

We became a little ashamed that we were unable to supply between us even a knighthood, the more so since one of the contestants for a place on the tour had been the son of Scotland's premier Duke. Many students clearly felt they had been cheated out of something. "I suppose you couldn't fly him over just for the weekend," said one heartrendingly beautiful sophomore from Wayne State.

The educational excellence of the Ivy League schools is unchallenged, but what interested us more was their social character. To an American ivy symbolizes genuine old age which *per se* is to admired. To a British gardener ivy signifies the destruction by slow suffocation of trees and shrubs. There is an element of truth in both these horticultural analogies.

At the University of Pennsylvania we were greeted by a student who, wihin two minutes of our arrival at the depôt where the Greyhound buses were kennelled, was saying in aggressive reply to our questions about the size of the campus and so on, "It's an Ivy League school, you know." He obviously felt that this label alone placed the University beyond the scope of investigation. He made it quite clear that visitors from England to an Ivy League school could worship if they liked, but ought not to ask too many questions. This student came from Texas (he informed us of this in the same breath as he informed us about his university being in the Ivy League, as though they were equal passports to excellence), and we soon began to wonder whether he wasn't suffering from an effortless inferiority complex. Certainly we never found anywhere else on the tour, as we found in Ivy League land, a kind of desire to involve us as Oxbridge graduates in the local mystique, a wish to prove without dispute that we and they were from the same stable.

There was superficially a devotion to Oxbridge traditions. Jonathan Edwards College, in which we stayed at Yale, with its pseudo quadrangles, greystone buildings and carefully cultivated ivy seemed to us to be almost an architectural parody. (Later on the tour we found a grandchild of the style at Duke University, North Carolina, called by its inmates "the Harvard of the South," where the campus, admittedly magnificent, was built in the fashion of the great Gothic revival of the 1930s.) Yale Hall, which is one of the campus dining rooms, is a very obvious forgery. One tolerates inconvenient serving arrangements, cramped and uncomfortable benches and the heavy lugubrious atmosphere of Christ Church Hall because transcending all these disadvantages one is conscious of a very real sense of Oxonian tradition and history. Yale Hall had all the disadvantages and none of the traditions. As we stood in Yale Hall in ye olde Oxford queue waiting fifteen minutes for our supper, we were sorry that the University had forsworn the opportunity to build one of the airy spacious cafeterias that we found on so many campuses. The stale marmalade on the tables as breakfast next morning had all the evocative significance of Proust's madeleine for the Oxford man.

At Harvard, moreover, there is a college system in operation, similarly an artificial creation since the traditions of the various houses date back only to the 1920s. Their intake is controlled by computers whose aim is to produce an equilibrium of social, athletic and scholastic virtues. The advantage of this mimicry is evident in the standards of comfort in some of the student quarters. Here it is the imaginary rather than the real Oxford that is copied in lavish suites, "The Oxford of the Hollywood movies," as one student neatly put it. It is not merely in architecture and structure that the New World pays homage to the Old. One Oxford expatriate currently attending the law school said that his every word was noted down by Anglodolatrous graduates. One day he asked the Professor sotto voce permission to go to the lavatory, and was rewarded by the sight of the whole class indulging in a buzz of speculation as to what gem had fallen from his English lips.

Ivy League universities cultivate their own special idiosyncrasies. Oxbride has produced the *Beyond the Fringe* team and *Private Eye*. At Harvard the satire magazine, the *Harvard Lampoon*, possesses a whole building to itself. Yale, we were told, is the only college where the campus newspaper has a gossip column. Certainly we never saw one anywhere else. The very collegiate clothing style in America is called Ivy League. Indeed at conservative Yale the students are presentable enough in their appearance to justify the great herds of male model recruiters who attend their commencement each year disguised as well-meaning uncles. (Or was this arch anecdote of a Michigan State graduate apocryphal? It reveals anyhow the resentments that one kind of student feels for the other.) On the other hand, there is a general tendency on the part of many Harvard and Columbia students to be as ill-kept as possible. There is a rule at Harvard that one must wear coat and tie to meals. It does not specify any particular standards from waist downwards, however, and we noticed the esoteric scruffiness of the jeans which contrasted so greatly with the well-fitting herringbone tweeds above. One Ohio State undergraduate was indeed heard to remark somewhat pathetically that "Guys around here are much Ivier than those slobs at Harvard."

The students at Columbia, Penn, Harvard and Yale struck us as much richer than their midwestern counterparts. They are in fact the chief national institutions, and, for example, the offspring of wealthy midwesterners are traditionally educated at Yale. With the students here we could discuss Athens, Paris and Rome; indeed for many the Grand Tour was an annual event. In the Midwest we were lucky if we found people who had visited Chicago. There were traces of real snobbery, name dropping of Rockefellers and Kennedys. At Columbia one of the debaters had been passed over for the presidency of his fraternity, for which he was clearly the most eligible and logical candidate, in favour of a Russian prince. We found too that Ivy League universities spurn with hauteur the idea of debates coaches—not that this notably improved the quality of their debating.

There were more sinister aspects of eastern seaboard culture. At Yale we were placed in a college guest room. "It's lucky you weren't in a house," said our host knowingly, "or you might have got mixed up with a gang-banging." This, it turned out, was a kind of communal copulation with as many as twenty couples sharing the same room. At Columbia we witnessed a still more extraordinary game. As we were walking along by the side of a dormitory we suddenly saw a student being dangled out of one window by a pair of room-mates, while from another window a torchlight was flashed on to his naked posterior, one buttock of which was painted blue. This, it was explained to us, was a "mooning session," the Ivy League version of tag. Instead of catching another player who then becomes "It," one gives him a view of one's nude behind. He then has to display a similar sight to the next "it." What we had seen was a local variation, called, for obvious reasons, blue-mooning. We left the Ivy League colleges, confident at least that they were different from other institutions of higher education.

Our travels took us next to Bates College, Maine, a small Liberal Arts school, where we were met off the aeroplane at Portland by a Bates student who seemed to personify all the virtues of a true scion of Ivy League land. He wore hunting boots and his complexion and gait were similar to those of Squire Western in *Tom Jones;* he shook hands with us in a vice-like grip, gave a hearty, braying laugh and exclaimed in tones of patronising pity "Welcome to New England."

As we drove from Portland Airport to Bates this jovial man of spirit (an accurate description, since he never stopped offering us and consuming himself vodka cocktails from a specially prepared flask) gave us his views on the current political situation. "I abhor both Goldwater and Johnson. . . . I did not think much of Kennedy either, he was just a mob raiser and his status among people who count was zero. . . . In my room I keep a picture of George Washington—it reminds me of the fact that our present leaders are nowhere near greatness. . . . We need a little more humility in our politics. . . . Incidentally,

I just can't understand how in England you can tolerate a Conservative Party of such violently left-wing inclinations."

For all his political bombast we took to this character in a big way. He had a great sense of humour and was very well read and knowledgeable about the arts. During the drive he outlined for us plans for the day. We were to be introduced to a speech professor, answer questions at a luncheon of the local Kiwanis and debate in the college chapel that night. Each of these functions was outlined in those unenthusiastic terms which only a true blasé can produce, generally ending with the comment: "And that'll be ghastlee, absolutely ghastlee."

We were duly introduced to the speech professor, who looked a sort of caricature nonagenarian Heath Robinson boffin, with droopy bloodhound eyes, a wisp of white hair and prince-nez spectacles perched precariously on the end of a beaky nose. He was evidently one of the old school academics, since he greeted us with "How do you do, Aitken. How do you do, Beloff" instead of the usual gush of "Hi Mike, hi Johnny" which came after the introductions from most speech professors. In fact, Professor Brooks Quimby was the doyen of American speech professors and later on in the day showed us his fascinating files of past tours that included a snapshot of the young Rab Butler in full tails in the middle of the 1924 expedition.

Meanwhile though, we had to extend our mission to a new environment. We were to be the guests of honour at the weekly lunch of the Auburn-Lewiston Kiwanis club, a kind of New World Rotary group. Our student hosts were clearly apprehensive about our reactions to this ordeal. "Oh my gawd," Squire Western kept saying. "The Kiwa-a-a-a-a-a-a-nis. Oh gawd." The luncheon was held in the cavernous *salle à manger* of the local YMCA. The Kiwanis turned out to be business men whose weekly meetings produced a feeling of good fellowship amongst them. In case one good fellow should forget the name of another good fellow, they all sported little badges proclaiming name, nickname and profession. "Dave Gutowski . . . Fatso . . . Stockbroker." Luckily we were not made to comply with this custom since Jonathan's aforementioned versatility of profession would have necessitated a dozen or so badges. After a rapid and somewhat tasteless meal a small man came to a microphone and with feverish zeal led the collected gathering in a few club chants. "God Save the Queen" opened the repertoire. We followed this up with the Kiwani drinking song, the Kiwani sweetheart song the Kiwani guest song. The tunes of these songs were in strong primary chords; and the words, quaint and simple, all conveyed a patriotic message. Alas, there was no new member to be initiated that day, and we were unable to sing the famous Kiwani initiation song whose words ran along these lines: "We are the Kiwanis. We are the Kiwanis. Now you are one, you son of a gun, so have some fun, pom, pom." The singing was carried out with great enthusiasm and after all were sweating profusely we were called upon to give our views on the political situation.

This week was apparently International Relations Week, so Michael was allowed to explain Harold Wilson to the assembled company. Then Jonathan unexplained him again. After short speeches a Colonel X, clearly the appointed buddy boy and spokesman of the group, fired a few questions at us, slapping his knee vigorously the while. A good time was had by all, but clearly it was American politics that interested them most and that evening the local newspaper carried a banner head-line "British Debaters Predict November Win for Johnson." Even now we remain disbelieving at our own foresight. After the meeting we were presented with Kiwanis Certificates of Appreciation—prophets honoured in another's country. Our student friends were impressed by our evident enjoyment of the whole affair, a brief glimpse at Babbit land. "Why," one exclaimed, "you ought to go to the Lions next. . . . They'll ro-ar-ar-ar-ar-ar-a-r-a-r-a-r-a-r-a-r at you." Should our enthusiasm turn out to be skin deep, however, Squire Western invited us to tea to revive us. Tea for him turned out to mean iced dry martinis at 4.30 in the after-noon. "I just couldn't survive without my cocktails," he drawled, "I am the most scungy boozehound." And in his company we spent a very enter-taining two days.

After Bates we went to debate at the Massachusetts Institute of Cor-rection. Since our friends from Yale had assured us that this was merely another name for Harvard we were somewhat surprised to discover that it was, in fact, Norfolk Prison, a pioneer centre of penal reform. Its inmates were voluntary transferees from the State jails, whose only qualifications had to be the attainment of a sufficient degree of criminal-ity. This exclusive character marked it out as an Ivy League Prison.

At the airport we were met by a hireling of the local television net-work, whose idea of the perfect interview was to talk to himself. After we had mutely assented to the proposition that we greatly looked forward to visting the Institution and had high hopes of being able to leave it, mutely dissented from the proposition that there was nothing in common between the natives of Norfolk and the natives of Oxford, and mutely consigned our tormentor to the seventh circle of Dante's Inferno, we were driven off in a Z (or as they would pronounce it "Zee") car towards our destination.

It was, we confess (or at least Michael confesses), with a certain amount of trepidation that we prepared ourselves for the debate. Al-though no one educated at Eton sees anything odd in living behind bars, our knowledge of etiquette on the "inside" was scanty. Should we, for example, pretend that our audience were free as air? "Oh, they know they're inside all right." How about some jests on their status? "Well, my boys are kinda sensitive. . . ." Tentative inquiries elicited the information that both our opponents were in for crimes of violence; one indeed had shot his sweetheart. Generously Michael made Jonathan a present of the "rape" joke for the evening, feeling modestly that an audience of hardened professionals would regard such amateur criminal pretensions as laughable, rather as members of the MCC would scorn a man who boasted of a half-century hit for his village team. Actually the applause with which the sally was eventually greeted showed that the prisoners were far from incredulous about the story. Evidently the image of Oxford in certain quarters of America is not all that it should be. Jonathan was clearly a little hurt since he believes that all his personal relationships are conducted on a purely voluntary basis.

We passed by the sentries, the searchlights, the looming walls with their fringes of barbed wire, and entered one by one through a massive metal door. A snack was provided by the prison chef, whom we complimented on his cuisine with unnatural vigour, the more so since as he handed us the fruit salad, he informed us that the general opinion was that though we might win the debate we would certainly lose the fight afterwards. To the sound of sonorous music from a giant organ we were led on to a wooden stage, concealed from the audience by a thick green curtain. Our sponsor and chairman, a programme informed us, was in charge of the prison arts, entertainment and religion. The organ music appeared to place our debate in the third category of his promotions.

After a few minutes in which we fidgeted and sweated, what seemed to be the entire contents of Congress Library were wheeled in on a trolley, and three prisoners arranged them on the table opposite. The music stopped and the curtain went up. We exchanged mutual glances with the audience. They were segregated into inmates and civilians, one group on either side of the gangway. To our horror we saw among them an old friend, John McDonnell, who had in fact been the Union's* last representative on the U.S.A. tour. Had he, we wondered, been incarcerated for losing the debate—or, worse still, for winning? At this moment our opponents waltzed on to tremendous cheers from the audience, half of whom were inspired by pride, the other half by fear. Their suave appearance, neat black cardigans, and general look of *bien aise* and cleanliness contrasted with our worn, unshaven greyness. It would have been easy for an outsider to pick out which pair of debaters were the violent criminals.

* Member of the debating team, Oxford Union Society.

The resolution that we were to debate that evening was that "The Power of the American Judiciary is Too Great." Thankfully the decision was to be made on the basis of the opinions of the judges and not of the audience, who, we felt, might have been swayed by a certain bias on that particular issue. There is a special technique for prison debates; and it is most important to remember that the stalest joke among free men has an almost unbearable freshness for the prisoner, for whom the clock has stood still since the date of his internment. Jonathan, who is temperamentally suited to prison debates since he has always believed that jokes like wines grow better as they grow older, and who has even been known to repeat a joke told earlier in the evening on the strength of its previous success, commenced in knockabout style. "This is the first time that I have ever had a captive audience; and it is also rare to be speaking opposite men who have the courage of their convictions." After all had recovered their breath some half hour later, the debate proceeded along its usual lines. Our opponents were extremely well read in the subject—they had after all more time at their disposal than most teams—and though we carried the day it was a close decision. One judge, infected by the criminal atmosphere, awarded us eighty points, the Norfolk team seventy-nine, and then the verdict to the latter!!

After the debate we attended a reception, whose enjoyment was only marred when John McDonnell (who turned out to be on a purely voluntary visit from nearby Harvard) asked some of the prisoners whether they had heard him two years previously, which, for men serving a life sentence, was not a wholly tactful question. Our feelings on the evening were best summed up by the Abbé Sièyes who, when asked what he had done during the French Revolution, replied "I survived."

Michael ambled across the sunlit slope of the campus at Bates College, Maine, and into the Senior Faculty Room. All along the tour Americans had expressed themselves anxious that we should share the pleasures of the classroom, and Michael, smitten by the blonde charms of his girl guide, had unanimously decided to offer himself up as a guinea pig. "Let's see if we've got anything to fit you," she said, as if she were offering him a choice of sports jackets rather than of classes to attend. "There's Latin, English literature—I don't suppose you want to be bothered with that. . . . You might try Professor M. though. He's just started on the Philosophy of History course."

"Glad to have you with us, Mike," said the Professor. All the teachers seemed to be Professor. Merit, not title, differentiates them in the eyes of their students. The class took some time to assemble, streaming in from all sides of the campus in their tee shirts and jeans, pony tails and crew cuts, acknowledging the presence of their teacher with an easy "Hiya Frank." We all sat round somewhat rickety tables. "Well, Dave," said the Professor, "I guess we'd better hear that paper of yours on 'Truth and Fact in History.' " There was a lot of coy chatter from Dave as if he had been asked to play a minuet at a Victorian Christmas party, and throughout his hurried reading he interspersed mock modest comments like "Gee, this ain't much good." Another student, Sam, was appointed inquisitor-in-chief and would break in with frequent contradiction. After twenty minutes of what at times developed into a Crosby-Hope routine rather than a Socratic dialogue the question was thrown open to the floor. There was a lot of joshing and joke-making. Most of the class, about twenty in all, were smoking. One girl knitted, her furrowed concentration ambiguously directed throughout. After a while Professor M. in his capacity as referee called "Break," and for the remaining few minutes read to us from various contemporary accounts of the Louisiana purchase to show how each participant had his own version of what had happened. Then after a short speech in summation he dispersed the class.

We cannot claim that this cosy experience is really typical for, in general, Americans carry to education the passion for size that distinguishes so much of what they do. The first thing we noticed about American education was that there was a lot of it. Boston is reputed to have as many colleges as Paris has brothels. There is, of course, great variety among the institutions. One typical establishment of the higher education is the Liberal Arts colleges, such as Bates in Maine, or Hiram, Wooster, and Denison in Ohio. As far as we could judge the connection with either liberalism or artiness was small, but an atmosphere of scholarship was more easily created on these small self-contained campuses which often housed as few as eight hundred students. Akin to these in size were the sectarian schools: Catholic colleges like La Salle or St. Josephs in Philadelphia, presided over by quick talking Jesuits with a good line in Irish ancestry and American jokes; or Protestant institutions like Eastern Nazarene, Boston, and Florida Presbyterian, with their somewhat tight-lipped approach to debates and life alike. At the other end of the scale were the huge States universities, like Ohio State, towns of some thirty thousand students, anonymous, sprawling, diverse. In between in size ranked the aristocratic colleges of the Ivy League, the rich uncles, and the Teachers' Training colleges, the poor cousins, of the system.

What all these institutions shared, and where they differed from at least the older English universities, was the concept of the Campus. Whether it was the red stone and white bricked buildings of the Liberal

Arts colleges or the bulky grey concrete edifices of the State universities their architecture was concentrated in one area. Sometimes, too, as in the Liberal Arts Colleges that we visited in Ohio, there would be nothing but scattered hamlets in the vicinity, and the nearest big town would be many miles away. In this they differ from almost every English university. Universities in America are self-contained, even self-centred. This naturally affects the attitudes of the students and often divorces them from life outside the campus. It may be a contributory factor to the general lack of political and social commitment. On the other hand, especially in the smaller universities, it certainly creates a sense of community and should, in theory at any rate, promote undistracted intellectual achievement.

The second factor that these colleges share, and that ours lack, is wealth. The libraries, always the centre-piece of any aspirant institution of learning, overwhelmed us everywhere with their munificence. The smallest Liberal Arts colleges would have libraries containing not only many thousands of books, but periodicals, magazines and newspapers from all over the world. And some of the libraries, like the Rare Books Library at Yale, or the Law Library at Harvard (which has, for example, a whole section devoted to the Law of Mediaeval Bulgaria) are among the greatest libraries of the world. At the other end of the spectrum of university activity we found much to admire in the way of sports facilities: the football stadia of the Midwestern State universities that would dwarf Highbury or White Hart Lane;* indoor gymnasia for the basketball team; rows of tennis courts for all weathers; rooms for massage and heat treatment. To give but one example: at Denison, Ohio, a college of less than fifteen hundred students, we found not only an athletics outdoor track, set deep in a small valley so that the hills around acted as natural windbreaks, but also an indoor track (how many are there in all Britain?), and an Olympic sized swimming pool (again, how many has Britain got?). No one could really believe us when we explained that Oxford University had neither a swimming pool nor gymnasium to call its own. "But it's the most famous university in the world," they would say. The Midwestern universities are so rich that they even employ teams of research workers to gather material for their debates squad, and computers to analyse the possible courses of argument Individual tape recorders for language students, closed circuit television for the larger classes, soundproof rooms for the experiments in the Speech Departments, model theatres for the drama students, printing presses for the embryo journalists, these are commonplace. At Purdue, Indiana, is the largest theatre in the world with an auditorium that

* Oxford University.

can seat six thousand. Ohio State university has not only its own television service, but also its own airport. For apart from state and federal subsidies and the accumulation of fees, the legacies and endowments given by alumni to their old colleges are often huge. The American cherishes the memory of his college days with the affection that in England is bestowed more frequently on the school. "I'm a Ball State Teachers' Training College man," one would hear someone say with pride, much as he might say in England, "I'm an Old Rugbeian."

The average American student thus lives in a seclusion that is often aesthetic; sleeps in dormitories with individual rooms, which will certainly have central heating and electric razor points, and in the more modern ones like those at Murry State, Kentucky, will run to showers and lavatories; eats in large cafeterias where the food, if not suited to the gourmet, at least satisfies the gourmand; has snack bars and soda fountains to satiate his extra-curricular appetites, and usually possesses every facility for study, sport and hobby that could be desired. (The one caveat might be about the degree of privacy obtainable.) Yet in the university land of milk and honey, the milk is turning sour and the honey is losing its sweetness.

It is clear that American education is undergoing a crisis similar in intensity, if different in kind, to that experienced in our own country. And yet the American university system possesses most of the features that appear to the radical educationalist in England most desirable: comprehensive schools; widespread rather than élite education beyond them; the equality of status of colleges of technology in the title of the degrees that they confer with the older established universities; syllabuses that break down the barriers between the two cultures; and syllabuses of a practical slant that draw on materials which in England would not be considered ripe for academic study at all. It was somewhat startling to discover that what we might have considered *Utopia* was considered by so many Americans to be *Purgatory*.

The root of the trouble is that it has proved impossible to maintain élite standards of education for a mass student population. The greatest difference that our conversations unearthed between the methods of teaching on either side of the Atlantic was the degree of professorial control over the studies of his pupils. During one week in our tour in early November our audiences suddenly fell off drastically as on campus after campus we hit the doldrums of the half-term exam days. One afternoon at Bates we were deserted by all our hosts as it was a "No Cut Class" day. The question that was most frequently posed to Michael, who had missed a term at Oxford to come on the tour, was not "How are you going to find time to make up the work?" but "How are you going to find time to make up your grades?" One's progress is apparently gauged by the number of classes one attends, not by the amount of knowledge that one imbibes. The concurrent passion for classification by examiners is of course anathema to anyone who belives that education is more than a matter of marks scored. In England we try to avoid this at the university level until the final degree. But in America, the teachers confessed, the large bulk of their classes have not the intellectual maturity or personal responsibility to be allowed to pursue their own course of studies with the same freedom that is enjoyed by their English counterparts. Examinations are used as much to weed out the weaker students as to evaluate the standards of the better ones. "The dormitories are absolutely crammed here at the moment," said the speech professor at Ball State Teachers' Training College, "but come the summer semester maybe as many as fifty percent will have dropped out. The wastage is enormous."

Another result of the invasion of the universities by swarms of semi-educated American boys and girls is the dilution of the syllabuses. This has two aspects. One is the introduction of courses, whose stimulus to mental activity is less than exiguous. The Schools of Journalism, of Business, of Speech, these are all admirable institutions in which America has pioneered an impressive route. But at a lower level a high sounding glossary conceals a multitude of idiocies. Domestic Economics (egg boiling *et al.*); Industrial Arts (carpentry); Driver Education (the syllabus of a British school of motoring). At one college in Florida we saw young gymnasts hurling themselves around on trapezes and trampolines and were told that they were graduates of the school of Circusology, presumably doing their homework. At Michigan State in the Kellog Centre, where we stayed, the waiters and room service stewards were all students engaged in becoming hoteliers. No one would dispute the value of training in all these matters; but whether a degree in them can be considered equal to a degree in some of the more established subjects is questionable. The fact is, though, that the Americans take these outward marks so seriously that in some places one cannot merely graduate, but even take a doctorate in these courses. *More* means not just *worse*, but positively *awful*.

The second aspect is the shunning of specialisation. Undergraduate courses in American universities are broadly based. Now if the purpose of this was to produce a race of Renaissance men, versed in all manner of subjects and cultures, it would be a worthy ideal. (It is easy to poke fun at some of the blinkered and ageing syllabuses that are taught in *our* older universities.) But that is not the purpose. Theses courses are not meant to accommodate the capable and the intelligent, but the backward and unintellectual. A little learning is a dangerous thing, and the average American student has a lot of little learning. There is more-over often no attempt to encourage a careful choice. A rapid course in World Culture will be followed by two years spent in the study of, say, Trigonometry, Moral Philosophy, and French Literature. Indeed, the American college student is more often than not pursuing in his undergraduate days a course of study that is no more advanced or de-manding than that followed by the English schoolboy preparing for the Advanced Certificate of Education.

Another result of the massive university expansion is the growth of the Factories of Learning. These are predominantly a West Coast phe-nomenon, but as, for example, we found at Ohio State not exclusively so. The sense of anonymity that this produced among the students was apparent. There are, it must be remembered, no colleges of the Oxford—with their professors or a greater change to live a truly communal Cambridge type to give the student a greater opportunity for contact life. "There are three great examples of mass production in the U.S.A. today," said one student to Michael. "At the stockyards in Chicago you can put in a pig at one end of a machine and get a sausage at the other. In the Ford works at Detroit you can put in a piece of metal ore at one end and get an auto at the other. And at a big State university you can put in an ignorant college kid at one end and get an ignorant graduate at the other." These students are often selected by computer, taught by disembodied figures from television screens, working with books which have been systematically filleted for examination purposes ("You could have a shorter *Othello* at one of these places that would cut out Iago," said a boy at Madison, Wisconsin) and lecture notes from lectures that they never went to but whose gist has been processed and sold in the college shops. This is a not very brave new world run riot.

A problem common to all spheres of higher education (though less prevalent in rich private institutions) is a shortage of teachers. "There's a kind of Gresham's law at work; bad teachers driving out good," said the speech profesor at Edinboro State Teacher's Training College, Erie, Penn. "And you get worse and worse people coming into teaching now-adays. They'd rather take any course than this." But of course the need must be supplied however poorly. "You can see the future," said one professor to Jonathan, "Half the population will end up teaching the other half."

The source of all the evil is the prevalent myth that every child born in the U.S.A. should have a college education, if it is possible. Constitu-ents believe it, so the State legislators must. Employers believe it, so therefore must potential employees. A college degree is no longer an added qualification for a profession: it is an indispensable one. But of course not everyone is taken in by the mere production of a B.A. Those people who in England inveigh against the "inferior status" of Colleges of Advanced Technology and Redbricks could do well to look at the American experience. The fact of conferring the title of university deceives no one. Until the value of the degree given by the new foundation can fairly be equated with that given by older ones, nothing has been achieved. The question now asked in America is not "Have you got a degree?" but "Where did you get your degree from?" or "What sort of a degree have you got?" Everyone knows that a B.A. in shark-fishing from the University of Miami is worth less than a B.A. in Liberal Arts from the University of Chicago and certainly less than the Harvard L.L.B.

The end product of all this is that well-known New World personality, the perpetual student. It is after all the most talented student who suffers the most from a system that panders to the least gifted. He is hampered in his academic enthusiasms by amorphous courses that he cannot bite on, by perpetual examinations that are only a source of irritation, by the company of colleagues who if literate are often barely so. ("I can't even get my kids to spell straight," said one disheartened faculty man at Kent State. "And I'm meant to be teaching them ethics.") At La Salle, Philadelphia, one of the debaters was on the Dean's list, which gave him the rare privilege of exemption from certain exams and permission to work more on his own. This kind of privilege would have been welcomed by many of the students whom we met, but the concept of differentiation is one that is born hard in the American mind. Thus, fettered by a system that has held him back since his school days (it was again alarming to hear teacher after teacher blame the comprehensive idea for the low standards of college freshmen), the gifted student is forced to take more and more higher degrees not only for the purpose of obtaining the first worthwhile and challenging course of education that he has ever received, but also to satisfy the demands of talent-scout employers. An English student who takes an advanced degree is usually training himself for an academic career; no such conclusion could be drawn in the case of his transatlantic counterpart. Five, seven, nine year college students—these were everywhere. But it is by no means certain that every country could afford either to educate or to dispense with the abilities of their best brains for so long.

Fortunately, most American graduate courses bear as little relation to undergraduate ones as a butterfly bears to a caterpillar. At this level at last the benefits of equipment and libraries, of imaginative breakthroughs into new fields of study, bear fruit. The testimony of Americans was less revealing than that of the numerous foreigners whom we met—

in both East and Midwest—from India, Germany, Nigeria, England, who claimed that the facilities and the teaching were superb and unrivalled. The experiences of those in the big law schools, Yale, Chicago, Columbia, were especially interesting to us as would-be lawyers. Not for them the esoteric ventures into obscure points of jurisprudence or the glossing of fragments of the Justinianic code. Theirs was a diet that was fed by practical study of tax statutes, company and union law. They would be more likely to be attending seminars on the problems raised in International Law by the invention of the Atom Bomb in the twentieth century than those raised by economic blockades in the nineteenth. There was much more mooting, far fewer lectures. This seemed to us to be relevant adaptation of study to contemporary needs.

But the glistening snow at the top of the mountain of education should not blind us to the moss-encrusted rock at the bottom. For while society demands that a teenager should be a college boy or girl, while it supplies him or her directly or indirectly with abundant facilities, it will not subsidise his education to the full. This aspect of the American belief in individual initiative is, alas, harmful to the smooth working of their university system. Of all the colleges that we visited, only at Queens in New York was the education wholly free; indeed the public universities of New York are unique in this respect. The result is that the less affluent students are forced to pay their own way through school. In Welfare State Britain no able student needs to work to earn his fees for tuition. Those who do take vacation employment do so to get "pocket-money." But in America many students are holding down jobs at the same time as they are working for their degrees. We found many examples of this. In Bates our rooms were swept out and cleaned by a student who said that his daily duties as janitor made him rise at six in the morning. Michael's date worked during the lunch hour as a college secretary. Naturally this puts a strain on these students; but if we queried the wisdom of this wastage of effort that should for the duration of one's college days be uniquely directed to the purpose in hand, we were told that this was "the American way."

It may be the American way, but the Americans might profit from trying some other. For one obvious result of the work-your-way-through-college principle is that American students by and large have none of that time for extracurricular or vacation reading that forms the basis of the English students' culture. Michael used to wax lyrical on the subject of the ideal Oxford man, conversant with the literature of his own and other countries, fluent in several languages, a lover of music and the fine arts, who would no more have needed a course in "European Civilisation in Four Lessons" than he would a ticket to Mars. Naturally this figment of his imagination bore about as much relation to the real person as did the American student, to whom he was addressing his remarks, to a Red Indian, but the airy persiflage cloaked a valid point. We believe much more in training than in merely filling the mind.

"I'm after grades, not knowledge," said one wordly-wise sophomore at Monmouth, Illinois. "The semi-educated teaching the wholly uneducatable. That's the future," said one world-weary professor at Akron, Ohio. "We aren't pursuing an ideal any more. It's running away with us." The progressive American teacher and student seems to be seeking just the opposite from his English counterpart; more streaming; more rigorous syllabuses; less sacrifice of the talented on the altar of uniform mediocrity. Whether he will succeed is another matter. But if he fails, it will be because of the power of the myth, not the lack of money. "You might as well give them a B.A. at birth," said our host at Pittsburgh cynically. With respect to its foremost philosopher, it is impossible any longer to remain Dewey-eyed about the state of American education.

Of course, American students, strictly controlled though their course of study may be, do not spend all their time in classroom or library. Indeed, the interest that the campus takes in the sporting activities of the college teams once more evokes the ideology of the English public school.

High among the rituals of American college life is the Big Football Game. In England the Dark Blue/Light Blue clashes on the Thames or at Twickenham evoke for a brief spasm of time the interests of sports enthusiasts and snobs alike.* Beyond that the world of university sport is a closed book, except to the expert. But imagine that the football game between Bangor and Aberystwyth were to be written up in the *Spectator*. Imagine that every Saturday afternoon David Coleman's nasal accents reported to the armchair fans not from Wembley, Aintree or Lords, but from Nottingham or Hull or Brighton University. Imagine that at the end of the gentlemanly encounter at Association Football between Oxford and Cambridge, instead of the teams coming off to a few "Jolly good show, Cambridge," or "Harry toughers, Percy old man," in the sight of millions of televiewers the Oxford captain was seen to be given a cheque for twenty thousand pounds and to sign professional forms for Tottenham Hotspur. Imagine all these things, transpose them, and you will see that college football in America is not so much a game, more a mass industry. Radicals may continue to gripe about the Keble** man, who reads (if the notion is not self-contradictory) the honours school of rowing. But in America the young illiterati of the university football world can pass from the amateur to the professional pitch without ever going by way of the classroom or the lecture hall.

* Oxford, Dark Blue, Cambridge, Light Blue, rowing and football sporting fixtures.
** Keble College, Oxford.

38

The U.S.: Mais Oui! Mais Non!

Let us face it. I should not write about the United States. I have now been teaching for five months at Stanford University in California; I have made a few quick trips—more to talk than to listen—and met a few people, politicians, and intellectuals; I have read books and newspapers. That is all, and that is not much with which to paint the picture of a country that is a continent unto itself.

But, I said to myself, if I am careful, if I confess the limits of my knowledge, why should I not pass on my observations to readers for whom the United States are all of a piece—readers often doubly misled by our French newspapers which, inevitably, quote only *The New York Times?* We are misled also by our politicians and our professors of law and political science who, in their discussions of the French regime, forever refer to the American as if he were nothing more than the relationship between President and Congress.

From Nursery School to University

Why is the psychiatrist king in the United States? I, for one, have found the answer: because human nature cannot endure the brutal change from too much freedom to too much conformity. I am joking, to be sure, but I believe there is a bit of truth in my "explanation."

The child is king. Nothing may impede the development of his personality. On the physical level to begin with—and here one must admire and envy—children are provided with playgrounds and swimming pools, campgrounds, the whole paraphernalia of sports. Olympic gold medals are but the incidental outcome of all this. It is significant that my five-year-old son, tall for his age and rather well-developed, seems singularly timid and awkward among his little American playmates.

Alfred Grosser, "The U.S.: Mais Oui! Mais Non!" in *Stanford Today* (Autumn, 1965), pp. 9–13. Reprinted by kind permission of the editors of *Stanford Today*, Palo Alto, California.

Author (1925–   ): Educated Lycee de Saint Germain-en-Laye, Faculty of Letters, Aix, and Paris; Director of Studies and Research at the National Foundation of Political Science in Paris and Professor at the Institute of Political Studies, University of Paris; during 1965 he held the Kratter Professorship in Modern European History at Stanford.

But no other impediments either, alas! To discipline is to create com-
plexes. Guidance is an assault on the personality. In Paris, at the *école
maternelle* (the only level of the French school system where any attention is paid to artistic education), that same son began to daub some
interesting watercolors. Here, at "nursery school," he produces quite
a few horrors. Nobody shows him anything, not even how to hold a
brush, for fear of hindering the free expression of his personality. How
many parents we see around us who are terrorized by their children
from their tenderest ages on! What cruelty we French parents practice
in inflicting upon our children the use of knife and fork or politeness
to their elders!

Only, when I have to fill out a recommendation so that a student
of mine may obtain a scholarship, I am faced with questions of the
sort: "Is he socially well-integrated?" Total freedom is supposed to lead
quite naturally to submission to very strict social rules. How can one
be surprised at the psychological difficulties that arise from a transition
which is in reality not natural at all?

One typical example, it seems to me, is furnished by sexual education.
I too am an advocate of plain information from an early age on. But
here one goes rather far. The highly respectable and conformist *Palo
Alto Times* the other day reviewed with admiration the lecture of a
professor who explained how he discussed with his students all con-
ceivable sexual perversions, and this "in the most natural manner." The
logical consequence of this passion for sexual education, this mania for
presenting what touches on sex as both important and without problems,
should really result in the destruction of the married couple and in
"free love." But there are probably few countries where all social
life is so geared to marriage and the family. The high divorce rate,
appearances to the contrary, corresponds. Often, actually, it is a
question of the divorce of young couples who had never envisaged, in
the course of their pleasant years as "teenagers," what formidable
material and psychological constraints would weigh upon them after
marriage.

All that, however, should be qualified. Extreme liberalism in pedagogy
is on the wane. And if a certain laissez-faire is the rule in elementary
school—contrasting rather happily with the intellectuality and severity
of the French system—the boy or girl who goes to high school hardly
has time to frolic if, as is more and more the case, he then wants to
enter a good university.

We are democratic in France. It would be strange to behold the
lycée graduate who did not automatically have the right to enter a university. And democratically, at the Faculty of Letters in Paris, for instance, he will be one of thirty thousand students looking for a place

to sit in a library with room for two hundred. In the United States, as in the Soviet Union and in Great Britain, how well a student has done in high school determines the kind of institution of higher learning to which he can gain admission—colleges being of very different levels and quality—and how well he does in his college studies will determine the quality of the university where he will work for the doctorate.

Ready as I am to point out the advantages of this system and, consequently, to approve of certain aspects of our government's reforms, I am obliged to point out two considerable drawbacks. If it is true that the proportion of young Americans who go to college is greater than that of young Frenchmen, if it is true that workers' children are better treated here than in France, there remains nevertheless the fact that, more and more, the cultural family background constitutes a trump card, since the "good" high school leads to the "good" college and the "good" college to the "good" graduate school, at Princeton or at Harvard. And soon only the good grammar school will lead to the good high school, and the good nursery school to the good grammar school. Certainly one has to do well in a good school, but, in order to go far, one must do exceptionally well in a school regarded as mediocre—and a child will do well far less on the strength of his own merit than that of the cultural background of his family.

The second drawback is that my students here are forever working under pressure. There are many examinations and grades. You have to succeed, which means not only to pass, but also to pass with the best grades. The pressure is both intellectual (to go to the best university) and financial (the best students get the best fellowships). While our dreadful system of competition is practically unknown in the United States, it is fair to say that American students live in a kind of climate of perpetual competition, even in areas where French universities know only the examination. The result is that students ingurgitate an incredible number of books and do not have the time to acquire culture, since what culture demands is a "waste of time" as far as preparing for examinations is concerned.

To the degree, however, to which culture is not merely an access to the heritage of the past, but an understanding of the world in which we live, American schools and universities have little to envy the French for. Sociology, anthropology, political science occupy an important place here. History is conceived in quite a different manner. I teach in the Department of History at Stanford. One of my courses is entitled "France from 1919 to 1965." As an examination question, students had the choice between the following subjects: "Assets and liabilities of the Popular Front," "The role of the French Communist party," "1940," "Compare the institutional life of the Fifth Republic with that of the Fourth."

No French faculty of letters would consider any of this as history. The result is that we owe to American universities the best books on the *Action française,* on management in France, on the history of contemporary French trade unionism, on the French Catholic movements, and alignments of the nineteen-fifties.

From this it should not be concluded that American students are very active in politics. There is nevertheless a growing interest in the world outside, whether it concerns racial integration, the war in Vietnam, or the misery of one third of the world's population. Even on the tranquil campus of Stanford (a private university more patrician than the neighboring state university at Berkeley) demonstrations about, and above all against, the war and its methods are multiplying. And among my best students the number of those who are preparing to go and rough it for two or three years in order to help Africans or South Americans is relatively large.

Society American Style

Students are never greatly representative of a society and no more so in the United States than elsewhere. This is particularly true of one essential: they do not have enough money or leisure to be full-fledged members of the famous "affluent society" of which the sociologists all speak, nor to let themselves get carried away by the torrent of advertisement which tends to convince Americans that happiness can be bought.

In France it is fashionable to be discontented and dissatisfied; friendliness and kindness do not grow on trees; we know well that "life is no joke." Here, discourtesy is both a social crime and a commercial mistake. And, above all, as Aldous Huxley had well foreseen in his *Brave New World* now almost forty years ago, the drive toward happiness is practically a duty. How many advertisements there are that invite you to feel exhilarated ("have a thrill") or be diverted ("have fun") by buying such and such a make of car or one washing machine rather than another!

I do not really know what my reaction is to the perpetual praise of the smile. On the one hand, this justification of things because they are fun, but on the other, this determination not to present a sullen face to life, including the service of humanity; on the one hand, a society where external success plays far too great a part, where it is no fun being poor, old, and sick; on the other, a society where people help one another with a smile, where, without fuss, they give large sums to innumerable good works for backward children or relapsed alcoholics. In France, we rely for all this on the state, protesting all the while against taxes and assessments. Surely that is no better.

This is all the more remarkable because—since recently, but before the French government—the American government has had the courage to admit frankly how little poverty has been conquered in an apparently prosperous society. The effects of the "war against poverty" launched by President Johnson will probably not make themselves felt right away. Perhaps there will even have to be recourse to less empirical methods. But the self-criticism has been made, not plaintively and with resignation, but by proposing at the same time some definite action.

It is true that the United States has resources that we lack: the wealth of a young country which has known neither the blood-lettings nor the ravages of wars, the time to experiment and to perfect, then to convince rather than to compel. There is a housing problem; there is a problem of school construction. But the situation is less catastrophic than in France and the analysis of given conditions less discouraging. This is even truer of the national problem number one, the integration of the Negroes. To those Frenchmen who are angered we must point out that much has been accomplished.

Two Parties Which Do Not Exist

Whether it be in local problems or a great national question such as racial integration, American politics should not be conceived as a permanent confrontation of two great parties. The American two-party system—how marvelous it would be in our country! There is only one drawback: the two American parties do not exist, except during the presidential campaigns. Regional and local parties abound, with a total dispersion of power, among the Democrats as well as among the Republicians. By comparison our own Radical Socialists and Independents seem like champions of a centralized discipline. The Speaker of the House in California is a conservative Democrat by local standards. He would be considered a liberal Democrat in most other states.

Momentarily troubled by the nomination of Barry Goldwater as Republican candidate, political analysts breathed easier at the sight of his total defeat. They were the ones who had been right, and not the Senator from Arizona. The mass of the electorate is located well in the center, and there are no reserves of abstainers that the extremes can mobilize. (Let us note in passing how the attitude of the English and German socialists is thereby justified: those who wish to attain to power must seek to reach the electorate where it is to be found in a developed and quiet society—that is to say, in the center.) One may surely speak—more because of the social stratification of the voters than because of their ideas—of a left of center and a right of center, but the idea, so widespread in French political circles, that the American two-party system permits a great and clear choice is totally false. Even the local dailies, firmly in the hands of one or the other tendency, do not follow a clear-cut "line."

Most striking here is the intensity of life on the regional and local level. I have just returned from some sessions of the Assembly and the Senate of the State of California, in Sacramento. In France, federalism is hard to imagine. There all, or almost all, the innumerable matters under discussion here would fall under the jurisdiction of the national Parliament and, more often, of the Administration. The local newspapers are constantly full of voter appeals for elections to posts which in France would be considered public functions and, therefore, come under government appointment. The American educational system? The American rules of the road? In a way, they do not exist. Laws vary from state to state, and great are the powers of the various men charged with enforcing them locally.

There we doubtless touch on one of the weaknesses, and at the same time the greatest strength, of American democracy. In France—though here too—people are shocked by the virtual impotence of President Johnson and federal power in general before a racial crime committed in Alabama. By the same token, every citizen has the possibility of influencing his local and regional authorities. Certainly few enough people vote (though here too one must be careful: many Americans cannot vote because they have not had the time to settle and register; a third of the population of California has been living at its present domicile for less than a year), but how many organizations everyone belongs to! And nothing will keep one from starting another for some specific purpose. Probably in no other country has the citizen such ample opportunity to compel competent authority to take matters of particular interest into consideration—provided he is willing to take the trouble, that is, to visit his neighbors, to organize meetings, to circulate petitions, and to call on his representatives (a threat to their electoral support). There is less grumbling than in France and more action, because action has a chance of succeeding and because one is used from childhood on to group life, to action as a group. A boy scout troop needs money? A door-to-door campaign is launched in which all members participate.

But from childhood on also one is accustomed here to regard the rules of the game as good, not to question a certain number of principles, or, more precisely, to consider them as so many axioms. Thus free enterprise; thus the virtues of the political and social system of the United States. Incitement against submission and training for conformity are inextricably mingled.

39

University and Community:
A Southern Exposure

It is startling how much one's reactions to events are conditioned by whether or not one has any first-hand knowledge of the places or people that the events are about. Eight months ago, the news that Dr. Martin Luther King had been murdered would have engendered feelings in me principally of shock—of horrified *surprise* more than anything else—but after a winter spent in Nashville, Tennessee, the element of shock at this tragedy is rather horribly diminished.

Before living in a Southern state of America, I had some idea of what Dr. King lived and worked for; now I feel I have far more of an idea about what that most noble and gentle man was up against. Trying to think calmly about it, I found myself repeating with savage bitterness: "So somebody *has* gone out and shot him a nigger." This was a phrase I heard used (in its future tense) three times seriously, and by different people during the four and a half months I spent in the South.

I went because my husband was invited to teach for the fall semester at one of the universities of Nashville.* We arrived with very ignorant—and open—minds; indeed, my husband chose this particular university from several other possibilities because we'd neither of us ever been to the South, and he felt that we ought to find out about it.

Perhaps, we said hopefully to each other on our way there, perhaps the Southerners, both colored and white, have found some way to deal peaceably and fairly with one another, perhaps the situation will turn out to be perfectly viable, undramatically okay and therefore not talked about very much except when there is some isolated instance of brutality or violence . . . Naive as these views may be, there is some advantage in going to a new and unknown place entirely without prejudice: you

Elizabeth Jane Howard, "Real Tragedy of the South" in *The Sunday Telegraph* (April 7, 1968). Reprinted by kind permission of the editors of the *Sunday Telegraph* (London).

Author (1923–   ): Educated London Mask Theatre, played repertory theatre; author, editor and reviewer; contributor to *Encounter*, and *The New Yorker*.
* Vanderbilt University.

are not only most properly trusting your own eyes and ears; you are starting with them and, with care, they can continue to be all you have got.

Nashville is the state capital of Tennessee: it has half a dozen universities, forty-seven Christian sects, and is the headquarters of guerrilla training for the Black Power group. It has about two hundred millionaires.

A great deal of the place is suburb: small, detached houses standing amid grass and trees; gardens and fences or hedges round them are rare, but the effect of space and privacy for each house is strikingly different from and better than any suburb I have seen in England. The distances for shopping, education or work mean that nearly everybody drives: that is, all white people and a fair number of Negroes. I once tried to shop walking, and felt immediately like the vulnerable character in a Hitchcock film.

There are two local newspapers, three television channels and I don't know how many radio stations. None of these informs the Tennesseans at all about what is going on outside the immediate vicinity, except for short but regular paragraphs about Vietnam and a very occasional statement about such items as Britain devaluing. But they will know that Dr. King is dead, not simply because Memphis is only a three-hour drive from Nashville, but because, one way or another, very few people in this university town will be actually indifferent to the event.

In a society that wants above all things not to have to consider its component parts, that makes openly, or covertly, a different (naturally much-inferior) species of the Negro, that suffers, I think, a feeling of mass inferiority in relation to Northern Americans ("those dam' Yankees; the war isn't over; the South will rise again; a Southerner's worth two Yankees," etc.—all heard by my ears and never a joke), the assassination by a white man of a Negro who systematically and patiently gave the lie to all their coarse, abusive, contemptuous, patronizing and downright disgusting views about his race will touch off many more emotions than grief. I can imagine a repeat celebration party being given by the person who celebrated Kennedy's assassination (his civil rights bill was not popular with some whites in the South).

But below—admittedly occasional—peaks of this kind of very frightening madness lies the bedrock of hysteria and prejudice, of bone-headed stupidity and sexual obsession (there is an extraordinary amount of sexual anxiety on the part of the whites about Negroes—very much on the "I make love, you perform, he rapes" basis). White women, whether they know it or not, have been conditioned to fear and dislike the Negro male. Illustration: wife of a university professor criticizing Olivier's film performance as Othello on the ground that he was too much like a

Negro: "His walk! And the way he carried his head! Who *could* love *that?*" No Desdemona, she.

In trying to understand these general attitudes of white Southerners to Negroes one comes back to the have, have-not aspect of the matter. White people, very much on the whole, that is to say 95 percent of the time, are richer, better educated, have access to better social services, get the right side of what often amounts to a double standard of justice, have more and better opportunities for jobs and so of course can do far more for their children and so on.

In situations where the haves live side by side for generation after generation with the have-nots, the haves certainly become emotionally brutalized. I have heard remarks made about and in front of Negroes that make Marie Antoinette's irresponsible suggestion about cake seem merely a piece of harmless, if fanciful, liberality. Possibly, in an unconscious effort not to feel guilty about one's fellow creatures having the rough edge of pretty well everything, there is a natural tendency to depersonalize them, to turn them into something else; Negroes are different from white people, you see. How? It was simple for Marie Antoinette and Co.: poor people were rabble, not much above animals—everybody knew that. But the white Southerner today cannot be so barefaced and simple. He is supposed to be living in a democracy; there was no constricting nonsense like that in eighteenth-century France. He has to be devious, merely imply the inferiority difference. Negroes' brains are much smaller than white men's; they are very simple people, best treated like children; they love me, because I know how to treat them! they're just longing for one person (me) to be loyal to; they aren't really capable of anything but simple, manual jobs . . . there is no end to the silly, nasty, dishonest propaganda that goes on and on.

Nauseating offshoots of this are the middle-aged ladies whose mythopeia prompts them to astonishing faded, jaded little accounts of their Youth and Gracious Living—with loyal, devoted mammies in the Great House—Times have Changed, but they Remember. After one or two of these sagas, I realized that none, anyway of these particular ladies, could possibly have had the childhood they were claiming, but that they put up with each other's lies for the sake of indulging in their own.

But apart from the depersonalizing and the mammy talk there is, of course, fear. White people are always afraid of what might happen to *them* if Negroes revolted against the present regime.

The emotional brutalizing the whites have suffered from or indulged in entails the inability to conceive of a living, working equality of rights and opportunities with a hitherto underprivileged society. They have sunk to, or have not evolved from, a simple jungle law: themselves *or* others—it cannot be both. (Of course we have all heard about this before, but actually to encounter it, to find it going on in 1968 is very different from hearing and reading about it.)

Surely a well-endowed university with the reputation for being one of the best in the South must entertain and propagate greater liberality? After a very few weeks there these hopes were certainly damaged. The students that I met were horrifyingly liable to remarks like this one: "I expect you've noticed that most of the trouble with Negroes is in the North: *we* know how to keep them in their place." This was an example of the young upon the old, old subject and it would seem that Daddy had known and was going to go on knowing best.

Were there any students who did not state or condone the attitude illustrated? I met one: a graduate student from Memphis, a young man of twenty-four who I can honestly say was the *only* person we met born and living in the south whose attitude and feeling about Negroes was natural, humane and honest. I am not saying that everyone at that university talked the standard racist rubbish on this subject; I'm saying that the ones I talked to about that did it to me.

And what about the faculty? I met one of them who said (but not to me and not in my hearing) that he could not find it in his heart to give an A to either a Negro or a Jew (it is safer to be liberal about one's illiberality—it gives people too much to get hold of, as it were). Another member of the faculty, when faced with a Fireside Chat (having your class to your house to discuss whatever anybody wants to talk about) found that his class included a Negro. He could not have a nigger in his house. ("Scratch a Southerner and you find a Southerner," my husband morosely remarked.)

Right: to do them justice, the whole class refused to go. But the damage had been done. The Negro knew why nobody was going to the Fireside Chat. If someone teaching in a respectable center for higher education behaves like that—and gets away with it—what is somebody colored, aged eighteen and clearly very bright or he would never have got there (a Negro getting into that sort of university is the equivalent of somebody with a cockney accent getting a commission in the Royal Navy—you have to be bloody extra good to make it), what *is* this young Negro to think—of the institution, the people who teach in it, and the society that supports this situation?

Well, then; what about all these Christian sects? At a large party one evening, I was accosted by a young couple who said they wanted to come and see me sometime about a problem. (I can't explain this suggestion; it was simply made.) They said that they were practicing

Christians; I don't think they told me what kind: their problem was that Negroes were not allowed in their church; they had protested several times about this, because they felt that Christ had not envisaged or intended such segregation: none of His teaching fitted this view and thus they felt that they had to *leave* their church and did I agree with them?

The points about this are that nobody else said anything of the kind to me, with the inference also that there really was nobody for them to say it *to:* they were falling back upon a total stranger.

I think it is necessary to say here that I am talking about a very reactionary—and *uneducated*—society. To teach Darwin in Tennessee was illegal until a very few years ago. I lectured once, largely about contemporary fiction in the English language, and the chief, indeed, almost wholesale reaction was "what a lot you *know*"—a reaction that would make any sane acquaintance of mine snort. This response came from people who taught, not people who were there to learn.

In the four and a half months we met a fair cross-section of white people in Nashville. We made only two lots of friends (excepting Northern importations—damn Yankees whom we'd known before) and with them, at least, we could argue, and did not have carefully to think before we spoke.

Even so, with one very intelligent man I remember a prolonged argument in which he was defending the progress of emancipation, and we were pressing him on what these freedoms amounted to. We could get no more from him than the following: ten years ago the Negro could ride only in the back seats of public buses; now, he could ride in any seat; he might not feel comfortable about it, but it could be done.

I have tried to confine myself to the positive statements and responses that we encountered during this short time. There is not room here for the lies, the lip-service to liberalism, the awful smarmy stuff that is an insult to any intelligence at all. I can't be bothered with it, in the same way that there is not room here to describe the sharp contrast in social circumstances between Negroes and whites that was immediately, and then continuously, apparent in Nashville.

Nobody living there could possibly give credence to the "it's all getting better all the time—all right really" stuff. Starting at the emotional top of the local pyramid there are the mad ones: the "shoot me a nigger, let's celebrate" ones. But then, and truly more frightening, are all those people who have genuinely been indoctrinated, and do not want to discover or change anything. They know, you see, that the Negro is a different (and inferior) creature.

But before we get too smug about this, let's remember that it is the attitude that very many men hold about many women: the rationalizations are equated with inferiority, and as anybody in the least interested in eugenics knows, you can breed and condition people to almost anything.

So: the untimely, disastrous tragic death of Dr. King has what effect in Tennessee? The young Black Power group are going to say that they *told* everybody so: what good could an old-fashioned, liberal Uncle Tom expect to do? They may, nonetheless, try to use Dr. King as a martyr: but other people will do that anyway: anybody who dies during the process of working without violence for a goal such as his exposes himself to this accolade or imprecation.

Not the least homage that should be paid to Dr. King is that he knew for many years that he was continuously vulnerable to the possibility of murder. A madman, many white Southern people will say, and of course they will be right; only a madman would have done something so violently silly. They haven't thought that this act stems from many years and thousands of people whose attitude on this subject, to say the least, has not really ever been sane. It is this chronic bulk of hysterical prejudice and fear that has made such an assassination possible.

Nevertheless, the act *is* a violently silly one. Leaving aside what many people may have thought about Dr. King in particular and what they have thought or now think about the racial problems in the United States in general, the fact remains that the repercussions of what could be considered as the homicidal and antisocial act of some individual maniac are likely to be world-wide for a long time to come.

But it seems to me necessary to make the possibly simple point that these maniacs—effective maniacs, at least—are very unlikely to stem from some social vacuum: if it takes all sorts to make a world, it takes certain sorts to make certain bits of it. Looking back on our time in Nashville, the most depressing conclusions are that this murder does not startle us, and that we can think of only three persons there whose reactions to it we would call honest, unhappy, and sane.

Bibliographical Notes

Introduction

The essays in Parts I and II of this book illustrate some of the many interpretations that can be placed, by foreign observers, on American education. The selection of references that follow in the bibliography also illustrate the rich storehouse of twentieth-century foreign commentary on the schools and the educational system of the United States. In addition, they illustrate many of the diverse comparative methods that can be employed in studying education. For a concise review of a cross section of these foreign commentaries and criticisms of American education, we recommend Willis Rudy's "Evaluations of American Education by Foreigners," Chapter 8 in *Schools in an Age of Mass Culture: An Exploration of Selected Themes in the History of Twentieth Century American Education* (1965).

The question of what foreigners think of American schools and universities is almost a perennial and certainly by now a standardized topic, and the United States Office of Education, and its predecessors, has at times taken upon itself the task of evaluating the efficacy of some of these foreign commentaries. But the Office of Education's last major effort in this regard was made a decade ago, in 1960, with the publication of notes from a conference it sponsored that was devoted to "Foreign Understanding and Interpretation of United States Education."[1] It is worthwhile noting, at this juncture, some of the more important recommendations made at this conference because many are still pertinent today, and some, unfortunately, have not been acted upon as yet.

Those recommendations (among the many of the conference) which appear to be the most noteworthy would include the following:[2]

1. A more active and intensive role should be taken by the United States Government and its cultural officers abroad in informing foreign educational officials and personnel about United States educational patterns and institutions.

2. Orientation programs should be available for United States cultural officers on education in the United States.

3. Appointments should be made to foreign posts of American educational attaches who would be experts on United States Education and who would report on and would interpret educational patterns and developments in other countries.

[1] Charles Hauch (ed.), *Foreign Understanding and Interpretation of United States Education*, Studies in Comparative Education OE 14059, Washington, D.C., U.S. Office of Education, 1960, p. 2.
[2] *Ibid.*, pp. 20, 21.

4. Qualified and highly trained educators and educational officials should be brought from foreign countries to the United States to observe and to study its educational system and institutions.

The above recommendations have been subjected to varying degrees of endorsement (or negligence, depending on one's point of view). Unfortunately, there is still a further major recommendation of considerable importance which has been acted upon only on an *ad hoc* and piecemeal basis and, then, primarily by but few interested scholars. Reference is made to the suggestion that the *"Compilation, perhaps by the Office of Education, of annotated bibliographies of publications or articles on United States education by educators and specialists from each country should be effected and, in this way, a summary of the output and the views of each country's education specialists on United States education would be available."*[3]

Unfortunately, a decade later, we cannot report any significant progress in this specific regard, and many of the United States Office of Education's comparative education research programs and studies of foreign education have been allowed to almost fall into abeyance. The few remaining specialists of comparative education in the Office of Education do maintain (when their other duties allow) a regional watching brief on foreign commentaries of United States education, especially, on those from the Soviet Union and other Communist countries. It is expected, however, that the recent establishment within the USOE of an *Institute of International Studies* will at last drastically reverse the downward trends of the past few years!

During the past decade, research into foreign commentaries within United States government circles has shown a preoccupation with an evaluation of the views of the foreign trainees who have been brought to America, and with analyzing the effectiveness of their educational programs in American universities. Outside of the varying, but specialized, United States governmental concern with foreign commentary, a small but increasing number of American social scientists and comparative educators have taken a particular interest in wider aspects of the topic.

Only infrequently can we consider directly the dialectics of an exchange of views and the cross-national evaluation of the efficacy of "foreign criticisms." However, during the 1960's it has been possible to identify what can be described as case studies in "the international ex-

---

[3] *Ibid.,* p. 21 (Italics and editing are the editor's, S.E.F.) This was the specific recommendation of William W. Brickman, Professor of Educational History and Comparative Education, Graduate School of Education, University of Pennsylvania.

change of educational opinion." Three of these are briefly mentioned below to illustrate the nature of these kinds of critical exchanges. They clearly show the differing viewpoints and, perhaps, some of the underlying educational and political prejudices of the relevant observers.

The first case study involves a southern community, the vitriolic and penetrating attacks on certain segments of that city's academic institutions, and the disparaging remarks made regarding the community at large. The author of this particular polemic was taken to task by the editor of one of the local newspapers, who carefully documented and refuted many of the charges made by the English visitor. This case study well illustrates the startling effectiveness of the journalistic approach in analyzing a community and its intellectual institutions. The exchange of views obviously did not come even close to suggesting solutions to the social, racial, and intellectual problems of this so-called "typical" southern city. But the journalistic exchanges and the spirited rebuttal by a local newspaper editor does illustrate the problems of a short-term, although sophisticated, visitor from Britain who was unable or unwilling to identify the presence of any social and ameliorative forces at work in the community, and who instead, produced a spectacularly sensational account of her educational visit.

The second case study in "cross foreign commentary," comes from two trans-Atlantic academics, both of whom, although at home with their own educational systems, are perhaps less so with the educational system in vogue on the other side of the Atlantic. Reference is made to the interesting and constructive exchange of views effected between a distinguished British historian and a well-known international university educator from the United States.

The last case study concerns the spirited and apparently interminable debate between educators from the U.S.S.R. and the U.S.A. as to *what system is best*. This debate, irrespective of its intellectual merits and the levels of scholarship involved, started long before the 1957 Sputnik and continues today unabated. It involves comparative education specialists of world standing and intellectual integrity on both sides of the well-developed "pedagogical curtain." This aspect of "cross" commentary is well documented, and the literature continues to flow from specialist researchers as well as journalistic pens.

Higher Education and a Southern City: Journalistic Brickbats Exchanged

On a spring Sunday morning, April 21, 1968, Nashville readers of the city's (pop. 450,000) only Sunday morning newspaper were able to read an intellectual condemnation of their fair city offered by an

English visitor, Elizabeth Jane Howard.[4] Miss Howard had spent nearly five months in Nashville while her husband, novelist Kingsley Amis, taught during the fall semester of 1967–1968 at Vanderbilt University. The shock impact of this article [see Reading No. 39] was considerable, and the vehemence of its tone drew much comment from many sections of the Nashville community, both "town and gown."

The city boasts of approximately a dozen colleges and universities, enrolling a student body of some twenty thousand with a faculty of more than two thousand. By a variety of indices, Nashville can be considered a "liberal" southern city with a number of civil-rights and community-educational entities that are attempting, with varying degrees of success, ameliorative work among "disenfranchised" groups in the community. Although the city has never been a national leader in civil-rights programs, during the past two decades, it has been in the forefront among southern cities of comparable size in advancing community racial relations. "No leader but no laggard" is the remark made by one African educator to the writer after an extended stay for the purpose of studying teacher education programs at the nearby internationally known George Peabody College for Teachers. This college, with Vanderbilt University, Scarritt College, and Fisk University, is involved in a number of cooperative ventures that constitute a condominium in the operation of academic programs in the Joint University Center. These four institutions, all private and ranging from an absence of religious involvement at Peabody to direct Methodist affiliation at Scarritt, constitute one major group of cooperative educational institutions in Nashville. However, it is primarily toward Vanderbilt University that Miss Howard's criticisms were directed. The occasion of her article was the assassination of the Reverend Dr. Martin Luther King in Memphis, Tennessee, a city 200 miles due west of Nashville that borders on the states of Arkansas and Mississippi. There is no record of the author's having visited Memphis extensively; however, Nashville was eminently suitable and close by for Miss Howard's purpose, which was to develop a sociological interpretation as to why the assassination could take place in the South. Thus, Nashville became the target for Miss Howard's writing, and for her it was a sufficient substitute for Memphis where the real tragedy took place.[5]

[4] See John Seigenthaler, "English Author Damns Vanderbilt," *The Nashville Tennessean* April 21 1968, pp. 16 and 36. The original article by Elizabeth Jane Howard was published in *The Sunday Telegraph* (London), April 7, 1968, and later in *Atlas: A Window on the World*, June 1968, pp. 22–25. See also Reading No. 39 in Part II of this book.
[5] It is apropos to note here that a memorial service was held for the Reverend Dr. Martin Luther King at Peabody College in Nashville shortly after his death; the commemorative service (called by the student body and the college administration) was attended by organizations of the various social, racial, religious, and academic persuasions of that institution. Similar services were held at the other collegiate institutions in Nashville, including Vanderbilt University.

The Editor of the Nashville Tennessean,[6] John Seigenthaler, took it on himself to offer an extensive rebuttal to Miss Howard's article, published in London on April 7. Mr. Seigenthaler has editorial responsibility for one of the more enlightened southern newspapers, at least, as far as its international and national news reporting and analysis is concerned.[7]

Miss Howard's complete article is included in Part II of this book because it illustrates a journalistic and sociological analysis of an American university and the community to which it directly relates. Her article, of course, aroused immediate response on the various Nashville campuses; among the more printable comments were those that simply said "Naive"—"she's been sold a bag of chitlins," or "another gullable Englishwoman." There were also several suggesting that she had "exposed a number of raw edges," or afforded "an overexaggerated account, but one in the right direction." Mr. Seigenthaler was disturbed because Miss Howard had apparently condemned the entire Vanderbilt University community for its so-called callous reaction to the murder of the Reverend Dr. King. For example, she had described (in her scathing indictment of Nashville) how Vanderbilt was a place where racism abounded, with a student body prejudiced towards Negroes, and a faculty grossly intolerant towards both Negroes and Jews. John Seigenthaler suggests that these 'views are going to jolt those Nashvillians who think of Vanderbilt as an institution that has turned sharply on a left-wing liberal course and is now 'interracial' before it is anything else."

Her evaluation of Vanderbilt is devastating where she graphically describes the anti-Negro prejudice of students, stating that they were "horrifying liable to remark . . . 'I expect you've noticed that most of the trouble with Negroes is in the North; *we* know how to keep them in their place.'" She also happily recounts that she had actually met a faculty member who admitted that he could never permit himself to give a course grade of *A* to either a Negro or a Jew!

Of her overall stay in Nashville and her acquaintance with Vanderbilt, she protested "surely a well-endowed university with a reputation for being one of the best in the South must entertain and propagate greater liberality. After a few weeks there, hopes were certainly damaged."

To this Mr. Seigenthaler replies: "Is this the Nashville or the Vanderbilt that anybody familiar with the campus or the city would possibly recognize? Is this the school, the students, the faculty, the community, that anybody with a passing acquaintance knows?" He says bluntly that

[6] See *The Nashville Tennessean,* "English Author Damns Vanderbilt," Nashville, April 21, 1968, pp. 16 and 36. The following notes and paraphrasing are taken directly from the sources mentioned without further documentation.
[7] It presents controversial news of differing political persuasions as Seigenthaler readily concedes, not attempting to compete with the *New York Times* (whose reporting services it uses) or newspapers such as the *Christian Science Monitor.*

"she is unfair—she exaggerates—she engages in sensational nonsense to write such a piece from such a distance at such a time and on the basis of a four-month stay in Nashville." The question Mr. Seigenthaler asks is why would she slander a school or a city and its people? Is the whole academic community damned because of the remarks of a few? Are there blatant racial antagonisms towards Negroes or Jews on the part of the faculty and student members of Nashville colleges and universities, but particularly those at Vanderbilt?

Mr. Seigenthaler produces illustrations of "liberal" behavior at Vanderbilt that evidently Miss Howard chose not to see, and he suggests that either she ignored evidence to the contrary or did not do her homework properly! As he says "Why would she ignore the fact that just a year—almost to the very day—before the tragic slaying in Memphis, Dr. King spoke at Vanderbilt Memorial Gymnasium to 5000 students? They gave a ringing accolade of applause and cheers to his oratorical condemnation of a society that, he said, had too long deprived Negroes of equal opportunities . . . his words brought a houseful of Vanderbilt students and faculty to their feet in thunderous ovation of endorsement." He asks "Are these the students that Miss Howard met? Is this the Vanderbilt Elizabeth Jane Howard visited? Is this the campus where she said folks indulged in "hysteria and prejudice, boneheaded stupidity and sexual obsession" about Negroes?" Mr. Seigenthaler goes on to note that Miss Howard also omitted to mention that just a few months prior to her arrival on Vanderbilt campus, Stokely Carmichael appeared on the campus—where "he was given an attentive ear, and by many, enthusiastic applause, a reaction which resulted in wholesale abuse being heaped on Vanderbilt, the likes of which was unprecedented before Miss Howard wrote her piece."[8]

It would appear that Miss Howard enjoyed, to some extent masochis-tically, the experience of living in the South; at least, it was possible for her and her husband to gather sufficient anecdotes, or what more appropriately would be called "mammy talk," for their literary purposes. Unfortunately, her journalistic touch combined with a novelist's flair

[8] It may also be apropos to mention that Eldridge Cleaver, a leader of the Black Panther Party, was invited to Vanderbilt to speak on November 21, 1968. The Vanderbilt University Student Association in conjunction with the Vanderbilt Afro-American Association, invited the black power advocate to the campus with Al Hubbard, Vanderbilt Student Association President noting that "There are two very important reasons for the invitation. . . . One is simply that he is a force in our society today, both as a leader of the Black Panther Party, and as a distinguished literary figure. The second is the highly relevant and important nature of the ideas that he presents." It should be noted, however, that he was unable to fulfill his speaking engagement at Vanderbilt because of various legal complications that occurred the day before concerning his parole status!

may have influenced many Englishmen to think that a prominent southern city such as Nashville abounds in racial hatred engendered by racially antagonistic university students led on by their professors who know little better. Miss Howard's controversial account concerning an American university and a southern city is not exactly unique in the long history of British commentaries on the American scene. Her predecessors were not uncritical nor passionate admirers of the total American picture, but their criticisms at times were tempered by more accurate reporting and reinforced by further research than that provided on the cocktail circuit or at faculty teas, which produced the "mammy talk" poured into a receptive vessel. But for Miss Howard and her British readers, Nashville exemplified a southern city that she characterized as "a very reactionary-and-uneducated society."

Transatlantic Comparisons: Anglo-American Exchanges

Some of the most significant and certainly some of the most sensitive analyses of American society, culture, and education have been made by European observers. The French are represented by such distinguished analysts as Alexis de Tocqueville, Gabriel Compayre, Jacques Maritain, André Maurois, Henri Peyre and, more recently, J. J. Servian-Schreiber. The German spokesmen include such scholars as Hugo Munsterberg, George Kerschensteiner, Franz Hilker, Friedrich Schneider, Erich Hylla, Friedrich Edding, and Walter Schultze.

But, perhaps, the British must be accorded a primary place of honor for sustained, though variegated, commentary in depth for a period of nearly two centuries. During the present century such commentators as Michael Sadler, James Bryce, H. G. Wells, Dennis W. Brogan, C. P. Snow, Geoffrey Crowther, Brian Holmes, Edmund King, and Arnold Toynbee have made for themselves a prominent place in the history of Anglo-American intellectual exchanges. Obviously, a few of the British commentaries, like those of other visitors, were uninformed, ephemeral and sometimes superficial. And it is just as obvious that, occasionally, distinguished scholars of worldwide renown if unversed in comparative techniques and ill-read in the field of pedagogy do not necessarily offer the most useful, penetrating, or succinct commentaries on another country's educational system.

Therefore, it is of some interest to study the exchange of views between Arnold Toynbee, the distinguished British historian, and James Davis, a leader in the field of international and higher education in the United States. The occasion for this exchange of views was a series of three articles written by Dr. Toynbee for the *London Observer* and published in the Toronto *Globe and Mail* in July 1963, and two rebuttal articles by Dr. James Davis in August 1963.[9] Dr. Davis, at the time of the publication of Toynbee's articles in Canada, was a visiting professor at the summer school of the Ontario College of Education, University of Toronto, where he was teaching a course in Comparative Education. Professor Davis, then Director of the International Center, University of Michigan, was induced to reply to Toynbee's articles and criticisms of American education. The extracts below are taken from the Toronto *Globe and Mail* of July and August 1963. Dr. Toynbee's three articles appear in full in this book and are to be found as Readings Nos. 17, 18, and 36.

Dr. Toynbee suggests that the "scholar" is not the typical present-day American student and believes that in America "the primary reason for going to a university is to acquire social experience and aplomb, intellectual work comes second to that."[10] Davis quickly responds by

[9] The following notes and paraphrasing are taken directly from the sources mentioned without futher documentation.

[10] Although this may have been true to some extent in 1963, it is still interesting to note some years later what Jean Partee, a "typical" American student believes to be the role of her university. Her letter to the *Nashville Banner* November 16, 1968, is in part reproduced below; obviously, such a clear-cut statement might go some way to support the generalization made by Dr. Toynbee five years earlier!

To the Editor of the *Banner*:

. . . Most of what we are learning comes under the heading of social acceptance—how to live in this world. This is what college is all about—learning to prepare ourselves to live and prosper in society. Our so-called education is really secondary . . . to our understanding of people and present-day society. At least, this is my opinion of what young people should be learning in college. All the mathematical formulas and English grammar in the world will not substitute for the basics of conducting our every-day existence.

Just this week I participated in a very meaningful and useful class discussion. The course is instruction in Television and Radio Announcing. However, this one morning my professor had read an article about pass-or-fail grading and television lectures in college and he wanted our views on the subjects. The discussion led to our opinions on "hippies" and the "establishment," marijuana, LSD, birth control and abortion laws. Was this discussion relevant to a broadcast speech course? No, but these subjects are very relevant to the college student in general. This discussion was worth more than any lecture on the proper French diction in radio music copy.

A Journalism professor teaching an editorial writing course was concerned that we frequently got off the subject in our class and discussed politics and current campus situations. But, I argued, we are not wasting time or getting off the subject. This is what Journalism is about, and this is what life is about.

Book knowledge is not sufficient. Our colleges and universities have many responsibilities toward their students and . . . themselves. Our sense of values, attitudes and goals are being formed in the college now. This, then, is what we are learning in college, or should be learning . . .

Jean Diane Partee
University of Tennessee,
Knoxville

pointing out that Toynbee seems to be comparing all the millions of students in American colleges and universities with the "fewer than twenty thousand scholars in Oxford and Cambridge Universities, to the detriment, of course, of the Americans." He suggests that Dr. Toynbee might make a fairer comparison by matching "two of twenty of the most distinguished American universities, of which ten would be public and ten private institutions."

Probably, the most illuminating, or spectacular, of Toynbee's pronouncements on American education concern the over-localization of educational control and the composition and "tyrannical" influence of school boards. Toynbee dismisses the school boards as "mostly small-scale bodies . . . the men elected to serve on them are, on the average, perhaps not fit to exercise the formidable power they wield." He also notes that "as virtually sovereign authorities . . . they behave as such—sometimes arbitrarily and tyrannically." Not undaunted in his generalizations he continues by suggesting that "the sovereign U.S. local school board is in fact a fortress of McCarthyism" or further that "a school teacher need have little fear of trouble for airing conservative or even Fascist views instead of liberal ones." To this, Davis replies that Toynbee erroneously views overall the local school boards as "repressive institutions which stifle the civic freedom of teachers" and according to Davis "this is just not so" and among some 90,000 school boards, "there are good boards and weak boards, but whatever they are, they are elected by the citizens of a locality to administer the policies under which schools are run. It means that the boards reflect citizen opinion about the school, and though McCarthyism, John Birchism and conservatism are perhaps present—they are not especially to be found in school boards."

The overall evaluation by Davis of Toynbee's excursion into comparative education is uncomplimentary. Furthermore, Davis makes a careful attempt to refute many of Toynbee's unfounded generalizations, without minimizing some of the more pressing problems that he notes concerning American education. For those who know Professor Davis and his contributions to international education, it will be quickly apparent that he is both a severe critic of his own country's educational system as well as a staunch "defender of the faith." As an influential member of the "international higher educational establishment" in the United States, for more than two decades he has been concerned directly with the introduction of American education to countless visiting scholars and foreign students. Accordingly, he does not take lightly what he regards as ephemeral and ill-founded commentaries by critical visitors, however distinguished they may be in the realms of scholarship outside of education. His rebuttal articles include interesting statements, suggesting that the historian, Toynbee, should confine his writing to the fields that he knows best. Davis states that "there are many problems in schools and colleges and universities of the United States. Toynbee has identified the wrong ones, analyzed them very poorly and offered the wrong solutions . . . There are many points in which Dr. Toynbee is uninformed. Numerous internal inconsistencies will appear to the careful reader of his articles. Some of his views are valid. But on the whole, he far misses the mark. It is not the kind of writing which adds to an understanding of U.S. education. Rather it is a biased and uninformed treatment which can lead only to misunderstanding."

The articles by Dr. Toynbee were published originally for a predominantly British audience. They probably, would not have been the subject of Anglo-American controversy if J. Bascom St. John of the *Toronto Globe and Mail* in his column *The World of Learning* had not decided that the pronouncements on education of a distinguished historian like Dr. Toynbee were important in helping "Canadians see differences between their own school systems and those of their neighbor." The presence of Professor Davis nearby, at the Ontario College of Education where he was teaching comparative education to a summer school class of Canadians, was opportune and led to the rebuttal articles. Perhaps, Professor Davis will obligate himself by writing succinctly on British history and the role of the contemporary observer on British universities! This, in turn, might permit Dr. Toynbee to reply in kind!

Cross Educational Commentary: The U.S.A. and U.S.S.R.

The cross-national evaluations of *school and society* between the United States and the Soviet Union did not start suddenly (as is popularly believed) in 1957 with the advent of Sputnik. There has been a long traditional analysis going back to the 1930's by educators of both these nations of the other nation's educational system. A brief list of commentators would reveal John Dewey, George Counts, Thomas Woody, William Johnson, William W. Brickman, Gerald Read, George Z. F. Bereday, Arthur S. Trace, Jr., Seymour Rosen, William Medlin, and Nicholas DeWitt, among others, lined up on the United States side, and Albert P. Pinkevitch, N. K. Goncharov, V. Strezikozin, I. K. Ekgolm, Zoya Malkova, S. Vishnersky, B. Vulfson, Yury Zhukov, Aleksei Markushevich, and Mikhail Prokofiev as members of the Soviet team.

The topics of interest range from a detailed analysis of educational goals (as one would expect) to the role of cybernetics in education. The comparisons, at times, become abrasive when the Americans are asked bluntly "Why Johnny Can't Read and Ivan can?" and when the Russians (understandably irritated) are chided and asked "Why are Soviet Jews not provided for both educationally as well as spiritually?" Both questions, of course, can be neatly balanced on top of a pile of *non sequiturs*, the answers to which would satisfy few, and rarely the poser of the questions!

Perhaps, the Americans at present are ahead in the writing of lengthy books, research treaties, and doctoral dissertations on Soviet education. And although there are few Soviet books or full-length treatises on American education, the same cannot be said for comprehensive Soviet journal articles, and in this field of research or polemic writing the Soviets are certainly competitive with their American counterparts. The bibliography includes some of the prominent writings by Soviet educators on what are termed "educational problems in the United States."

Guidelines: Analyzing Foreign Commentary on American Education

In recent years, published critiques of American education emanate from a variety of sources, including foreign journalists, visiting professors, exchange teachers, and foreign students. Occasionally, comments from visiting businessmen, embassy officials or cultural attaches, and even tourists, are printed, as all too rarely, are the findings of distinguished scholars from abroad, several of whom have devoted a lifetime to studying the United States, its educational "systems," and its intellectual and academic communities.

Although journalistic and popular reports are plentiful, there is, a dearth of comprehensive works written by foreigners who specifically comment on and evaluate American education.[11] Although periodical articles in educational journals do appear quite regularly, they range from scholarly essays and professionally comparative analyses[12] to super-

---

[11] See W. H. G. Armytage, *The American Influence on English Education*, London, Routledge and Kegan Paul, 1967. Peripheral but important comment on American education and its economic and political effects is afforded by such writers as J. J. Servian-Schreiber, *The American Challenge*, New York, Atheneum, 1968, and James McMillan and Bernard Harris, *The American Takeover of Britain*, New York, Hart Publishing Company, Inc., 1968.

[12] A perusal of the following pubications will be particularly fruitful in pursuing this topic further: *Comparative Education Review* (New York); *Comparative Education* (Oxford); *International Review of Education* (Hamburg); *Phi Delta Kappan* (Bloomington); *School and Society* (New York); *Soviet Education* (translations, New York); *The Times Educational Supplement* (London); *The Educational Forum* (West Lafayette, Indiana); *Universities Quarterly* (London); *Universities Review* (London); *The Asian Student* (San Francisco).

ficially "popular" but entertaining accounts.[13] These journals publish articles illustrative of the wide range of "approaches" that may be utilized in analyzing and in presenting educational comparisons. The professional journals of interest to the comparative specialist, such as the *Comparative Education Review*, will generally publish material that differs greatly in content, methodology, and intellectual approach from a general interest educational journal, such as the *Peabody Journal of Education* or the NEA Journal, *Todays Education*.

But before perusing the comments of visiting teachers and professors it is worthwhile to ascertain the following:

(a) The extent of professional training and "technical" competence of the foreign observer; an evaluation of his general education and skill as a "comparativist" as well as, perhaps, his standing in his own discipline or profession.

(b) The foreign educational community from which he has come and the American school constituency towards which he directs his commentary: that is, the degree of "contrast" and personal idiosyncracies of the social, political, and educational system that constitutes the observers own datum point.

(c) The extent of his stay in the United States, the range of intellectual and educational experiences; whether nationwide travel or localization, the level and intensity of visits to teaching and research institutes, primary and secondary schools, colleges and universities.

It is necessary to carefully evaluate the comments of foreign observers in the various contexts in which they may have been made. Constructive and fair criticism are both enlightening and revealing. Likewise, it is important to note and to understand inaccuracies in fact as distinguished from those of interpretation. The thoughtful student of education also should be prepared to provide intelligent answers to criticisms, actual or implied.

American educators, however, should be prepared to analyse those criticisms and should know how to discuss them frankly and intelligently. They should also remember that, in fact, most of the more critical statements by foreigners are the ones that are made vociferously by American educators themselves. However, too often, it is the critical statements by visitors, which irritate, that are remembered on balance, instead of

---

[13] Books of interest under this category would also include W. Kenneth Richmond, *Education in the U.S.A.: A Comparative Study*, New York, Philosophical Library, Inc., 1956; Jonathen Aitken and Michael Beloff, *A Short Walk on the Campus*, London, Secker and Warburg Ltd., 1966, and Jacques Lusseyran, *Douce trop douce Amérique: les étudiants et leurs professeurs aux États-unis;* Paris, Editions Gallimand, 1968.

those of a more positive or favorable nature. Accordingly, it is of greater utility to understand these criticisms, and the American teacher and student should be prepared not only to understand them but also to answer the critics, and be able perhaps, to pose the following questions:

1. Are these comments and criticisms merely superficial and unfounded?
2. Are they applicable to only segments of American education? If so, to what segments?
3. Are they constructive and worthy of further analysis and study?
4. What constitutes the "educational base" from which the critic is approaching American education?
5. What constructive criticisms or suggestions could be made, in reply, regarding the critic's own educational system?

Selected Bibliography*

The bibliography includes nearly a thousand alphabetically arranged references, beginning with the year 1900. For the most part the items are derived from English language sources, and there is a concentration on Anglo-American references. Accordingly, for a more comprehensive treatment of this topic, this bibliography should be used in conjunction with other language sources on "foreign commentaries." The bibliography focuses principally on foreign criticisms, commentaries, and comparisons, found in a variety of journal articles, books, and newspapers reporting on education in the United States. Although the majority of the authors listed are not American by birth, there are some American scholars and anthologists included, who have either edited collections of writings by foreigners or, who have conducted extensive cross-cultural research on foreign visitors and students in the United States. The country of birth, education, or domicile of the author, if foreign, is generally included in parentheses after the annotation. Some authors included in the bibliography have foreign origins and are so classified, although they now may be United States citizens. Their works are included because of the special insight they bring to the analysis of American education in foreign perspectives.

Abass, Abdul Majid. "As Visiting Statesmen See Our Schools," edited by William J. Ellena, *Nation's Schools*, Vol. 67, No. 6 (June, 1961), pp. 51–55. [Iraq] [IV]

Adam, Ronald F. "American Schools Television," *Journal of Education* (London), Vol. 89, No. 1061 (December, 1957), pp. 514–516. [Britain] [IV]

Adams, John. "Advancement of Education in the United States," Chapter IV in *Educational Advancement Abroad*. London: George G. Harrap & Co., Ltd., 1925, pp. 56–68. [Britain] [IV]

* This bibliography has been compiled with the assistance of Dorothy Reeves and Allan Peterson, Research Associates, Peabody International Center. Grateful acknowledgement is made of their assistance and collaboration. Some of the references from German educational sources are derived, with kind acknowledgments to Val Dean Rust's study, *German Interest in Foreign Education Since World War I*, No. 13, University of Michigan Comparative Education Dissertation Series, 1968.

Originally this bibliography included detailed annotations and unpublished doctoral dissertations to facilitate the specialist or functional interests of readers. These have been omitted because of publication and editorial restrictions imposed on the editor. In view of this fact and because some titles do not sufficiently inform as to content, each reference has been given a general classification to assist the reader: Elementary [I], Secondary [II], Tertiary [III], and Education:General [IV].

Adams, John. "Advancement of Education in the United States of America," *Journal of Education* (London), Vol. 56, No. 657 (April 1, 1924), pp. 237–239. [Britain] [IV]

Adamson, John William. *A Short History of Education.* Cambridge: Cambridge University Press, 1930. 371 pp. [Britain] [IV]

Aigner, Lucien. "The New Air Age: Developments in the American School," *Times Educational Supplement* (London) No. 1453 (March 6, 1943), p. 113. [I]

Aitken, Jonathan and Michael Beloff. *A Short Walk on the Campus.* London: Secker and Warburg, Ltd., 1966. 208 pp. [Britain] [III]

Allen, George C. "The American 'Project English'," *Trends in Education* (London), No. 3 (July, 1966), pp. 34–38. [Britain] [II]

Allen, George C. "As Others See Us: An Interview After the Fact," (Interview by Robert F. Hogan.) *English Journal,* Vol. 55, No. 5 (May, 1966), pp. 531–540. [Britain] [II]

Allen, Harry Cranbrook and C. P. Hill. *British Essays in American History.* London: E. Arnold, 1957. 348 pp. [IV]

The American Embassy. *The Exchange of Persons: An Evaluation of the Experiences and Training of Individual Grantees under Fulbright and Technical Cooperation Programs.* New Delhi, India: December, 1953. 93 pp. [IV]

The American Embassy. *Report on a Survey of the Department of State Exchange of Persons Program in Austria.* Vienna, Austria, March, 1955. 190 pp. [IV]

The American Embassy. *Study of Impressions and Disseminations by Information Specialists and Students from the Exchange of Persons Program.* Bonn, Germany, December, 1955. 48 pp. [IV]

Anderson, Charles C. "A Canadian Critic on Teacher Education in Western U.S.A.," *School and Society,* Vol. 88, No. 2173 (April 23, 1960), pp. 204–207. [Canada] [III]

Anderton, Arthur. "Report of Mr. Arthur Anderton," *Reports of the Mosely Educational Commission to the United States of America.* London: The Co-operative Printing Society Limited, 1904, pp. 1–6. [Britain] [IV]

Andrews, E. B. and A. L. Bowley. "The Public School System of Chicago," *Board of Education, Special Reports on Educational Subjects* in *Education in the United States of America, Part I.* Vol. X. London: H.M.S.O., 1902. [Britain] [I]

Angell, Melvin. *A Descriptive Analysis of the Academic Achievement of Selected Samples of Foreign Students from Non-English Speaking Countries at Fresno State College.* Fresno: Fresno State College, 1960. [III]

Antin, Mary. *The Promised Land.* Boston and New York: Houghton Mifflin Company, April, 1912. 373 pp. [Russia] [IV]

Appelmann, Anton H. "Amerikanisches Schulwesen," *Monatschift fuer Hoehere Schulen,* Vol. XIX (1919), p. 311ff. [Germany] [IV]

Apsler, Alfred. "Contrasts in European and American Secondary Education," *The School Review*, Vol. 54, No. 5 (May, 1946), pp. 295–298. [Austria] [II]

Archer, R. L. "Educational Psychology, American and British," *British Journal of Educational Psychology* (Birmingham, England), Volume II, Part 2 (June, 1941), pp. 128–134. [Britain] [IV]

Armfelt, Roger. "From Across the Atlantic," *Educational Forum*, Vol. XX, No. 3 (March, 1956), pp. 361–363. [Britain] [II]

Armstrong, Henry E. "Report of Professor Henry E. Armstrong," *Reports of the Mosely Educational Commission to the United States of America*. London: The Co-operative Printing Society Limited, 1904, pp. 7–25. [Britain] [IV]

Armytage, W. H. G. *The American Influence on English Education*. London: Routledge and Kegan Paul, 1967. 118 pp. [Britain] [IV]

Ascher, Mary K. "A Comparison of Education and National Ideals in Germany and the United States," *The School Review*, Vol. 45, No. 5 (May, 1937), pp. 368–380. [Germany] [IV]

Ashby, Eric. "Education As Investment in Man," *Overseas*, Vol. III, No. 7 (March, 1964), pp. 8–14. [Britain] [IV]

Ashley, Percy. "Some Notes on American Universities," *Board of Education, Special Reports on Educational Subjects* in *Education in the United States of America, Part II*. Vol. XI. London: H.M.S.O., 1902. [Britain] [IV]

Atlas. "The World Looks at the U.S.A.: The Closed School Doors," (July, 1966), pp. 37–38. [Translated from *Laiko Vima*, Gjinokastër, Albania [I]

Auberry, Pierre. "Myths and Realities," *Atlas*, Vol. VI, No. 4 (October, 1963), pp. 231–233. [Translated from *Le Monde*, Paris]. [France] [III]

Aydelotte, Frank. *The American Rhodes Scholarships: A Review of the First Forty Years*. Princeton: Princeton University Press, 1946. 208 pp. [III]

Ayrton, William Edward. "Report of Professor W. E. Ayrton," *Reports of the Mosely Educational Commission to the United States of America*. London: Co-operative Printing Society Limited, 1904, pp. 26–37. [Britain] [III]

Babbel, Rosemarie. "Impressions from Abroad," *NEA Journal*, Vol. 39, No. 1 (May, 1950), p. 30. [Germany] [IV]

Bachtier, Adam with Martin J. Bartels. "Indonesian Schools See Contradictions in American Education," *Nation's Schools*, Vol. 48, No. 1 (July, 1951), pp. 37–38. [Indonesia] [IV]

Bailey, C. W. "Some American Sketches," Part I, *Educational Outlook*, Vol. 6, No. 3 (March, 1932), pp. 153–157. [Britain] [III]

Bailey, C. W. "Some American Sketches," Part II, *Educational Outlook*, Vol. 6, No. 4 (May, 1932), pp. 193–198. [Britain] [III]

472

Bailyn, Lotte and Herbert C. Kelman. "The Effects of a Year's Experience in America on the Self-Image of Scandinavians," *Journal of Social Issues*, Vol. XVIII, No. 1 (1962), pp. 30–40. [III]

Bannister, S. J. "Co-education and the Position of Women in the Educational World in the United States," *Journal of Education* (London), Vol. 30, No. 470 (September, 1908), pp. 641–642. [Britain] [III]

Barclay, Thomas. "Report of Mr. Thomas Barclay," *Reports of the Mosely Educational Commission to the United States of America*. London: Co-operative Printing Society Limited, 1904, pp. 394–400. [Britain] [II]

Barnes, Donald. "Quality and the Masses—Continuing American Dilemma," *Times Educational Supplement* (London), No. 2617 (July 16, 1965), p. 115 [Britain] [IV]

Baron, George. "British View of Brimstone," *Teacher's College Record*, Vol. 65, No. 8 (May, 1964), pp. 667–670. [Britain] [III]

Baron, George. "Mid-West High Schools," *Journal of Education* (London), Vol. 87, No. 1031 (June, 1955), pp. 259–260; 262. [Britain] [II]

Bartels, Martin H. "Indonesian Schools See Contradictions in American Education," *Nation's Schools*, Vol. 48, No. 1 (July, 1951), pp. 37–38. [IV]

Basaran, Mehmet. "Hands Off Our Schools," *Atlas*, Vol. IV, No. 6 (December, 1962), pp. 464–465. [Turkey] [IV]

Bastide, Charles. *Les écoles et les Universités*. Paris: La Renaissance du Livre, 1921. [France] [II]

Baumgarten, Eduard. "Dewey—Die Idee der Demokratie, die Auseinandersetzung mit dem deutschen Idealismus," *Internationale Zeitschrift fuer Erziehung*, Vol. V (1963), pp. 81ff, 407ff. [Germany] [IV]

Baumgarten, Eduard. "John Dewey—Theorie der menschlichen Natur," *Internationale Zeitschrift fuer Erziehung*, Vol. VI (1937), p. 177ff. [Germany] [IV]

Beadle, Margaret. "What's Happening in Education," *PTA Magazine*, Vol. 56, No. 5 (January, 1962), p. 14. [Britain] [IV]

Beals, Ralph L. and Norman D. Humphrey. *No Frontier to ·Learning: The Mexican Student in the United States*. Minneapolis: University of Minneapolis Press, 1957. 148 pp. [III]

de Beauvoir, Simone, "L'Amerique au jour le jour." Paris: Gallimard, 1954. 376 pp. (Translated and reprinted: "American Day by Day," *Modern America Through Foreign Eyes*. Boston: Heath, 1959, pp. 44–47.) [France] [III]

Beck, Earl R. "The German Discovery of American Education," *History of Education Quarterly*, Vol. 5, No. 1 (March, 1965), pp. 3–13. [IV]

Beck, Friedrich. *Americana Paedagogica: Bericht über eine studienveise nach den Vereinigten Staaten von Nordamerika*. Leipzig: Klinkardt, 1912. [Germany] [III]

Beeby, C. Edward. "As Visiting Statesmen See Our Schools," *Nation's Schools*, Vol. 67, No. 106 (June, 1961), pp. 51–55. [New Zealand] [IV]

Beloff, Max. "American Universities: Some Impressions and Reflections," *Universities Quarterly* (London), Vol. III, No. 2 (February, 1948), pp. 571–580. [Britain] [III]

Beloff, Michael and Jonathan Aitken. *A Short Walk on the Campus*. London: Secker & Warburg, Ltd., 1966. 208 pp. [Britain] [III]

Bennett, Arnold. "Your United States," *Harper's Monthly Magazine*, Vol. 125, No. 749 (October, 1912), pp. 675–682. [Britain] [IV]

Bennett, Arnold. *Your United States: Impressions of a First Visit*. New York and London: Harper and Brothers, October, 1912. 191 pp. [Britain] [IV]

Bennett, Arnold. *Those United States*. London: Martin Secker, 1912. 246 pp. [Britain] [IV]

Bennett, Arnold. *Things That Have Interested Me*. New York: George H. Doran Company, 1910. 332 pp. [Britain] [IV]

Bennett, Jack Arthur Walter. "English as You Teach It in America," *College English*, Vol. 2, No. 7 (April, 1941), pp. 675–681. [New Zealand] [III]

Bennett, John W. "Cross-Cultural Education Research and the Study of National Acculturation," *Annals of the American Academy of Political and Social Science*, Vol. 297 (March, 1957), p. 198 [III]

Bennett, John W. and Robert K. McKnight. "Liberation or Alienation: The Japanese Women Student in America," *IIE News Bulletin*, Vol. 31, No. 7 (1956), pp. 38–47. [III]

Bennett, John W. and Robert K. McKnight. "Misunderstandings in Communication between Japanese Students and Americans," *Social Problems*, Vol. III (April, 1956), pp. 243–256. [III]

Bennett, John W., Herbert Passin, and Robert K. McKnight. *In Search of Identity. The Japanese Overseas Scholar in America and Japan*. Minneapolis: University of Minnesota Press, 1958. 368 pp. [III]

Bennett, John W., Herbert Passin, and Robert K. McKnight. "The Japanese Overseas Student," *IIE News Bulletin*, Vol. 31, No. 4 (1956), pp. 30–34. [III]

Benson, Adolph Burnett. *Farm, Forge and Philosophy*. Chicago: Swedish Pioneer Historical Society, 1961. 162 pp. [Sweden] [III]

Bentzen, Anna. "Individual Report," (Chapter XXVIII) *Report of the Commissioner of Education, 1901*, Vol. 2. Washington, D.C.: U.S. Government Printing Office, 1902, pp. 1273–1275. [Norway] [I]

Berger, Max. *The British Traveller in America, 1836–1860*. New York: Columbia University Press, 1943. 239 pp. London: P. S. King and Staples, Ltd. [IV]

Bereday, George Z. F. "American and Soviet Education at Mid-Century," *Wisconsin Journal of Education*, Vol. 92, No. 6 (January, 1960), pp. 19–23. [Poland] [IV]

474

Bereday, George Z. F. "Comparative Education and Ethnocentrism," *International Review of Education,* Vol. 7, No. 1 (1961), pp. 24–34. [Poland] [IV]

Bereday, George Z. F. with Bonnie B. Stretch. "Political Education in the U.S.A. and the U.S.S.R." *Comparative Education Review,* Vol. VII, No. 1 (June, 1963), pp. 9–16. [IV]

Bergson, M. E. "En l'honneur des universities Columbia et Harvard, " *Revue Internationale de l'Enseignement,* Vol. LXVI, No. 8 (August 15, 1913), pp. 91–109. [France] [III]

Bernard, Roger, Henry J. G. Collis, and Rudolf Bringmann. "The Plus and Minus of American Education," *IIE News Bulletin,* Vol. 29, No. 9 (June, 1954), pp. 53, 54. [France, Britain, Germany] [IV]

Besuden, Heinrich. *Helen Parkhursts Dalton–Plan in den Vereinigten Staaten.* Oldenburg: R. Sussmann, 1955. [Germany] [IV]

Bigelow, Karl W. "Some British Views on American Education," *Teacher's College Record,* Vol. 60, No. 7 (April, 1959), pp. 369–377. [IV]

Birmingham, George A. (pseud). *From Dublin to Chicago: Some Notes on a Tour in America.* New York: George H. Doran Company, 1914. 320 pp. [Britain] [III]

Black, A. W. "Report of Mr. A. W. Black," *Reports of the Mosely Educational Commission to the United States of America.* London: Co-operative Printing Society Limited, 1904, pp. 38–39. [Britain] [IV]

Blai, Boris. "Working in Wood, Stone, and Clay." *Progressive Education,* Vol. 8, No. 2 (February, 1931), pp. 120–126. [Russia] [I]

Blair, Isobel. "Observations of an Innocent Abroad," *The American Teacher,* Vol. XXXI, No. 5 (February, 1947), pp. 18–19. [Britain] [I]

Blair, Robert. "Report of Mr. Robert Blair," *Reports of the Mosely Educational Commission to the United States of America.* London: Co-operative Printing Society Limited, 1904, pp. 40–63. [Britain] [II]

Blair, Robert. *Some Features of American Education.* Dublin: Alexander Thom and Company, 1904. 184 pp. [Britain] [II]

Blauth, Heinrich. "A Newcomer Looks at American Students," *World Education,* Vol. 5, No. 3 (July, 1940), pp. 324–327. [Germany] [I]

Board of Education. *Special Reports on Educational Subjects* in *Education in the United States of America, Part I.* Vol. X. London: H.M.S.O., 1902. [IV]

Board of Education. *Special Reports on Educational Subjects* in *Education in the United States of America, Part II.* Vol. XI. London: H.M.S.O., 1902. [IV]

Boas, Frederick S. "Some British Impressions of American Universities," *School Life,* Vol. 9 (March, 1924), p. 164. [Britain] [III]

Bolivian Institute of Public Opinion Survey. *A Study of Former Bolivian Grantees in the United States.* La Paz, Bolivia, March, 1959. 94 pp. [IV]

Bollerup, Henning. "The American High School Through European Eyes," *Phi Delta Kappan*, Vol. 43, No. 9 (June, 1962), pp. 395–398. [Denmark] [II]

Bonser, Friedrick G. "Werktaetige Erziehung in den Vereinigten Staaten," *Paedagogisches Zentrablatt*, Vol. VIII (1928), p. 561ff. [Germany] [IV]

Bose, Sudhindra. *Fifteen Years in America*. Calcutta: Kar, Majumder and Co., 1920. 479 pp. [India] [IV]

Bowden-Smith, Alice Georgette. *An English Student's Wander-Year in America*. London: Edward Arnold Publishers, Ltd., 1910. 328 pp. [Britain] [III]

Bowers, David F. *Foreign Influences on American Life: Essays and Critical Bibliographies*. New York: Peter Smith, 1952. 254 pp. [IV]

Bowley, A. L. "Summary Account of the Report of the Educational Commission of the City of Chicago, 1898," *Board of Education, Special Reports on Educational Subjects* in *Education in the United States of America, Part I*. Vol. X. London: H.M.S.O., 1902. [Britain] [IV]

Bowley, A. L. "The Constitution of the City School Systems of the United States," *Board of Education, Special Reports on Educational Subjects* in *Education in the United States of America, Part I*. Vol. X. London: H.M.S.O., 1902. [Britain] [IV]

Bowley, A. L. "The Public School System of Boston," *Board of Education, Special Reports on Educational Subjects* in *Education in the United States of America, Part I*. Vol. X. London: H.M.S.O., 1902. [Britain] [IV]

Bowley, A. L. "The Public School System of the City of New York," *Board of Education, Special Reports on Educational Subjects* in *Education in the United States of America, Part I*. Vol. X. London: H.M.S.O., 1902. [Britain] [IV]

Bowley, A. L. "The Public School System of St. Louis, Missouri," *Board of Education, Special Reports on Educational Subjects* in *Education in the United States of America, Part I*. Vol. X. London: H.M.S.O., 1902. [Britain] [IV]

Brace, W. S. "An English Schoolmaster Looks at American Mathematics Teaching," *The Mathematics Teacher*, Vol. 49, No. 4 (April, 1956), pp. 241–249. [Britain] [II]

Braddon, Henry Yule. *American Impressions*. Sydney: Angus and Robertson Ltd., 1920. 120 pp. [Australia] [IV]

Bradford, John Rose. "Report of Mr. John Rose Bradford," *Reports of the Mosely Educational Commission to the United States of America*. London: Co-operative Printing Society Limited, 1904, pp. 64–78. [Britain] [III]

Bravo, R. S. "America Creates Favorable Impressions Upon Chilean Teacher," *School Life*, Vol. 13, No. 3 (November, 1927), p. 43. [Chile] [IV]

Breier, Helmut. "Probleme des Erziehungswesens in dens U.S.A.," *Die Hoehere Schule*, Vol. X (1958), p. 131ff. [Germany] [IV]

476

Brenner, Anton. "Bilder aus dem amerikanischen Schulleben," *Die Schulwarte,* Vol. II (1949), p. 296ff. [Germany] [IV]

Brereton, Cloudesley. "A Bird's Eye View of American Education," *Monthly Review.,* Vol. V (December, 1901), pp. 57–68. [Britain] [IV]

Brereton, Cloudesley. "A Bird's Eye View of Educational Reform," *Nineteenth Century,* Vol. LXXXI (June, 1917), pp. 1300–1312. [IV]

Briant, Keith. *Oxford Limited.* London: Michael Joseph, Ltd., 1937, 320 pp. and New York: Frarrar and Rinehart, 1938. 306 pp. [Britain] [III]

Brickman, William W. "An Historical Survey of Foreign Writings on American Educational History," *Paedagogica Historica,* Vol. II, 1962, pp. 51–21. [IV]

Bringmann, Rudolf. "The Plus and Minus of American Education," *IIE News Bulletin,* Vol. 29, No. 9 (June, 1954), pp. 54–56. [Germany] [IV]

Brinkmann, Carl. *Demokratie und Erziehung in Amerika.* Berlin: Fischer, 1927. [Germany] [IV]

Brittan, Leon. "The Oxbridge Style on Tour," *Overseas,* Vol. 1, No. 9 (May, 1962), pp. 9–12. [Britain] [III]

Britton, Philip J. "What America Taught Me About Music," *Music Educator's Journal,* Vol. 29 (April, 1963), pp. 79–82. [South Africa] [II]

Broderick, William. "Sick Schools," *The Age* (Melbourne, Australia) (November 24, 1965), pp. 13, 15. [Australia] [II]

Brogan, Denis William. "American Education," Chapter IV in *America in the Modern World.* New Brunswick, New Jersey: Rutgers University Press, 1960, pp. 73–81. [Britain] [IV]

Brogan, Denis William. "Unity and Liberty," Chapter V in *The American Character.* New York: Alfred A. Knopf, 1944, pp. 135–138. [Britain] [IV]

Brogan, Denis William. *U.S.A.: An Outline of the Country, Its People, and Institutions.* London: Oxford University Press, 1941. 143 pp. [Britain] [IV]

Brooke, Rupert. "Boston and Harvard" in *Letters from America* with a preface by Henry James, London, Sidgwick and Jackson, Ltd., 1916, pp. 35–46. [Britain] [III]

Brooks, Edward. "The Public School System of Philadelphia," *Board of Education, Special Reports on Education Subjects* in *Education in the United States of America, Part I.* Volume X. London: H.M.S.O., 1902. [Britain] [I]

Brooks, John Graham. *As Others See Us: A Study of Progress in the United States.* New York: The Macmillan Company, 1909. 365 pp. [IV]

Brown, Ralph A. and Marian R. Brown (editors). *Impressions of America.* New York: Harcourt, Brace and World, Inc., 1966, Vol. I, 257 pp; Vol. II, 274 pp. [IV]

Browne, George Stephenson. *Contemporary Education: A Comparative Study of National Systems.* New York: Harcourt Brace and World, Inc., 1956. Revised edition, 1965, pp. 55–56; 228–263. [Australia] [coauthored with J. F. Cramer] [IV]

Bruce, G. "Fairer Examinations—British and U.S. Ideas," *Times Educational Supplement* (London), No. 2584 (November 27, 1964), p. 987. [Britain] [I]

Bryce, James. "The Mission of State Universities," "What a University May do for a State," "Special and General Education in Universities," in *University and Historical Addresses.* New York: The Macmillan Company, 1913, pp. 151–170; 229–245; 301–315. [Britain] [III]

Bryce, James. "The Problem of National Education in England and Wales," *Introduction* in *The Parliamentary History of the Education Act of 1902.* London: The Liberal Publication Department, 1903, pp. 1–4. [Britain] [III]

Bryce, James. "America Revisited: The Changes of a Quarter-Century, Parts I and II," *Outlook*, Vol. LXXIX (March 25, 1905; April 1, 1905), pp. 733–740 and pp. 846–855. [Britain] [III]

Bryce, James. *University and Historical Addresses.* New York: The Macmillan Company, 1913. 433 pp. [Britain] [III]

Buisson, Ferdinand. "Valuable Suggestions," *Journal of Education,* Vol. 82, No. 19 (November 25, 1915), pp. 515–520. [France] [IV]

Bulletin of the International Bureau of Education. "Soviet Educationists in the United States," Vol. XXXIV (First quarter, 1960), p. 17. [IV]

Bureau of Social Science Research. *An Analysis of Attitude Change Among German Exchanges.* Washington, D.C.: The American University, August, 1951. 126 pp. [IV]

Burgess, Tyrrell. "Anglo-American Exchanges: Brickbats," *Overseas,* Vol. II, No. 2 (October, 1962), pp. 6–9. [Britain] [III]

Burnor, Duane, James M. Davis, and Russell G. Hanson. *IIE Survey of the African Student: His Achievements and His Problems.* New York: Institute of International Education, 1961. 71 pp. [IV]

Burstall, Sara A. *Impressions of American Education in 1908.* London: Longmans, Green and Co., 1909. 329 pp. [Britain] [IV]

Busbey, Katherine G. *Home Life in America.* London: Methuen & Co., Ltd., 1910. 410 pp. [IV]

Buyse, Omer. "American Schools as Seen by a Belgian Educator," *Elementary School Teacher,* Vol. IX (February, 1909), pp. 322–326. [Belgium] [I]

Buyse, Omer. *Méthodes américaines d'education, générale et technique.* Paris: Dunod and Pinat, 1908. [Belgium] [IV]

Cajoleas, Louis P. "The American-Educated Foreign Student Returns Home," *Teachers College Record,* Vol. 60, No. 4 (1959), pp. 191–197. [Lebanon] [III]

478

Cakmakcioglu, Adnan. "Visitors from other Lands View our Schools and the Convention," *Nation's Schools*, Vol. 53 (March, 1954), pp. 71–78. [Turkey] [IV]

Cambon, Victor. *États-Unis, France*. Paris: Pierre Roger et Cie, 1917. [France] [I]

Campos, Maria dos Reis. "Education in Brazil," *School and Society*, Vol. 31, No. 801 (May 3, 1930), pp. 585–589. [Brazil] [I]

Cannon, John G. *Comments on Education in the United States of America and Victoria, Australia*. Melbourne: Melbourne University Press, 1933. 58 pp. [Australia] [IV]

Caselmann, Christian. "Colleges and Universitaeten, Hoehere Schulen in U.S.A.," *Die Schulwarte*, Vol. II (1949), p. 604ff. [Germany]

Casparis, Hans. "A Swiss Educator Looks at American Education," *School and Society*, Vol. 65, No. 1690 (May 17, 1947), pp. 362–364. [Switzerland] [IV]

del Castillo, Benjamin E. *Dos Américas*. Valencia: F. Sempere y Compañiá, 1910. [Venezuela] [II]

Caullen, Maurice. *Les universités et la vie scientifique aux États-Unis*. Paris: Colin, 1917. [France] [III]

Central Research Services, Inc. *Evaluation Study of Japanese Returned Fulbright Grantees*. Tokyo, Japan, January, 1958. 194 pp. [IV]

Cespedes, Francisco. "I Like American Secondary Education," *Secondary Education*, Vol. 11, No. 3 (April, 1943), p. 13. [Panama] [II]

Cestre, Charles. "Chronique de l'enseignement:" (Section on) "Harvard University, 1907–1909," *Revue Internationale de l'Enseignement*, Vol. LXI, No. 5 (May 15, 1911), pp. 444–447. [France] [III]

Cestre, Charles. "Oeuvres pour les etudiants a l'Universite Harvard," *Revue Internationale de l'Enseignement*, Vol. XLII, No. 7 (July 15, 1901), pp. 26–33. [France] [III]

Cestre, Charles. "Universités americaines." Section, "Chronique de l'enseignement," *Revue Internationale de l'Enseignement*, Vol. LIX, No. 1 (January 15, 1913), pp. 77–79. [France] [III]

Champlin, Carrol D. "European Criticism of American Education," *School and Society*, Vol. 41, No. 1059 (April 13, 1935), pp. 509–511. [IV]

Chang Chih-tung. *China's Only Hope: An Appeal by Her Greatest Viceroy, Chang Chih-tung, With the Sanction of the Present Emperor, Kwang Su*. Trans. by Samuel I. Woodbridge. New York: Fleming H. Revell Co., 1900. 148 pp. [China] [IV]

Chapman, Colin. "A Briton Views American Schools," *American Education*, Vol. 3, No. 6 (June, 1967), pp. 23–26. [Britain] [II]

Chatterjee, M. N. "An Indian on Education," *The Survey*, Vol. LIX, No. 10 (February 15, 1928), pp. 638–640. [India] [III]

Chen, Theodore Hsi-En. "As Visiting Statesmen See Our Schools," *Nation's Schools*, Vol. 67, No. 6 (June, 1961), pp. 51–55. [China] [IV]

Chen, Theodore Hsi-En. "Is American Education Good for China?" *Educational Review* (China Christian Education Association), Vol. 16, No. 3 (July, 1929), pp. 260–263. [China] [IV]

Chetcuti, Rita. "Impressions from Abroad," *NEA Journal*, Vol. 39, No. 1 (May, 1950), p. 351. [Malta] [IV]

Chien, Hsun-li. *Some Phases of Popular Control of Education in the United States.* Shanghai: The Commercial Press, Ltd., 1927. [China] [IV]

China Institute in America. *A Survey of Chinese Students in American Universities and Colleges in the Past One Hundred Years.* New York: National Tsing Hua University Research Fellowship Fund and China Institute in America, 1954. 68 pp. [III]

Chon, Siryoon. "Depends Upon the Posture," *The Asian Student* (Spring, 1963), p. S–6. [Korea] [III]

Chu, Don-Chean. "The Tasks of American Colleges," *Educational Forum*, Vol. XXVIII (May, 1964), pp. 457–462. [China] [III]

Clark, Wilfrid. "We Must Exercise the Genes of Patience," *Saturday Review* (September, 1961), pp. 54–55. [Britain] [IV]

Coelho, George V. *Changing Images of America: A Study of Indian Students' Perceptions.* Glenco, Illinois: Free Press of Glencoe, 1958. 145 pp. [III]

Cohen, Sol. "English Writers on the American Common School, 1884–1904," *The School Review*, Vol. 76, No. 2 (June, 1968), pp. 127–146. [I]

Cohen, Sol. "Sir Michael E. Sadler and the Sociopolitical Analysis of Education," *History of Education Quarterly*, Vol. 7, No. 3 (Fall, 1967), pp. 281–294. [IV]

Colville, Derek. "British and American Schools," *Harper's Monthly Magazine*, Vol. 215, No. 1289 (October, 1957), pp. 58–62. [Britain] [II]

Commager, Henry Steele (editor). *America in Perspective: The United States Through Foreign Eyes.* New York: The New American Library of World Literature, Inc., 1948. 336 pp. [IV]

Commission of Chief Education Officers on behalf of the National Association of Education Officers. *Education in Relation to Industry: A Report on Technical, Trade, Applied Art, Manual Training, Domestic, Commercial, and Public Schools in Canada and the United States.* Leeds, England: E. J. Arnold & Son, Ltd., c. 1911. 187 pp. [II]

Compayre, Gabriel. "La coeducation des sexes aux États-Unis," *Revue Pedagogique*, Vol. 40 (October 15, 1906), pp. 325–326. [France] [IV]

Compayre, Gabriel. "School Exhibits and Pedagogical Monographs From the United States at the Paris Exposition," *Education*, Vol. 21, No. 7 (1901), pp. 420–435. [France] [IV]

480

Compayre, Gabriel. "School Exhibits and Pedagogical Monographs from the United States at the Paris Exposition," *Report of the Commissioner of Education for the Year 1900*, Vol. 2. Washington, D.C.: U.S. Government Printing Office, 1901, pp. 1684–1687. [France] [IV]

Cook, Stuart W. and Claire Selltiz. "Factors Influencing Attitudes of Foreign Students toward the Host Country," *Journal of Social Issues*, Vol. XVIII, No. 1 (1962), pp. 7–23. [III]

Cooke, Alistair. "The American—Image and Reality," *Overseas*, Vol. II, No. 1 (September, 1962), pp. 2–5. [Britain] [IV]

Cooper, Susan. *Behind the Golden Curtain: A View of the U.S.A.* New York: Charles Scribner's Sons, 1966. 244 pp. [Britain] [IV]

Correas, Edmundo. *Public Instruction in the United States of America.* Mendoza, Argentina: Universidad Nacional de Cuyo, 1942. [Argentina] [I]

Costello, Anthony. "As Another Sees Us," *Senior Scholastic*, Vol. 65, No. 6 (October 20, 1954), p. 5. [Britain] [II]

Cotner, Thomas E. "What They Say About Us," *School Life*, Vol. 43 (June, 1961), pp. 7–11. [IV]

Cove, W. G. "Impressions of America," *NEA Journal*, Vol. 12, No. 1 (January, 1923), pp. 11–12. [Britain] [IV]

Coward, Harry. "Report of Mr. Harry Coward," *Reports of the Mosely Educational Commission to the United States of America.* London: Co-operative Printing Society Limited, 1904. pp. 79–99. [Britain] [IV]

Cramer, John Francis. "As Others See Us," *School and Society*, Vol. 38, No. 989 (December 9, 1933), pp. 770–772. [IV]

Crespi, Leo. "Germans View the U.S. Re-orientation Program," *The International Journal of Opinion and Attitude Research*, Vol. V, No. 2 (Summer, 1951), pp. 179–190. [IV]

Crist, June R., Stuart W. Cook, Joan Havel and Claire Selltiz. *Attitudes and Social Relations of Foreign Students in the United States.* Minneapolis: University of Minnesota Press, 1963. [III]

Cross, Livingston with Amirbahar H. Jaafar. "America Will Stand; The Democratic Ways Are the Durable Ones," *Educational Forum*, Vol. XXVIII, No. 3 (March, 1964), pp. 335–336. [Philippines] [IV]

Crowther, Geoffrey. "English and American Education: Depth versus Breadth," *The Atlantic Monthly*, Vol. 205, No. 4 (April, 1960), pp. 37–42. [Britain] [IV]

Cummings, Ivor G. and Ruth C. Sloan. *A Survey of African Students Studying in the United States.* New York: Phelps-Stokes Fund, 1949. 78 pp. [III]

Cunningham, Kenneth Stewart. "The Educational Situation in the U.S.A.," *Educational Observations and Reflections.* Melbourne, Australia: Melbourne University Press, 1934, pp. 7–21. [Australia] [IV]

Cunningham, Kenneth Stewart and G. E. Phillips. *Some Aspects of Education in the United States of America.* Melbourne, Australia: Melbourne University Press, 1930. 104 pp. [Australia] [IV]

Curwen, Spencer. "American Women Teachers in South Africa," *Journal of Education* (London), Vol. 22, No. 372 (July, 1900), p. 462. [Britain] [III]

von Czihak, D. R. "German Views of American Education, with Particular Reference to Industrial Development," *U.S. Bureau of Education Bulletin.* Series No. 361, No. 2. Washington, D.C.: U.S. Government Printing Office, 1906, pp. 16–17; 26–29. [Germany] [II]

Daiches, David. "Through Cambridge Eyes—Views on American System," *Times Educational Supplement* (London), No. 2314 (September 25, 1959), p. 326. [Britain] [III]

Davidsen, Oluf M. and William H. Sewell. "The Adjustment of Scandinavian Students," *Journal of Social Issues,* Vol. XII, No. 1 (1956), p. 11. [III]

Davidsen, Oluf M. and William H. Sewell. *Scandinavian Students on an American Campus.* Minneapolis: University of Minnesota Press, 1961. [III]

Davies, Sarah J. "On Education of Teachers," *Carnegie Visitor's Reports Nos. 32–37* (Pretoria, South Africa), No. 37 (1940), pp. 1–36. [South Africa] [III]

Dawes, Sally Freeman. "Random Notes of an English Exchange," *Education* (January, 1934), pp. 265–266. [Britain] [II]

D'Constant, H. B. D'Estournells. *America and Her Problems.* New York: The Macmillan Company, 1918. [France] [IV]

Dehmelt, Bernhard. "Food for Thought," *Midland Schools,* Vol. 63, No. 8 (April, 1949), pp. 8–9. [Germany] [III]

Demiashkevich, Michael. "National Characteristics and Comparative Education," *Educational Forum,* Vol. I, No. 1 (November, 1936), pp. 5–14. [Russia] [III]

Demiashkevich, Michael. "The Value of Comparative Education for the Training of Teachers," *Educational Outlook,* Vol. 10, No. 2 (January, 1936), pp. 65–72. [Russia] [III]

Demiashkevich, Michael. "Why Comparative Education," *Peabody Journal of Education,* Vol. 9, No. 1 (July, 1931), pp. 41–45. [Russia] [II]

Dent, H. D. "A Visitor's Impressions of the United States," *Educational Forum,* Vol. XIII, No. 1 (November, 1948), pp. 13–18. [Britain] [I]

DeVault, M. Vere. "Targets for Criticism," *Childhood Education,* Vol. 11 (November, 1963), pp. 125–127. [I]

DeWitt, Nicholas. "Strategic Problems of Educational Policy in the Soviet Union and the United States," *Comparative Education Review,* Vol. VII, No. 1 (June, 1963), pp. 4–8. [III]

Dickey, Frank G. "An Outsider Looks at American Education," *Kentucky School Journal,* Vol. 20 (December, 1941), pp. 14–15. [IV]

Diels, P. A. "Dutch View of the Dalton Plan," *School Life,* Vol. 9, No. 9 (May, 1924), p. 198. [Netherlands] [IV]

Diem, Le Van. "The American As I See Him," *IIE News Bulletin*, Vol. 30 (December, 1954), pp. 52–54. [Vietnam] [III]

Diggle, Margaret. "Secondary Education in the U.S.A. and Britain," *Journal of Education* (London), Vol. 83, No. 986 (September, 1951), pp. 476–477. [Britain] [II]

Dillon, Wilton Sterling. *American Intellectual Cooperation with Japanese: Some Recommendations Based on Studies of Japanese Students and Scholars in the United States.* New York: The Japan Society, Inc., 1956. [III]

Dindorf, Wojciech. "A Polish Educator's Observations," *Educational Forum*, Vol. XXIX, No. 2 (January, 1965), pp. 189–198. [Poland] [IV]

Dingwall, Eric John. *The American Woman: A Historical Study.* London: Gerald Duckworth & Co., Ltd., 1956. 286 pp. [Britain] [IV]

Donald, W. P. *et al. Education in Relation to Industry: A Report on Technical, Trade, Applied Art, Manual Training, Domestic, Commercial, and Public Schools in Canada and the United States.* Leeds, England: E. J. Arnold and Son, Ltd., c. 1911. 187 pp. [Britain] [II]

Donaldson, James. *Addresses Delivered in the University of St. Andrews from 1886 to 1910.* Edinburgh: The University of St. Andrews, 1911. 663 pp. [Britain] [III]

Dorner, Otto with Earl R. Beck. "The German Discovery of American Education," *History of Education Quarterly*, Vol. 5, No. 1 (March, 1965), pp. 3–13. [Germany] [IV]

Douarche, Leon. "L'enseignement superieur aux États-Unis, Universités et Colleges, (Part I). *Revue Internationale de l'Enseignement*, Vol. LXI, No. 6 (June 15, 1911), pp. 481–510. [France] [III]

Douarche, Leon. "L'enseignement superieur aux États-Unis, Universités et Collèges" (Part II). *Revue Internationale de l'Enseignement*, Vol. LXII, No. 7 (July 15, 1911), pp. 12–26. [France] [III]

Doumic, Rene (*et al*). "En l'honneur des universites Columbia et Harvard," *Revue Internationale de l'Enseignement*, Vol. LXVI, No. 8 (August 15, 1913), pp. 91–109. [France] [III]

Dovie, Charles. "American Universities Face Their Problems," *Journal of Education* (London), Vol. 78, No. 412 (April, 1946), p. 412. [Britain] [III]

Downey, Lawrence W. "The Task of the Public School in the United States and Canada," *Comparative Education Review*, Vol. IV, No. 2 (October, 1960), pp. 118–120. [IV]

Dryland, Ann. "Polytechnical Education in the USA and the USSR," *Comparative Education Review*, Vol. IX, No. 2 (June, 1965), pp. 132–138. [Britain] [IV]

DuBey, R. E. (editor) with Srihanouwong, Inthompadit, Souphida. "Our Laotian Educators," *Ohio Schools*, Vol. 39 (April, 1961), pp. 8–9. [Laos] [IV]

Dubois, Cora. *Foreign Students and Higher Education in the United States.* Washington, D.C.: American Council on Education, 1956. 221 pp. [III]

DuBois, Cora. "Motivations of Students Coming to the United States," *IIE News Bulletin*, Vol. 29, No. 9 (June, 1945), pp. 2–7. [III]

DuBois, Cora. "Research in Cross Cultural Education," *IIE News Bulletin*, Vol. 28, No. 9 (June, 1953), pp. 5–8, 60–64. [III]

Dugdale, John. "Mass Education in America," *Current History*, Vol. XXXII, No. 1 (April, 1930), pp. 71–75. [Britain] [III]

Duncan, Ernest R. "Teaching Arithmetic in the United States and New Zealand," *Comparative Education Review*, Vol. V, No. 1 (June, 1961), pp. 59–62. [New Zealand] [I]

Duncan, Ernest R. "The Effect of Administrative Systems on the Education of Gifted Children: U.S.A. and New Zealand," Chapter Two in *The Year Book of Education*. New York: Harcourt, Brace and World, Inc., 1961, pp. 220–226. [New Zealand] [IV]

Dunker, D. R. "German Views of American Education with Particular Reference to Industrial Development," *U.S. Bureau of Education Bulletin*. Series No. 361, No. 2. Washington, D.C.: U.S. Government Printing Office, 1906, pp. 9–12. [Germany] [II]

Eagle, Hazel. "School in America," *Spectator*, Vol. 209, No. 7018 (December 28, 1962), pp. 1000–1001. [Britain] [I]

Ebbitt, F. H. "Wandering Scholar Visits Uncle Sam," *Times Educational Supplement* (London), No. 2685 (November 4, 1966), p. 1074. [Britain] [IV]

Eccles of Chute. "Anglo-American Exchanges: Bouquets," *Overseas*, Vol. II, No. 2 (October, 1962), pp. 2–5. [Britain] [III]

Eckert, Georg and Otto-Ernst Schueddekopf. *Die U.S.A. imdeutschen Schulbuch*. Braunschweig: Limpert, 1958. [Germany]

Eckstein, M. A. "The Elitist and the Popular Ideal," *International Review of Education*, Vol. 12, No. 2 (1966), pp. 184–195. [Britain] [IV]

Educational Review. "Notes and News: The London 'Times' on American Education," Vol. 24 (October, 1902), pp. 317–319. [IV]

Egger, Eugene and Raymond P. Whitfield. "School Attendance of Swiss and American Children," *School and Society*, Vol. 93 (April 17, 1965), pp. 254–256. [IV]

Ehrentreich, Alfred. "Auslesegrundsaetze fuer Schulleiter in U.S.A.," *Bildung und Erziehung*, Vol. VI (1953), p. 355ff. [Germany] [IV]

Ehrentreich, Alfred. "Wesenszuege und Probleme der amerikanischen High School," *Die Sammlung*, Vol. VIII (1953), pp. 217ff, 309ff. [Germany] [IV]

Ekgolm, I. K. and B. Strezikozin with E. Salgaller. "Two Soviet Views of American Education," *Education*, Vol. 85, No. 1 (September, 1964), pp. 42–46. [USSR] [II]

Ekstein, Rudolf. "A Refugee Teacher Looks on Democratic and Fascist Education," *Education*, Vol. 60, No. 2 (October, 1939), pp. 101–109. [Austria] [IV]

Elecheroth, Joseph. "Impressions from Abroad," *NEA Journal,* Vol. 39, No. 1 (May, 1950), p. 351. [Luxemburg] [I]

Elementary School Journal. "Comparison of Educational Achievement of American and Scottish Pupils," Vol. 35, No. 8 (April, 1935), pp. 564–566. [I]

Elford-Gulley, Henry. "Bungalow Built by School Children," *School Life* (May, 1921), p. 3. [Britain] [I]

Eliot, T. S. "Britain and America: Promotion of Mutual Understanding," *Times Educational Supplement* (London), No. 1540 (November 4, 1944), p. 532. [Britain] [IV]

Elliot, Alice. "As Others See Us," *Virginia Journal of Education,* Vol. 40, No. 6 (February, 1947), p. 289. [Britain] [II]

Elliot, Alice. "Briton in a Bear Garden," *Time Magazine,* Vol. XLIX, No. 1 (January 6, 1947), p. 58. [Britain] [II]

Emerson, T. L. W., *et al.* "Some Observations on American Education," *Education News* (Sydney, Australia), Vol. IX, No. 2 (April, 1963), pp. 3–4. [Australia] [IV]

Emmanuel, Pierre. "Americans as Students," *The Atlantic Monthly,* Vol. 194, No. 2 (August, 1954), pp. 59–62. [France] [III]

English Journal. "As Others See Us: An Interview After the Fact with G. C. Allen," Vol. 55 (May, 1966), pp. 531–540. [Britain] [IV]

Enock, Charles Reginald. *Farthest West: Life and Travel in the United States.* New York: D. Appleton and Company, 1910. 332 pp. [Britain] [IV]

Ensor, Beatrice. "The New Education in Europe," *Progressive Education,* Vol. 3, No. 3 (July, August, September, 1926), pp. 222–229. [Britain] [I]

Etter, Leo. "My Americanization," *Educational Outlook,* Vol. 5, No. 4 (May, 1931), pp. 243–245. [Russia] [IV]

Evans, Robert Crispin. "Empire and Foreign News—United States," *Journal of Education* (London), Vol. 84, No. 990 (January, 1952), pp. 24–28. [Britain] [IV]

Evans, W. D. Emrys. "Year in the Bronx," *High Points,* Vol. 46, No. 9 (December, 1964), pp. 22–28. [Britain] [II]

Everett, Samuel. "Transatlantic Comparison," *Times Educational Supplement* (London), No. 2343 (April 15, 1960), p. 769. [Britain] [IV]

Ewing, Irene R. "Schools in England and America," *The Volta Review,* Vol. 48 (November, 1946), pp. 706–709. [Britain] [I]

Ewing, John L. "Visitors from Other Lands View Our Schools and the Convention," *Nation's Schools,* Vol. 53 (March, 1954), pp. 71–78. [New Zealand] [I]

Faij, M. Bernard. "Education in the United States—A French View," *The American Review of Reviews,* Vol. LXIX (May, 1924), pp. 548–549. [France] [II]

Farrar, P. M. "American Influence on the Movement for a National System of Elementary Education in England and Wales, 1830–1870," *British Journal of Educational Studies* (London), Vol. XIV, No. 1 (November, 1965), pp. 36–47. [Britain] [I]

Ferber, Ellen. "A School That Smiles," *American Education*, Vol. 1 (September, 1965), pp. 8–10. [I]

Ferrari, Pedro. "Americans and American Schools Find Favor with Uruguayan Visitor," *School Life*, Vol. 14, No. 2 (October, 1928), p. 24. [Uruguay] [IV]

Figueroa, John J. "Post-graduate Teacher Education: Some Experiments in the U.S.," *Universities Quarterly* (London), Vol. XIII, No. 1 (November, 1958), pp. 75–82. [B. W. Indies] [III]

Findlay, Joseph John (editor). *Educational Essay by John Dewey*. London: Blackie and Sons, Limited, 1910. 168 pp. [Britain] [IV]

Findlay, M. E. "The Training of Teachers in the United States of America," *Board of Education, Special Reports on Educational Subjects* in *Education in the United States of America, Part I*. Vol. X. London: H.M.S.O., 1902. [Britain] [III]

Finlay, T. A. "Report of the Reverend T. A. Finlay," *Reports of the Mosely Educational Commission to the United States of America*. London: Co-operative Printing Society Limited, 1904, pp. 100–105. [Britain] [IV]

Fischer, Curt. "Americanization and the German Secondary School," *Journal of Secondary Education*, Vol. 40, No. 7 (November, 1965), pp. 325–330. [II]

Fischer, Hugo. "Idee und Entwicklung der amerikanischen hoeheren Schulen," *Die Hoehere Schule*, Vol. III, No. 5 (1950), p. 1f. [Germany] [II]

Fisher, Herbert A. L. "An Englishman Criticizes American Education," *The World's Work*, Vol. 49, No. 5 (March, 1925), pp. 462–464. [Britain] [IV]

Fisher, Herbert A. L. "Former British Minister of Education on American Education," *The School Review*, Vol. 33, No. 3 (March, 1925), pp. 162–165. [Britain] [IV]

Fisher, Herbert A. L. "Mr. H. A. L. Fisher on American Education," *School and Society*, Vol. 21, No. 526 (January 24, 1925), pp. 101–102. [Britain] [IV]

Fitch, Joshua Girling. "Teachers' Institutes and Conventions in America," Chapter VIII in *Educational Aims and Methods*. Cambridge: Cambridge University Press, 1900, pp. 249–271. [Britain] [III]

Fitch, Joshua Girling. "The Educational Problem," *Nineteenth Century* (London), Vol. LI, No. 299 (January, 1902), pp. 24–38. [Britain] [III]

Fitch, Joshua Girling. "The Study of American Education: Its Interest and Importance to English Readers," *Board of Education, Special Reports on Educational Subjects* in *Education in the United States of America, Part I*. Vol. X. London: H.M.S.O., 1902. [Britain] [III]

Fitzpatrick, Albert E. "Seis Messes en Akron," *American Education,* Vol. 1 (September, 1965), pp. 6–7. [II]

Fletcher, W. C. "Report of Mr. W. C. Fletcher," *Reports of the Mosely Educational Commission to the United States of America.* London: Cooperative Printing Society Limited, 1904, pp. 130–146. [Britain] [II]

Floud, Jean. "Studying Higher Education in Britain and America," *Universities Quarterly* (London), Vol. XVII, No. 2 (March, 1963), pp. 126–138. [Britain] [III]

Floyd, Elizabeth R. "What Misconceptions do Foreign Students Have About U.S.," *Senior Scholastic,* Vol. 84 (February 28, 1964), p. 9. [III]

Fonrobert, Leo. "Die amerikanische High School," *Die Hoehere Schule,* Vol. XI (1959), p. 144ff. [Germany] [II]

Foot, Stephen Henry. "The Future of the Public Schools," *Nineteenth Century.* Vol. CVII, No. 635 (January, 1930), pp. 17–25. [Britain] [IV]

Ford, Edith A. "Exchange of Teachers With the U.S.A.," *Journal of Education* (London), Vol. 81 (June, 1949), pp. 336–338. [Britain] [III]

Foster, T. Gregory. "Report of Professor T. Gregory Foster," *Reports of the Mosely Educational Commission to the United States of America.* London: Co-operative Printing Society Limited, 1904, pp. 106–127. [Britain] [III]

Fox, George L. "A Comparison Between the English and American Secondary Schools," *Board of Education, Special Reports on Educational Subjects in Education in the United States of America, Part II.* Vol. XI, London: H.M.S.O., 1902. [Britain] [II]

Fox, Ray. "Ethiopian Students Appraise American Education," *Clearing House,* Vol. 41, No. 3 (November, 1966), pp. 183–185. [II]

Francis, Alexander. *Americans: An Impression.* New York: D. Appleton and Company, 1909. 256 pp. [Britain] [III]

Fraser, Stewart E. (editor). *Governmental Policy and International Education.* New York: John Wiley and Sons, 1965, 370 pp. [III]

Fraser, Stewart E. and William W. Brickman. *A History of International and Comparative Education: Nineteenth Century Documents.* Glenview, Illinois: Scott, Foresman and Company, 1968. 495 pp. [IV]

Froese, Leonard. "Die Ueberwindung des Deweyismus in den U.S.A.," *Internationale Zeitschrift fuer Erziehung,* Vol. XII (1966), p. 34ff. [Germany] [IV]

Fussing, Ellen Munroe. *And the Streets are Covered with Gold.* New York: Willard Publishing Company, 1950. 194 pp. [III]

Gager, Delaye. *French Comment on American Education.* New York: Columbia University Press, 1925. 151 pp. [IV]

Galleymore, Harry. "How the Other Half . . . Technical Education in America," *Times Educational Supplement* (London), No. 2455 (June 8, 1962), p. 1184. [Britain] [II]

Gallup, George and Evan Hill. "Is European Education Better Than Ours?" *Saturday Evening Post,* No. 233 (December 24 and 31, 1960), pp. 59–76. [IV]

Galt, Russell. "European vs. American Education for the Orient," *School and Society,* Vol. 38, No. 972 (August 12, 1933), pp. 217–220. [IV]

Gardner, Percy. "Educational Ideas, Abroad and at Oxford," Chapter I in *Oxford at the Cross Roads: A Criticism of the Course of Litterae Humaniores in the University.* London: Adam and Charles Black, 1903, pp. 1–18. [Britain] [III]

Garrett, John. "Do American Schools Educate?" *The Atlantic Monthly,* Vol. 191, No. 2 (February, 1953), pp. 69–72. [Britain] [II]

Gaskell, W. H. "Report of W. H. Gaskell," *Reports of the Mosely Educational Commission to the United States of America.* London: Co-operative Printing Society Limited, 1904, pp. 147–161. [Britain] [III]

Gauba, Kanhaya Lal. *Uncle Sham: Being the Strange Tale of a Civilization Run Amok.* Lahore, India: The Times Publishing Company, 1929. 214 pp. [India] [IV]

Gavrilov, Nikandr and I. Bagrova. "A Soviet View of American Libraries," *Library Journal,* Vol. 87, No. 4 (February 15, 1962), pp. 703–711. [USSR] [IV]

Geck, L. H. Ad. "Die soziale Schulung der Ingenieure in Frankreich, U.S.A. und Deutschland," *Internationale Zeitschrift Erziehung,* Vol. IV (1933/34), p. 518ff. [Germany] [IV]

Gerard, Raymond. "L'echo des sports," *Literary Digest,* Vol. XXXXIII (June, 1927), p. 19. [France] [IV]

Gezi, Khalil Ismail. "Arab Students' Perceptions of American Students," *Sociology and Social Research,* Vol. 45, No. 4 (July, 1961), pp. 441–447. [III]

Gezi, Khalil Ismail. *The Acculturation of Middle Eastern Arab Students in Selected American Colleges and Universities.* New York: American Friends of the Middle East, 1959. Monograph. 102 pp. [III]

Ghadiali, Dinshah P. *American Sex Problems.* Malaga, New Jersey: Spectro-Chrome Institute, 1929. 242 pp. [India] [IV]

Gibbs, Philip Hamilton (editor). *Bridging the Atlantic.* Garden City, New York: Doubleday, Doran and Company, 1944. 274 pp. [Britain] [III]

Gil, Enrique. *Por que envie a mi hijo a una escuela de los Estados Unidos.* Buenos Aires, Argentina: Publicaciones del Instituto Cultural Argentino-Norte Americano, 1939. [Argentina] [IV]

Gilgallen, Alice. "Trading Ideas Through Exchange Teachers," *The American Teacher,* Vol. XXXIV (March, 1950), pp. 11–13. [Britain] [IV]

Gillett, Margaret. "Orientation of Foreign Students in the United States," *Overseas Education,* Vol. 33, No. 4 (January, 1962), pp. 171–175. [Australia] [III]

Glaap, Albert-Reiner. "Kritische Stellungnahme zu Reformtendenzen im amerikanischen Schulwesen," *Die Hoehere Schule*, Vol. XIV (1963), p. 234ff. [Germany] [IV]

Glavas, Christos B. "Impressions from Abroad," *NEA Journal*, Vol. 39, No. 1 (May, 1950), p. 350. [Greece] [IV]

Glum, Friederich. "Political Education: A Survey of France, U.S.A., Great Britain, and Germany," *International Review of Education*, Vol. 1, No. 2 (1955), pp. 166–168. [Germany] [II]

Gommes, Antoinette. *A travers les écoles d'Amérique*. Paris: Les Presses d'Ile de France, 1947. [France] [IV]

Gooch, George Peabody. "Some Notes on Elementary and Secondary Education in the United States," *Westminster Review* (London), Vol. LII (September, 1901), pp. 294–301. [Britain] [IV]

Goodhart, Philip (editor). *Exchange Teacher*. London: Conservative Political Centre, 1960. [Britain] [III]

Gorer, Geoffrey. "The All American Child," Chapter III in *The Americans: A Study in National Character*. London: The Cressent Press, 1948, pp. 50–78. [Britain] [IV]

Gottschalk, Herbert. "Amerikas grosser Erzieher," *Unsere Schule*, Vol. VII (1952), p. 625ff. [Germany] [IV]

Gottschalk, R. "Amerikanica Paedagogica," *Die Deutsche Schule*, XVII (1913), 138ff. [Germany] [IV]

Gowrie, Earl of. "Assault on Knowledge: A Briton Looks at Buffalo," *Times Educational Supplement* (London), No. 2543 (February 14, 1964), p. 381. [Britain] [III]

Graell, C. Arrocha. "Inter-American Educational Relations: A Visitor Looks at Our Schools," *Education for Victory*, Vol. 1, No. 23 (February 1, 1943), p. 30. [Panama] [IV]

Graham, Grace. "Foreign Teachers Look at American Secondary Schools," *California Journal of Secondary Education*, Vol. 29, No. 2 (February, 1954), pp. 65–68. [I]

Grant, Cecil. "Can American Co-education be grafted upon the English Public School System?" *Board of Education, Special Reports on Educational Subjects* in *Education in the United States of America, Part II.* Vol. XI. London: H.M.S.O., 1902. [Britain] [II]

Grant, Donald. "The American Scene: Is the U.S.A. a Foreign Country?" *Times Educational Supplement* (London), No. 1374 (August 30, 1941), p. 408. [Britain] [IV]

Gray, Herbert Branston. *America at School and at Work*. London: Nisbet and Company, 1918. 172 pp. [Britain] [III]

Gray, Herbert Branston. "Report of the Reverend Herbert Branston Gray," *Reports of the Mosely Educational Commission to the United States of America*. London: Co-operative Printing Society Limited, 1904, pp. 162–173. [Britain] [III]

Grier, Lynda. *Achievement in Education: The Work of Michael Ernest Sadler, 1885–1935.* London: Constable, 1952. 267 pp. [Britain] [IV]

Grosser, Alfred. "The U.S.: Mais Oui! Mais Non!" *Stanford Today.* Series 1, No. 14. Palo Alto, California: Publications Service of Stanford University, Autumn, 1965, pp. 9–13. [France] [III]

Groser, W. P. *Education and Industrial Success.* London: Hazell, Watson, and Viney, Ltd., 1904. 32 pp. [Britain] [III]

Groser, W. P. "Report of Mr. W. P. Groser," *Reports of the Mosely Educational Commission to the United States of America.* London: Co-operative Printing Society Limited, 1904, pp. 174–197. [Britain] [III]

Guddat, Kurt. "A German Teacher Observes American Education," *New Mexico School Review,* Vol. XXXI (September, 1951), pp. 4–6. [Germany] [IV]

Guijarro, L. Garcia. *Notas Americanas.* Madrid: Fontanet, 1913. [Spain] [IV]

Gullahorn, John T. and Jeanne E. *Foreign Student Leaders on American Campuses: An Experiment in Cross-Cultural Education.* Lawrence: University of Kansas Press, 1958. [III]

Gutiérrez, Alberto. *Notas e impresiones de los Estados Unidos.* Santiago de Chile: Imprenta Cervantes, 1904. [Chile] [IV]

Gyi, Shirley. "Out of the Mouths of Students," *NEA Journal,* Vol. 46 (December, 1957), p. 609. [Burma] [II]

Hailmann, William Nicholas. *German Views of American Education with Particular Reference to Industrial Development.* U.S. Bureau of Education Bulletin. Series No. 2. Washington, D.C.: U.S. Government Printing Office, 1906. 55 pp. [II]

Haldane, Richard Burdon. *Education and Empire.* London: John Murray, 1902. 198 pp. [Britain] [IV]

Hamano, Masao. "Impressions of Musical Education in the United States," *Etude,* Vol. 75, No. 2 (February, 1957), pp. 14, 43, 64. [Japan] [IV]

Hamilton, C. J. "Secondary Education in America," Part I, Chapter IV in *The Higher Education of Boys in England.* Cyril, Norwood and Arthur H. Hope (editors). London: John Murray, 1909, pp. 128–152. [Britain] [II]

Hanauer, Simon W. "A German View of United States Development," *Report of the Commissioner of Education, 1800–1900.* Vol. 2. Washington, D.C.: U.S. Government Printing Office, 1901, p. 1438. [Germany] [IV]

Handlin, Oscar. *This Was America: True Accounts of Peoples and Places, Manners and Customs as Recorded by European Travellers to the Western Shore in the Eighteenth, Nineteenth, and Twentieth Century.* New York: Harvard University Press and Harper and Row, 1949, 1964. 602 pp. [IV]

Hänninger, Nils. "Some Contrasts Between Swedish and American Schools," *School Life,* Vol. 8, No. 3 (November, 1922), pp. 55–57. [Sweden] [IV]

Hans, Nicholas. "English Pioneers of Comparative Education," *British Journal of Educational Studies* (London), Vol. I (November, 1952), pp. 84–105. [IV]

Hans, Nicholas. "The Educational System of the USA," Chapter XIV in *Comparative Education: A Study of Educational Factors and Traditions.* Third edition. London: Routledge and Kegan Paul, Ltd., 1958, pp. 273–289.

Hans, Nicholas. "Two Aspects of Humanism in England and America," *Comparative Education Review*, Vol. VII, No. 2 (October, 1963), pp. 113–118. [Britain] [IV]

Hanus, Paul H. "Secondary Education in a Democratic Community," *Board of Education, Special Reports on Educational Subjects* in *Education in the United States of America, Part II.* Vol. XI. London: H.M.S.O., 1902. [Britain] [II]

Harrison, Frederic. "Impressions of America," *Nineteenth Century*, Vol. XLIX, No. 292 (June, 1901), pp. 913–930. [Britain] [III]

Harrison, Tom. "The Future of British Sociology," *International Journal of Opinion and Attitude Research*, Vol. 1, No. 1 (1947), pp. 47–62. [Britain] [IV]

Hartog, P. J. "Commercial Education in the United States," *Board of Education, Special Reports on Educational Subjects* in *Education in the United States of America, Part II.* Vol. XI. London: H.M.S.O., 1902. [Britain] [II]

Harvey, A. "American Teacher Shortage," *Journal of Education* (London), Vol. 87, No. 1027 (February, 1955), pp. 62–64. [Britain] [III]

Hauch, Charles (editor). *Foreign Understanding and Interpretation of United States Education.* Studies in Comparative Education, OE 14059. Washington, D.C., U.S. Office of Education, 1960. [III]

Hawnt, J. Stuart. "American Journey," *Ulster Education*, Vol. IX, No. 2 (January, 1953), pp. 7–14. [Britain] [IV]

Heape, Joseph R. "Report of Alderman Joseph R. Heape," *Reports of the Mosely Educational Commission to the United States of America.* London: Co-operative Printing Society Limited, 1904, pp. 198–210. [Britain] [I]

Heindel, Richard Heathcote. *American Influences Abroad* (Papers and remarks of the annual meeting of the American Historical Association, Boston, December 30, 1940). New York: Carnegie Endowment for International Peace, 1940. 51 pp. [IV]

Heindel, Richard Heathcote. "British Teachers and the United States," *School and Society*, Vol. 45, No. 1172 (1937), pp. 821–826. [II]

Heindel, Richard Heathcote. *The American Impact on Great Britain, 1898–1914: A Study of the United States in World History.* Philadelphia: University of Pennsylvania Press, 1940. 439 pp. [IV]

Heli, Karsten. "Eleven Weeks in the U.S.A.," *Phi Delta Kappan*, Vol. 30, No. 3 (November, 1948), pp. 91–94. [Norway] [IV]

Helms, Erwin. "Die amerikanische Lehrerbildung," *Die Deutsche Schule*, Vol. LVI (1964), p. 441ff. [Germany] [IV]

Henn, T. R. "Some American Universities as Seen Through British Eyes," *Harvard Educational Review*, Vol. 24, No. 3 (Summer, 1954), pp. 202–221. [Britain] [III]

Hennig, Willi. "Schule und Wehrgeist im Ausland: Italien, Japan und Amerika," *Die Deutsche Hoehere Schule*, Vol. III (1936), p. 224ff. [Germany] [IV]

Henning, Karl. "Deutsch oder amerikanisch?" *Die Deutsche Schule*, Vol. XVIII (1914), p. 237ff. [Germany] [IV]

Henry, Denis. "Are Headmasters Necessary? American System Compared," *Times Educational Supplement* (London), No. 21391 (March 17, 1961), p. 525. [Britain] [IV]

Hermansson, Ester. *Amerikanska Skolor*. Göteborg: Elander, 1941. [Sweden] [IV]

Heseltine, Harry. "An Australian Looks at America," *IIE News Bulletin*, Vol. 30, No. 2 (November, 1954), pp. 26–31. [Australia] [IV]

Higginson, J. H. "English Education Between the United States and the U.S.S.R.," *Comparative Education Review*, Vol. II, No. 1 (June, 1958), pp. 16–19. [Britain] [IV]

Higginson, J. H. *Sadler's Studies of American Education*. Monograph No. 1. Leeds, England: The University of Leeds, Institute of Education, 1955. 86 pp. [Britain] [IV]

The High School Journal. "A Foreign Visitor's Impressions of American Schools," Vol. 25 (January, 1942), pp. 14–17. [II]

Highet, Gilbert. "The American Student as I See Him," *The American Scholar*, Vol. 10, No. 4 (Autumn, 1941), pp. 416–427. [Britain] [III]

Hilker, Franz. "Paedagogische Amerikafahrt," *Paedagogisches Zentralblatt*, Vol. VIII (1928), p. 529ff. [Germany] [IV]

Hingorani, D. K. "The Strange Business of Teaching Strangers," *Saturday Review*, Vol. 39, No. 39 (September 29, 1956), pp. 9–10; 27–28. [India] [III]

Hirshler, Eric E. (editor). *Jews from Germany in the U.S.* New York: Farrar, Straus and Cudahy, 1955, pp. 142–143. [IV]

Hockey, S. L. "Reflections After Visiting the U.S.A.," *West African Journal of Education*, Vol. 6, No. 2 (June, 1962), pp. 66–68. [Britain] [II]

Holbrook, David. "American Schools Television," *Journal of Education* (London), Vol. 90, No. 1063 (February, 1958), p. 433. [Britain] [IV]

Holme, E. R. *The American University; An Australian View*. Sydney: Angus and Robertson, Ltd., 1920. [Australia] [III]

Holmes, Brian. "Teacher Training and the Profession of Education (U.S.A.)," Chapter VIII in *Problems in Education: A Comparative Approach*. London: Routledge and Kegan Paul, Ltd., 1965, pp. 191–220. [Britain] [III]

Hood, D. W., *et al.* "Some Observations on American Education," *Education News* (Sydney, Australia), Vol. IX, No. 2 (April, 1963), pp. 7–8. [Australia] [IV]

Hooper, Frederick and James Graham. "The Position in the United States in 1901," *Commercial Education at Home and Abroad.* London: The Macmillan Company, 1901, pp. 135–159. [Britain] [II]

Horn, Ewald. "Amerikanisches Schulwesen," *Monatschrift fuer Hoehere Schulen,* Vol. III (1904), p. 592ff. [Germany] [IV]

Horwill, Herbert W. "Politics in American Education," *Quarterly Review* (London) Vol. 7, No. III (April, 1909), pp. 275–287. [Britain] [IV]

Horwill, Herbert W. "Private Secondary Schools in America," *Journal of Education* (London), Vol. 27, No. 434 (September, 1905), pp. 637–638. [Britain] [II]

Horwill, Herbert W. "The Monastic Danger in Higher Education," *The Forum,* Vol. 32, No. 2 (October, 1901), pp. 244–254. [Britain] [III]

Hosius, Carl. "Aus Amerikas klassischen Schulen," *Monatschrift fuer Hoehere Schulen,* Vol. XXXV (1926), p. 188ff. [Germany] [II]

Howard, Alvin W. "Hassan Kissed Me," *Clearing House,* Vol. 35 (September, 1960), pp. 3–6. [IV]

Howard, Elizabeth Jane. "Real Tragedy of the South," *Sunday Telegraph* (London), April 7, 1968. [Britain] [III]

Hsiung, James C. "All, Not Just a Part," *The Asian Student* (Spring Semester, 1963), pp. S–3. [China] [III]

Hsunli-Chien. *Some Phases of Popular Control of Education in the United States.* Shanghai: The Commerical Press, Ltd., 1927. [China] [IV]

Huang, Chi-Ren. "Visitors from Other Lands View Our Schools and the Convention," *Nation's Schools,* Vol. 53 (March, 1954), pp. 71–78. [China] [II]

Hubertson, Amanda Labarca. *La escuela secundaria en los Estados Unidos.* Santiago, Chile: Universo, 1919. [Chile] [II]

Hughes, James L. and Louis Richard Klemm. "The United States," Chapter XI in *Progress of Education in the Century.* London: W. & R. Chambers, Limited. Toronto and Philadelphia: The Linscott Publishing Co., 1901, pp. 335–354. [Britain and Germany] [IV]

Hughes, Robert Edward. "National Types and Educational Ideals," Chapter I in *The Democratic Ideal in Education.* London: Charles and Dible, 1903, pp. 9–21. [Britain] [IV]

Hughes, Robert Edward. "The Half-Way House: A Study in Comparative Education," Chapter I in *Schools at Home and Abroad.* London: Swan Sonnenschein and Company, Ltd., 1901, pp. 1–51. [Britain] [IV]

Hughes, Robert Edward. *The Making of Citizens: A Study in Comparative*

Education. London and Newcastle-on-Tyne: The Walter Scott Publishing Co., Ltd., 1902. 405 pp. [Britain] [IV]

Humphrey, Darlow W. "Views of an English Visitor," *Nation's Schools,* Vol. 24, No. 2 (August, 1939), pp. 55–56. [Britain] [II]

Humphrey, William Gerald. "Schools in America," *Spectator* (London), Vol. 171, No. 6023 (December 3, 1943), p. 525. [Britain] [IV]

Huq, Azizul. "Small and Completely Interdependent," *The Asian Student* (Spring Semester, 1960), p. S–7. [Pakistan] [III]

Hurry, Charles D. "Foreign Students on the American Campus," *Educational Record,* Vol. XVIII (October, 1937), pp. 374–379. [Britain] [III]

Husen, Torsten. "Social Determinants of the Comprehensive School," *International Review of Education,* Vol. 9, No. 2 (1963–1964), pp. 158–173. [Sweden] [II]

Huxley, Julian S. "America Revisited: American Universities," *Spectator* (London), Vol. 133, No. 5033 (December 13, 1924), pp. 924–926. [Britain] [III]

Huxley, Julian S. "America Revisited: Backgrounds," *Spectator* (London), Vol. 133, No. 5029 (November 15, 1924), pp. 732–733. [Britain] [IV]

Huzayyin, S. *Some Comparisons Between Universities.* Oxford, England: Basil Blackwell, 1944, pp. 28–30. [Egypt] [III]

Hylla, Erich. "Die Erziehung zum Buche in den Vereinigten Staaten," *Die Deutsche Schule,* Vol. XXXII (1928), p. 14ff. [Germany] [IV]

Hylla, Erich. "Die paedagogische Forschung in den Vereinigten Staaten," *Paedagogisches Zentralblatt,* Vol. VIII (1928), p. 601ff. [Germany] [IV]

Hylla, Erich. *Die Schule der Demokratie.* Langensalza: Beltz, 1928. [Germany] [IV]

Hylla, Erich. "Schule und Leben in den Vereinigten Staaten," *Paedagogisches Zentralblatt,* Vol. X (1930), p. 29ff. [Germany] [IV]

Iddesleigh, Walter Stafford. "The American Preparatory School," *Contemporary Review,* Vol. CXXXIII (January-June, 1928), pp. 632–636. [Britain] [II]

IIE News Bulletin. "American Colleges Viewed by a European," Vol. 10, No. 5 (February, 1935), pp. 4–6.

Institute for Social Research. *A Study of Intercultural Contact: Norwegian Fulbright Grantees Visiting the United States.* Oslo, Norway: August, 1954. Vol. I, 108 pp; Vol. II, 236 pp. [III]

Institute of International Education. *African Students in the United States.* New York: Committee on Educational Interchange Policy, December, 1960, 30 pp. [III]

Institute of International Education. *A Foreign Student Program for the Developing Countries During the Coming Decade.* New York: Committee on Educational Interchange Policy, June, 1962. 30 pp. [III]

494

Institute of International Education. *Chinese Students in the United States, 1948–55.* New York: Committee on Educational Interchange Policy, March, 1956. [III]

Institute of International Education. *Foreign Professors and Research Scholars at U.S. Colleges and Universities.* New York: Committee on Educational Interchange Policy, October, 28 pp. 1963. [III]

Institute of International Education. *Hungarian Refugee Students and United States Colleges and Universities.* New York: Committee on Educational Interchange Policy, March, 1957. [III]

Institute of International Education. *Hungarian Refugee Students and United States Colleges and Universities: One Year Later.* New York: Committee on Educational Interchange Policy, June, 1958. [III]

Institute of International Education. *The Foreign Student: Exchangee or Immigrant?* New York: Committee on Educational Interchange Policy, May, 1958, 17 pp. [III]

Institute of Sociology. *Finnish Fellowship Students in the United States.* Helsinki, Finland: University of Helsinki, July, 1964. 134 pp. [III]

EMNID. International Institute for Public Opinion and Market Research. *Impressions of State Department Grantees from Burma.* Bielefeld, Germany: April, 1961. [III]

International Public Opinion Research, Inc. *Evaluation of International Exchange Experiences of Brazilian Grantees.* New York: International Public Opinion Research, Inc., September, 1953. 128 pp. [III]

International Public Opinion Research, Inc. *German Exchangees: A Study in Attitude Change.* New York: International Public Opinion Research, Inc., August, 1953. 58 pp. [III]

International Public Opinion Research, Inc. *Interviews with Six Brazilians Who Came to the United States Under the International Exchange Program.* New York: International Public Opinion Research, Inc., February, 1952. 30 pp. [III]

International Public Opinion Research, Inc. *Interviews with Twenty Mexican Teachers to Help Evaluate the Teacher Exchange Program.* New York: International Public Opinion Research, Inc., June, 1953. 95 pp. [III]

International Research Associates, Inc. *Italian Exchangees: A Study in Attitude Change and Diffusion.* New York: International Research Associates, Inc., March, 1955. 39 pp. [III]

International Research Associates, Inc. *The Thai Student Exchangee: An Evaluation Report.* New York: International Research Associates, Inc. August, 1955. 122 pp. [III]

International Research Associates, S.A. de C.V. *A Study of Reactions to the State Department Exchange Program Among Returned Mexican Grantees.* Mexico City: International Research Associates, January, 1959. 136 pp. [III]

The International Teacher Development Program. "Comments on American Educational Practices," OE–14118 (1964), p. 11+. [IV]

Jaafar, Amirbahar H. "America Will Stand. The Democratic Ways are the Durable Ones," *Educational Forum,* Vol. 28, No. 3 (March, 1964), p. 335. [Philippines] [IV]

Jacabson, Dan. *No Further West: California Visited.* London: Weidenfeld and Nicolson, 1959. 127 pp. [Britain] [IV]

Jacks, Lawrence Pearsall. *My American Friends.* New York: The Macmillan Company, 1933. 263 pp. [Britain] [IV]

Jackson, Alice M. "An Interesting American Normal School," *Journal of Education* (London), Vol. 32, No. 488 (March, 1910), pp. 215–216. [Britain] [III]

Jacobson, Edward S. "Scottish Impressions of American Education," *Clearing House,* Vol. 36, No. 7 (March, 1962), pp. 403–407. [Britain] [IV]

James, Eric. "American Reflections," *Times Educational Supplement* (London), No. 2216 (November 8 and 15, 1957), pp. 1434, 1461. [Britain] [II]

Jastrow, J. "Higher Education for Businessmen in the United States and Germany," *Report of the Commissioner of Education, 1905.* Vol. I. Washington, D.C.: U.S. Government Printing Office, 1907, pp. 97–110. [Germany [III]

Jenictz, Alice K. "Britishers on America," *Times Educational Supplement* (London), No. 2492 (February 22, 1963), p. 351. [III]

Jephson, A. W. "Report of the Reverend A. W. Jephson," *Reports of the Mosely Educational Commission to the United States of America.* London: Co-operative Printing Society Limited, 1904, pp. 211–234. [Britain] [IV]

Johnson, J. B., *et al. Education in Relation to Industry: A Report on Technical, Trade, and Applied Art, Manual Training, Domestic, Commercial, and Public Schools in Canada and the United States.* Leeds, England: E. J. Arnold & Son, Ltd., c. 1911. 187 pp. [Britain] [IV]

Johnson, John Francis. "A New Zealander's View of American Education," *School Life,* Vol. 41, No. 6 (April, 1959), p. 5. [New Zealand] [II]

Joseph, Franz M. (editor). *As Others See Us: The United States Through Foreign Eyes.* Princeton, New Jersey: Princeton University Press, 1959, 360 pp. [IV]

Kalen, Herbert. "A Swede Looks at Business Education in the U.S.A.," *The National Business Education Quarterly,* Vol. 20, No. 1 (October, 1951), pp. 35–40. [Sweden] [II]

Kandel, Isaac Leon. "The American System of Education," Chapter I in *Education and Society: Some Studies of Education Systems in Europe and America.* Introduction and Forward by John Sargent. London: Phoenix House, Ltd., 1955, pp. 9–44. [IV]

496

Kandel, Isaac Leon. "Visit to America of Sir Michael Sadler," *School and Society*, Vol. 31, No. 792 (March 1, 1930), pp. 290–291. [IV]

Kartzke, Georg. *Das amerikanische Schulwesen.* Leipzig: Quelle and Meyer, 1928. [Germany] [IV]

Kataoka, Jenitaro. "Visitors from Other Lands View Our Schools and the Convention," *Nation's Schools*, Vol. 53, No. 3 (March, 1954), pp. 71–78. [Japan] [IV]

Katz, Joseph. "What is Good About American Education: A Canadian Educator's View," *Teachers College Journal*, Vol. 36, No. 1 (October, 1964), pp. 57–59. [Canada] [IV]

Kazamias, Andres M. and Byron G. Massialas. *Tradition and Change in Eudcation: A Comparative Study.* Englewood Cliffs, New Jersey: Prentice-Hall, Inc., 1965. 182 pp. [IV]

Kellermann, Fritz. "Grundlagen des amerikanischen Schulwesens," *Die Erziehung*, Vol. IV (1929), p. 702ff. [Germany] [IV]

Keolouangkhot, Tay. "Visitors from Other Lands View Our Schools and the Convention," *Nation's Schools*, Vol. 53, No. 3 (March, 1954), pp. 71–78. [Laos] [I]

Kerschensteiner, Georg. "A Comparison of Public Education in Germany and in the United States." Series No. 534, No. 24. Washington, D.C.: U.S. Government Printing Office, 1913, pp. 5–15. [Germany] [I]

Kerschensteiner, Georg. "Das oeffentliche Unterrichtswesen in Deutschland und in den Vereinigten Staaten," *Paedagogisches Zentralblatt*, Vol. VI (1926), p. 1f. [Germany] [I]

Kerschensteiner, Georg. "Notes and News: Dr. Kerschensteiner on American Schools," *Educational Review*, Vol. 43 (April, 1912), pp. 428–431. [Germany] [I]

Kershaw, John B. C. "Some Fallacies and the Education Bill," *Monthly Review*, Vol. IV (July, 1901), pp. 30–49. [Britain] [IV]

Keyserling, Hermann Alexander. *America Set Free.* London: Jonathan Cape, 1930. [Germany] [I]

Kiehle, D. L. "A Sketch of the Development and present Condition of the System of Education in the State of Minnesota, with an Appendix dealing with Minneapolis and St. Paul," *Board of Education, Special Reports on Educational Subjects* in *Education in the United States of America, Part I.* Vol. X. London: H.M.S.O., 1902. [Britian] [I]

Kim, Dong Hwan. "An American Education for Asians: Does it Meet the Need?" *IIE News Bulletin,* Vol. 33, No. 9 (May, 1958), pp. 33–36. [Korea] [IV]

Kim, Young Chum. "Through the Eyes of a Korean," *California Teachers Association Journal*, Vol. 50, No. 6 (September, 1954), pp. 20–21. [Korea] [II]

King, Edmund J. *Society, Schools and Progress in the U.S.A.* New York: Pergamon Press, 1965. 241 pp. [Britain] [IV]

King, Edmund J. "The United States of America: A Nation on Wheels," Chapter 5 in *Other Schools and Ours: A Comparative Study for Today.* Third edition. New York: Holt, Rinehart and Winston, Inc., 1967, pp. 159–216. [Britain] [IV]

Kiriro, Amos. "An African Student Studies Us," *New York Times Magazine,* Section 6 (December 10, 1961), pp. 16, 114, 116. [Kenya] [III]

Kirpal, Prem. "Fascination for Studies Abroad," *The Educational Quarterly,* Vol. VII, No. 65 (March, 1965), pp. 7–10. [India] [III]

Klein, Felix. *In the Land of the Strenuous Life.* Chicago: A. C. McClurg & Company, 1905. 387 pp. [France] [IV]

Klemm, Louis R. *Public Education in Germany and in the United States.* Boston: R. G. Bodger, 1911. [Germany] [I]

Knortz, Karl. *Die amerikanische Volksschule.* Tübingen: Laupp, 1904. [Germany] [I]

Kobayashi, Victor N. "The Quest for Experience: Zen, Dewey, and Education," *Comparative Education Review,* Vol. V, No. 3 (February, 1962), pp. 217–222. [Japan] [IV]

Koch, Heinrich. "Vom Auftrag der Schulen in den Vereinigten Staaten," *Unsere Schule,* Vol. VIII (1953), p. 755ff. [Germany] [IV]

Koh, Eng Kiat. "American Educational Policy in the Philippines and British Policy in Malaya," *Comparative Education Review,* Vol. IX, No. 2 (June, 1965), pp. 139–146. [IV]

Köhler, Wolfgang. "The Scientists and Their New Environment," *The Cultural Migration: The European Scholar in America.* Philadelphia: The University of Pennsylvania Press, 1953, pp. 112–137. [Germany] [III]

Kreuzer, Siglinde. "Public Education in Amerika," *Die Sammlung,* Vol. X (1955), p. 95ff. [Germany] [III]

Kuehnemann, Egon. "Die Zusammenarbeit von Schule und Elternhaus in den Vereinigten Staaten von Nordamerika," *Paedagogisches Zentralblatt,* Vol. X (1930), p. 205ff. [Germany] [IV]

Kunz, W. "Thank You, American Friends," *The Volta Review,* Vol. 40, No. 3 (March, 1938), pp. 140–142. [Switzerland] [II]

Kurani, Habib A. "Near Eastern Student and his Problems on Transfer to American Universities," *Registrar's Journal,* Vol. XXIV (July, 1940), p. 182.

Kurz, Karl. *Aus dem amerikanischen Erziehungsleben, Beobachtungen und Anregungen.* Bielefeld: F. Eilers, 1950. [Germany] [IV]

Kuypers. "German Views of American Education, with Particular Reference to Industrial Development," *U.S. Bureau of Education Bulletin.* Series No. 2. Washington, D.C.: U.S. Government Printing Office, 1906, pp. 12–16. [Germany] [II]

Lacombe, Maria Isabel. "The Dream Come True," *School Arts,* Vol. 47, No. 8 (April, 1948), pp. 285–286. [Brazil] [III]

498

Laird, M., *et al.* "En l'honneur des universites Columbia et Harvard," *Revue Internationale de l'Enseignement,* Vol. LXVI, No. 8 (August 15, 1913), pp. 91–109. [France] [III]

Lambert, Richard D. (editor). "America Through Foreign Eyes," *Annals of The American Academy of Political and Social Science,* Vol. 295 (September, 1954), pp. 1–145. [IV]

Lambert, Richard D. and Marvin Bressler. *Indian Students on an American Campus.* Minneapolis: University of Minnesota Press, 1956. 122 pp. [III]

Lambert, Vvedale. "Some Comparisons Between British and American Education," *National Association of Secondary School Principals Bulletin,* Vol. 34, No. 1 (January, 1950), pp. 95–100. [Britain] [II]

Lambert, Wallace E. and Otto Klineberg. *Children's Views of Foreign People.* New York: Appleton-Century-Crofts, 1967. 319 pp. [I]

Landé, Walter. "Family and School in Europe and America," *IIE News Bulletin,* Vol. 12, No. 6 (March 1, 1937), pp. 4–6. [Germany] [IV]

Lanson, Gustave. "Le langue francaise aux États-Unis," *Revue Internationale de l'Enseignement,* Vol. LIX, No. 1 (January 15, 1913), p. 27 [France] [II]

Lanson, Gustave. "The Problems of National Education: Citations from an Article by M. Gustave Lanson," *Report of the Commissioner of Education, Year 1900,* Vol. 2 (1901), pp. 1688–1691. [France] [II]

Lanson, Gustave. *Trois mois d'énseignement aux États-Unis.* Paris: Libraire Hachette et Cie, 1912. [France] [II]

Laski, Harold J. "American Education," Chapter 8 in *The American Democracy: A Commentary and an Interpretation.* New York: The Viking Press, 1948, pp. 323–392. [Britain] [III]

Laue, Franz, "Amerikanische Schulverhaeltnisse unter dem Gesichtspunkt der Einheitschule," *Deutsches Philologen-Blatt,* Vol. XXIV (1916), p. 501ff. [Germany] [IV]

Lauwerys, Joseph A. "General Education in a Changing World," *International Review of Education,* Vol. II, No. 4 (1965), pp. 385–403. [Britain] [IV]

Lauwerys, Joseph A. "The Philosophical Approach to Comparative Education," *International Review of Education,* Vol. 5, No. 3 (1957), pp. 281–296. [Britain] [IV]

Leacock, Stephen. "Education by the Acre-Impressions of an Exchange Teacher," *Times Educational Supplement* (London), No. 19443, Part I (February 7, 1943), p. 100. [Britain] [II]

Leao, A. Carneiro. *A Educacaõ nos Estados Unidos.* Rio de Janeiro: Jornal de Commercio, 1940. [Brazil] [IV]

Ledov, A. "Anticommunist Jungles and Moscow Woods," *The Current Digest of the Soviet Press,* Vol. XV, No. 22 (June 26, 1963), p. 23. [USSR] [IV]

Leont'ev, A. N. and P. Ia. Gal'perin. "Programmed Instruction," *Soviet Education,* [trans.] Vol. 7, No. 5 (March, 1965), pp. 7–15. [USSR] [IV]

Leroi, Helene. "Amerika erizieht sum Militarismus," *Die Neue Erziehung,* Vol. IX (1927), p. 922ff. [Germany] [IV]

Li, P'ei Yu. *A Critical Study of Group Instruction in American Schools.* Shanghai, China: Comacrib Press, 1937, pp. 199–224. [China] [IV]

Liang, Shang-yung. "A Study on the State Educational Foundation Programs of the United States," *The National Chengchi University Journal* (Taiwan), Vol. 10 (December, 1864), pp. 293–310. [China] [IV]

Lietzmann, Walter. "Die Unterrichtsmethoden in den Schulen der Vereinigten Staaten," *Paedagogisches Zentralblatt,* Vol. XI (1931), p. 251ff. [Germany] [II]

de Lignereux, Saint-Andre. *L'Amerique au XXth Siecle.* Paris: Librairie Illustree, 1908. [France] [IV]

Lindsay, Kenneth, "British American Relations: Towards an Educational Link," *Times Educational Supplement* (London), No. 1537 (October 14, 1944), p. 496. [Britain] [III]

Lindsay, Kenneth. "Mr. Kenneth Lindsay, M. P.," *Some Comparisons Between Universities.* (Education Association of University Professors). Oxford: Basil Blackwell, 1944, pp. 61–62. [Britain] [III]

Linhoff, Lieselotte. "Impressions from Abroad," *NEA Journal,* Vol. 39, No. 1 (May, 1950), p. 351. [Germany] [I]

Lippitt, Ronald and Jeanne Watson. "Cross-Culture Learning: A Study Among a Group of German Leaders," *IIE News Bulletin,* Vol. 30, No. 9 (June, 1955), pp. 2–5. [IV]

Lippitt, Ronald and Jeanne Watson. *Learning Across Cultures: A Study of Germans Visiting America.* Ann Arbor: University of Michigan Press, 1955. [IV]

The Living Age. "A Year Amongst Americans: Co-education and Secular Education," Vol. XL (Seventh Series), No. 3340 (July 11, 1908), pp. 75–80. [IV]

Locher, Theodore J. G. "Your Education Versus Mine," *The Journal of Higher Education,* Vol. XXIV, No. 8 (November, 1953), pp. 395–402. [Netherlands] [III]

Lockwood, Geoflrey. "Admissions to Harvard and Yale," *Universities Quarterly* (London), Vol. XIX, No. 4 (September, 1965), pp. 365–377. [Britiain] [III]

Lockwood, Geoffrey and Barry Supple. "Admissions Policies and Procedures in the United States," *Universities Quarterly* (London), Vol. XXI, No. 4 (September, 1967), pp. 415–437. [III]

Lockyer, Norman. *Education and National Progress: Essays and Addresses 1870–1905*. London: The Macmillan Company, Limited, 1906. 269 pp. [Britain] [III]

Loebner, Heinrich. *Die Grundzüge des Unterrichts-und Erziehungswesens in den Vereinigten Staaten von Nordamerika*. Vienna: Deuticke, 1907. [Austria] [IV]

London, H. H. "Russia Takes a Look at Vocational Education, U.S.A.," *American Vocational Journal*, Vol. 35, No. 4 (April, 1960), pp. 25–26. [II]

Long, Lewis M. K. "An Image of America, Changing Democratic Orientations in Brazilian Students Studying in America," *The Journal of Higher Education*, Vol. XXIX, No. 1 (January 1958), p. 31. [IV]

Loomis, Charles P. and Edgar A. *Acculturation of Foreign Students in the U.S.* East Lansing: Michigan State College Social Research Service, 1948, 34 pp. [IV]

Loram, Charles T. "Education in the United States and in South Africa," *Educational Outlook*, Vol. 7, No. 4 (May, 1933), pp. 193–199. [South Africa] [IV]

Loram, Charles T. "Influence Abroad of American Education," *School Life*, Vol. 21, No. 7 (April, 1936), pp. 209–210. [South Africa] [IV]

Love, Enid. "A European View of American Educational T.V.," *IIE News Bulletin*, Vol. 36, No. 2 (October, 1960), pp. 33–37. [Britain] [IV]

Lowe, John. "Impressions of Adult Education in the United States," *Adult Education*, Vol. XII, No. 3 (Spring, 1962), pp. 183–189. [Britain] [III]

Lowe, John. "Lessons from America," *Adult Education: The Tutor's Bulletin* (London), Vol. XXXV, No. 4 (November, 1962), pp. 203–207. [Britain] [III]

Ludwig, Emil. "Why I Shall Send My Son to an American College," *American Magazine*, Vol. CXII, No. 4 (October, 1931), pp. 29, 96, 98; 100. [Germany] [III]

Lusseyran, Jacques. *Douce trop douce Amérique: 'les étudiants et leurs professeurs aux États-Unis'*. Paris: Editions Gallimand, 1968. 264 pp. [France] [III]

Lykes, Richard W. "Teachers From Abroad Take a Look at America," *American Education*, Vol. 2 (September, 1966), pp. 14, 15–19. [IV]

Lysgaard, Sveere. "Adjustment in a Foreign Society: Norwegian Fulbright Grantees Visiting the United States," *International Social Science Bulletin*, Vol. 7 (1955), pp. 45–51. [Norway] [IV]

Majid, Abdul. "As Visiting Statesmen See Our Schools," *Nation's Schools*, Vol. 67 (June, 1961), pp. 51–55. [Iraq] [IV]

Makowski, Erich. *Staatsbuergerliche Erziehung der Schuljugend in den Vereinigten Staaten von Nordamerika*. Paderborn: Ferdinand Schoeningh, 1932. [Germany] [IV]

Malkova, Zoya. "The American Comprehensive High School Today," *International Review of Education,* Vol. 11, No. 3 (1965), pp. 257–264. [USSR] [II]

Malkova, Zoya. "Critique of Western Educational Theory: Pragmatism and Pedagogy," *Soviet Education,* [trans], Vol. 5, No. 7 (May, 1963), pp. 42–45. [USSR] [II]

Malkova, Zoya. "In The Schools of America (Notes of a Soviet Educator), Part I," *Soviet Education,* [trans], Vol. 5, No. 4 (December, 1962), pp. 50–59. [USSR] [II]

Malkova, Zoya. "In The Schools of America (Notes of a a Soviet Educator), Part II," *Soviet Education,* [trans] Vol. 5, No. 4 (February, 1963), pp. 55–62. [USSR] [II]

Malkova, Zoya. "What I Think the American Schools Should Teach About the Soviet Union," *Teachers College Journal,* Vol. 35, No. 2 (December, 1963), pp. 104–106. [USSR] [II]

Mani, Korah M. "Visitors from Other Lands View Our Schools and the Convention," *Nation's Schools,* Vol. 53, No. 3 (March, 1954), pp. 71–78. [India] [IV]

Mann, Kathleen. "The Backgrounds of English and American Education Today," *Elementary School Journal,* Vol. 48, No. 8 (April, 1948), pp. 405–412. [Britain] [I]

Manning, E. A. "As Others See Us," *The School Review,* Vol. 35, No. 10 (December, 1927), pp. 726–727. [IV]

Manny, Frank A. "American Schools As Seen by Belgian Educator," *Elementary School Teacher,* Vol. IX, No. 6 (February, 1909), pp. 322–326. [I]

Mansuro, N. S. "Social Psychology and Pedagogical Science," *Soviet Education,* [trans] Vol. 8, No. 4 (February, 1966), pp. 33–52. [USSR] [IV]

Marchan, Maximiliano Salas. "American Equipment Is an Example and Inspiration," *School Life,* Vol. 9, No. 7 (March, 1924), p. 166. [Chile] [IV]

Marinosci, Ibis Edith. "My Year in the United States," *Ohio Schools,* Vol. 38, No. 7 (October, 1960), pp. 10–11. [Argentina] [II]

Mark, Harry Thiselton. "The American and the English Public Elementary School," *Educational Review,* Vol. 23 (March, 1902), pp. 250–263. [Britain] [IV]

Mark, Harry Thiselton. "Education and Industry in the United States," *Board of Education, Special Reports on Educational Subjects* in *Education in the United States of America, Part II.* Vol. XI. London: H.M.S.O., 1902. [Britain] [IV]

Mark, Harry Thiselton. *Individuality and the Moral Aim in American Education.* London and New York: Longmans, Green and Company, 1901. 298. pp. [Britain] [IV]

Mark, Harry Thiselton. *Modern Views on Education.* Baltimore: Warwick and York, Inc., 1914. 264 pp. [Britain] [IV]

Mark, H. Thiselton. "Moral Education in American Schools; with Special Reference to the Formation of Character and to Instruction in the Duties of Citizenship," *Board of Education, Special Reports on Educational Subjects* in *Education in the United States of America, Part I.* Vol. X. London: H.M.S.O., 1902. [Britain] [IV]

Markushevich, Aleksei I. "Through Soviet Eyes," *School Life,* Vol. 41, No. 4 (January-February, 1959), pp. 8–10; 23. [USSR] [II]

Marousky, W. C. "Why is public education in the United States not as successful as it is in Germany," *Educational Review,* Vol. 33 (March, 1907), pp. 217–244. [Germany] [IV]

Marshall, Enrique. "A Chilean Looks at American Education," *The Texas Outlook,* Vol. 31, No. 9 (September, 1967), p. 19. [See also *Minnesota Journal of Education,* Vol. 23, No. 3 (November, 1967), p. 127, and *Kentucky School Journal,* Vol. XXVI, No. 5 (January, 1968), pp. 7–8.] [Chile] [IV]

Martin, G. Currie. "International Activities," Chapter XIII in *The Adult School Movement: It's Origin and Development.* London: National Adult School Union, 1924, pp. 319–341. [Britain] [III]

Martin, Monica E. "Not Enough Indians," *Times Educational Supplement* (London), No. 2444 (March 23, 1962), p. 552. [Britain] [I]

Mason, Henry. "Foreign Interest in American Schools," *Education,* Vol. 20 (September, 1899–1900), pp. 441–446. [IV]

Mason, Peter. "American School Counsellor: Teacher's Role Usurped?" *Times Educational Supplement* (London), No. 2598 (March 5, 1965), p. 673. [Britain] [II]

Matsumine, Ryuzo. "Impression from Abroad," *NEA Journal,* Vol. 39, No. 1 (May, 1950), p. 351. [Japan] [IV]

Mauersberger, Ernst. *Die amerikanische Bildungsleiter.* Dortmund: W. Cruewell, 1928. [Germany] [IV]

Maurois, Andre. "A Frenchman Appraises U.S. Schools," *Saturday Review,* Vol. 44, Part 1 (April 15, 1961), pp. 54–55; 75. [France] [II]

Mboya, Tom. "African Higher Education: A Challenge to America," *The Atlantic Monthly,* Vol. 208, No. 1 (July, 1961), pp. 23–26. [Kenya] [III]

Meador, Peter E. "Two Months in America: An Educational Survey," *Times Educational Supplement* (London), No. 928 (February 11, 1933), p. 44. [Britain] [IV]

Medley, J. D. G. "An Australian's View of American Education," *Elementary School Journal,* Vol. 44 (February, 1944), p. 318. [Australia] [IV]

Meiring, J. Murray. "The American High School," *Carnegie Visitor's Reports Nos. 1–8* (Pretoria, South Africa), No. 4 (1930), pp. 1–53. [South Africa] [II]

Melby, John F. and Elinor K. Wolf. *Looking Glass for Americans: A Study of the Foreign Students at the University of Pennsylvania.* Philadelphia: National Council on Asian Affairs, 1961. [III]

Mesick, Jane Louise. *The English Traveler in America, 1785–1835.* New York: Columbia University Press, 1922. 370 pp. [IV]

Métraux, Guy S. *Exchange of Persons: The Evolution of Cross-Cultural Education.* Pamphlet No. 9. New York: Social Science Research Council, 1952. 53 pp. [IV]

Michigan State University. *Greek Fulbright Research Project: A Study in Cross-Cultural Education.* East Lansing: Michigan State University, June, 1956. 143 pp. [IV]

Micocci, Antonio. "Teachers from Cuba—A Cultural Import," *NEA Journal,* Vol. 51 (December, 1962), pp. 38–39. [Cuba] [IV]

Miller, Ezechiel H. *L'éducation des Noirs aux États-Unis d' Amérique.* Dijon: Bernigaud & Privat, 1937. [France]

Miller, Helen Rand. "Interpreting American Education," *School and Society* Vol. 66, No. 1705 (August 30, 1947), pp. 160–161. [IV]

Millgate, Michael. "Englishman on Campus," *IIE News Bulletin,* Vol. 35, No. 6 (February, 1960), pp. 23–27. [Britain] [III]

Minssen, Fredrich. "What's Good About American Education: A German Educator's View," *Teachers College Journal,* Vol. 36, No. 1 (October, 1964), pp. 52–54. [Germany] [II]

Mitchell, George H. "Impressions from Abroad," *NEA Journal,* Vol. 39, No. 1 (May, 1950), p. 351. [New Zealand] [II]

Mitsuhashi, Setsuko. "Conceptions and Images of the Physical World: A Comparison of Japanese and American Pupils," *Comparative Education Review,* Vol. VI, No. 2 (October, 1962), pp. 142–147. [Japan] [II]

Mohrt, Michel. "Time Lag in American Schools," *Atlas,* Vol. 2, No. 5 (November, 1961), pp. 380–381. (Translated from *Nouvelles Litteraires,* February 23, 1961.) [France] [II]

Mohsenin, Nuri. "The 'Lost' Student: Cause and Cure," *Overseas,* Vol. II, No. 3 (November, 1962), pp. 2–6. [Iran] [III]

Monaghan, Frank. *French Travellers in the United States, 1765–1932.* New York: Antiquarian Press, Limited, 1961. [First published by the New York Public Library, 1933]. [IV]

Moore, Roy. "Impressions of An American University," *Times Educational Supplement* (London), No 2450 (May 4, 1962), pp. 878–879. [Britain] [II]

Morize, Andre. "French and American Education," *School and Society,* Vol. 15, No. 382 (April, 1922), p. 444. [France] [II]

Morris, Helen L. "A Kiwi in a Kentucky Classroom," *Kentucky School Journal,* Vol. 42, No. 8 (April, 1964), pp. 34, 42–43. [New Zealand] [II]

Morris, Richard T. "National Status and Attitudes of Foreign Students," *Journal of Social Issues,* Vol. XII, No. 1 (1956), p. 20. [III]

Morris, Richard T. *The Two-Way Mirror: National Status in Foreign Students' Adjustment.* Minneapolis: University of Minnesota Press, 1960. [IV]

504

Morris, Robert W. "Education in the United States," *Educational Record,* Vol. XLIII (October, 1962), pp. 272–279. [Britain] [II]

Mosley, Alfred. "A British View of American Schools," *The World's Work,* Vol. 7, No. 4 (February, 1904), pp. 4484–4487. [Britain] [IV]

Mosse, Hilde L. "Reading Disorders in the United States," *The Reading Teacher,* Vol. XVI, No. 2 (November, 1962), pp. 90–94. [Germany] [I]

Moyle, Nicholas P. "Registers a Protest," *New York State Education,* Vol. 50, No. 9 (June, 1963), p. 15. [Britain] [II]

Muir, Ramsay. *America the Golden: An Englishman's Notes and Comparisons.* London: Williams and Norgate, Ltd., 1927. 141. pp. [Britain] [IV]

Mukherjee, L. "Education in the United States of America," Chapter 4 in *Comparative Education for Students and Educationists.* Allahabad, India: Kitab Mahal, 1959, pp. 79–125. [India] [IV]

Mukherjee, Prithwindra. "Music East and West," *Indo-Asian Culture,* (New Delhi), Vol. XIV, No. 1. (January, 1965), pp. 12–20. [India] [IV]

Munsterberg, Hugo. *American Traits.* New York: Houghton, Mifflin and Company, 1901. [Germany] [IV]

Munsterberg, Hugo. *Die Amerikaner. (The Americans* translated by E. B. Holt. New York: McClure, Philips and Company, 1905.) [Germany] [IV]

Munsterberg, Hugo. "School Reform," *The Atlantic Monthly,* Vol. 85, No. 511 (May, 1900), pp. 656–669. [Germany] [II]

Murray, Gilbert. "American Schools," *Journal of Education* (London), Vol. 44, No. 516 (July, 1912), pp. 497–498. [Britain] [III]

Muthesius, D. R. "German Views of American Education with Particular References to Industrial Development," *U.S. Bureau of Education Bulletin.* Series No. 316, No. 2. Washington, D.C.: U.S. Government Printing Office, 1906, p. 26. [Germany] [II]

Myrdal, Gunnar. "The Negro School," Chapter 41 in *An American Dilemma: The Negro Problem and Modern Democracy.* New York: Harper and Row, 1944, and The McGraw-Hill Book Company, 1964, pp. 879–907. [Sweden] [IV]

MacDonald, John. "The Social Ideas of Canadian Educators," *Comparative Education Review,* Vol. IX, No. 7 (February, 1965), pp. 38–45. [Canada] [IV]

MacGregor, Gregor. "A Comparison of the Educational Achievement of Scottish and American Pupils," *The Elementary School Journal,* Vol. 35, No. 8 (April, 1935), pp. 564–568. [Britain] [I]

Maclean, Magnus. "Report of Mr, Maclean," *Reports of the Mosely Educational Commission to the United States of America.* London: Co-operative Printing Society Limited, 1904, pp. 235–245. [Britain] [II]

MacNaughton, Donald A. "Utilitarian Secondary Education," *Contemporary Review*, Vol. LXXXVII (January, 1905), pp. 51–64. [Britain] [II]

MacRae, Helen and Donald G. "American Schools Surprised Us," *NEA Journal*, Vol. 48, No. 8 (November, 1959), pp. 59–60. [Britain] [I]

MacVicar, Winifred. "A British Teacher Views the American School," *National Association of Secondary School Principals*, Vol. 33, No. 162 (April, 1949), pp. 109–114. [Britain] [II]

McAulay, J. D. "U.S. Prestige in Australia, New Zealand and Other Countries," *Peabody Journal of Education*, Vol. 37, No. 4 (January, 1961), pp. 220–224. [Australia] [IV]

McCleary, G. F. "The Infant Welfare Movement in America," Chapter IV in *The Early History of the Infant Welfare Movement*. London: H. K. Lewis and Co., Ltd., 1933, pp. 53–69. [Britain] [I]

McMillan, James and Bernard Harris. *The American Takeover of Britain*. New York: Hart Publishing Company, Inc., 1968. 253 pp. [Britain] [IV]

McRae, C. R. *An Australian Looks at American Schools*. Melbourne, Australia: Melbourne University Press, Australian Council for Educational Research, Series No. 20, 1933, [Australia] [I]

Nation's Schools. "An Interview with Seven Journalists from Northern Europe," Vol. 52, No. 3 (September, 1953), pp. 43–47. [IV]

Nation's Schools, "As Visiting Statemen See Our Schools," Vol. 67, No. 6 (June, 1961), pp. 51–55. [IV]

Naylor, Phyllis. "Seen Through Yorkshire Eyes," *Virginia Journal of Education*, Vol. 44, No. 8 (April, 1951), pp. 24–25, 34. [Britain] [I]

Neidle, C. S. *The New Americans*. New York: Twayne Publishers, Inc., 1967. 342 pp. [IV]

Nemes, Marthe M. "A Hungarian Progressive School," *Progressive Education*, Vol. 3, No. 3 (July, August, September, 1926), pp. 260–263. [Hungary] [IV]

Nencioni, Giovanni. "An Italian Educator Looks at our Schools," *High Points*, Vol. 32, No. 1 (January, 1950), pp. 5–8. [Italy] [II]

Neuhaus, Ilse. "A German Teacher's Estimate of a New York High School," *High Points*, Vol. 35, No. 9 (November, 1953), pp. 5–7. [Germany] [II]

Neumann, Franz L. "The Social Sciences," in *The Cultural Migration: The European Scholar in America*. Philadelphia: University of Pennsylvania Press, 1953, pp. 4–26. [Germany] [III]

Neumann, Gerhard and Gerhard Schellenberg (editors). *Begegnung mit dem Erziehungswesen der U.S.A.* Munich: Max Hueber, 1961. [Germany] [IV]

Nevins, Allan. *America Through British Eyes*. New York: Oxford University Press, 1948. 530 pp. [IV]

Nevins, Allan. *American Social History as Recorded by British Travellers*.

New York: H. Holt and Company, 1923. 577 pp. See also. *America Through British Eyes*, 1948. [IV]

New Era (London). "Education in the U.S.A.," Vol. 24 (1943), pp. 92–93. [IV]

New York-Times. "Foreign Students End a Year in U.S.," Vol. 69 (August 5, 1962), p. 3. [IV]

New York Times. "Germans on Tour Hail U.S. Schools," Vol. 13 (June 8, 1962), p. 2. [IV]

New York Times. "Japanese Teachers Laud System Here," Vol. 12 (October 21, 1960), p. 6. [VI]

Nicholas, Herbert George. "The Ideals of American Education," *Times Educational Supplement* (London), Part I, No. 1375 (September 6, 1941), p. 420; Part II, No. 1377 (September 20, 1941), p. 444. [Britain] [IV]

Nichols, A. E. "Impressions of American Education," *National Association of Secondary School Principals Bulletin* Vol. XIX, No. 12 (December, 1935), pp. 2–26. [Britain] [II]

Nicolson, Harold. "Marginal Comment," *Spectator*, Vol. 167, No. 5907 (September 12, 1941), p. 258. [Britain] [IV]

Nicolson, Harold. "Marginal Comment," *Spectator*, Vol. 167, No. 5922 (December 26, 1941), p. 597. [Britain] [IV]

Nisbet, John D. "American Education," *The Scottish Educational Journal* (Edinburgh). Vol. 47, No. 50 (December 11, 1964), pp. 1141–1142. [Britain] [III]

Nitobe, Inazo (Ota). *The Japanese Nation: Its Land, Its People, and Its Life, with Special Consideration to Its Relations with the United States.* New York and London: G. P. Putnam's Sons, 1912. 334 pp. [Japan] [IV]

Noble, Ben. "A Mathematician, U.S.-Bound," *Universities Quarterly* (London), Vol. XIX, No. 1 (December, 1964), pp. 5–22. [Britain] [III]

Norwood, Cyril. *The English Tradition of Education.* London: John Murray, 1929. 340 pp. [Britain] [IV]

Novrup, Johannes. "A Dane Looks at American Education," *Clearing House*, Vol. 9, No. 8 (April, 1935), pp. 476–479. [Denmark] [IV]

Nowlin, Mabel. "What American Education is Doing for Me," *Educational Review* (Shanghai), China Christian Educational Association, Vol. 21, No. 3 (July, 1929), pp. 266–268. [China] [I]

Nuechter, Friedrich. "Klasseneinteilung und Vorruecksysteme in Amerika," *Die Deutsche Schule*, Vol. XIX (1915), p. 91ff. [Germany] [II]

Nunn, Percy. "American and English Education," *School and Society*, Vol. 23, No. 576 (January 9, 1926), p. 37. [Britain] [IV]

Ohlinger, Gustavus. *The German Conspiracy in American Education.* New York: George H. Doran Company, 1919. 113 pp. [IV]

Oliver, Richard Alexander Cavaye. "English Plans and American Practice," *Times Educational Supplement* (London), Part I, No. 1452 (February

27, 1943), p. 100; Part II, No. 1453 (March 6, 1943), p. 113. [Britain] [IV]

Ono, Takaharu. "Impressions of American Business Education," *American Business Education,* Vol. XXI, No. 2 (December, 1955), pp. 110–113. [Japan] [II]

O'Rafferty, Terrence. "Some Impressions of Education in the U.S.A.," *The High School Journal,* Vol. 45, No. 3 (December, 1961), pp. 98–118. [Ireland] [II]

Osburn, Worth James. *Foreign Criticism of American Education.* U.S. Bureau of Education Bulletin, 1921, No. 8. Washington, D.C.: U.S. Government Printing Office, 1922. 158 pp. [IV]

Senior Scholastic. "Ourselves As Others See Us," Vol. 64, No. 10 (April 14, 1954), pp. 7–8. [IV]

Owen, John Elias. "How Delinquent are Our Juveniles," *Educational Forum,* Vol. XXI, No. 2, Part 1 (January, 1957), pp. 203–206. [Britain] [IV]

Pabst, Alwin. "Amerikanische Schulen, aus den Volksschulen in Boston," *Die Deutsche Schule,* Vol. XI (1907), p. 301ff. [Germany] [II]

Pabst, Alwin. "Amerikanische Schulen, das Pratt Institute in Brooklyn," *Die Deutsche Schule,* Vol. XI (1907), p. 634ff. [Germany] [II]

Pabst, Alwin. "Beobachtungen und Bemerkungen ueber die Koeducation in Amerikanischen Schulen," *Die Deutsche Schule,* Vol. XII (1908), p. 15ff. [Germany] [II]

Pan, Y. C. "The American Junior College," *Malaysian Journal of Education,* Vol. 4, No. 1 (June, 1967), pp. 74–80. [Malaysia] [II]

Panholzer, Herbert. "A Foreign Exchange Teacher Looks at Each Pupil's International Responsibility," *Journal of Secondary Education,* Vol. 37, No. 3 (March, 1962), pp. 175–178. [Austria] [II]

Panneerselvan, Sri A. "Teachers from Abroad Take a Look at America," *American Education,* Vol. 2 (September, 1966), pp. 14–19. [India] [IV]

Panofsky, Erwin. "The History of Art," in *The Cultural Migration: The European Scholar in America.* Philadelphia: University of Pennsylvania Press, 1953, pp. 82–111. [Germany] [III]

Papillon, T. L. "Report of the Rev. T. L. Papillon," *Reports of the Mosely Educational Commission to the United States of America.* London: Co-operative Printing Society Limited, 1904, pp. 246–255. [Britain] [IV]

Park, No-Yong. "A Chinese View of American Education," *School and Society,* Vol. 37, No. 942 (January 14, 1933), pp. 63–65. [China] [IV]

Parker, Henry T. *The Background of American Education as an Australian Sees It.* Melbourne, Australia: Melbourne University Press, 1935. 48 pp. [Australia] [IV]

Part, Antony. "An Englishman Looks at American Public Schools—And Asks Some 'Critical Questions'," *The School Executive,* Vol. 71 (October, 1951), pp. 69–70. [Britain] [I]

Pasch, Dorothy with Katherine Edbrooke. "English Exchange Teacher Speaks," *Ohio Schools*, Vol. 15 (1937), p. 314. [III]

Paterson, W. J., *et al.* "Some Observations on American Education," *Education News* (Sydney, Australia), Vol. IX, No. 2 (April, 1963), pp. 3–8. [Australia] [II]

Paton, John Lewis. "Education as a Link Between Great Britain and America," *Journal of Education* (London), Vol. 73, No. 6 (June 2, 1941), pp. 227–228. [Britain] [IV]

Paton, John Lewis. "The Public School Idea in America," *Spectator*, Vol. 152, No. 5519 (April 6, 1934), pp. 533–534. [Britain] [IV]

Percy, Eustace. "Education in the Doldrums," *Spectator*, Vol. 150, No. 5454 (January 6, 1933), pp. 7–8. [Britain] [IV]

Perrino, Pedro-Fidel. "Foreign Teens View the U.S.," *Senior Scholastic*, Vol. 82, No. 14 (May 8, 1963), pp. 14–15. [Spain] [II]

Peterson, Alexander Duncan Campbell. *A Hundred Years of Education*. London: Duckworth, 1952. 272 pp. (Second Edition, New York: The Macmillan Company, 1960.) [Britain] [IV]

Peterson, H. Munkholm. "What I Saw in American Schools," *Wisconsin Journal of Education*, Vol. 84, No. 1 (September, 1951), pp. 6–7. [Denmark] [II]

Peyre, Henri Maurice. "A French Professor's Remarks on American Education," *Quality and Quantity in American Education*, 46th Annual Schoolmen's Week Proceedings (edited by Frederick C. Gruber), Vol. XLVI. Philadelphia: University of Pennsylvania Press, 1958, pp. 55–61. [France] [IV]

Peyre, Henri Maurice. "A Frenchman's View of American Education," *Man, Science, Learning, and Education* (edited by S. W. Higginbotham). Houston, Texas: William Marsh Rice University, 1963, pp. 185–200. [France] [IV]

Peyre, Henri Maurice. "French and American Education," *IIE News Bulletin,* Vol. 26, No. 6 (March, 1951), pp. 12–14. [France] [III]

Peyre, Henri Maurice. "The Study of Literature," in *The Cultural Migration: The European Scholar in America*. Philadelphia: University of Pennsylvania Press, 1953, pp. 27–81. [France] [III]

Picavet, Francois. "Relations intellectuelles et universitaries entre la France et les États-Unis de l'Amerique du nord," *Revue Internationale de l'Enseignement*, Vol. LXII, No. 11 (November 15, 1911), pp. 449–452. [France] [III]

Pickles, J. E., *et al. Education in Relation to Industry: A Report on Technical, Trade, Applied Art, Manual Training, Domestic, Commercial, and Public Schools in Canada and the United States*. Leeds, England: E. J. Arnold & Son, Ltd., c 1911. 187 pp. [Britain] [II]

Platt, William J. "Distinction in American Education," *Teachers College Journal*, Vol. 38 (January, 1966), pp. 38–42. [Britain] [IV]

Polanyi, Karl. "Education for Politics—in England and the United States," *School and Society*, Vol. 45, No. 1161 (March 27, 1937), pp. 447–450.

Pollachek, Walter. "German Schools: A Pupil Who has Studied in America and German Schools Notes Some Differences," *Clearing House*, Vol. 19, No. 3 (November, 1944), pp. 182–183. [Germany] [II]

Ponsonby, Montague Vernon. *The Preposterous Yankee*. London: Limpus, Baker & Company, 1903. 281 pp. [IV]

Potier, André. *Un Français a L'École Américaine*. Paris: Amiot, Dumont, 1951.[France] [IV]

Prantl, Rudolf. "Dewey als Paedagog," *Vierteljahresschrift fuer wissenschaftliche Paedagogik*, Vol. I (1925). [Germany] [II]

Presdome, Carlo. "Visitors from Other Lands View Our Schools and the Convention," *Nation's Schools*, Vol. 53 (March, 1954), pp. 71–78. [Italy] [IV]

Price, Mary R. "Visit to America," *Journal of Education* (London), Vol. 81, No. 958 (May, 1949), pp. 260, 262. [Britain] [III]

Priestley, Kenneth E. "The Layman and Education in the U.S.A.," *Journal of Education* (London), Vol. 86, No. 1015 (February, 1954), pp. 68–70. [Britain] [II]

Priestley, Kenneth E. "An Englishman's View of School Administration, U.S.A.," *Nation's Schools*, Vol. 54, No. 6 (December, 1954), pp. 47–49. [Britain] [II]

Priestley, John Boynton. *Rain Upon Godshill*. New York: Harper and Brothers, 1939. 308 pp. [Britain] [IV]

Priestley, John Boynton. *Midnight on the Desert*. New York: Harper and Brothers, 1937. 310 pp. [Britain] [IV]

Prokofiev, Mikhail. "Soviet Views," *Scholastic*, Vol. 76, No. 9 (April 6, 1960), pp. 1–2; 6 [USSR] [IV]

Pudlowski, Zalmen with Alice Kalousdian. "Education Through the Eyes of a New American," *High Points*, Vol. 28 (January, 1946), pp. 57–59. [Poland] [IV]

Putt, S. Gorley (editor). *Cousins and Strangers: Comments on America By Commonwealth Fund Fellows from Britain, 1946–1952*. Cambridge, Massachusetts: Harvard University Press, 1956. 222 pp. [III]

Quadt, Max. "Erziehung der Massen in den Vereinigten Staaten," *Monatschrift fuer Hoehere Schulen*, Vol. XXVII (1929), p. 544ff. [Germany] [IV]

Qvamme, Borre. "Education in Norway and the United States: A Comparison," *The American-Scandinavian Review*, Vol. 19, No. 10 (1931), pp. 615–616. [Norway] [II]

Rarditsa, Bogdan. "American v.s. European Education," *The Texas Outlook*, Vol. 40, No. 4 (April, 1956), p. 9. [IV]

Rangiscuta, Pragao, Sawasdi Singhaphong, and Aree Walanakul. "Visitors From Other Lands View Our Schools and the Convention," *Nation's*

Schools, Vol. 53, No. 3 (March, 1954), pp. 71–78. [Thailand] [IV]

Rathbone, Herbert R. "Report of Mr. Herbert R. Rathbone," *Reports of the Mosely Educational Commission to the United States of America.* London: Co-operative Printing Society Limited, 1904, pp. 256–273. [Britain] [I]

Ratcliffe, S. K. "The Spectacle of America," *Contemporary Review,* Vol. CXXXIV (July–December, 1928), pp. 12–19. [Britain] [IV]

Rathore, Naeem Gul. *The Pakistan Student: His Desire to Study in and Preconceptions of the U.S., His Problems and Evaluation of His Experience in the U.S. and Upon Return to Pakistan.* New York: American Friends of the Middle East, 1957. [Pakistan] [III]

Ravenhill, Alice. "Educational Tendencies in the United States," *Journal of Education* (London), Vol. 24, No. 397 (August, 1902), pp. 508–510. [Britain] [IV]

Ravenhill, Alice. "School Training for the Home Duties of Women," *The Teaching of "Domestic Science" Board of Education, Special Reports on Educational Subjects* in *Education in the United States of America,* Part I. Vol. XV. London: H.M.S.O., 1905. [Britain] [IV]

Ravenhill, Alice. "Some Points of Educational Interest in the Schools of the United States," *Board of Education, Special Reports on Educational Subjects* in *Education in the United States of America,* Part I. Vol. X. London: H.M.S.O., 1902. [Britain] [IV]

Ravi-Booth, Vincent. "A New College for Women," *Progressive Education,* Vol. 2, No. 3 (July, August, September, 1925), pp. 138–145. [Italy] [III]

Raymont, T. "An English View of American Education," *Journal of Education and School World* (London). Reprinted in *The School Review,* Vol. 36 (December, 1928), pp. 731–732. [Britain] [IV]

Raymont, T. "A Scottish Estimate of American Education," *Journal of Education* (London), Vol. 65, No. 773 (December, 1933), pp. 763–764. [Britain] [IV]

Raymont, T. "Aspects of American Education," *Journal of Education* (London), Vol. 70 (1938), p. 710. [Britain] [IV]

Reed, Edward Bliss (editor). *The Commonwealth Fund Fellows and Their Impressions of America.* New York: The Commonwealth Fund, 1932. 143 pp. [III]

Rees, T. J. "What I Saw in the Schools of United States," *The High School Teacher,* Vol. VII, No. 8 (October, 1931), pp. 283; 316–317. [Britain] [II]

Reeves, Marjorie. "Liberal Arts Colleges: Part I—An American Paradox," *Times Educational Supplement* (London), No. 2386 (February 10, 1961), p. 251. [Britain] [III]

Reeves, Marjorie. "Liberal Arts Colleges: Part II—American Experience Relevant," *Times Educational Supplement* (London), No. 2387 (February 17, 1961), p. 302. [Britain] [III]

Reichel, H. R. "Report of Professor H. R. Reichel," *Reports of the Mosely Educational Commission to the United States of America*. London: Co-operative Printing Society Limited, 1904, pp. 274–309. [Britain] [III]

Reimers, Hans. "As Visiting Statesmen See Our Schools," *Nation's Schools*, Vol. 67, No. 6 (June, 1961), pp. 51–55. [Germany] [II]

Rendell, Stanley. "Secondary Education in England and America," *Ohio Schools*, Vols. 13–14, No. 5 (May, 1936), pp. 167, 199. [Britain] [II]

Retsch, Traudl. "International Looking Glass: My First American Football," *IIE News Bulletin*, Vol. 29, No. 4 (January, 1954), pp. 47–48. [Germany] [II]

Rhys, John. "Report of Professor Rhys," *Reports of the Mosely Educational Commission to the United States of America*. London: Co-operative Printing Society Limited, 1904, pp. 310–329. [Britain] [IV]

Richmond, W. Kenneth. *Education in the U.S.A.: A Comparative Study*. New York: Philosophical Library, Inc., 1956. 227 pp. [Britain] [IV]

Richmond, W. Kenneth. "Hazards in Segregating the Able Few," *Crucial Issues in Education*. New York: Holt, Rinehart and Winston, 1959, pp. 320–322. [Britain] [II]

Ripper, W. "Report of Mr. W. Ripper," *Report of the Mosely Educational Commission to the United States of America*. London: Co-operative Printing Society Limited, 1904, pp. 330–343. [Britain] [III]

Riske, Marcus. "As Another Sees Us," *The Mathematics Teacher*, Vol. 54, No. 1 (1961), pp. 40–43. [New Zealand] [II]

Robinson, Harry Perry. *The Twentieth Century American*. New York: G. P. Putnam's Sons, 1908. 463 pp. [Britain] [IV]

Robson, Ernest Smith Awmack. *Report of a Visit to American Educational Institutions*. London: Sherratt and Hughes, 1905. 166 pp. [Britain] [II]

Roehrs, Hermann. "Die amerikanische Schule in der gegenwaertigen Diskussion," *Zeitschrift fuer Paedagogik*, Vol. V (1959), p. 274ff. [Germany] [IV]

Rogge, Heinz. "Das amerikanische Erziehungs-und Bildungswesen," *Die Sammlung*, Vol. XIII (1958), p. 98ff. [Germany] [IV]

Rosen, Seymour M. "Soviet Interpretation of U.S. Higher Education," *Higher Education*, Vol. XVIII, No. 3 (December, 1961), pp. 8–11. [III]

Rosowsky, Andre. "Beyond the Far Horizon," *Phi Delta Kappan*, Vol. 35 (November, 1953), pp. 121–122. [France] [IV]

Roth, Heinrich. "Was Kann die amerikanische Paedagogik zur Loesung unserer Erziehungsprobleme beitragen," *Bildung und Erziehung*, Vol. IV (1951), p. 27ff. [Germany] [IV]

Rowley, Charles. "Report of Mr. Charles Rowley," *Reports of the Mosely*

Educational Commission to the United States of America. London: Co-operative Printing Society Limited, 1904, pp. 344–350. [Britain] [III]

Rudy, Willis. "Evaluations of American Education by Foreigners," *School and Society,* Vol. 93, No. 2255 (February 6, 1965), pp. 93–104. See also Chapter 8 in *Schools in an Age of Mass Culture: An Exploration of Selected Themes on the History of Twentieth Century American Education,* Englewood Cliffs, New Jersey: Prentice-Hall, Inc., 1965, pp. 284–308. [IV]

Russell, Bertrand. "News and Comments," *Progressive Education,* Vol. 1, No. 2 (July, August, September, 1924), pp. 97–98. [Britain] [II]

Rust, Val Dean. *German Interest in Foreign Education Since World War I.* University of Michigan Comparative Education Dissertation, Series No. 13. Ann Arbor: School of Education, University of Michigan, 1968. 251 pp. [IV]

Ruttmann, W. J. "Amerikanische Kindervereine und Kinderlesehallen," *Die Deutsche Schule,* Vol. XIV (1910), p. 696ff. [Germany] [I]

Sadler, Michael Ernest. "A Contrast Between German and American Ideals in Education," *Board of Education, Special Reports on Educational Subjects* in *Education in the United States of America, Part II.* Vol. XI. London: H.M.S.O., 1902. [Britain] [IV]

Sadler, Michael Ernest. "The Education of the Coloured Race," *Board of Education, Special Reports on Educational Subjects* in *Education in the United States of America, Part II.* Vol. XI. London: H.M.S.O., 1902. [Britain] [IV]

Sadler, Michael Ernest. "The Ferment in Education on the Continent and in America," *Proceedings of the British Academy, 1903–1904.* London: Oxford University Press, 1904, pp. 81–94. [Britain] [IV]

Sadler, Michael Ernest. *Outlook in Secondary Education.* New York: Bureau of Publications, Teachers College, Columbia University, 1930, p. 56. [Britain] [II]

Sadler, Michael Ernest. "Impressions of American Education," *Educational Review,* Vol. 25, No. 3 (March, 1903), pp. 217–231. [Britain] [IV]

Sadler, Michael Ernest (editor). *Moral Instruction and Training in Schools: Report of an International Inquiry.* Vol. II. New York & London: Longmans, Green, and Company, 1910. [Britain] [IV]

Sadler, Michael Ernest. "Education for Life and Duty," *International Review of Missions,* Vol. 10 (1921), pp. 449–466. [Britain] [IV]

Sadler, Michael Ernest. "The School in Some of its Relations to Social Organization and to National Life," *Educational Review,* Vol. 29, No. 2 (April, 1905), pp. 338–342. [Britain] [IV]

Sadler, Michael Ernest (editor). *Continuation Schools in England & Elsewhere: Their Place in the Educational System of an Industrial and Commercial State.* Manchester: Manchester University Press, 1908. [Britain] [IV]

Sadler, Michael Ernest. "The English Ideal of Education and Its Debt to America," in *National Education Association Journal of Proceedings and Addresses* (July 7–11, 1902), pp. 75–83. [Britain] [IV]

Salgaller, Emanuel (editor). "Two Soviet Views of American Education," *Education*, Vol. 85, No. 1 (September, 1964), pp. 42–46. [IV]

Salve, Ujjwala. "Not of Things but the Self," *The Asian Student* (Spring Semester, 1960), p. S–3. [India] [III]

Samonte, Quirico S. "Some Problems of Comparison and the Development of Theoretical Models in Education," *Comparative Education Review,* Vol. VI, No. 3 (February, 1963), pp. 177–181. [Philippines] [II]

Sampaio, Maria S. L. "Comments on American Educational Practices," *The International Teacher Development Program,* No. OE–14118. Washington, D.C.: United States Office of Education, 1964, p. 11. [Brazil] [II]

Sanchez, Luis Alberto. "On Education in Both Americas," *Teachers College Record,* Vol. 65, No. 1 (October, 1963), pp. 1–10. [Peru] [IV]

Sanford, D. S. "The Curriculum of the American Secondary School (High School)," *Board of Education, Special Reports on Educational Subjects* in *Education in the United States of America, Part II.* Vol. XI. London: H.M.S.O., 1902. [Britain] [II]

Sara, Nathir G. "Shared by All Nations," *The Asian Student* (Spring Semester, 1963), p. S–7. [Iraq] [III]

Sargent, John (editor). *Education and Society: Some Studies of Education Systems in Europe and America.* London: Phoenix House, Ltd., 1955. 176 pp. [Britain] [IV]

Sayiadain, K. G. *Education for International Understanding.* Bombay: Hind Kitab, Ltd., 1948, pp. 26–29. [India] [IV]

Scarfe, N. V. "Is American Education Undemocratic?" *School and Society,* Vol. 89, No. 2036 (June 26, 1954), pp. 193–196. [Canada] [IV]

Scarangello, Anthony. *American Education Through Foreign Eyes.* New York: Hobbs Dorman and Company, Inc., 1967. 138 pp. [IV]

Schild, Erling O. "The Foreign Student as Stranger Learning the Norms of the Host Culture," *Journal of Social Issues,* Vol. XVIII, No. 1 (1962), pp. 41–54. [III]

Schafer, Joseph. "Public Schools One Hundred Years Ago As Seen Through Foreign Eyes," *Wisconsin Magazine of History,* Vol. 22 (June, 1936), pp. 435–459. [IV]

Schlee, E. (Excerpts) "From Report of Dr. E. Schlee of the Realgymnasium of Altona, Prussia, delegate to the Educational Congress at Chicago," Chapter XXVIII in *Report of the Commissioner of Education 1900–1901,* Vol. II. Washington, D.C.: U.S. Government Printing Office, 1902, pp. 1267–1269. [Germany] [II]

Schneider, Friedrich. "Von Geist und Wirklichkeit amerikanischer Paedagogik," *Pharus,* Vol. XX (1929), p. 241ff. [Germany] [IV]

School Life. "Noted British Educator Visits America," Vol. 15, No. 9 (May, 1930), pp. 170–171. [IV]

School Life. "Through Soviet Eyes," Vol. 41, No. 4 (January-February, 1959), pp. 8–10; 23. [USSR] [IV]

The School Review. "Educational News and Editorial Comment: An English View of American Education in the Depression," Vol. 43, No. 9 (November, 1935), pp. 649–652. [IV]

The School Review. "The London 'Times' on 'Low Standards' in our Schools," Vol. 45, No. 3 (March, 1937), pp. 161–164.

The School Review. "Our Schools to English Eyes," Vol. 42, No. 10 (December, 1934), pp. 721–727. [IV]

School and Society. "Quotations: The Standards of American Schools," Vol. 45, No. 1157 (February 27, 1937), pp. 295–297. [IV]

Schreiber, Carl F. "Das amerikanische Schulwesen," *Deutsches Philologen-Blatt,* Vol. XXXVI (1928), p. 621ff. [Germany] [IV]

Schroeteler, Joseph. "Die Loesung der Schulfrage in den Vereinigten Staaten von Nordamerika," *Die Erziehung,* Vol. VI (1930/31), p. 507ff. [Germany] [IV]

Schule und Gegenwart. *Drittes Ergaenzungsheft: das Schulwesen der U.S.A. Bericht einer deutschen Studienkommission,* 1948. [Germany] [IV]

Schultze, Ernst. "Spielplaetze der Schulen in den Vereinigten Staaten," *Die Deutsche Schule,* Vol. XV (1911), p. 431ff. [Germany] [IV]

Schwarz, Sebald. "Amerikanisches," *Die Neue Erziehung,* Vol. XI (1929), p. 125ff. [Germany] [IV]

Schwarz, Sebald. "Amerika und wir," *Die Erziehung,* Vol. V (1930/31), p. 469ff. [Germany] [IV]

Shwarz, Sebald. "Bilder aus amerikanischen Schulen," *Paedagogische Warte,* Vol. XXXVIII (1931), p. 256ff. [Germany] [IV]

Schwarz, Sebald. "Etwas vom math. Anfangsunterricht in Amerika," *Die Neue Erziehung,* Vol. XI (1929), p. 369ff. [Germany] [IV]

Schwarz, Sebald. "Was ist fuer uns in Amerika zu lernen," *Deutsches Philologen-Blatt,* Vol. XXXVI (1928), p. 630ff. [Germany] [IV]

Scott, Franklin D. *The American Experience of Swedish Students: Retrospect and Aftermath.* Minneapolis: University of Minnesota Press, 1956. 129 pp. [III]

Scott, F. W. "Social Studies in America," *Journal of Education* (London), Vol. 83, No. 988 (November, 1951), pp. 597–598. [Britain] [IV]

Selby, Henry A. and Clyde M. Woods. "Foreign Students at a High Pressure University," *Sociology of Education,* Vol. 39, No. 2 (Spring, 1966), pp. 138–154. [III]

Sellitz, Charles. *Attitudes and Social Relations of Foreign Students.* Minneapolis: University of Minnesota Press, 1963. 434 pp. [III]

Senior Scholastic. "Education for What? . . . A Foreign View," Vol. 78, No. 3 (February 15, 1961), pp. 13–14; 20–21. [II]

Senior Scholastic. "Foreign Teens Sound off: What We learned in the United States," (excerpts of an annual forum under auspices of the *New York Herald Tribune,* 1961), Vol. 79, No. 3 (September 27, 1961), pp. 17–18. [II]

Senior Scholastic. "What's Wrong with American High Schools?" Vol. 70, No. 8 (March 22, 1957), pp. 7–10. [II]

Servan-Schreiber, J. J. *The American Challenge.* New York: Atheneum Publishers, 1968. 291 pp. [France] [IV]

Shadwell, Arthur. *Industrial Efficiency.* London: Longmans, Green, and Company, 1906. 488 pp. [Britain] [IV]

Sharp, Percival, *et al. Education in Relation to Industry: A Report on Technical, Trade, Applied Art, Manual Training, Domestic, Commercial, and Public Schools in Canada and the United States.* Leeds, England: E. J. Arnold & Son, Ltd., c. 1911. 187 pp. [Britain] [IV]

Sharples, Hedley. "Diversity in Democracy: Some Abroad Thoughts From at Home," *Teachers College Journal,* Vol. 36, No. 1 (October, 1964), pp. 56–57. [Britain] [IV]

Shenoy, G. Keshay. "An Indian Teacher in America," *NEA Journal,* Vol. 53, No. 9 (December, 1964), p. 50. [India] [II]

Shepheard, A. J. "Report of Mr. A. J. Shepheard," *Reports of the Mosely Educational Commission to the United States of America.* London: Cooperative Printing Society Limited, 1904, pp. 351–359. [Britain] [II]

Sherif, Muzafer. "Some Methodological Remarks to Experimentation in Social Psychology," *International Journal of Opinion and Attitude Research,* Vol. I, No. 2 (1947), pp. 71–93. [Turkey] [IV]

Shih, Hsio-Yen. "A Legacy of Understanding," *The Asian Student* (Spring Semester, 1960), p. S–6. [China] [III]

Shils, Edward. "Observations on the American University," *Universities Quarterly* (London), Vol. XVII, No. 2 (March, 1963), pp. 182–193. [Britain] [III]

Shimkin, Demitri B. "Soviet—U.S. Education," *Science News Letter,* Vol. 75, No. 15 (April 11, 1959), pp. 234–235. [USSR] [II]

Shipley, A. E. *The Voyage of a Vice Chancellor: A Diary of a Tour in America.* Cambridge: Cambridge University Press, 1919. 139 pp. [Britain] [III]

Shuaibi, M. N. "Visitors from Other Lands View Our Schools and the Convention," *Nation's Schools,* Vol. 53, No. 3 (March, 1954), pp. 71–78. [Nigeria] [IV]

Silbermann, Peter A. *Aus New Yorks Hoeheren Schulen.* Berlin: Hans Market, 1927. [Germany] [IV]

Sillars, Malcolm O. (editor). "Shop Talk," *Quarterly Journal of Speech,* Vol. L, No. 1 (February, 1964), pp. 93–95. [III]

Simon, Ernest. "American Universities—Some Facts and Figures," *Times Educational Supplement* (London), Vol. 1943, Part 2 (August 14, 1943), p. 388. [Britain] [III]

Simon, Ernest. "The Provision for University Education and Research in U.S.A.," *Some Comparisons Between Universities.* Oxford: Basil Blackwell, 1944, pp. 6–9. [Britain] [III]

Simpson, Alexander B. "A Chiel's Amang Ye," *New York State Education,* Vol. 52, No. 7 (April, 1965), pp. 24–25. [Britain] [II]

Singhaphong, Sawasde. "Visitors from Other Lands View Our Schools and the Convention: Thailand Visitors Reflect on our Teachers' Work and Worry," Interview by Sylvia Ciernick. *Nation's Schools,* Vol. 53, No. 3 (March, 1954), pp. 71–78. [Thailand] [IV]

Skantz, Per. "Educational Matters, Swedish and American," *School Life,* Vol. 9, No. 3 (November, 1923), pp. 53–54. [Sweden] [IV]

Skantz, Per. "As a Swedish Schoolmaster Views American Education," *School Life,* Vol. 9, No. 8 (April, 1924), pp. 185–186. [Sweden] [IV]

Sleight, Walter Guy. *The Organization and Curricula of Schools.* London: Edward Arnold, 1920. 264 pp. [Britain] [IV]

Smith, Ronald A. "A Britisher Looks at Our Schools," *Wisconsin Journal of Education,* Vol. 88, No. 3 (November, 1955), pp. 11–12. [Britain] [II]

Smuts, Adriaan J. "Trends and Novelties in Modern Education: A South African's Views on European and American Schools," *Internationale Zeitschrift fuer Erziehung,* Vol. VII (1938), pp. 343–345. [South Africa] [IV]

Snow, Charles P. "C. P. Snow on American Education," *School and Society,* Vol. 90, No. 2210 (May, 1962), p. 209. [Britain] [III]

Snow, Charles P. "Higher Education in America," *NEA Journal,* Vol. 53, No. 4 (April, 1964), p. 11. [Britain] [III]

Snow, Charles P. "Soviet System Best," *Times Educational Supplement* (London), No. 2336 (February 26, 1960), p. 384. [Britain] [III]

Snowden, J. "European View of American Education," *Educational Forum,* Vol. XXIII (March, 1959), pp. 243–249.

Son, Leminh. "Foreign Teens View the U.S.," *Senior Scholastic,* Vol. 82 (May 8, 1963), pp. 14–15. [Vietnam] [II]

Spalding, E. N. *The Problem of Rural Schools and Teachers in North America.* Pamphlet No. 13. London: Education Department, H.M.S.O., 1908. [Britain] [I]

Spectator. "America and Ourselves," Vol. 121 (July 6, 1918), pp. 4–5. [IV]

Spectator. "Education and the English-Speaking People," Vol. 138 (January 29, 1927), p. 142. [IV]

Spectator. "Educational Progress," Vol. 169 (September 11, 1942), p. 320. [IV]

Spectator. "Modern Methods in Education," Vol. 140 (June 2, 1928), p. 821. [IV]

Spectator. "The Necessities of Education," Vol. 164 (February 9, 1940), p. 169. [IV]

Spence, Christine. "Hoosick Falls Central School Hosts Visitors From Thailand, Canada, Malaysia," *Journal of School Health,* Vol. 37, No. 6 (June, 1967), pp. 307–308. [II]

Spender, A. Edmund. "Report of Mr. A. Edmund Spender," *Reports of the Mosely Educational Commission to the United States of America.* London: Co-operative Printing Society Limited, 1904, pp. 360–375. [Britain] [III]

Spender, John Alfred. *The America of Today.* London: Ernest Benn Limited, 1928. 269 pp. [Britain] [III]

Stabler, Ernest. "The Current Scene in Teacher Education," Chapter I in *Education of the Secondary School Teacher.* Middletown, Connecticut: Wesleyan University Press, 1962, pp. 3–21. [Canada] [III]

Steitz, Wilhelm. "Education for Life in American High Schools," *The School Review,* Vol. 21, No. 4 (April, 1913), pp. 282–284. [*Germany*] [II]

Sterling, Charles I. Loram. "Influence Abroad of American Education," *School Life,* Vol. 21 (April, 1936), pp. 209–210. [South Africa] [IV]

Stevens, Kate. "Impressions of Education in America," *Journal of Education,* Vol. 66, No. 7 (August 22, 1907), pp. 171–173. [Britain] [II]

Stevens, P. D. "Lessons and Warnings: What Can We Learn from America?" *Modern Languages,* Vol. XLVII, No. 1 (March, 1966), pp. 25–35. [Britain] [II]

Stewart, Jean. "English Schools Are Different," *Wisconsin Journal of Education,* Vol. 79, No. 9 (May, 1947), pp. 451–452. [Britain] [IV]

Strachan, James. *New Zealand Observer.* New York: Columbia University Press, 1940. [New Zealand] [II]

Strachan, James. "Vocational Training in American High Schools," *Times Educational Supplement* (London), No. 1395 (January 24, 1942), p. 40. [New Zealand] [II]

Strachey, J. St. Loe. *American Soundings.* New York: D. Appleton and Company, 1926. 256 pp. [Britain] [III]

Strecher, Reinhard. "German on American Schools," *The Living Age,* Vol. CCCXVII, No. 4118 (June 9, 1923), pp. 559–560. [Germany] [I]

Strezikozin, V. and I. K. Ekgolm with E. Salgaller. "Why Does Ivan Know More than Johnny?" *Soviet Education* [trans], Vol. 5, No. 2 (December, 1962), pp. 59–63. [USSR] [I]

Tanner, M. E. "Education in the American Dependencies," *Board of Educa-*

tion, Special Reports on Educational Subjects in *Education in the United States of America, Part II.* Vol. XI. London: H.M.S.O., 1902. [Britain] [IV]

Tanner, M.E. "The Holiday Course for Cuban Teachers at Harvard," *Board of Education, Special Reports on Educational Subjects* in *Education in the United States of America, Part II.* Vol. XI. London: H.M.S.O., 1902. [Britain] [III]

Taskiran. "As Turks See Us," *Scholastic,* Vol. 5, No. 51 (September 24, 1952), p. 215. [Turkey] [IV]

Tate, Frank. "Introduction," *Educational Observations and Reflections* (edited by Kenneth S. Cunningham). Melbourne, Australia: Melbourne University Press, 1934, pp. v–x. [Australia] [IV]

Tate, Frank. *Preliminary Report of the Director of Education.* Melbourne, Australia: Education Department of Victoria, 1908. [Australia] [IV]

Taura, Takeo, *et al.* "A Japanese View: Recent Development in Reconstructionists' Theory," *Phi Delta Kappan,* Vol. 48, No. 3 (November, 1965), pp. 150–152. [Japan] [IV]

Thierbach, Hans. "Amerikanisches und sowjetisches Schulwesen," *Unsere Schule,* Vol. X (1955), p. 209ff. [Germany] [IV]

Thomas, Glyn W. "A Pedagogue Abroad: Some Reactions of a British Exchange Teacher in an American High School," *Educational Outlook,* Vol. 22 (March, 1948), pp. 153–158. [Britain] [II]

Thompson, W., *et al.* "Some Observations on American Education," *Education News* (Sydney, Australia), Vol. IX, No. 2 (April, 1963), pp. 4–6. [Australia] [II]

Thomson, David Cleghorn. "America and the Academic Exiles," *The Scottish Educational Journal,* Vol. 22 (June 30, 1939), pp. 801–803. [Britain] [III]

Thomson, J. J. *Recollections and Reflections.* New York: The Macmillan Company, 1937. 451 pp. [Britain] [III]

Thormälen, E. "German Views of American Education, with Particular Reference to Industrial Development," *U.S. Bureau of Education Bulletin.* Series No. 361, No 2 (1906). 28 pp. [Germany] [II]

Tillich, Paul. "The Conquest of Theological Provincialism," in *The Cultural Migration: The European Scholar in America.* Philadelphia: University of Pennsylvania Press, 1953, pp. 138–156. [Germany] [III]

Time Magazine. "Schools: Quality, U.S. vs. British," Vol. LXXXVI, No. 23 (December 3, 1965), p. 48. [IV]

Times Educational Supplement (London). "American Education in the Melting Pot," Vol. 25, No. 1061 (August 31, 1935), pp. 301–303. [IV]

Times Educational Supplement (London). "America's Military Schools," No. 2671 (July 29, 1966), p. 250. [II]

Times Educational Supplement (London). "American Tendencies Surveyed:

Some Changes in Organization," Vol. 25, No. 1014 (October 6, 1934), p. 337. [IV]

Times Educational Supplement (London). "American Tendencies Surveyed—II," Vol. 25, No. 1015 (October 13, 1934), p. 345. [IV]

Times Educational Supplement (London). "An English Teacher Comments to a Conference of American School Teachers at East St. Louis, Missouri, U.S.A.," No. 1297 (March 23, 1940), p. 107. [IV]

Times Educational Supplement (London). "Aspects of America: Exchange Teachers' Seminar," No. 2410 (July 28, 1961), p. 116. [III]

Times Educational Supplement (London). "Contrasts in Education: Some Thoughts on Schools in U.S.A.," No. 1754 (December 11, 1948), p. 697. [IV]

Times Educational Supplement (London). "Cousins Compared: Americans Catch Up," No. 2634 (November 12, 1965), p. 1025. [I]

Times Educational Supplement (London). "Education by the Acre: Impressions of an Exchange Teacher," No. 1452 (January 27, 1943), p. 100. [IV]

Times Educational Supplement (London). "English Schools and American Practice: Experience of a Sister Democracy," No. 1530 (August 26, 1944), p. 412. [IV]

Times Educational Supplement (London). "English Teaching in America: A Visitor's Comparisons," No. 1299 (March, 1940), p. 107. [IV]

Times Educational Supplement (London). "Flight of the Scientists—'U.S. Can Offer More'," No. 2543 (Friday, February 14, 1964), p. 379. [III]

Times Educational Supplement (London). "In the Sweet South," No. 2347 (May 13, 1960), p. 965. [IV]

Times Educational Supplement (London). "Letter from America," No. 2703 (March 10, 1967), p. 797. [IV]

Times Educational Supplement (London). "On Exchange in the U.S.," No. 2672 (August 5, 1966), p. 283. [I]

Times Educational Supplement (London). "Science Teacher Shortage, Lesson from America," No. 2459 (July 6, 1962), p. 17. [II]

Times Educational Supplement (London). "Task of the American Schools: A Democratic Attitude to Life," No. 1353 (April 5, 1941), p. 156. [IV]

Times Educational Supplement (London). "University For Everybody—North American System Examined," No. 2434 (January 12, 1962), p. 40. [III]

Times Educational Supplement (London). "We Can Teach U.S.A.," No. 2468 (September, 1962), p. 235. [IV]

Times Educational Supplement (London). "Year in the Bronx," No. 2544 (February 21, 1964), p. 433. [II]

Timmermans, Jean. "On the Organization of Scientific Research," *Some Com-*

parisons Between Universities. Oxford: Basil Blackwell, 1944, pp. 1–5. [Belgium] [III]

Towgan, Hamdan. "Visitors from Other Lands View Our Schools and the Convention," *Nation's Schools,* Vol. 53, No. 3 (March, 1954), pp. 71–78. [Iraq] [IV]

Toynbee, Arnold. "A British View of U.S. Education," *The Globe and Mail,* (Toronto). July 24, 1963. [Britain] [III]

Toynbee, Arnold. "School Boards Run System," *The Globe and Mail,* (Toronto). July 30, 1963. [Britain] [III]

Toynbee, Arnold. "Typical Student in U.S. University Not Scholar," *The Globe and Mail,* (Toronto). July 31, 1963. [Britain] [III]

Traude, Franz. "Das amerikanische Eriziehungs und Bildungswesen," *Paedagogische Rundschau,* Vol. IX (1954/55), p. 72ff. [Germany] [IV]

Trevelyan, Charles. "The Equalization of Education," *Fortnightly Review* (London), Vol. CLIII (March, 1940), pp. 266–270. [Britain] [IV]

Tricker, R. A. R. "Impressions of the Teaching of Science in Schools in the United States of America," *School Science and Mathematics,* Vol. 62, No. 1 (January, 1962), pp. 3–21. [Britain] [II]

Triulzi, Alessandro. "An Italian View of the U.S. Campus," *Overseas,* Vol. III, No. 2 (October, 1963), pp. 10–13. [Italy] [III]

Trumble, Hazel. "Educators from Europe Praise Freedom in American Schools," *Michigan Education Journal,* Vol. 32 (October, 1954), pp. 65–67. [IV]

Turner, John. "Some Aspects of British and American Education," *Education,* Vol. LXXXVI, No. 1 (September, 1965), pp. 52–55. [Britain] [II]

Tuulikki, Terttu. "Comments on American Educational Practices," *The International Teacher Development Program,* No. OE–14118. Washington, D.C.: United States Office of Education, 1964. 11 pp. [Finland] [II]

Tweedie, Ethel Brilliana. *America As I Saw It: or America Revisited.* London: Hutchinson and Company, 1913. 395 pp. [Britain] [IV]

Twentyman, A. E. "Note on School Attendance in the Public Schools of the United States," *Board of Education, Special Reports on Educational Subjects* in *Education in the United States of America, Part I.* Vol. X. London: H.M.S.O., 1902 . [Britain] [I]

van Uden, A. "Observations on the Education of the Deaf in the Netherlands and the U.S.A." *The Volta Review,* Vol. 62, No. 1 (January, 1960), pp. 10–14. [Netherlands] [II]

Uder, Azize. "Comments on American Educational Practices," *The International Teacher Development Program,* No. OE–14118. Washington, D.C.: United States Office of Education, 1964. 11 pp. [Turkey] [II]

University of Hawaii. *The Evaluation of the Japanese and Thai grantees of Their Orientation Experiences.* Honolulu: University of Hawaii, June, 1955. 58 pp. [IV]

University of Hawaii. *Reactions of Asiatic Grantees to Orientation in Hawaii.* Honolulu: University of Hawaii, November, 1954. 41 pp. [III]

Urena, Pedro Henriquez. "Quotations: A Latin-American Criticism of North American Education," *School and Society,* Vol. 14, No. 366 (December 31, 1921), pp. 641–643. [IV]

U.S. Department of Health, Education, and Welfare. "Comments on American Educational Practices," *The International Teacher Development Program, Office of Education.* Washington, D.C.: U.S. Government Printing Office, pp. 11–12. [II]

U.S. Department of State, Bureau of Intelligence and Research. *Cross-cultural Education: A Bibliography of Government-Sponsored and Private Research on Foreign Students and Trainees in the U.S. and in other Countries, 1946–1964: A Selective Bibliography.* Washington, D.C.: U.S. Department of State, External Research Staff, April, 1965, 61 pp. [IV]

U.S. Department of State. "The Near East and South Asia—Other Foreign Visitors," *Educational and Cultural Diplomacy—1964.* Publication No. 7979. Washington, D.C.: U.S. Government Printing Office. 67 pp. [III]

U.S. Department of State. "Western Europe—Foreign Leaders," *Educational and Cultural Diplomacy—1964.* Publication No. 7979. Washington, D.C.: U.S. Government Printing Office, pp. 42–43. [III]

Useem, John and Ruth Hill. *The Western-Educated Man in India: A Study of His Social Role and Influence.* New York: Dryden Press, 1955. 237 pp. [IV]

Vakil, K. S. "Impressions of American Education by a Visitor from India," *NEA Journal,* Vol. 17, No. 5 (May, 1928), p. 163. [India] [IV]

Vakil, K. S. "Impressions of a Foreign Observer of American Education," *Elementary School Journal,* Vol. 28, No. 8 (April, 1928), pp. 603–605. [India] [IV]

Valeur, Robert and Jacques Barzun. "The French Lycee: Its Roots and its Fruits," *Columbia University Quarterly,* Vol. 24 (1932), pp. 402–427. [II]

Valko, Laszlo. "What Do We Expect from America," *IIE News Bulletin,* Vol. 7, No. 5 (February, 1932), pp. 4–5. [Hungary] [IV]

Vallete, Jean José. "Impressions from Abroad," *NEA Journal,* Vol. 39, No. 1 (May, 1950), p. 350. [France] [IV]

Vallins, Dorothy, "Peace is One and Indivisible: Conclusions of a British Teacher," *NEA Journal,* Vol. 36, No. 5 (May, 1947), p. 374. [Britain] [I]

Vanderschmidt, Fred. *What the English Think of Us.* New York: Robert M. McBride and Company, 1948. 213 pp. [IV]

Van Reesema, C. Philippi-Siewertsz. *Pioniers der volksopvoeding: Bijdrage tot de geschiedenis van het ontstaanende ontwikkeling van het onderwijs in de Verenigde Staten [Pioneers of Public Education: Contributions*

Toward the History of the Origin and Development of Instruction in the United States]. The Hague, Netherlands: Martinus Nijhoff, 1949. 604 pp. [IV]

Velichansky, Leonid. "Literaturnaya Assails U.S. Institutes Studying Russia," *The Current Digest of the Soviet Press,* Vol. XV, No. 21 (1963), pp. 19–21. [USSR] [III]

Vera, Fernando Antonio. "Graduate Study in the United States and in Latin America," *IIE News Bulletin,* Vol. 23, No. 5 (March, 1948), pp. 11–12. [Paraguay] [III]

Vial, Jacques. "Democracy, the Hard Lesson," *Atlas,* Vol. VII (June, 1964), pp. 262–263. [France] [III]

Vickers, Steve B. "American and English Schools Compared," *Virginia Journal of Education,* Vol. 40, No. 7 (March, 1947), pp. 312–313. [Britain] [I]

Vickers, Steve B. "To Our Mutual Advantage," *School and Society,* Vol. 66, No. 1710 (1947), pp. 268–270. [Britain] [I]

Vishnevsky, S. "Lenin's Ideas Grip the Imagination," *The Current Digest of the Soviet Press* (Pravda), Vol. XV, No. 21 (1963), p. 20. [USSR] [IV]

Vissec, Lucien de. "La formation du peuple americain par l'ecole," *Le Musee Social* (memoires et documents), (1912). [France] [IV]

Vogel, Adolf. "Das amerikanische College und die deutsche Oberstuf," *Die Sammlung,* Vol. VI (1951), p. 305ff. [Germany] [III]

Vogt, Karl. "What Do We Expect from America?" *IIE News Bulletin,* Vol. 7, No. 2 (November, 1931), pp. 6–8. [Germany] [IV]

Vosberg-Rekow, Dr. "Comments of Dr. Vosberg-Rekow," Chapter XXVII in *Report of the Commissioner of Education, 1900.* (Reported by Simon W. Hanauer), Vol. II. Washington, D.C.: U.S. Government Printing Office, 1901, p. 1438. [Germany] [II]

Wagner, Charles. *My Impressions of America.* (Trans. by Mary Louise Hendee). New York: McClure, Phillips and Company, 1906. 301 pp. [France] [I]

Wallace, R Hedger. " 'Nature Study' in the United States", *Board of Education, Special Reports on Educational Subjects* in *Education in the United States of America, Part I.* Vol. X. London: H.M.S.O., 1902. [Britain] [I]

Wallas, Graham. "The Universities and the Nation in America and England," *Contemporary Review,* Vol. CV (January–June, 1914), pp. 783–790. [Britain] [III]

Wangombe, Mariga T. "An African Studies Our Schools," *NEA Journal,* Vol. 52, No. 2 (February, 1963), pp 21–22. [Kenya] [II]

Ware, Fabian. "The American Educational Exhibit at Manchester," *Journal of Education* (London), Vol. 23, No. 381 (April, 1902), pp. 235–236. [Britain] [IV]

Waterfall, Edith Anna. *The Day Continuation School in England: Its Function and Future.* London: George Allen & Unwin, Ltd., 1923. 221 pp. [Britain] [I]

Watson, Jack M. "Hosting Foreign Educators," *Music Journal,* Vol. 20 (January, 1962), pp. 67–68. [IV]

Webb, William H. *School Planning at Home and Abroad: A Resume of English and Continental Practice.* London: The Sanitary Publishing Company, Ltd., 1911. [Britain] [I]

Wedge, Bryant M. *Visitors To The United States And How They See Us.* Princeton, New Jersey: D. Van Nostrand Company, Inc., 1965. 168 pp. [IV]

Weigand, Karl. "Schools Across the Sea," *IIE News Bulletin,* Vol. 27, No. 8 (May, 1952), pp. 20–23. [Germany] [IV]

Weinaug, Catherine T. "Portrait: Japanese Boy in American School," *Childhood Education,* Vol. 42, No. 4 (December, 1965), pp. 225–228. [I]

Weinrich, Ernest F. "German Educators Look at Our Schools," *NEA Journal,* Vol. 38, No. 5 (May, 1949), p. 359. [IV]

Wells, Herbert George. *The Future in America.* New York and London: Harper and Row, Publishers, 1906. 259 pp. [Britain] [IV]

Wells, Herbert George. *The New America.* New York: The Macmillan Company, 1935. 78 pp. [Britain] [IV]

Wenke, Hans. "Das amerikanische Erzehungswesen," *Die neue Sammlung,* Vol. I (1961), p. 314ff. [Germany] [IV]

Wessling, Wilhelm. "Amerikanische Stimmen zur High School," *Die Hoehere Schule,* Vol. XI (1959), p. 26ff. [Germany] [II]

Wessling, Wilhelm. "Zehn Jahre deutsch-amerikanischer Austausch," *Bildung und Erziehungen,* Vol. XV (1962), p. 30ff. [Germany] [IV]

Weulersse, M. "L'education publique aux États-Unis," *Revue Internationale de l'Enseignement,* Vol. XLVII, No. 2 (February 15, 1904), pp. 128–132. [France] [II]

Whitburn, John. "Report of Councillor John Whitburn, of the Newcastle-upon-Tyne Education Committee," *Reports of the Mosely Educational Commission to the United States of America.* London: Co-operative Printing Society Limited, 1904, pp. 376–393. [Britain] [I]

Whitehead, Howard J. and G. P. Gooch. *Wider Aspects of Education.* Cambridge: Cambridge University Press, 1924. [Britain] [IV]

Whitely, J. "Thoughts on Education in the United States and Great Britain," *Phi Delta Kappan,* Vol. 39, No. 5 (February, 1958), pp. 223–226. [Britain] [I]

Wielenga, Gurt. "A Dutch Teacher Sees American High Schools," *The Bulletin of the National Association of Secondary School Principals,* Vol. 34, No. 167 (January, 1950), pp. 85–94. [Netherlands] [II]

Wilhelm, Theodor. "Die Zukunft der amerikanischen Schule," *Internationale Zeitschrift fuer Erziehung*, Vol. VII (1938), p. 298ff. [Germany] [IV]

Willers, Georg. *Das Bildungswesen der U.S.A.* Munich: Ehrenwirth, 1965. [Germany] [IV]

Williams, M. Atkinson. "The Place of English in the American Elementary School," *Journal of Education* (London), Vol. 29, No. 456 (July, 1907), pp. 497–499. [Britain] [I]

Willich, Johanna. "Building the Bridge Between America and Europe," *Journal of the American Association of University Women*, Vol. XXV, No. 1 (October, 1931), pp. 32–33. [Germany] [II]

Willoughby, Hugh. *Amid the Alien Corn: An Intrepid Englishman in the Heart of America*. Indianapolis: The Bobbs-Merrill Company, Inc., 1958. 159 pp. [Britain] [III]

Wilson, Garnet D. "A Glimpse at American Schools," *The Scottish Educational Journal*, Vol. VIII, Part I, No. 7 (February 13, 1925), pp. 162–163; Part II, No. 8 (February 20, 1925), pp. 186–187. [Britain] [II]

Wilss, Wolfram. "Dewey im Wandel," *Die Hoehere Schule*, Vol. XIII (1961), p. 25ff. [Germany] [IV]

Winch, H. W. "The Curriculum of American High Schools," *Journal of Education* (London), Vol. 30, No. 469 (August, 1908), pp. 524–526. [Britain] [II]

Wittlin, Alma S. "The Social Value of Museum Education in the United States," *Journal of Education* (London), Vol. 83, No. 982 (May, 1951), pp. 247–249. [Britain] [IV]

Wolff, Georg. "Der Dalton Plan," *Monatschrift fuer Hoehere Schulen*, Vol. XXVIII (1929), p. 566ff. [Germany] [II]

Wolff, Georg. "Die High Schools der Vereinigten Staaten im Spiegel der Mathematik und der Naturwissenschaft," *Monatschrift fuer Hoehere Schulen*, Vol. XXVII (1928), p. 131ff. [Germany] [II]

Wolff, Georg. "Neuere Stroemungen im Schulleben der Vereinigten Staaten," *Deutsches Philologen Blatt*, Vol. XXXVI (1928), p. 113ff. [Germany] [IV]

Wolff, Georg. "Zur Unterrichtsreform in den Vereinigten Staaten," *Die Erziehung*, Vol. IV (1929), p. 60ff. [Germany] [IV]

Wood, Myfanwy. "A Brief Comparison Between the Universities of China and Those of Europe and the U.S.A.," *Some Comparisons Between Universities*. Oxford: Basil Blackwell, 1944, pp. 44–45. [Britain] [III]

The Woodrow Wilson School of Public and International Affairs. *Cultural Contacts Project*. 3 vols. *An Evaluation of the Longtime Effects of International Educational Exchange in Belgium*, Vol. I, 208 pp; *Opinions Belges*, Vol. II, 219 pp. *Summary and Conclusions*, Vol. III, 67 pp. Princeton, New Jersey: Princeton University, 1951. [IV]

Woods, Alice. "Co-education in America," *Journal of Education* (London), Vol. 40, No. 471 (October, 1908), pp. 705–706. [Britain] [IV]

Wu, Ting fang. "American Education," *America Through the Spectacles of an Oriental Diplomat.* New York: Frederick A. Stokes Company, 1914, pp. 54–65. [China] [IV]

Yakobson, Helen B. "Russian Language Teaching in American Secondary Schools," *School and Society,* Vol. 87, No. 2149 (1959), pp. 108–111. [IV]

Yalman, Ahmet Enin. "An Experience with Progressive Education in America and in Turkey," *Progressive Education,* Vol. 17, No. 3 (March, 1940), pp. 206–208. [Turkey] [IV]

Yamamoto, Taneshiro. "A Student From Japan at Bowdoin," *IIE News Bulletin,* Vol. 36, No. 9 (May, 1961), pp. 27–30. [Japan] [III]

Yaqzan, Abdul. "On the Basis of Achievement," *The Asian Student* (Spring Semester, 1958), pp. S–6. [Pakistan] [III]

Yung, Wing. *My Life in China and America.* New York: Henry Hiel, 1908. 286 pp. [China] [III]

Ziegler, W. "Der Dalton Plan," *Die Schulwarte,* Vol. IV (1951), p. 292ff. [Germany] [II]

Ziemer, Gregor. "Education for Life—American Education Challenged," in *Education for Death—The Making of the Nazi.* New York: Oxford University Press, 1941, pp. 193–200. [Germany] [IV]

Ziertmann, Paul. *Das amerikanische College und die deutsche Oberstufe. Vergleichende Erziehung,* Heft 2. Wiesbaden: Metopen, 1950. [Germany] [III]

Zimbel, Max. "World from Abroad," *NEA Journal,* Vol. 39 (April, 1950), p. 246. [Germany] [IV]

Zorn, Walter. "Eriziehungsziele in England und Amerika," *Monatschrift fuer Hoehere Schulen,* Vol. XXX (1931), p. 739ff. [Germany] [IV]